PUBLIC ADMINISTRATION
IN CANADA

PUBLIC ADMINISTRATION IN CANADA

A Text

Kenneth Kernaghan
David Siegel

Nelson Canada

© Nelson Canada
A Division of International Thomson Limited
Published in 1989 by
Nelson Canada
A Division of International Thomson Limited
1120 Birchmount Road
Scarborough, Ontario M1K 5G4

Originally published by Methuen Publications in 1987.

All rights reserved. No part of this work covered by
the copyrights hereon may be reproduced or used in
any form or by any means-graphic, electronic or
mechanical, including photocopying, recording,
taping or information storage and retrieval systems-
without the prior written permission of the publisher.

Canadian Cataloguing in Publication Data
Kernaghan, Kenneth, 1940-
    Public administration in Canada : a text

Includes bibliographical references and indexes.
ISBN 0-17-603480-3

1. Public administration - Canada.   2. Canada -
Politics and government.   3. Civil service -
Canada.   I. Siegel, David.   II. Title.

JL108.K45 1989   354.71   C89-094566-7

Printed and bound in Canada
1 2 3 4 5   THB   5 4 3 2 1 0 9

To Helgi, Kevin, Scott and Kris
and
To Nancy and Sarah

CONTENTS

DETAILED TABLE OF CONTENTS

PREFACE

This book is designed as a basic comprehensive text which will promote better understanding of the study and practice of public administration in Canada. We hope to enhance our readers' knowledge of the unique nature of administration in the public sector and their appreciation of the challenges and opportunities of a career in the public service. We anticipate that the audience for this text will include university and college students in public administration courses, public servants engaged in training and development courses in all spheres of Canadian government, and knowledgeable lay readers.

The scope of the field of public administration is so vast that an all-inclusive text would be a multi-volume work. In determining the content of this single volume, therefore, we have sought advice from many quarters in an effort to cover the major topics in the field. We have attempted also to provide a balanced treatment of the diverse features of public administration by relating theoretical considerations to practical experience, by examining both the political and managerial dimensions of the field, and by covering enduring as well as current issues. The content of the book unavoidably reflects the fact that writings on public administration in Canada have focussed primarily on the federal government. We have, however, made a special effort to cover provincial and municipal public administration by supplementing secondary research materials with our own research.

Material in this book that has been published previously has been revised and updated. This material appeared originally either in scholarly journals, in the book entitled *Public Administration in Canada: Selected Readings*, or in monographs published by the Institute of Public Administration of Canada. For permission to reprint previous work, we are grateful to the Institute and to the journals *Canadian Public Administration*, *Canadian Public Policy*, *Public Administration* (Britain), and *Public Administration* (Australia).

For the scholarly foundation on which this book is based, we are greatly indebted to the many academics and practitioners who have contributed to our understanding of the discipline and practice of public administration in Canada and elsewhere. The written contributions of most of these persons are acknowledged in the book's footnotes and bibliography. However, we wish to recognize also the wealth of information and insights we have gained from formal and informal discussions with our academic colleagues and with public servants from all spheres of Canadian government. We express appreciation to students past and present who have shared — or endured — our fascination with the field of public administration. This text is in large part a response to the frequent lament of these students that a comprehensive text on Canadian public administration has been unavailable.

We acknowledge also our gratitude to those public servants and university colleagues who have improved the quality of this book by commenting on various chapters in draft form. In particular, we express warm appreciation to Barbara Carroll, Nicolas Baxter-Moore, Terry Downie, Ed Farren, Wilbur Grasham, Donald Higgins, Bill Hull, Margaret Johnston, P. K. Kuruvilla, Rick Loreto, Bruce Macnaughton, Brian Marson, Robert McLaren, Ross Murray, Allan O'Brien, Randy Olling, Tom Plunkett, and Trevor Price. We alone, of course, are responsible for any errors that remain.

Kenneth Kernaghan
David Siegel
December 1986

INTRODUCTION

THE IMPORTANCE OF PUBLIC ADMINISTRATION

During this century, and especially since the beginning of the Second World War, there has been an enormous expansion in the activities of Canadian governments. The present scope and the continuing growth of responsibilities in all spheres of Canadian government — whether federal, provincial, or municipal — have a great impact on the daily lives and future prospects of Canadian citizens. The degree of happiness and prosperity or misery and poverty experienced by Canadians is affected by the countless decisions made each day by our governments. The range of governmental activities includes the traditional functions of administration of justice, the conduct of external relations, and the defence of the country, as well as such newer responsibilities as medicare, environmental protection, and atomic energy research.

The two major areas of government action are *the provision of services* and *the enforcement of regulations*. The *service* functions include the maintenance of streets and highways, mail delivery, and grants and loans for new housing and for urban renewal. Among the *regulatory* functions are the setting of standards for food and drugs, the prevention and restraint of restrictive trade practices, and the enforcement of fair housing and employment regulations. In order to carry out these and other responsibilities as effectively as possible, governments are actively engaged in research on matters ranging from the inspection of food and drugs to scientific and medical research. Virtually every government department and agency is involved in research related to its service or regulatory functions. Research activities are a costly, but essential, component of the total responsibilities of government.

Very few Canadians are aware of the importance and the magnitude of their governments' operations. Canadians, like citizens of other countries, tend to be conscious of only those government activities that affect them directly and significantly — for example, the collection of taxes, the provision of family allowances, or the payment of unemployment insurance benefits. Many important functions of government, such as the preservation of internal law and order or the administration of justice, are taken for granted unless the services are discontinued or disrupted for some reason. An excellent example is the awakened public concern about postal operations when normal service is disrupted by labour disputes.

The impact of government activities on the lives of Canadians during a typical working day is vividly demonstrated by the following example from the sphere of government regulation:

> In the morning the clock radio awakens us with the sound of music subject to Canadian content regulations. The price, at the farm gate, of the eggs we eat for breakfast has been set by a government marketing board. We drive to work on tires that must meet federal minimum safety standards and in a car whose exhaust is subject to pollution emission regulations. At lunch, the restaurant in which we eat has been subject to the scrutiny of public health inspectors. The monthly rate for the telephone we use at the office is set by a federal or provincial regulatory agency. Shopping in the supermarket on the way home, we note the unpronounceable names of certain chemical preservatives that, by government regulation, are disclosed to us on a finely printed label. As we turn down the thermostat before retiring, we are confident that a government agency has protected our purse by setting the price we will be charged by the monopoly supplier of natural gas. Putting on our sleepwear, we are secure in our knowledge that it is not impregnated with a hazardous substance . . . . If we live in certain cities, we approach our rest reassured that the smoke detector we were required to install will stand on guard throughout the night.[1]

What do these extensive and pervasive activities of Canadian governments have to do with public administration? A great deal! Public administration is concerned with the ways and means by which governments formulate and implement policies to fulfil their onerous service and regulatory responsibilities. These ways and means are in large part provided by what is called the public bureaucracy. This term is not used here in a pejorative sense; rather, it refers to a system for achieving government objectives. Elected representatives, especially political executives (e.g., Cabinet ministers, city mayors), are, of course, centrally involved in the making of public policies. However, we shall see in later chapters that bureaucrats (also called public servants, civil servants, or government employees) have considerable influence on the content of these policies and make most of the decisions required to implement them. Thus, while a recurring theme in this book is the importance of relations between the political and bureaucratic realms of government, the role of the bureaucracy is the major focus of attention.

THE APPROACH AND ORGANIZATION OF THE BOOK

This book is organized so as to cover the field of public administration in a logical, coherent fashion. The organization of the book flows from our conviction that the study of public administration requires the use of concepts and insights from several disciplines, most notably political science and organiza-

---

[1]Economic Council of Canada, *Responsible Regulation* (Ottawa: Supply and Services, 1979), p. xi.

tion theory. Wamsley and Zald argue persuasively that "organization analysis can provide a rigour and conceptual sophistication currently lacking in public administration; political science brings an awareness of political influences and environmental pressures upon public agencies . . . that often seems slighted in organization theory and analysis; and public administration reminds us of the range of tasks and organizational problems of public agencies."[2]

Thus, Part I of this book explains the importance for the study and practice of public administration of theories of bureaucracy, organization, management, decision making, and policy making. Chapter 1 examines the meaning of public administration and compares public and private administration; it describes the growth of public bureaucracy in Canada and the environment within which it operates; and it reviews the evolution and the major theories of public bureaucracy. Chapters 2 and 3 are concerned with the relationship between public administration and organization theory, with particular reference to the Canadian context. Chapter 4 builds in part on the work of some of these organization theorists to discuss the closely related management issues of motivation, leadership, and communication. Finally, Chapter 5 examines theories of policy making and policy implementation and the practical implications of these theories for Canadian public administration.

On the basis of some of the organization theories and principles discussed in Part I, Part II covers the structure and standard method of operation of the main organizational forms employed in parliamentary governments. The theme which ties these chapters together is what we call *the choice of organizational form*. We are concerned here with how the various organizational forms differ from one another and why governments choose a particular organizational form to carry out a particular responsibility. Therefore, each chapter deals with the characteristics of a different organizational form and with the advantages and disadvantages of the use of each form. Chapter 6 focusses on the most commonly used organizational form — the operating department — and on central agencies. Chapter 7 discusses Crown corporations, and Chapter 8 deals with regulatory agencies. Chapter 9 examines a number of important, but less widely used, organizations and instruments — Royal commissions, task forces, advisory councils, and white and other coloured papers.

Part III builds on Parts I and II. The insights provided in Part I are utilized to develop a frame of reference for examining interactions between bureaucrats working in the organizations described in Part II and other political actors. Chapter 10 explains the institutional and value frameworks which provide the conceptual and organizational basis for the chapters in Part III. Then, Chapters 11 and 12 examine in turn the perennial and interrelated themes of bureaucratic power and responsibility. These themes are pervasive in the next seven chapters on the relations between bureaucrats on the one hand and political executives, legislators, the courts, bureaucrats in other governments, pressure groups, political parties, the public, and the media on the other. The final chapter

---

[2]Gary L. Wamsley and Mayer N. Zald, *The Political Economy of Public Organizations* (Bloomington, Indiana: Indiana University Press, 1976), p. 83.

in this part, Chapter 20, reinforces the importance of the primary administrative values and examines the issue of administrative ethics.

The explanation in Part III of the relations between bureaucrats and other political actors provides an essential base of knowledge for the examination in Part IV of the management of organizational resources. Many of the administrative organizations and administrative values discussed in Part III appear again in our examination of public personnel management and collective bargaining in Chapters 21 and 22 and of the budgetary process and financial management in Chapters 23 and 24.

Finally, Part V contains a single chapter on public administration in the local government setting. References are made in various chapters to public administration in the municipal sphere of Canadian government, but this sphere is so distinctive compared to the federal and provincial spheres that it merits separate treatment.

Bibliographies at the end of each chapter contain valuable references for further reading on particular subjects. For a comprehensive bibliography on Canadian public administration, readers should consult W. E. Grasham and Germain Julien, *Canadian Public Administration Bibliography*,[3] including supplements 1–4.

At the end of most chapters is a list of case studies that can be used to relate the theoretical and descriptive material in the text and in formal lectures to actual administrative situations. The cases are drawn from three sources. The book of case studies entitled *Canadian Cases in Public Administration*[4] contains twenty-four relatively brief cases and a subject index of the primary issues covered by the cases. A second book entitled *Canadian Cases in Business-Government Relations*[5] contains twenty somewhat longer cases dealing with such matters as the regulation and takeover of business by government. A large number of more lengthy cases has been published in the *Case Program in Canadian Public Administration* by the Institute of Public Administration of Canada.

Some readers may wish to use the various chapters of this book in an order which suits their own purposes. We have, therefore, tried to make each chapter as self-contained as possible and to give cross-references to other chapters which elaborate on certain subjects. It is notable, however, that we have provided a definition and/or detailed explanation of new and unfamiliar terms the first time they appear in the text. If the chapters are used in some other order, readers may wish to consult the Glossary at the end of the book for both a definition and a page reference to where key terms are discussed in more detail.

---

[3](Toronto: Institute of Public Administration of Canada, 1972) and supplements 1–4 dated 1974, 1977, 1980, and 1985 respectively.

[4]Kenneth Kernaghan, *Canadian Cases in Public Administration* (Toronto: Methuen Publications).

[5]Mark C. Baetz and Donald H. Thain, *Canadian Cases in Business-Government Relations* (Toronto: Methuen, 1985).

I

INTRODUCTION TO PUBLIC ADMINISTRATION

1

Public Administration
and Public Bureaucracy

This chapter examines in turn the study and practice of public administration, the environment and growth of public bureaucracy, and the evolution and interpretation of the concept of bureaucracy.

THE PRACTICE AND THE STUDY OF PUBLIC ADMINISTRATION

What is Public Administration?

Public administration is a term that can more easily be explained than defined. This fact has not discouraged several scholars from trying to capture the meaning of the term in a single sentence. Among the typical one-sentence definitions of public administration are these:

> The study and practice of the tasks associated with the conduct of the administrative state.[1]

> All processes, organizations and individuals (the latter acting in official positions and roles) associated with carrying out laws and other rules adopted or issued by legislators, executives and courts.[2]

> The coordination of individual and group efforts to carry out public policy.[3]

> The application of organizational decision-making, and staffing theory and procedures to public problems.[4]

These brief definitions indicate the scope and purpose of public administration, but they are necessarily incomplete in their coverage and very general in their wording. The emphasis in these and most other definitions of public administration is on the implementation of policy; there is insufficient recognition of the role of bureaucrats in policy development. Moreover, these definitions contain abstract words and terms that tend to leave the reader with more questions than answers. For example, what *are* the tasks associated with the conduct of

[1]Ivan L. Richardson and Sidney Baldwin, *Public Administration: Government in Action* (Columbus, Ohio: Charles E. Merrill, 1976), p. 3.

[2]George J. Gordon, *Public Administration in America* (New York: St. Martin's Press, 1978), p. 8.

[3]John M. Pfiffner and Robert Presthus, *Public Administration*, 5th ed. (New York: Ronald Press, 1967), p. 7.

[4]Thomas Vocino and Jack Rabin, *Contemporary Public Administration* (New York: Harcourt Brace Jovanovich, 1981), p. 4.

the administrative state? What *are* the relationships between bureaucrats and such institutions as legislatures, executives, and courts? Is public administration confined to the *carrying out* of public policy? What is distinctive about organization and management in public administration as opposed to private administration? This book provides answers to these and many other questions about public administration, with particular reference to Canadian governments.

The terms public administration and public bureaucracy are often used interchangeably, but they do not mean the same thing. Public bureaucracy is the system of authority, people, offices, and methods that government uses to achieve its objectives. Public administration, by way of contrast, refers to a field of practice (or an occupation) *and* to a field of study (often referred to as a discipline). Public bureaucracy is the means whereby the practice of public administration is carried on; it is also the main focus of the study of public administration. In this book, the term public administration refers to its practice unless we indicate otherwise by specific reference to its study. The book as a whole is devoted to studying the practice of public administration as that practice is conducted through the system known as public bureaucracy.

The scope of the practice and study of public administration is so broad that it is difficult to achieve general agreement on where the boundaries of the field should be drawn. The breadth of the field could be demonstrated simply by listing the hundreds of departments and agencies at all levels of Canadian government which collectively carry out an enormous array of activities. It could be demonstrated also by showing the range of concerns shared by teachers and practitioners of public administration. For example, the themes discussed in recent years at the national seminars of the Institute of Public Administration of Canada[5] have included the administration of such public policy fields as transportation, energy, and criminal justice, as well as the implications for public administration of such matters as intergovernmental relations, public sector collective bargaining, pressure group activity, program evaluation, and information management. Moreover, among the issues covered during a recent two-year period in *Canadian Public Administration*, the learned journal of the Institute of Public Administration of Canada, are the policy and expenditure management system in the federal government, quasi–public service agencies in British Columbia, fiscal constraints and user-fees in Canadian municipalities, the administration of regional economic development policy, human resources planning, affirmative action, administrative law reform, public policy making, and the accountability of senior public servants.

Public Administration versus Private Administration

The meaning of public administration can also be clarified by comparing it to private (or business) administration. A widely quoted statement on this subject is Wallace Sayre's assertion that "business and government administration are

---

[5]The Institute of Public Administration of Canada is an association of public servants from all levels of government and of academics that is devoted to improving the study and practice of public administration in Canada.

alike in all unimportant respects."[6] There is in fact much that is similar in public and private administration. Administration in all organizations involves cooperative group action. Moreover, all large organizations, whether they are government departments, hospitals, universities, labour unions, factories, or commercial enterprises, must provide for the performance of such functions of general management as planning, organizing, staffing, and budgeting. There is, however, much that is different in the administration and management of public sector organizations, and these differences have enormously important implications for the study and practice of public administration. At the very least, the differences suggest the need for caution in transferring practices and technologies from private sector organizations to public sector organizations.

In contemporary Canadian society the line between public and private administration is somewhat blurred. Public and private sector organizations can usefully be depicted on a continuum running from typical operating departments of government to private sector corporations largely free from governmental control or assistance. In the middle section of this continuum is a variety of organizations characterized by a mix of public and private elements. These organizations include public corporations (Air Canada, Eldorado Nuclear) which compete with and operate much like private corporations; mixed enterprise corporations which are owned or controlled by different governments (the Saint John Harbour Bridge Authority) or by governments and private organizations (Canarctic Shipping); and private sector organizations which are subject to close government regulation (e.g., pharmaceutical companies), which depend heavily on government financial assistance (e.g., textile firms), or which do 100 per cent of their business with government (e.g., defence contractors). Despite this public-private "grey area," we can for analytical purposes make a broad distinction between the public and private spheres of administration.

Two major characteristics of government account in large part for the differences between public administration and private administration. These are (1) the vast scope and complexity of government activities, and (2) the political environment within which these activities are conducted.

The first and most frequently cited difference is that the overall mission of public administration is service to the public, whereas the primary raison d'être of private administration is profits or what is often described as "the bottom line." The service orientation of public administration results from the need for bureaucrats to assist elected politicians to respond to public demands and requirements for government services. Private administration is profit-oriented because the survival of private sector organizations depends ultimately on making a profit. A Canadian business executive with senior public service experience has noted that

> in the business world. . . the focus is on output and efficiency. The judge of success is the market place and the measure of success is profitability. In government, the focus is more complicated and uncertain. Considerations

---

[6]Quoted in Joseph L. Bowen, "Effective Public Management," *Harvard Business Review*, vol. 55 (March–April 1977), p. 132.

of efficiency have to be traded off against various other considerations such as equity, . . . political and legal feasibility; administrative capacity; and so on. The judge of success is the electorate, which renders its verdict at the ballot box every few years.[7]

It is commonly argued that a second difference, which follows directly from the service versus profit distinction, is that public administration operates less efficiently than private administration. It is suggested that since government departments receive their funds largely through annual appropriations from the public treasury they do not have to worry about profits; thus they have less incentive to cut costs and operate efficiently. Business organizations are motivated to operate efficiently because they must compete in the market place; most government operations, however, are monopolistic (e.g., the police) so that the public does not have a choice among competing organizations for the delivery of services. It is argued that public organizations are less inclined to be efficient because they do not have to be as sensitive as private organizations to the preferences and grievances of their "consumers." Finally, many services are provided by government because they would not produce sufficient profits to interest private sector organizations. A considerable body of public opinion argues that when government activities produce a profit they should be turned over to private enterprise.

Governments also provide what are called "public" goods; these are goods, such as control of water pollution, which are funded through the general tax system rather than on the "user-pay" principle that is characteristic of "private" goods (e.g., a bottle of milk). The benefits of public goods are available to many persons, and the benefits are not easily measured. Indeed, it is very difficult to measure the efficiency of many government expenditures (e.g., on health services).

It is true that public administration does not have the measuring rods of prices and profits which are so central to efficiency considerations in the private sector. Nevertheless, government departments and agencies do have incentives to operate efficiently. For example, the many administrative units within government compete with one another for public funds; this competition is especially vigorous during a period of financial restraint in government. In recent times, treasury officials have paid much more attention to the economy, efficiency, and effectiveness of departmental operations, and an increasing number of government programs are operated on a cost-recovery basis. Another spur to efficiency in government is the threat of public criticism which may embarrass elected politicians and, in turn, damage the career prospects of the government employees involved.

The achievement of business-like efficiency in government is greatly affected — and often hampered — by the demands of the political environment in which it is pursued. In a major study of productive management in the public sector, Canada's Auditor General noted that departmental recommendations to cut operating costs are sometimes incompatible with political priorities. He observed that "private sector firms are not required, to the same extent as the public

---

[7]Grant Reuber, "Better Bureaucracies," *Policy Options*, vol. 3 (September–October 1982), p. 11.

sector, to reconcile questions of productive management with concerns such as national unity, regional development and national well-being."[8]

Efficiency in government is also hindered by a third difference between public and private administration, namely the greater emphasis in the public sector on accountability. The Auditor General concluded that a major constraint on productive management "is the body of administrative regulations and the conflicting accountability requirements that limit managerial authority and autonomy."[9] The lines of authority and responsibility tend to be much clearer in private sector organizations. In government, such factors as the scale and complexity of operations, the desire for political control over the bureaucracy, and the search for consistency and coordination have resulted in a proliferation of accountability mechanisms which lengthen and complicate the decision-making process. For example, deputy ministers in the federal government are typically accountable to the Prime Minister, their minister, the Public Service Commission, the Auditor General, and a number of central agencies, including Treasury Board, the Comptroller General, the Department of Finance, the Privy Council Office, and so on. In addition to this direct accountability, deputy ministers are indirectly accountable through their minister to Parliament and the public. While excessive and conflicting accountability requirements are most evident at the senior levels of the bureaucracy, they affect the middle levels as well. The negative impact of these requirements on efficiency in government is demonstrated by the Auditor General's concern that "when constraints become a spider's web of rules, regulations, directives, prohibitions and controls, managers lose sight of value-for-money concerns."[10] For example, the pursuit of efficiency through speedy program implementation may be hampered by numerous financial and personnel constraints.

A fourth difference is that the personnel management system is much more complicated and rigid in government than in private sector organizations. In general, it is harder both to hire and to fire government employees. In the public sector, the merit system, which is the mechanism for hiring and promoting employees, includes several criteria which go well beyond the idea of technical proficiency. In the federal government, these criteria are efficiency and effectiveness, sensitivity and responsiveness, equality of access to public service employment and equity in employment policies and practices. To promote sensitivity and responsiveness to the needs of a certain minority group, for example, the government may hire a person from that group who is not as well qualified as other candidates in terms of education and experience. The complexity and inflexibility of public personnel management systems result also from the general emphasis on accountability. Indeed, three of the top ten constraints on management productivity identified by federal public service managers lie squarely in the personnel field, that is, in the areas of job classification, personnel rules, and staffing.[11]

---

[8]Auditor General, *Annual Report–1983* (Ottawa: Supply and Services, 1983), p. 57.
[9]Ibid., p. 60.
[10]Ibid.
[11]Ibid., p. 62. See also Chapter 21 in this book.

Fifth, and finally, the "public" nature of public administration requires that much of it be conducted in a "goldfish bowl" of publicity. Many government deliberations are conducted behind closed doors, but compared to the private sector, many more government decisions are subjected to public scrutiny. Taxpayers insist on the right to know how much public money is being spent and for what purposes. Thus a government decision to construct a new airport in a particular area will probably receive much more public and media examination than a decision by a major manufacturer to construct or close a plant in the same area, even if the latter decision has a greater economic or social impact on the area in question. The media will report on the effects of such private sector decisions, but they do not expect these decisions to be made in public. An important consequence of public scrutiny of government activities is greater emphasis in the public sector on such considerations as responsiveness and accountability. This emphasis explains in part the presence of what is popularly described as bureaucratic "red tape" and the consequent slowness in decision making.

Given the size, complexity, and political imperatives of government, the issue of whether public or private administration is more efficient is not the most relevant concern. The critical question is whether public administration is conducted as efficiently as can reasonably be expected.

The Study of Public Administration

The systematic study of public administration in North America is a relatively recent development. In the United States, the study of the field is generally acknowledged to date from the publication in 1887 of Woodrow Wilson's celebrated essay "The Study of Administration."[12] In Canada, no single date or publication marks the formal beginning of the study of public administration. There are, however, several noteworthy developments in the evolution of the formal study of Canadian public administration.[13]

Several of the twenty-three volumes on *Canada and Its Provinces*, written by A. Shortt and A. G. Doherty and published in 1914, covered aspects of public administration and public bureaucracy in Canada. Then, in 1918, the first work focussing on a particular problem in Canadian public administration was written by two American scholars.[14] The earliest general work in the field was R. McGregor Dawson's *The Civil Service of Canada*, published in 1929.[15] It was not until 1936 that Luther Richter and R. A. Mackay established the first degree program in Canadian public administration at Dalhousie University. Carleton College (now Carleton University) graduated students with a Bachelor of Public Administration degree in 1946, and the university's School of Public Adminis-

[12]Reprinted in Peter Woll, ed., *Public Administration and Policy* (New York: Harper and Row, 1966), pp. 15–41.

[13]For an account of the development of the study of public administration in Canada, see A. Paul Pross and V. Seymour Wilson, "Graduate Education in Canadian Public Administration: Antecedents, Present Trends and Portents," *Canadian Public Administration*, vol. 19 (Winter 1976), pp. 515–541.

[14]H. S. Villard and W. W. Willoughby, *The Canadian Budgetary System* (New York: Appleton, 1918).

[15]R. McGregor Dawson, *The Civil Service of Canada* (Oxford: Oxford University Press, 1929).

tration was established in 1952. Moreover, it was not until the early 1950s that a handful of academic scholars[16] made the first of their many contributions to the literature on public administration in Canada. *Canadian Public Administration*, the learned journal devoted to the study of public administration, commenced publication in 1958.

The academic study of public administration really began to flourish in the late 1960s. Indeed, progress in the study of Canadian public administration since 1970, as measured by research, publications, teachers, and programs, has been greater than all the preceding years combined. This greatly increased attention to research and teaching in public administration is in large part a direct response to the growth in the operations, expenditures, and size of the federal, provincial, and municipal bureaucracies. It also coincided with the expansion of Canadian universities and colleges, which were thereby able to devote more resources to teaching and research in public administration.

The study of public administration is commonly described as a discipline, but it is not a discipline in the restrictive sense of an intellectual endeavour with a body of coherent and accepted theory. Even if the term discipline is defined less rigorously as a field of study with a nucleus of unifying beliefs, public administration has not yet achieved agreement on what those beliefs are. The matter is complicated by what has often been called the field's "crisis of identity" which arises from two distinct and largely countervailing developments. The first is the evolution of public administration under the parentage of political science. The second is the continuously expanding dimensions of the study and practice of public administration and the increasingly interdisciplinary approach to its study and teaching. A critical issue bearing on the status of public administration is whether the subject should properly be considered a subdiscipline (or subfield) of political science or of administrative science (i.e., organization theory and management science). The administrative science approach involves considerable borrowing from such disciplines as economics, sociology, and psychology.

Political Science or Administrative Science?

The two opposing positions on the appropriate theoretical base for the organization of studies in public administration have been succinctly expressed as follows:

> Any tendency for public administration to break away from the parent discipline must ultimately weaken both political science as a whole and the study of public administration. It will weaken political science by removing the part of it which brings the teacher into closest relationship with the practical business of government. It will weaken the study of public administration by divorcing it from political theory and the principles of government which underlie political and administrative institutions.[17]

---

[16]Prominent among these scholars were Albert Abel, Roch Bolduc, J. E. Hodgetts, J. R. Mallory, D. C. Rowat, and Malcolm Taylor.

[17]William Robson, *The University Teaching of Social Sciences: Political Science* (UNESCO, 1954), p. 47.

> The greatest promise for study of public administration in the universities will be in association with the growth of an integrative, organizing, generic concept of administration. From the nucleus of general administrative studies, it may be possible to interrelate more meaningfully the study of administration to the various disciplines and professions. In the modern world, no clear line separates administration in government from the administrative processes of the total society. The organization of administrative studies in the university must ultimately correspond to this reality.[18]

There are sound theoretical grounds for teaching public administration as part of political science. Knowledge of the administrative structures of government and of the political and legal environment in which the public administrator works is essential to a sound understanding of the political system. In addition, the bureaucracy plays a central role in the political system through its active involvement in the making, enforcement, and adjudication of laws and regulations. Less evident, but extremely significant, intellectual bonds between public administration and political science lie in their shared concern for inquiry into such key theoretical concepts as responsibility, authority, and the public interest. Political theorists who fail to explore the meaning of these themes in the particular milieu of public administration omit a perspective essential to adequate analysis. All these factors attest to the status of public administration as an integral part of the study of political science.

The most productive approach for political scientists may be to treat public administration as a *subdiscipline* on the basis of existing organizational patterns and theoretical links between public administration and political science. Political scientists may resolve the identity crisis, at least to their own satisfaction, by ceasing to agonize over the vast scope of public administration and by seeking agreement on achievements made towards a general theory of public administration.

Those who view public administration as a part of administrative science contend that the study of administration may be most fruitfully pursued by dividing the general field of administration into public, business, hospital, educational, police, and other types of administration. To proponents of this view, the similarities between these various forms of administration are greater than their differences. This belief has led to the establishment of "professional" schools or faculties of administrative studies.

Moreover, some scholars are convinced that intellectual developments are moving inexorably in the direction of a rigorous *discipline* of administrative studies. This discipline will be interdisciplinary and integrative in its subject content and teaching approach. Its program will be characterized by a flowing together for mutual enrichment of the present "academic" and "professional" streams in administrative studies. Discussion of the distinctive nature of "public" administration will be founded on a solid base of knowledge about the concepts and techniques of administration generally. All students, regardless of the type of

---

[18]Lynton Caldwell, "Public Administration and the Universities: A Half Century of Development," *Public Administration Review*, vol. 25 (March 1965), p. 60.

administration in which they are primarily interested (e.g., public, business, educational), will be required to take a group of "core subjects" in administration. The "core subjects" will normally include organizational behaviour, accounting, micro-economics, macro-economics, and quantitative methods. Later specialization in a particular type or problem of administration will be founded on this base of common knowledge.

Public Administration as Public Administration

Given the absence of a Ph.D. program in public administration at any Canadian university, most teachers and scholars in the field will continue to receive a substantial portion of their education in political science or economics supplemented by some practical experience in the public service. However, a variety of structural arrangements exists for the master's level education of current and aspiring public servants. Programs leading to a Master of Public Administration (M.P.A.) degree or to a degree in political science or public sector management are available in departments of political science or in schools or faculties of administrative studies. However, the most common route to an M.P.A. degree is through one of the several specialized schools of public administration which have grown rapidly during the last fifteen years. These schools offer an interdisciplinary approach with a professional emphasis. Programs are designed to accommodate students proceeding directly from their bachelor's degree as well as mid-career public servants. The schools require a similar group of core courses (e.g., government structure and organization, policy formulation, quantitative methods, applied economics, the management process in government, and public sector financial management and accounting) and a range of elective courses in specialized areas such as local government administration and intergovernmental relations.

Most of the schools have adopted a policy-management approach to program content which combines political science and administrative science with an examination of public policy. This approach focusses on public administration as a distinct field of study rather than as a subdiscipline or subfield of political science or administrative science.

THE ENVIRONMENT AND EXPANSION OF CANADIAN BUREAUCRACY

Environmental Factors

Public administration is greatly influenced by the broad environment within which it is conducted. J. E. Hodgetts, in his discussion of environmental influences on the public service, notes that the most persistent influences in Canadian society are the geographical and economic settings, technological change, and culture.[19] The influence of *geography*, which has been manifested largely

[19]J. E. Hodgetts, *The Canadian Public Service: A Physiology of Government* (Toronto: University of Toronto Press, 1973), p. 17. See also, by the same author, "Challenge and Response: A Retrospective View of the Public Service of Canada," *Canadian Public Administration*, vol. 7 (December 1964), pp. 409–421.

by the need to disperse government operations and personnel across the country, is discussed in Chapter 2 of this book. Perhaps the most important of the *economic* factors affecting the public service has been the reliance in the Canadian economy on exploiting and marketing such staple products as fish, fur, wheat, timber, minerals, and pulpwood. Several of the original departments of the federal government (e.g., Agriculture, Marine and Fisheries) were created to deal with problems connected with the production, transportation, and trade of staple products, and several existing departments are still concerned with these problems.

Another important economic influence has been the growth during this century of large industrial and commercial organizations (e.g., General Motors, IBM) and of large and powerful labour organizations (e.g., the Canadian Automobile Workers, the Canadian Labour Congress). Employer-employee disputes over such matters as wage levels and the effects of technological change on existing jobs can result in lengthy strikes. Such strikes may not only bring much personal strife and misfortune to those directly involved in the dispute, but may also have an injurious impact on innocent third parties and on the economy as a whole. To protect the public interest, governments have been increasingly obliged to regulate the activities of business and labour organizations and to arbitrate disputes between them.

The environment within which contemporary governments work has also been greatly affected by *technological* developments. The problems for government arising from the widespread use of such inventions as the automobile, the airplane, and television have become more critical as transportation routes have become snarled, airports have become too small for huge jetliners, and intercontinental television transmission has become possible. The opportunities brought about by more recent technological developments involving automation, computers, and atomic energy have created such problems as technological unemployment, invasion of privacy, and possible misuse of atomic energy. Scientific and technical advances, such as increasing numbers of human tissue transplants, test-tube babies, and instruments of instant communication, also present challenging issues for government concern and involvement. The internal management and operations of the public service have, of course, been transformed by technological developments in such areas as word processing and communications systems.

Cultural factors have also been influential in moulding the public service. For example, the powerful influence of the United States on Canadian culture has led to such measures as "Canadian content" regulations in radio and television broadcasting. Both the United States and Britain have exercised significant influence on the organization and administrative arrangements of the public service in Canada. Finally, the public service has been required to adapt to an extremely important cultural factor within Canada itself — the constitutional guarantees to the use of the English and French languages.[20]

---

[20]See the discussion in Chapter 22 of francophone representation in the public service.

Aside from these geographic, economic, and technological factors, the influence of *demographic* factors on the public service deserves special mention.

Rapid population growth in Canada (from 5.4 million in 1901 to 24.9 million
in 1986) was, until recently, accompanied by a movement of Canadians from
rural-agricultural areas to urban-industrial centres. The urban population in
Canada rose from 19.6 per cent in 1871 to 76.1 per cent in 1971, but declined
slightly to 75.7 per cent in 1981. Over 70 per cent of Canadians now live in
cities, towns, and villages of 1,000 or more persons, and approximately 52 per
cent of the population is found in urbanized areas of more than 100,000 inhabi-
tants (called census metropolitan areas). This urbanization of the Canadian
population has brought enormous problems for governments in the form of inadequate housing and air and water pollution. The resolution of these problems
continues to require large government expenditures and close cooperation
between governments. It is notable that a counter-urbanization movement began
in the early 1970s. More people have been moving to rural from urban areas
than the reverse. Medium-sized urban areas are growing faster than large and
small ones. The total population of the metropolitan areas is the same now as in
1971, and within these areas, people are selecting the semi-urban and rural
fringes rather than the core districts. This population redistribution, if it continues, will require reconsideration of land development and environmental protection policies because the trend to ruralization will increase demand for the
limited supply of arable land.[21] Moreover, these people tend to bring with them
"urban tastes" in the form of demands for improved services in such fields as
transportation, recreation, and education.

Another demographic factor with enormous implications for public administration is the changing age composition of the Canadian population.[22] The percentage of Canadians over sixty-five years of age rose from 5.0 per cent in 1901
to 8.6 per cent in 1976 and is projected to rise to 13.3 per cent by 2011 and to
22.2 per cent by 2031.[23] As the number of elderly persons increases, their needs
for health, housing, and community services of various kinds will also increase.
There will be, indeed there already is, a need for different orders of government
and different administrative units within each order of government to find the
financial and personnel resources to meet these needs.

This brief discussion of environmental factors shows that the operations of
governments are extremely complex and the demands on government are constantly changing. Governments must provide rapid solutions to urgent current
problems while planning for the solution or avoidance of future problems. They
must be conscious of the widespread ramifications of major governmental decisions on various sectors of Canadian society. For example, the federal government must assess the probable impact on Canada of changes in the economic
policies of other nations and decide how to counteract the adverse effects these

---

[21]For an examination of urbanization in Canada, see Statistics Canada, *Urban Growth in Canada*
(Ottawa: Supply and Services, 1984).

[22]See Kenneth Kernaghan, "Politics, Public Administration and Canada's Aging Population,"
Canadian Public Policy, vol. 8 (Winter 1982), pp. 69–79.

[23]These figures are taken from ibid., p. 70.

changes may have on provincial and municipal governments, on the level of employment, on the prosperity of businesses, and so on. After an evaluation of the likely consequences has been made, the government may have to alter its existing plans and programs to take account of these changes. Clearly, governments operate in a constant state of flux and must have the capacity and the inclination to adapt quickly to change.

The Growth of Public Bureaucracy

In Canada, as elsewhere, expansion in the scope and complexity of government activities has been accompanied by a striking growth in expenditures and in the number of government employees. Expressed as a percentage of the Gross National Product (i.e., the total output of final goods and services without allowance for depreciation), government expenditures rose from 29.6 per cent in 1960 to 43.1 per cent in 1982. As shown in Table 1.1,[24] the relative percentage of total government expenditures made by the three levels of government has altered substantially since 1947.

Table 1.1
EXPENDITURES BY LEVEL OF GOVERNMENT
SELECTED YEARS
(AS % OF GNP)

Year	Federal	Provincial	Local
1947	14.1	5.2	4.4
1950	11.5	5.7	4.9
1955	15.3	5.2	5.8
1960	15.0	7.3	7.3
1965	12.9	6.8	8.1
1970	13.8	10.2	9.4
1975	16.8	12.2	8.8
1980	16.5	12.7	8.6
1981	17.5	12.4	8.5
1982	20.1	13.6	9.4

Source: Richard M. Bird, *Financing Canadian Government: A Quantitative Overview* (Toronto: Canadian Tax Foundation, 1979) and calculated from *Economic Review 1982*, Tables 3, 52, 57, and 59 and *Economic Review 1983*, Tables 4, 51, 56, and 58.

Before the outbreak of the Second World War, each sphere of government spent about the same amount of money on the provision of goods and services to the public. During the war, the federal government took control of the economy to promote the war effort with the result that, by the end of the war, federal expenditures of public funds had risen to 82 per cent of total government

[24]From Dan Butler and Bruce D. Macnaughton, "More of Less for Whom? Debating Directions for the Public Sector," in Michael S. Whittington and Glen Williams, eds., *Canadian Politics in the 1980s*, 2nd ed. (Toronto: Methuen, 1984), p. 9.

expenditures. During the post-war period, the total amount of money spent by all levels of government has increased greatly. The federal percentage of total expenditures, however, has declined steadily, while provincial and municipal expenditures have increased. The substantial increase in expenditures by the ten provincial governments combined is a result of the increased demand for services within the constitutional jurisdiction of the provinces, particularly in the areas of education, health, and social welfare, and of the increasing revenue available to the resource-rich provinces.

Most Canadians are more interested in what the various spheres of government do with the money they receive from taxpayers than in what percentage of total expenditures is made by each level of government. To indicate the primary areas of government spending, Table 1.2[25] shows the changes over time in the expenditures of Canadian governments on particular activities. All figures are expressed as a percentage of GNP. Note in particular the steady increases in expenditures on social welfare, education, and health. Expenditures on defence, as a percentage of GNP, have declined substantially since 1960.

Table 1.2
GOVERNMENT EXPENDITURES BY MAJOR ACTIVITY
SELECTED YEARS
(AS % OF GNP)

Major Activity	1933	1950	1960	1970	1974	1977
Social Welfare	3.8	3.5	4.5	6.8	9.2	9.9
Education	3.0	2.5	4.3	7.0	6.1	6.6
Health	0.9	1.3	2.3	4.9	5.1	5.3
Transportation and Communications	2.6	2.6	5.0	3.8	4.2	3.7
Natural Resources	1.0	1.1	1.6	0.6	1.4	2.6
Debt Charges (Interest)	8.4	2.6	2.4	3.1	3.2	3.7
General Government and Protection	1.2	1.8	2.5	3.9	4.6	5.0
International Aid	—	0.1	0.2	0.3	0.4	0.5
Other	4.1	3.0	2.9	4.3	5.2	4.4
Total Civilian	25.0	18.2	24.9	34.7	39.4	41.7
Defence	1.8	4.5	5.0	2.0	1.6	1.7
Total	26.8	22.7	29.9	36.7	41.0	43.4

Source: 1933–1960: Richard M. Bird, *Growth of Government Spending in Canada* (Toronto: Canadian Tax Foundation, 1970), Tables 9 to 11, Appendix C; 1970–1977: Statistics Canada, *Consolidated Government Finance* (Ottawa: Information Canada, 1973, 1977, and 1980).

[25]Based on Table 2.3 in Douglas J. McCready, *The Canadian Public Sector* (Toronto: Butterworths, 1984), p. 18.

The rapid increase in total expenditures at all levels of Canadian government has been accompanied by a related growth in the number of public employees required to carry out these increasing governmental responsibilities. Table 1.3[26] shows the growth in the number of public employees at each level of government for selected years between 1960 and 1982.

Much public criticism has centred on the size and growth of public sector employment in Canada, especially at the federal level of government. Certainly the absolute size of public sector employment has increased greatly since 1945. The public sector, broadly defined, now employs roughly one-quarter of the total labour force. But the fact is that public sector employment, as a percentage of total employment, has increased very little since 1960. The hiring of public sector employees has been especially slow since the mid-1970s as a result of restraint programs and hiring freezes imposed on government departments and agencies. Indeed, Table 1.3 shows that between 1975 and 1982 government employment, as a proportion of the total labour force and as defined by Sutherland and Doern, actually declined from 20.3 per cent to 17.9 per cent. It is particularly notable that the federal public service constitutes a comparatively small proportion of total public sector employment, and that since the mid-1960s growth has been slower in the federal than in the provincial and municipal governments.

Related to the growth in the number of government employees is the variety and change in the occupational composition of the public service. Virtually every occupation, trade, and skill can be found in the public service. The Royal Commission on Government Organization in Canada (the Glassco Commission) noted that the occupations in the federal public service range "from actuaries and anthropologists through bee keepers, dry dock riggers, map compilers and pharmacists, to veterinarians and X-ray operators. An element of mystery is created by the listing of such intriguing operations as insect sampling, . . . receivers of wreck, . . . strippers and layouters."[27] Clearly, a wide variety of job opportunities is available to those who aspire to become Canadian public servants.

The increasingly complex and technical nature of government operations noted earlier has brought about a significant qualitative change in the public service. Especially over the past few decades, the rate of growth in the administrative, professional, scientific, and technical occupational categories has been more rapid than that in the traditional clerical and operational categories. This change in the occupational make-up of the public service is often referred to as the "professionalization" of the service. One result of this development is that students must not only spend a longer time in school to obtain the education neces-

[26]From Sharon L. Sutherland and G. Bruce Doern, *Bureaucracy in Canada: Control and Reform.* Volume 43 of Research Studies for the Royal Commission on the Economic Union and Development Prospects for Canada (Ottawa: Supply and Services, 1985), pp. 134–135. Reproduced with permission of the Minister of Supply and Services. Chapter 3 of this book contains very useful data on the growth and characteristics of government employment in Canada.
[27]Canada, *Report of the Royal Commission on Government Organization*, vol. 1 (Ottawa: Queen's Printer, 1962–1963), p. 21.

Table 1.3
TOTAL GOVERNMENT EMPLOYMENT

	1960	% LF	1965	% LF	1970	% LF	1975	% LF	1980	% LF	1982	% LF
Labour Force (000s)	6,430	—	7,185	—	8,329	—	9,923	—	11,522	—	11,743	—
Federal												
General[a]	203,013	3.2	211,913	3.0	251,237	3.0	323,902	3.3	335,375	2.9	351,295	3.0
Enterprise	131,118	2.0	129,916	1.8	123,906	1.5	132,046	1.3	157,988	1.4	138,281	1.2
Total	334,131	5.2	341,829	4.8	375,143	4.5	455,948	4.6	493,363	4.3	489,576	4.2
Provincial												
General[b]	139,434	2.2	168,536	2.3	216,475	2.6	288,937	2.9	311,634	2.7	317,407	2.7
Enterprise	63,444	1.0	70,281	1.0	95,520	1.1	134,513	1.4	143,105	1.3	159,260	1.4
Total	202,878	3.2	238,817	3.3	311,955	3.7	423,450	4.3	459,739	4.0	476,667	4.1
Local[c]												
General	149,403	2.3	162,901	2.3	201,425	2.4	247,199	2.5	274,126	2.4	287,103	2.4
Enterprise	23,187	0.4	25,860	0.4	31,976	0.4	39,242	0.4	43,517	0.4	45,577	0.4
Total	173,121	2.7	188,761	2.7	233,401	2.8	286,441	2.9	317,643	2.8	332,680	2.8
Total Government												
General	491,850	7.6	543,350	7.6	669,137	8.0	860,038	8.7	921,135	8.0	955,805	8.1
Enterprise	218,280	3.4	226,057	3.2	251,402	3.0	305,801	3.1	349,610	3.0	343,118	2.9
Total	710,130	11.0	769,407	10.8	920,539	11.0	1,165,839	11.8	1,270,745	11.0	1,298,923	11.0
Education Sector												
Teaching	160,800[d]	2.5	211,463[d]	2.9	291,624	3.5	313,341	3.1	328,975	2.9	314,201	2.7
Non-teaching[e]	99,696	1.6	131,107	1.8	180,807	2.2	194,271	2.0	203,965	1.8	194,805	1.7
Total	260,496	4.1	342,570	4.7	472,431	5.7	507,612	5.1	532,940	4.7	509,006	4.4
Hospital Sector[f]	183,189	2.8	251,511	3.5	319,826	3.8	339,517	3.4	299,388	2.6	297,195	2.5
Grand Total	1,153,815	17.9	1,363,488	17.9	1,712,796	19.0	2,012,968	20.3	2,103,073	18.3	2,105,124	17.9

a. Excludes federal hospital care workers. They are reflected in the hospital sector totals.
b. Excludes provincial hospital care workers. They are reflected in the hospital sector totals. Also excludes local school teachers from New Brunswick who were included 1975–82. Excludes teachers from CAATs (Ontario) and CEGEP (Quebec) who were included from 1975–82. Public college teachers who were included in 1975 are excluded from provincial totals. These employees are reflected in the education sector totals. Estimates for Quebec in 1960 and B.C. from 1960–75 are included in the totals.
c. Local general employment totals for 1960 and 1965 are estimated. Local enterprise totals are estimated for 1960–82.
d. Excludes Community College teachers.
e. Non-teaching personnel are estimated for 1960–82.
f. The 1979–80 hospital statistics were used for 1980 total. The 1980–81 statistics were used as estimates for 1982 total.
Source: Tables 3-5, 3-5, 3-15, 3-16, 3-19, 3-20, and 3-23, in Sutherland and Doern, *Bureaucracy in Canada: Control and Reform.*

sary for appointment to the public service, but also must return to school in later years to keep informed about new developments affecting their jobs.

To fulfil the growing responsibilities of government, additional administrative units have been created in the form of new departments, new sections of existing departments, and new agencies, boards, and commissions enjoying varying degrees of independence from political (i.e., Cabinet and parliamentary) control. There are now twenty-seven federal government departments, including, for example, the Departments of Agriculture, Consumer and Corporate Affairs, External Affairs, Justice, Labour, National Defence, National Health and Welfare, and National Revenue. Among the government agencies, boards, and commissions, of which there are more than four hundred, are such Crown corporations as the Canadian Broadcasting Corporation, the Canadian National Railways, and Air Canada, and such regulatory agencies as the Canadian Radio-television and Telecommunications Commission and the Canadian Transport Commission.

A variety of explanations has been offered for the growth of the public sector. The three main types of explanatory models suggested by Butler and Macnaughton are the socio-economic, organizational, and political models.[28] *Socio-economic* explanations for public sector growth focus on external social and economic influences such as inflation, population growth rates, demographic change, and the level of real personal disposable income. *Organizational* explanations emphasize pressures that emerge within the bureaucracy itself, including responsiveness to clientele demands, bureaucratic empire building and incremental decision making. *Political* explanations stress the pressures to expand government expenditures and employment which result from such factors as electoral competition, party ideology, and pressure group demands.

The growth of government during the 1960s and 1970s has been substantial, but it has often been exaggerated. Popular myths about the extent of this growth, especially in the federal government, help to explain the heightened public criticism of the bureaucracy in recent decades. We shall see in the next section that complaints about bureaucracy actually extend over several centuries.

THE EVOLUTION AND INTERPRETATION OF PUBLIC BUREAUCRACY

Origins and Criticisms of Public Bureaucracy

Many of the central features of contemporary public bureaucracy (e.g., chain of command, specialization, delegation of authority) were evident in the ancient civilizations of Egypt and China. In the West, many characteristics of present-day public bureaucracy existed during the period of the Roman Empire. After the fall of the Empire and the onset of the Dark Ages, some of the Roman achieve-

---

[28]Butler and Macnaughton, " More of Less for Whom?" pp. 17–22. For a more detailed treatment of the causes of growth in public expenditure, see Chapter 23 in this book. See also Richard Bird, *The Growth of Public Employment in Canada* (Montreal: Institute for Research on Public Policy, 1979), ch. 8.

ments in administration were kept alive by the Roman Catholic Church. It is generally acknowledged, however, that the modern type of administrative system began to develop in the seventeenth century after the emergence of nation-states from the feudal societies of Europe. It was not until the 1800s that continental Europe, Great Britain, the United States, and Canada developed their distinctive systems of public bureaucracy which in broad outline have endured to the present.

Despite the long history of bureaucratic forms of administration, use of the word bureaucracy is comparatively recent. It appears to have been first used in eighteenth-century France by Vincent de Gournay to signify a form of government in which appointed officials play a central role. In France at this time the word "bureau" referred not only to a writing-table (or, according to some scholars, a cloth covering the desks of government officials); it also referred to a place where officials worked. A Greek word meaning "rule" was added as a suffix to "bureau," and by 1798 the Dictionary of the French Academy defined bureaucracy as "power, influence of the heads and staff of governmental bureaux."[29] An indication of the subsequent pejorative interpretations of the term was provided by the Academy's approval of the term bureaucratic to signify "the influence of governmental bureaux, and also a regime where bureaux multiply without need."[30] Use of the term spread quickly to other European countries and eventually throughout the world.

During the past two centuries, the term bureaucracy has been interpreted in a striking variety of ways. We noted earlier that in this book the word bureaucracy will be used to refer to a system of authority, people, offices, and methods that government uses to achieve its objectives. Large business and other non-governmental organizations are often described as bureaucracies, but the concept of bureaucracy is so closely associated with government that the terms "bureaucracy" and "public bureaucracy" are commonly used interchangeably.

Regardless of this neutral meaning we have assigned to the term bureaucracy, we must acknowledge that the most frequent usage of the term throughout history and in current everyday conversation is a pejorative one. The word bureaucracy normally conjures up images of government employees and organizations characterized by unresponsiveness, inaccessibility, inflexibility, inefficiency, arbitrariness, and empire building.

Among those groups whose negative views on the bureaucracy have been most widely disseminated are novelists, journalists, politicians, business people, and academics. As early as 1836, in his novel Les Employés, Honoré de Balzac described bureaucracy as "the great power wielded by pygmies" and noted that bureaucracy was organized "under a constitutional government with a natural kindness for mediocrity, a predilection for categorical statements and reports, a government as fussy and meddlesome, in short, as a small shopkeeper's wife."[31] And in 1885, the English novelist Charles Dickens wrote in Little Dorrit about

---

[29]Martin Albrow, Bureaucracy (London: Macmillan, 1970), p. 17.
[30]Ibid., pp. 17–18.
[31]Translated by E. Marriage as Bureaucracy, 1898, p. 84. Cited in ibid., p. 18.

the Circumlocution Office where "numbers of people were lost." In this office, "unfortunates with wrongs, or with projects for the general welfare . . . , who in slow lapse of time and agony had passed safely through other public departments; who, according to rule, had been bullied in this, over-reached by that, and evaded by the other; got referred to the Circumlocution Office, and never reappeared in the light of day."[32] Similar anti-bureaucratic sentiments have pervaded a great deal of fictional literature during the past century.

Novelists have been joined by satirists, whose works on bureaucracy include *Parkinson's Law*, *When in Doubt: Mumble*, and *Cover Your Ass*. In *The Completely Civil Servant*, a Canadian author writing under the pseudonym of G. Arthur Sage describes his book as "the bible for survival, therapy and reform" for public servants and as a means by which "the taxpayer will get an insider's view of the practices that have mushroomed under the justification of improved service to a demanding citizenry."[33] Movies, public affairs shows on television (e.g., "Ombudsman," "The Fifth Estate") and on radio (e.g., "As It Happens"), popular magazines and professional journals all engage with varying degrees of intelligence and intensity in the national sport of bashing bureaucrats. Journalists make a major contribution to the bureaucracy's negative image through provocative headlines and through news stories that trumpet the bureaucracy's deficiencies and failures. Many of these headlines and stories reflect attacks on bureaucrats by politicians. An enduring theme of election campaigns at all levels of Canadian government is the need to control the bureaucracy, to make it more efficient, and to reduce its size. Journalists and politicians find a very receptive audience for anti-bureaucratic assertions among the general public, and especially among business people. The kind of distorted picture of bureaucracy painted by some business publications is illustrated in a recent issue of *Canadian Business* where a writer is discussing the problems of running a restaurant:

> A restaurant . . . is the natural prey of petty bureaucrats who will obstruct and complicate everything you do. All of them will hunt you down, and any of them, on a whim, can shut you down. A mouse in the house, you get a cat. A mouse in a restaurant, you get a visit, an hour's lecture and a warning notice (this time about the cat); and a series of visits and letters from the building inspector who wants to see the drawings for the cat box.[34]

In addition to these journalistic and popular accounts, there have been serious scholarly analyses of bureaucracy. The bureaucracy has received mixed reviews from the academic community. Victor Thompson refers to "bureaupathic" behaviour in large-scale organizations which takes the form of "excessive aloofness, ritualistic attachment to routines and procedures, and resistance to change; and associated with these behavior patterns is a petty insistence upon rights of authority and status."[35]

[32]Cited in E. N. Gladden, *The Essentials of Public Administration* (London: Staples Press, 1964), p. 66.

[33]G. Arthur Sage, *The Completely Civil Servant* (n.p.: Eden Press, 1985).

[34]James Barber, "Cordon Blues," *Canadian Business* (June 1981), p. 116.

[35]Victor Thompson, *Modern Organization* (New York: Knopf, 1961), pp. 152–153.

Other scholars sing the bureaucracy's praises. Charles Perrow contends that "the sins generally attributed to bureaucracy are either not sins at all or are consequences of the failure to bureaucratize sufficiently."[36] For example, the impersonality and rigid adherence to rules found in bureaucracies are frequently criticized. However, the fact that a bureaucrat responds to people according to the objective merits of their case rather than to factors such as their skin colour or religion is a very positive aspect of bureaucracy. A bureaucratic response based on prejudice or other inappropriate considerations would, in Perrow's view, be evidence of "failure to bureaucratize sufficiently."

One of the strongest proponents of the positive elements of bureaucracy is Charles T. Goodsell. In his book *The Case for Bureaucracy*,[37] he argues that bureaucracy in the United States has been the victim of unfortunate stereotyping and incorrect myths. He notes that while people rail against the evils of bureaucracy in the abstract, when they are asked how *they* have been treated by bureaucrats in specific situations, they tend to see the bureaucrats as being fair and helpful. After reviewing a great deal of evidence, he concludes that while bureaucracy is not perfect by any means, it does have an enviable record of providing services.

Goodsell's point about the contradictory nature of the public's perception of the bureaucracy is supported by two major studies[38] of Canadian attitudes towards the federal public service. The two studies demonstrate that despite favourable personal interactions with bureaucrats, many Canadians have a negative image of the bureaucracy as a whole. For example, when asked about their personal experience, more than 80 per cent of those Canadians surveyed in 1978 indicated that public servants had been helpful and courteous, and 75 per cent indicated that their problems had been handled promptly; however, when asked about their view of public servants in general, only 65 per cent of the respondents expected courteous treatment, only 50 per cent expected public servants to be helpful, and only 40 per cent expected prompt handling of their problems.[39] After analysing the survey data, David Zussman concluded that "in the final assessment, it appears that the public weighs more heavily media and other reports of government inefficiencies than their own experiences with government services and public servants."[40]

Bureaucratic Theories

We turn now to an examination of major scholarly contributions to our understanding of the phenomenon of bureaucracy. On the basis of an exhaustive study

[36]Charles Perrow, *Complex Organizations: A Critical Essay*, 2nd ed. (Glenview, Illinois: Scott, Foresman, 1979), p. 5.

[37]Charles T. Goodsell, *The Case for Bureaucracy*, 2nd ed. (Chatham, New Jersey: Chatham House, 1985).

[38]Task Force on Government Information, *To Know and Be Known* (Ottawa: Queen's Printer, 1969) and *Task Force on Service to the Public, Surveys Among the Public on the Quality of Service to the Public from the Federal Government* (unpublished report, 1978).

[39]David Zussman, "The Image of the Public Service in Canada," *Canadian Public Administration*, vol. 25 (Spring 1982), p. 77.

[40]Ibid., p. 78.

of interpretations and theories of bureaucracy, Martin Albrow has set forth seven "modern concepts of bureaucracy." These concepts and some of the major scholars associated with each are shown below:

1. The concept of bureaucracy as *rational organization* views bureaucracy as a means of achieving organizational efficiency; this definition is also closely linked to Max Weber's ideal-type of bureaucracy, which is discussed in Chapter 2 of this book.

2. In direct contrast to this first concept is the interpretation of bureaucracy as *organizational inefficiency*, which has been accepted not only by a large portion of the general public, but also by such scholars as Marshall Dimock, E. Strauss, Robert Merton, and Michael Crozier.[41]

3. The conceptualization of bureaucracy as *rule by officials* has been supported by Harold Laski and Herman Finer and has been carefully studied by such other writers as Harold Lasswell and Abraham Kaplan.[42]

4. The interpretation of bureaucracy as *public administration* has been analytically convenient in broad comparative studies conducted by such theorists as Fritz Morstein Marx, S. N. Eisenstadt, and Fred Riggs.[43]

5. Bureaucracy as *administration by officials* is a neutral, non-pejorative use of the term which is in accord with Max Weber's general concept of bureaucracy (not his ideal-type) as administration through appointed officials. Other representatives of this school of thought are Reinhard Bendix and Peter Blau.[44]

6. Interpreting bureaucracy as *the organization* follows the lead of scholars such as Talcott Parsons and Herbert Simon[45] who tend to equate bureaucracy with organizations in general.

7. The very broad interpretation of bureaucracy as *modern* society is based on the view that "the growth of organizations involves the bureaucratization of society, and that is tantamount to society becoming bureaucracy."[46] Exponents of this interpretation are James Burnham and Robert V. Presthus.[47]

[41]M. E. Dimock, "Bureaucracy: Self Examined," *Public Administration Review*, vol. 4 (1944), pp. 197–207; E. Strauss, *The Ruling Servants* (London: Allen and Unwin, 1961); R. K. Merton, "Bureaucratic Structure and Personality," in R. K. Merton, et al., eds., *Reader in Bureaucracy* (Glencoe, Illinois: The Free Press, 1952), pp. 361–371; Michael Crozier, *The Bureaucratic Phenomenon* (London: Tavistock, 1964).

[42]Harold Laski, "Bureaucracy," *Encyclopedia of Social Sciences*, vol. 3 (New York: Macmillan, 1930), pp. 70–74; Herman Finer, "Critique of 'bureaucracy,' " *Political Science Quarterly*, 60 (1945), pp. 100–112; Harold Lasswell and Abraham Kaplan, *Power and Society* (New Haven: Yale University Press, 1950).

[43]F. Morstein Marx, *The Administrative State* (Chicago: University of Chicago Press, 1957); S. N. Eisenstadt, "Bureaucracy and Bureaucratization," *Current Sociology*, vol.7 (1958), pp. 97–164; Fred Riggs, "Agraria and Industria — Toward a Typology of Comparative Administration" in W. J. Siffin, ed., *Toward the Comparative Study of Public Administration* (Bloomington, Indiana: Indiana University Press, 1957), pp. 23–116.

[44]Reinhard Bendix, *Work and Authority in Industry* (New York: John Wiley, 1956); Peter Blau, *Bureaucracy in Modern Society* (New York: Random House, 1956).

[45]Talcott Parsons, *Structure and Process in Modern Societies* (Glencoe, Illinois: The Free Press, 1960); Herbert Simon, *Administrative Behaviour* (New York: Macmillan, 1957).

[46]Albrow, *Bureaucracy*, p. 105.

[47]James Burnham, *The Managerial Revolution* (Middlesex: Penguin Books, 1962); R. V. Presthus, *The Organizational Society* (New York: Knopf, 1962).

The brief treatment of these concepts provided here cannot capture fully their complexity or their differences; it does, however, demonstrate the diverse interpretations of bureaucracy and its centrality to the study of large-scale organizations, especially government organizations. The meaning and importance of the term are examined further in the following section, which reviews major theories (and theorists) of bureaucracy. These theories set the subject of bureaucracy within the much broader framework of theories of society; they are especially concerned with the effects of bureaucracy on the power structure of society. The next chapter covers, among other topics, managerial theories of organization; these theories are more narrowly focussed on the internal management of organizations.

Karl Marx (1818–1883)

Marx's ideas on bureaucracy must be examined in the context of his theory of class conflict in capitalist societies and the advent of communism. According to Marx, the state in capitalist societies does not represent the general interest, but rather the interests of the dominant or ruling class. He regards the state as "nothing more than the form of organization which the bourgeois necessarily adopt . . . for the mutual guarantee of their property and interests."[48] The bureaucracy of the state is viewed as an instrument by which the dominant class exercises its power over other social classes. Bureaucracy is in fact one of the primary means for perpetuating class division and consolidating the power of the dominant class. The bureaucracy also serves as a general interest smoke screen which obscures the domination of the exploited by the exploiters. The state becomes more oppressive as class conflict intensifies. For Marx, the increasing bureaucratization of the state under capitalism accompanies the intensification of the class struggle.

This class struggle eventually leads to a proletarian revolution and the gradual development of a classless society. With the advent of communism, the state and the exploitative elements of the bureaucracy will ultimately wither away. Administrative tasks will be everyone's concern and will involve the administration of things rather than of people.

In his early writings, Marx argued that bureaucracy contributes to the general process of alienation in society; it becomes an autonomous and oppressive force beyond the control of the people. He asserted also that bureaucracy is characterized by secrecy, incompetence, empire building, and self-interest. In his later writings, Marx downplayed the idea of bureaucracy as an autonomous social force by referring to bureaucracy simply as part of the state that would wither away with the state itself. Allowing for the possibility of bureaucracy exercising autonomous power would have been inconsistent with his later view that "nothing could prevent economic forces producing the polarization of society into bourgeoisie and proletariat."[49]

---

[48]K. Marx, from K. Marx and F. Engels, *The German Ideology*, p. 78. Cited in Albrow, p. 70.
[49]Albrow, *Bureaucracy*, p. 70.

Robert Michels (1876–1936)

In striking contrast to Marx, Robert Michels, a major representative of what are called oligarchic or elite theories of bureaucracy, views bureaucracy as inevitable in the modern state. Through bureaucracy, the politically dominant classes secure and preserve their power. They use, indeed they expand, positions in the bureaucracy to provide security for middle-class intellectuals who in turn support the state. The bureaucracy tends to oppress the rest of society. Lower-level bureaucrats in particular suppress individual liberty and initiative. Michels notes:

> In every bureaucracy we may observe place-hunting, a mania for promotion, and obsequiousness towards those upon whom promotion depends; there is arrogance towards inferiors and servility towards superiors . . . the more conspicuously a bureaucracy is distinguished by its zeal, by its sense of duty, and by devotion, the more also will it show itself to be petty, narrow, rigid and illiberal.[50]

Michels's major focus was not, however, on the state bureaucracy, but on the internal political structures of large-scale organizations. On the basis of his study of political parties and trade unions, he formulated his famous "iron law of oligarchy" according to which large-scale organizations are necessarily oligarchic because they tend to develop a bureaucratic structure which precludes internal democracy. In Michels's words, "who says organization, says oligarchy." Power becomes concentrated at the top of the organization and is wielded in a dictatorial manner by an organizational elite.

There are several interrelated reasons for the development of these oligarchic bureaucratic structures. The large size and increasing complexity of modern organizations mean that it is extremely difficult for the rank and file to participate in decision making. The consequent need to delegate authority to leaders is followed by a concentration of decision-making power in their hands so as to ensure that decisions are made quickly and with sufficient expertise. Leaders begin to associate their own continuation in office with the future well-being of the organization. This causes them to monopolize and manipulate information to weaken the position of potential rivals and to acquire knowledge and political skills which make them virtually irreplaceable. All of this is made easier by the realization of the rank and file that continuity of leadership is desirable and by their general apathy regarding active involvement in organizations. Finally, the leaders seek to consolidate their power; they do this in part by sacrificing the objectives of the rank and file to their own interests.

For Michels, the iron law of oligarchy has broad implications in that oligarchic bureaucratic structures undermine the democratic institutions of society as a whole. The eventual result is an oligarchic political regime which resists demands for change made by the general populace.

Max Weber (1864–1920)

Max Weber, a German scholar, has had more influence on the study of bureaucracy than any other theorist. He was quite possibly the last renaissance man in

---

[50]Robert Michels, *Political Parties*, trans. by E. and C. Paul (London: Jarrold, 1915), p. 200.

that during his tragically short and troubled life he studied such diverse fields that it is impossible to categorize him neatly. He studied law in university, but he never practised it, and he spent only short periods actually working in the government — a common career choice for law graduates at that time. He is usually considered to be a sociologist, and his works are studied more in sociology than in any other discipline. However, he was also an astute student of religion, politics, and ancient history. His writings reflected his eclectic interests in that he was always searching for connections between various modern phenomena. For example, he related certain religious beliefs to the development of both the modern state and capitalism, which he linked in turn to the development of modern bureaucracy.

Weber did not agree with Marx that bureaucracy would eventually wither away. Indeed, he predicted that bureaucratic administration would pervade all forms of organization, whether in the religious, educational, or economic spheres of life. He asserted that "the needs of mass administration make (bureaucratic administration) completely indispensable. The choice is only that between bureaucracy and dilletantism in the field of administration."[51] Weber also disagreed with Michels's view that bureaucratic domination of elected politicians was inevitable. But Weber was ambivalent on this matter of the power of the bureaucracy. Support can be found in his writings both for the view that in a democracy the bureaucracy must be subordinate to elected politicians and for the view that in certain circumstances bureaucrats could dominate their political superiors.

Like Marx and Michels, Weber set his ideas on bureaucracy within the context of a study of the power structure of society. He examined the concept of bureaucracy within a broad and complex framework of political sociology. Unlike Marx and Michels, he treated bureaucracy as the central concept in his analysis and as a general phenomenon in modern society.

Weber related bureaucracy to his analysis of three sources of authority which he distinguished on the basis of their claim to legitimacy. Under *traditional* authority, the right to rule is legitimated by such factors as heredity, religious beliefs or divine right (as in absolute monarchies). *Charismatic* authority is based on the outstanding personal characteristics of an individual (for example, Jesus, Adolph Hitler, John Kennedy). Finally, *legal* authority is legitimated by laws and regulations obeyed by both the rulers and the ruled. In this system, "obedience is owed not to a person — whether a traditional chief or charismatic leader — but to a set of impersonal principles."[52] Each of the types of authority is associated with different administrative arrangements; the usual administrative system under legal authority is bureaucracy.

From his knowledge of Western European bureaucracies, notably the German and the British, Weber developed his celebrated ideal-type of bureaucracy, which is discussed in the next chapter.

---

[51]Max Weber, *Economy and Society* (New York: Bedminster Press, 1968), p. 223.
[52]Peter Blau and Richard W. Scott, *Formal Organizations* (San Francisco: Chandler, 1962), p. 32.

Frederich A. Hayek (1899–) and Milton Friedman (1912–)

Aside from the classical theories of bureaucracy explained to this point, it is worth noting the more contemporary views of two Nobel prize–winning economists — Frederich Hayek and Milton Friedman. In the tradition of Adam Smith and John Stuart Mill, Hayek and Friedman are concerned about the threat which the expansion of government activities and of the bureaucracy poses for economic liberty. Indeed, they argue that this expansion threatens political as well as economic liberty.

Frederich Hayek's best-known book, *The Road to Serfdom*,[53] which was published in 1944, is based on principles of nineteenth-century economic liberalism. He argues that economic liberty is possible only in a capitalist system and that all forms of collectivism (e.g., socialism) are incompatible with democracy because the social planning involved in collectivism tends to destroy both political and economic freedom. Hayek is not opposed to the idea of a welfare state, but he is concerned that the machinery of the welfare state may be used to bring about a much greater degree of collectivism than intended by the designers of welfare programs. He contends that even the moderate planning involved in creating a welfare state will have consequences neither foreseen nor desired by the planners and will put the state on the road to serfdom, that is, to totalitarianism. Moreover, the bureaucracy will play a critical role in putting the state on this road.

Hayek notes that economic planning and regulation in the welfare state lead to very substantial growth in the size and power of the bureaucracy, some of whose members exercise extensive discretionary powers over individual citizens. In addition, the bureaucracy is composed of persons whose careers depend significantly on the expansion of government services. According to Hayek, in the welfare state the rule of law is breached in that bureaucrats are delegated powers to make decisions which discriminate between individuals and against which appeal is very difficult. Efficiency is also reduced in that the welfare system doesn't really help those for whom it was designed; for example, a progressive income tax benefits middle-income persons rather than the poor. More than a decade after the publication of *The Road to Serfdom*, Hayek argued that economic planning by the British Labour government had led to "a despotism exercised by a thoroughly conscientious and honest bureaucracy for what they sincerely believe is the good of the country. But it is nevertheless an arbitrary government, in practice free from effective parliamentary control; and its machinery would be as effective for any other than the beneficent purposes for which it is now used."[54]

Milton Friedman's best-known books include *Capitalism and Freedom*,[55] published in 1962, and *Free to Choose*,[56] published in 1980. Like Hayek, Friedman worries about the threat to economic and political liberty from the expansion of government activities and of bureaucracy. This expansion is the unavoidable

---

[53](Chicago: University of Chicago Press, 1944).
[54]Foreword to ibid., 17th impression, 1963.
[55](Chicago: University of Chicago Press, 1962).
[56](New York: Harcourt Brace Jovanovich, 1980).

result of the growth of the welfare state which, in his view, diverts important economic resources away from the private sector of the economy and creates a kind of government paternalism that undermines the very foundations of the capitalist system. Among government activities to which he objects are rent control, legal minimum wage rates, legal maximum prices, detailed regulation of industries, and public housing.[57]

Friedman warns that the the United States is moving in the same direction as other countries that have lost their economic and political liberty as a consequence of the expansion of the welfare state. He cites the examples of Chile, Britain, and New York City to support his view that the expanded role of the state, the increased volume of government regulations, and the growth of government spending, no matter how well intended, threaten individual liberty. He contends that "the Welfare State's fundamental fallacy, which leads to both financial crisis and the destruction of freedom, is the attempt to do good at someone else's expense."[58] This happens because nobody spends someone else's money with as much care as his or her own. Moreover, to do good at someone else's expense, you have to take the money away from that person. Thus, the use of force and coercion which destroy freedom is necessary to do good at somebody else's expense.

Friedman distinguishes between the economic market where you get what you vote (pay) for and the political market where there is very little relation between what you vote for and what you get. In the economic market, "each man can vote, as it were, for the colour of the tie he wants and get it; he does not have to see what colour the majority wants and then, if he is in the minority, to submit."[59] One of the myths about the political market is that a government bureaucrat can be distinguished from someone in private enterprise on the ground that the bureaucrat serves a *public* interest rather than a *private* interest. Friedman contends that "a government bureaucrat is seeking to serve his private interest just as much as you or I or the ordinary businessman."[60] In the economic market, our self-interest motivates us to serve our customers' interests, but in a government bureaucracy the customers have nowhere else to go. Thus, the bureaucrats can serve their self-interest at their customers' expense by expanding their empire and reducing their workload. Another myth is that the political market actually operates on a one-person/one-vote system; the fact is that some people have much more influence on government decisions than others, and that a small group can pressure the government to support its *special* interest as opposed to serving the *general* interest.

The school of thought represented by such thinkers as Hayek and Friedman is called Libertarianism. This school of thought has had a great deal of influence on the views of those who are associated with the neo-conservative movement.

---

[57]*Capitalism and Freedom*, pp. 35–36.
[58]Milton Friedman, "The Threat to Freedom in the Welfare State," *Business and Society Review* (Spring 1977), pp. 8–16.
[59]Ibid., p. 15.
[60]Ibid., p. 12.

The term *neo-conservatism*[61] emerged in the mid-1970s to describe the views of a group of American intellectuals (e.g., Irving Kristol, Nathan Glazer, and Norman Podhoretz)[62] who believe that big government is a threat to freedom and economic prosperity and who tend to ally themselves with business interests on many political and economic issues. Neo-conservatism has had very significant influence on the Reagan administration in the United States and on the Thatcher government in Britain. It also has followers in Canada (e.g., Michael Walker of the Fraser Institute in Vancouver, writer Barbara Amiel, and John Bulloch of the Canadian Federation of Independent Business). A practical application of neo-conservative thinking can be seen in efforts over the last decade in Canada and elsewhere to reduce government spending and the size and influence of the bureaucracy.

The theories of Marx, Michels, Weber, Hayek, and Friedman explained above are concerned with the role of the bureaucracy vis-à-vis the state. The next chapter focusses on the characteristics of bureaucracy as a formal organization.

---

[61]See Peter Steinfels, *The Neoconservatives* (New York: Simon and Schuster, 1979).
[62]Kristol and Glazer are the editors of *The Public Interest* and Podhoretz is the editor of *Commentary*.

BIBLIOGRAPHY

Public Administration — General

Baker, R. S. *Administrative Theory and Public Administration*. London: Hutchinson, 1972.

Bernstein, Samuel J., and Patrick O'Hara. *Public Administration*. New York: Harper and Row, 1979.

Chapman, Brian. *The Profession of Government*. New York: Macmillan, 1959.

Dunsire, A. *Administration: The Word and the Science*. New York: Wiley, 1973.

Gordon, George J. *Public Administration in America*. New York: St. Martin's Press, 1978.

Heady, Ferrel. *Public Administration: A Comparative Perspective*. 2nd ed. New York: Marcel Decker, 1979.

Henry, Nicholas. *Public Administration and Public Affairs*. 2nd ed. Englewood Cliffs, N.J. : Prentice-Hall, 1980.

Hodgson, J. S. *Public Administration*. Toronto: McGraw-Hill, 1969.

Kramer, Fred A. *Dynamics of Public Bureaucracy*. 2nd ed. Cambridge, Mass.: Winthrop Publishers, 1981.

Marini, Frank, ed. *Toward a New Public Administration: The Minnowbrook Perspective*. Scranton, Pa.: Chandler, 1971.

McCurdy, Howard E. *Public Administration: A Synthesis*. Menlo Park, Calif.: Cummings, 1977.

Miewald, Howard F. *Public Administration*. New York: McGraw-Hill, 1978.

Mosher, Frederick C. *Democracy and the Public Service*. New York: Oxford University Press, 1968.

Nigro, Felix A., and Lloyd A. Nigro. *Modern Public Administration*. 5th ed. New York: Harper and Row, 1980.

Ostrom, Vincent. *The Intellectual Crisis in American Public Administration*. University of Alabama, 1973.

Presthus, R. V. *Public Administration*. 6th ed. New York: Ronald Press, 1975.

Pursley, Robert D., and Neil Snortland. *Managing Government Organizations*. Belmont, Calif.: Wadsworth, 1980.

Rehfuss, John. *Public Administration as Political Process*. New York: Charles Scribner's Sons, 1973.

Richardson, Ivan L., and Sydney Baldwin. *Public Administration*. Columbus, Ohio: Charles E. Merrill, 1976.

Self, Peter. *Administrative Theories and Politics*. 2nd ed. London: George Allen and Unwin, 1977.

Sharkansky, Ira. *Public Administration: Agencies, Politics and Policies*. San Francisco: W. H. Freeman, 1982.

Simmons, Robert H., and Eugene P. Dvorins. *Public Administration*. Port Washington, N.Y.: Alfred Publishing, 1977.

Simon, Herbert A., D. W. Smithburg, and V. A. Thompson. *Public Administration*. New York: Knopf, 1950.

Starling, Grover. *Managing the Public Sector*. Homewood, Illinois: Dorsey Press, 1977.

Stein, Harold. *Public Administration and Policy Development: A Casebook*. New York: Harcourt Brace, 1952.

Vocino, Thomas, and Jack Rabin, eds. *Contemporary Public Administration*. New York: Harcourt Brace Jovanovich, 1981.

Waldo, Dwight. *The Administrative State: A Study of the Political Theory of American Public Administration*. New York: Ronald Press, 1948.

Waldo, Dwight, ed. *Public Administration in a Time of Turbulence*. Scranton, Pa.: Chandler, 1971.

Public Administration—Canada

Adie, Robert F., and Paul G. Thomas. *Canadian Public Administration: Problematical Perspectives*. Scarborough, Ont.: Prentice-Hall, 1982.

Borgeat, Louis, René Dussault, and Lionel Ouellet. *L'administration Québecoise: organisation et fonctionnement*. Québec: Presses de l'Université du Québec, 1984.

Cole, Taylor. *The Canadian Bureaucracy, 1939–1947*. Durham, N.C.: Duke University Press, 1949.

Dawson, R. McGregor. *The Civil Service of Canada*. Oxford: Oxford University Press, 1929.

Doerr, Audrey. *The Machinery of Government in Canada*. Toronto: Methuen, 1980.

Garant, Patrice. *La fonction publique: Canadienne et Québecoise*. Québec: Les Presses de l'Université Laval, 1973.

Gow, Iain, ed. *Administration publique québecoise*. Montréal: Librairie Beau-chemin Limitée, 1970.

Hodgetts, J. E. "Challenge and Response: A Retrospective View of the Public Service of Canada." *Canadian Public Administration*, vol. 7 (December 1964): 409–421.

Hodgetts, J. E. *The Canadian Public Service: A Physiology of Government, 1867–1970*. Toronto: University of Toronto Press, 1973.

Hodgetts, J. E. "The Public Service: Its Past and the Challenge of its Future." *Canadian Public Administration*, vol. 17 (Spring 1974): 17–25.

Hodgetts, J. E., and D. C. Corbett, eds. *Canadian Public Administration*. Toronto: Macmillan, 1960.

Kernaghan, Kenneth. "An Overview of Public Administration in Canada Today." *Canadian Public Administration*, vol. 11 (Fall 1968): 291–308.

Kernaghan, Kenneth, ed. *Bureaucracy in Canadian Government*. 2nd ed. Toronto: Methuen, 1973.

Kernaghan, Kenneth. "Canadian Public Administration: Progress and Pros-pects." *Canadian Public Administration*, vol. 25 (Winter 1982): 444–456.

Kernaghan, Kenneth, ed. *Canadian Public Administration: Discipline and Pro-fession*. Toronto: Butterworths, 1983.

Kernaghan, Kenneth, ed. *Public Administration in Canada: Selected Read-ings*. 5th ed. Toronto: Methuen, 1985. (1st ed., 1968; 2nd ed., 1971; 3rd ed., 1977; 4th ed., 1982.)

Laframboise, H. L. "The Future of Public Administration in Canada." *Cana-dian Public Administration*, vol. 25 (Winter 1982): 507–519.

McCready, Douglas J. *The Canadian Public Sector*. Toronto: Butterworths, 1984.

Sutherland, Sharon L., and G. Bruce Doern. *Bureaucracy in Canada: Control and Reform*. Research Study no. 43 for the Royal Commission on the Eco-nomic Union and Economic Prospects for Canada. Toronto: University of Toronto Press, 1985.

Wilson, V. Seymour. *Canadian Public Policy and Administration*. Toronto: McGraw-Hill Ryerson, 1981.

Critiques and Theories of Bureaucracy

Albrow, Martin. *Bureaucracy*. London: Macmillan, 1970.

Blau, Peter M., and Marshall W. Meyer. *Bureaucracy in Modern Society*. 2nd ed. New York: Random House 1971.

Blau, Peter M., and Richard W. Scott. *Formal Organizations*. San Francisco: Chandler, 1962.

Burnham, James. *The Managerial Revolution*. Middlesex: Penguin Books, 1962.

Crozier, Michael. *The Bureaucratic Phenomenon*. Chicago: University of Chi-cago Press, 1964.

Downs, Anthony. *Inside Bureaucracy*. Boston: Little, Brown, 1967.

Friedman, Milton. *Capitalism and Freedom*. Chicago: University of Chicago Press, 1962.

Friedman, Milton. "The Threat to Freedom in the Welfare State." *Business and Society Review* (Spring 1977): 8–16.

Goodsell, Charles T. *The Case for Bureaucracy*. 2nd ed. Chatham, New Jersey: Chatham House, 1985.

Hayek, Frederich A. *The Road to Serfdom*. Chicago: University of Chicago Press, 1944.

Hummel, Ralph P. *The Bureaucratic Experience*. New York: St. Martin's Press, 1977.

Merton, Robert K., et al., eds. *Reader in Bureaucracy*. Glencoe, Illinois: The Free Press, 1953.

Michels, Robert. *Political Parties*. Translated by E. and C. Paul. London: Jarrold, 1915.

Morstein Marx, F. *The Administrative State*. Chicago: University of Chicago Press, 1957.

Mouzelis, Nicos P. *Organisation and Bureaucracy: An Analysis of Modern Theories*. Chicago: Aldine, 1968.

Perrow, Charles. *Complex Organizations: A Critical Essay*. 2nd ed. Glenview, Ill.: Scott, Foresman, 1979.

Thompson, Victor A. *Modern Organization*. New York: Knopf, 1961.

Thompson, Victor A. *Bureaucracy and the Modern World*. Morristown, N.J.: General Learning Press, 1976.

Weber, Max. *From Max Weber: Essays in Sociology*. Edited and translated by H. H. Gerth and C. Wright Mills. New York: Oxford University Press, 1946.

Weber, Max. *The Theory of Social and Economic Organization*. Translated by A. M. Henderson and Talcott Parsons. Fair Lawn, N.J.: Oxford University Press, 1947.

Weber Max. *Economy and Society*. New York: Bedminister Press, 1968.

2

Public Administration and Organization Theory: The Structural Foundation

Organizations have existed for a very long time. The first cave-dwellers who decided to join forces and divide responsibilities to improve their chances in hunting wild animals probably created the first organization. Given this lengthy history of organization in general, it is surprising that bureaucracy as we know it today has had a relatively short history. As noted in Chapter 1, bureaucratic forms existed as early as ancient China and in the medieval Roman Catholic Church. While these organizations had certain characteristics in common with modern forms of bureaucracy, they all lacked one or more of the essential attributes usually found in modern bureaucracies. This chapter and the next will discuss a number of theories which have been used to explain bureaucracy or to attempt to improve its operation. The approach will be roughly chronological, beginning with the earliest theorists and moving in the next chapter to some contemporary writers.

It is useful to begin by explaining why something which sounds as dry and other-worldly as organization theory is worth studying. Frequently, theory is contrasted with action, and not surprisingly, most managers seem to prefer the latter and disdain the former. This is unfortunate because it masks a very important consideration. Every member of society approaches organizations, fellow members of society, and tasks to be accomplished with a particular bundle of attitudes. Most people would be surprised to think of those attitudes as constituting a theory of organization, but they do. Whether we realize it or not, commonly heard conventional expressions such as, "If I didn't watch my employees all the time, they'd just goof off," or "My boss treats me like a child; if he just let me decide how I wanted to do the work, I could do it much better," are really important parts of rather highly developed organizational theories. The problem with disparaging any systematic study of good theory is that members of organizations hold attitudes which are theories and which they use in the operation of their organizations. This chapter will discuss some of the early theories of organization to provide the basis for some of the more modern theories studied in the next chapter. However, the theories studied in this chapter are also important in their own right because they provide a good description of the manner in which modern bureaucracy works.

MAX WEBER AND CLASSICAL BUREAUCRATIC THEORY

It would be difficult to locate the first bureaucratic organization, but the most noted person who systematically studied the emerging phenomenon of bureaucracy was Max Weber (1864–1920). As explained in the previous chapter, Weber was a brilliant scholar whose interests spanned many fields. The first chapter dealt with his views on the role of bureaucracy in society; this chapter will focus mainly on his discussion of the internal organization of bureaucracies.

The Characteristics of Weberian Bureaucracy

Weber's empirical study of the German bureaucracy suggested to him that the modern bureaucratic form consisted of a number of interrelated characteristics. When these characteristics were all combined in the same organization, this resulted in what he called the "ideal-type" bureaucracy. The main components of this "ideal-type" were:[1]

• hierarchical structure;
• unity of command;
• specialization of labour;
• employment and promotion based on merit;
• full-time employment;
• decisions based on impersonal rules;
• importance of written files; and
• bureaucratic employment totally separate from the bureaucrat's private life.

Hierarchical structure. A bureaucratic organization is arranged in a series of superior-subordinate relationships, at the pinnacle of which is one, and only one, superior. Thus Weber identified what is now a commonplace characteristic of an organizational chart. He further pointed out that this hierarchy required a clear division of duties among the various individuals within the organization. In particular, it required *unity of command*, which means that for each position in the hierarchy, there was one, and only one, supervisor. The clear line of authority produced by unity of command was one reason why Weber felt that bureaucracy was more efficient than previous forms of organization, but there were other reasons for this belief as well.

Specialization of labour. The purpose of the hierarchical structure was to allocate responsibilities to subordinates in a clear and unambiguous fashion. The significance of this division of responsibilities is that a person will become very efficient when he or she can concentrate on a specific job. Writing a century before Weber, Adam Smith opened his classic *The Wealth of Nations* with the argument that:

> The greatest improvement in the productive powers of labour, and the greater part of the skill, dexterity, and judgment with which it is any where

---

[1]Weber's famous discourse on bureaucracy, originally published in his *Wirtschaft und Gesellschaft*, has been translated and published in many places, but one of the most commonly cited references is *From Max Weber: Essays in Sociology*, ed. and trans. H. H. Gerth and C. Wright Mills (New York: Oxford University Press, 1946), pp. 196–244.

[sic] directed, or applied, seem to have been the effects of the division of labour.[2]

Smith then explained how the employees of a pin factory had increased their output 240-fold by moving from individual production to specialization of labour. However, specialization of labour is not enough if the employees are not qualified to perform the work.

Employment and promotion based on merit. In earlier times people often obtained organizational positions through either heredity or outright purchase. Obviously, this method of staffing provided no guarantee that the person in a particular position was the best person for the job, or even a competent one. Without some assurance of competence, no organization could operate in an efficient manner. In the German bureaucracy which Weber studied, employment and promotion based on an objective test of merit provided this assurance and, therefore, increased the efficiency of operation.

Full-time employment. An important principle related to employment based on merit was that employment in the bureaucracy was the full-time activity and major source of income of the official. This ensured that the official would develop allegiance to the bureaucracy and that the bureaucrat's hierarchical superior could exercise real *control* over the day-to-day activities of the official. The superior needed effective control to force the subordinate to abide by organizational regulations in the carrying out of his or her duties. This led to another important characteristic of modern bureaucracy.

Decisions based on impersonal rules. Bureaucrats are bound by certain rules in dealing with the public. These rules are "impersonal" in the sense that they apply equally to all clients in a similar situation. Thus, bureaucrats cannot properly substitute their own set of rules for those legitimately proclaimed by superiors. If a particular benefit is to be provided without regard to race or religion, then a member of a bureaucracy would risk severe penalties if he or she allowed personal prejudice to affect the decision made. Reliance on impersonal rules in dealings between the bureaucracy and the general public increases confidence in the bureaucracy by establishing a regime of certainty in dealings.

Importance of written files. The importance of these rules leads to the importance of written files. If the bureaucrat must prove that he or she has abided by the rules in making decisions, then it is important to maintain written records, first, of the rules themselves, and then of all decisions made and the rationale for those decisions. It is worth noting here that the bureaucrat's allegiance to the rules takes precedence over allegiance to his or her superior. A superior can exercise judgement in an area that is unclear under the rules, but he or she cannot order a subordinate to violate those rules.

Bureaucratic employment is totally separate from the individual bureaucrat's private life. This is a recognition both of the autonomous nature of the bureaucracy as an organization and of the fact that the bureaucrat does not "own" his or her position and the rights which go with it. Bureaucrats possess very power-

---

[2]*An Inquiry into the Nature and Causes of the Wealth of Nations*, R. H. Campbell and W. B. Todd, eds. (Oxford: Clarendon Press, 1976), p. 13.

ful authority. In the case of members of a government bureaucracy, this could be highly coercive authority. However, it is always clear that that power attaches to the position, rather than to the individual. This was not a distinction that was always obvious among members of the monarch's retinue in pre-bureaucratic times. An obvious result of this division is that the bureaucrat is not permitted to obtain any personal gain, other than a fixed salary, from his or her position.

Weber seems to have had a rather difficult love-hate relationship with this new organizational form called bureaucracy. As a serious, objective scholar, he documented the characteristics of the German bureaucracy as he saw them without favourable or critical comment. Beyond that, he seems to have been of two minds about bureaucracy. On the one hand, he argued that bureaucracy was the most efficient method of organization — a position for which he has been attacked by some contemporary critics. In fairness to Weber, he was likely suggesting that bureaucracy was more efficient than any *previous* system — an argument which would be difficult to refute. However, Weber did foresee many of the problems which contemporary critics find in bureaucracy.

> This passion for bureaucratization . . . is enough to drive one to despair. It is . . . as though we knowingly and willingly were *supposed* to become men who need "order" and nothing but order, who become nervous and cowardly if this order shakes for a moment and helpless when they are torn from their exclusive adaptation to this order. That the world knows nothing more than such men of order — we are in any case caught up in this development, and the central question is not how we further and accelerate it but what we have to *set against* this machinery, in order to preserve a remnant of humanity from this parcelling-out of the soul, from this exclusive rule of bureaucratic life ideals.[3]

In this quotation, Weber touched upon the crucial aspects of bureaucracy which still confound us today. On the one hand, it seems to be the most efficient way of arranging a large number of offices and accomplishing complex, repetitive tasks. But, on the other hand, we condemn the impersonal, mind-numbing aspects of its operation.

Criticisms of Weber

The general criticism of Weber's work is that he dwelt too much on the structural aspects of bureaucracy and not enough on the human side of organization. It is suggested that because Weber viewed bureaucrats as mere cogs in the mechanism, he both overstated the efficiency of bureaucracy and overlooked the effect which it would have on its members.

Robert Merton was concerned about the effect which the Weberian "ideal-type" of bureaucracy would ultimately have on the personality of the individual bureaucrat. He noted that situations occurred in which the application of general rules to the specific case produced either inefficient results or results which

[3]*Gesammelte Aufsatze zur Sozial und Wissenschaftslehre*, as quoted in Arthur Mitzman, *The Iron Cage: A Historical Interpretation of Max Weber* (New York: Alfred A. Knopf, 1970), p. 178. (Emphasis in Mitzman.)

seemed unfair to the client. In this situation, the Weberian bureaucrat must either abide by the general rule and produce an undesirable result or violate the rule and produce a desirable result. The bureaucrat who really values his or her career has little choice but to follow the rules. Thus, there is an inevitable tendency towards "an over-concern with strict adherence to regulations which induce timidity, conservatism, and technicism."[4]

Philip Selznick questioned the presumed efficiency of Weberian bureaucracy. He argued that the informal system of worker relationships could be just as important and influential as the formal system established in the rules of the organization.[5] To illustrate this point, he first distinguished between professed and operational goals. The professed goals are the original, overarching goals of the organization as a whole. The operational goals relate to the day-to-day functions and needs of the workers within the organization. He gave the example of a boys' reformatory which had adopted progressive ideals of rehabilitation as its professed goal, but continually slipped into the use of such techniques as discipline, regimentation, and spying to solve its practical, day-to-day problems. Thus, operational goals can easily diverge from professed goals and so weaken the efficiency of the organization.

He suggested that these two kinds of goals can come into play in any case where there is delegation of function — an important part of bureaucratic operation. This delegation has a tendency to create a "*bifurcation of interest* between the initiator of the action and the agent employed."[6] The initiator wants a particular thing done in a particular manner (the professed goal), but the agent who must deal with practical problems frequently is unable to do exactly what is desired and so must do something else instead (the operational goal). This raises the question of *control*, which Weber implies is automatically attained, as a very serious issue. The initiator will not always be able to control absolutely the agent. The struggle for control leads to the creation of an informal system in which rank and file workers interact to attempt to control their work environment and fend off any capricious demands of senior officials.

In another of his works, Selznick provided a second, related criticism of the classical notion of the efficiency of bureaucracy. He argued that the division of labour which Weber thought was so beneficial could become detrimental because it establishes separate units with their own goals which might not be consistent with the goals of the organization as a whole. This divergence of goals then sets up the possibility of conflict and competition within the organization.[7]

Warren G. Bennis and Philip E. Slater take a radical stance in arguing that bureaucracy is currently outmoded as a form of organization.[8] They suggest

---

[4]Robert K. Merton, "Bureaucratic Structure and Personality," *Social Forces*, vol. 18 (May 1940), p. 564.

[5]"An Approach to the Theory of Bureaucracy," *American Sociological Review*, vol. 8 (February 1943), pp. 47–54.

[6]Ibid., p. 51. (Emphasis in original.)

[7]*TVA and the Grass Roots* (New York: Harper & Row, 1966), p. 256 and passim.

[8]*The Temporary Society* (New York: Harper & Row, 1968), ch. 3.

that modern trends such as rapid change and the increasing professionalization of the workforce make bureaucracy with its emphasis on rigid rules and hierarchy of control obsolete.

The next chapter examines contemporary theories of organization which purport to maintain the positive aspects of bureaucracy and circumvent its less desirable aspects. However, it is useful first to examine an American contemporary of Weber who was also very influential in the study of organizations.

FREDERICK W. TAYLOR AND SCIENTIFIC MANAGEMENT

Max Weber was a philosopher who could stand at arm's length from organizations and describe in broad terms their general characteristics. By contrast, Frederick Winslow Taylor (1856–1915) was a mechanical engineer who began his career working as a technician on the factory floor and spent much of his later working life in either a supervisory or advisory capacity dealing with problems of production management. His major concern was the proper arrangement of the human and mechanical resources of the factory so as to minimize waste, particularly waste of workers' time.

Taylor's experience in the factory showed him that a great deal of "soldiering," i.e., slacking off, was taking place, and that there were two reasons for this. One was what he regarded as the natural tendency of employees to do as little work as possible. The second was that work was sometimes arranged in such an awkward manner that no reasonable human being, regardless of how ambitious or honest he or she was, could physically perform what was expected by superiors. Since "soldiering" constituted the squandering of a national resource, it was important for management to end it. Taylor argued that the increased productivity that would result would benefit both employers and employees.

The employee's natural tendency towards soldiering could be eliminated if the employer used scientific methods rather than "rule-of-thumb" methods to determine an employee's appropriate workload. Some "soldiering" was caused by the employee's rational reaction to the method of piece-work payment which was prevalent in Taylor's time. Employees knew that in the short run they could earn more by working hard and producing above standard, but they realized that in the long run this was counter-productive because employers simply raised the standard. Therefore, it was better to work at a steady pace and receive adequate pay than to be a "rate-buster." The basic problem was that employers had no idea what an employee *could* do in an average shift. Therefore, most employers used rules of thumb to establish standards, and so did not have the confidence of their employees. The obvious solution to the problem was to establish *scientific standards* based on the proven physical capacities of workers and then refrain from adjusting those standards arbitrarily.

Taylor's usual approach in establishing these scientific standards was to select employees who performed a particular task exceptionally well, i.e., moving the most pig iron, shovelling the most coal. Then, a trained management employee would carefully scrutinize the actions of these employees, watching and *timing* their every movement. This was the beginning of the time and motion study which has stirred so much controversy on factory floors. The purpose of these studies was to learn from the most efficient employees the ideal method of performing a particular task. This is the "one best way" employed by Frank and Lillian Gilbreth and popularized with humorous effect by their children in the book and movie *Cheaper by the Dozen*.[9] When the best set of physical motions was determined, then it was the responsibility of certain managers to teach this technique to all employees.

The second cause of "soldiering" was the simple inability of workers to maintain the pace which was expected of them because of the manner in which the work was organized. Taylor pointed out that workers could be more productive if management took greater care in organizing the work. He laid particular emphasis on things such as determining the optimal working rhythm necessary to maximize output. The next time you are working in the garden or shovelling snow it might be useful to know that, according to Taylor, the greatest tonnage per day can be shovelled when the worker moves twenty-one pounds on each shovel load.[10]

Taylor felt that it was important to have a clear division of duties between management and labour. It was the job of management to select employees for specific jobs in a scientific manner so that the physical and mental characteristics of the individual fit the job, and then it was the role of management to teach labourers the optimum way to perform their duties. It was the job of labourers to supply strong backs, but since in Taylor's mind a strong back connoted a weak mind, it would be impossible for labourers to arrange their own duties.

Taylor also emphasized the importance of financial factors as a motivating force. However, he eschewed the crude principle of piece-work, because he knew that workers could easily manipulate the standard. Instead, he singled out the best workers for the privilege of working in a higher-paid group. By examining their actions as described above, he was able to determine in a scientific manner how much work should be accomplished. In one experiment, workers who had met the standard in their previous day's work were given white slips at the beginning of their next shift, while those who had not were given yellow slips. Those receiving yellow slips obviously did not understand fully how their job should be done, so it was the responsibility of management to provide additional training. The consistent receipt of yellow slips would cause one's return to the lower-paid gang.[11] This was Taylor's method of using financial incentives without the drawbacks identified with piece-work.

Some writers suggest that Taylor showed a lack of concern for the workers. It is clear that he saw management as very enlightened and he viewed workers in a

---

[9]Frank B. Gilbreth, Jr. and Ernestine Gilbreth Carey, *Cheaper by the Dozen* (New York: Thomas Y. Crowell, 1948).

[10]Frederick Winslow Taylor, *The Principles of Scientific Management* (New York: W. W. Norton, 1967), p. 65.

[11]Ibid., pp. 67–68.

rather condescending manner. This attitude is exemplified in unintended humour in this quotation:

> Now one of the very first requirements for a man who is fit to handle pig iron as a regular occupation is that he shall be so stupid and so phlegmatic that he more nearly resembles in his mental make-up the ox than any other type. . . . Therefore the workman who is best suited to handling pig iron is unable to understand the real science of doing this class of work. He is so stupid that the word "percentage" has no meaning to him, and he must consequently be trained by a man more intelligent than himself into the habit of working in accordance with the laws of this science before he can be successful.[12]

Given this attitude, it is not surprising that Mr. Taylor was once advised by some of his employees that it might be unsafe for him to take a particular route home in the evening.[13]

However, Taylor did strive for harmony between management and workers, and he was sensitive to the need not to alienate unions. He always argued that cooperation was the best way to maximize productivity — but one gets the impression that it would be cooperation on management's terms. Furthermore, he was strongly opposed to overworking employees in sweat-shop conditions. Although this might well have been more for reasons of productivity than humanity, it apparently was still a fairly radical idea for his time.

Taylor did not confine his emphasis on improvement and innovation simply to the factory floor. An avid tennis player, he and Clarence M. Clark won the first United States Lawn Tennis Association doubles championship in 1881. Not content to just play the game, he also invented an improved tennis net and the sprocket device which is still used to tighten the net. These changes were quickly accepted, but his spoon-shaped racket was just as quickly made the subject of ridicule.[14]

However, his main leisure-time activity was the rehabilitation of the old estate near Philadelphia where he went into semi-retirement at the age of forty-five. His main accomplishment on the estate was the successful transplanting of twelve hundred feet of a hundred-year-old box hedge. He did this by designing a mechanism to go under the root system and lift entire sections of the hedge — roots, soil, and all — and move them. Each section was thirty feet long, nine feet wide, six feet high, and weighed thirty tons.[15] This was not just idle self-indulgence on the part of a rich man. This same principle is still employed by highways departments to save large trees in the path of road construction.

Taylor's main contribution to organization theory was his emphasis on the scientific approach to work management — the "one best way" — and his emphasis

---

[12]Ibid., p. 59.
[13]Ibid., pp. 51–52. See also, Frank Barkely Copley, *Frederick W. Taylor: Father of Scientific Management* (New York: Augustus M. Kelley, 1969), vol. 1, pp. 166–167.
[14]Copley, op. cit., vol. 1, p. 143.
[15]Ibid., vol. 2, p. 191 ff.

on the important role of management in organizing the work. However, there were certain problems with the manner in which Taylor's ideas were implemented. Management, in some cases, used time and motion studies to attempt to extract the maximum possible production from workers. This led to worker resistance to the entire concept. The idea of the narrow subdivision of work into its smallest components created monotony, which led to further unrest on the part of workers. All of these problems in the application — some might say misapplication — of Taylor's ideas became evident eventually, but not before his ideas were tried in a number of places, including the Canadian federal government.

THE CANADIAN EXPERIENCE: FROM PATRONAGE TO MERIT

The Canadian federal government gradually began adopting some of Taylor's ideas as an expedient in moving from a patronage-based public service to a merit-based one, thus simultaneously moving also towards the Weberian concept of bureaucracy.

The Civil Service Commission (CSC) was established in 1908 to act as guardian of the merit principle. The CSC was the outgrowth of a number of reports which indicated that the prevalence of patronage appointments in the Canadian civil service was having a detrimental impact on its efficiency. The CSC began the process of entrenching the merit principle by administering competitive examinations for applicants for government positions. However, it soon discovered that a serious problem existed in that the duties of specific positions within the departments were usually not well defined. Without a clear delineation of duties associated with a position, a meaningful competitive examination was somewhat problematic.

Gradually the powers and responsibilities of the CSC evolved until in 1918 it was given the power to actually make appointments and to reorganize departments, whether this was sought by the department or not. This legislation seemed to be influenced by officials of the CSC who were in turn influenced by the principles of scientific management which were so prevalent at the time.[16]

The commissioners and the executive secretary of the CSC hired the American consulting firm of Arthur Young & Co. to introduce the principles of scientific management into the Canadian federal government. The exercise began with the systematic description and classification of fifty thousand positions. The positions had to be described in great detail because this was the starting point for the mechanistic process of matching the person possessing the proper qualifications with the appropriate position. The next step was to be a sweeping reorganization of the entire governmental bureaucratic apparatus, which involved streamlining and reducing the number of departments and agencies. Obviously, the idea of government reform is not as radical and new as some think.

Arthur Young & Co.'s involvement became bogged down in a series of problems, and as a result the reorganization did not occur. The sole but significant

[16]J. E. Hodgetts, et al., *The Biography of an Institution* (Montreal: McGill-Queen's University Press, 1972), ch. 4.

result of the exercise was an extensive and systematic classification of all government positions. Not everyone was pleased with the result. The basis of the scientific management approach to job classification was that it was possible to match
in a mechanical fashion the skills required in a particular job with the skills
possessed by a particular person. When the match was complete, presumably
the process would be like plugging the appropriate size plug into a wall socket — an
automatic perfect connection which would last until it was unplugged. Not everyone was impressed by the neatness of this arrangement. For example, R. McGregor
Dawson observed:

> All positions are deemed to call for special talents, and each is filled through
> an examination of its own designed to test those special qualifications. But
> therein lies its basic weakness. Some civil servants — a plumber, a chemist,
> a stenographer, an entomologist, an accountant, an engineer — should
> unquestionably be chosen because of the special knowledge or skill which
> they happen to possess at the moment of their candidature; but for others,
> such as a clerical or administrative official, the knowledge of their duties
> which they might have at entrance is comparatively unimportant. The really
> vital question is their inherent ability and what they will be capable of doing
> after they have been trained by years of experience in the department.[17]

The above words could have been written as easily in 1986 as they were in
1936. The classification system has undergone a number of thorough revisions
since the original exercise. The most recent was in the late 1960s in preparation
for the beginning of collective bargaining. However, each revision has brought
forth complaints about the complexity and inflexibility of the system. As will be
discussed in Chapter 21, some flexibility has been introduced into the most senior
layer of positions, but for the vast majority of positions below these, the job
description and classification process is still the spiritual successor of the original Arthur Young work.

At roughly the same time that Taylor and consultants such as Arthur Young
were concerned with the classification and arrangement of individual jobs, there
was a movement afoot to consider broader questions of the appropriate overall
structure of organizations.

GULICK AND URWICK AND THE SCIENTIFIC
THEORY OF ORGANIZATION

In the 1930s in the United States, the work of the President's Committee on
Administrative Management spurred a great deal of interest in trying to develop a
scientific theory of organization. Taylor's work dealt with how to organize the
work on the factory floor, but people such as Luther Gulick and Lyndall Urwick
were concerned with developing broader theories about the ideal structure for

---

[17]R. McGregor Dawson, "The Canadian Civil Service," *Canadian Journal of Economics and Political Science*, vol. 2 (August 1936), p. 293.

any organization. Their basic concerns were span of control and the proper alignment of related functions.

The Scientific Theory of Organization

Span of control refers to the number of subordinates who report to one supervisor. There has long been controversy about what that ideal number should be. From the standpoint of adequacy of supervision, obviously the smaller the span of control the better, but too narrow a span of control leads to too many supervisors and too much overhead.

This point is illustrated in Figure 2.1, which compares two different organizations, both of which have sixty-four production workers. In Figure 2.1a, the span of control in every case is four. This narrow span of control results in a total organization of eighty-five employees with two intermediate levels of management between the chief executive and the workers. In Figure 2.1b, the span of control is eight. This results in a total of seventy-three employees and only one intermediate level of management between the chief executive and the workers. In the latter case, not only are there fewer total employees and therefore less cost, but also the presence of only one intermediate level of management makes communication considerably easier. However, the intangible cost in following this route is that supervisors cannot supervise eight people as closely as they can four. This could lead to production problems. McLaren points out the nature of this dilemma quite well:

> Small spans of control may appear to tighten control for the superior-subordinate relationship, but they loosen the overall control of the organization by extending the number of levels and thereby making the top that much more removed from the bottom. To cut down on the number of levels will reduce the distance between top and bottom, but the resulting increase in the span of control at each level will lessen the control that each level can maintain.[18]

The question as to the appropriate span of control is still answered much as it was in Gulick and Urwick's time: It all depends. It depends on the interaction of several things:

- the nature of the work supervised (routine procedures allow for a broader span of control, but supervision of several heterogeneous activities requires a narrower span of control);
- the level of training of the subordinates;
- the extent of geographical decentralization of the work; and
- the overall stability of the organization.[19]

Aside from span of control, Gulick and Urwick were concerned with the problem of the ideal arrangement of duties within the organization. They argued

---

[18]Robert I. McLaren, *Organizational Dilemmas* (Chichester, U.K.: Wiley & Sons, 1982), pp. 45–46.

[19]Luther Gulick, "Notes on the Theory of Organization," in Luther Gulick and L. Urwick, eds., *Papers on the Science of Administration* (New York: Augustus M. Kelley, 1969), pp. 7–9.

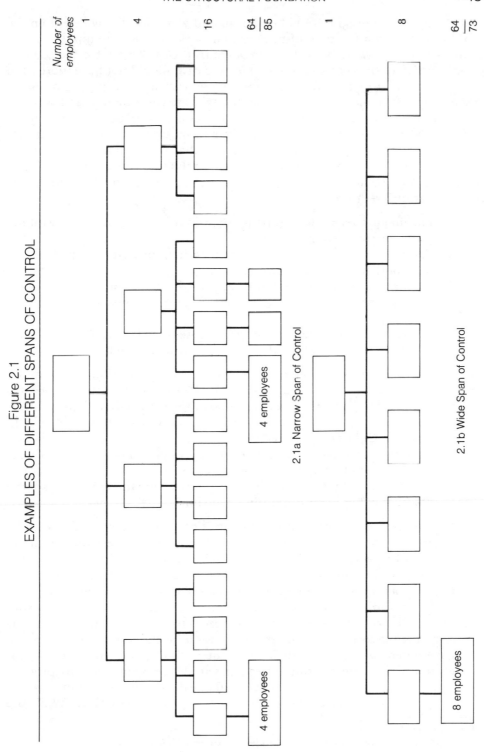

Figure 2.1
EXAMPLES OF DIFFERENT SPANS OF CONTROL

2.1a Narrow Span of Control

2.1b Wide Span of Control

that the process of organizational design should work simultaneously from the top-down and from the bottom-up.[20] When working from the top-down, the primary criterion was to limit the span of control. Gulick reflected the conventional wisdom of the time that the senior executive should not have more than three direct subordinates. Working from the bottom-up, the important factor was to combine homogeneous activities to facilitate coordination and supervision. The analyst then simply built in both directions until the two were joined.

The important point in working from the bottom-up was an appropriate definition of homogeneity. Obviously, it suggests that people doing similar work ought to be grouped together, but on further analysis this idea is more difficult to apply than it seems. Gulick suggested that each worker could be characterized in four different ways:

1. The major *purpose* he is serving, such as furnishing water, controlling crime, or conducting education;
2. The *process* he is using, such as engineering, medicine, carpentry, stenography, statistics, accounting;
3. The *persons or things* dealt with or served, such as immigrants, veterans, Indians, forests, mines, parks, orphans, farmers, automobiles, or the poor;
4. The *place* where he renders his service, such as Hawaii, Boston, Washington, the Dust Bowl, Alabama, or Central High School.[21]

In designing an organization, employees who had all four things in common would be grouped together in the same organizational unit. If an employee was different in one category — for example, if he or she worked in a slightly different location — then that would be some evidence that he or she ought to be in another unit, but Gulick emphasized the importance of pragmatism and judgement applied to individual cases. Where employees had only one or two things in common they would likely be in separate units.

Given that there are four possibilities, the question remains as to which of the four should be the dominant organizing principle.

> Each of the four basic systems of organization is intimately related with the other three, because in any enterprise all four elements are present in the doing of the work and are embodied in every individual workman. Each member of the enterprise is working for some major purpose, uses some process, deals with some person, and serves or works at some place.
>
> If an organization is erected about any one of these four characteristics of work, it becomes necessary to recognize the other characteristics in constructing the secondary and tertiary divisions of the work. For example, a government which is first divided on the basis of place will, in each geographical department, find it necessary to divide by purpose, by process, by clientele, or even again by place; and one divided in the first instance by purpose, may well be divided next by process and then by place. While the

---

[20]Ibid., pp. 11–12.
[21]Ibid., p. 15. (Emphasis in original.) Reproduced by permission.

first or primary division of any enterprise is of very great significance, it must none the less be said that there is no one most effective pattern for determining the priority and order for the introduction of these interdependent principles. It will depend in any case upon the results which are desired at a given time and place.[22]

For example, this problem comes up in a very practical way in deciding how to arrange the legal services function in a large, multi-function organization. If there is one legal department containing all lawyers, then that is a process form of organization. If instead the lawyers are divided and assigned to the units which handle the programs, then that is organization by purpose. At first glance, one arrangement seems to have as many advantages and disadvantages as the other. Gulick admitted that the lack of empirical evidence made serious discussion difficult, but he did suggest some of the pros and cons of each particular method of organization.[23]

It is often very difficult to resolve this question of the best method of organization. For example, in general it can be said that provincial governments are organized by purpose, i.e, departments of health, education, social assistance, and so forth. However, recently there has been a trend in some provinces to establish departments having a special mandate to look after the unique problems of the northern areas of those provinces. In some cases these new departments have some role in delivering the services provided by the "purpose" departments in the south, and in others they act as coordinating bodies. There is usually some tension between this new "place" department and the traditional "purpose" department over what the appropriate role of each ought to be.

Gulick also dealt with the appropriate activities of the executive. He argued that words like "administration" and "management" had lost their specific content. He felt that the job of the executive could be summed up by the acronym POSDCORB,[24] which stood for the following activities:

- planning;
- organizing;
- staffing;
- directing;
- coordinating;
- reporting;
- budgeting.

Carrying out all of these diverse functions as a part of managing a complex organization posed a very difficult problem, particularly as each of these functions was becoming more complex in itself. Urwick noted that one way in which many organizations were dealing with this problem was by the use of separate *line and staff functions*.[25] In some cases, it is difficult to define these terms precisely, but a line function is usually considered to be directly involved in produc-

---

[22]Ibid., pp. 31–32. Reproduced by permission.
[23]Ibid., pp. 21–30.
[24]Ibid., p. 13.
[25]"Organization as a Technical Problem," in ibid., pp. 47–88.

ing and distributing the goods or services provided by the organization. A classic example would be the manufacturing section of an industrial organization. Some typical examples in government would be public health nurses, social workers, or officers dealing directly with social assistance claimants. A staff function is a function which aids, advises, and supports the employees providing the line function, usually without dealing directly with the clients or output of the organization. The obvious examples are accounting, legal, and personnel services.

Some writers distinguish between three categories — line, staff, and auxiliary.[26] The basic difference is that auxiliary is used to refer to such repetitive, "housekeeping" kinds of activities as personnel and accounting, while staff refers to such non-repetitive functions as policy advice and coordination. This distinction has some value, but it can be difficult to make these kinds of distinctions in practice, which is probably the reason that one is more likely to see the two-fold distinction used in organizations.

When organizations are structured in this typical line-staff manner, the organization chart resembles Figure 2.2. Ideally, the two functions work together closely to further the objectives of the organization. The staff units can provide specialized advice to the line units about handling unusual situations. This means that line officers can concentrate on their standard repetitive tasks and do not have to be trained to cope with every eventuality. Another function frequently provided by staff employees is specialized record keeping. Again, this relieves the line officers of the responsibility for a routine, repetitive task and allows them to concentrate on their major function. Thus, one would expect a smooth, complementary relationship between these two functions, and in fact this is the case in many organizations.

When problems do crop up in the line-staff relationship they usually concern the answer to the question: Is the staff function a *service* or a *control* function? If the answer to the question is the ambiguous "yes" sometimes favoured by comedians, then there can be serious problems. The organization chart in Figure 2.2 illustrates that the presence of the staff function could lead to a violation of the principle of unity of command. The regional director in Halifax is responsible to the assistant deputy minister, field operations, for most things, but he or she is also responsible to the various staff officers for certain things as well. In some cases the staff department will render advice which the line department would rather not hear or act upon. Line officials argue that to carry out their duties appropriately, they cannot be constrained by the whims of some group that does not really understand the operation of the organization. The line manager might even point out the amount of profit or units of production which his or her unit has contributed to the organization and ask rhetorically how much the staff units have contributed.

The real problem for senior management arises from the fact that the staff unit usually has equally good arguments grounded in the long-term future good of the organization. For example, at the moment it might seem expedient to

---

[26]J. E. Hodgetts, *The Canadian Public Service: A Physiology of Government, 1867–1970* (Toronto: University of Toronto Press, 1973), ch. 9.

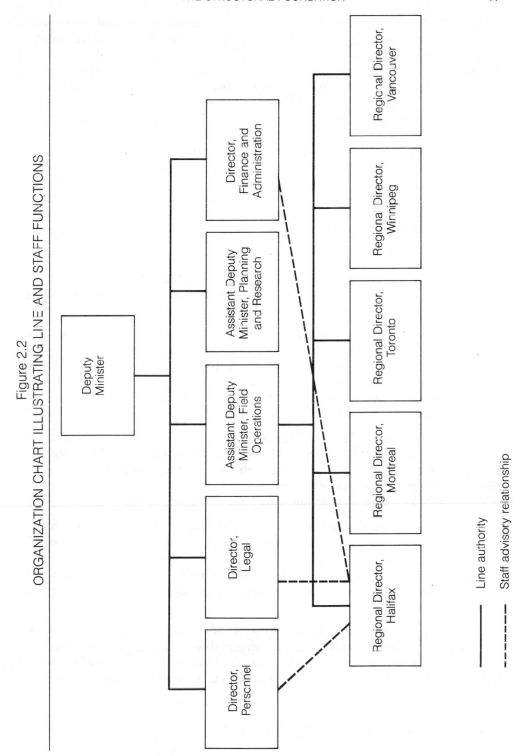

Figure 2.2
ORGANIZATION CHART ILLUSTRATING LINE AND STAFF FUNCTIONS

Deputy Minister

Director, Personnel

Director, Legal

Assistant Deputy Minister, Field Operations

Assistant Deputy Minister, Planning and Research

Director, Finance and Administration

Regional Director, Halifax

Regional Director, Montreal

Regional Director, Toronto

Regional Director, Winnipeg

Regional Director, Vancouver

——— Line authority

- - - - Staff advisory relationship

ignore the advice of the legal department, but this might prove short-sighted if in a few years the organization starts facing legal action. Organizations usually try to resolve this difficulty by establishing clear lines of authority and procedures to be followed in particular cases. The problem is that these procedures seldom anticipate every circumstance. Obviously, both line and staff functions are important in an organization. How well they work together is frequently what separates good organizations from those which simply limp along from one crisis to the next.

The contribution of Gulick and Urwick to organizational behaviour was the synthesis and dissemination of ideas which had been developed by other people. Nevertheless, these two men made a valuable contribution both in forcing others of their time to think about management in a systematic manner and in beginning to set out certain principles — many of which are still seen as beneficial guides to action today. However, not everyone treated these scientific principles with reverence.

Herbert Simon and the Proverbs of Administration

Herbert Simon is a prolific writer on many topics of administration. One of his most widely quoted passages deals with the scientific principles of administration:

> It is a fatal defect of the current principles of administration that, like proverbs, they occur in pairs. For almost every principle one can find an equally plausible and acceptable contradictory principle. Although the two principles of the pair will lead to exactly opposite organizational recommendations, there is nothing in the theory to indicate which is the proper one to apply.[27]

One commonly heard example of this kind of problematic pair of proverbs is: "Look before you leap" and "He who hesitates is lost." If the so-called scientific principles of management could be seen to have similar flaws, then their continued validity was in doubt.

One example Simon gives is the juxtaposition of two principles:

> Administrative efficiency is supposed to be enhanced by limiting the number of subordinates who report directly to any one administrator to a small number — say six. . . .
>
> Administrative efficiency is enhanced by keeping at a minimum the number of organizational levels through which a matter must pass before it is acted upon.[28]

Obviously, it cannot be both ways. Earlier in this chapter, Figure 2.1 demonstrated that a narrow span of control always results in a large number of layers in the organization. A truly scientific principle of management would not leave one with this sort of dilemma. If the solution to this conundrum is that one must

---

[27]*Administrative Behavior* (New York: The Free Press, 1957), p. 20.
[28]Ibid., p. 26.

exercise judgement and discretion in achieving a blend of the two rules, then the rules are not very scientific.

Simon saves most of his attack for the idea of organizing by purpose, process, people, or place. He points out that not only is the overall idea contradictory in that one of the four must take precedence, but that the concepts themselves are somewhat fuzzier than Gulick had suggested so that some of them shade into one another.

Presumably, the rebuttal could be made here that Simon is being too fussy. The principles are simply guides to action; they are considerations to be taken into account before acting. They are used to shape our judgement and guide our discretion. The rebuttal might well be valid, but the crucial point is: If judgement and discretion are so important in applying these principles, then can they really be called "scientific"?

Simon's solution recognizes this point. He argues that these ideas should not be discarded because all of them have real value in certain cases. The trick is to find the proper combination of them that works in different cases. To accomplish this, Simon argues that good empirical work on the efficiency of existing organizations is needed more than additional theoretical mulling.

CENTRALIZATION/DECENTRALIZATION

Gulick and Urwick's discussion of methods of organization opened the way for a serious discussion of an issue of major significance in the Canadian environment. Decentralization of government services is a very important issue in a country as large and heterogeneous as Canada. The size and diversity of most provinces, and even some of our larger cities, makes it an issue in provincial and municipal governments as well.

An important distinction must be made between decentralization and deconcentration. The difference between the two lies in the amount of real decision-making authority which is vested in the outlying unit. *Decentralization* suggests a vesting of real discretionary authority in the outlying unit. In some cases this might mean that the unit will also be physically removed from the centre to facilitate an understanding of local conditions, but physical dispersal is not a prerequisite for decentralization. *Deconcentration*, on the other hand, suggests a physical dispersal of members of the organization with only very limited delegation of decision-making authority. Obviously, the line between the two is sometimes unclear. Even in deconcentration there is virtually always some limited amount of discretion vested in field officials, just as in decentralization there are always some kinds of decisions which can only be made after consultation with head office. It is sometimes the case that authority to deal with matters of an operational nature will be decentralized, while matters of a policy or program nature will be retained within the control of head office.

It is probably the large size and diversity of Canada which usually causes Canadians to think of decentralization in terms of the physical dispersal of operating units. This is one entirely appropriate use of the term, but it has a more general meaning as well. Geographic decentralization is decentralization by place, but decentralization can also be based on any of Gulick and Urwick's other classical methods for organization — process, purpose, or people.[29] Even an organization with all of its divisions located in the same building can be decentralized, if real decision-making authority is vested in each of the separate units. Within the federal government, a similar situation exists in the Ministry of Transport. The air, land, and marine units of the ministry operate quite independently of one another even though their headquarters are all in the same building.

More than two-thirds of federal employees in regular government departments work outside the National Capital Region (that is, the Ottawa-Hull area). These employees are spread across the vast expanse of Canada in field units that vary greatly in purpose, size, and organization. This deconcentration of the federal government's operations is essential to the successful development and implementation of its policies and programs.

The present balance in each department or agency between the number and level of employees at headquarters and in the field is a culmination of the interplay over more than a century of political, administrative, economic, and geographical factors. In the earliest days of the Canadian federation, it was necessary to establish outposts for such government services as the post office and customs. The subsequent geographical dispersal of the public service is a complicated story of government response to the challenge of providing a broad range of services to a population spread across a continent. Virtually all government departments now have field units of substantial but differing size. In late 1983, the percentage of employees located outside the National Capital Region ranged from 0.4 per cent in Finance and 14.4 per cent in Energy, Mines and Resources to 87.7 per cent in Fisheries and Oceans and 88.4 per cent in Employment and Immigration.[30]

Whether this represents decentralization or deconcentration, the basic problem remains the same. There needs to be a balance between *accountability* to rules specified in head office and *responsiveness* to regional needs. Officials in the field always feel two contradictory pulls. On the one hand, the rules and procedures set out by head office must be followed. On the other hand, field workers are sufficiently close to clientele in their everyday work that they frequently perceive an injustice in the manner in which the general rule must be applied to the specific case. The pressures to bend the rule are sometimes irresistible.

From the standpoint of head office, the problem is to maintain mechanisms to ensure that officials in the field are complying with head office rules and procedures without unnecessarily restricting the freedom of field officials to be responsive to local conditions. After all, it is these officials who are closest to the situation and are most knowledgeable about what should be done. However, they cannot be given carte blanche to do whatever they like without regard to the overall objectives of the department.

---

[29]McLaren points out that decentralization can occur in several dimensions. *Organizational Dilemmas*, ch. 2.

[30]These percentages were calculated on the basis of data provided by the Public Service Commission of Canada.

In balancing accountability and responsiveness, it can be argued that deconcentration is most likely to promote accountability, while decentralization is most likely to promote responsiveness. However, the real problem in organizations is to balance accountability and responsiveness so that both of these important principles are maintained in adequate amounts.

Specific approaches to departmental decentralization in Canada will be discussed in Chapter 6, but at this point it is worth considering the general form which decentralization or deconcentration can take. In any organization serving a large geographic area, there must be some form of decentralization. Oversimplifying somewhat, this decentralization can take one of two forms. Figure 2.3 illustrates the two possibilities for an organization carrying out three different functions across the country.[31]

Figure 2.3a illustrates decentralization by place. This style of decentralization is more likely to be true decentralization rather than deconcentration. In this case there is one main office in each region, and that office is subdivided based on the three functions. This kind of structure will tend to improve coordination between the three functions within each region. Because of this ease of coordination and because of the orientation towards place, the regional office of an organization of this kind is likely to be highly responsive to the needs of its geographic area. In fact, with this kind of structure there is usually some concern that officials will become too sensitive to their geographic area and possibly deviate from the national objectives of their programs. For this reason, there is usually a group of staff advisors in head office who have some sort of functional authority over the people delivering the programs in the regional offices. This is illustrated by the dotted lines in Figure 2.3a. This is necessary to ensure uniformity of the programs across the country. However, it can create the sort of line-staff problems discussed earlier in this chapter. In sum, the strong points of this form of organization are good coordination within each region and responsiveness to regional needs. The weak points are possible departures from national objectives and a complex form of organization.

Figure 2.3b illustrates decentralization based on purpose, although this same form would also be applicable to decentralization based on process or people. This form is more likely to result in deconcentration than decentralization. In this case, the primary division is by purpose, with the managers of each function remaining in head office. Within each branch there is a subdivision by region, although the geographic areas covered by the regions are not necessarily the same for each branch. This reflects the fact that some programs might be relatively more important in certain areas of the country than in others. Because each branch and each regional office specialize in providing only one function, it is relatively easy to ensure uniformity of administration across the entire country and to accomplish this without the awkward organizational structure required in the case of decentralization by place. The strong points of this style of organization are the simpler form of organization and the uniformity of administra-

---

[31]McLaren's enlightening treatment takes a slightly different approach, but deals with the same issues. *Organizational Dilemmas*, pp. 12-17.

Figure 2.3
TWO TYPES OF ORGANIZATIONAL STRUCTURES

2 possibilities for one organization carrying out 3 different functions.

2.3a Organization by Place

2.3b Organization by Purpose

tion of the program across the country. Its weak points are a lack of coordination of the programs at the regional level and a weaker responsiveness to regional needs.

The style of organization which is preferable depends upon the nature of the programs to be delivered and the need for regional responsiveness. If good coordination between programs at the regional level and a sensitivity to regional needs is important, then the preferable style is decentralization by place, as illustrated in Figure 2.3a. An example of this kind of program would be one aimed at regional economic development. Uniform administration across the country is less important than responsiveness to local conditions. On the other hand, if the uniform administration of the program across the country is more important than regional sensitivity, then deconcentration by program as illustrated in Figure 2.3b would be preferable. The word deconcentration is used here because, if there is uniformity of administration across the country, then, by definition, there will be little scope for decision making within each region. An example of this kind of organization would be a tax collection organization where fairness and equity demand that the same rules apply to everyone in the country.

CONCLUSION

The ideas of Weber and Taylor and even the later contributions of Gulick and Urwick viewed good management from the standpoint of devising an optimal organizational structure to maximize output. They took little account of the needs and desires of the workers themselves. In these early theories, the worker is just like any other interchangeable machine part to be moved at the whim of management in order to create a better organization chart. Taylor, in particular, seemed to view the worker as simply an extension of the machine. Gradually a different approach to management emerged — one that took a more human and humane view of the worker. This later approach will be the subject of the next chapter.

BIBLIOGRAPHY

Bennis, Warren G., and Philip F. Slater. *The Temporary Society*. New York: Harper & Row, 1968.

Copley, Frank Barkely. *Frederick W. Taylor: Father of Scientific Management*. 2 vols. New York: Augustus M. Kelley, 1969.

Dawson, R. McGregor. "The Canadian Civil Service." *Canadian Journal of Economics and Political Science*, vol. 2 (August 1936): 288–300.

Gilbreth, Frank B., Jr. and Ernestine Gilbreth Carey. *Cheaper by the Dozen*. New York: Thomas Y. Crowell Company, 1948.

Gulick, Luther, and L. Urwick, eds. *Papers on the Science of Administration*. New York: Augustus M. Kelley, 1969.

Hodgetts, J. E., William McCloskey, Reginald Whitaker, and V. Seymour Wilson. *The Biography of an Institution*. Montreal: McGill-Queen's University Press, 1972.

McLaren, Robert I. *Organizational Dilemmas*. Chichester, U.K.: Wiley & Sons, 1982.

Merton, Robert K. "Bureaucratic Structure and Personality." *Social Forces*, vol. 18 (May 1940): 560–568.

Mitzman, Arthur. *The Iron Cage: A Historical Interpretation of Max Weber*. New York: Alfred A. Knopf, 1970.

Selznick, Philip. "An Approach to the Theory of Bureaucracy." *American Sociological Review*, vol. 8 (February 1943): 47–54.

Selznick, Philip. *TVA and the Grass Roots*. New York: Harper & Row, 1966.

Simon, Herbert. *Administrative Behavior*. 2nd ed. New York: The Free Press, 1957.

Smith, Adam. *An Inquiry into the Nature and Causes of the Wealth of Nations*. Edited by R. H. Campbell and W. B. Todd. Oxford: Clarendon Press, 1976.

Taylor, Frederick Winslow. *The Principles of Scientific Management*. New York: W. W. Norton & Company, 1967.

Weber, Max. *From Max Weber: Essays in Sociology*. Edited and translated by H. H. Gerth and C. Wright Mills. New York: Oxford University Press, 1946.

CASES

In Kenneth Kernaghan, *Canadian Cases in Public Administration* (Toronto: Methuen Publications):

Dr. Stockfield's Resignation
The Shared Authority
The Frustrated Purchasing Agent
The Vague Purchasing Assignment
The Resigning Engineer

3

Public Administration and Organization Theory: The Humanistic Response

Gradually, organization theory began to emphasize the human rather than the mechanical nature of workers. The theories in the previous chapter focussed on how employees fit into the structure of the organization, with only slight attention to the needs of the workers. Later, more humanistic theories centred on the needs of the workers and the role of the organization in fulfilling those needs. This chapter will trace the history of organization theory from the original humanistic, but still highly paternalistic, approach to some present-day theories which emphasize genuine worker participation in organizational decision making.

ORGANIZATIONAL HUMANISM

Just as scientific management bore the imprint of Frederick Taylor, the production engineer, organizational humanism or the human relations school bore the imprint of the social psychologists who were its prime movers. Taylor focussed on what *should* happen in the factory to maximize production. The organizational humanists focussed instead on what actually *did* happen on the factory floor. Their basic finding seems rather unspectacular now, but it totally upset scientific management. They found that in addition to the formal system of authority in the factory through which management controlled workers, there was an informal system of worker control which was in some cases more powerful than the formal system. The informal system was characterized by the network of friendships, friendly banter, and informal sanctions which occur in every work setting. The devastating impact that this had on scientific management theory was obvious. Of course, Taylor and his disciples could continue to set their standards, but workers would simply not comply with them if it meant the ostracism that is frequently accorded the "rate-buster." This meant that Taylor's emphasis on scientific principles to set the work pace and on financial incentives to improve productivity was somewhat misplaced. While these factors had some value, it was becoming clear that another route to increased productivity lay with the informal system.

Mary Parker Follett
One of the first people to understand the importance of the informal system was not a conventional researcher, but rather a very perceptive student of human nature. Mary Parker Follett (1868–1933) did not study organizations systemati-

cally in the ordinary sense, but she did use every opportunity to discuss organizational questions with everyone from senior executives to factory workers. From these discussions, she developed a number of important ideas.

Her basic philosophy stemmed from the fact that she rejected the conventional use of raw power in organizations. She felt that its use was either futile or in some cases totally counter-productive. Instead, she focussed on two related points — circular response and integration.

Circular response was her way of rejecting the biological concept of unidirectional stimulus-response relationships as inapplicable in the human setting. Instead, she emphasized shared interaction.[1] No one unilaterally acts on someone else; rather, people interact with one another in ways that influence both people. It was this view which caused her to reject the idea of power as a one-way street.

Integration referred to the need to combine diverse elements into a useful whole. In some ways, this could be seen as simply a restatement of the old idea of division of labour, but Follett's contribution was that she realized that integration was a dynamic concept and not simply the static arrangement of slots on an organization chart. She understood that conflict would inevitably develop in any organization because of the existence of circular response and the informal organization.

> It was, however, the particular genius of Mary Follett's contribution that she recognized and held fast to the notion that the process of change that generates conflict also provides the opportunity for the further changes necessary to resolve that conflict. Each solution contains the seeds of new differences, but these differences also contain the seeds of new solutions. What they need is freedom to grow within a milieu of intelligent and sympathetic cultivation.[2]

This latter point was a very important one for Follett. She frequently emphasized the importance of executives exercising leadership rather than wielding power. She felt that the way to motivate employees was through a rational appeal to a person's higher instincts rather than a reliance on fear or threats.

Follett was an important influence because she lectured very widely and knew many of the senior business people of her time, but it is questionable whether her rather unscientific views had any influence on some of the more scientific researchers of her time. For this reason, her role in the development of the human relations school is sometimes overlooked.

Roethlisberger and Dickson and the Hawthorne Experiments

The beginnings of the human relations school are usually traced to a very conventional experiment conducted with workers at the Hawthorne Works (near Chicago) of Western Electric in 1924. The idea was to test the impact of dif-

---

[1]Mary Parker Follett, *Creative Experience* (New York: Peter Smith, 1951), ch. 3; Mary Parker Follett, *The New State* (Gloucester, Mass.: Peter Smith, 1965), pp. 25–26.
[2]Mary Parker Follett, *Dynamic Administration: The Collected Papers of Mary Parker Follett*, Elliot M. Fox and L. Urwick, eds. (London: Pitman Press, 1973), p. xxv.

ferent levels of lighting on employee productivity. The experiments were organized and conducted by an industrial psychologist from Harvard, F. J. Roethlisberger, and a Western Electric management employee, William J. Dickson. They were later joined by another Harvard professor, Elton Mayo.[9] The experimenters assumed that improving physical working conditions by increasing levels of lighting would increase productivity. The research was poorly designed and the results inconclusive because production tended to move erratically up or down without much regard to changes in the level of lighting. The experimenters had to discard their original hypothesis because the ambiguity of the results indicated that the physical conditions surrounding work did not have the paramount influence that had been assumed.

The Hawthorne experiment was followed by a series of experiments which tested many other changes in physical conditions in the workplace which it was felt could produce changes in the level of output. Again, the results were ambiguous. This caused experimenters to begin to think about a characteristic of the experiments that they had not considered previously. In every case, the tests were conducted using a group of people who were selected from the workroom, moved to a special place and singled out for significant amounts of attention from researchers. This led experimenters to focus on the *Hawthorne* or *sympathetic observer effect* — the idea that workers singled out for special attention will experience an increase in morale which will lead to greater productivity. This finding has been criticized widely over the years.[4] Some critics have pointed to the poor design of the research, and others have argued that the findings of the research do not support the conclusions usually drawn from them. However, this did not seem to matter at the time. The human relations school grew and thrived over these years.

The human relations school attracted a number of adherents, not all from academic circles. Its ideas were also discussed very widely by practising business executives.

Chester Barnard and the Importance of Cooperation

Chester Barnard was a career business executive who rose to become president of the New Jersey Bell Telephone Company. In 1938, after his retirement, he wrote his landmark work, *The Functions of the Executive*.[5] His crucial idea was that an organization is a cooperative system held together by a good communication system and by the continuing desire of individual members to see the organization thrive. Members of the organization make *contributions* to it, but only when they receive adequate *inducements* to encourage them to continue to do so. The important thing is the balancing of contributions and inducements. If inducements exceeded contributions, this would lead to business failure. On

---

[3]Their work is described in great detail in Roethlisberger and Dickson's book *Management and the Worker* (Cambridge, Mass.:Harvard University Press, 1964).

[4]Two of the more trenchant critics are: Charles Perrow, *Complex Organizations: A Critical Essay* (Glenview, Ill.: Scott, Foresman, 1972), pp. 97–106; Amitai Etzioni, *Modern Organizations* (Englewood Cliffs, N.J.: Prentice-Hall, 1964), pp. 39–49.

[5](Cambridge, Mass.: Harvard University Press, 1962).

the other hand, if inducements were inadequate, then workers would cease making contributions. The inducements offered workers could be in the form of monetary rewards, but Barnard felt that other forms of inducement such as loyalty, good working conditions, and pride in the work and in the organization were probably more effective.

Barnard tried to be sensitive to the needs of workers, but in the final analysis it must be said that his basic attitude towards workers was somewhat patronizing. The title of his book, *The Functions of the Executive*, did not come about by accident. He felt that workers were rather docile, uninspired creatures who depended upon leadership to accomplish anything. It was the responsibility of the executive to establish good communications systems which would, in turn, instil the appropriate company spirit in employees.

He recognized that there was an informal organization which could thwart the desires of management, but he argued that it was the responsibility of management to use the idea of cooperation to harness that informal system for the benefit of the organization.

Abraham Maslow's Hierarchy of Needs

Scientific management focussed on the idea of monetary rewards as an incentive for good work performance. Maslow argued that this was too simplistic and that, in fact, people are motivated by a hierarchy of five categories of needs ranging from the physiological to self-actualization. The idea of the hierarchy is that a person will first be motivated by a desire to satisfy the most basic physiological needs, but as these are satisfied, then the person will strive to meet the next level of needs, and so on up the hierarchy. As an employee attains each succeeding level in the hierarchy, he or she will no longer be motivated by rewards directed at the more basic needs. The five levels in the hierarchy are:

1. *Physiological* — food, shelter, clothing, sex, and sleep;
2. *Safety* — security, stability, freedom from fear;
3. *Belongingness and Love* — friendship, love, membership in some community;
4. *Esteem* — achievement, competence, independence, prestige, status;
5. *Self-actualization* — self-fulfilment, attaining ultimate goals in life.[6]

Maslow's important finding and management's crucial problem is that there is no "one best way" to motivate people. Instead, management must be sensitive to the fact that people have a variety of needs beyond the simple need for money. In particular, thinking about employee needs such as esteem, self-esteem, and self-actualization posed serious problems for managers who were accustomed to thinking in simple piece-work terms.

Maslow's more complex theory of motivation does seem to strike a more responsive note than the simpler, unidimensional approach of the scientific management school. It squares with the usual observation that different people are motivated by different kinds of things, and even the same person is motivated by different things at different times.

---

[6]Abraham H. Maslow, *Motivation and Personality* (New York: Harper & Row, 1970), ch. 4.

Douglas McGregor's Theory X and Theory Y

McGregor built on Maslow's ideas and related them to the attitudes of individual managers. He noted that some managers basically do not trust and respect their employees. These Theory X managers make the following assumptions about their employees:

1. *The average human being has an inherent dislike of work and will avoid it if he can. . . .*
2. *Because of this human characteristic of dislike of work, most people must be coerced, controlled, directed, threatened with punishment to get them to put forth adequate effort toward the achievement of organizational objectives. . . .*
3. *The average human being prefers to be directed, wishes to avoid responsibility, has relatively little ambition, wants security above all.*[7]

On the other hand, Theory Y managers are more positive and more respectful of their employees' needs. These managers operate under the assumptions that:

1. *The expenditure of physical and mental effort in work is as natural as play or rest.* The average human being does not inherently dislike work. Depending upon controllable conditions, work may be a source of satisfaction (and will be voluntarily performed) or a source of punishment (and will be avoided if possible).
2. *External control and the threat of punishment are not the only means for bringing about effort toward organizational objectives. Man will exercise self-direction and self-control in the service of objectives to which he is committed.*
3. *Commitment to objectives is a function of the rewards associated with their achievement.* The most significant of such rewards, e.g., the satisfaction of ego and self-actualization needs, can be direct products of effort directed toward organizational objectives.
4. *The average human being learns, under proper conditions, not only to accept but to seek responsibility.* Avoidance of responsibility, lack of ambition, and emphasis on security are generally consequences of experience, not inherent human characteristics.
5. *The capacity to exercise a relatively high degree of imagination, ingenuity, and creativity in the solution of organizational problems is widely, not narrowly, distributed in the population.*
6. *Under the conditions of modern industrial life, the intellectual potentialities of the average human being are only partially utilized.*[8]

McGregor's basic message was that employees react differently depending upon how they are treated. If managers convey the impression that they believe

---

[7]Douglas McGregor, *The Human Side of Enterprise* (New York: McGraw-Hill, 1960), pp. 33–34. (Emphasis in original.) Reproduced by permission.
[8]Ibid., pp. 47–48. (Emphasis in original.) Reproduced by permission.

that their employees are Theory X types of workers, then the workers will likely meet those expectations. On the other hand, managers who treat employees in a Theory Y manner will likely be more successful.

Summary of Principles of Organizational Humanism

The important, key beliefs which characterize the organizational humanists are:
- respect for workers as complex human beings with diverse sets of needs;
- distrust of simple, unidimensional theories of motivation;
- recognition that the informal organization can be as influential as the formal one in setting work rules.

CRITICISMS OF ORGANIZATIONAL HUMANISM

There have been many criticisms of the philosophy of the human relations school. The most significant are based on the idea that the presumed community of interest between workers and management simply does not exist, and therefore the entire human relations concept is simply a method to manipulate employees to behave in the interests of management.

It is obviously in management's interest to extract as much work as possible from employees. This is what the profit motive is all about. On the other hand, it is in the employees' interest to restrict their output to what they can do in physical comfort. Employees are also aware that the amount of work to be done is usually finite and that their reward for working hard might be a lay-off slip when the work is completed. When one views the workplace in this way, the cooperation which the organizational humanists treasure is somewhat illusory.

The critics charge that this is precisely the point where the theories developed by the organizational humanists become important. How does management convince workers to behave in the best interests of management rather than in their own best interests? The human relations response is to establish a feeling of caring and unity in the workplace that can then be used to manipulate employees. Critics like to point to one aspect of the work done at Hawthorne which involved hiring three hundred employees to wander the factory floor and listen to complaints of other employees. Management never did anything about the complaints and never intended to do anything; the sole purpose of this action was to create an *impression* that management actually cared about workers.[9]

There was also a management-oriented critique of the human relations approach. Some managers were concerned that this approach was *too* employee-centred. Their criticism was that in its revulsion from scientific management, it tipped the balance too far in the other direction. Some derisively referred to human relations as "country club" management, meaning that the ideal work-place for some ought to resemble a country club. Others suggested that for human relations the "one best way" was employee satisfaction rather than concern for production.

---

[9]Perrow, *Complex Organizations*, p. 100.

In the face of this criticism from both sides, organizational humanism had to evolve. The next step was a cluster of ideas that attempted to meet both kinds of criticisms. These varying concepts can all be loosely grouped under the heading of participatory management.

PARTICIPATORY MANAGEMENT

Gradually it began to be accepted that there was an innate tension and conflict in the workplace. This could centre around universal issues such as rates of pay and speed of the production process or specific issues such as the attitude of a particular supervisor or the quality of food served in the lunchroom. Organizational humanism tried to cover over this tension by "bribing" employees to accept management views. The participatory theories held that the tension could be controlled and directed, but probably not totally eliminated, by allowing workers a real role in decision making in the workplace.

There are many different approaches to participatory management. Two recent and important approaches are discussed here by way of illustration.

Management by Objectives

Peter Drucker is usually considered the founder of management by objectives (MBO).[10] Drucker's basic argument stood Weber's views of bureaucracy on their head. Drucker argued that the very things which Weber saw as such powerful engines of *efficiency* — bureaucracy, hierarchical structures, and specialization — were, in fact, powerful forces for *misdirection*. He felt that in large organizations managers and employees became too involved in their specialty and had a tendency to emphasize this at the expense of the overall good of the organization. For example, if the purchasing department emphasizes buying at low prices rather than the high quality of the product or security of supply, then the production department can suffer precisely because the purchasing department is doing its job well — at least, in the view of people in that department. Thus, it frequently happens that inefficiency and misdirection occur *because* of hierarchy and specialization of labour. The problem is the inability to focus on the overall organizational goal; the solution is management by objectives.

George S. Odiorne was another of the early gurus of management by objectives. He described MBO in this manner:

> In brief, the system of management of objectives can be described as a process whereby the superior and subordinate managers of an organization jointly identify its common goals, define each individual's major areas of responsibility in terms of the results expected of him, and use these measures as guides for operating the unit and assessing the contribution of each of its members.[11]

---

[10]Peter F. Drucker, *The Practice of Management* (New York: Harper & Row, 1954).
[11]*Management By Objectives* (New York: Pitman Publishing, 1965), pp. 55-56.

There is no one standard way in which MBO is always implemented. On the contrary, the literature is filled with debate about the ideal, precise steps to be followed. However, there seems to be general agreement that the rough framework consists of six steps:

1. Consultation between top managers and their immediate subordinates to determine the broad goals of the organization. This should be a truly participative exercise during which subordinates can state their views and have them considered seriously by top management. It should not be an exercise in which top management sells its ideas to subordinates.

2. Statement by top management of the overall results expected in the upcoming year. This makes it clear that, while there is meaningful participation, in the final analysis the responsibility for setting objectives rests with senior management.

3. Top managers and their subordinates then meet again to parcel out the responsibility for these results to individual organizational units. It is an important part of this exercise that these responsibilities are not simply imposed upon subordinate managers, but rather that they agree that they will be able to fulfil the goals set. As a part of this exercise, three types of objectives are set for each unit. *Routine objectives* are the results expected from the normal operating activities of each unit — number of files processed, number of widgets manufactured. The *problem-solving objective* deals with clearing up some past problem. This might be the difficulty experienced between the purchasing and production departments mentioned above. The *innovative objective* should lead to some results beyond the anticipated goals. For example, this could be a new production process. The purpose of having three different kinds of objectives is to force managers to look beyond immediate problems. The usual tendency is for a manager to concentrate on one kind of objective, usually the routine, until some crisis develops which then forces him or her to devote full time to the crisis and neglect the routine, production function. The MBO approach encourages managers to deal with problems before they become crises.

4. Repeat the process of parcelling out the responsibilities outlined in step 3 throughout the organization. After each of the managers reporting to top management receives his or her parcel of the work to be accomplished in the coming year, then it is his or her responsibility to further subdivide that parcel among his or her subordinates using the same consultative techniques mentioned in the earlier steps. This process continues down through the various hierarchical levels. As a result of this exercise, a plan showing the assigned role of each organizational unit is developed.

5. Management reviews this plan for consistency and to ensure that the desired goals are met.

6. Year-end comprehensive performance review. The significance of this review is that managers are evaluated according to goals which they helped to set and to which they agreed at the beginning of the year. Thus, no manager is able to duck substandard results by saying that the goals were unrealistic or were unfairly imposed by top management.

MBO has been used extensively in both business and government organizations. It is particularly well suited for use by government because the objectives do not have to be stated in financial terms. However, it has not been without its critics. One stream of criticism suggests that MBO is simply organizational humanism with a few bells and whistles attached. This view suggests that the participation which occurs is not really meaningful because top management always makes the final decisions. Clearly, some attempts to implement MBO have foundered on this very problem, but there is some question about whether this is a criticism of MBO as a concept or simply a criticism of errors in the way some organizations have attempted to implement it. Another criticism raises the difficulty of establishing meaningful, easily measurable objectives. Clearly, this can be a problem in some organizations, but not an insurmountable one. Still another criticism is that the implementation and operation of MBO consumes significant amounts of time and other organizational resources. The proponents of MBO point out that this is more of a problem in the first year of operation than in subsequent years when people are more familiar with the functioning of the system.

The general consensus about MBO is that it is a useful tool, but only when implemented in a sensitive manner. There is a general understanding that all of the criticisms discussed above are valid if implementation is not properly handled.

Organizational Development

Organizational development is also a participative approach to management, but it is considerably more all-encompassing than MBO. The basic concern addressed by organizational development (OD) is that all organizations tend to become very rigid or "frozen." As the environment of the organization changes while the organization remains rigid, this has serious consequences. What usually happens is that conditions gradually deteriorate until some serious crisis occurs which causes either radical restructuring or even the collapse of the organization. The purpose of OD is to locate the barriers to change and to show the organization how to engage in planned, goal-directed change, not directionless evolution or radical revolution.

The basic problem is that all organizations have a history which creates an organizational culture. In some cases this can be a good thing, but in many cases it is not. And even if the existing culture is desirable now, that does not mean that it will be functional in the future. This history or culture develops as a result of the organization's past successes and failures. For example, when someone responds to a new proposal by saying, "We can't do that because we tried something like it ten years ago and it didn't work," that is an example of history at work. Of course, the fact that something similar was unsuccessful ten years earlier might or might not be relevant now, but in many cases this kind of argument will carry the day. Some history is more formal and becomes embodied in "standard operating procedures." Most people know about numerous examples of procedures which are still followed simply because they were established years earlier, even though they are no longer relevant. When the culture or history of an organization has this kind of negative influence, it is referred to as "drag."

The practitioners of OD warn that these patterns and procedures which create drag are merely symptoms of a more serious underlying problem embedded in the culture. It is pointless to change these patterns and procedures without also changing the underlying culture. Such changes would meet strong resistance, and inappropriate new patterns could possibly be imposed on an unfriendly environment.

Figure 3.1
BLAKE AND MOUTON'S MANAGERIAL GRID®

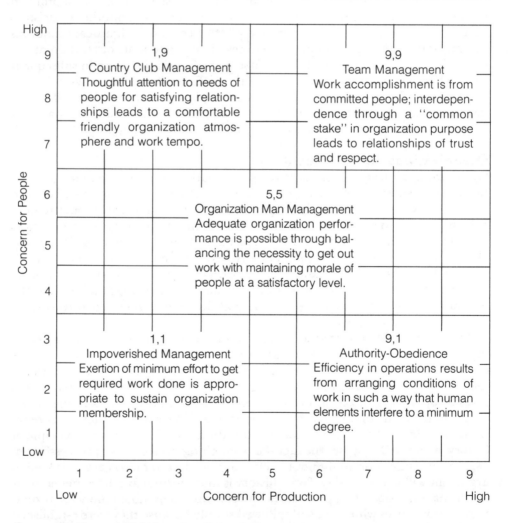

Source: The Managerial Grid figure from Robert R. Blake and Jane S. Mouton, *The Managerial Grid III* (Houston: Gulf Publishing Company, 1985), p. 12. Copyright © 1985, and not to be reproduced without written permission of the authors. Reproduced by permission of the authors and the publisher.

The objective of OD is to "un-freeze" the organization, locate and eliminate those elements causing drag, determine what the organization should look like under ideal conditions, and then set about creating those ideal conditions. A number of researchers have developed different ways of accomplishing these objectives, but few have been as successful and prolific as Robert R. Blake and Jane S. Mouton.

Their approach centres around the "Managerial Grid"® (Figure 3.1). The Grid measures concern for production along one axis and concern for people along the other. The attitude of any individual manager or of an organization as a whole can be located within the Grid. Blake and Mouton suggest that scientific management is 9,1 in that it shows high concern for production, but low concern for people. Human relations falls in the opposite corner because it values concern for people over concern for production. As discussed earlier in this chapter, either of these extreme orientations can lead to problems. Blake and Mouton suggest that it is possible to develop a 9,9 management style — high concern for both production and people.

The six phases in OD as developed by Blake and Mouton are:[12]

1. *Initiation*. All managers in the organization participate in a week-long seminar to describe the concept of the Grid and discuss where they as individual managers and the organization as a whole fit on the Grid.

2. *Team Building*. Within each unit of the organization, the senior manager works with subordinates to discuss barriers to better teamwork and to plan their ideal working arrangement. The objective is to establish better working relationships *within* groups.

3. *Intergroup Development*. This involves discussions between people from organizational units which must cooperate with one another. The objective is to break down intergroup barriers to communication and establish better working arrangements *between* groups.

4. *Designing an Ideal Strategic Organization Model*. Top managers decide the future strategies and activities of the firm. This includes decisions about goods or services provided, clientele served, management relations with employees, and so forth. Blake and Mouton emphasize the need to use "pure business logic" in this exercise and so rise above the previous organizational culture.

5. *Implementing Development*. This involves comparing the existing organization with the ideal developed in phase 4 and preparing a blueprint of what changes need to be made to attain that ideal. Note that this does not necessarily involve destroying the entire organization. It is simply a careful review of those things which need to be changed.

6. *Consolidation*. This consists of a review of the ongoing implementation process to detect any unanticipated problems which are developing and a monitoring of the environment to find any other changes which should be made.

One of the criticisms frequently levelled at the participative approaches is that they require a huge commitment of resources on the part of the organiza-

---

[12]Robert R. Blake and Jane S. Mouton, *The Managerial Grid III* (Houston: Gulf Publishing, 1985), ch. 12.

tion and that they are so disruptive that they can lead to rather lengthy periods of turmoil. The entire idea of the approach is that virtually all employees of the organization must become involved, and in some cases, for fairly lengthy periods. This imposes a real cost on the organization in addition to the usual hefty consulting fees charged by the outside consultants.

There is also almost always a psychological cost to the organization from undergoing this kind of radical surgery. Even though the actual organizational changes themselves can be planned in an incremental and minimally disruptive manner, the rumour mill which always works full time in these situations can wreak havoc on morale. The obvious response to this criticism is that the end result is worth the short-term trauma, and in many cases this has proven correct. However, given the cost and turmoil engendered in the short run, management's frequent reluctance to become fully involved in a participative management exercise is understandable.

Many of the criticisms of the idea of participative management echo those directed against the organizational humanists. There always seems to be a lingering concern that the process is not really and truly participative, but rather is guided — not to say manipulated — by management. As mentioned above, this stands more as a criticism of the manner in which the process has been applied in certain cases than a basic criticism of the process itself. However, this does raise a difficult conundrum. In a true hierarchical setting, those at the pinnacle of the hierarchy have authority over those at lower levels. Some things have not changed since Weber. Given this obvious fact, is real participation possible?

Both MBO and OD have been used in various government organizations. It might be worthwhile at this point to examine some of these practical experiences to consider the value of these techniques.

THE CANADIAN EXPERIENCE: FROM TAYLOR TO MBO

In the previous chapter, the status of scientific management in the federal government was considered. Since then many other styles of management have been discussed, but there has been no comment on their impact on Canadian governments. The reason is quite simple — they seem to have had little impact. V. S. Wilson describes the impact which the organizational humanists had in the United States, and then addresses the Canadian situation in this manner:

> In Canada no developments of this sort surfaced in the public sector. The federal government, for example, continued in its well-established role as omnipotent employer. Institutions of employer-employee relationships created during this time . . . had as their central focus "the problems of the government as employer and not those of the employees."[13]

---

[13]V. Seymour Wilson, "The Influence of Organization Theory in Canadian Public Administration," *Canadian Public Administration*, vol. 25 (Winter 1982), pp. 553–554. The quotation within the quotation is from J. E. Hodgetts, et al., *The Biography of an Institution* (Montreal: McGill-Queen's University Press, 1972), p. 194.

It might be a bit unfair to say that nothing of the organizational humanist school filtered into the Canadian public sector. Since the human relations school is in large part a prescription for changes in the actions of individual managers, it is possible that certain managers did follow the advice of the organizational humanists without there being any system-wide documentation of the practice. But, Wilson is surely correct in his overall assessment of the situation. Throughout the time of the organizational humanists, Canadian governments continued to exhibit rigid hierarchies, inflexible job classification structures, and the other trappings of scientific management.

However, when the participatory style of management came into full flower, it found easier acceptance. The way was made ready by the gradual emergence after the Second World War of the personnel function as a legitimate and important staff activity providing advice to management. Referring to this time, a later chairman of the Public Service Commission stated that "the use of the title personnel officer or training officer would have been sufficient to have one tried for witchcraft."[14] Gradual change occurred between the end of the war and the early 1960s, but in the face of many negative comments on the quality of management, including a ringing indictment by the Royal Commission on Government Organization in 1962, changes began occurring very rapidly in the 1960s.

The name of the Civil Service Commission was changed to the Public Service Commission (PSC) in 1967, but there was much more than just a change in name occurring. Without in any way abandoning its former role as guardian of the merit principle, the PSC moved into more active areas of personnel management such as human resource planning and training. Similar changes were occurring within operating departments as personnel officials became both more numerous and more influential. The effect of this was that there was more emphasis on training managers in management skills. Courses with titles such as "supervisory skills" and "effective motivation" became very popular as offerings of both the PSC and educational institutions. Governments were belatedly discovering the marvels of the organizational humanists at the same time that they were experimenting with participatory management.

Changes started coming so quickly that there were real fears that managers would not be able to cope with them all. H. L. Laframboise's insightful article on the "saturation psychosis" became required reading for every manager. Laframboise argued that the implementation of major management reforms, the introduction of collective bargaining, and the movement to a truly bilingual public service — all at the same time — were making it very difficult for managers to cope with their rapidly changing environment.[15]

The major management reforms discussed by Laframboise involved a more systematic approach to managing both financial and human resources. This led to a more sophisticated approach to planning in both operating depart-

[14]Sylvain Cloutier, as quoted in Wilson, "The Influence of Organization Theory in Canadian Public Administration," p. 554.

[15]"Administrative Reform in the Federal Public Service: Signs of a Saturation Psychosis," *Canadian Public Administration*, vol. 14 (Fall 1971), pp. 303–325.

ments and central agencies, which will be discussed in more detail in a later chapter, but one of the most commonly used reforms was management by objectives or some similar technique with a slightly different name.[16] Many departments experimented with MBO with some degree of success. Most managers treaded a bit more warily around organizational development,[17] but some became involved in it in a big way.

These various reforms have probably produced a higher quality of management, but they have also created problems. The basic problem is that as the new innovations have been implemented, few of the trappings of the older systems have been discarded. The entire arrangement is reminiscent of one of those old European buildings with a basic structure from one era and many succeeding additions, each bearing the architectural style of the era in which it was added. There is nothing wrong with each separate part, but it creates a very unusual overall impression. For example, team-building exercises which emphasize flexibility and cooperation have been piled on top of lengthy, complicated job descriptions which emphasize rigidity and differentiation of duties.

On balance though, the system has improved over the last few years. The mere fact that there is a greater attempt to keep in step with modern management development sets the current period off from earlier times. Large governmental organizations will probably always suffer from rigidities which will hamper their rapid employment of new techniques, but at least there is now an awareness of the need for improvement.

While such practical changes as MBO and OD were being imported into the Canadian scene, progress continued apace in the theoretical study of organizations. Many of these new approaches were significant improvements in organizational theory, but were still basically embellishments of ideas coming from the participatory approach.

KATZ AND KAHN'S OPEN SYSTEMS APPROACH

One such theory is the open systems theory. Some social psychologists such as Robert Merton, Talcott Parsons, Daniel Katz, and Robert L. Kahn became disenchanted with the earlier organizational theories because they placed too much emphasis on activities of individuals within organizations and on the activities of the organization as a monolithic body without a consideration of the environment within which the organization operated. These people criticized

---

[16]For one example, see: J. S. Hodgson, "Management by Objectives — The Experience of a Federal Government Department," *Canadian Public Administration*, vol. 16 (Fall 1973), pp. 422–431. There have been other programs which are similar to MBO, such as: Ontario, The Management Board of Cabinet, *Manager's Guidelines to Managing by Results* (Toronto: The Management Board of Cabinet, 1982).

[17]For the history of a largely unsuccessful attempt in some Ontario municipalities, see the various documents prepared as a part of the Local Government Management Project, such as *The LGMP Experience: Guidelines for Organizational Change in Local Government* (Toronto: Ministry of Treasury, Economics and Intergovernmental Affairs, 1977).

this kind of thinking as the "closed-system" approach because, in their eyes, it considered the organization only as a closed system and not as a part of its environment.

Followers of this school were influenced by biological models that dealt with both the internal organization of organisms and the manner in which they interacted with their environment. Natural scientists did this by thinking in terms of inputs-throughputs-outputs-feedback. To continue in existence, any organism must receive certain inputs from its environment. It then converts these to outputs which, through feedback, help it to attain more inputs. In the case of simple one-cell organisms, this means capturing some nourishment, converting it to energy, which it in turn uses to move about to capture more nourishment. Human beings operate on the same principle, only with a more complex interaction system. Human beings need nourishment, shelter, and psychic encouragement, which they convert to work effort which can be sold for cash or traded to satisfy such needs as food, shelter, and psychic encouragement.

The open systems theorists felt that organizations could be approached in the same manner. Organizations need inputs in the form of labour power, raw material, and so forth. These are then converted to finished products which are sold for cash so that more inputs can be purchased. Not-for-profit organizations do not follow exactly the same cycle in that their products are usually not sold, but they still must produce some acceptable output so that some organization such as a government will provide inputs to them.

Katz and Kahn argued that successful organizations arrange the input-throughput-output process so as to reverse the normal entropy to which all organisms are subject. Entropy is the process through which all organisms are subject to deterioration. In complex physical systems, as the size of the system becomes larger, the individual parts of the system become more disorganized until they are no longer able to sustain the organization as a whole. At this point, the system perishes. A successful organization overcomes this process by developing *negative entropy*, which is the process of importing and storing more energy than it expends. This allows the organization to expand and to survive in difficult times by drawing on the stored reserve.[18] This stored reserve could take several forms. An obvious one is cash and other hard assets, but some other forms of stored energy could be the trust and goodwill of important people or a high quality management team.

The crucial lesson for managers in open systems theory is its reminder that all organizations are a part of their environments. Previous thinkers such as Frederick Taylor and, to a lesser extent, the organizational humanists attempted to see the organization as a closed system unaffected by its environment. The open system concept should remind managers that in addition to managing the internal aspects of their organization, they must also be sensitive to the rapidly changing environment which affects things such as the acceptance of their product, their relationship with their clientele, and the attitudes of their employees.

---

[18]Daniel Katz and Robert L. Kahn, *The Social Psychology of Organizations* (New York: John Wiley & Sons, 1966), ch. 2.

CONTINGENCY THEORY

One of the most recent theories of organizational structure argues that there is no "one best way" of structuring an organization. Instead, contingency theory suggests that the best way to structure a particular organization is contingent on a number of factors such as the attitudes of the managers and employees, the nature of the task performed by the organization, and the nature of the environment. For example, one would not expect an organization performing a routine, repetitive task to be structured in the same way as an organization performing original scientific research. Similarly, a Theory X manager would not structure an organization in the same manner as a Theory Y manager. Following McGregor, there is a tendency to look at the Theory X manager as always being the "bad guy." In fact, the problem might stem more from a lack of congruence between the attitude of the manager and the organizational structure than something which is innately wrong with Theory X management. It is possible that Theory X management might be quite functional in some cases.

There have been a number of empirical tests of the importance of the congruence of organizational structure, environmental factors, and efficiency. The usual procedure is to hypothesize some defined relation between factors such as decentralization of decision making or destandardization of work procedures and the structure of the organization.

> Enterprises with highly predictable tasks perform better with organizations characterized by the highly formalized procedures and management hierarchies of the classical approach. With highly uncertain tasks that require more extensive problem solving, on the other hand, organizations that are less formalized and emphasize self-control and member participation in decision making are more effective. In essence, according to these newer studies, managers must design and develop organizations so that the organizational characteristics *fit* the nature of the task to be done.[19]

The usual procedure in conducting empirical inquiries into the validity of contingency theory is to use survey research to compare a large number of organizations. Sometimes the investigator will select a number of organizations engaging in the same activity, but with varying degrees of success, and sometimes the investigator will choose organizations engaged in very different kinds of activity. In the former case, the hypothesis is that successful organizations will possess congruence and unsuccessful ones will not. In the latter approach, the hypothesis is that organizations engaged in different kinds of activities will be structured differently and have different approaches to management.

In general, the results of these inquiries have been mixed. An early study conducted by Morse and Lorsch consisted of a study of four firms — two engaged in predictable manufacturing tasks and two in unpredictable research and development tasks. Their results strongly supported contingency theory in that

---

[19]John J. Morse and Jay W. Lorsch, "Beyond Theory Y," *Harvard Business Review* (May–June 1970), p. 62. (Emphasis in original.)

for each pair the one with congruence between the nature of its task and its organizational structure was the more effective performer. More recent studies employing larger samples have usually not produced such unambiguous results. Many have found, at most, moderate support of the linkages posited in contingency theory.[20]

Probably the safest thing that can be said about contingency theory is that the jury is still considering the final verdict. Almost all of the studies do find some kinds of linkages, although they seldom find all of the ones expected and the ones found are sometimes weaker than expected. The authors of the various studies usually conclude with a plea for more research in this area to search out other variables or refine measurement techniques. It is likely that contingency theory has some value, although it probably does not hold out the promise suspected initially.

One of the strengths of contingency theory is that, unlike many of the other theories which have been discussed, it is a dynamic approach to organizations. Managers must be aware constantly that there is no "one best way" to organize their operation. The structure which was highly successful last year might be a dismal failure with the changed conditions of the new year. This emphasis on the need to adjust to the rapidly changing environment is something all modern organizational theories have in common. Therefore, it is not surprising that this need to adapt to a changing world also plays a role in writings about the future of organizations.

THE FUTURE OF ORGANIZATIONS

Alvin Toffler's book *Future Shock*[21] was one of the most influential books on the future written in the 1970s. His basic idea is that permanence is disappearing so that the only permanent thing in the future will be constant change. He notes trends ranging from wedding dresses that convert easily to curtains after the wedding to the increasingly rapid way in which people move from one house and even one family to another. Obviously, this situation of constant change will have an effect on organizations.

He argues that we do not have to worry about the crushing impact of bureaucracy so feared by some because bureaucracy is already in the process of cracking under the influence of the new rapidly changing society. He predicts that bureaucracy will be replaced by "ad-hocracy."[22] Bureaucracy worked well in reasonably stable times, when the environment was predictable and the bureaucracy could be "programmed" to respond in predictable ways. The rapid change occurring in recent years has destroyed the efficiency of bureaucracy.

---

[20]A good review of many of the studies which have been conducted can be found in Claudia Bird Schoonhoven, "Problems with Contingency Theory: Testing Assumptions Hidden within the Language of Contingency 'Theory,' " *Administrative Science Quarterly*, vol. 26 (September 1981), pp. 349–377.
[21](Toronto: Bantam Books, 1970).
[22]Ibid., ch. 7.

When change is accelerated, more and more novel first-time problems arise, and traditional forms of organization prove inadequate to the new conditions. They can no longer cope.[23]

Increasingly, organizations are adopting a task force form of organization to deal with these complex, non-repetitive problems. Unlike bureaucracy, the task force has a finite existence — until the problem is solved — after which the members of the task force will scatter to other task forces elsewhere. The members of the task force will be a diverse group of individuals bringing a diverse group of skills to the problem to be addressed. One of the most significant things about this new form of organization is that it blurs or possibly even destroys the lines of hierarchy. With a task force of people drawn from different units of the organization or even from outside the organization, it becomes very difficult to "supervise" their operations in the usual sense of that word. Even the recommendations of the task force are likely to cut across traditional organizational lines in such a manner that traditional hierarchical structures are blurred.

Of course, there will always be some repetitive type of work which needs to be done and could fit the bureaucratic mould. However, this is exactly the kind of work which is most susceptible to being done by sophisticated automatic production techniques such as the computer or robot. Therefore, while there will likely always be some people working in bureaucratic types of environments, their relative numbers will probably decline in future years.

One innovation already in relatively common use that is similar to what Toffler predicted is the idea of matrix management. In this style of management, employees are permanently assigned to a specific group, but are actually on continuous loan to work on some particular project or other. This violates the principle of unity of command in that a person is reporting to two supervisors — one in the long-term and one when dealing with a particular project. In places where matrix management has been used it creates some of the expected tensions and problems, but it is frequently seen as the best method of dealing with complex projects where sophisticated expertise is needed for only limited periods of time.[24]

Figure 3.2 shows the organization of a computer systems design and programming operation. In terms of permanent structures, employees report to one of three supervisors — systems design, business programming, or scientific programming. However, in terms of actual location of work, some people from each of these groups will be assigned to each project as they are needed. This form of organization means that there is flexibility in assigning people to perform the task for which they are most qualified. Matrix organizations are by their nature dynamic organizations in that the organization chart could easily change tomorrow when people are reassigned to different projects. The supervisors of the various projects do not have any employees reporting to them on a

---

[23]Ibid., p. 135.

[24]A more extensive description of the advantages and disadvantages of matrix management is provided in Robert I. McLaren, *Organizational Dilemmas* (Chichester, U.K.: John Wiley & Sons, 1982), pp. 34–36.

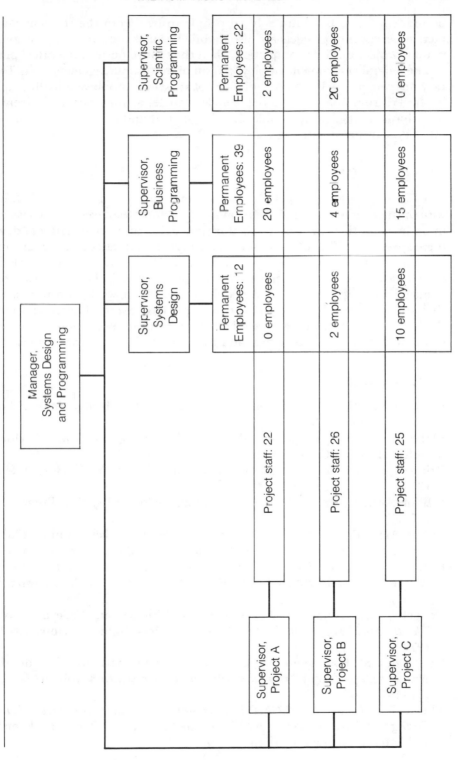

Figure 3.2
MATRIX ORGANIZATION

permanent basis, but must rely on people drawn from the relevant pool. In fact, supervisors of projects are also mobile because they are assigned to a particular project until its completion, then they move on to some other project.

The federal government employs a form of matrix management in its Temporary Assignment Pool. Members of the pool are senior people nominally employed by the Treasury Board, but actually on loan to departments on a relatively long-term basis to engage in trouble-shooting or to handle reorganizations or any other type of non-recurring task.

CONCLUSION

The history of organizational theory is rather lengthy and convoluted. It begins with the mechanistic views of Weber and Taylor and progresses to the considerably more humanistic views of the social psychologists and organizational development specialists. The thread that runs through all of these theories is an emphasis on motivating employees to perform better. No organizational "quick fix" or even long-term structural reform can ever be effective if the most basic components of any organization — the people who make it work — do not carry out their duties in an efficient and effective manner. The next chapter will continue the focus on the behaviour of people in organizations by examining the related issues of motivation, leadership, and communication in organizations.

BIBLIOGRAPHY

Barnard, Chester. *The Functions of the Executive*. Cambridge, Mass.: Harvard University Press, 1962.

Blake, Robert R., and Jane S. Mouton. *The Managerial Grid III*. Houston: Gulf Publishing Company, 1985.

Drucker, Peter F. *The Practice of Management*. New York: Harper & Row, 1954.

Etzioni, Amitai. *Modern Organizations*. Englewood Cliffs, N.J.: Prentice-Hall, 1964.

Follett, Mary Parker. *Creative Experience*. New York: Peter Smith, 1951.

Follett, Mary Parker. *The New State*. Gloucester, Mass.: Peter Smith, 1965.

Follett, Mary Parker. *Dynamic Administration: The Collected Papers of Mary Parker Follett*. Edited by Elliot M. Fox and L. Urwick. London: Pitman Press, 1973.

Hodgetts, J. E., William McCloskey, Reginald Whitaker, and V. Seymour Wilson. *The Biography of an Institution*. Montreal: McGill-Queen's University Press, 1972.

Hodgson, J. S. "Management by Objectives — The Experience of a Federal Government Department." *Canadian Public Administration*, vol. 16 (Fall 1973): 422–431.

The LGMP Team. *The LGMP Experience: Guidelines for Organizational Change in Local Government*. Toronto: Ministry of Treasury, Economics and Intergovernmental Affairs, 1977.

Katz, Daniel, and Robert L. Kahn. *The Social Psychology of Organizations*. New York: John Wiley & Sons, 1966.

Laframboise, H. L. "Administrative Reform in the Federal Public Service: Signs of a Saturation Psychosis." *Canadian Public Administration*, vol. 14 (Fall 1971): 303 325.

McGregor, Douglas. *The Human Side of Enterprise*. New York: McGraw-Hill Book Company, 1960.

McLaren, Robert I. *Organizational Dilemmas*. Chichester, U.K.: John Wiley & Sons, 1982.

Maslow, Abraham H. *Motivation and Personality*. New York: Harper & Row, 1970.

Mintzberg, Henry. *Structure in Fives: Designing Effective Organizations*. Englewood Cliffs, N. J.: Prentice-Hall, 1983.

Morse, John J., and Jay W. Lorsch. "Beyond Theory Y." *Harvard Business Review* (May–June 1970): 61–68.

Odiorne, George S. *Management By Objectives*. New York: Pitman Publishing Corporation, 1965.

Ontario. The Management Board of Cabinet. *Manager's Guidelines to Managing by Results*. Toronto: The Management Board of Cabinet, 1982.

Perrow, Charles. *Complex Organizations: A Critical Essay*. Glenview, Ill.: Scott, Foresman, 1972.

Roethlisberger, F. J., and William J. Dickson. *Management and the Worker*. Cambridge, Mass.: Harvard University Press, 1964.

Schoonhoven, Claudia Bird. "Problems with Contingency Theory: Testing Assumptions Hidden within the Language of Contingency 'Theory.' " *Administrative Science Quarterly*, vol. 26 (September 1981): 349–377.

Toffler, Alvin. *Future Shock*. Toronto: Bantam Books, 1970.

Wilson, V. Seymour. "The Influence of Organization Theory in Canadian Public Administration." *Canadian Public Administration*, vol. 25 (Winter 1982): 545–563.

CASES

In *Case Program in Canadian Public Administration* (Toronto: Institute of Public Administration of Canada):

Bureaucratie, by Guy Demers

Case Studies in Government Operations and Procedures, by R. I. McLaren

A Taxing Problem, by Roy S. Gunn

In Kenneth Kernaghan, *Canadian Cases in Public Administration* (Toronto: Methuen Publications):

Dr. Stockfield's Resignation

The Difficult Supervisor

The Health of Mr. Cole

4

Motivation, Leadership, and Communications

The previous two chapters have focussed on organizations as organizations much more than on the actions and motivations of the people within those organizations. This chapter moves the focus to a concern with the individual members of the organization. It is frequently argued that the most important resource that any organization possesses is its human resources — its employees. Yet, it is shocking how carefully some organizations husband their other resources, but neglect their human resources. This chapter will first consider two important aspects of motivation — communications and leadership — and then tie these together with a discussion of some general theories concerning the motivation of employees.

COMMUNICATIONS

Communications are the lifeblood of any organization; one of the main purposes of communication is to effect coordination between the various elements of an organization. If an organization is to function properly, people in the organization must understand what is taking place in other parts of it. Communication takes place in several ways. At one extreme are the formal written instructions which one finds in an organization manual or a list of standard operating procedures. At the other extreme, communication can be by example. When senior managers all dress very conservatively, work long hours, and take short breaks, they are communicating something very significant to those below them in the hierarchy — without saying a word.

Pursley and Snortland capture the full subtlety of the situation when they define communication as "the transfer and reception of information, emotions, ideas, and orders."[1] Notice that this definition considers communication as a two-step process; communication is not just the sending of a message, but the reception of that message as well. We are all aware of situations where the message that was sent was not the same message received — either accidentally or intentionally. There are a number of different kinds of communication as well as a number of obstacles to communications.

---

[1] Robert D. Pursley and Neil Snortland, *Managing Government Organizations: An Introduction to Public Administration* (North Scituate, Mass.: Duxbury Press, 1980), p. 218.

Different Kinds of Communications

Formal and informal communications. The previous chapter discussed formal and informal organizations. In many ways, formal and informal communications parallel the formal and informal organization.

All organizations provide certain formal communications to members. These take such forms as the orientation package for new employees, training material, and operating manuals. These set out the formal rules of the organization and tell people what is expected of them. However, as new employees become socialized in an organization they also receive many informal communications which modify communications they have received through the formal channels. For example, the operating manual might say that employees are entitled to be paid for all overtime worked at a premium rate. However, the informal channel of communications might suggest to you that if you value your future in the organization and want to be seen as a "team player," you will simply work the overtime and not bother to ask for the extra pay. In many cases, the information conveyed through the informal communication system can be as important as that conveyed through the formal one.

Management should attempt to keep track of communication flowing through the informal system. It will frequently provide advance notice of employee dissatisfaction or other problems in lower levels of the organization. There is also much misinformation which is passed through the "grapevine." This can be a sign that the more formal methods of communication are not adequate. An "organization's informal communications network begins to hum whenever the formal channels are silent or ambiguous on subjects of importance to its members."[2] Management must be conscious of this tendency and head it off by providing a steady flow of accurate formal communication. Thus, if the formal system communicated that there was soon to be a major reorganization and then went silent, the informal system might then begin to buzz with information about imminent huge lay-offs. However, if senior management used the formal system to keep employees informed about the reorganization, there would be less misinformation in the informal system.

Downward communications involve the communication of official organizational pronouncements from the top levels of the hierarchy down to operating employees. Downward communication is used by senior management to coordinate the activities of lower level employees. This is usually done through formal communications such as policy directives, operating manuals, or notices on bulletin boards, but as mentioned earlier, downward communication can also be informal.

Great care must be taken to ensure that the message sent by senior managers is the same one which is received by operating employees. This problem increases with the number of levels in the hierarchy and with functional specialization. One of the barriers to communication which will be discussed below is that the

---

[2]Eugene Walton, "How Efficient Is the Grapevine?" *Personnel*, vol. 38 (March–April 1961), p. 45.

language spoken varies at different levels in the organization and in different functional areas. A communication which begins at the top level of the organization as a one-page statement about the need for better safety in the factory will be "translated" as it passes down the chain of command into lengthy statements about who must wear safety shoes, hard hats, and protective glasses, when they must be worn, and how they will be paid for. In this translation process, the policy as implemented on the factory floor may or may not be the same one articulated by senior management.

Upward communications, sometimes called *feedback*, are messages from lower levels of the organization to higher levels. This is the most unnatural form of communication in the organization because it runs counter to the normal chain of command, but it can also be the most important. Operating level employees are in a much better position to know about problems as they are developing than are senior managers. Operating level employees deal with clients on a daily basis and so have immediate feedback about dissatisfaction among clients; factory employees see how a product is being assembled and so can frequently point to quality control problems and bottlenecks in operations.

Senior managers should always encourage upward communication, but this is easier said than done. Lower level employees are sometimes reticent to discuss problems with senior employees, either because of the social distance involved, or the unnaturalness of upward communications, or for fear that managers will "kill the messenger bearing the bad news." The major inhibition on the upward flow of information is simply that lower level employees do not want to pass upward information that can be used against them.

Thus, there is a natural tendency to pass upward positive information, but not negative information. The cumulative impact of this tendency can be so severe that senior managers are totally out of touch with what is actually happening at the operating level. David Halberstam suggests that the American involvement in Vietnam in the 1960s was characterized by this attitude of telling superiors what they wanted to hear. He states that one journalist felt that senior officers in the military "had created an elaborate machine to lie to them, only to become prisoners of their own lies."[3] Wartime situations bring about extreme cases, but it is not unusual for senior managers to be forced to deal quickly with a crisis that could have been headed off if they had had some advance warning, but for which junior officials did not provide advance warning because they tried to hide the problem.

Some companies have formal programs such as suggestion boxes or plans which reward employees for ideas that improve productivity, but these plans frequently meet with mixed success. One interesting method of stimulating upward communication is "management by wandering around" (MBWA).[4] MBWA, also called "the technology of the obvious," urges managers to put aside computer print-

---

[3] *The Best and the Brightest* (Greenwich, Conn.: Fawcett Publications, 1973), p. 771.
[4] Tom Peters and Nancy Austin, *A Passion for Excellence: The Leadership Difference* (New York: Random House, 1985), ch. 2 and passim.

outs and marketing surveys periodically and escape from their offices simply to wander about and see their product or service as customers see it and experience their work environment as their employees do. Some managers' findings when they attempted this were obvious, basic and brilliant at the same time. One manager insisted on cleaner washrooms in the factory because he did not see how a sense of pride in their work could be instilled in employees when they had to put up with the stench from stinking washrooms on the assembly line.[5] Some of the things which have the greatest effect on working conditions never find their way into computer printouts.

Lateral communication "takes place among workers of the same level in the hierarchy, or among individuals of different levels who are not in a superior-subordinate relationship."[6] *Most* communication in organizations could well be of the lateral variety, although it is impossible to measure this precisely. Some kinds of lateral communication are encouraged by the formal organization, but some kinds are discouraged or even prohibited.

Lateral communication between employees within the same work team is usually encouraged because it promotes coordination. It is impossible for standard operating procedures to foresee every future working condition; lateral communication between employees fills this void by facilitating informal solutions to work problems.

However, lateral communication between employees in different organizational units is more problematic. Strictly speaking, all communication within an organization should flow "through channels." This means that people at the same level, but reporting to different supervisors, do not consult directly with one another. Figure 4.1 shows the proper formal communication route in a bureaucracy. If X desires to communicate with Y, X passes the communication up the hierarchy until it reaches someone who has line authority over both X and Y. This person then makes some decision and passes that decision down.

However, people working in organizations quickly discover the difficulties with this communication "through channels." Not only is it time consuming, but there is also a risk that relatively small issues will be caught up in larger concerns of "office politics" or territoriality. Subordinates learn quickly that it is much faster and easier to resolve minor problems through informal lateral communication than through the hierarchy. Thus, the rigid standard operating procedures found in formal communications are frequently modified in practice because people at lower levels in the organization have found better ways to coordinate their activities.

There is some risk to subordinates in ignoring the chain of command. If it is really a small matter which does not affect others, then it will be acceptable, but if something larger goes awry as a result of these informal agreements, then subordinates can be in a great deal of trouble for not keeping their bosses informed.

---

[5]Ibid., pp. 228–229.
[6]Felix A. Nigro, *Modern Public Administration* (New York: Harper & Row, 1965), p. 197.

Figure 4.1
BUREAUCRATIC FLOW OF COMMUNICATION

proper bureaucratic flow
of information

lateral communication

Some organizations see real value in encouraging lateral communication. It can smooth out many problems quickly and be a source of innovation. Henri Fayol developed the idea of the "gang plank," which allows lateral communications to occur while still preserving the concept of the chain of command. He strongly urged that lateral communications were highly preferable to the round-about method of following channels as long as the communicators' immediate supervisors were kept informed of what was happening.[7]

Lateral communication can also occur between different organizations. This can be routine, such as when someone in a regional office communicates directly with a head office counterpart, or it can involve the transfer of major innovations from one organization to another. People performing the same function in different organizations frequently belong to associations that allow them to meet and discuss changes in their field. These can be as formal as the provincial engineers or accountants associations, or as informal as a periodic breakfast meeting of personnel officers employed in municipal governments in a certain area. One of the activities in which these people engage is lateral communication about new activities in their organizations. This allows for dissemination of new ideas to different organizations.

[7]*General and Industrial Management*, trans. Constance Storrs (London: Pitman Publishing, 1971), pp. 35–36.

Lateral communications can have substantial value in certain cases. They aid problem solving and can foster new innovation and the dissemination of innovative ideas. However, some organizations are fearful of this form of communication because it can appear to subvert the formal chain of command.

Obstacles to Communication

Good, clear lines of communication are important in coordinating activities and ensuring organizational effectiveness, but there are a number of factors which inhibit effective communications.

Territoriality and other organizational tensions occur in organizations where there is a climate that encourages managers to think solely about the furtherance of their own aims and those of their department. In this environment, communication is discouraged because managers do not want to tip their hands too early and allow other departments to know what they are doing. This attitude is clearly dysfunctional to organizational health, but it is found all too often in organizations.

Language differences exacerbate problems which might already exist between various occupational specialties and organizational units. Andrew Dunsire compares a typical organization to a high-rise building which he calls the "Babel house." Each ascending floor is a higher level in the hierarchy; and the horizontal separation on each floor represents different functional specialties.

> The building is a Tower of Babel because a different tongue (concepts, vocabulary) is talked on each floor — amounting to a considerable linguistic disparity between top-floor speech and ground-floor speech — and different jargons and dialects are spoken on any one floor, in each of the corners and other areas. As between one floor and the next, or as between one office and its neighbour on the same floor, differences in language and habitual style of doing business can usually be noted, though it is quite easy for adjacent ranks, and denizens of adjacent offices, to understand one another. Messages from distant locations in any direction — from a far-away corner, or from a much higher or much lower floor — do not, by contrast, make much sense on first hearing or reading: the more distant, the less intelligible.[8]

These different languages and dialects come about as a result of professional and functional specialization. For example, both economists and accountants talk about "depreciation" and "rents," but the two groups have different meanings for those same terms, which are in turn different from their more common usage by members of the public. In a factory, a document that is clearly identified on its face as "Form No. C31-a" might be called a "requisition form" or "green sheet" in different parts of the plant.

---

[8]*Implementation in a Bureaucracy* (Oxford: Martin Robertson, 1978), p. 176.

Communications overload occurs when there are so many communications taking place that they overload the channels for processing them and so cause organizational dysfunctions. In the popular novel and film *The Day of the Jackal*, the French authorities know that the Jackal has entered the country to assassinate President de Gaulle. And someplace in the elaborate French bureaucracy they have the information which they need to track him down. The problem is that they also have so much other information that they are unable to locate the relevant bits.

This sort of thing is a relatively frequent occurrence in large organizations. Senior executives are inundated with communications so that it is difficult for them to decide which are the most relevant ones.

Noise or *distortion* occurs when messages are altered as they pass through the various steps in the hierarchy. Almost everyone has played the game which involves telling one individual something who, in turn, passes the information to someone else, and so forth until it has passed through many people. The message in its final form usually bears little relationship to its original statement. This problem can be even more severe in large organizations when there is the possibility that territoriality or language differences can add to the distortion.

Organizations can attempt to minimize these distortions by relying on formal, written communications, hoping that there is less likelihood of misinterpretation of written documents than of word-of-mouth communication. However, even written documents can suffer from poor translation as intents are passed from senior managers down the hierarchy.

One of the other factors which can be used to coordinate activities within any organization is good leadership. It can be used to supplement communications in that unclear or distorted communications can be put back into perspective by sound leadership.

LEADERSHIP

Leadership is usually considered to be a very important factor in the motivation of employees. It is necessary to be a good leader in order to be a good manager, but the words are not synonymous. Managers possess power as a result of their organizational position; leaders possess power as a result of the concurrence of their subordinates. Some managers are leaders in the sense that their relationship with subordinates is such that subordinates comply with their requests, not just out of fear for the consequences, but because they are willing followers. Katz and Kahn "consider the essence of organizational leadership to be the influential increment over and above the mechanical compliance with the routine directives of the organization."[9] Pursley and Snortland provide a more detailed distinction between a leader and a manager:

---

[9] Daniel Katz and Robert L. Kahn, *The Social Psychology of Organizations*, 2nd ed. (New York: John Wiley & Sons, 1978), p. 528.

Managers are appointed and have formal authority within an organization; leaders may be elected, appointed, or merely emerge from within a group. A manager has a formal position; a leader may or may not have a formal position. A manager usually can expect people to follow proper, official orders; leaders may be able to move people to do things far beyond the call of duty. Although every manager should be a leader, not all leaders are managers. A manager is expected to be able to organize, plan, and evaluate; some leaders may not be able to perform these management tasks. A manager's formal authority provides the resources that the manager may be able to use to influence the behavior of people — in short, to lead. However, not every manager is a leader or even understands the importance of leadership.[10]

The difficulty of defining leadership in an unequivocal manner is evidenced by the fact that Stogdill, in his compendium review of the literature on leadership, devotes an entire chapter to definitions in which he lists eleven different categories of definitions.[11] However, this lack of a precise definition has not restricted the amount of research undertaken in the area of leadership.

This voluminous research has yielded a number of different perspectives on the issue of leadership. One of the earliest approaches was to attempt to locate those *traits* which always seemed to be present in a successful leader. This was followed by a trend towards research to determine which *skills* were most likely to be of use to leaders. The difference between traits and skills is that the former are seen to be almost genetically a part of the individual, whereas skills can be learned and developed. The switch to an emphasis on skills led to a concern for the development of an ideal leadership *style* — democratic, authoritarian, or laissez-faire. Finally, there has been a trend in recent years to a belief that there is no one ideal style, but that the most appropriate style is a function of the relationship between, on the one hand, both traits and skills of leaders and, on the other hand, the characteristics of followers and the environment of the organization. This has led to the *contingency* theory of leadership, which holds that different situations bring forth different kinds of leaders. Each of these approaches to the study of leadership will be discussed in this chapter.

Leadership Traits or Skills

One of the earliest approaches to the study of leadership was an analysis of a group of people who were commonly regarded as successful or "natural leaders" to determine what traits these individuals possessed in common. The basis of this research was that there were certain inherited traits which would always mark a leader. Some studies suggested that leaders tended to be older, taller, weigh more, and have greater athletic and speaking ability than non-leaders.[12]

---

[10]Pursley and Snortland, *Managing Government Organizations*, p. 186.

[11]Ralph M. Stogdill, *Handbook of Leadership: A Survey of Theory and Research* (New York: The Free Press, 1974), ch. 2.

[12]Ibid., ch. 5.

However, this line of research fell on hard times when the results produced were not consistent.[13]

A second wave of research began to apply some of the same techniques used in the earlier studies to locate the traits and skills common to successful leaders in the workplace — managers and supervisors in hierarchical organizations. This focus was considerably more productive. Stogdill has summarized the findings of these studies:

> The leader is characterized by a strong drive for responsibility and task completion, vigor and persistence in pursuit of goals, venturesomeness and originality in problem solving, drive to exercise initiative in social situations, self-confidence and sense of personal identity, willingness to accept consequences of decision and action, readiness to absorb interpersonal stress, willingness to tolerate frustration and delay, ability to influence other persons' behavior, and capacity to structure social interaction systems to the purpose at hand.[14]

A more recent study of two thousand managers in twelve organizations identified twelve common characteristics usually found in successful managers: efficiency orientation, proactivity, diagnostic use of concepts, concern with impact, self-confidence, use of oral presentations, conceptualization (middle level managers and executives only), use of socialized power, managing group process (middle level managers and executives only), perceptual objectivity, self-control, and stamina and adaptability.[15]

Some commentators see the situation more simply and suggest that management abilities can be identified in two or three clusters of skills. Katz's three-skills typology was first developed in 1955, but is considered still relevant:

> *Technical Skills*: "An understanding of, and proficiency in, a specific kind of activity, particularly one involving methods, processes, procedures, or techniques. . . . Technical skill involves specialized knowledge, analytical ability within that specialty, and facility in the use of the tools and techniques of the specific discipline."[16]
>
> *Human Skills*: "The executive's ability to work effectively as a group member and to build cooperative effort within the team he leads. As *technical* skill is primarily concerned with working with 'things' (processes or physical objects), so *human* skill is primarily concerned with working with people."[17]

---

[13]Dorwin Cartwright and Alvin Zander, "Leadership and Performance of Group Functions: Introduction," in Dorwin Cartwright and Alvin Zander, eds., *Group Dynamics: Research and Theory*, 3rd ed. (New York: Harper & Row, 1968), p. 303; Gary A. Yukl, *Leadership In Organizations* (Englewood Cliffs, N.J.: Prentice-Hall, 1981), pp. 68–69.

[14]Stogdill, *Handbook of Leadership*, p. 81.

[15]Richard A. Boyatzis, *The Competent Manager: A Model for Effective Performance* (New York: John Wiley & Sons, 1982), p. 229.

[16]Robert L. Katz, "Skills of an Effective Administrator," *Harvard Business Review*, vol. 33 (January-February 1955), p. 34. Copyright © 1955 by the President and Fellows of Harvard College; all rights reserved.

[17]Ibid. (Emphasis in original.)

Conceptual Skills: "The ability to see the enterprise as a whole; it includes recognizing how the various functions of the organization depend on one another, and how changes in any one part affect all the others; and it extends to visualizing the relationship of the individual business to the industry, the community, and the political, social, and economic forces of the nation as a whole. Recognizing these relationships and perceiving the significant elements in any situation, the administrator should then be able to act in a way which advances the over-all welfare of the total organization."[18]

All managers must possess these skills to some degree, but managers at different levels in the organization need different quantities of each. The first-line supervisor must be high on technical skills because he or she must be able to advise workers on production problems. First-line supervisors must also possess human relations skills because it is necessary to maintain satisfaction and motivation among group members and direct them towards organizational goals. Conceptual skills are less necessary for first-line supervisors because the problems facing them are fairly well defined and recurring and usually involve problems within the organization, rather than in its environment.

The skill needs of senior managers are reversed. Technical skills are not very important because there are large numbers of skilled operatives at lower levels to solve those kinds of problems. Conceptual skills are much more important for senior managers because they are constantly facing new and unstructured problems involving relationships between different units of the organization or the organization and its environment.

One of the outcomes of this type of research was a debunking of the conventional wisdom that "leaders are born, not made." If the traits and skills commonly found in good leaders could be identified, then these same characteristics could be nurtured in other promising people, so that possibly good leaders — or at least passable managers — could be developed.

This idea led many organizations to establish what are called *assessment centres*. These centres administer a battery of various kinds of tests to current and potential managers to locate the most promising new managers and point out the skills which they need to develop. This battery of tests usually lasts for several days and ranges from objective intelligence tests to role-playing exercises to determine human relations skills. Intended or accidental bias is reduced by the use of multiple testing instruments and multiple human evaluators.

These assessment centres are used quite widely in the private sector, and there is some evidence that they are effective in identifying managers.[19] However, government organizations have been somewhat slower to adopt this concept because of the rigidities imposed by the mechanistic application of the merit system discussed in Chapters 2 and 3. The assessment centre technique can be construed as identifying "high flyers" and providing them with preferential training and development. This identification of "high flyers" runs counter to the mechanis

---

[18]Ibid., pp. 35–36.
[19]James R. Huck, "Assessment Centres: A Review of the External and Internal Validities," *Personnel Psychology*, vol. 26 (Summer 1973), pp. 191–212.

tic application of the merit principle, which requires that individuals be matched to jobs for which they possess the necessary skills right now.

The study of leadership traits and skills led to a realization that leadership was not something contained only in the leader, but rather that leadership described a reciprocal relationship between the leader and followers. The next approach to leadership studied the exchange relationship between these two.

Styles of Leadership: Authoritarian, Democratic, Laissez-faire

Many studies have focussed on the consequences of different leadership styles — authoritarian, democratic, and laissez-faire. The *authoritarian* style involves the leader making all decisions and communicating work tasks to followers in a highly detailed manner so that followers have no role in making decisions or organizing the work. The *democratic* or participative style of leadership involves a more open relationship in which leaders encourage followers to work together in seeking and implementing solutions. Leaders guide the group by advising on alternative possibilities. The *laissez-faire* style allows followers to "do their own thing" with no direction or even involvement on the part of the leader. In a sense, it is a corruption or a misapplication of the democratic style.[20]

The relative effectiveness of these different styles has been tested many times, and the results have always been very similar. The laissez-faire style is universally rejected as having no redeeming value. It results in groups deteriorating into chaos and produces neither organizational effectiveness nor member satisfaction. The democratic leadership style seems to further member satisfaction and group cohesion more than the other two. The evidence is less clear-cut concerning the effect of leadership style on group productivity. Stogdill's comprehensive review of studies suggests that leadership style (authoritarian or democratic) had little impact on productivity.[21]

However, some researchers began to delve a bit more deeply into this issue.[22] They found that authoritarian styles seemed to be more functional in cases where the task to be accomplished was clearly defined and could be well structured,

---

[20]These depictions of the styles come from one of the earliest studies: Ronald Lippitt and Ralph K. White, "The 'Social Climate' of Children's Groups," in Robert G. Barker, Jacob S. Kounin, and Herbert F. Wright, eds., *Child Behavior and Development: A Course of Representative Studies* (New York: McGraw-Hill, 1943), pp. 485–508. See also the more widely cited Ralph K. White and Ronald Lippitt, *Autocracy and Democracy* (Westport, Conn.: Greenwood Press, 1972), pp. 26–27.

[21]*Handbook of Leadership*, ch. 32.

[22]A good review of a number of these different approaches is contained in J. D. Williams, *Public Administration: The People's Business* (Boston: Little, Brown, 1980), pp. 147–148; Richard H. Hall, *Organizations: Structure and Process*, 3rd ed. (Englewood Cliffs, N.J.: Prentice-Hall, 1982), pp. 163–166; Alan C. Filley and Robert J. House, *Managerial Process and Organizational Behavior* (Glenview, Ill.: Scott, Foresman, 1969), pp. 401–405. Some of the specific studies which support this view are Fred E. Fiedler, "Personality and Situational Determinants of Leadership Effectiveness," in Cartwright and Zander, eds., *Group Dynamics*, 3rd ed. (New York: Harper & Row, 1968), pp. 362–380; Kurt Lewin, Ronald Lippitt, and Ralph K. White, "Patterns of Aggressive Behavior in Experimentally Created 'Social Climates,'" *Journal of Social Psychology*, vol. 10 (1939), p. 273.

e.g., factory assembly line. Democratic styles were more productive where tasks were ill-defined and non-repetitive, e.g., research laboratory. This was one of the findings which led to the idea that there was no "one best way" of establishing leadership, but that different leadership styles were more effective in different situations.

Contingency Theories

The contingency theory of organization discussed in Chapter 3 holds that the ideal structure for an organization is a function of a number of factors such as the backgrounds of employees in the organization and the task to be accomplished. The contingency theory of leadership borrows this in arguing that the best style of leadership is a product of a number of factors relating to *characteristics of the leader, characteristics of the members of the group*, and the *situation or environment*. A number of different researchers have developed different forms of contingency theory. Paul Hersey and Kenneth H. Blanchard's situational leadership theory will be discussed here to provide an example of the general idea of contingency theory.[23]

Hersey and Blanchard suggest that all leadership activity is of one of two types — task behaviour or relationship behaviour. Task behaviour is directed at carrying out the day-to-day work and accomplishing the organization's goal. Relationship behaviour is directed at motivating subordinates and moulding the group. Leaders can engage simultaneously in both kinds of activity, but this is rather difficult; usually, one must be emphasized at the expense of the other.

The status of subordinates can be measured in terms of their "maturity" in relation to a particular task. Maturity is defined as "the capacity to set high but attainable goals (achievement-motivation), willingness and ability to take responsibility, and education and/or experience of an individual or group."[24] Some people are more willing and able to work than others, and the former type of person needs less close supervision than the latter. But, maturity in this case also refers to a person's ability to carry out a *specific task*, regardless of his or her level of motivation. A young engineer could be perfectly capable of supervising construction of a particular section of highway without detailed supervision, but would need close supervision in the construction of an elaborate system of bridges and overpasses. Thus, the same person could be "mature" with regard to one task, but not another.

Hersey and Blanchard's basic thrust in situational leadership theory is that leaders must vary their mix of task versus relationship behaviour depending upon the level of maturity of subordinates in a particular situation. Figure 4.2 illustrates this relationship diagramatically. For immature subordinates, a high task orientation is necessary. Since the subordinate will have relatively little ability to perform the work on his or her own, it is necessary for the leader to become

---

[23]*Management of Organizational Behavior: Utilizing Human Resources*, 3rd ed. (Englewood Cliffs, N.J.: Prentice-Hall, 1977), ch. 7 and passim.
[24]Ibid., p. 161.

Figure 4.2
HERSEY AND BLANCHARD'S SITUATIONAL LEADERSHIP THEORY

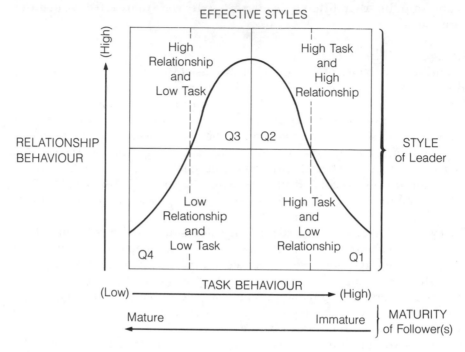

Source: Paul Hersey and Kenneth H. Blanchard, *Management of Organizational Behavior: Utilizing Human Resources*, 3rd ed. (Englewood Cliffs, N.J.: Prentice-Hall, © 1977), p. 164. Reprinted by permission.

heavily involved in the work itself. As the worker becomes more mature, he or she will need less advice on how to carry out the work and more encouragement and emotional support to stimulate motivation and build confidence. Finally, when the worker is very mature in relationship to the work, he or she needs little task advice or emotional support, and when they are needed they can be provided by members of the peer group rather than the leader.

Situational leadership theory reminds managers that they must be aware of where particular subordinates stand on this continuum at any time and shift their leadership style appropriately. This can be difficult, because a subordinate who is mature with regard to one task can be at the opposite end of the continuum for another task. Thus, managers must be flexible enough to constantly shift management styles as they move from one subordinate to another and from one task to another.

Hersey and Blanchard's approach to contingency theory has been criticized as being a bit too simplistic because it focusses on only the one variable — maturity.[25] Other approaches are considerably more complex in that they incorporate

---

[25]Yukl, *Leadership in Organizations*, pp. 143–144 and ch. 6.

more variables which managers ought to take into account in choosing a leadership style,[26] but situational leadership theory is a good illustration of the concept of contingency theory.

However, leadership is not something to be valued in itself. Leadership must have some purpose; one of the main purposes of leadership is to improve organizational effectiveness by motivating employees. The next section of this chapter reviews some theories of motivation.

MOTIVATION

Earlier ideas of motivation were rather simple. Bosses simply told workers what to do and they did it — or were fired. Henry Ford is purported to have said that the best incentive to an employee is the presence of unemployed workers outside the factory gate. Chapters 2 and 3 described how earlier ideas of external motivation based on fear of punishment or monetary or other rewards have recently been replaced with ideas of the importance of internal motivators such as self-actualization or pride in accomplishment. Traditional forms of motivation based on punishment have fallen into disuse for a number of reasons. The strength of unions and recent changes in labour laws to protect workers have reduced the unilateral power which employers once had to discipline employees. However, research indicates that motivation by fear of punishment is not a very efficient motivator, anyway.[27] Negative forms of motivation might well encourage employees to do just enough to avoid being disciplined without really striving for excellence; this could result in a continual game of employees trying to find out how much they can "get away with" before they are disciplined. This could then lead to escalation on the part of both employer and employees as management continually imposes new controls and restrictions and employees find ways of circumventing them. Positive methods of motivating people are probably much more effective.

Chapters 2 and 3 discussed some of the motivating mechanisms employed in various schools of management. Table 4.1 summarizes some of the main points made in those chapters. This chapter will build on some of the general findings presented earlier and provide additional details on motivating mechanisms.

Chris Argyris's Maturity-Immaturity Theory
Chris Argyris points out that all social organizations are composed of individuals and a formal structure, but that tensions inevitably develop because there is a basic incongruence between the behaviour pattern of mature individuals and the needs of the formal organization.

He suggests that the characteristics of a maturing individual are increasing activity or self-determination, independence rather than dependence, multi-

---

[26]A good review of the contingency theories of leadership is found in ibid., chs. 6 and 7.
[27]Leonard R. Sayles and George Strauss, *Managing Human Resources* (Englewood Cliffs, N.J.: Prentice-Hall, 1977), p. 132.

Table 4.1
SUMMARY OF MOTIVATING MECHANISMS

Management School	Communication Style	Leadership Style	Motivating Mechanism
Weberian	Formal Downward	Authoritarian	Commands Authority
Scientific Management (Taylor)	Formal Downward	Authoritarian	Authority Financial Rewards
Human Relations (Theory X–Theory Y) (Hierarchy of Needs)	Upward Downward Lateral	Democratic Potentially Laissez- faire	Self-actualization
Participative (Organizational Development)	Upward Downward Lateral	Democratic	Self-actualization Participation

facetted behaviour, deepening interest in stimulating challenges, longer time perspective, feelings of equality with peers, and self-awareness.[28]

He goes on to point out that formal organizations are based on such principles as task or work specialization, chain of command, unity of direction, and span of control.[29] Most of these principles require not mature, but *immature*, behaviour on the part of the individual. For example, mature individuals capable of complex behaviour and interested in challenges are placed in jobs which require boring, repetitive actions. "Organizations are willing to pay high wages and provide adequate seniority if mature adults will, for eight hours a day, behave in a less than mature manner!"[30]

It is quite normal for individual employees to react negatively when confronted with this situation. They could simply leave the organization. Or they could stay in the organization and become apathetic and/or establish an informal work group which could have a detrimental effect on production. Or they could resolve to work their way up the organizational ladder, because the incongruence between personality and organizational demands are less at the higher levels.[31]

In a later work, Argyris presents some tentative suggestions for resolving this basic incongruence.[32] He suggests that organizations of the future will emphasize the pyramidal organizational structure less, and recognize that there are other, less formal structures in place which are important as well. He strongly supports a form of job enlargement (discussed in more detail below) which would ensure that employees develop a greater understanding of, and concern for, the activities of the *entire* organization, rather than only their narrow portion of it. This should be supplemented by employees meeting in small groups to discuss

---

[28]*Personality and Organization: The Conflict Between System and the Individual* (New York: Harper & Row, 1957), pp. 50–51.
[29]Ibid., ch. 3.
[30]Ibid., p. 66.
[31]Ibid., ch. 4.
[32]*Integrating the Individual and the Organization* (New York: John Wiley & Sons, 1964).

problems of the organization and possibilities for improvement. He argued that autocratic leadership styles should be replaced by what are now called contingency approaches to leadership — different types of employees and situations call forth different leadership styles. Control mechanisms should be less negatively oriented towards detecting transgressions and more oriented towards helping individuals achieve greater "self-responsibility and psychological success."[33]

A standard criticism of Argyris's approach is that he views human nature as too homogeneous. His view that *everyone* is mature and wants interesting, challenging work is too simplistic. Robert Presthus argues that different personalities react differently to bureaucratic structures. He labels the three different bureaucratic personality types as "upward mobiles," "indifferents," and "ambivalents."[34] One might disagree with the specifics of Presthus's categories, but it does seem to be the case that different individuals behave differently in bureaucratic settings; most seem to hate the boredom, but some find things about even the most boring job to relish.[35] It is possible that it is the characterization of "bureaucracy" as homogeneous which misses the mark. The characteristics of particular jobs can vary quite widely; an employee's positive or negative feelings might have more to do with how the employee views his or her job than with how he or she relates to the overall bureaucracy.

Frederick Herzberg's Motivation-Hygiene Theory

Frequently people assume that the factors which cause *satisfaction* in the work environment are the same factors which cause *dissatisfaction*. Frederick Herzberg tested this conventional wisdom by asking a number of employees to describe work occurrences that led to satisfaction and dissatisfaction. In many cases, the factors causing satisfaction were very different from those causing dissatisfaction.[36] For example, Table 4.2 indicates that the presence of a feeling of achievement tended to satisfy workers, but its absence did not make them dissatisfied; it simply reduced their satisfaction. Conversely, company policy and administration were a frequent source of dissatisfaction, but correcting problems in this area merely lessened dissatisfaction; it did not increase satisfaction.

One important caveat about Herzberg's approach is that it focusses predominantly on employee satisfaction; it says nothing about productivity, unless you assume that there is some relationship between satisfaction and productivity — a contentious point, at best.

Herzberg referred to those factors which led to dissatisfaction as *hygiene factors* because "they act in a manner analogous to the principles of medical hygiene. Hygiene operates to remove health hazards from the environment of man. It is

---

[33]Ibid., p. 275.

[34]*The Organizational Society*, rev. ed. (New York: St. Martin's Press, 1978).

[35]Henry Mintzberg, *Structure in Fives: Designing Effective Organizations* (Englewood Cliffs, N.J.: Prentice-Hall, 1983), pp. 178–179.

[36]The results of this research were reported in detail in: Frederick Herzberg, Bernard Mausner, and Barbara Bloch Snyderman, *The Motivation to Work* (New York: John Wiley & Sons, 1959). A more elaborate discussion and further verification of the theory is contained in Frederick Herzberg, *Work and the Nature of Man* (Cleveland: World Publishing Company, 1966).

Table 4.2
HERZBERG'S MOTIVATION AND HYGIENE FACTORS

Motivators	*Hygiene*
Achievement	Company Policy & Administration
Recognition	Supervision—Technical
Work Itself	Salary
Responsibility	Interpersonal Relations—Supervision
Advancement	Working Conditions

not curative; it is, rather, a preventive."[37] The factors which led to satisfaction, Herzberg labelled *motivators* because they had a highly positive effect on people's feelings about their job.

Herzberg noted a very interesting difference between the hygiene and motivating factors. The hygiene factors all relate to the work environment, while the motivating factors are all intrinsic to the nature of the job itself. The implications of Herzberg's theory for management are clear. The general work environment should be pleasant enough to avoid dissatisfaction, but any major improvements in motivation can be made only through changes in the nature of the job itself.

The specific remedy suggested by Herzberg was job redesign or job enrichment.

Job Redesign

The theories of both Argyris and Herzberg focussed on the ability to improve motivation through careful job design. A number of different approaches to improving the quality of the job itself have been tried.

Job rotation involves keeping the job descriptions for all positions the same, but shifting the people who fill the positions. This could be done for only a half-day at a time or for a few weeks. It adds some variety to a person's workday and could increase a person's sense of accomplishment and responsibility if he or she knows how to do several jobs instead of just one.

The rigidities introduced into the workplace by collective agreements and the merit system can limit the possibility of job rotation. Moving a person into a job temporarily could be seen as giving that person an advantage in any future competition for that job. Employees also sometimes resist job rotation on the basis that it is no more interesting to do two boring jobs than to do one boring job.

Job enlargement tries to relieve the boredom in a job by expanding the size of the job. Instead of spending all day simply examining and filing forms, an employee might also be responsible for working at a counter and helping members of the public fill out forms. Having broader responsibilities and being able to see more of the total process should increase an employee's sense of belonging and accomplishment.

---

[37]Herzberg, et al., *The Motivation to Work*, p. 113.

Job enlargement has been tried in many places and has been quite successful,[39] but again, bureaucratic rigidities can cause problems. A job description with more duties probably means that the job will receive a higher rate of pay. If this is the case, management will likely want to stay away from job enlargement.

Job enrichment or *vertical job loading* is a variant of job enlargement proposed by Argyris and Herzberg, among many others. Herzberg, in particular, emphasized the importance of expanding jobs not just by arbitrarily adding more duties, but also by considering the needs of the mature employee. He pointed out the difference between horizontal job loading, which meant simply loading a person with more work, and vertical job loading, which meant expanding the job through such means as:[39]

- removing some detailed controls and making the employee more responsible for his or her own work,
- carving out a "natural unit of work" for the person and granting him or her additional responsibility for dealing with all problems in that area, and
- introducing more specialized and difficult tasks.

Herzberg felt that these improvements in the job itself would improve an employee's satisfaction, but other theories argue that more extensive changes in the overall work environment are beneficial.

Quality of Working Life

In recent years workers have become more vocal and more sophisticated in their complaints about their work environment. This has been reflected in such problems as more militant union actions, demands for higher pay and improved working conditions, and greater employee dissatisfaction evidenced through high absenteeism, and alcohol and drug abuse. Quality of working life (QWL) has come to signify a number of different specific programs all directed at "renovat[ing] working patterns and environments in order that there might be a better fit between what people *expected* from their jobs and what they actually *found* in their jobs."[40]

The purpose of QWL is to analyse the reasons for the discrepancy between employee expectations and actual conditions and prescribe what ought to be done to correct that discrepancy.

> QWL techniques or approaches cannot be purchased as one buys candy from a store, with thought given only to the sweetness of the commodity. The choice of the "candy" must be integrated with the needs of the organization's social and technical system. A "best fit" between the two must be sought.[41]

---

[38]Roy W. Walters, "Job Enrichment Isn't Easy," *Personnel Administration and Public Personnel Review*, vol. 1 (September–October 1972), p. 61.

[39]Frederick Herzberg, "One More Time: How Do You Motivate Employees?" *Harvard Business Review*, vol. 46 (January-February 1968), pp. 59-62.

[40]"Introduction," in J. B. Cunningham and T. H. White, eds., *Quality of Working Life: Contemporary Cases* (Ottawa: Minister of Supply and Services Canada, 1984), p. 2. (Emphasis in original.)

[41]Eric Trist, Preface in ibid., p. x.

The innovations adopted as a result of a QWL undertaking could consist of anything from minor changes in job descriptions to major organizational development projects. Barry A. Stein provides a list of some of the possible changes: employee opinion surveys, all-employee meetings, management by objectives, open-door policies, flexible schedules, team building, job enrichment, and self-managed work teams.[42]

However, the purpose of a good QWL exercise is not to "molly-coddle" employees and make their work easier. The intent of QWL is to improve both worker satisfaction and organizational productivity. As has been mentioned a number of times in this and earlier chapters, these two do not always go together. The potential for QWL to accomplish both of these elusive goals seemed so good that between 1978 and 1986 the federal Department of Labour undertook a major project involving research into certain aspects of QWL and dissemination of information about successful QWL projects.[43]

The processes of carrying out a QWL project can vary as widely as the resultant outputs, but there are a few common elements. A prime consideration is that the project must be jointly "owned" and managed by the union (or employees) and management. There is already a risk that some changes will be seen as a method of exploiting employees; a lack of meaningful employee involvement in the process will add weight to that charge. The project is usually managed by a steering committee composed of representatives of the employees and management.

The process itself can be seen as having five phases.[44] The first phase, *initiation*, requires that labour and management become familiar with QWL concepts and decide whether they want to proceed with the project. An important aspect of this phase is the building of trust between the parties; this can be particularly difficult in environments where there is a long history of labour-management strife. This is why an outside facilitator (sort of a marriage counsellor) is sometimes useful at this point and throughout the process.

The *set-up* phase involves the preparation of an agreement and a plan of action. The written agreement is a key part of the process because it provides a test of how committed the two sides are and how far they are willing to go. It sets out areas of expected change as well as "untouchable" areas. The agreement is not legally binding, but a serious violation of it would constitute a show of bad faith.

The project would usually not be implemented in all units of the organization. The steering committee will select the work unit or units in which the project will commence. The unit selected should be reasonably representative of the

---

[42]*Quality of Work Life In Action: Managing for Effectiveness* (New York: American Management Associations, 1983), pp. 32–34.

[43]This project was responsible for a number of the publications mentioned in this section as well as the very interesting and useful periodical publication *Quality of Working Life: The Canadian Scene*, which described current innovations in the QWL scene.

[44]Carl P. Johnston, Mark Alexander, and Jacquelin Robin, *Quality of Working Life: The Idea and its Application* (Ottawa: Minister of Supply and Services Canada, 1980), pp. 15–32.

overall organization and should also offer a good chance of successful application.

The third phase is *work/situation analysis*. This involves "socio-technical analysis," which is a fancy way of saying that both the social and technical aspects of specific jobs and the general work environment will be studied in depth to determine if they can be improved. The project team will ask these questions:

> How can the job be changed, in order that the job incumbent can find more challenge in it, an opportunity to learn, to be involved in the decisions that affect the job without significantly reducing job outputs?

> How can the environmental factors that surround that job (management and communication processes, measurement systems and personnel policies and practices) be changed in order to make the work situation a better place, not only in terms of human satisfaction, but also operational effectiveness?

> How can the technology be changed in order to allow the individual to have more control and better serve the needs of that individual?[45]

The next phase is the *design and implementation* of the improvements identified in the third phase. These could involve an infinite number of changes, such as those listed above.

The fifth phase is *evaluation and diffusion*. To this point, the project has been implemented in only a limited number of units in the organization. Now, the steering committee assesses the results of the exercise[46] and decides whether it wants to cancel the whole project or proceed to extend the exercise throughout the organization or into selected other areas.

This sounds a great deal like the concept of organizational development discussed in Chapter 3. One of the major differences is that QWL is not concerned purely with organizational effectiveness; it is also interested in improving the employees' work environment. Also, OD almost invariably implies major highly disruptive changes in the organization; QWL begins in only a limited number of units, and its outcome could involve anything from minor shifts in responsibilities or job descriptions to the major changes which frequently come from OD.

QWL is a way of effecting change so that employees will be better motivated. There are some other management systems which also promise better motivation and organizational performance. The remainder of this chapter will look at two of these.

Theory Z—Japanese Management

One of the great success stories of recent years has been the performance of the Japanese economy. Japanese companies are both envied and feared by their North American competitors. Japan is a country with virtually no natural

---

[45]Ibid., p. 24.
[46]D. A. Ondrak and M. G. Evans, *Quality of Working Life: Evaluation and Measurement* (Ottawa: Minister of Supply and Services Canada, 1981).

resources, but its companies have shown an ability to enter almost any market and produce a very high quality product at a competitive price. This success is usually linked to the high productivity of the Japanese worker. This has produced an interest in Japanese management techniques to determine if some of them can be exported.[47] This section will discuss some of those techniques and some of the impediments to their use in Canada.

Lifetime Employment. The large firms that employ approximately one-third of the labour force in Japan virtually guarantee lifetime employment to their management workforce. New employees are recruited once each year from that year's crop of university graduates. These people are not recruited to fill specific positions, but rather employers seek to hire a group of employees whose interests and temperament are compatible with the milieu of the firm. In some cases, there might not be a position available immediately for a new recruit, but this is not a concern because it is more important to hire good people for the long run than to fill specific positions in the short run.

After someone is hired, he (even today, Japanese firms tend not to hire women managers[48]) has a virtual guarantee that he will not be laid off or fired for anything short of a criminal offence. This is one of the things which creates the system of trust on which much of Japanese management is based. Ouchi points out a number of situations in which managers agree to do things which benefit the firm, but leave them very vulnerable personally.[49] Canadian managers would be loathe to put themselves in this position, but in the Japanese system, managers trust that their sacrifices for the firm will be remembered and rewarded in the long run. After all, if you know that you will be spending the rest of your working life with a person, it would not do to take advantage in the short term.

The fact that a person has lifetime tenure with an organization does not eliminate any sort of incentive to perform. On the contrary, good performance is very important to attain promotions and to maintain your credibility with your lifelong peer group.

Non-specialized Career Paths. The new recruit to the firm embarks on an orientation program which involves rotation through a number of different units in the company. In a Japanese firm, no one spends an entire career specializing in one function; people are systematically rotated through a number of different functions. There is a cost to doing this; Japanese firms do not have people with a high degree of specialization in particular functions. What they have instead is an entire workforce which understands the total operation of the organization, the problems encountered in other organizational units, and a great many of the people working in those units. This is another method of engendering the

---

[47]Most of the following commentary is derived from one of the most prolific writers on Theory Z. William G. Ouchi, *Theory Z: How American Business Can Meet the Japanese Challenge* (New York: Avon Books, 1981).
[48]Ibid., p. 21.
[49]Ibid., pp. 5, 16–17, 40.

trust mentioned above, as well as a concern for the total company rather than only one portion of it.

Slow Evaluation and Promotion. After the new employee is hired, he moves through a number of different assignments, usually with progressively more responsibility, but he will not receive a formal evaluation or a promotion until he has been with the firm approximately ten years. This focus on the long term has a number of consequences.

Everyone has heard stories of the dysfunctional corporate "game playing" in Canadian companies — managers play tricks to make themselves look good in the short term and win a promotion. If evaluation is done only after ten years, there is simply no point in this kind of behaviour. Also, managers being evaluated over such a long term can take the risk of being innovative and experimenting with new ideas; they know that one project gone sour will not destroy a career.

The fact that a person does not receive a formal promotion does not mean that he is not given additional responsibilities. Canadians are sometimes confused in dealing with Japanese firms because titles — which are so important to Canadians — are frequently not commensurate with responsibility in Japanese firms. Promotions, once given, are seldom reversed. Therefore, potential senior managers are given great scope for decision making while still at apparently junior levels in order to test their abilities before they are given the title to go with the responsibility.

Large Bonuses Based on Total Company Performance. As much as one-third of a Japanese manager's annual pay can come in the form of a bonus. The most significant aspect of the bonus is that all employees receive the same percentage which is based on *total company performance* and not personal, or even divisional, performance. Here is another example of an incentive system which encourages managers to place the performance of the overall company ahead of their own personal good.

Slow, Collective Decision Making. In Canadian companies, there is frequently a sense of individual responsibility for decisions. Managers take pride in saying: "The buck stops here." The Japanese system requires collective decision making, but a form of collective decision making which goes far beyond the standard prescriptions of participative management discussed in the previous chapter. A small team is assigned to prepare a report; its members must consult very widely in the organization. The decision finally made reflects the needs and interests of a broad cross-section of employees. The system works well in Japanese firms because all employees are socialized to have a greater concern for the overall good of the company than for their own unit.

Canadians dealing with Japanese companies are frequently frustrated at the slow pace at which this kind of decision making proceeds. However, the slowness in decision making can be more than offset in the speed of implementation because everyone understands the aims of the decision and is in agreement with it.

A *quality circle* consists of a small group of employees who meet on a *voluntary* basis to discuss work-related concerns. Because of the title, there is usually an incorrect assumption that quality circles are concerned with quality control. The group could discuss work factors which would improve quality control, but this is only one aspect of their concerns. Group discussions could involve "increasing output, improving work procedures, utilizing equipment better, and even improving product design. Quality circles also discuss ways to improve job satisfaction or morale."[50]

Can Theory Z Work in Canada?

Most of the reservations about the adoption of the Japanese management system in Canada revolve around the belief that it is culture-bound, i.e., it works in Japan because of certain aspects of its culture which are not present elsewhere.[51] For a variety of reasons, Japanese society is considered to be characterized by a degree of trust between individuals and concern for the collective good which does not seem to exist in other societies.[52] This is reflected in management techniques. The Japanese management system built on trust contrasts rather sharply with the Canadian one built on elaborate labour laws and collective agreements. Ouchi suggests that these obstacles can be overcome, but the distance to be traversed by labour and management is significant.

Certain aspects of the Japanese system might not sit well with other aspects of the Canadian value system. By Canadian standards, the Japanese system could be considered frankly exploitative. It works well for shareholders and, to a lesser extent, for the — predominantly male — managers. It does not work so well for others. The fact that managers receive such a large portion of their incomes in the form of a bonus gives the company a nice cushion in difficult times. Bonuses are reduced so that managers, not shareholders, bear the risks. However, the male managers fare better than the female operating employees. The lifetime guarantee of security of employment applies only to managers; operating employees are laid off and recalled very quickly in response to market demands.

The Japanese system has worked very well — in Japan. There is also evidence that some of the best-managed American companies have adopted some of its ideas.[53] Canadians would be foolish not to examine it and consider the lessons which it holds. However, it can be very difficult to adapt motivational techniques from other societies. It could well be that there are lessons to be learned from experiences closer to home.

---

[50]Jan P. Muczyk, Eleanor Brantley Schwartz, and Ephraim Smith, *Principles of Supervision: First- and Second-Line Management* (Columbus, Ohio: Charles E. Merrill, 1984), p. 206. See also Richard J. Schonberger, *Japanese Manufacturing Techniques* (New York: The Free Press, 1982), ch. 8.

[51]Ouchi, *Theory Z*, pp. 54–57.

[52]S. Prakash Sethi, Nobuaki Namiki, and Carl L. Swanson, *The False Promise of the Japanese Miracle* (Boston: Pitman, 1984).

[53]Ouchi, *Theory Z*, pp. 57–59.

In Search of Excellence

One of the most widely read books of the 1980s on management has been Thomas J. Peters and Robert H. Waterman, Jr.'s *In Search of Excellence*.[54] These two management consultants set out on a major project to determine the factors which created maximum organizational effectiveness. Their first approach was to begin tinkering with organizational structures, but their research quickly told them that there were more important factors in organizational effectiveness than rearranging boxes on an organization chart.

Their work considered far more than just motivation, but since many of their findings dealt with the relationship between the organization and its people, it is logical to discuss these findings in conjunction with employee motivation.

They conducted extensive research on forty-three excellent American companies in various industries. The companies were selected on the basis of their financial performance, their financial position in comparison to other companies in the industry, and a subjective assessment of their innovativeness. The research indicated that these companies possessed eight factors which contributed to their excellence.

A Bias for Action. This sounds obvious, but Peters and Waterman contrast the kind of organization which appoints a huge team to study all of the implications of a change and report back in two years with the once-and-for-all solution with companies which are continually innovating and experimenting on a small scale. The former kind of organization seems to experience either total success or, usually, abject failure because it invariably ends up putting all of its eggs in one basket. Excellent companies assign several small task forces to a problem and emphasize the need to respond quickly. They are able to experiment with a number of innovations in a limited way. Because they are experimenting and doing *something*, they are more likely to hit on the best solution than the slow, stodgy company which will not move until it has weighed all of the possibilities.

Close to the Customer. Again, this sounds like an obvious point, but the researchers were surprised at how frequently it was overlooked. All companies are concerned with customers when they are selling their products; there is nothing special about that. However, Peters and Waterman found that the excellent companies continually curried the favour of their customers by emphasizing service and by going beyond the minimum that had to be done to complete the sale.

Excellent companies also spend time talking — and more important, *listening* — to customers. Customers know better than suppliers the problems with existing products and the innovative new products which are needed. Closeness to customers keeps innovators on the cutting edge and prevents them from producing "white elephants."

---

[54](New York: Warner Books, 1982).

Autonomy and Entrepreneurship. Bureaucracies can stifle creativity and inno-vation. Excellent companies ensure that some people in the organization are insulated from this problem. The main technique employed is to decentralize the organization in such a manner that it masks the huge size of the total organization.

> It eventually became clear that all of these companies were making a pur-poseful trade-off. They were creating almost radical decentralization and autonomy, with its attendant overlap, messiness around the edges, lack of coordination, internal competition, and somewhat chaotic conditions, in order to breed the entrepreneurial spirit. They had forsworn a measure of tidiness in order to achieve regular innovation.[55]

It is noteworthy that one of the factors inherent in this and some of the previ-ous characteristics is a frank acceptance of failure. Taking action instead of ruminating is inviting failure. Excellent companies accept the fact that one of the costs of major success is a series of smaller failures. This means that the company's incentive system must not punish people who make legitimate, cre-ative efforts and fail. Excellent companies remember the importance of having good people and sticking with them.

Productivity Through People. Excellent companies treat their employees as though they were responsible, trustworthy human beings. That does not sound like such a radical idea, but many organizations send strong signals which indi-cate their lack of trust in their employees. Peters and Waterman emphasize that the concern for people must be genuine and that there is no one best way to accomplish that. MBO, quality circles, open door policies are all useful, but none of them really works if management is not genuinely concerned about workers.

Hands-on, Value Driven. Excellent companies have a company philosophy in which employees can take pride. This tends to mould people into a cohesive group. It helps if the goal is something that can create interest and enthusiasm among employees. It is much easier to get excited about a high concern for service or quality than maximizing earnings per share.

Stick to Your Knitting. One of the executives interviewed stated it quite simply: "Never buy a business you don't know how to run."[56] There is nothing wrong with diversification per se. In fact, excellent companies tended to diversify while staying within one general area. The biggest problems come about when compa-nies diversify into areas where they have no experience.

Simple Form, Lean Staff. Complex management structures confuse people and divide their efforts. In the matrix management structure discussed in Chapter 3, it can be unclear to whom an employee is responsible. Some problem in this

---

[55]Ibid., p. 201.
[56]Ibid., p. 15.

area could involve several senior executives in the exchange of many memoranda. A large, strong staff organization can intervene too much and so distract operating employees from the performance of their primary duties. The excellent companies surveyed had small headquarters staffs and simple organization structures.

Simultaneous Loose-tight Properties. This refers to "the co-existence of firm central direction and maximum individual autonomy."[57] This apparent paradox means that excellent companies give their employees a great deal of operating autonomy as long as they do not violate certain strongly held central tenets of the organization. IBM employees are encouraged to experiment with all sorts of new ideas as long as they do not forget that "IBM Means Service."

Even though this research was done exclusively in the private sector, there are some lessons for public sector organizations. There are limits on the appropriate entrepreneurship of public administrators; initiating new programs is clearly the job of politicians. However, if administrators stayed closer to their clients (customers) they would probably have a much better understanding of problems in service delivery, and they would also be able to provide better policy advice to their political masters. The high concern for employees is fairly readily adaptable to public organizations, although the scope in public sector organizations for decentralization and "messiness" can be somewhat limited. Some of the lessons contained in *In Search of Excellence* are not relevant to the public sector, but many are.

CONCLUSION AND AN ASSESSMENT

The general thrust of the theories on motivation discussed in this chapter is the need for greater flexibility in leadership styles, organizational structures, and job design. There is substantial evidence that suggests that this flexibility is highly conducive to achieving organizational effectiveness and worker satisfaction.

How do Canadian governments rate in terms of their use of the techniques mentioned in this chapter. The answer is simple: very poorly. At a time when all the evidence points towards greater flexibility, most Canadian governments are bolstering their skills at writing detailed job descriptions and tightening reporting requirements. These steps do not bode well for attempts at job redesign, contingency approaches to leadership, or quality of working life projects. The termination of the federal Department of Labour's Quality of Working Life project in 1986 is only one signal, but an important one.

In fairness to governments, they face certain environmental constraints not faced in the private sector. The most significant of these is the comparative openness of government. This openness makes governments hypersensitive about failure and about gaps in their systems of control because government failures are so public and are handled so brutally by the media. This sensitivity to failure influences many characteristics of government organization. It creates a

---

[57]Ibid., p. 318.

bias for *in*action and constant study; it gravitates against autonomy; it gravitates in favour of strong central control agencies. Because of government's basic concern for failure, there would be a great deal of difficulty in establishing the characteristics which Peters and Waterman see as essential for excellence in government organizations.

One should not conclude on a totally negative note. There are many bright spots in government departments where individual managers have realized the importance of improving the system. The problem is that there has been little attention to system-wide initiatives in this area.

BIBLIOGRAPHY

Argyris, Chris. *Integrating the Individual and the Organization*. New York: John Wiley & Sons, 1964.

Argyris, Chris. *Personality and Organization: The Conflict Between System and the Individual*. New York: Harper & Row, 1957.

Argyris, Chris, with Roger Harrison. *Interpersonal Competence and Organizational Effectiveness*. Homewood, Ill.: Richard D. Irwin, 1962.

Blau, Peter M., and W. Richard Scott. *Formal Organizations: A Comparative Approach*. San Francisco: Chandler Publishing Company, 1962.

Boyatzis, Richard A. *The Competent Manager: A Model for Effective Performance*. New York: John Wiley & Sons, 1982.

Cartwright, Dorwin, and Alvin Zander, eds. *Group Dynamics: Research and Theory*. 3rd ed. New York: Harper & Row, 1968.

Cunningham, J. B., and T. H. White, eds. *Quality of Working Life: Contemporary Cases*. Ottawa: Minister of Supply and Services Canada, 1984.

Dubin, Robert, George C. Homans, Floyd C. Mann, and Delbert C. Miller. *Leadership and Productivity*. San Francisco: Chandler Publishing Company, 1965.

Dunsire, Andrew. *Implementation in a Bureaucracy*. Oxford: Martin Robertson, 1978.

Fayol, Henri. *General and Industrial Management*. Translated from the French by Constance Storrs. London: Pitman Publishing, 1971.

Fiedler, Fred A. *A Theory of Leadership Effectiveness*. New York: McGraw-Hill Book Company, 1967.

Fiedler, Fred A., Martin M. Chemers, with Linda Mahar. *Improving Leadership Effectiveness: The Leader Match Concept*, rev. ed. New York: John Wiley & Sons, 1977.

Filley, Alan C., and Robert J. House. *Managerial Process and Organizational Behavior*. Glenview, Ill.: Scott, Foresman and Company, 1969.

Hall, Richard H. *Organizations: Structure and Process*. 3rd ed. Englewood Cliffs, N.J.: Prentice-Hall, 1982.

Hersey, Paul, and Kenneth H. Blanchard. *Management of Organizational Behavior: Utilizing Human Resources*. 3rd ed. Englewood Cliffs, N.J.: Prentice-Hall, 1977.

Herzberg, Frederick. "One More Time: How Do You Motivate Employees?" *Harvard Business Review*, vol. 46 (January–February 1968): 53–62.

Herzberg, Frederick. *Work and the Nature of Man*. Cleveland: World Publishing Company, 1966.

Herzberg, Frederick, Bernard Mausner, and Barbara Bloch Snyderman. *The Motivation to Work*. New York: John Wiley & Sons, 1959.

Huck, James R. "Assessment Centres: A Review of the External and Internal Validities." *Personnel Psychology*, vol. 26 (Summer 1973): 191–212.

Johnston, Carl P., Mark Alexander, and Jacquelin Robin. *Quality of Working Life: The Idea and its Application*. Ottawa: Minister of Supply and Services Canada, 1980.

Katz, Robert L. "Skills of an Effective Administrator." *Harvard Business Review*, vol. 33 (January–February 1955): 33–42.

Katz, Daniel, and Robert L. Kahn. *The Social Psychology of Organizations*. 2nd ed. New York: John Wiley & Sons, 1978.

Lewin, Kurt, Ronald Lippitt, and Ralph K. White. "Patterns of Aggressive Behavior in Experimentally Created 'Social Climates.' " *Journal of Social Psychology*, vol. 10 (1939): 271–299.

Likert, Rensis. *The Human Organization*. New York: McGraw-Hill Book Company, 1967.

Likert, Rensis. *New Patterns of Management*. New York: McGraw-Hill Book Company, 1961.

Lippitt, Ronald, and Ralph K. White. "The 'Social Climate' of Children's Groups." In *Child Behavior and Development: A Course of Representative Studies*, edited by Robert G. Barker, Jacob S. Kounin, and Herbert F. Wright. New York: McGraw-Hill Book Company, 1943, pp. 485–508.

Mintzberg, Henry. *Structure in Fives: Designing Effective Organizations*. Englewood Cliffs, N.J.: Prentice-Hall, 1983.

Muczyk, Jan P., Eleanor Brantley Schwartz, and Ephraim Smith. *Principles of Supervision: First- and Second-Line Management*. Columbus, Ohio: Charles E. Merrill Publishing Company, 1984.

Nigro, Felix A. *Modern Public Administration*. New York: Harper & Row, 1965.

Ondrak, D. A., and M. G. Evans. *Quality of Working Life: Evaluation and Measurement*. Ottawa: Minister of Supply and Services Canada, 1981.

Ouchi, William G. *Theory Z: How American Business Can Meet the Japanese Challenge*. New York: Avon Books, 1981.

Peters, Thomas J., and Robert H. Waterman, Jr. *In Search of Excellence*. New York, Warner Books, 1982.

Peters, Tom, and Nancy Austin. *A Passion for Excellence: The Leadership Difference*. New York: Random House, 1985.

Presthus, Robert. *The Organizational Society*, rev. ed. New York: St. Martin's Press, 1978.

Pursley, Robert D., and Neil Snortland. *Managing Government Organizations: An Introduction to Public Administration*. North Scituate, Mass.: Duxbury Press, 1980.

Quality of Working Life: The Canadian Scene. (A periodical published by the federal Department of Labour from 1978 to 1986.)

Sayles, Leonard R., and George Strauss. *Managing Human Resources*. Englewood Cliffs, N.J.: Prentice-Hall, 1977.

Schonberger, Richard J. *Japanese Manufacturing Techniques*. New York: The Free Press, 1982.

Scott, William G., Terence R. Mitchell, and Philip H. Birnbarum. *Organization Theory: A Structural and Behavioral Analysis*. 4th ed. Homewood, Ill.: Richard D. Irwin, 1981.

Sethi, S. Prakash, Nobuaki Namiki, and Carl L. Swanson. *The False Promise of the Japanese Miracle*. Boston: Pitman, 1984.

Stein, Barry A. *Quality of Work Life In Action: Managing for Effectiveness*. New York: American Management Associations, 1983.

Stogdill, Ralph M. *Handbook of Leadership: A Survey of Theory and Research*. New York: The Free Press, 1974.

Tannenbaum, Robert T., and Warren H. Schmidt. "How to Choose A Leadership Style." *Harvard Business Review*, vol. 36 (March–April 1958): 95–101.

Walters, Roy W. "Job Enrichment Isn't Easy." *Personnel Administration and Public Personnel Review*, vol. 1 (September–October 1972).

Walton, Eugene. "How Efficient Is the Grapevine?" *Personnel*, vol. 38 (March–April 1961): 61–66.

White, Ralph K., and Ronald Lippitt. *Autocracy and Democracy*. Westport, Conn.: Greenwood Press, 1972.

Williams, J. D. *Public Administration: The People's Business*. Boston: Little, Brown and Company, 1980.

Yukl, Gary A. *Leadership in Organizations*. Englewood Cliffs, N.J.: Prentice-Hall, 1981.

CASES

In *Case Program in Canadian Public Administration* (Toronto: Institute of Public Administration of Canada):

    The Administrative In-Basket Case, by C. Lloyd Brown-John

    The Police Chief's In-Basket, by R. I. McLaren

    Trying to Fire the Medical Officer of Health: A Case Study, by Alison McGear, Ted Darby, and Raisa B. Deber

In Kenneth Kernaghan, *Canadian Cases in Public Administration* (Toronto: Methuen Publications):

    Dr. Stockfield's Resignation

    The Shared Authority

    Dr. Aphid's Accident

    The Frustrated Purchasing Agent

    The Vague Purchasing Assignment

    The Successful Leader

    This Hour Has Seven Days

    The Difficult Supervisor

    The Health of Mr. Cole

    The Auditor's Lament

    The Renfrew Group

    The Resigning Engineer

    The Foot and Mouth Disease Epidemic, 1952

5

Making and Implementing
Public Policy

The previous chapters have discussed some of the theories of organizing and motivating employees. These theories are not ends in themselves; rather, they assist in the making and implementing of public policy which is the real core of government activity. There are a number of theories about how government policies are made. This chapter will first review some of these theories and then discuss a relatively new area of study in public administration — policy implementation. In the past, the area of policy implementation was simply not studied because there seemed to be an implicit assumption that once policy was articulated, implementation was automatic, with little friction or tension. In the last decade, there has been a growing awareness that the relationship between making and implementing policy is not always so smooth.

MODELS OF POLICY MAKING

Political scientists and other students of public policy have developed several models of how public policies are made. These models are ways of describing how policy makers, such as Cabinet ministers and legislators, think about public policy and interact in the policy-making process. However, policy makers usually do not consciously think about these models when they are making policy; the models have been developed by academics and others who analyse policy decisions after they have been made.

Models of public policy can be divided into normative and descriptive models. *Normative* models prescribe how decisions *should* be made. Thus, a normative model is an ideal model of how a particular theorist feels that the policy process *ought* to work. *Descriptive* models attempt to explain how decisions *are* made in practice. The formulation of a descriptive model involves the study of how a number of policies have been made and some generalization about how the system works. As will be discussed below, some models purport to be both normative and descriptive.

There are a number of different definitions of the phrase "public policy." This book will use Thomas R. Dye's simple, yet effective, definition that "public policy is whatever governments choose to do or not do."[1] He explains that:

> Governments do many things. They regulate conflict within society; they organize society to carry on conflict with other societies; they distribute a

---

[1] *Understanding Public Policy*, 5th ed. (Englewood Cliffs, N.J.: Prentice-Hall, © 1984), p. 1.

great variety of symbolic rewards and material services to members of the society; and they extract money from society, most often in the form of taxes. Thus, public policies may regulate behavior, organize bureaucracies, distribute benefits, or extract taxes — or all of these things at once. . . .

Public policies may deal with a wide variety of substantive areas — defense, energy, environment, foreign affairs, education, welfare, police, highways, taxation, housing, social security, health, economic opportunity, urban development, inflation and recession, and so on. They may range from the vital to the trivial — from the allocation of tens of billions of dollars for a mobile missile system to the designation of an official national bird.[2]

Several aspects of this definition are important. First, unlike other definitions of public policy, there is no discussion of "goals" or "objectives." Policies are specific courses of actions; the adoption of a policy does not imply that all those who agree on a specific policy share the same goals. In fact, some policies come about, not because of an agreement on goals, but because several groups all favour a particular policy, but for totally different reasons. This phenomenon will be discussed in more detail later.

Second, Dye's definition recognizes that policies are reflected in choosing *not* to act as well as in choosing to act. These "non-decisions" can be as important as decisions, especially for groups attempting to effect change.

This definition also suggests that a policy can be either *a specific action* by a government (e.g., the decision by a municipality to allow development in a particular area), or *the result of a series of diverse decisions* (e.g., health care policy, which is really the combination of a large number of decisions, and non-decisions, by many different governments).

The other point about public policy which will be emphasized in this book is that policy is not merely a *statement* by a government about some problem; rather, policy is what is actually *implemented*. Thus, Dye's definition refers to what governments "do," not what they say they want to do or plan to do. Peter Aucoin takes this into account in his definition of public policy: "Public policy must be considered to encompass the actual activities undertaken by a government, whether or not a government's objectives and strategies are explicit, or are congruent with its activities."[3] As explained later in this chapter, there can be significant slippage between policy statements and actual policy, and then further slippage between policy as adopted and policy as implemented.

This section will consider different models of the policy-making process; most of the major models will be reviewed, but this is not meant to be comprehensive.

Comprehensive Rationality

The comprehensive rationality model suggests that policies are subjected to a multi-step analysis before a decision is made. Different writers list slightly different steps, but Anderson's list is typical:

---

[2]Ibid., pp. 1–3. Reprinted by persmission.

[3]"Public-Policy Theory and Analysis," in G. Bruce Doern and Peter Aucoin, eds., *Public Policy in Canada* (Toronto: Macmillan of Canada, 1979), p. 2.

1. The decision-maker is confronted with a given problem that can be separated from other problems or at least considered meaningfully in comparison with them.
2. The goals, values, or objectives that guide the decision-maker are clarified and ranked according to their importance.
3. The various alternatives for dealing with the problem are examined.
4. The consequences (costs and benefits, advantages and disadvantages)
   that would follow from the selection of each alternative are investigated.
5. Each alternative, and its attendant consequences, can be compared with
   the other alternatives.
6. The decision-maker will choose that alternative, and its consequences,
   that maximizes the attainment of his or her goals, values, or objectives.[4]

The attractions of this style of decision making are obvious. It has an aura of
careful forethought and scientific precision which contrasts with some of the
more rudderless models of policy making that will be discussed below. Some of
the techniques used in rational decision making are operations research, cost-
effectiveness, and cost-benefit analysis. Because comprehensive rationality
involves careful analysis, it ought to provide a solution which produces the desired
result with the most efficient use of resources.

However, there are many criticisms of this model. Most of them flow from the
second step identified above — clarification and ranking of goals. In democratic,
pluralistic societies, it is very difficult to rank "goals, values, or objectives" in
order of priority. The question becomes whose goals and whose values will be
reflected in the final decision. The best technical analysis available is useless if
there is no agreement on this point, and there seldom is. Dunn points out this
problem by suggesting that there are at least five different types of "rationality"
which are frequently in conflict with one another.[5]

Even if there were agreement on goals, the requirement for *comprehensive*
analysis would introduce severe complications. The model requires that the decision maker find and compare *all* potential solutions. At what point can the
decision maker be confident that he or she has actually identified *all* possible
solutions? And how far must one go in identifying all consequences (desirable
and undesirable) of a decision? Because of these problems, comprehensive rationality is sometimes dismissed as "paralysis by analysis."

Given these difficulties, it is not surprising that the concept of comprehensive
rationality is not applied very often in practice.

With the possible exception of those few instances when there is the appearance of a full-scale review and analysis of policy alternatives, the empirical
investigation of the making of a public policy usually tends to illustrate

---

[4]James R. Anderson, *Public Policy-Making*, 3rd ed. (New York: Holt, Rinehart and Winston,
1984), p. 8. Copyright © 1984 by CBS College Publishing. Reprinted by permission.
[5]William N. Dunn, *Public Policy Analysis* (Englewood Cliffs, N.J.: Prentice-Hall, 1981), pp.
225-226.

how logical procedures were overrun by a dominant political leader, a pressure group of some sort, or perhaps an influential section of the bureaucracy.[6]

It is difficult to think of examples of public policy decisions made in a purely rational manner, although most decisions are subjected to some limited form of rational analysis at some stage in the decision-making process. For example, in government purchasing decisions, the many alternatives available are frequently reduced to a smaller number on a fairly rational basis, e.g., minimum cost, security of supply, but "non-rational" elements, such as the number of jobs provided in particular areas of the country, frequently intrude on the final decision.

Incrementalism

Charles E. Lindblom argued that not only is comprehensive rationality impossible, but he also pointed out that policies are seldom changed radically as a result of extensive reviews.[7] In effect, he suggested that comprehensive rationality failed as both a normative and a descriptive model. Instead, he argued that policies are changed incrementally as a result of "successive limited comparisons" between the status quo and some very close alternatives. If some improvement on the status quo is desired, policy makers do not really search far and wide for the best possible alternative. Instead, they usually find some marginal improvement which makes the policy more acceptable to those affected by it.

Lindblom further argued that this "successive limited comparisons" approach was not only an accurate descriptive model, but also a normatively desirable one. He pointed out that comprehensive rationality tends to ignore the fact that new policies must be accepted by existing organizations and clientele groups. It might well be true that some radically different policy would be ideal if there were no ingrained ideological or institutional biases. However, these biases invariably exist. If a new policy recommendation is not acceptable to established players, then it will be very difficult to implement.

This is one of the reasons why Lindblom argues that the best test of the worth of a policy is its acceptance by most relevant actors, and not its rigid conformance to some preset objectives. It is difficult enough to implement policies when all are in agreement; if there is no consensus, then the problems are magnified greatly.

Incrementalism also recognizes that policy making is an ongoing process.[8] When a particular decision is made it will not be carved in stone to remain

---

[6]Peter Aucoin, "Theory and Research in the Study of Policy-Making," in G. Bruce Doern and Peter Aucoin, eds., *The Structures of Policy-Making in Canada* (Toronto: Macmillan of Canada, 1971), p. 24.

[7]Lindblom's ideas on incrementalism have been elaborated in a number of different places. The shortest and most succinct is in "The Science of 'Muddling Through,' " *Public Administration Review*, vol. 19 (Spring 1959), pp. 79-88. Some of the other more thorough treatments are: David Braybrooke and Charles Lindblom, *A Strategy of Decision* (New York: The Free Press, 1970); Charles Lindblom, *The Policy-Making Process* (Englewood Cliffs, N.J.: Prentice-Hall, 1968); Robert A. Dahl and Charles E. Lindblom, *Politics, Economics, and Welfare* (New York: Harper & Row, 1953).

[8]Braybrooke and Lindblom, *A Strategy of Decision*, pp. 99-102.

unchanged for the next hundred years. On the contrary, the policy-making process proceeds slowly by successive small iterations. If a particular marginal adjustment does not seem to move the policy in the desired direction, then a different change is made.

The incremental model also has its critics. Etzioni has expressed the fear that incrementalism goes too far in buttressing the established order.[9] If the status quo is satisfactory, then there is no point in searching widely for improvements. However, if the status quo is not acceptable to major groups in society, then incrementalism is a less suitable guide to action. It assigns too great a role to established and powerful interest groups and does not recognize the need to protect those who are unorganized.

Incrementalism does not lend itself very well to some kinds of "all or nothing" decisions. If a society favours a system of state-run unemployment insurance, then incrementalism provides a mechanism to determine such details of the plan as conditions for eligibility, amounts of payment, and so forth. Incrementalism does not work very well on such "all or nothing" decisions as going to war, capital punishment, or abortion. Moreover, incrementalism also does not work very well in dealing with new problems. For example, it does not help very much in dealing with new scientific breakthroughs such as genetic engineering or *in vitro* fertilization.

In practice, incrementalism explains some kinds of decisions better than others. Lindblom is right that *most* decisions are simply minor variations from previous decisions, but some *very important* decisions are not. It would be rather difficult to argue that the establishment of the Canada and Quebec Pension Plans or the founding of the Canadian Radio Broadcasting Commission and Trans-Canada Airlines were incremental decisions. It is true that a *small* number of decisions fit in this category, but they are almost all very important decisions.

Yehezkel Dror is concerned about incrementalism because it provides a rationale for the inertia and lack of innovation which are too frequently found in large organizations, anyway. He argues that incrementalism acts

> as an ideological reinforcement of the pro-inertia and anti-innovation forces prevalent in all human organizations, administrative and policy making. The actual tendency of most organizations is to limit the search for alternatives to the minimum; there is little danger in real life then, that administration will become bogged down in exhaustive search for all alternatives and full enumeration of consequences, in order to achieve "rational-comprehensive" policy making. The "rational-comprehensive" model has at least the advantage of stimulating administrators to get a little outside their regular routine, while Lindblom's model justifies a policy of "no effort."[10]

Given the various shortcomings identified in both the rational comprehensive

[9]"Mixed-Scanning: A 'Third' Approach To Decision-Making," *Public Administration Review*, vol. 27 (1967), p. 387.

[10]"Muddling Through — 'Science' or Inertia?" *Public Administration Review*, vol. 24 (1964), p. 155.

and incremental approaches, it is not surprising that a number of attempts have been made to synthesize certain elements of the two into a better model.

Bounded Rationality and Satisficing

Herbert Simon argued that in practice people do not really spend huge amounts of time searching for the *ideal* solution to a problem, and even if they did, their attempts at rationality would fail because of the complexity of the problem.

> It is impossible for the behavior of a single, isolated individual to reach any high degree of rationality. The number of alternatives he must explore is so great, the information he would need to evaluate them so vast that even an approximation to objective rationality is hard to conceive. Individual choice takes place in an environment of "givens" — premises that are accepted by the subject as bases for his choice; and behavior is adaptive only within the limits set by these "givens."[11]

The presence of these "givens" and the innate limitations on human abilities provide boundaries which define the search for alternatives. In the real world, when people determine that the status quo is no longer working, they begin their search for alternatives by starting with solutions which are very similar to the status quo and gradually move further and further away, searching only until they find a *satisfactory*, not an ideal, solution. Simon coined the term "satisficing" to describe this type of behaviour.

> *Most human decision-making, whether individual or organizational, is concerned with the discovery and selection of satisfactory alternatives; only in exceptional cases is it concerned with the discovery and selection of optimal alternatives.* . . . To optimize requires processes several orders of magnitude more complex than those required to satisfice. An example is the difference between searching a haystack to find the *sharpest* needle in it and searching the haystack to find a needle sharp enough to sew with.[12]

Bounded rationality or *optimal policy making* uses the *process* identified with comprehensive rationality, but instead of searching for *all* possible alternatives, it searches for alternatives only within some limited range.[13] Also, it does not seek the *best* possible policy, but rather searches for an *optimal* policy. For example, when a politician says, "We must find a better solution to this problem, but we can't afford to increase our expenditure on it," that is a request for bounded rationality. Alternatively, the boundary could be a structural one in that a desire to improve the delivery of a service would be "bounded" by a need to retain the basic structure of the organization currently delivering the service.

Bounded rationality is obviously considerably easier to accomplish than comprehensive rationality, and it does not simply give up any hope of furthering

---

[11]*Administrative Behavior*, 2nd ed. (New York: The Free Press, 1957), p. 79.

[12]James G. March and Herbert A. Simon, *Organizations* (New York: John Wiley & Sons, 1958), pp. 140–141. (Emphasis in original.)

[13]Yehezkel Dror, *Public Policymaking Reexamined* (Scranton, Pa.: Chandler Publishing, 1968), chs. 13–15 and passim.

rationality as do some of the models to be discussed below. However, it does require the difficult and stressful agreement on goals and objectives mentioned as a problem with comprehensive rationality.

Mixed Scanning

Amitai Etzioni has developed a different way of combining rationalism and incrementalism. He argues that governments really make two different kinds of decisions — fundamental and incremental. Fundamental (or "contextuating") decisions are radical changes in policy, while incremental decisions are used either to pave the way for fundamental decisions or to fine-tune fundamental decisions after some of their consequences have been identified.

> Fundamental decisions are made by exploring the main alternatives the actor sees in view of his conception of his goals, but — unlike what rationalism would indicate — details and specifications are omitted so that an overview is feasible. Incremental decisions are made but within the contexts set by fundamental decisions (and fundamental reviews). Thus, each of the two elements in mixed-scanning helps to reduce the effects of the particular shortcomings of the other; incrementalism reduces the unrealistic aspects of rationalism by limiting the details required in fundamental decisions, and contextuating rationalism helps to overcome the conservative slant of incrementalism by exploring longer-run alternatives.[14]

Etzioni cites the history of the United States' space program as an example of how this system operates.[15] First, the Congress made a *fundamental* decision to embark on a space program. Over the years, it has made a number of related *incremental* decisions to provide more or less funding, to proceed rapidly with some parts of the program, and to scrap other parts. This illustrates the interaction between fundamental and incremental decisions.

The framework of incremental and rational decisions and the many models in between are still used quite extensively, but there are some newer models of policy making which do not rely so heavily on these concepts.

Public Choice

Public choice is one of the newest models of public policy making and probably for this reason it seems to mean a number of different things to different writers. The basic element of public choice is the application of economic styles of thinking to the analysis of political behaviour. "Public choice can be defined as the economic study of nonmarket decisionmaking, or simply the application of economics to political science."[16] Public choice uses the concept of the market except that, instead of seeing a market for tangible goods and services, public

---

[14]Etzioni, "Mixed Scanning," pp. 389–390.
[15]Ibid., p. 388.
[16]Dennis C. Mueller, *Public Choice* (Cambridge: Cambridge University Press, 1979), p. 1.

choice theorists think in terms of a market for votes and for specific public policies.[17]

In the public choice model, the basic building block of political action is the self-interested, utility-maximizing individual — "economic man." The aim of the public choice model is "to explain collective decisions (about what are often thought to be political matters) in terms of the self-seeking behaviour of rational individuals."[18] The desire to maximize income, security, or, more generally, utility is the motivating force behind all actions — including voting. "Each citizen . . . votes for the party he believes will provide him with a higher utility income than any other party during the coming election period."[19]

Of course, citizens can participate in the political process in ways other than voting. Breton suggests that individuals will begin to participate more actively in the political process when their perceived costs as a result of government policies exceed their benefits from them. The nature and intensity of their organizing efforts are a function of the distance between costs and benefits.[20]

This "market" for votes and other political activity leads politicians who want to be elected to espouse policies which will please voters — but not just any voters. Politicians would be advised to ignore committed voters — regardless of whether they are committed for or against the politician or party in question. It would be a better use of resources to try to sway undecided voters, since this is the group which normally determines electoral outcomes.[21]

This might explain the continuing allegation that both the Liberal and Progressive Conservative parties are more concerned about voters in eastern Canada than in western Canada. The Liberals do not bother to curry the favour of westerners because it is clear that westerners always vote Conservative; the Conservatives can ignore westerners for the same reason.

Public choice can also explain the actions of public servants. Public servants will ordinarily attempt to increase their department's mandate and the sizes of its staff complement and budget because this will increase the individual public servant's income and status.[22] This desire for increased status will also cause public servants to favour particular kinds of policies. For example, Breton and

---

[17]One of the clearest statements of the public choice approach is in M. H. Sproule-Jones, *Public Choice and Federalism in Australia and Canada* (Canberra: Centre for Research on Federal Financial Relations, The Australian National University, 1975), ch. 2; see also Mark Sproule-Jones, "Institutions, Constitutions, and Public Policies: A Public-Choice Overview," in Michael M. Atkinson and Marsha A. Chandler, eds., *The Politics of Canadian Public Policy* (Toronto: University of Toronto Press), pp. 127–150.

[18]D. G. Hartle, *A Theory of the Expenditure Budgetary Process* (Toronto: University of Toronto Press, 1976), p. 12.

[19]Anthony Downs, *An Economic Theory of Democracy* (New York: Harper & Row, 1957), pp. 38–39.

[20]Albert Breton, *The Economic Theory of Representative Government* (Chicago: Aldine Publishing, 1974), ch. 5 and passim. One of the most complete formulations of public choice theories of collective action is contained in Mancur Olson, *The Logic of Collective Action* (Cambridge: Harvard University Press, 1965).

[21]Hartle, *A Theory of the Expenditure Budgetary Process*, p. 65.

[22]William A. Niskanen, Jr., *Bureaucracy and Representative Government* (Chicago: Aldine-Atherton, 1971), ch. 4.

Wintrobe have argued that income and price controls are imposed by governments, not because they are successful, and not because politicians or citizens want them, but because they make it easier for bureaucrats to obscure accountability and so take credit for successes and shift blame for failures.[23]

Public choice explains the behaviour of individual voters, politicians, and bureaucrats, but it can also be used to explain the interactions of these groups. Hartle discusses budget making as a series of interacting games. In rather picturesque language he suggests that there are four games going on as a part of the establishment of the expenditure budget:

> The political game, the bureaucratic game, the special interest group game, and the media game. Each game has its own set of rules. These sets of rules constitute the incentive systems under which the individuals and teams operate.[24]

For example, the bureaucratic game involves eleven rules, but these three provide the general idea:[25]

- Senior bureaucrats are friendly adversaries. They can compete with one another for positions, but they never do anything to damage the system as a whole.

- It is acceptable for a public servant to prescribe a short-term solution which does not really solve a problem, if that is what the minister wants. However, it would be wise for the bureaucrat to change jobs before the underlying problems become obvious. Then, difficulties can be blamed on his or her successor.

- Public servants try to increase their prestige by gaining a monopoly in some area, e.g., providing a particular kind of policy advice. However, monopoly positions are constantly under attack from other senior bureaucrats.

The overall policy game consists of the interaction of these four games, because everyone in the system needs everyone else. Media people need politicians to give them "scoops," but politicians also need media people to help establish their image. However, not all players in the game are equal; depending on the issue at stake and the resources (financial or other) of the various players, different outcomes can be expected. Thus, public policy is the result of the interaction of these games.

One of the problems with the public choice model is that it presents few testable hypotheses. People are presumed to act based on certain motivations, but since these are subjective motivations, they cannot be measured or tested. For example, it is clear that some people do not always seem to act in the self-interested, rational manner posited by the model. Public choice theorists would

---

[23]Albert Breton and Ronald Wintrobe, *The Logic of Bureaucratic Conduct* (Cambridge: Cambridge University Press, 1982), pp. 146–154. For a similar point, see also Breton, *The Economic Theory of Representative Government*, p. 163.

[24]*A Theory of the Expenditure Budgetary Process*, p. 67.

[25]Ibid., pp. 73–74.

suggest that such a person is, in fact, acting in some longer-term self-interest or taking additional things into account. This sounds suspiciously like "saving the hypothesis," but it is impossible to counter.

Governmental or Bureaucratic Politics

Public choice theory attempts to explain virtually all political actions in society as a result of the actions of various groups and their involvement in the making of major policy decisions. The governmental or bureaucratic politics model has some factors in common with public choice, but the bureaucratic politics model is generally confined more narrowly to a discussion of public policy making.

Various elements of this model have been the subject of much discussion, but these elements were drawn together and the model was given greater recognition as a full-blown theory of policy making by Graham Allison in his book *Essence of Decision.*[26]

In many ways this model is the exact opposite of the rational model. The rational model sees "the government" as a monolithic actor guided by a dedication to efficiency, effectiveness, and rationality, however those concepts might be defined. The governmental or bureaucratic politics model sees government as composed of a number of different departments and agencies, each with its own goals and each trying to mould policy to further its own interests. Thus, government is a coalition of various interests; and government policies are the outcome of the interactions of these various entities. For that reason, this model is sometimes referred to as the *bargaining* model.

When a decision needs to be made, each government entity could well have a different perspective on it. For example, if Canada were called upon to act because one country had invaded another, there could be a number of different responses. The military might propose some sort of retaliation or other military solution. External Affairs might propose such diplomatic initiatives as international negotiations or actions through the United Nations, including possibly a trade embargo. Industrial development officials might propose that there be an embargo on food products, since Canadian manufacturers should not suffer. The Department of Agriculture might favour an embargo on manufactured goods so that Canadian farmers would not suffer. Each organization sees the problem and the solution in a different way depending on how its interests are affected. This gives rise to the statement: "Where you stand depends on where you sit."[27]

There is no question of disloyalty to the public interest or the common good in different entities adopting different positions. All of these organizations are firmly committed to the public interest, but they all see that interest being served in a different manner.

The decision ultimately taken is the outcome of compromise and negotiation between the various interested parties, and thus is heavily influenced by the relative power of the various organizations. In almost every policy area, there is a "lead ministry" which is most directly involved in the area and whose opinions

[26](Boston: Little, Brown, 1971), ch. 5.
[27]Ibid., p. 176.

carry the greatest weight, but there are a number of other departments interested in the area that also have some influence in the final policy.

> Government decisions are made, and government actions are taken, neither as the simple choice of a unified group, nor as a formal summary of leaders' preferences. Rather, the context of shared power but separate judgments about important choices means that politics is the mechanism of choice. Each player pulls and hauls with the power at his discretion for outcomes that will advance his conception of national, organizational, group, and personal interests.[28]

This theory is easier to see at work in the open presidential system of the United States than in the Canadian parliamentary system, where decisions tend to be made in Cabinet behind closed doors and Cabinet solidarity prevails after the decision has been made. However, this model has been used to describe the federal budgetary process[29] and intergovernmental policy making in a number of areas.[30] Nossal has suggested that it could also be used to analyse the making of Canadian foreign policy.[31]

Socio-economic Determinants

The socio-economic determinants model of public policy suggests that policies evolve in response to certain changes in the socio-economic environment of a society. It does not suggest that individuals and groups are powerless in the policy process, but it does suggest that their scope for autonomous action is severely limited by the environmental constraints which they face.

Ronald Manzer has developed one of the most interesting and innovative approaches to relating socio-economic development to changes in public policy. He has divided the economic history of Canada into three broad phases, and he argues that each phase has been characterized by different kinds of policy.

The first phase (sixteenth century to early twentieth century) was identified by what Manzer calls "economic growth by resource appropriation,"[32] which is economic growth as a result of "private individual enterprise in settling and developing the land and exploiting its resources."[33] This is characterized by individualistic units of production in such areas as fishing, fur trading, and lumbering. The individualistic culture of the time meant that government income

---

[28]Ibid., p. 171.

[29]Richard D. French, *How Ottawa Decides* (Toronto: James Lorimer, 1980), ch. 2 and passim.

[30]Richard J. Schultz, *Federalism, Bureaucracy, and Public Policy* (Montreal: McGill-Queen's University Press, 1980); Simon McInnes, "Federal-Provincial Negotiation: Family Allowances 1970–1976" (Ph.D. diss., Carleton University, 1978); David Siegel, "Provincial-Municipal Relations in Ontario: A Case Study of Roads" (Ph.D. diss., University of Toronto, 1984).

[31]Kim Richard Nossal, "Allison through the (Ottawa) Looking Glass: Bureaucratic Politics and Foreign Policy in a Parliamentary System," *Canadian Public Administration*, vol. 22 (Winter 1979), pp. 610–626.

[32]*Public Policies and Political Development in Canada* (Toronto: University of Toronto Press, 1985), p. 22.

[33]Ibid.

security policy was rudimentary at best.[34] Short-term unemployment, such as it existed at all, was mitigated by family and charitable or religious organizations. Government programs were limited to institutional care for "children and old people with no family or friends to support them" and "insane or physically disabled persons whose requirements for care exceeded the simple facilities of family homes."[35]

The next stage identified by Manzer is "economic growth by capital accumulation"[36] (late nineteenth century to 1930s or 1940s), which is characterized by the growth of large industrial enterprise and the mass market needed by this form of industrial organization. This period was also characterized by mass migration from rural to urban areas, with the attendant weakening of family ties. The dependence of labour on large enterprises for jobs increased unemployment, and the weakening of family support mechanisms made this unemployment a societal, and not just a family or community, problem. Government was forced to become more involved in providing real income security programs. These programs changed from institutional care to such income transfers as mothers' allowance, workers' compensation, and old age pensions.[37]

Manzer's third stage is "economic growth by economic stabilization."[38] This stage is the maturing of the second stage with the economy being almost totally driven by large enterprise, which needs economic stability to function smoothly. Government must respond to this need for stability by employing economic tools "to minimize fluctuations in the level of economic activity"[39] and so keep the economy running smoothly. Government income security policy in this period is characterized by what are commonly called welfare state programs — de facto guaranteed income levels through programs such as unemployment insurance that have a counter-cyclical impact in that they automatically increase in times of high unemployment and so stimulate the economy.

The important point of Manzer's argument is that there have been distinct stages in Canada's economic development which have produced distinctive public policies that are a product of those times. This flies in the face of much analysis that focusses on the importance of partisan and ideological factors in policy making.

The conventional wisdom which one reads in some political science textbooks and most popular journalism is that public policies are a product of the ideology of the political party in power or possibly of the configuration of the present legislature, e.g., weak minority government. Anyone who spends a great deal of time and energy studying the political system (such as political scientists and journalists) would like to believe that these political factors are highly influential. However, in the last twenty years the evidence has begun to mount in a

---

[34]Manzer illustrates his argument with references to a number of different policy areas; the examples here will be drawn strictly from the one field of income security.
[35]Manzer, *Public Policies and Political Development*, p. 52.
[36]Ibid., p. 29.
[37]Ibid., pp. 54–59.
[38]Ibid., p. 39.
[39]Ibid., p. 40.

Figure 5.1
ALTERNATE MODELS OF THE POLICY PROCESS

5.1a Traditional "Politics" Model

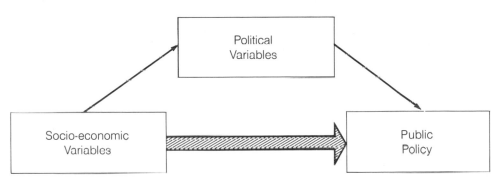

5.1b Socio-economic Variables Model

number of jurisdictions that socio-economic variables are more important determinants of public policy than political ones.

Figure 5.1a illustrates the conventional wisdom about the central role of political factors in policy making. It suggests that there are certain socio-economic
factors which influence the decisions of voters to support a particular political
party. For example, union members vote for the NDP; wealthy business people
vote for the Conservatives. The political party elected would then make policies
which supported the political predispositions of those who voted for it. Over
time, these socio-economic factors change, e.g., increase in union membership,
a fact which could put a different political political party in power and so bring
about changes in public policy. Not only does this sound like the way in which a
democratic system "ought" to work, but it coincides nicely with the legal arrangements of the situation.

Quantitative studies, first in the United States, then in a number of other
countries including Canada, indicate that in fact political variables may be less
influential than had been thought. The general argument is that Figure 5.1b is

a more accurate depiction of the process than Figure 5.1a. Note that this refinement does not suggest that "politics doesn't matter," but it does suggest that political variables matter somewhat less than certain socio-economic variables.

The evolution of this style of thought can be illustrated by a brief discussion of how the idea developed in the United States. At one time, there was a widely held view that the level of interparty competition in state politics had a major impact on the level of public expenditure, particularly in such functions as education and social welfare.[40] This was supported by comparing southern states with little party competition and low expenditures with New England states with high competition and high expenditure. The rationale for this was that where there was a high level of competition for office, the party in power was forced to provide "goodies" to the public to increase its chance of re-election.

However, one could also note that these two groups of states differed not just in level of interparty competition, but also in such socio-economic factors as per capita income, levels of adult literacy, education, urbanization, and industrialization. This finding led to the use of such quantitative techniques as partial correlation and multiple regression to test the relative power of political versus socio-economic variables as explanatory agents. In the various tests, the strength of the relationship has varied, but the overall conclusion of these studies has almost invariably been that socio-economic factors have a greater influence on public policy than political factors.

Falcone and Whittington have conducted a comprehensive study of this question in Canada.[41] They tested the strength of such political variables as party in power, minority versus majority government, and social background of legislators. Their Canadian findings were substantially in agreement with the American ones reported above. They found that such socio-economic variables as income and urbanization had a greater influence on levels of public expenditure than the political variables.

However, it is important to note that none of these studies has found that all changes in public policy can be explained by socio-economic factors. As Richard Simeon has pointed out, the environment determines what issues will move to the forefront of the agenda, what constraints decision makers will face, and what resources will be available to them, but environment does not determine exactly what response they will make to an issue. "Urbanization generates the need to move people around, it does not tell us how the costs will be distributed."[42] *Politics does matter*, but probably not as much as some have believed in the past.

On further analysis, this should not be so surprising. In Canada, political parties seldom disagree on basic societal values. For example, all major parties

---

[40]A good general history of this approach is contained in Dye, *Understanding Public Policy*, ch. 12.

[41]David J. Falcone and Michael S. Whittington, "Output Change in Canada: A Preliminary Attempt to Open the 'Black Box.'" (Paper presented to the Annual Meeting of the Canadian Political Science Association, Montreal, Quebec, June 4, 1972).

[42]"Studying Public Policy," *Canadian Journal of Political Science*, vol. 9 (December 1976), p. 567.

believe in economic prosperity shared by all, lower inflation, lower unemployment, more equitable distribution of wealth, sunny weather in summer, and good snow on the ski slopes in winter. The strongest arguments at election times usually revolve around which party is more adept at furthering the basic societal values on which all agree. Richard Rose described this phenomenon in British politics:

> Parties can compete with each other by claiming to be more proficient in achieving goals generally valued by the electorate. For example, the Conservative and Labour parties do not compete by one party favouring full employment, and the other unemployment, or one favouring inflation and the other price stability. The parties compete by each claiming to be *better* qualified to achieve both full employment and stable prices. Instead of taking different positions, the parties take the same position, but differ in boasting of their competence in handling . . . conditions commonly valued by the majority of the electorate.[43]

Therefore, it should not be surprising that *all* parties are more likely to be influenced by general societal trends than by rigid, historical ideological positions. For example, in recent years all parties have seen the value of privatizing Crown corporations — the Social Credit in British Columbia, the Conservatives in the federal, Alberta, and Saskatchewan governments, and even the provincial Liberal governments in Ontario and Quebec, in spite of the presumed Liberal ideological support for big government.

One reason for the similarity of policies is that parties, once in power, face a similarity of external constraints. In commenting on the British situation, Richard Rose points out that whichever party is in power is so constrained in the making of economic policy by the power of big business and big labour, export policies of foreign governments, and the price of North Sea oil that it has great difficulty engaging in a policy significantly different from its predecessor which faced the same constraints. Thus, parties tend to arrive at the same policies regardless of their ideological differences.

> To emphasize the force of a relatively consensual electorate and powerful secular trends is *not* to assert that the beliefs and interests of Conservative and Labour politicians are identical. Similarity in behaviour need not imply an identity of values. It can occur in spite of underlying differences if the specifics of a given circumstance are sufficiently powerful to lead people with different perspectives to arrive at the same conclusion about what must be done. *Necessity more than ideological consensus is the explanation for similarities in behaviour.*[44]

In sum, the thrust of the socio-economic determinants model of policy making is that variables relating to the stage of a society's socio-economic development are more important in determining the types of policies formulated than

---

[43]*Do Parties Make A Difference?* (London: Macmillan Press, 1980), p. 12. (Emphasis in original; footnote omitted.)

[44]Ibid., p. 145. (Emphasis in original.)

are some of the political variables which are discussed so frequently. The Marxist theory of the state also emphasizes the significance of socio-economic factors.

Marxist Analysis

Marxists feel that the ultimate aim of the capitalist state is to organize society in such a manner as to ensure that the economic elite will be able to exploit the working class. Neo-Marxists argue that the state has three roles — fostering accumulation, providing legitimation, and imposing social order.[45]

In the Marxist view, the overriding concern of the state is assisting capitalists in *accumulating* large amounts of wealth and power. The state can aid in accumulation directly through such means as the provision of industrial development grants to wealthy corporations; or it can act indirectly through labour laws which inhibit unionization; or it can act through "non-decisions" such as refusal to enforce aggressively pollution or occupational health and safety laws. All of these policies result in what has been described as the privatization of profit and the socialization of costs or public costs and private benefits.[46]

However, neo-Marxists argue that accumulation must be restrained somewhat, and capitalists must be saved from themselves, i.e., too much heavy-handed pure exploitation would incite armed rebellion or at least concerted actions on the part of workers. The state could use its coercive force to prevent such action, but that could be dysfunctional.

> The state must try to maintain or create the conditions in which profitable capital accumulation is possible. However, the state also must try to maintain or create the conditions for social harmony. A capitalist state that openly uses its coercive forces to help one class accumulate capital at the expense of other classes loses its legitimacy and hence undermines the basis of its loyalty and support.[47]

Therefore, the state also attempts to illustrate to workers the value of the present system by providing *legitimation*, which is in a sense the benevolent face of capitalism. To convince workers that the existing system is legitimate and in their own best interests, the state softens the jagged edges of capitalism by providing an adequate, but not abundant, social welfare safety net, by sometimes enforcing laws against pollution, and by providing some services which benefit working class people.

However, if workers cannot be kept in line through the persuasion inherent in legitimation, then the state stands ready to use *coercion to impose the appropriate social order*, such as legislation making union organization more difficult (the so-called "Michelin law" in Nova Scotia) and limitations on the right to picket during strikes.

---

[45]Leo Panitch, "The Role and Nature of the Canadian State," in Leo Panitch, ed., *The Canadian State: Political Economy and Political Power* (Toronto: University of Toronto Press, 1977), p. 8 and passim.

[46]Rick Deaton, "The Fiscal Crisis of the State and the Revolt of the Public Employees," *Our Generation*, vol. 8 (October 1972), pp. 11–51.

[47]James O'Connor, *The Fiscal Crisis of the State* (New York: St. Martin's Press, 1973), p. 6.

The role of the state, and by extension of public policy, in the Marxist view is to mediate between the various conflicting interests present in society. However, this is not a neutral style of mediation. In the Marxist view, the state always acts in the long-term interests of the capitalist class. This might involve taking actions which have a short-term detrimental effect on accumulation and so are opposed by the capitalist class, e.g., extension of workers' compensation or unemployment insurance plans. However, these are necessary for legitimation and so benefit the capitalist class in the long run. In this sense, the role of the state is to maintain a relative autonomy[48] from *all* classes so that it can save the capitalist class from its own greed.

Evidence to support the Marxist model of the state can be seen in tax laws which provide generous benefits to people able to invest large sums while taxing wage-earners on the basis of each dollar earned. Another example is the case of the legislators who have great difficulty passing legislation preventing business combinations that limit competition, but have no such difficulty passing legislation ordering the end of legal strikes and the jailing of union leaders. Not many Canadians accept this Marxist view of the state, but it seems to be a valid explanation of certain actions of the state.

This section has discussed some of the theories of policy making. This is a partial, but reasonably representative, explanation of the various theories. However, it is not enough for a government simply to make a policy; policies are only truly relevant when they are implemented. The next section discusses what happens during the implementation phase.

IMPLEMENTATION

Traditionally, political scientists have been predominantly concerned with the study of political institutions, e.g., Cabinets or legislatures, and their impact on policy making. The general implication was that after policy decisions were made, they were simply automatically carried out so that there was nothing of interest to political scientists in the implementation process. At best, there were a few questions of organization and motivation, which were considered to be more properly in the realm of those who study administration than of those who study important things like political science.

This attitude began to change in the 1970s, at least partly as a result of an increasing interest in policy impact studies. These studies found that public policies frequently did not have the impacts that were envisaged when they were first formulated by the executive or legislature. For example, it was discovered that children were not learning as much in school as some thought they should be, that poverty was no closer to elimination in spite of the expenditure of significant amounts of money, and that courts were experiencing such a backlog that justice was seriously delayed. This led to a clear understanding that there was some slippage between policy making and policy impact; this, in turn, led

---

[48]Nicos Poulantzas, *Political Power and Social Classes* (London: Verso Editions, 1978), p. 255ff. and Part IV passim.

to greater concern for studying the policy implementation process as an important part of the overall political process.

The Implementation Process

One of the keys to understanding the implementation process is a better grasp of the complex relationship between those who make policy and those who implement it. Nakamura and Smallwood suggested that there could be five different styles of linkage between them.[49]

The *"classical" technocratic* linkage closely approximates the Weberian ideal-type. It assumes that formulators state goals clearly and unequivocally and delegate the technical responsibility for carrying out those goals to implementers, and that implementers automatically carry out those duties in the desired manner.

The *instructed delegate* approach is similar to the classical technocratic approach in that formulators specify goals and implementers agree with those goals, but it differs in that formulators delegate a somewhat broader area of discretion to the implementers. Implementers are not simply automatons; they have limited authority to make decisions about programs during the implementation process.

In the *bargaining* approach, the formulators and implementers do not agree on policy goals. However, since each needs the cooperation of the other in order to carry out any program, bargaining occurs. "The final outcome of bargaining between policy makers and implementers is determined by the distribution of relative power resources (actual or perceived) among the two groups."[50] This plays havoc with the traditional Weberian notion of bureaucracy in that it suggests that implementers could have some influence over formulators.[51]

The *discretionary experimenter* approach occurs when formulators can decide on broad general goals, but do not have enough knowledge to specify precise goals or directions. In this case, formulators have little choice but to convey general goals to implementers and to provide them with a grant of wide discretionary powers to carry out these general abstract goals.

The *bureaucratic entrepreneur* approach turns the traditional relationship between formulators and implementers on its head. In this style of interaction, implementers begin by formulating their goals and then marshalling support for those goals among various significant groups. After this is done, the implementers then approach the formulators to obtain the necessary resources, including legitimation, to undertake the program. This is the most radical approach, but it is also a very common one. Samuel H. Beer had this sort of relationship in mind when he made this comment on the political process in the United States:

> I would remark how rarely additions to the public sector have been *initiated* by the demands of voters or the advocacy of pressure groups or the plat-

---

[49]Robert T. Nakamura and Frank Smallwood, *The Politics of Policy Implementation* (New York: St. Martin's Press, 1980), ch. 7.

[50]Ibid., p. 122.

[51]This phenomenon of subordinates' power over superiors is also considered in Donald S. Van Meter and Carl E. Van Horn, "The Policy Implementation Process: A Conceptual Framework," *Administration & Society*, vol. 6 (February 1975), pp. 454–458.

forms of political parties. On the contrary, in the fields of health, housing, urban renewal, transportation, welfare, education, poverty, and energy it has been, in very great measure, people in government service, or very closely associated with it, acting on the basis of their specialized and technical knowledge, who first perceived the problem, conceived the program, initially urged it on the President and Congress, went on to help lobby it through to enactment, and then saw to its administration.[52]

The closed nature of the parliamentary system makes it difficult to see this process at work in Canada, but cases can be cited where implementers have in fact had a major role in formulating policies.[53]

As mentioned above, one of the keys to good implementation is understanding the relationship between policy makers and policy implementers, and also understanding how problems develop in the implementation of a policy. The next section of this chapter focusses on some of these problems.

Difficulties of Implementation

Implementation is frequently much more difficult than it is perceived to be at a distance. All sorts of problems develop during implementation that were only dimly seen when the original policies were made.

Communications Problems. Chapter 2 discussed the Weberian idea of bureaucracy, which held that senior officials gave orders and subordinates simply carried them out. Chapters 3 and 4 went on to suggest that it was not quite that simple. Subordinates are not programmed automatons; they have minds of their own and are capable of misunderstanding or misinterpreting (either accidentally or intentionally) the desires of senior officials. The need to communicate between policy formulators and policy implementers presents problems.

> Communications linkages within any policy system can be replete with potential pitfalls. Mishaps can occur because of (1) garbled messages from the senders; (2) misinterpretation by the receivers; or (3) system failure in terms of transmission breakdowns, overload, "noise," and inadequate follow-through or compliance mechanisms.[54]

These possible problems can be magnified by the presence of organizational and other kinds of systematic bias on the part of implementers.

Organizational Rigidities. These communication difficulties raise the possibility of some sort of selective perception on the part of implementers. There are cases

---

[52]"Federalism, Nationalism and Democracy in America," *American Political Science Review*, vol. 72 (March 1978), p. 17. (Emphasis in original.)

[53]H. L. Laframboise, "Moving a Proposal to a Positive Decision: A Case Study of the Invisible Process," *Optimum*, vol. 4, no. 3 (1973), pp. 31–41; J. L. Granatstein, *The Ottawa Men* (Toronto: Oxford University Press, 1982); Kenneth Kernaghan and T. H. McLeod, "Mandarins and Ministers in the Canadian Administrative State," in O. P. Dwivedi, ed., *The Administrative State in Canada* (Toronto: University of Toronto Press, 1982), pp. 17–30.

[54]Nakamura and Smallwood, *The Politics of Policy Implementation*, p. 24.

where this is deliberate and malicious, but that need not be the case. Most people have a strong predisposition to handle particular problems in a particular manner. When confronted with new problems there is a tendency to continue to respond in the old manner. For example, most professions possess what has been described as a "trained incapacity." Professional training teaches people one specific way to deal with a problem and so makes them unable to develop new approaches. In the 1960s and 1970s when there were acrimonious disputes about expressways versus public transit, it was suggested that one of the problems was that engineers had been trained in one way of moving people — private cars on roads; they had developed a "trained incapacity" to see that other ways of moving people could be developed.

Policy makers frequently ignore the existence of these organizational biases when they are deciding on new policies. This means that policies are produced under the assumption that organizations will change to implement the policies; in fact, it is more likely that policies will be changed to fit the organization.

Insufficient Resources. Even when people are willing and able to implement policies, there can still be difficulties if adequate resources are unavailable. This problem is sometimes compounded when policy makers who are instrumental in the adoption of a policy tend to underestimate the resources needed to implement it because this will facilitate adoption of the policy. Implementers then suffer from a shortage of funds, but this is not the only resource necessary to implement some policies. In the case of scientific programs in particular, there are sometimes not enough people with appropriate training to carry out a project, regardless of the funds available to pay them.

Implementers also complain that they do not receive enough political support at key points in the implementation phase. Frequently, politicians lose interest in a particular policy after it has been approved; they simply assume it will be implemented properly. However, implementers can frequently have difficulty battling inertia or even hostile forces in the environment. Without continuing political support, implementers can be left like the proverbial explorers up the creek without a paddle. Political support is particularly necessary when there are a number of different organizations involved in implementation.

Interorganizational Complexity. Implementing programs which have intergovernmental or interorganizational implications are given a special place in the literature on implementation because of the great difficulties encountered. These problems arise because of the number of different organizations involved and because each of these organizations has different goals. At times, the raw numbers alone can be devastating. Pressman and Wildavsky's analysis of an economic development program found that it was necessary to arrive at seventy different agreements involving fifteen different organizations. They calculate that with this number of agreements needed, if each has an 80 per cent probability of success, then the probability that all seventy would be arrived at successfully is .000000125. One would have to assume a 99 per cent probability of success for each contract to have close to a 50 per cent chance of having all seventy contracts completed successfully.[55] They also point out the importance of speed in arriving at agreements, because agreements once made can still be abrogated if later decisions are not made promptly:

> It could be said that the EDA public works program was characterized by the slow dissolution of agreement. As one delay succeeded another, the major individual participants changed and so did the understandings they had with one another. Agreements were reached, eroded, and remade. The frequent calls for coordination . . . reflected the inability of the machinery for implementation to move fast enough to capture the agreements while they lasted. Allow enough time to elapse in a rapidly changing external world and it is hard to imagine any set of agreements remaining firm.[56]

Fullness of Time. One of the things that many people do not understand about implementation is that you can't produce a child in one month by impregnating nine women. When a large organization with many accumulated organizational structures and biases is being asked to accept a new idea, it takes a while for that idea to sink in. This is particularly important because in "the implementation process . . . politics appears primarily *defensive*. Actors seem more concerned with what they in particular might lose than with what all in general might gain."[57] Many times the best implementation strategy is a very low-key one which involves simply mentioning a new idea that is currently being floated without activating defence mechanisms by suggesting it be adopted. Then, after there has been some discussion of it, the idea begins to seem more palatable. Finally, it comes to be accepted by most people in the organization, and the time is ripe for implementation. A great deal of damage can be done by trying to ram through a new idea without taking time to let people feel comfortable with it.

Inadequate Participation. The importance of participation was discussed in Chapters 3 and 4, but it is important to realize that participation is not just therapeutic for the individual; there is some evidence that it can have real benefits for the organization. Some studies have indicated that when people have the opportunity to participate in the early stages of policy design, the implementation process works much more smoothly.[58] There are at least two reasons for this. First, people who have been consulted about a policy will feel that they

---

[55]Jeffrey L. Pressman and Aaron B. Wildavsky, *Implementation* (Berkeley and Los Angeles: University of California Press, 1974), p. 92.

[56]Ibid.

[57]Eugene Bardach, *The Implementation Game: What Happens After a Bill Becomes a Law* (Cambridge, Mass.: MIT Press, 1977), p. 42. (Emphasis in original.)

[58]In spite of many pious protestations about the positive value of participation, the hard evidence is not clear on this point. For a good review of this literature, see Neal Gross, Joseph B. Giacquinta, and Marilyn Bernstein, *Implementing Organizational Innovations: A Sociological Analysis of Planned Educational Change* (New York: Basic Books, 1971), pp. 25–29.

own a part of the policy and will feel comfortable with it during the implementation phase; the defence mechanisms mentioned above will never be activated. Second, early consultation with administrators will allow them to identify certain problems that can be corrected sooner rather than later.

Choice of Governing Instrument

In recent years there has been an emerging literature in the field of what has come to be called the "choice of governing instrument." This approach to public policy making recognizes that policy making is not simply the choice of a policy objective, but rather it also involves a decision about *how* the policy will be implemented. Doern and Phidd define governing instruments as "the major ways in which governments seek to ensure compliance, support and implementation of public policy."[59]

When most people think of government policy, they tend to think very quickly of the more visible aspects of government activity, usually government expenditure or regulation. However, in attempting to implement some policies, governments have a number of techniques or instruments at their disposal. Doern and Phidd categorize these under a number of headings:

- exhortation,
- expenditure,
- taxation,
- regulation, and
- public enterprise.[60]

Note that these instruments are listed in order from the least coercive to the most coercive. Exhortation and symbolic policies are not coercive in that they could involve a statement of concern by the government, appointment of a commission to study something, or reorganization of a department to illustrate government concern.

When governments make policy decisions, they are actually making two decisions — what the policy ought to be and how the policy ought to be implemented. Doern and Wilson have suggested that the implementation portion of the decision is made with a keen eye on public acceptability and that the public will more easily accept persuasive rather than coercive measures:

> This hypothesis would suggest that politicians (especially the collective cabinet) have a strong tendency to respond to policy issues (any issue) by moving successively from the *least coercive* governing instruments to the *most coercive*. Thus they tend to respond first in the least coercive fashion by creating a study, or by creating a new or reorganized unit of government, or merely by uttering a broad statement of intent. The next least coercive governing instrument would be to use a distributive spending approach in which the resources could be handed out to various constituencies in such a

---

[59]G. Bruce Doern and Richard W. Phidd, *Canadian Public Policy: Ideas, Structure, Process* (Toronto: Methuen, 1983), p. 110.
[60]Ibid.

way that the least attention is given as to which taxpayers' pockets the resources are being drawn from. At the more coercive end of the continuum of governing instruments would be a larger redistributive programme, in which resources would be more visibly extracted from the more advantaged classes and redistributed to the less advantaged classes. Also at the more coercive end of the governing continuum would be direct regulation in which the sanctions or threat of sanctions would have to be directly applied. It is, of course, obvious that once a policy issue has matured and been on the public agenda for many years, all or most of the basic instruments could be utilized.[61]

Examples of the movement from less coercive policies to more coercive ones can be seen in a number of areas. The issue of equality for women has been dealt with first by the use of a Royal commission to highlight the fact that there was a problem. Next, governments took action to improve the ability of women to compete in the labour force by providing innovative kinds of job training and encouraging employers not to discriminate against women. These kinds of policies benefited women without imposing an obvious cost on anyone. Next, legislation was passed to force employers to provide equal pay to women. This confers a benefit on women and imposes an obvious cost on only one limited group — employers. To this point, Canadian policy makers have stopped short of employment quotas, which would be the most coercive form of policy in that they would clearly benefit women and impose a cost on men. Thus, we see a movement along Doern and Phidd's hierarchy from exhortation to expenditure to regulation. Similar examples could be found in the approach to bilingualism, inflation, and foreign ownership.

However, not all policy areas fit so neatly into this picture. In the field of passenger air transportation, the government's first approach to the development of this field was the establishment of a Crown corporation. Fifty years later with the introduction of deregulation, the government now seems to be moving from more coercive to less coercive instruments.

Michael Trebilcock, et al. have adopted a different approach, which combines the idea of the choice of governing instrument with the public choice approach discussed earlier in this chapter. They argue that politicians choose governing instruments not on the basis of policy rationality or efficiency, but rather to improve their electoral position. For example, they point out that there is a tendency for politicians to assign the administration of programs which impose significant costs on voters to "independent" agencies so that the actions of these agencies are not directly associated with politicians.[62]

Another general rule which they suggest will be followed by politicians is that benefits will be conferred on a concentrated group of uncommitted voters, while

---

[61]G. Bruce Doern and V. Seymour Wilson, "Conclusions and Observations," in G. Bruce Doern and V. Seymour Wilson, eds., *Issues in Canadian Public Policy* (Macmillan of Canada, 1974), p. 339. Reprinted by permission of the authors.
[62]*The Choice of Governing Instrument* (Ottawa: Minister of Supply and Services Canada, 1982), p. 33.

costs will be spread as widely as possible. This strategy could be supplemented by control of information so that the benefit side could be emphasized and the cost side obscured.[63]

This approach could be used to explain the growing use of tax expenditures as policy instruments. Tax expenditures are benefits in the form of reduced taxes to taxpayers who do (or refrain from doing) something desired by government. Their obvious attraction is that they provide low-visibility benefits, while spreading the cost (in increased taxes to others) so widely that people do not feel coerced.[64]

It is clear that the choice of governing instruments approach has a great deal of value in illuminating certain characteristics of public policy. First, it emphasizes that policy making is not simply choosing a desired end, but rather it also involves a selection of means to accomplish that end — implementation. Second, it points out that there is a substitutability between the various instruments. Several instruments could potentially be used to accomplish the same ends; if one does not succeed, then policy makers might try another.

In the next section of this book, we borrow this concept of choice of governing instrument and apply it to the choice that governments make with regard to organizational form. When confronted with a particular task, governments must choose the appropriate organizational form for accomplishing the task. They have available such forms as operating departments, Crown corporations, and regulatory agencies. We will discuss the various characteristics of these organizational forms, with particular reference to why governments would choose one form over the others available to deal with a particular problem.

---

[63]Ibid.

[64]Kenneth Woodside, "The Political Economy of Policy Instruments: Tax Expenditures and Subsidies in Canada," in *The Politics of Canadian Public Policy*, pp. 175–176 and passim.

BIBLIOGRAPHY

Allison, Graham. *Essence of Decision: Explaining the Cuban Missile Crisis*. Boston: Little, Brown, 1971.

Anderson, James R. *Public Policy-Making*. 3rd ed. New York: Holt, Rinehart and Winston, 1984.

Atkinson, Michael M., and Marsha A. Chandler, eds. *The Politics of Canadian Public Policy*. Toronto: University of Toronto Press, 1983.

Bardach, Eugene. *The Implementation Game: What Happens After a Bill Becomes a Law*. Cambridge, Mass.: The MIT Press, 1977.

Beer, Samuel H. "Federalism, Nationalism and Democracy in America." *American Political Science Review*, vol. 72 (March 1978): 9–21.

Braybrooke, David, and Charles Lindblom. *A Strategy of Decision*. New York: The Free Press, 1970.

Breton, Albert. *The Economic Theory of Representative Government*. Chicago: Aldine Publishing Company, 1974.

Breton, Albert, and Ronald Wintrobe. *The Logic of Bureaucratic Conduct*. Cambridge: Cambridge University Press, 1982.

Dahl, Robert A., and Charles E. Lindblom. *Politics, Economics, and Welfare*. New York: Harper & Row, 1953.

Deaton, Rick. "The Fiscal Crisis of the State and the Revolt of the Public Employees." *Our Generation*, vol. 8 (October 1972): 11–51.

Doern, G. Bruce, and Peter Aucoin. *Public Policy in Canada*. Toronto: Macmillan of Canada, 1979.

Doern, G. Bruce, and Peter Aucoin. *The Structures of Policy Making in Canada*. Toronto: Macmillan of Canada, 1971.

Doern, G. Bruce, and Richard W. Phidd. *Canadian Public Policy: Ideas, Structure, Process*. Toronto: Methuen, 1983.

Doern, G. Bruce, and V. Seymour Wilson, eds. *Issues in Canadian Public Policy*. Macmillan of Canada, 1974.

Downs, Anthony. *An Economic Theory of Democracy*. New York: Harper & Row, 1957.

Dror, Yehezkel. "Muddling Through — 'Science' or Inertia?" *Public Administration Review*, vol. 24 (1964): 153–158.

Dror, Yehezkel. *Public Policymaking Reexamined*. Scranton, Pa.: Chandler Publishing Company, 1968.

Dunn, William N. *Public Policy Analysis*. Englewood Cliffs, N.J.: Prentice-Hall, 1981.

Dunsire, Andrew. *Implementation in a Bureaucracy*. Oxford: Martin Robertson, 1978.

Dye, Thomas R. *Policy Analysis: What Governments Do, Why They Do It, and What Difference It Makes*. University, Ala.: The University of Alabama Press, 1976.

Dye, Thomas R. *Understanding Public Policy*. 5th ed. Englewood Cliffs, N.J.: Prentice-Hall, 1984.

Etzioni, Amitai. "Mixed-Scanning: A 'Third' Approach To Decision-Making." *Public Administration Review*, vol. 27 (1967): 385–392.

Falcone, David J., and Michael S. Whittington. "Output Change in Canada: A Preliminary Attempt to Open the 'Black Box.'" Paper presented to the Annual Meeting of the Canadian Political Science Association, Montreal, Quebec, June 4, 1972.

Granatstein, J. L. *The Ottawa Men*. Toronto: Oxford University Press, 1982.

Gross, Neal, Joseph B. Giacquinta, and Marilyn Bernstein. *Implementing Organizational Innovations: A Sociological Analysis of Planned Educational Change*. New York: Basic Books, 1971.

Hartle, D. G. *A Theory of the Expenditure Budgetary Process*. Toronto: University of Toronto Press, 1976.

Kernaghan, Kenneth, and T. H. McLeod. "Mandarins and Ministers in the Canadian Administrative State." In *The Administrative State in Canada*, edited by O. P. Dwivedi. Toronto: University of Toronto Press, 1982, pp. 17–30.

Laframboise, H. L. "Moving a Proposal to a Positive Decision: A Case Study of the Invisible Process." *Optimum*, vol. 4, no. 3 (1973): 31–41.

Lindblom, Charles E. *The Policy-Making Process*. Englewood Cliffs, N.J.: Prentice-Hall, 1968.

Lindblom, Charles E. "The Science of 'Muddling Through.' " *Public Administration Review*, vol. 19 (Spring 1959): 79–88.

Manzer, Ronald. *Public Policies and Political Development in Canada*. Toronto: University of Toronto Press, 1985.

March, James G., and Herbert A. Simon. *Organizations*. New York: John Wiley & Sons, 1958.

McInnes, Simon. "Federal-Provincial Negotiation: Family Allowances 1970–1976." Ph.D. diss., Carleton University, 1978.

Mueller, Dennis C. *Public Choice*. Cambridge: Cambridge University Press, 1979.

Nakamura, Robert T., and Frank Smallwood. *The Politics of Policy Implementation*. New York: St. Martin's Press, 1980.

Niskanen, William A., Jr. *Bureaucracy and Representative Government*. Chicago: Aldine-Atherton, 1971.

Nossal, Kim Richard. "Allison through the (Ottawa) Looking Glass: Bureaucratic Politics and Foreign Policy in a Parliamentary System." *Canadian Public Administration*, vol. 22 (Winter 1979): 610–626.

O'Connor, James. *The Fiscal Crisis of the State*. New York: St. Martin's Press, 1973.

Olson, Mancur. *The Logic of Collective Action*. Cambridge: Harvard University Press, 1965.

Panitch, Leo. "The Role and Nature of the Canadian State." In *The Canadian State: Political Economy and Political Power*, edited by Leo Panitch. Toronto: University of Toronto Press, 1977.

Poulantzas, Nicos. *Political Power and Social Classes*. London: Verso Editions, 1978.

Pressman, Jeffrey L., and Aaron B. Wildavsky. *Implementation*. Berkeley and Los Angeles: University of California Press, 1974.

Rose, Richard. *Do Parties Make A Difference?* London: Macmillan Press, 1980.

Schultz, Richard J. *Federalism, Bureaucracy, and Public Policy*. Montreal: McGill-Queen's University Press, 1980.

Siegel, David. "Provincial-Municipal Relations in Ontario: A Case Study of Roads." Ph.D. diss., University of Toronto, 1984.

Simeon, Richard. "Studying Public Policy." *Canadian Journal of Political Science*, vol. 9 (December 1976): 548–580.

Simon, Herbert. *Administrative Behavior*. 2nd ed. New York: The Free Press, 1957.

Sproule-Jones, M. H. *Public Choice and Federalism in Australia and Canada*. Canberra: Centre for Research on Federal Financial Relations, The Australian National University, 1975.

Treblicock, M. J., R. S. Prichard, D. G. Hartle, and D. N. Dewees. *The Choice of Governing Instrument*. Ottawa: Minister of Supply and Services Canada, 1982.

Van Meter, Donald S., and Carl E. Van Horn. "The Policy Implementation Process: A Conceptual Framework." *Administration & Society*, vol. 6 (February 1975): 445–488.

CASES

In *Case Program in Canadian Public Administration* (Toronto: Institute of Public Administration of Canada):

L'Affaire Caloil, by Michel Paquin

The Draft Memorandum to Cabinet, by Douglas G. Hartle

The Elusive IPB System, by Walter Baker

The Toronto Airport(s), by Sandford F. Borins

Assessing Housing Needs in Manitoba's Remote Communities, by Nelson Wiseman

Policy Analysis: A Case Study, by David Zussman

Implementing Bilingual Air Traffic Control in Quebec, by Sandford F. Borins

Screening the Boat People? Case Studies in Health Policies, by Peter Owen, Peggy Purvis, and Raisa B. Deber

All Things to All People: Government and Its Client Groups, by Sharon Bider and Peter McNaughton

We'll Take You On, Mr. Toyota: A Case Study on Japanese Imports and the Future of the Canadian Automobile Industry, by Sandford F. Borins, John M. Curtis, R. Moroz, and Tony R. Washington

The Allocation of a National Housing Budget, by Barbara Carroll

The Commissioner's Dilemma: Body Cavity Searches in the Canadian Penitentiary Service, by Edd LeSage

In Kenneth Kernaghan, *Canadian Cases in Public Administration* (Toronto: Methuen Publications):

The Renfrew Group

The Foot and Mouth Disease Epidemic, 1952

II

THE CHOICE OF ORGANIZATIONAL FORM

6

Government Departments and Central Agencies

THE CHOICE OF ORGANIZATIONAL FORM

In the first part of this book, the emphasis was on the development of certain general principles or theories. The major purpose of the second part is to build on those general ideas and discuss how they apply in the Canadian context. Each chapter in this part covers the structure and standard method of operation of one of the main organizational forms employed in parliamentary governments. Chapters 6, 7, and 8 deal respectively with government departments, Crown corporations, and regulatory agencies. Chapter 9 covers a miscellany of other forms of organization such as Royal commissions and task forces.

The theme that ties these chapters together is the *choice of organizational form*, that is, how the various organizational forms differ from one another and why governments choose a particular organizational form to carry out a particular responsibility.

Chapter 5 pointed out that when a government is confronted with a problem it has a number of alternative ways of dealing with that problem. The main instruments which government could employ were summarized as:

- exhortation,
- expenditure,
- taxation,
- regulation, and
- public enterprise.[1]

In some cases, the instrument to be employed is fairly obvious. For example, taxation is likely to work better than exhortation in raising revenue. However, in many cases there are a variety of instruments that could be used to accomplish a particular end.

If a government wishes to promote indigenous cultural activity, it can engage in public ownership, as in the case of the Canadian Broadcasting Corporation or the National Film Board; provide direct subsidies to theatre groups; finance granting institutions (e.g. the Canada Council); provide tax incentives, such as capital cost allowance on films or an expense allowance for advertising; and engage in regulation (e.g. through the Canadian

---

[1]G. Bruce Doern and Richard W. Phidd, *Canadian Public Policy: Ideas, Structure, Process* (Toronto: Methuen, 1983), p. 110.

Radio-Television and Telecommunications Commission's broadcasting content rules).[2]

In general, it could be said that in carrying out any function the government has available to it a broad range of organizational forms. When governments organize, or reorganize, they are not simply deciding to carry out a particular function, but they are also making a strategic choice about *how* that function ought to be carried out. In most cases, the choice of the appropriate strategy for implementation can be a key determinant of how well the government's objective will be met.

One of the key choices which a government makes in this regard is the choice of the organizational structure — operating department, Crown corporation, regulatory agency or other structure — in which responsibility for the function will be lodged. There are a number of factors which could influence governments in choosing a particular organizational form. It will not be suggested here that this decision is always made according to the tenets of comprehensive rationality. In many cases, governments simply "follow the leader" in adopting the kind of structure which is already employed for the same or similar purposes in other jurisdictions. However, in some cases, governments make conscious decisions about organizational forms. For example, if a particular function is very much like a commercial operation, such as operating an airline or oil company, then the Crown corporation form is likely to be chosen. If a function requires an arm's length relationship with government, such as regulating broadcasting, then the regulatory agency will likely be the preferred form. Each chapter in this section will consider the unique characteristics of one of the organizational forms.

This chapter starts by examining the departmental form of organization. It begins with a discussion of the legal foundations of departments, which requires an examination of interactions between departments, the legislature, and the political executive (that is, the Cabinet).[3] The relationship of departments to central agencies such as the Prime Minister's Office and the Privy Council Office is also discussed. The organizational structure of a typical department is illustrated, and finally, some new forms of departmental organization in the federal and provincial spheres of government are described.

THE LEGISLATURE, THE EXECUTIVE, AND DEPARTMENTS

It is customary to speak of three branches of government — legislative, executive, and judicial. The judicial branch, which consists of the law courts and related institutions, is not discussed in this chapter, but is considered in Chapter 16. In Canada, the legislative branch of the federal government consists of the Queen and two houses or chambers — the House of Commons and the Senate. Each of the provincial legislatures has only one house (e.g., the National Assembly in Quebec, the Legislative Assembly in several western provinces).

[2]Michael J. Trebilcock, et al., *The Choice of Governing Instrument* (Ottawa: Minister of Supply and Services Canada, 1982), p. 1.

[3]A more detailed treatment of these interactions is contained in Chapters 13 to 15.

The executive branch is technically headed by the Queen as represented in Canada by the Governor General and the Lieutenant Governors of the various provinces. In practice, neither the Queen nor any of her vice-regal representatives ever acts except on the advice of the government of the day as embodied in the Prime Minister (or provincial Premier) and the Cabinet. This means that the responsibilities of the executive branch are carried out collectively by Cabinet, or what is commonly called "the government." All public servants act under the direction and control of the Cabinet, and are included, therefore, as part of the executive branch. Thus, in this book, the practical, working definition of the executive is the Cabinet and the public service.

One sometimes hears that something is done by the "Governor General in Council" or the "Lieutenant Governor in Council." This means that the Governor General or Lieutenant Governor has taken some legal action after consultation with the Cabinet. It actually means that the Cabinet has taken some action; the Governor General's or Lieutenant Governor's signature is a formality.

The congressional system of government in the United States is characterized by a balance of powers between the three branches so that no one branch has authority over any other. In parliamentary systems, like Canada's, it is an important principle that the executive branch is accountable to the legislative branch, i.e., the branch most directly responsible to the general public. The two branches are, in fact, joined because Cabinet ministers are almost invariably members of the legislative branch. This institutional arrangement helps the legislature to hold the executive accountable for its actions.

Definition of a Department

It is difficult to establish a precise, working definition of a department. Legal definitions can be found in both the Financial Administration Act[4] and the Public Service Employment Act.[5] Not only are these two legislative definitions different, but since their purpose is to determine which organizations will be subject to a particular regime of financial or personnel administration, they do not capture the essence of a department.

The definition used in this book is that of J. E. Hodgetts, who states that:

> A department is an administrative unit comprising one or more organizational components over which a minister has direct management and control. This definition restricts our terms of reference to major ministerial portfolios and thereby excludes subordinate units such as Insurance and Public Printing and Stationery that in law actually carry the title "department." Since we are also concerned with the ways in which programs are allocated to these units, we can disregard cabinet portfolios to which no duties are assigned: thus the customary minister without portfolio will be excluded from the list.[6]

---

[4]R.S.C. 1970, c. F-10, s. 2.

[5]R.S.C. 1970, c. P-32, s. 2(1).

[6]*The Canadian Public Service: A Physiology of Government* (Toronto: University of Toronto Press, 1973), p. 89.

One characteristic which should be emphasized in distinguishing operating departments from regulatory agencies and Crown corporations is that of "direct management and control" by the minister. The constitutional convention is that the minister should very closely and directly control the actions of an operating department. This differs from the minister's relationship with regulatory agencies and Crown corporations in which there are certain understood limits on the direct involvement of the minister in the specifics of their day-to-day management.

Classification Systems for Departments

There are so many departments with so many specialized responsibilities that a number of writers have tried to facilitate the understanding of their roles by grouping them in some way. Hodgetts's classification system is based on the *general policy fields* addressed or functions carried out by the department, such as "public works, communications, and transportation" and "conservation, development, and promotion of physical resources."[7]

Doern focusses on the *relative power* of different departments by developing a classification system which considers size of budget, responsibility for coordination, and knowledge or research capability.[8] He argues that all three of these factors are sources of power, although different kinds of power. Thus, it is very difficult to compare the importance of a department with a large budget, such as National Health and Welfare, and one with a small budget but a broad coordinating role, such as Treasury Board. He identifies four types of departments — traditional horizontal coordinative, new horizontal coordinative, administrative coordinative, and vertical constituency. A contemporary application of Doern's classification scheme results in the grouping of departments shown in Table 6.1.

The *traditional horizontal coordinative portfolios* tend to be the most politically influential:

> They have inherent high policy influence because of the formal authority they possess and because they afford their occupants the highest number of strategic opportunities to intervene in almost any policy issue if the occupant wishes. They each deal respectively with the traditionally most basic horizontal or cross-cutting dimensions of government policy, namely overall political leadership and strategy, foreign policy and the foreign implications of domestic policy fields, aggregate economic and fiscal policy, the basic legal and judicial concepts and values of the state, and the overall management of government spending programmes.[9]

These portfolios tend to be weak in terms of size of budget, but very strong in the other two dimensions.

---

[7]Ibid., ch. 5.

[8]G. Bruce Doern, "Horizontal and Vertical Portfolios in Government," in G. Bruce Doern and V. Seymour Wilson, eds., *Issues in Canadian Public Policy* (Macmillan of Canada, 1974), pp. 310-319. This same idea is also developed in Doern and Phidd, *Canadian Public Policy*, pp. 206-209.

[9]Doern, "Horizontal and Vertical Portfolios in Government," pp. 316-317.

Table 6.1
DOERN'S CLASSIFICATION OF DEPARTMENTS AND CENTRAL AGENCIES

Traditional Horizontal Coordinative Portfolios
    External Affairs
    Finance
    Justice
    Privy Council Office
    Federal-Provincial Relations Office
    Treasury Board
New Horizontal Coordinative Portfolios
    Ministry of State for Science and Technology
    Ministry of State for Forestry
    Ministry of State for Mines
    Ministry of State for Tourism
    Ministry of State for Youth
    Minister of International Trade
    Ministry of State for Fitness and Amateur Sport
    Ministry of State for Small Business
    Ministry of State for Multiculturalism
Administrative Coordinative Portfolios
    National Revenue
    Public Works
    Supply and Services
Vertical Constituency Portfolios
    Agriculture
    Communications
    Consumer and Corporate Affairs
    Employment and Immigration
    Energy, Mines and Resources
    Environment
    Fisheries and Oceans
    Indian Affairs and Northern Development
    Insurance
    Labour
    National Defence
    National Health and Welfare
    Regional Industrial Expansion
    Secretary of State
    Solicitor General
    Transport
    Veterans Affairs

Source: Based on G. Bruce Doern, "Horizontal and Vertical Portfolios in Government," in G. Bruce Doern and V. Seymour Wilson, eds., *Issues in Canadian Public Policy* (Toronto: Macmillan of Canada, 1974), pp. 315–316, but updated to reflect changes since the table was originally prepared.

The *new horizontal coordinative portfolios* are the hardest to assess because they have been the least stable. These are basically the ministries of state, which will be discussed in more detail later in this chapter. These portfolios have little power in terms of funds spent or operating programs administered. Their main lever of influence comes from a sometimes rather vague mandate to coordinate the work of other departments. Conceptually, this gives them the right to intervene in the activities of many other departments. However, in practice, their small size and lack of financial and program resources have weakened their ability to influence the stronger operating departments.

The *administrative coordinative portfolios* are usually felt to be the least influential in that they are assumed to be the "nuts and bolts" departments which provide the wherewithal for other departments to operate. However, even these departments have some political and policy-making significance. The Department of National Revenue — Taxation has caused a stir in the past because of its assessment and collection practices, and it is sometimes suggested that the purchasing policy of the Department of Supply and Services could be used as a tool for economic development.

The *vertical constituency portfolios* are generally involved in providing services directly to the public. These are high-profile departments from the standpoint of the general public in that they have the largest budgets and deal with a large constituency. In general, they lack the power to intervene in the affairs of other departments, which comes with the responsibility to coordinate, but their large budget and vocal constituency give these departments a significant amount of power. It is difficult for the horizontal coordinative portfolios to intervene too much in the affairs of these departments without raising the ire of the large number of constituents who are dependent on the department for service.

While it is possible to group portfolios according to a number of characteristics, it is considerably more difficult to rank these portfolios or the ministers who hold them in order of importance. A minister's relative position in Cabinet is determined in part by his or her portfolio, but also in large part by such other factors as regional power base, personal diplomatic and judgemental skills, and relationship with the Prime Minister. In short, no portfolio can be deemed unimportant. All portfolios have significant roles, and they can all lead to substantial embarrassment for the government if the occupant of a portfolio is careless or incompetent.

Departments are the most closely controlled of all government agencies. Other entities such as regulatory agencies and Crown corporations are deliberately insulated to some extent from direct control by the legislature and the executive, but departments have no such insulation. It is important to consider some of those avenues of legislative and executive control.

The Legislature and Government Departments

This section will discuss the various methods that the legislature uses to control government departments. (A more complete description of the interactions between the legislature and the bureaucracy is contained in Chapter 15.) This control begins at the time of the creation of a new department, because a new department can be created only by an Act of Parliament. This enabling legislation sets out the responsibilities of the department and the limits of its authority. The statute establishing the federal Department of Communications is typical in that it is only two pages long and its very general wording imposes only rather broad conditions on the department's operation. The statute provides in part that:

> 2. (1) There shall be a department of the Government of Canada called the Department of Communications over which the Minister of Communications appointed by commission under the Great Seal shall preside.
>
> (2) The Minister of Communications holds office during pleasure and has the management and direction of the Department of Communications . . . .
>
> 4. The duties, powers and functions of the Minister of Communications extend to and include all matters over which the Parliament of Canada has jurisdiction, not by law assigned to any other department, branch or agency of the Government of Canada, relating to
>
> > (a) telecommunications; and
> >
> > (b) the development and utilization generally of communications undertakings, facilities, systems and services for Canada.[10]

In some provinces this kind of legislation is considerably longer and more detailed and restrictive. In any case, the executive has fairly broad prerogatives to arrange the internal structure of departments. Under the federal Public Service Rearrangement and Transfer of Duties Act,[11] the executive also has the power to transfer responsibilities between departments.

In addition to the initial, enabling legislation, Parliament sometimes passes other legislation affecting departments. This includes both specific legislation, such as that setting up a new program and assigning it to a department, and general legislation, such as the Financial Administration Act or the Public Service Employment Act which binds all departments in certain matters. Thus, Parliament can specify a department's mandate as loosely or as tightly as it wants, although the usual practice is to provide a broad mandate that allows maximum flexibility to the executive.

Another important element of Parliament's relationship to the executive is the annual budget. Each year the executive must seek parliamentary approval to spend funds in the upcoming year. At a minimum, the members of Parliament, particularly Opposition members, use this opportunity to question ministers and public servants about the operation of their departments and programs. In extreme cases, Parliament could decide to reduce or even entirely eliminate an appropriation for a department.

While these methods by which the legislature can affect departmental operations are, legally speaking, correct, realism requires some modification in prac-

---

[10]R.S.C. 1970, c. C-24.
[11]R.S.C. 1970, c. P-34.

tice. When the government party holds a majority of seats in the legislature, the government has fairly effective control over the legislation passed. Members of the Opposition can introduce amendments to proposed legislation, including reductions of appropriations, but these are unlikely to be passed. In the case of a minority government, the situation is more complex, but the government usually finds some method of exercising a certain amount of control over activities in the legislature.[12] Obviously, if it cannot exert sufficient control, it will not govern long.

However, this should not be taken to mean that the government can totally dominate the legislature. Opposition members have certain tools at their disposal to thwart arbitrary government actions. The legislature is a highly public forum, and the government is very sensitive to the embarrassment which it can suffer when the Opposition rallies public opinion behind it in response to some unpopular action of the government. The government, particularly in a majority situation, has a strong position, but not an absolutely commanding one. Opposition parties still have means of holding a government accountable for its actions.

This is where the doctrine of *individual ministerial responsibility* becomes important.[13] Conceptually, the principle of ministerial responsibility holds that a minister is responsible for all actions carried out by his or her department. This means that even if the minister did not approve an action in advance or had no knowledge of it, he or she still must accept responsibility for the action. This principle is an important element in a system of responsible government because the minister is the only link between the legislature and the operating department. If the minister could avoid responsibility for the actions of his or her department, then the legislature would have no effective way of holding the executive accountable for its actions. Since the minister is accountable for the actions of his or her department, it is important that there are adequate methods available for the minister to control the department.

The Executive and Government Departments

In the first place, the minister is the political head of the department and so has line authority over all public servants in the department. Within the provisions of relevant legislation, he or she has full authority to assign duties to departmental employees and to supervise their activities. In Chapters 2, 3, and 4, there was some discussion of the difficulties of administrative superiors holding subordinates truly accountable for their actions. The large size and geographical decentralization of most departments, and the incredible demands made on ministers' time in the legislature and in constituency work, make the enforcement of true accountability particularly problematic. However, ministers have a number of tools to assist them in controlling the activities of operating departments.

---

[12]For a description of how the Ontario Progressive Conservative Party managed this, see Vaughan Lyon, "Minority Government in Ontario, 1975–1981: An Assessment," *Canadian Journal of Political Science*, vol. 17 (December 1984), pp. 685–705.

[13]For a more complete discussion of ministerial responsibility, see Chapters 13 and 15.

All ministers have a small, personal staff. The members of this staff are selected personally by the minister and are not considered to be public servants; rather, they are the minister's political assistants. They are selected partly for their administrative competence, but unlike public servants, they are also selected for their partisan affiliation. Their roles are difficult to define because each minister uses them in somewhat different ways; however, one role they all have in common is assisting the minister to exercise political control over the bureaucracy.[14]

Ministers also have more formal, legal means of controlling their departments. The legislation establishing departments and programs seldom specifies in precise detail how all activities are to be carried out, in large part because the legislature is simply unable to foresee every future possibility. There is usually a clause in this kind of legislation which allows either the minister or the Governor in Council (that is, the Cabinet) to make certain regulations as long as they are consistent with the terms of the enabling legislation. In some cases, this is done in strict legal form through an *order in council*. This is a formal regulation approved by the Governor in Council and, in the case of the federal government, published in the *Canada Gazette*, which is a bi-weekly listing of official announcements prepared by the government. All provincial governments have similar official publications.

These orders in council frequently establish the ground rules governing relationships between public servants and members of the public affected by their actions and decisions. For example, there are lengthy orders in council specifying the rules for the operation of charter aircraft flights. They impose certain restrictions on the charter operator, but they also make it clear that if the operator complies with these regulations, the public servants must grant the appropriate licences. In this sense, regulations are an important means of controlling the actions of public servants.

In a less formal manner, ministers frequently issue internal departmental regulations. These are also binding on all departmental officials, provided that the regulations are within the terms of the enabling legislation. It is these regulations — covering such matters as which form is to be completed in a particular case and how a particular situation is to be treated — which are the lifeblood of most large organizations. Over the years, these regulations can accumulate to several volumes.

Ministers have an individual, personal responsibility in managing their departments, but there is also a collective Cabinet responsibility in managing the total affairs of the government. This means that the Cabinet collectively must have some assurance that departments are being managed well and that coordination between departments is being handled properly. It is to help ensure these objectives that central agencies have developed as mechanisms of *Cabinet control of government* activities.

---

[14]The general roles of these staff members and, in particular, their use under Prime Minister Mulroney is discussed in more detail in Chapter 14.

CENTRAL AGENCIES

Rationale for Central Agencies

The discussion in Chapter 2 of span of control drew attention to the fact that as the number of units reporting to the same person increases, that person has more difficulty maintaining control of the units and coordinating their activities. The organization chart of the government of Canada in this book demonstrates that Cabinet's span of control is very broad. The organization charts of most provinces show only a slightly smaller span of control. This broad organizational structure requires some method of coordinating the activities of the separate departments and preventing overlap and working at cross-purposes. One of the methods employed in Canada is the central agency.

There are other ways of dealing with this problem. In Britain, there are many departments headed by ministers who are not members of Cabinet. The ministers heading related departments are then grouped under a senior minister who is a member of Cabinet. This creates a situation where the span of control is reasonable for both Cabinet, with a relatively small number of senior ministers, and for the senior ministers, each of whom has a reasonable number of non–Cabinet ministers reporting to him or her. It provides for both reasonable spans of control and a relatively small Cabinet.

It is this latter characteristic which precludes the use of this system in Canada. In Canada, the concept of the *representative Cabinet* is very important. This principle means that many diverse interests must be represented in the federal Cabinet. It requires the selection of Cabinet members to provide an appropriate balance of geographic, religious, ethnic, linguistic, gender, and certain other criteria. As a result, the Cabinet must be fairly large to ensure that all groups are represented adequately.

The principle of a representative Cabinet also requires adherence to the concept that all Cabinet ministers are equal. If there were a distinction between Cabinet and non–Cabinet ministers, it would be impossible to achieve the appropriate representative balance with a limited number of senior ministers. The Clark government of 1979–80 had a small, powerful "inner Cabinet," but Opposition members delighted in pointing out to residents of certain provinces that they had no representative within the important "inner Cabinet." The practice has not been resurrected by subsequent governments.

Definition of a Central Agency

These conventions of representative Cabinet and equality of Cabinet ministers require the wide span of control illustrated in the organization chart, and the wide span of control requires the presence of some mechanism to coordinate and control the activities of the operating departments. This is the role of the central agencies. *A central agency is any agency that has a substantial amount of continuing legitimate authority to intervene in and direct the activities of departments.*

The application of any definition, particularly one which contains words such as "substantial" and "continuing," is somewhat arbitrary, but it is widely acknowledged in the mid-1980s that there are six full-fledged central agencies in the government of Canada — the Prime Minister's Office, the Privy Council Office, the Federal-Provincial Relations Office, the Treasury Board Secretariat, the Office of the Comptroller General, and the Department of Finance.[15] The claims of other administrative units to central agency status will be considered at the end of this section.

Central agencies obtain their power from either legislative authority to operate in a particular area, or proximity to someone with legitimate authority, such as the Prime Minister. They usually do not have a large number of employees, although most of the staff employed are relatively high-level, professional people. Table 6.2 shows the number of people employed in these six agencies and some of the largest and smallest departments in the fiscal year ended March 31, 1985. Even the smallest departments have more employees than the central agencies, and the largest departments completely dwarf them.

Table 6.2
EMPLOYEES IN SELECTED DEPARTMENTS AND AGENCIES
(FISCAL YEAR ENDED MARCH 31, 1985)

Prime Minister's Office	91
Privy Council Office	150
Federal-Provincial Relations Office	59
Treasury Board Secretariat	767
Office of the Comptroller General	156
Department of Finance	706
Department of Labour	1,039
Department of Justice	1,986
Department of Transport	22,976
Department of Employment and Immigration	24,823
Department of the Solicitor General	32,462
Department of National Defence	37,018

Source: Canada, *Estimates for the Fiscal Year Ended March 31, 1985, Part II* (Ottawa: Supply and Services Canada, 1984).

All six agencies discussed in this section have either been created or experienced significant change as a result of the style of government brought to office by Prime Minister Trudeau in 1968.[16] Trudeau's predecessor, Prime Minister Pearson, never had a majority government and so had to be concerned with conciliation and fire-fighting. Trudeau, with a majority government in his first term, had the luxury of focussing on specific goals he wanted to accomplish and using such newly fashionable rational tools as cost-effectiveness and systems

[15]This list coincides with the list used in the most recent comprehensive study of central agencies: Colin Campbell and George J. Szablowski, *The Superbureaucrats* (Toronto: Macmillan of Canada, 1979).

[16]G. Bruce Doern, "Recent Changes in the Philosophy of Policy-making in Canada," *Canadian Journal of Political Science*, vol. 4 (June 1971), pp. 243–266.

analysis to attain those goals. His limited experience in working in large organizations could have made him somewhat uncomfortable in a bureaucratic environment. As a result, Trudeau wanted *competing sources of information* so that he did not have to rely solely on the traditional information sources of the operating departments. This was not evidence of distrust of the traditional organizational structures; rather, it was the logical desire to obtain more than one point of view on an issue before acting.

Thus, another major role for central agencies developed in addition to the coordinating role discussed above. Trudeau began to use these agencies as competing sources of information. As the agencies began to adopt a much more significant role in policy development, they began to attract to their ranks people who brought with them "rational" tools such as cost-benefit analysis, systems analysis, and economic modelling. The style of Prime Minister Trudeau, the need for competing sources of information, and the presence of, and confidence in, these rational techniques significantly increased the role of these central agencies in the 1970s.

When Prime Minister Mulroney came to office, he brought with him a different style of governing, which has been characterized as brokerage politics — focussing more on accommodating varying interests than Trudeau's search for rationality. Peter Aucoin argues that this different style is reflected in a different approach to the use of the Cabinet committee system and the central agencies. For example, Mulroney has been less interested in competing sources of information and more interested in bringing power closer to him so that he has the necessary levers to engage in accommodation. Specifically, this has resulted in the ascendancy of the Prime Minister's Office (the PM's personal political advisors) at the expense of the Privy Council Office composed of public servants left over from the Liberal era.[17]

It is important to understand that each Prime Minister has placed his own personal stamp on the government bureaucracy, but there has been enough consistency that it is still possible to generalize about the duties of the central agencies. They have two related roles. They are responsible for the coordination of political and administrative activities of line departments. They are also involved in advising the Prime Minister and Cabinet on policy initiatives and shepherding these initiatives through the decision-making and implementation processes. Van Loon argues that the ascendancy of central agencies

> derives from the continuing attempt within the federal government to impose financial and qualitative discipline and a notion of collective responsibility on what was hitherto a rather undisciplined policy process.[18]

These roles and responsibilities can be illustrated best by a discussion of the activities of each of these six agencies.

---

[17]Peter Aucoin, "Organizational Change in the Machinery of Canadian Government: From Rational Management to Brokerage Politics," *Canadian Journal of Political Science*, vol. 19 (1986), p. 22 and passim.

[18]R. Van Loon, "Stop the Music: The Current Policy and Expenditure Management System in Ottawa," *Canadian Public Administration*, vol. 24 (Summer 1981), p. 176.

The Prime Minister's Office

The Prime Minister's Office (PMO) works directly for the Prime Minister and has an unabashedly partisan political role.[19] Its major responsibilities are to serve the Prime Minister by providing advice on how policy initiatives will be viewed politically in the country, and to assist in other ways which will cast the Prime Minister in the best political light. Specifically, these responsibilities include planning and coordinating major new policy initiatives, providing liaison with the party machinery in the provinces, maintaining good relations with the media, writing speeches, advising on appointments and nominations, and briefing the Prime Minister concerning issues that could come up during question period and debate. Because these functions are all overtly political activities, the small number of people in the PMO who are involved in them are political appointees. This means that they hold their positions at the pleasure of the Prime Minister and always resign when there is a change of government.

The PMO has other important activities of a "housekeeping" nature, such as making travel arrangements and answering the huge volume of mail for the Prime Minister. The largest number of employees in the PMO are employed in carrying out the latter function. The recent growth in the size of the office has been severely criticized, but much of that growth has occurred in this correspondence function.

It is difficult to generalize about the relationship between the PMO and operating departments. The PMO has no statutory authority of its own; it derives its power from the fact that it is headed by the Prime Minister, through whom it must act in taking initiatives with departments. Its contact with departments is largely limited to consulting about new policy initiatives or dealing with political problems. There is some idea that the PMO would like to become more involved in policy matters, but its small size and other responsibilities prevent it from doing so. In sum, the PMO usually chooses not to become too involved with the activities of operating departments, but it has a significant amount of power which it can exercise on the authority of the Prime Minister.

The Privy Council Office

The Privy Council Office (PCO) is a relatively small organization which provides policy advice and administrative support to the Prime Minister, to Cabinet as a whole, and to Cabinet committees. The title of the office comes from the fact that the formal name for Cabinet is the Queen's Privy Council.[20] The status of the PCO is illustrated by the fact that the senior public servant in the agency, who is called the clerk of the Privy Council and the secretary to the Cabinet, is usually considered to be the most senior federal public servant.

Unlike the PMO, the PCO is staffed by career public servants rather than political appointees. However, the kind of advice provided by PCO, while not overtly political in the partisan sense, is certainly sensitive to the political pulse of the

[19]Marc Lalonde, "The Changing Role of the Prime Minister's Office," *Canadian Public Administration*, vol. 14 (Winter 1971), pp. 509–537.
[20]Technically, the Queen's Privy Council consists of all previous and present federal Cabinet ministers plus a limited number of others on whom the honour has been bestowed.

nation. A former clerk of the Privy Council described the roles of the PMO and the PCO in this manner:

> The Prime Minister's Office is partisan, politically oriented, yet operationally sensitive. The Privy Council Office is non-partisan, operationally oriented yet politically sensitive.[21]

The Privy Council Office has a number of different roles, including some which are assigned to it by the Prime Minister on a temporary basis. For example, after the election of the Parti Québécois in 1976, the position of deputy secretary (coordination) was established.[22] Its main role was to coordinate the activities of all government departments in dealing with Quebec. After a time, when this role seemed less important, this separate unit was eliminated. The PCO is the obvious locus for such sensitive tasks.

However, the major, continuing activities of the PCO fall into the two categories of support for the Cabinet and its committees, and advice on machinery of government.[23] Each of these categories is discussed below.

The PCO provides several different kinds of support for Cabinet committees. Organizationally, the office is divided so that there is a small secretariat attached to each Cabinet committee, except Treasury Board which has its own secretarial arm. Each secretariat monitors the general policy environment in the area for which its committee is responsible. The secretariat advises on new policy initiatives or responses to ongoing problems and ensures that all proposals that go before a Cabinet committee are in good order. Among other things, this means that the interdepartmental aspects have been discussed and any problems resolved. This aspect of the PCO has prompted some to refer to it as a "gatekeeper," although this might be something of an overstatement. PCO also assists in the preparation of the agenda of Cabinet committee meetings and in briefing the chairperson of the committee. At the housekeeping level, PCO also arranges for meeting space and maintains the minutes of the meetings.

The machinery of government group in the PCO advises the Prime Minister on the reallocation of programs between departments and on the reorganization of government departments and agencies. This also involves the handling of jurisdictional disputes between ministers or departments and an analysis of the operation of the Cabinet committee system.

The machinery of government section of the PCO also advises the Prime Minister and Cabinet about senior appointments within the federal bureaucracy. It is concerned with moving highly competent public servants through senior postings so that they are always employed in a capacity where their talents can be best used and can gain experience for their next position. The PCO is involved in

---

[21]Gordon Robertson, "The Changing Role of the Privy Council Office," *Canadian Public Administration*, vol. 14 (Winter 1971), p. 506.
[22]Audrey D. Doerr, *The Machinery of Government in Canada* (Toronto: Methuen, 1981), p. 33.
[23]For a good discussion of the role of PCO see ibid., pp. 30–34 and Richard D. French, "The Privy Council Office: Support for Cabinet Decision Making," in Richard Schultz, Orest Kruhlak, and John C. Terry, eds., *The Canadian Political Process* (Toronto: Holt, Rinehart and Winston, 1979), pp. 363–394.

advising only about employment of public servants; advice about more political kinds of appointments comes from the PMO.

The PCO provides a good example of central agency activities and the general position of central agencies in the organizational structure. The duties of the PCO give it the legitimate right to become involved in the activities of every other department of government. It does not have line authority over those departments, but its position as "gate-keeper" and its proximity to Cabinet mean that operating departments always consider very carefully advice offered by the PCO. This helps to explain the very complex love-hate relationships which operating departments usually have with central agencies.

Federal-Provincial Relations Office

The Federal-Provincial Relations Office (FPRO) has a relatively long history as a unit within the PCO, but its existence as a separate unit dates only from the late 1970s. It was elevated in response to a growing concern over the general state of federal-provincial relations and to provide the federal government with a better way to manage its approach to dealing with the provinces.[24]

The FPRO maintains liaison with federal and provincial officials who are involved in the operation of federal provincial programs. It is most concerned with policy issues and the overall operation of the federal-provincial structure, and not as concerned about the details of individual programs.

The status of the FPRO is clear from the fact that it reports directly to the Prime Minister and is headed by the secretary to Cabinet (Federal-Provincial Relations) whose status is only slightly below that of the clerk of the Privy Council.

Like the PCO, the FPRO has many opportunities to become involved in the activities of operating departments, i.e., in any area in which a department operates an intergovernmental program. This engenders some of the same love-hate relationship between departments and FPRO as was mentioned above in connection with PCO.

Treasury Board

Treasury Board (TB) is a Cabinet committee consisting of the President of Treasury Board, the Minister of Finance, and four other ministers appointed by the Prime Minister. TB differs from other Cabinet committees in two respects. It is the only Cabinet committee that is enshrined in legislation — the Financial Administration Act — and it is the only Cabinet committee that has a large bureaucracy reporting to it. In fact, it controls two administrative units — Treasury Board Secretariat (TBS) and, since 1978, the Office of the Comptroller General (OCG). A former secretary of the Treasury Board has written that the Treasury Board is one committee, but it has a dual role. It functions as both the Cabinet's committee on the expenditure budget and the Cabinet's committee on manage-

---

[24]For an interesting explanation of the creation of the FPRO, see Colin Campbell, *Governments Under Stress* (Toronto: University of Toronto Press, 1983), p. 90.

ment.[25] The Treasury Board itself considers these matters in the final analysis, but in practice, most of the preparatory work is done by TBS and OCG.[26]

Treasury Board Secretariat. TBS has gradually accumulated many, seemingly diverse responsibilities. The one factor which ties them together is that they all relate to ensuring the efficient and effective use of government resources, both human and financial.

TBS is responsible for the preparation of the expenditure budget that the government proposes in the House of Commons each year. It receives general guidelines from the Cabinet Committee on Priorities and Planning and the Department of Finance, which allow it, in turn, to set guidelines for expenditure by operating departments. This requires TBS to negotiate with departments about starting new programs or cutting back or eliminating existing ones.

TBS is also responsible for certain aspects of personnel administration, such as negotiating from the employer's position in collective bargaining, approving the organizational structure of operating departments, exercising control over the addition of new positions to the staff complement of departments, and classifying all positions to ensure that employees performing similar duties in all departments will receive the same rate of pay. TBS also monitors the implementation of the government's official languages policy to ensure that positions have been classified properly as bilingual, unilingual English, unilingual French, or either English or French.

TBS has a shared role with the Office of the Comptroller General in ensuring that sound administrative practices are followed in all government activities. It is responsible for making regulations dealing with administrative matters such as purchasing, entering into contracts, and receiving and spending public funds. The general thrust of these duties is to ensure that proper controls are in effect concerning government assets and that adequate safeguards are in place before funds are spent.

Office of the Comptroller General. The Comptroller General is considered the chief financial officer of the government of Canada. As mentioned above, the OCG shares certain duties with the TBS in making regulations concerning receipt and disbursement of public money, accounting procedures, and the form of financial statements. The OCG has a special interest in ensuring the quality of all departmental financial officers and the integrity of the internal audit function. It is also responsible for evaluating the quality of government programs and discussing the results of the evaluation with the department to help it improve its management and, with Treasury Board, to aid it in the budget process.

In sum, Treasury Board, supported by its two secretariats, has numerous responsibilities, but they all relate to ensuring the wise use of resources — both human and financial — within federal government departments. This involves ensur-

---

[25]A. W. Johnson, "The Treasury Board of Canada and the Machinery of Government of the 1970's," *Canadian Journal of Political Science*, vol. 4 (September 1971), p. 346.

[26]The duties of these two organizations will be discussed in more detail in Chapters 23 and 24.

ing that prudence and probity are always observed in government transactions and attempting to ensure uniformity in areas such as levels of pay across all government departments.

From the standpoint of operating departments, Treasury Board is easily the most active — some might say intrusive — of the central agencies, simply because there are so many points of contact and so many specific activities for which TB clearance must be obtained. In the article mentioned earlier, a former secretary of Treasury Board compares the board to the castle in Franz Kafka's novel *The Castle*. The analogy is good in the sense of the looming presence that the castle had over the town, but the analogy breaks down at one point. The land-surveyor's major frustration was that his actions were ignored by officials from the castle; officials in operating departments often wish that they had the same difficulty with Treasury Board.

Department of Finance
The Department of Finance is responsible for advising Cabinet on matters of economic policy. Thus, the department has an exceedingly broad mandate. It advises on questions of fiscal policy, international trade policy (including tariffs), domestic industrial policy, taxation policy, and the preparation of the revenue and expenditure budgets.[27]

The Department of Finance could potentially intervene in the activities of any department involved in policies that touch upon any of the above areas. And, given the breadth of those areas, it is difficult to think of a department which does not. The role of Finance does not bring it into the same kind of obtrusive, day-to-day contact with operating departments as they experience with TBS, but its concern with economic policy allows it to intervene at strategic points in the policy development process. Its role in the preparation of the expenditure budget helps determine whether the upcoming year will be a lean or a fat one for government agencies. Finance also has a role as the budgetary gatekeeper. Indeed, it has traditionally provided the strongest opposition to new spending programs.[28] This brings Finance into fairly frequent conflict with operating departments.

Other Possible Central Agencies
A number of other departments, such as External Affairs and Regional Industrial Expansion, sometimes claim central agency status because they have a certain amount of cross-cutting authority which allows them to intervene in the internal affairs of other departments in limited ways. Their claims to central agency status are not entirely without merit, but they are somewhat overstated. They have not been included here because their mandate to intervene is frequently as limited as their success in using it. These claims should be taken

[27]For a more detailed description of the responsibilities of the Department of Finance, see Richard W. Phidd and G. Bruce Doern, *The Politics and Management of Canadian Economic Policy* (Toronto: Macmillan of Canada, 1978), ch. 7.
[28]Ibid., p. 224.

more as an indication of the desire of these departments to attain central agency status than as a legitimate claim to that status.

Central Agencies in the Provinces

It is obvious that the functions performed by central agencies in the federal government will also be necessary in provincial governments. However, the smaller size of the provincial governments usually means that organizational structures are less complex and differentiated. In most provinces, the functions of the PMO, the PCO, and sometimes the TB are all carried out in the Premier's Office. However, there is a general movement towards the establishment of a separate organization with duties similar to those carried out by TB at the federal level.[29] For example, the duties of the Management Board of Cabinet in Ontario are very similar to those of TB. The functions of the Department of Finance are carried out in most provinces by a Treasury Department headed by the provincial treasurer.

ORGANIZATION OF A TYPICAL OPERATING DEPARTMENT

Figure 6.1 is an organization chart of the federal Department of Indian and Northern Affairs. The minister, of course, is at the top of the pyramid. The political staff of the minister is shown immediately below, but it should be noted that these people do not have direct line authority within the department. They advise the minister and frequently consult on the minister's behalf with public servants, but they must always act through the minister in seeking action by public servants.

The next link in the chain of accountability is the deputy minister. Deputy ministers are the administrative (as distinct from political) heads of departments. They are permanent heads of departments in that they do not usually leave when governments change. Unlike ministers, who are politicians, deputy ministers usually work their way up through the ranks of the public service, although in some cases they are brought in directly from other governments or from the private sector.

In some senses, deputy ministers have the most difficult positions in the entire system, because they must act as a link between the political desires of the minister and the administrative concerns of the public servants in the departments. Of course, ministers are not totally insensitive to administrative concerns, any more than public servants are totally insensitive to political ones, but each side brings a different dimension to the issue at hand. Ministers, particularly if they represent a new government, often feel under pressure from colleagues to make changes in programs and activities. It would not be appropriate for public servants to oppose these changes, but public servants are frequently more attuned to the administrative problems posed by change than to its political benefits. Good deputy ministers must stand between these two concerns and not be afraid

---

[29]Marsha A. Chandler and William M. Chandler, *Public Policy and Provincial Politics* (Toronto: McGraw-Hill Ryerson, 1979), pp. 101–105.

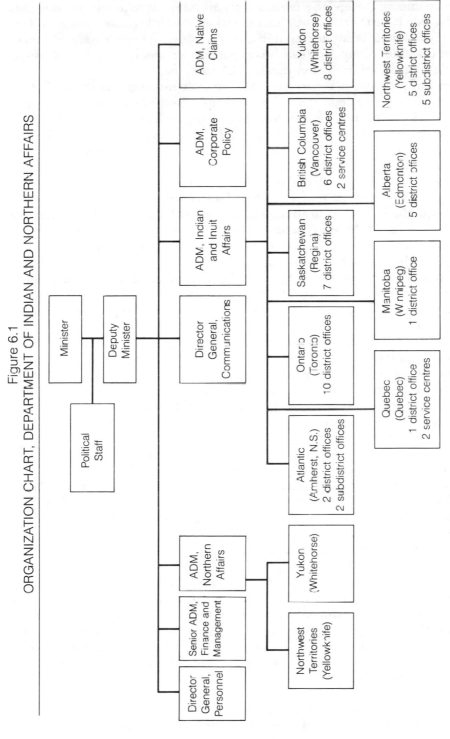

Figure 6.1
ORGANIZATION CHART, DEPARTMENT OF INDIAN AND NORTHERN AFFAIRS

Source: Adapted from Canada, Department of Indian and Northern Affairs, *1982–83 Annual Report* (Ottawa: Minister of Supply and Services Canada, 1983). p. 6.

either to impose change on a reluctant organization or to advise ministers fully and frankly if their actions will lead to serious administrative problems. However, if this advice is not delivered in a very sensitive and diplomatic manner, it can be taken for disloyalty. Because the role of the deputy minister is so important, it is described in greater detail in Chapter 14.

One word of caution is necessary. The term deputy minister is not used consistently throughout departments. For example, in the Department of External Affairs, where the minister is referred to as the secretary of state for external affairs, the senior public servant is called the undersecretary, while in Treasury Board, where the minister is called the president, the senior public servant is called the secretary. Confused? In most government publications, the term deputy head is used to cover all of these senior people. In normal discussion around government offices, one frequently hears reference to "the deputy."

Beneath the level of deputy minister, the nomenclature can become even more confusing. Usually, there will be several assistant deputy ministers (ADMs) reporting to the DM. Sometimes the superior status of one of these positions will be established by designating it as associate deputy minister or senior assistant deputy minister. This is usually a sign that the position carries a heavier weight of duties or responsibilities than the other ADM positions. In the Indian and Northern Affairs example in Figure 6.1, there are four assistant deputy ministers and one senior assistant deputy minister.

Also, in this department, there are two directors general reporting directly to the DM — one for Personnel and one for Communications. These positions have almost the same status as the ADM in that they report directly to the DM, but their title indicates that their ranking is slightly lower, usually because they have less weighty responsibilities. The director general of Personnel has a very important role in the organization, but he or she has less important responsibilities and fewer administrative problems than the ADM, Indian and Inuit Affairs.

At this point, it is useful to relate this organization chart to some of the material about organizational behaviour covered in Chapter 2.

In terms of the line-staff distinction, there are two line units — Northern Affairs, and Indian and Inuit Affairs — and five staff functions — Personnel, Finance and Management, Corporate Policy, Native Claims, and Communications. A more complete organization chart would also illustrate the functional lines of authority between the line and staff functions.

An attempt to apply the principles of organization by purpose, process, place, or people illustrates some of the ambiguities in these concepts. The Northern Affairs unit seems to be organized by place, but since the responsibility of this unit is to guide and control northern development, one could make an argument for organization by purpose, as well. By the same token, Indian and Inuit Affairs sounds at first like organization by people, but given the mandate of the unit to deal with the particular rights and problems of these two groups, it could also be organization by purpose.

The organization structure of the federal Department of Indian and Northern Affairs is typical of the organization of a traditional operating department. It is replicated across the federal government and in all provinces. However, there have been numerous organizational innovations implemented in several jurisdictions. Some of the most important innovations will be considered in the last section of this chapter.

SOME INNOVATIVE ORGANIZATIONAL STRUCTURES

Some recent organizational innovations have involved a wholesale reorganization of an entire government, while others have involved experimentation within only one department. This section will deal first with some very broad changes in the Ontario and federal governments, and then move to a discussion of the reorganization of the federal Ministry of Transport.

The Ontario Committee on Government Productivity

In the late 1960s, it became clear to Premier John Robarts that the government of Ontario had certain fundamental, structural problems. Rising demand for and costs of government services were outstripping the increase in revenue. The heightened demand for services was also causing such a rapid increase in the size of government departments that they were becoming difficult to manage using the traditional means. Related to these trends was a greater interdependence of departments. Actions taken within one department sometimes had unexpected impacts on other departments. All these developments pointed to the need for better coordination of government activity. At the same time, some way was needed to lessen the ministers' heavy burden of departmental, party, and constituency work.

To seek solutions to these problems, Premier Robarts appointed the Committee on Government Productivity (COGP) in 1969 to

> inquire into all matters pertaining to the management of the Government of Ontario and to make such recommendations as in its opinion will improve the efficiency and effectiveness of the Government of Ontario.[30]

One basic recommendation of the COGP was both substantive and semantic. The word "ministry" replaced "department" to emphasize the intent that the new organizational units were to include not just operating departments, but also all agencies, boards, and commissions reporting to a minister.

The main group of recommendations of the committee involved the arrangement of these new operating *ministries* in *policy fields* around a new kind of research and coordinating *provincial secretariat*.[31] Three provincial secretariats were created — Social Development, Resource Development, and Justice. Figure 6.2 illustrates the structure as it existed in 1984. It was largely based on the

---

[30]Order in Council 4689/69 (December 23, 1969) as reproduced in Ontario, Committee on Government Productivity, *Interim Report Number Three* (1971), p. 63.

[31]Ibid., passim. See also the discussion in: James D. Fleck, "Restructuring the Ontario Government," *Canadian Public Administration*, vol. 16 (Spring 1973), pp. 55–68; and James D. Fleck, "Reorganization of the Ontario Government," *Canadian Public Administration*, vol. 15 (Summer 1972), pp. 383–385.

Figure 6.2
ORGANIZATION CHART OF ONTARIO POLICY FIELD SYSTEM

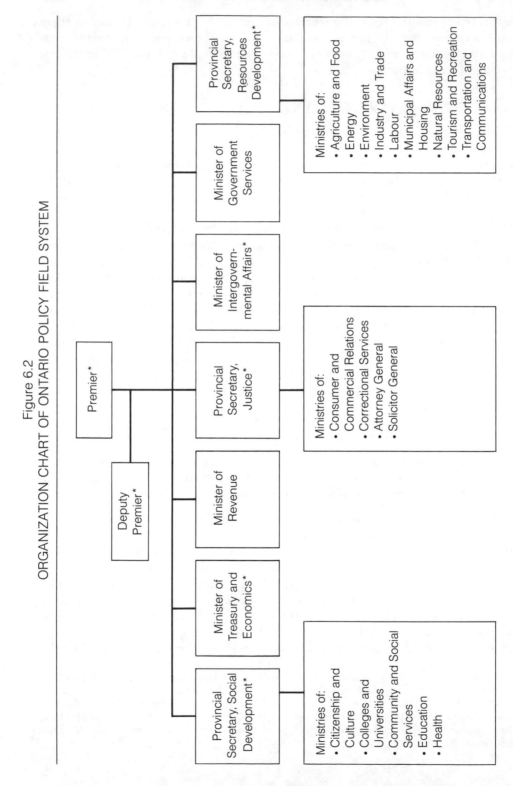

Source: Adapted from Ontario, Ministry of Government Services, *KWIC Index to Your Ontario Government Services, 1984* (Toronto: Ministry of Government Services, 1984), p. 2.

*Member of Policy and Priorities Board

COGP recommendations, but has changed somewhat over time.[32] Each of these secretariats was to be headed by a very senior Cabinet minister called a provincial secretary (soon dubbed "super minister" by the media). The provincial secretary chaired a Cabinet committee consisting of all of the ministers within his or her policy field. A number of other Cabinet committees continued in existence, but these were not affected by the reorganization and so will not be discussed here.

The relationship between the provincial secretaries and the ministers within their policy fields was rather delicate. The provincial secretaries did not have line authority over these other ministers; rather, they were supposed to provide leadership and guidance within their policy fields through influence rather than control. The secretary had access to a number of tools for exercising this influence. First, it was envisaged that the secretary would always be a very senior minister. Second, the fact that the secretary was the permanent chairperson of one of the policy field Cabinet committees made him or her a member of the highly influential Policy and Priorities Board discussed below. Third, the secretary had access to the research activities of the public servants in the provincial secretariat. These resources were intended to allow the secretary to coordinate activities within his or her policy field.

Each provincial secretariat consisted of a small number of public servants involved in policy making and research activities and in coordinating the work of the departments in its policy field. The provincial secretariats were not ordinarily responsible for operating programs.

The purpose of this reorganization was to increase coordination between operating departments. Not only would all related ministers be on the same Cabinet committee, but there would also be a secretariat charged with examining the entire policy field and suggesting rearrangements of responsibilities between ministries, which would improve coordination and/or achieve cost savings. This arrangement would improve policy making by relieving the provincial secretaries of program responsibilities and freeing them to think more about overall policies in their areas. It was hoped that this would reduce some of the time demands made on ministers, because the primary responsibility for policy making would be separated from the primary responsibility for program delivery. It would also reduce the workload of Cabinet, because it was presumed that certain sectoral problems could be worked out in the Cabinet committees and not require the time of the full Cabinet.

The new system was topped off by the Policy and Priorities Board, which was a type of inner Cabinet composed of the Premier and various senior ministers always including the three provincial secretaries.

Many of the recommendations of the COGP were instrumental in improving significantly the quality of management, but a number of problems began to emerge very quickly. The idea that the previous departments could become "min-

---

[32]For a good discussion of the evolution of Cabinet structures both before and after COGP, see Richard A. Loreto, "The Structure of the Ontario Political System," in Donald C. MacDonald, ed., *The Government and Politics of Ontario*, 3rd ed. (Scarborough, Ont.: Nelson Canada, 1985), pp. 18–33.

istries" that also included agencies, boards, and commissions never really worked out as fully as was planned.[33] Most of these organizations remained as autonomous as they were before COGP.

Problems also developed in the role of the provincial secretary. Specifically, these so-called "super ministers" were really more like "mini-ministers."[34] The architects of the new system forgot that ministers score political points by administering programs, dealing with the media, and having a high profile in the legislature; they do not score political points by sitting in their offices and ruminating about policy making and coordination. Therefore, it became clear to ambitious politicians that it was much better to be a minister with an operating ministry than to be a provincial secretary. This meant that senior ministers were simply not interested in becoming provincial secretaries. Without the presence of senior ministers in these key positions, the ability of the policy secretary to influence through suasion was considerably limited.

Over time, the role of the provincial secretaries and their secretariats gradually, but steadily, eroded until Premier Peterson abolished them when he came to office in 1985. However, the concept should not be seen as totally discredited. There were specific reasons why it did not work as well as expected in this case, but this approach could well be employed in a different form elsewhere and work better. In fact, the existing structure of the Quebec government would seem to be based to a certain extent on these principles.[35]

Ministries and Ministers of State in the Federal Government

In 1970, the federal government adopted certain organizational revisions which are sometimes referred to as a ministry system, but the federal reforms were considerably less far-reaching than the Ontario ones.

After Prime Minister Trudeau came to power in 1968, he made a number of changes in the way Cabinet and the bureaucracy were organized. One of the major innovations was embodied in the Ministries and Ministers of States Act.[36] Trudeau wanted more flexibility in the size of Cabinet and in the appointment of Cabinet ministers. In particular, he wanted to be able to bring people into Cabinet to consider problems which did not fit neatly into the existing departmental structure. This was difficult under the legislative arrangements that prevailed at that time. He also sought some way of easing the managerial burden which some ministers were feeling in managing the more rapidly growing and diverse departments. And finally, he recognized that to maintain the idea of representative Cabinet, all this had to be accomplished without creating a hierarchy of senior and junior ministers.

---

[33]Kenneth Bryden, "Executive and Legislature in Ontario: A Case Study on Governmental Reform," *Canadian Public Administration*, vol. 18 (Summer 1975), p. 243.

[34]This and many other highly accurate predictions were made in J. R. Mallory, "Restructuring the Government of Ontario: A Comment," *Canadian Public Administration*, vol. 16 (Spring 1973), pp. 69–72.

[35]See Louis Borgeat, et al., *L'administration Québécoise: organisation et fonctionnement* (Presses de l'Université du Québec, 1984), ch. 2.

[36]R.S.C. 1970 (2nd supplement), c. 14, ss. 13–24.

This reorganization resulted in four different kinds of ministers. It is important to remember that, even though these different types of ministers have different levels of responsibility, they are all equal in terms of their formal position in Cabinet.

Departmental Ministers. These are the conventional ministers, who head operating departments. They derive their authority from the statutes which created their departments and are not really affected by the 1970 legislation.

Ministers of State for Specified Purposes. This was the major innovation in this legislation. The Prime Minister could appoint an unlimited number of new ministers in this category by an order in council approved by a vote of the House of Commons. This was a considerably easier and less formal mechanism than seeking legislation to establish a department. The idea was that this type of minister would head a Ministry of State, a small department oriented to the consideration of some specific problem. It would be a "think tank" with some responsibility for coordinating activities of departments, but no responsibility for operating programs. It was understood that this kind of ministry could be a temporary organization which would analyse a problem, propose a solution and then be put out of business.

The first two ministries created were the Ministry of State for Urban Affairs (MSUA) and the Ministry of State for Science and Technology (MOSST). The former ministry was created in response to a presumed urban crisis. It conducted a significant amount of research on urban problems, but its abilities to coordinate the activities of operating departments in urban affairs proved to be somewhat limited. It was eliminated in 1979 as a cost saving move and as a concession to the provinces, which resented any federal involvement in municipal affairs. MOSST is still active in coordinating the activities of public and private sector organizations in scientific research, although the Mulroney government has substantially reduced its funding level.

There were two other short-lived ministries of state. The Ministry of State for Economic and Regional Development (MSERD) and the Ministry of State for Social Development (MSSD) were created in 1979 and 1980, respectively, to be secretariats to the relevant Cabinet committees and to coordinate the activities of operating departments in their areas. They were abolished by Prime Minister Turner when he took office in 1984, ostensibly as a cost-saving measure.

In sum, the ministries of state established to this point have not lived up to their expectations. The ministry concept was born at a time when the catchphrase was "knowledge is power." It was expected that these ministries would obtain their power from their superior knowledge in particular policy areas. In retrospect, it seems that the ability to control programs and spend money is considerably more powerful than knowledge.[37] The ministries of state had very few successes in using their knowledge and suasion to affect the policies of operating departments. Since these ministries did not have programs, they could

---

[37]Peter Aucoin and Richard French, *Knowledge, Power and Public Policy* (Ottawa: Information Canada, 1974), ch. 3 and passim.

never develop a committed clientele. Therefore, when cost-saving or a sop to provincial autonomy was needed, these ministries were the easiest places in which to make cuts.

Minister of State to Assist a Minister. Originally, the idea of this type of portfolio was that some departments were so large and their duties so diverse that it seemed a single minister could not adequately manage the entire department. The solution to this problem was to "hive off" or divide one portion of a minister's department and make that the responsibility of a minister of state. The longest-standing such ministry is the Ministry of State for Fitness and Amateur Sport. Administratively, this organization is a part of the Department of National Health and Welfare, but politically it is the responsibility of a separate minister of state. The objective of this kind of arrangement is both to relieve some of the work pressure on the minister responsible for the department and to signal the intentions of the government to give a particular policy area a higher priority. This position has also been used to test the abilities of new ministers and to groom them for more weighty responsibilities.

Recently, the roles of some of these ministers have gone beyond the original idea of hiving off portions of a department and expanded to include managing responsibilities that span several departments. A large number of different organizational arrangements have been employed in using the minister of state to assist.[38]

A distinction should be made between a parliamentary secretary and a minister of state to assist a minister. The parliamentary secretary usually does not have continuing responsibilities in a defined area, but rather does as much or as little as requested by the minister to whom he or she is assigned. The major difference between the two positions is that the parliamentary secretary is not a member of Cabinet and so cannot speak for the government in the House or answer questions on behalf of the minister. The minister of state to assist a minister is a member of Cabinet and so speaks for the government in the House and is conceptually equal to all other ministers.

A recent evaluation of this type of minister has produced a rather mixed judgement. Chenier suggests that there have been some problems in the manner in which it has been employed, but that some valuable lessons were learned which, if applied in future, could make this a very useful organizational form.[39]

Minister without Portfolio for Designated Purposes. This kind of minister ordinarily has no program responsibilities. Instead, his or her role is to speak in Cabinet for a particular group to ensure that it is appropriately treated by *all* departments and agencies of the government. He or she can be seen as a kind of informal ombudsman for the interests of the group. This is usually a two-way street in that this type of minister is expected to carry the message about the value of government programs to the group. The longest-standing position in this category is in the field of multiculturalism.

---

[38]John A. Chenier, "Ministers of State to Assist: Weighing the Costs and the Benefits," *Canadian Public Administration*, vol. 28 (Fall 1985), pp. 400–403.
[39]Ibid., pp. 403–411.

This type of minister of state has probably fulfilled the expectations for it better than the others, but comparisons are difficult because much less was expected of these kinds of ministers.

Ministry of Transport

A distinction is usually made between a minister's department and his or her portfolio. An operating department was defined above as an administrative unit over which a minister has direct control. The minister's *portfolio* is considerably broader in that it can include regulatory agencies, Crown corporations, and miscellaneous boards and commissions, as well as the operating department. For example, in the organization chart in this book, one could compare the complex structure reporting to the Minister of Transport or Secretary of State with the rather simple structure reporting to the Minister of National Revenue.

The federal Minister of Transport has long had one of the most difficult portfolios to manage, because it contains so many diverse elements and so many large and important organizations that are outside the normal departmental structure, such as Air Canada, Canadian National Railways, and the Canadian Transport Commission. One possible solution in such cases is to divide the entity, but the nature of transportation planning is such that this solution was considered inappropriate. Therefore, it was decided that some radically new way of managing not just the department, but the minister's entire portfolio, would have to be devised.[40]

Figure 6.3a is a partial organization chart illustrating the extent of the minister's responsibilities before the change. It is the usual structure of an operating department, with the minister at the top, the deputy minister immediately below, and a number of units reporting to the deputy minister. However, the real problem was not in managing the department, but in managing the non-departmental organizations. The major problem was that the minister needed some way of managing and coordinating *the entire portfolio*.

Figure 6.3b illustrates the solution adopted. The department was reorganized into three large line administrations, each one responsible for one mode of transportation — marine, surface, and air. The minister's span of control was reduced somewhat by moving some Crown corporations to reporting relationships within the department, e.g., the National Harbours Board and the St. Lawrence Seaway Authority reported to the administrator, marine, after the reorganization. This also provided for better coordination within the various modes of transport.

Every non-departmental structure could not be moved into the department, so the minister was provided with some better tools for managing those which continued to report directly to him or her. The minister, deputy minister, and two senior assistant deputy ministers formed the ministry executive, which was responsible for managing the minister's entire portfolio. The minister was also assisted in the management of his portfolio by the staff advisors included in the

---

[40]The best description of this reorganization can be found in John W. Langford, *Transport in Transition* (Montreal: McGill-Queen's University Press, 1976).

Figure 6.3
COMPARISON OF MINISTER OF TRANSPORT'S PORTFOLIO

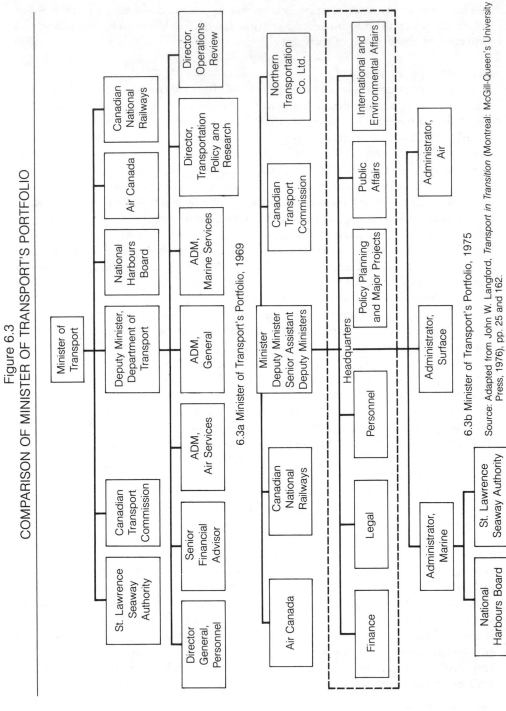

6.3a Minister of Transport's Portfolio, 1969

6.3b Minister of Transport's Portfolio, 1975

Source: Adapted from John W. Langford, *Transport in Transition* (Montreal: McGill-Queen's University Press, 1976), pp. 25 and 162.

block labelled "Headquarters." For example, within the Finance and Legal sec
tions, there are individuals who function as Crown corporation advisors.

The other innovation introduced to improve coordination was the Transportation Council. This council was chaired by the minister and consisted of senior
managers from within the department and from most of the non-departmental
organizations. The council was to function as a sort of "Cabinet" for the making
of transportation policy, providing advice to the minister from diverse perspectives before a final decision was made.

The consensus is that the reorganization was beneficial in providing coordination in a very difficult policy area. The weak point has always been the Transportation Council. From the beginning, senior officials of some agencies felt
that they should not be a part of the regular deliberations of the council because
their legislation required independence from departmental activities. The Canadian Transport Commission, which is a regulatory agency, probably has the
strongest claim in this regard. Less than full participation means that the council has never functioned as well as was initially hoped.

These are just a few examples of innovations in governmental organizational
arrangements. There are many other interesting structural changes in both the
federal and provincial spheres, but the ones cited here are those that are the
most widely discussed and, therefore, the most likely to be emulated in other
jurisdictions.

CONCLUSION

This chapter has described the main characteristics of the departmental form
of organization. This form is usually preferred when the situation calls for strong
ministerial control. There are other cases in which it is better for an agency to
function at arm's length from the direct control of the minister. The next two
chapters will deal with two organizational forms which ensure this distance
— the Crown corporation and the regulatory agency.

BIBLIOGRAPHY

Aucoin, Peter, and Richard French. *Knowledge, Power and Public Policy*.
    Ottawa: Information Canada, 1974.

Borgeat, Louis, René Dussault, Lionel Ouellet avec la collaboration de Patrick
    Moran, Marcel Proulx. *L'administration Québécoise: organisation et fonc-
    tionnement*. Presses de l'Université du Québec, 1984.

Bryden, Kenneth. "Executive and Legislature in Ontario: A Case Study on Gov-
    ernmental Reform." *Canadian Public Administration*, vol. 18 (Summer 1975):
    235–252.

Campbell, Colin. *Governments Under Stress*. Toronto: University of Toronto
    Press, 1983.

Campbell, Colin, and George J. Szablowski. *The Superbureaucrats*. Toronto:
    Macmillan of Canada, 1979.

Chandler, Marsha A., and William M. Chandler. *Public Policy and Provincial Politics*. Toronto: McGraw-Hill Ryerson, 1979.

Chenier, John A. "Ministers of State to Assist: Weighing the Costs and the Benefits." *Canadian Public Administration*, vol. 28 (Fall 1985): 397–412.

Doern, G. Bruce. "Horizontal and Vertical Portfolios in Government." In *Issues in Canadian Public Policy*, edited by G. Bruce Doern and V. Seymour Wilson. Toronto: Macmillan of Canada, 1974, pp. 310–336.

Doern, G. Bruce. "Recent Changes in the Philosophy of Policy-making in Canada." *Canadian Journal of Political Science*, vol. 4 (June 1971): 243–266.

Doern, G. Bruce, and Richard W. Phidd, *Canadian Public Policy: Ideas, Structure, Process*. Toronto: Methuen, 1983.

Doerr, Audrey D. *The Machinery of Government in Canada*. Toronto: Methuen, 1981.

Fleck, James D. "Reorganization of the Ontario Government." *Canadian Public Administration*, vol. 15 (Summer 1972): 383–385.

Fleck, James. "Restructuring the Ontario Government." *Canadian Public Administration*, vol. 16 (Spring 1973): 55–68.

French, Richard D. "The Privy Council Office: Support for Cabinet Decision Making." In *The Canadian Political Process*, edited by Richard Schultz, Orest Kruhlak, and John C. Terry. Toronto: Holt, Rinehart and Winston, 1979, pp. 363–394.

Hockin, Thomas A. *Apex of Power*. 2nd ed. Scarborough, Ont.: Prentice-Hall, 1977.

Hodgetts, J. E. *The Canadian Public Service: A Physiology of Government*. Toronto: University of Toronto Press, 1973.

Jackson, Robert J., Doreen Jackson, and Nicolas Baxter-Moore. *Politics in Canada: Culture, Institutions, Behaviour and Public Policy*. Scarborough, Ont.: Prentice-Hall, 1986.

Johnson, A. W. "The Treasury Board of Canada and the Machinery of Government of the 1970's." *Canadian Journal of Political Science*, vol. 4 (September 1971): 346–366.

Lalonde, Marc. "The Changing Role of the Prime Minister's Office." *Canadian Public Administration*, vol. 14 (Winter 1971): 509–537.

Langford, John W. *Transport in Transition*. Montreal: McGill-Queen's University Press, 1976.

Loreto, Richard A. "The Structure of the Ontario Political System." In *The Government and Politics of Ontario*, 3rd ed, edited by Donald C. MacDonald. Scarborough, Ont.: Nelson Canada, 1985, pp. 17–47.

Lyon, Vaughan. "Minority Government in Ontario, 1975–1981: An Assessment." *Canadian Journal of Political Science*, vol. 17 (December 1984): 685–705.

Mallory, J. R. "Restructuring the Government of Ontario: A Comment." *Canadian Public Administration*, vol. 16 (Spring 1973): 69–72.

Ontario, Committee on Government Productivity. *Interim Report Number Three*, 1971.

Phidd, Richard W., and G. Bruce Doern. *The Politics and Management of Canadian Economic Policy*. Toronto: Macmillan of Canada, 1978.

Robertson, Gordon. "The Changing Role of the Privy Council Office." *Canadian Public Administration*, vol. 14 (Winter 1971): 487–508.

Trebilcock, Michael J., Douglas G. Hartle, J. Robert S. Prichard, and Donald N. Dewees. *The Choice of Governing Instrument*. Ottawa: Minister of Supply and Services Canada, 1982.

Van Loon, Richard. "Stop the Music: The Current Policy and Expenditure Management System in Ottawa." *Canadian Public Administration*, vol. 24 (Summer 1981): 175–199.

Van Loon, Richard J., and Michael S. Whittington. *The Canadian Political System: Environment, Structure, and Process*. 3rd ed. Toronto: McGraw-Hill Ryerson, 1981.

CASES

In *Case Program in Canadian Public Administration* (Toronto: Institute of Public Administration of Canada):

Case Studies in Government Operations and Procedures, by R. I. McLaren
A Taxing Problem, by Roy S. Gunn

In Kenneth Kernaghan, *Canadian Cases in Public Administration* (Toronto: Methuen Publications):

The Minister and the Doctor

7

Crown Corporations

This chapter will focus on the form of government organization traditionally known as the Crown corporation or public enterprise. This organizational form is very commonly used by government to deliver commercial types of services. Crown corporations affect us virtually every day, for example, when we receive our mail, use electricity in our homes, or ride to work in a public transit vehicle operated or manufactured by a public enterprise. D. P. Gracey illustrates the importance of Crown corporations in the Canadian economy:

> Roughly 25 per cent of Canada's net fixed assets fall under the control of federal or provincial Crown corporations. Crown corporations' contribution to the gross national product (GNP) is somewhere between 10 and 12 per cent. Six federal Crown corporations and 4 provincial Crown corporations are listed in the *Financial Post's* top 100 corporations. All, or virtually all, of Canada's electrical generation and distribution, water and liquor distribution, mail distribution and overseas telecommunications, and a significant portion of all domestic telecommunications, railways and air transportation are provided by Crown corporations.[1]

This chapter first defines public enterprise and then discusses the rapid growth of this form of government structure. In keeping with the theme of this part of the book — the choice of organizational form — there will be an analysis of why the corporate form of organization is chosen over other forms. Then, concerns such as methods of control of the corporation and its internal structure and method of operation will be considered. Finally, some of the criticisms of the corporate form and related proposals for reform will be discussed.

DEFINITION OF A CROWN CORPORATION

A number of different terms are used to denote the corporate form. The most common are "Crown corporation," "mixed enterprise," and "public enterprise." Sometimes, these terms are used interchangeably, but this section will provide different definitions of each one.

Separating the corporate form from other forms of government organization is relatively easy.[2] Crown corporations are established either through their own

---

[1]"The Real Issues in the Crown Corporations Debate," in Kenneth Kernaghan, ed., *Public Administration in Canada: Selected Readings*, 5th ed. (Toronto: Methuen, 1985), p. 122.

[2]One of the most thoughtful considerations of the definition problem is found in M. J. Trebilcock and J. R. S. Prichard, "Crown Corporations: The Calculus of Instrument Choice," in J. Robert S. Prichard, ed., *Crown Corporations in Canada: The Calculus of Instrument Choice* (Toronto: Butterworths, 1983), pp. 8–15. John W. Langford also does an admirable job of grappling with

legislation or through incorporation under the federal or provincial companies legislation in exactly the same way as any private sector corporation. Determining what constitutes a corporate form as distinct from other organizational forms is not difficult; the difficult part is determining what constitutes a *Crown corporation.*

Patrice Garant suggests:

> *Crown corporations* are companies in the ordinary sense of the term, whose mandate relates to industrial, commercial or financial activities but which also belong to the state, are owned by the government or the Crown or whose sole shareholder is the government or the Crown. This also includes wholly owned subsidiaries. Such companies must be considered part of the governmental public sector: they belong to the state and are exclusively controlled by it.
>
> On the other hand, institutions that are really administrative bodies rather than companies should be excluded from the family of Crown corporations: for example, organizations concerned with economic or social regulation, administrative management and consultation. On the other hand, semi-public companies, that is, majority or even minority subsidiaries in which there is co-participation of public and private capital, are not Crown corporations, although they are often similar to them.[3]

This definition leaves out certain non-commercial entities which are defined as Crown corporations in the federal Financial Administration Act; these include the Unemployment Insurance Commission, the Agricultural Stabilization Board, and the Economic Council of Canada. While there are valid financial and political reasons for separating these organizations from their related departments, they are excluded from this definition because their *method of operation* is much more like an operating department than a corporation.

A *mixed enterprise* is a corporation "in which the federal government has taken a direct equity position in common with other participants for the purposes of implementing a public policy or satisfying a public need."[4] These "other participants" could be provincial or foreign governments or private sector organizations. Some examples of mixed enterprises are Telesat Canada, the Canada Development Corporation, and the Asian Development Bank. The mixed enterprise is not a unique organizational form; it is simply a standard business corporation in which governments own a certain number of the shares.

---

this same difficult question in "The Identification and Classification of Federal Public Corporations: A Preface to Regime Building," *Canadian Public Administration*, vol. 23 (Spring 1980), pp. 76–104. For a different, but equally plausible, definition, see Royal Commission on Financial Management and Accountability, *Final Report* (Hull: Minister of Supply and Services Canada, 1979), ch. 16.

[3]"Crown Corporations: Instruments of Economic Intervention — Legal Aspects," in Ivan Bernier and Andrée Lajoie, eds., *Regulations, Crown Corporations and Administrative Tribunals*, research study for the Royal Commission on the Economic Union and Development Prospects for Canada (Toronto: University of Toronto Press, 1985), p. 4. (Emphasis added.)

[4]Canada, Royal Commission on Financial Management and Accountability, *Final Report*, pp. 358–359.

Public enterprise is the most general term and encompasses both Crown corporations and mixed enterprises.

This chapter will focus predominantly on Crown corporations, although there will be some discussion of mixed enterprise as well. This focus was chosen because the Crown corporation is a distinctive organizational form with its own problems of structure and accountability.

THE GROWTH OF CROWN CORPORATIONS

Governments have grown very rapidly in recent years, and it is not surprising that public enterprise has followed suit. In fact, by some accounts the corporate sector of government has grown more rapidly than the traditional forms of government organization. This section will discuss the overall growth of the corporate sector in both federal and provincial orders of government, and some of the more specific trends within that overall growth.

The Federal Scene

For the federal government, the first problem confronted in measuring the growth of Crown corporations stems from the somewhat embarrassing fact that there is no central listing of all Crown corporations. Since this fact was first publicized by the Auditor General in 1976,[5] various agencies have attempted to assemble this information, and by 1980 a list of 464 "corporations in which the government has an interest" was prepared.[6] Langford and Huffman made some changes in this list and identified 454 corporations and subsidiaries, which they then grouped by degree of government ownership as illustrated in Table 7.1.

Table 7.1
FEDERAL CROWN CORPORATIONS BY METHOD OF OWNERSHIP

	Parent Corporations	Subsidiaries	Total
Owned Directly and Solely	81	161	242
Owned Jointly with Other Governments, Private Organizations and Individuals	20	174	194
Membership Interest	18	—	18
Total	119	335	454

Source: John W. Langford and Kenneth J. Huffman, "The Uncharted Universe of Federal Public Corporations," in J. Robert S. Prichard, ed., *Crown Corporations in Canada: The Calculus of Instrument Choice* (Toronto: Butterworths, 1983), pp. 233–273.

---

[5]*Report of the Auditor General of Canada to the House of Commons for the Fiscal Year Ended March 31, 1976* (Ottawa: Minister of Supply and Services Canada, 1976), p. 51.

[6]Canada, Office of the Comptroller General, "Corporations in which the Government Has an Interest," (photocopy).

There is no definitive count of the number of Crown corporations; the figures employed by different commentators usually flow from different definitions employed. The federal government produced a report in 1984 which identified 336 Crown corporations.[7] It seems unlikely that any widely acknowledged "right" number will emerge from this discussion. The most salient fact is that everyone agrees that the numbers are very high, the relationships generated very complex, and the scope of their activities is very broad.

This complexity is indicated by the fact that in their listing of corporations, Langford and Huffman must use symbols such as [SSSSS] to indicate "a subsidiary of a subsidiary of a subsidiary of a subsidiary of a sub-subsidiary corporation" and [SSSAS] "a subsidiary of a sub-subsidiary of an associate of a subsidiary corporation." The scope of these entities runs from the fairly well known ones, such as the Canada Mortgage and Housing Corporation and the Canadian Broadcasting Corporation, to such exotic organizations as the Canada-France-Hawaii Telescope Corporation.

Commenting on the growth of public corporations is very difficult because there are at least three measures of growth that could be used — number of corporations, assets owned, number of employees.

Table 7.2

FEDERAL CROWN CORPORATIONS BY METHOD OF OWNERSHIP AND DATE OF INCORPORATION

	Sole		Joint		Membership		Total	
	N	%	N	%	N	%	N	%
1970–79	21	26	8	40	13	72	42	35
1960–69	18	22	8	40	3	17	29	24
1950–59	13	16	2	10	1	6	16	13
1940–49	13	16	1	5	0	0	14	12
1930–39	6	7	1	5	0	0	7	6
1908–29	10	12	0	0	1	6	11	9
	81	100	20	100	18	100	119	100

Source: John W. Langford and Kenneth J. Huffman, "The Uncharted Universe of Federal Public Corporations," in J. Robert S. Prichard, ed., *Crown Corporations in Canada. The Calculus of Instrument Choice* (Toronto: Butterworths, 1983), p. 275

Table 7.2 indicates that the majority of Crown corporations that were in existence when Langford and Huffman were doing their research (early 1980s)[8] were incorporated since 1960, and over one-third have been incorporated since 1970. The other interesting fact indicated in Table 7.2 is the shift in the type of

[7]Treasury Board of Canada Secretariat, *Crown Corporations and Other Canadian Government Corporate Interests* (Ottawa: Minister of Supply and Services Canada, 1984), p. 3.

[8]This excludes the large number of Crown corporations which were established during the Second World War to assist in supplying the war effort and wound up shortly after the war. See Sandford F. Borins, "World War Two Crown Corporations: Their Wartime Role and Peacetime Privatization," *Canadian Public Administration*, vol. 25 (Fall 1982), pp. 380-404.

corporation from the traditional solely owned entity to the jointly owned or membership type of entity.

The above information would suggest that the last few years have been the golden age of Crown corporations, but a consideration of the other possible measures of growth — assets and employees — produces a different result.

Figure 7.1 illustrates the growth of public enterprise in Canada. The line showing the number of corporations confirms what was discussed earlier, i.e., the *number* of enterprises grew fairly slowly in the early years, but has increased rapidly during the 1960s and 1970s. The other two lines in Figure 7.1 indicate that the largest corporations (in 1978) are those created in the earlier years. Fifty per cent of employees of Crown corporations work for corporations owned prior to 1938, and 50 per cent of assets are held by corporations owned prior to 1946. The really large increments in these areas came as a result of the 1919 creation of Canadian National Railways and the 1934 takeover of the Bank of Canada. More recent acquisitions have not added as much in terms of assets or employees. Of course, this chart would look somewhat different if it were extended beyond 1979 to include the addition of more than 54,000 postal workers in 1981.

The activities in which federal Crown corporations have been involved have changed over the years. In the years immediately after Confederation, the federal government was most concerned with nation building, and so focussed on transportation undertakings which would unify the diverse parts of the country. During the Second World War, the major theme of public policy changed from national unity to national defence with the creation of many new corporations to supply the war effort. Since the end of the war, federal Crown corporations have become more involved in the areas of finance, insurance, and real estate. Marsha Gordon describes the changes in the 1960s and 1970s in this manner:

> Corporations designed to implement the federal government's lending programs have expanded rapidly over the past two decades. The most prominent lending companies are the Canada Mortgage and Housing Corporation (CMHC), the Farm Credit Corporation (FCC), the Export Development Corporation (EDC), and the Federal Business Development Bank (FBDB). CMHC has grown considerably since it was established in 1945. Today it insures and makes mortgage loans, is active in land assembly, and promotes urban renewal. The FCC, which has been used to support farm incomes, offers long-term mortgage loans to farmers and makes loans for the purchase of farm machinery. The EDC insures and finances exports, including transportation and communications equipment, airplanes and nuclear reactors. The FBDB assists firms unable to find financing elsewhere and provides management services to small business.[9]

Federal Crown corporations have diversified quite widely into areas of energy exploration and sales (Petro-Canada), manufacture of aircraft (Canadair), medi-

---

[9]*Government in Business* (Montreal: C. D. Howe Institute, 1981), p. 13.

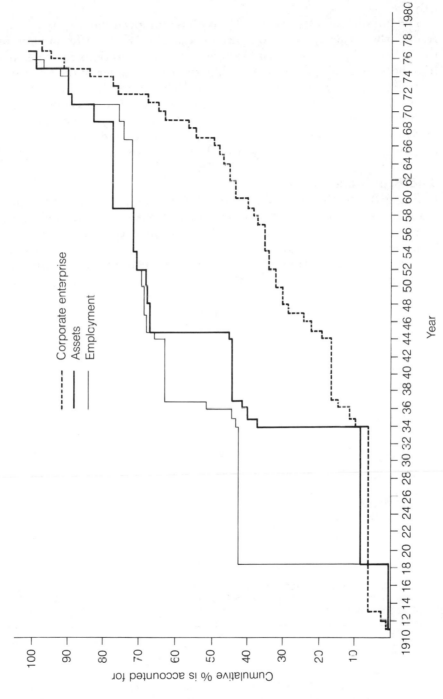

Figure 7.1
GROWTH OF CORPORATE ENTERPRISE, ASSETS AND EMPLOYMENT,
1911–1978

Source: John W. Langford and Kenneth J. Huffman, "The Uncharted Universe of Federal Public Corporations," in J. Robert S. Prichard, ed., *Crown Corporations in Canada: The Calculus of Instrument Choice* (Toronto: Butterworths, 1983), p. 298.

cal supplies (Canada Development Corporation), and rubber, plastics, and chemicals (Polysar).

The question of which political party has employed the corporate form more frequently has always been contentious. Langford and Huffman point out that the Liberals have created an average of two corporations for each year they have been in power, which is more than twice the average of the Conservatives.[10] And the Liberal years of the 1960s and 1970s certainly saw the creation of a large *number* of Crown corporations. However, the Conservatives have created such major corporations as the Canadian Broadcasting Corporation, the Bank of Canada, Canadian National Railways, and the Canadian Wheat Board. This topic is likely to remain a subject of lively partisan debate.

The Provincial Scene

Defining the public enterprise sector is even more difficult in the provincial than in the federal sphere. The ten jurisdictions each have slightly different definitions of Crown corporations, so the data collection and comparability problems are significantly multiplied. Nevertheless, Vining and Botterell have concluded an excellent survey in which they identified 233 provincial Crown corporations distributed geographically as illustrated in Table 7.3.

Table 7.3
PROVINCIAL CROWN CORPORATIONS BY PROVINCE

Province	N	%
Newfoundland	42	18
Prince Edward Island	10	4
Nova Scotia	10	4
New Brunswick	9	4
Quebec	35	15
Ontario	27	12
Manitoba	13	6
Saskatchewan	25	11
Alberta	20	9
British Columbia	36	15
Northwest Territories	2	1
Yukon	2	1
Regional	2	1
TOTAL	233	100

Source: Aidan R. Vining and Robert Botterell, "An Overview of the Origins, Growth, Size and Functions of Provincial Crown Corporations," in J. Robert S. Prichard, ed., *Crown Corporations in Canada: The Calculus of Instrument Choice* (Toronto: Butterworths, 1983), p. 325.

[10]John W. Langford and Kenneth J. Huffman, "The Uncharted Universe of Federal Public Corporations," in Prichard, ed., *Crown Corporations in Canada: The Calculus of Instrument Choice*, p. 276.

The growth of provincial Crown corporations has been similar to the federal trend. There has been a large growth in the *number* of corporations since 1960, but the major growth in assets occurred in the periods 1900–1920 and 1940–1960.[11]

Provinces have adopted the Crown corporation form in a number of different functional areas. Table 7.4 indicates that industrial development, liquor sales, housing, power generation and research and development are the most popular in terms of the number of provinces employing them. In terms of the total value of assets controlled, the two major fields are electrical power and banking, followed by housing, education, and telephone and communications. These five functions account for just over 80 per cent of total assets.[12]

Table 7.4

NUMBER OF PROVINCES EMPLOYING CROWN CORPORATIONS BY FUNCTION

Function	Number of Provinces
Industrial Development	10
Liquor	10
Housing	9
Power Utility	8
Research and Development	8
Forest Development and Manufacturing	7
Miscellaneous Marketing and Brokerage Facilities	7
Agricultural Development	6
Mineral Mining and Development	6
General and Auto Insurance	5
Municipal Finance Corporations	5
Oil and Gas Production	5
Telephones and Communications	5
Transport Facilities	5
Transport Systems	5
Banking, Saving, and Investment	4
Government Computer Services	4
Miscellaneous Manufacturing	4
Government Buildings	3
School and Hospital Financing	3
Lotteries (also two regional corporations)	2
Shipyards	2
Steel Production	2
Water Supply	2

Source: Aidan R. Vining and Robert Botterell, ''An Overview of the Origins, Growth, Size and Functions of Provincial Crown Corporations,'' in J. Robert S. Prichard, ed., *Crown Corporations in Canada* (Toronto: Butterworths, 1983), pp. 328–334. (Note that this is the number of *provinces* which utilize Crown corporations in this area, not the number of corporations.)

[11] Aidan R. Vining and Robert Botterell, "An Overview of the Origins, Growth, Size and Functions of Provincial Crown Corporations," in ibid., p. 320.

[12] Ibid., p. 340.

The major activities in which provincial Crown corporations have been involved have changed over the years. In the early years, one function was dominant — power generation.[13] This gave way to diversification into the trade, finance, insurance, and real estate sectors. More recently, provincial Crown corporations have become involved in industrial and resource development areas, with the newest area being insurance.[14]

Comparisons between federal and provincial Crown corporations are difficult because of the problems of different universes and data collection techniques, but it is usually suggested that provincial Crown corporations are both considerably larger and have grown more rapidly in recent years than federal Crown corporations.[15]

Marsha Chandler's work suggests that this recent growth is the result of the presence of more left-wing (NDP and Parti Québécois) governments in provincial capitals. Her data indicate that left-wing governments not only use the corporate form more often, but they also use it for different purposes from those of their right-wing counterparts. "Non-socialist governments have used public ownership almost exclusively to facilitate economic development,"[16] e.g., hydro-electric and industrial development corporations. Left-wing governments have been more likely to use the corporate form for redistributive ends and to supplant private sector corporations, e.g., insurance and natural resources.

THE RATIONALE FOR THE CREATION OF CROWN CORPORATIONS

One of the major themes of this section of the book is the choice of organizational form — a consideration of the reasons why governments would choose one organizational form over others. This section will consider some of the factors inherent in the structure of Crown corporations which make this organizational form superior to others in accomplishing certain goals.[17]

There is one important factor that distinguishes Crown corporations in Canada from similar entities in many other countries. In some countries, public enterprises are referred to as "nationalized industries" because they were at one time private sector corporations which have since been taken over as a result of

---

[13]For a discussion of the early history of the hydro-electric companies and their uneven development in different provinces, see Aidan Vining, "Provincial Hydro Utilities," in Allan Tupper and G. Bruce Doern, eds., *Public Corporations and Public Policy in Canada* (Montreal: The Institute for Research on Public Policy, 1981), pp. 152–175.

[14]Gordon, *Government in Business*, pp. 14–15.

[15]Ibid., pp. 11–12.

[16]"State Enterprise and Partisanship in Provincial Politics," *Canadian Journal of Political Science*, vol. 15 (December 1982), p. 735.

[17]One of the best treatments of these factors is contained in M. J. Trebilcock and J. R. S. Prichard, "Crown Corporations: The Calculus of Instrument Choice," in Prichard, ed., *Crown Corporations in Canada: The Calculus of Instrument Choice*, pp. 39–75. Two other articles in this book are also useful in considering this area: Thomas A. Borcherding, "Toward a Positive Theory of Public Sector Supply Arrangements," pp. 99–184; and Marsha A. Chandler, "The Politics of Public Enterprise," pp. 185–218.

some degree of coercion by the state. The phrase "nationalized industries" is not usually employed in Canada because this has not been the ordinary mode of establishing Crown corporations. In most cases, Crown corporations have been started from scratch. In some recent cases, governments have taken over existing entities, but seldom with any overt coercion. In other cases, the takeover has involved picking up the pieces of a failed or near-failed company and continuing to operate it to provide jobs, or purchasing a publicly traded company on the open market, such as Alberta's purchase of Pacific Western Airlines[18] or the numerous purchases made by Petro-Canada.[19]

Corporations have been created for many different reasons; there are probably as many different reasons as there are corporations. "It cannot be said that any unifying philosophy underlies the use of the public corporation in Canada: the whole development has been piece-meal and pragmatic."[20] However, several attempts have been made to categorize a few of the diverse reasons for employing the corporate form.[21] A number of these reasons are discussed below.

Nation Building (or Province Building) and Community and Economic Development

Trebilcock and Prichard suggest that this is the most common rationale for the creation of public enterprises. They suggest that it usually involves two components:

(i) Integrating the country by making infrastructure investments and providing essential services, which private business is unable or unwilling to provide; and

(ii) Promoting Canadian nationalism, i.e., developing a national identity and preserving Canadian control over certain services and sectors of the economy.[22]

There are numerous examples of both of these elements. The earliest Crown corporations were begun to develop infrastructure in areas where the private sector was unable or unwilling to become involved. Some of the more obvious examples are in transportation (canals, railways, and even Trans-Canada Air

---

[18]The circumstances surrounding this acquisition are described in Allan Tupper, "The Nation's Businesses: Canadian Concepts of Public Enterprise" (Ph.D. diss., Queen's University, 1977), pp. 99–113.

[19]There have been a few exceptions to this happy picture in which government takeover attempts have been the subject of much consternation. Some of these are mentioned in Garant, "Crown Corporations," p. 6.

[20]J. E. Hodgetts, "The Public Corporation in Canada," in W. Friedmann and J. F. Garner, eds., *Government Enterprise: A Comparative Study* (London: Stevens & Sons, 1970), p. 202. (Footnote omitted.)

[21]V. Seymour Wilson, *Canadian Public Policy and Administration: Theory and Environment* (Toronto: McGraw-Hill Ryerson, 1981), pp. 365–370; C. A. Ashley and R. G. H. Smails, *Canadian Crown Corporations: Some Aspects of their Administration and Control* (Toronto: Macmillan of Canada, 1965), pp. 3–10; Tupper, "The Nation's Businesses," pp. ii–iv and passim; Chandler, "State Enterprise and Partisanship in Provincial Politics," pp. 727–735.

[22]Trebilcock and Prichard, "Crown Corporations: The Calculus of Instrument Choice," p. 53.

Lines) and energy (the provincial hydro-electric utilities). In general, these projects either required large sums of money which were difficult to raise on the open market, or were sufficiently risky that private investors were reluctant to invest in them. In some cases, public enterprise was chosen simply because the general populace had more confidence in government than in private sector investors. Ontario Hydro was a product of the desire of local business people to have assured power at low rates, something which they could not be assured of if private power magnates controlled the industry.[23]

Business people frequently complain about the Crown corporation form because they feel that it is inappropriate and unfair for government to compete with the private sector; there are many cases where this competition exists. However, Crown corporations have frequently been established to provide support to private sector corporations. The provincial power generation utilities and the federal Export Development Corporation are prime examples.

Economic development motives are present in some more modern forays into public enterprise. The creation of Petro-Canada was in part a recognition of the need for an assured supply of energy at reasonable prices, something which Canada could not be certain that foreign-controlled energy companies would provide.

Provinces use the Crown corporation instrument to engage in province building and to attain what they see as their rightful position in the national economic structure. There are examples of this in all provinces, but Bernard Landry, Quebec's former Minister of State for Economic Development, expressed the concern well: "Part of our global strategy is to be less dominated. . . . We don't want to own everything, but we want to have real power in some firms. It is not that we want the power in government hands, we want it in Quebecers' hands."[24]

Also in this category are the increasing number of cases which involve rescuing failed or floundering private companies to preserve jobs. This could involve supporting a company in a geographic area where unemployment is already a serious problem. This was the rationale for the creation of the Cape Breton Development Corporation and the Canadian Saltfish Corporation. Or, it could mean providing a continuing Canadian presence in a sensitive industry. This is the usual reason cited for the takeover of de Havilland and Canadair in the airline industry.

Economic development can be one of the soundest motives for creating a Crown corporation. There is little doubt that Canada has benefited from the presence of the large hydro-electric companies able to undertake huge capital projects and keep the cost of energy low. However, there is also some evidence that this argument is one of the most abused. Governments have usually not been very successful in "rescue efforts." Even referring to some of these as economic development is a misnomer; they frequently come about in areas where little development is likely to occur.

---

[23]H. V. Nelles, *The Politics of Development: Forests, Mines & Hydro-electric Power in Ontario, 1849–1941* (Toronto: Macmillan of Canada, 1974).

[24]As reported in *The Financial Post*, September 19, 1981, p. S14.

The danger inherent in state rescues, whatever their form, is that, because they are designed to subvert market forces, they can lead to costly misallocation of economic resources. State intervention may prevent the shift of capital and labor away from unproductive activities to newer (and more productive) ones. In such circumstances the state may end up supporting increasingly inefficient enterprises — those that may have become obsolete because of technological and/or market changes. Moreover, by backing inefficient operations, the state makes them dependent on government aid, and this dependence can become progressively more difficult to break. In the eyes of dependent interests, government assistance becomes their social right.[25]

It is a very humane government policy to provide subsidies to continue jobs for workers about to become unemployed. However, it might be that using the corporate form to do something which is basically humanitarian rather than commercial puts the entire corporate sector under an unfortunate cloud.

Cultural nationalism has also had a role in the creation of some Crown corporations. Canada's proximity to the overwhelming magnetism of the United States has prompted a conscious desire to maintain a unique Canadian culture, but has simultaneously raised doubts about the ability of the private sector alone to accomplish this. The Canadian Broadcasting Corporation and some more recent initiatives in the film industry are examples of corporations geared to developing a national identity and promoting community development.

Allan Tupper has summed up well the nation-building and community and economic development arguments:

Provincial public ownership in the fields of transportation, communications, and power is an important means of promoting economic growth. It has contributed to the development of natural resources and has facilitated intra- and extraprovincial commerce. State enterprise has also been used to bind together disparate provincial communities and subprovincial economies. Provincial governments, like their federal counterparts, have also used public ownership to ensure provincial, rather than private, control over particular firms or industries.

The community development seeks to influence the output of goods and services in several ways. For example, Air Canada and the Canadian Broadcasting Corporation were created to provide national services which private enterprise had been tardy in establishing. On the other hand, the case of the Canadian National Railways illustrates how public enterprise was dictated by the importance for the community at large of the continued provision of vital transportation services. The CBC, telephone companies in the Prairie provinces, and Saskatchewan Transport were established to extend services to previously neglected regions. Ontario Hydro and Hydro-Quebec were prompted by the state's desire to make electric power widely

---

[25]Gordon, *Government in Business*, p. 151.

available at lower rates than charged by private enterprise. Nationalization in 1963 of the entire hydro-electric industry in Quebec was also dictated by the state's desire to provide high-quality service to all parts of the province.[26]

Herschel Hardin has argued in a similar, but more extreme, vein that, contrary to the popular myth, it has not been private enterprise which has been instrumental in the development of Canada, but rather such public enterprises as the canals, railways, and the CBC. He argues that the public corporation has been so important to Canada that it has spawned a "Canadian public enterprise culture."[27]

Separation from Political Control

It is important that an organization which carries out government policy is closely controlled by the political executive. However, when an organization has a predominantly commercial mandate, it is possible that political concerns could interfere with that commercial mandate. For example, it has been argued that the commercial objectives of Amtrack (the United States public passenger railway) have suffered because it has been forced to modify its route system because of political, not commercial, concerns.[28]

The Crown corporation form places the organization under the control of a board and at arm's length from government control. This is beneficial from the standpoint of assisting the corporation in furthering its commercial activities, but one of the problems discussed below is that Crown corporations can become *too* independent of legislative and government control.

The corporate form can also be beneficial to governments in providing insulation from the potentially embarrassing or irritating actions of some Crown corporations. Recent federal governments are probably quite pleased that they can no longer be held directly responsible for the labour turmoil and other problems of the Canada Post Corporation.

Diverse Representation on the Board

Crown corporations are headed by Boards of Directors which allow for the presence of geographic, consumer, ethnic, language, and other types of representation. This differs from an operating department headed by a single minister. In the Crown corporation form, a number of people representing interested groups are actively involved in the decision-making process, thus ensuring that these diverse interests are considered in the making of important decisions. For example, it is traditional that the Board of Directors of the Canadian Broadcasting Corporation contain balanced representation from the various geographic areas of the country.

[26]Tupper, "The Nation's Businesses: Canadian Concepts of Public Enterprise," pp. 77-78.

[27]Herschel Hardin, *A Nation Unaware: The Canadian Economic Culture* (Vancouver: J. J. Douglas, 1974), part II.

[28]Robert Kent Weaver, "The Politics of State Enterprise: Railroad Nationalization in the United States and Canada" (Unpublished Ph.D. diss., Harvard University, 1982), pp. 505-508.

Provide a "Window" on the Private Sector

Some kinds of activities are usually carried out by the private sector, but are still immensely important to the overall public well-being. In these cases, governments sometimes feel a need to use the corporate form to obtain a "window" on this particular industry, so that the government can ensure that the industry will act in the national interest.

Prior to the creation of Petro-Canada, almost all petro-chemical trading was done in the private sector. As a result of the energy crisis of the early 1970s, governments were urged to take a stronger hand in this field, but the solution was clearly not to nationalize the entire industry. Instead, Petro-Canada was established so that the federal government could enter the field in a fairly small way (initially), and develop an understanding of how the industry operated so that it could regulate the industry in a responsible manner. The presence of Petro-Canada as a source of information about the industry was important.

> The petroleum industry is one in which information is highly specialized and complex and is almost exclusively in the hands of the participants in the industry. Furthermore, to the extent that industry voluntarily or in response to regulatory demands releases information, it is information which is very difficult for non-industry sources to verify. A growing lack of confidence in the quality of information provided by the industry to the National Energy Board and other regulatory bodies involved in the industry through the 1960s and early 1970s led to increasing demands for the creation of a Crown corporation which would be able to independently generate information about the industry which could be used as a standard for evaluating the claims made by private firms. Only armed with this information would the other regulatory instruments already in place in the industry be made effective, since the other regulatory techniques, including tax incentives, export regulations, and price setting, all depend for their efficacy on the quality of the information on which they are based. Therefore the creation of Petro-Canada can be primarily understood as responding to the information deficiencies facing the government which plagued its ability to use any of the other instruments of regulation.[29]

Freedom from Central Agency and Other Controls

Operating departments frequently complain that they experience difficulties in fulfilling their mandate because of the strict financial and personnel restrictions imposed by organizations such as the Treasury Board and the Public Service Commission. The argument is frequently made that entities engaging in commercial activities would be at a competitive disadvantage if they were subject to the same regulations. Thus, the corporate form is frequently employed in cases where competitive pressures require more flexibility than is provided in other organizational forms.

This freedom from controls is one reason that the postal unions argued strongly

---

[29]Trebilcock and Prichard, "Crown Corporations: The Calculus of Instrument Choice," p. 70.

in favour of the post office becoming a Crown corporation. Labour relations in departments are governed by the Public Service Staff Relations Act, which limits the items which are subject to bargaining. Crown corporations are governed by the same legislation as any other corporation which allows for a broader scope of bargaining.

Attract Business People to Management

One of the most important keys to success for any organization is attracting good people as directors and managers. Successful business people frequently have much to offer to government organizations, but they are sometimes uncomfortable coming into an unfamiliar management structure such as an operating department with a political head, central agency controls, and the other trappings of government. These people feel more comfortable in a setting familiar to them such as the corporate form. Therefore, it is sometimes suggested that one of the benefits of the Crown corporation is an increased ability to attract successful business people as managers.

Low Visibility Taxation

Crown corporations pay dividends to their shareholders, i.e., government, in the same manner as private sector corporations. In some cases, governments use Crown corporations as sources of income, which might be considered a form of scarcely concealed taxation. For example, all of the provincial liquor sales agencies make significant profits that are passed along to provincial governments.

Political or Bureaucratic Opportunism

Richard Carter has examined many of the economic rationales for the creation of Crown corporations stated above and notes that most of them could be accomplished as easily through regulation or taxation as through government ownership. He uses the ideas of vote maximization and concern for self-interest, which are a part of the public choice approach discussed in Chapter 5, to argue that the corporate form of government intervention is most likely to be chosen for two reasons.

First, this form is the most visible and, therefore, could lead to the capture of the maximum number of votes from people who are interested in a particular policy area. For example, if a government provided a grant to a private corporation to create jobs, this might be overlooked or forgotten at election time; it is more difficult to forget that your town's major employer is a Crown corporation.

The second possible reason for the creation of Crown corporations is the desire on the part of public servants to improve their positions:

> The political power and the income, if not the prestige, of the bureaucrat is often greater if he is the manager of a public enterprise rather than the supervisor of regulatory or taxation measures affecting the enterprise in question.[30]

---

[30]"Les enterprises publiques: pourquoi et pour qui?" *Canadian Public Administration*, vol. 26 (Summer 1983), p. 251. (Translation by authors.)

Carter suggests further that this replacement of private managers by state managers has little effect on the operation of the enterprise, except possibly to reduce profit, and it does not increase the control of legislators or citizens over the enterprise in question. Therefore, he is led to conclude that the sole reason for the use of the corporate form is political or bureaucratic opportunism.

Joint Undertakings

Governments frequently engage in joint ventures. These could be between governments within Canada, such as the Western Canada Lottery, or internationally, such as the Asian Development Bank, or they could be between governments and private sector organizations, such as Telesat Canada (a joint undertaking of the federal government, CN/CP Telecommunications and a small number of other shareholders). The corporate form is the obvious one to employ in these cases because it creates an autonomous entity separate from any of the governments involved in the entity.

This is not a comprehensive list of the reasons for the use of the Crown corporation form. However, it does provide the major rationales which are usually given when a new corporation is being formed. Given the many different reasons for the creation of Crown corporations, it is not surprising that they exhibit many different characteristics. Therefore, not all Crown corporations are treated the same way for purposes of politicial accountability.

CLASSIFICATION OF CROWN CORPORATIONS

Most governments have a classification system which determines the type and amount of political control to which particular groups of corporations will be subject. For example, the federal Financial Administration Act has four schedules which define the accountability regime of federal organizations. Schedule A lists the operating departments. Schedule B lists those entities which have separate corporate status, but which perform "administrative, research, supervisory, advisory or regulatory functions of a governmental nature."[31] These organizations, such as the Canada Employment and Immigration Commission and the National Research Council, do not meet the criteria of a Crown corporation specified at the beginning of this chapter. Some of the Schedule B organizations function in a manner almost identical to departments, and some are advisory councils, which will be discussed in more detail in Chapter 9.

Schedule C-II lists the names of each corporation which "(a) operates in a competitive environment; and (b) is not ordinarily dependent on appropriations for operating purposes."[32] These are the high-profile corporations such as Air Canada, Canadian National Railways, and Canada Development Investment Corporation.

Schedule C-I lists those corporations which do not meet one of the two criteria mentioned in the preceding paragraph. Some of these are not commer-

---

[31]Financial Administration Act, S.C. 1984, c. 31, s. 3.
[32]S.C. 1984, c. 31, s. 11.

cially oriented, e.g., Canada Museums Construction Corporation Inc.; but most of them fail to meet the second criterion — financial viability, e.g., VIA Rail Canada Inc.

The purpose of the classification system is to establish different accountability regimes for corporations in the different schedules. Moving from Schedule A to Schedule C-II is moving from the least to the most autonomous type of entity.

Eight Crown corporations are not covered by this new legislation. The Bank of Canada, the Canadian Wheat Board, the International Development Research Centre, the Canadian Institute for International Peace and Security, and the Canada Council are each governed by their own legislation. The Canadian Broadcasting Corporation, the National Arts Centre, and the Canadian Film Development Corporation will be governed by a new "cultural agencies act" which is being prepared.[33] This new legislation will recognize the importance of maintaining the independence of these cultural organizations from direct government control.

POLITICAL CONTROL OF CROWN CORPORATIONS

One of the reasons for the use of the Crown corporation form of organization is to separate the organization from direct political control. However, a Crown corporation is a creature of the government, carries out government objectives, and in many cases, uses government funds. Therefore, a Crown corporation cannot behave in a totally autonomous manner, but the precise method of political control is awkward because of the need for some limited amount of autonomy.

There is a detectable pendulum swing between emphasis on control and autonomy. In the last few years the pendulum has been swinging towards greater control. The beginning of this trend is usually identified as the Auditor General's report for the fiscal year ending March 31, 1976.[34] This report contains an extensive review and critique of Crown corporations. In the first place, the Auditor General found that there was no focal point for the control of Crown corporations and therefore no single listing of all Crown corporations. Of the Crown corporations that he was able to identify and audit, his conclusion was devastating:

> In the majority of the Crown corporations audited by the Auditor General, financial management and control is weak and ineffective. Moreover, coordination and guidance by central government agencies of financial management and control practices in these Crown corporations are virtually nonexistent.[35]

In the face of such strong criticism it is not surprising that responses from both the government and Parliament were quick in coming. In 1977, the Privy Council Office issued a document commonly referred to as the "blue paper"

---

[33]Gracey, "The Real Issues in the Crown Corporations Debate," p. 128.
[34]*Report of the Auditor General of Canada to the House of Commons for the Fiscal Year Ended March 31, 1976,* ch. 5.
[35]Ibid., p. 49.

which contained a number of proposals and draft legislation geared to improving the control and accountability of Crown corporations.[36] At the same time, the House of Commons Public Accounts Committee, which examines the Auditor General's annual reports, produced a report containing its recommendations for solving the problems.[37] The Royal Commission on Financial Management and Accountability, which reported in 1979, devoted an entire section of its report to Crown agencies.[38] A number of abortive bills were introduced between 1979 and 1984, when major amendments were finally made to the Financial Administration Act which changed the accountability regime of Crown corporations. This section will examine how the system of political control, as modified by these amendments, functions.

Establishing the Crown Corporation

Public enterprises can be established in three ways: by separate enabling legislation, under the relevant companies legislation, and through the purchase of the shares of a going concern.[39]

The first method provides the greatest legislative control and accountability. The legislature passes a specific law for each new corporation, specifying the mandate of the corporation, i.e., the activities in which it can engage, and its accountability regime to the legislature, for example, annual reports, method of financing. Thus, the accountability relationship can be as tight or as loose as members of the legislature desire. In most cases, the corporations created in this manner do not have any share capital because they are controlled directly by the government. Some of the federal corporations which have been established by separate legislation are the Canadian Broadcasting Corporation[40] and the Canada Post Corporation.[41]

Alternatively, governments can incorporate companies under the relevant federal or provincial companies legislation in the same manner as any private citizen. A minister or even a public servant simply prepares the necessary documentation, and in due course, the Crown corporation is in business. These companies have share capital which is legally vested in either the minister or the Crown.

Finally, the government can enter into any sort of contract, which means that it may decide to purchase the shares of a company on the open market or through a private arrangement. The shares so obtained are then vested in either the minister or the Crown. This same heading covers those relatively rare situations in which governments have forcibly nationalized companies against the will of

---

[36]*Crown Corporations: Direction — Control — Accountability* (Minister of Supply and Services Canada, 1977).

[37]Canada, House of Commons, Standing Committee on Public Accounts, *Minutes of Proceedings and Evidence*, no. 22, April 11, 1978.

[38]*Final Report*, Part IV.

[39]For a good overview of the legal and practical aspects of the use of these different methods, see Garant, "Crown Corporations," pp. 14–22.

[40]R.S.C. 1970, c. B-11, s. 34(1).

[41]S.C. 1980–81, c. 54, s. 4.

the previous shareholders. This requires enabling legislation and usually provokes a court challenge. The most recent examples of this are the actions of the Quebec government with regard to the asbestos industry[42] and the Saskatchewan government with regard to the potash industry.[43]

The creation of Crown corporations through the companies legislation and direct purchase has come under attack recently because of questions concerning proper accountability. There have been occasions when a Crown corporation has been created by either a minister or a public servant deciding that this was desirable, finding available funding, and either establishing or purchasing a corporation. Parliamentary and even Cabinet approval was not necessary, and in some cases was not obtained. The problem in these cases is that there is no established regime of accountability. This was a part of the cause of the embarrassing situation in which the federal government was not able to determine how many corporations it owned.

The 1984 amendments to the Financial Administration Act have changed this situation considerably. It is now illegal for any person to establish a new corporation or purchase the shares of a corporation without Cabinet approval,[44] and it is illegal for an existing Crown corporation to establish a subsidiary corporation without approval of the Governor in Council, i.e., the Cabinet.[45]

The Federal Financial Administration Act

This Act establishes a general framework for the allowable activities and accountability of Crown corporations. The purpose of the Act is to provide some uniformity in the treatment of Crown corporations, but this uniformity is tempered by the provisions of the various Acts which created the corporations. The Crown corporation provisions of the Act changed little from its original proclamation in 1952 until the major amendments of 1984.[46] The specific provisions of these amendments are discussed elsewhere in this chapter, but their general thrust was to tighten considerably the accountability regime for Crown corporations. In one sense, this is clearly beneficial because there were certain problems with the accountability structure that definitely needed improvement. However, there could be a negative side to this as well. Increasing accountability will lessen a corporation's autonomy and innovativeness. It might be less easy than some think to force all of the disparate kinds of Crown corporations into one mould.

Ministerial Responsibility

All corporations report to Parliament through a minister. In the case of corporations established by special legislation, this minister is specified in the legisla-

---

[42]Pierre Fournier, "The National Asbestos Corporation of Quebec," in Tupper and Doern, eds., *Public Corporations and Public Policy*, pp. 353–364.

[43]Jeanne Kirk Laux and Maureen Appel Molot, "The Potash Corporation of Saskatchewan," in ibid., pp. 189–219.

[44]S.C. 1984, c. 31, s. 11. (Section 100, as amended.)

[45]S.C. 1984, c. 31, s. 11. (Section 101, as amended.)

[46]S.C. 1984, c. 31.

tion. In the case of corporations with share capital, the minister usually holds the government's shares in trust for the Crown.

The concept of ministerial responsibility was discussed in the chapter on government departments because the ability to hold the minister accountable for bureaucratic actions is a very important control mechanism over operating departments. The concept of ministerial responsibility is not as strong with regard to the Crown corporation form of organization. It is clear that ministers are not accountable for the day-to-day activities of corporations which report to them; but when a Crown corporation has been created by the government, crucial appointments have been made by government, and subsidies are provided by government, then the government cannot escape some measure of responsibility for the actions of that corporation.[47]

This dilemma could present itself with regard to almost any Crown corporation, but some examples from the Canadian Broadcasting Corporation can highlight the nature of the problem. Most would agree that the government should not interfere with the operations of the CBC; this would smack of censorship or news management. Not only would it destroy the credibility of the CBC, but it would also open the government to severe criticism.

However, should the government step in when the CBC crosses over the boundaries of appropriate morality or good taste? Members of the Opposition have raised questions in the House of Commons concerning such matters as inappropriate conduct on a news show,[48] cancellation of a popular television series,[49] and even the broadcasting of the World Series in northern areas.[50] The minister's position in all of these cases is very difficult. On the one hand, the CBC cannot take public money and engage in activity which is repugnant to the general public. On the other hand, if the minister becomes too deeply involved in the activities of the CBC, he or she will be open to the charge of political interference, or even censorship. There is no obvious solution to this problem; ministers must simply learn to walk a tightrope on each issue.

Memorandum of Understanding

In Ontario, some Crown agencies are required to prepare a *memorandum of understanding*, which is approved by the agency's board, the responsible minister, and Management Board of Cabinet (the Ontario equivalent to the federal Treasury Board). The purpose of this memorandum is "to clarify the objectives, priorities and performance expectations of an agency and to set out the operat-

[47]This dilemma is not new; it was discussed extensively in Parliament in the 1920s. Ashley and Smails, *Canadian Crown Corporations*, ch. 5.

[48]This can be a relatively common occurrence. For example, see the question by Mr. Cossitt in Canada, House of Commons, *Debates*, June 1, 1981, 10119-20. The most tumultuous example of this kind of controversy surrounded the controversial show, "This Hour Has Seven Days." The controversy is described in K. Kernaghan, *Canadian Cases in Public Administration* (Toronto: Methuen, 1977), pp. 48-54.

[49]Canada, House of Commons, *Debates*, March 9, 1973, p. 2067.

[50]Canada, House of Commons, *Debates*, October 13, 1983, p. 27986.

ing relationships between the agency and its parent Ministry."[51] It also sets out "the degree and nature of a minister's control over a particular agency and thereby the degree of his accountability to the legislature for the agency."[52]

In practice, these memoranda have not lived up to expectations. The major problem is that "the objectives, priorities and performance expectations" have usually not been clearly set out in the memorandum.[53] Because these memoranda are tabled in the legislature, governments have been loath to be too specific about this information lest they provide too much ammunition to the Opposition parties.

Scrutiny of Corporate Plans and Annual Reports

As a result of the 1984 amendments to the Financial Administration Act, all federal Crown corporations are now required to submit an annual corporate plan for the minister's approval. This plan must include:

(a) the objects or purposes for which the corporation is incorporated . . .
(b) the corporation's objectives for the period . . .
(c) the corporation's expected performance for the year . . . as compared to its objectives for that year . . . .[54]

After the plan is approved by the minister, it is tabled in Parliament in summary form for information purposes.

All Crown corporations are also required to submit year-end annual reports of their operations. These reports must include:

(a) the financial statements of the corporation . . .
(b) the annual auditor's report . . .
(c) a statement on the extent to which the corporation has met its objectives for the financial year,
(d) such quantitative information respecting the performance of the corporation, . . . relative to the corporation's objectives as the Treasury Board may require to be included therein, and
(e) such other information as is required by this or any other Act of Parliament, or by the appropriate Minister, the President of the Treasury Board or the Minister of Finance, to be included therein . . . .[55]

Members of Parliament have traditionally been dissatisfied with the lack of any method of reviewing the general operations of Crown corporations. The requirement for the corporate plan and the year-end report is certainly a step in the right direction, because they allow Parliament to assess the performance of

---

[51]Quotation from an Ontario Management Board of Cabinet document in John Eichmanis and Graham White, "Government by Other Means: Agencies, Boards and Commissions," in Donald C. MacDonald, ed., *The Government and Politics of Ontario* (Scarborough, Ont.: Nelson Canada, 1985), p. 94.
[52]Ibid.
[53]Ontario, Agencies, Boards and Commissions Project, *First Report* (July 1985), pp. 18–19.
[54]S.C. 1984, c. 31, s. 11. (Section 129(3), as amended.)
[55]S.C. 1984, c. 31, s. 11. (Section 152(3), as amended.)

the corporation against its stated objectives. It is too early to assess the real worth of these reports. In the private sector, it is fairly well understood that these kinds of reports are largely public relations exercises frequently designed to hide as much as they reveal. The worth of these reports will depend on the goodwill of those preparing them and on the desire of the legislators and members of the public to demand better accounting.

Power to Issue Directives

A directive issued to a corporation would require it to do something even if its Board of Directors and/or management was opposed. As a result of the 1984 amendments to the federal Financial Administration Act, the Governor in Council may issue directives to any Crown corporation covered by the Act, after consultation with the board.[56] The government followed the advice of the Lambert Commission in requiring that all directives be public.[57] This ensures that these directives will be tested in the court of public opinion and so will not be used for any nefarious purpose.

If the directive approach were used frequently and in anger, it would indicate heightened tension between the corporation and the government, and would likely provoke resignations from the Board of Directors and/or senior management of the corporation. The Lambert Commission suggests that the directive function will more likely be used in a friendly manner in two situations.[58] If the government wanted the corporation to act against its own economic interests for some political reason, the board might request that the government issue a directive to this effect so that the board would be absolved of any guilt for the consequences.[59] The second way a directive could be used would be to clarify details of the corporation's mandate.

Method of Funding

Crown corporations receive the funding they need to carry on their operations in a wide variety of ways.[60] In some cases, a corporation will need only a lump sum at its inception similar to the amount provided by shareholders at the creation of a private corporation. In other cases, corporations will need start-up funds as well as periodic infusions of additional funds. These infusions could come directly from government in the form of grants or loans, from the private sector in the form of loans guaranteed by the government, or from non-guaranteed loans.

The classification system of Crown corporations discussed earlier usually determines the type of financial control which the government and legislature have over particular Crown corporations. By way of illustration, Table 7.5 provides a

---

[56]S.C. 1984, c. 31, s. 11. (Section 99(1), as amended.)
[57]S.C. 1984, c. 31, s. 11. (Section 99(4), as amended.)
[58]Royal Commission on Financial Management and Accountability, *Final Report*, pp. 337–338.
[59]This is the effect of the recent amendments to the Financial Administration Act, S.C. 1984, c. 31, s. 11. (Sections 99.(3) and 124, as amended.)
[60]See Garant, "Crown Corporations," p. 18.

Table 7.5

FINANCIAL ACCOUNTABILITY OF SCHEDULE C CROWN CORPORATIONS

	Part I	Part II
Corporate plan	Approved by minister and Governor General in Council; summary tabled in Parliament	Same as Part I
Operating budget	Approved by minister and Treasury Board; summary tabled in Parliament	Not required by legislation
Capital budget	Approved by minister and Treasury Board; summary tabled in Parliament	Same as Part I
Borrowing	Approval of minister and Minister of Finance required	Same as Part I
Audit	Audit required by Auditor General (begins January 1, 1989)	Audit required (not necessarily by Auditor General)

summary of the regime of financial accountability for Schedule C corporations. This table compares the accountability regime of Schedule C-I and C-II corporations, but the factor which probably has the greatest impact on a corporation's autonomy is whether it is self-financing. If the corporation must return to the public treasury on an annual basis and steer its request for funding through the surveillance of an operating department, the Treasury Board, a legislative committee, and ultimately the legislature, then it has little more autonomy than an operating department. On the other hand, if a corporation is self-funding, it has a much greater amount of autonomy.

Appointment and Removal of Directors

Like private sector corporations, a Crown corporation is under the control of a Board of Directors, which determines the general direction of the corporation. The board of a Crown corporation has a particular responsibility to act as a buffer between the corporation's management and the political concerns of the shareholder, i.e., the minister.

These directors are appointed (and removed) by the minister, after consultation with Cabinet.[61] There is no recent comprehensive analysis of the backgrounds of board members, but they seem to be mainly business and professional people. Public servants and, in some provinces, ministers also serve as board members. These positions have also been used for purposes of political patronage. This situation diminishes the status of the board and limits its credibility in policy making.[62]

There is a dilemma concerning the advisability of appointing public servants or ministers to be members of boards. The appointment of a public servant to a board could improve coordination between the corporation and the public servant's department, but it could also place the public servant in a conflict

---

[61]S.C. 1984, c. 31, s. 11. (Section 114(1), as amended.)
[62]John Langford, "Crown Corporations as Instruments of Policy," in G. Bruce Doern and Peter Aucoin, eds., *Public Policy in Canada* (Toronto: Macmillan of Canada, 1979), p. 257.

situation. For example, should the public servant advise the corporation if his or her department is considering regulatory changes that will affect it? In general, one of the main functions of the board is to provide a buffer between corporation and government activities and:

> It would appear that the board's function of acting as a buffer between those responsible for day-to-day administration and external political pressures is adversely affected by this trend to elevate managerial officials to top-ranking positions on the board.[63]

The presence of ministers on boards of Crown corporations is even more problematic. This mechanism has never been employed in the federal government and is rapidly falling into disfavour in the provinces.

However, even at best there can be problems with the operation of these boards. Just as in the private sector, there is some question about whether these part-time directors really effectively control the full-time, professional management of the corporation. In the case of Crown corporations, this difficulty is exacerbated by the role of the minister. The minister (or full Cabinet) usually retains some of the powers which the Board of Directors in a private sector corporation would have. Chief among these are the power to issue directives and appoint senior management.

Scrutiny by Legislative Committees

Crown corporations are subject to the same kind of scrutiny by the various legislative committees as are the operating departments. Hearings are sometimes instituted as a result of information generated by the Auditor General or by public concerns about some controversial actions. This is an important element of control, but its usefulness is somewhat limited. Elected members have many responsibilities and little assistance in meeting them. This makes it very difficult for them to use the committee system in an optimal manner. This situation is exacerbated in the case of Crown corporations because they see themselves as somewhat removed from detailed political control, anyway. Furthermore, unless a corporation needs additional funding or a change in its legislation, there is no automatic mechanism to bring its affairs before a committee and no incentive on the part of the corporation to be totally forthcoming.

In 1978, British Columbia created a legislative Committee on Crown Corporations which

> will, not less than every three years and more often if it or the legislature desires, examine the directors and officers of the [four major B.C. Crown corporations]. Unique in Canada, the committee will have a status beyond that of the normal legislative committee, in the middle ground between a legislative committee and a House or Senate committee in the United States. It is designed to more or less perform the function of the annual general meeting required of investor-owned corporations.[64]

---

[63]J. E. Hodgetts, "The Public Corporation in Canada," p. 220.
[64]Don Gracey, "Public Enterprise in Canada," in André Gélinas, ed., *Public Enterprise and the Public Interest* (Toronto: The Institute of Public Administration of Canada, 1978), p. 47.

The committee had a full-time staff to assist it, and the members were developing some expertise and gradually expanding the committee's mandate[65] when it was terminated because, in the words of one observer, it was "taking unto itself some of the functions the government saw as its own prerogatives."[66] That sounds like another way of saying that the committee was axed because it was *too effective* at carrying out its role.

The Accountability-Autonomy Conundrum

Establishing the appropriate amount of control over the activities of a Crown corporation is an awkward dilemma. On the one hand, the corporation is an emanation of government and uses government funds, and so cannot be allowed to operate completely outside government control. On the other hand, too much control defeats the purpose of using the corporate form.

> Parliament and even the responsible Minister must show confidence in the corporation by refraining from breathing down the neck of management. On the other hand, the Canadian system of parliamentary government can impose responsibility only on the Ministers of the Crown. Hence the public corporation cannot be used as a means of evading ultimate responsibility. Where to draw the line between the claims of managerial autonomy and the claims of parliamentary responsibility remains for Canada a problem that has been seriously posed rather than solved by contemporary use of the public corporation.[67]

Crown Management Board of Saskatchewan

Since 1946, Saskatchewan has had a unique way of dealing with this accountability-autonomy dilemma, which has leaned decidedly in the direction of accountability. It is based on the concept of the "holding company" borrowed from the private sector. A holding company is a company established for the sole purpose of holding the shares of other companies; it usually does not engage in any business activity of its own.

The Crown Management Board of Saskatchewan (CMB) is a holding company that owns the shares of fourteen companies grouped in three sectors — resources, utilities, and finance and service.[68] These are such major provincial Crown corporations as Saskatchewan Oil and Gas Corporation, Saskatchewan Telecommunications, and Saskatchewan Government Insurance.

Traditionally, the role of the CMB and its predecessors has been to enhance the *accountability* of Crown corporations to Cabinet. This has been done through three mechanisms.

---

[65]John W. Langford and Neil A. Swainson, "Public and Quasi-Public Corporations in British Columbia," in O. P. Dwivedi, ed., *The Administrative State in Canada* (Toronto: University of Toronto Press, 1982), pp. 84–85.

[66]Gracey, "The Real Issues in the Crown Corporations Debate," p. 136.

[67]Hodgetts, "The Public Corporation in Canada," p. 226.

[68]Crown Management Board of Saskatchewan, *Annual Report 1984* (Regina: Crown Investments Corporation of Saskatchewan, 1985), p. 5.

First, Cabinet ministers have traditionally served as chairpersons of the Boards of Directors of Crown corporations. This has provided a direct link between the corporation and Cabinet that is lacking in other governments. This has also created a direct linkage between the corporations and the legislature. In Saskatchewan, ministers do not escape responsibility for the actions of Crown corporations as do their colleagues in other provinces. Recently, the tendency has been to appoint ministers as vice-chairpersons. This reflects a greater concern for business-like efficiency and less emphasis on political accountability.

Second, the Board of Directors of CMB is composed of a majority of Cabinet ministers so that it functions as a Cabinet committee or as a kind of central agency concerned with Crown corporations. The board controls the capital budgets of subsidiary corporations and plays a major role in determining the amount of funds appropriated to particular corporations. The board also has a small staff which provides advice to Crown corporations in such areas as industrial relations, accounting policy, and public relations.

Third, there is a Crown Corporations Committee of the legislature which reviews the annual reports and financial statements of all Crown corporations. Its work can involve calling ministers before it to discuss the activities of their corporations.

In the last few years, there has been a general trend towards appointing individuals with a private sector background to the boards of Crown corporations and a greater emphasis on business-like efficiency. This could have the effect of diminishing the direct lines of accountability which historically existed, but the holding company model as implemented in Saskatchewan remains a unique instrument of accountability.

STRUCTURE AND OPERATION OF CROWN CORPORATIONS

The internal structure and operation of Crown corporations resemble those of private sector corporations so much that little elaboration is necessary. As discussed above, the role of the minister and/or Cabinet complicates the picture somewhat, but the general direction of the corporation is the responsibility of the Board of Directors and the senior officials of the corporation. The members of the board, except sometimes the chairperson, serve on a part-time basis, and their main involvement is attending meetings several times a year at which important policy issues are considered. The Governor in Council, i.e., Cabinet, appoints (and can remove) the chief executive officer after consultation with the board, but all other senior appointments are the responsibility of the board and senior management. The senior officials of the corporation then carry on the activities of the corporation on a day-to-day basis, very much as they would if they were working for a private sector corporation.

One significant feature of the operation of Crown corporations is that they possess some limited immunities which flow from their status as agents of the Crown and the traditional maxim that "the Crown can do no wrong."[69] At the

---

[69]The legal principles underlying this are discussed in Peter W. Hogg, *Constitutional Law of Canada* (Toronto: The Carswell Company, 1985), pp. 217-221 and ch. 10 passim.

extreme, this could mean that Crown corporations are immune from any civil or criminal court actions, from having their property seized, from the application of most legislation and regulations, and from taxation by another sphere of government.[70]

In practice, many of these immunities have been whittled away over the years. In the first place, they apply only to those corporations that are "Crown agents," which does not include all Crown corporations. Also, many of these immunities have been reduced somewhat in practice by the courts. The main ones which remain are the exemption from regulation and taxation by other spheres of government. For example, this immunity from regulation has allowed Eldorado Nuclear and Uranium Canada Ltd. to ignore provisions of the Combines Act,[71] and the federal Freshwater Fish Marketing Corporation to ignore Saskatchewan and Winnipeg anti-pollution legislation.[72]

SOME CRITICISMS OF CROWN CORPORATIONS

The next two sections examine some of the major problems identified with Crown corporations and some of the reforms which have been proposed.

Many of the long-standing problems with regard to federal Crown corporations were remedied by the 1984 amendments to the Financial Administration Act, but some problems have proven more resistant to easy solution. Also, the positions of the provinces vary. Some had enough foresight that many of these problems were headed off in advance, but other provinces have not yet addressed the problems identified in the last few years by the federal government.

Proliferation of New Corporations and Subsidiaries
One of the most basic criticisms of the existing arrangement is that there are simply too many corporations, and many of them constitute an inappropriate use of the corporate form.

A review of the list of Crown corporations reveals

> a bewildering array of corporations, including business corporations (Air Canada, CNR), cooperatives (Canadian Wheat Board), advisory bodies (Economic Council of Canada), regulatory agencies (Atomic Energy Control Board), granting councils (Canada Council), research organizations (National Research Council), theatres (National Arts Centre), museums (National Museums Corporation) and departmental corporate shells (the National Battlefields Commission). The business corporations can be further subdivided into monopolies, oligopolies and competitive corporations spanning the transportation, manufacturing, communications, insurance and banking sectors.[73]

---

[70]Garant, "Crown Corporations," pp. 22–38.

[71]Jean Brazeau and Cathy Schutz, "Crown Corporations and Competition Policy," in *Government Enterprise: Roles and Rationale* (Papers presented at a symposium sponsored by the Economic Council of Canada in Ottawa, September 1984), pp. 424–446.

[72]Garant, "Crown Corporations," p. 36.

[73]Gracey, "The Real Issues in the Crown Corporations Debate," p. 132.

This is not a purely theoretical concern; the expanding mandate of some corporations has led to clashes between different governments, and between the public and private sectors.

Intergovernmental Conflict

Public enterprise can be a vehicle for cooperation between different governments, but provincial governments also view Crown corporations as tools for province building, and there have been incidents in which this has resulted in intergovernmental conflicts.

When the government of Alberta purchased Pacific Western Airlines, it was the cause of some discord between the federal and Alberta governments over the right of a provincial government to purchase an airline without seeking prior federal approval, and between the British Columbia and Alberta governments when the airline's head office was moved from Vancouver to Calgary. Some Crown corporations are not simply passive investments, but rather are tools of province building. Alberta wanted to purchase PWA to ensure that Edmonton remained the "gateway to the north." If the federal government desired a different transportation policy, it would be rather difficult for it to enforce its view.

Unfair Competition with the Private Sector

Crown corporations receive financial support from government to become established and in some cases to meet operating deficits. In other cases, the support is less direct; for example, the government may provide loan guarantees so that money can be borrowed at a lower interest rate, or the Crown corporation could be the beneficiary of some regulatory preference. For example, for a number of years the Canadian Transport Commission ruled that Air Canada must have the majority of the transcontinental market, even though CP Air felt that it could have captured more of the market if this artificial restraint did not exist. These kinds of preferences can be very frustrating for independent entrepreneurs who are already in, or would like to enter, the same market as the Crown corporation.

Increasing Financial Power of Crown Corporations

The trend on the part of Crown corporations to be more involved in financial activities was discussed earlier. In some cases, the effect of this has been to create a very large pool of capital which could be used in any number of, sometimes controversial, ways. Quebec's Caisse de dépôt et placement and the Alberta Heritage Savings Trust Fund are two examples of these kinds of corporations.

The Caisse is the main repository of funds collected by the Quebec Pension Plan and some other large provincial pension plans and insurance funds. This money must be invested by the Caisse so that it earns a return adequate to pay these pensions in future years. Traditionally, organizations such as this have been "passive investors," i.e., they have not attempted to control or influence the companies in which they have invested. However, in recent years the Caisse has become a more active investor and attempted to obtain seats on the Boards of Directors of companies in which it invests. This raised concern on the part of some businesses that the Caisse could become a political tool of the Quebec government and so force these corporations to make decisions based on political, rather than business, considerations.[74] There is little evidence that the Caisse *has* used its power in this way[75]; but, it is clear that it and similar organizations in other provinces *could* wield significant power if they chose to do so.

Profits or Public Purpose? — Problems of Accountability

One of the most basic problems facing a Crown corporation is whether it ought to function to make a profit or to serve a public purpose. There can easily be conflicts between these two. For example, VIA Rail can maximize profit by terminating long-distance runs and reducing services to smaller towns and, instead, focussing on high-volume routes, e.g., the Quebec–Windsor corridor. However, whenever it proposes this, various interests point out VIA's requirement to serve the public interest.

Determining the amount of control which the government should have over the activities of a Crown corporation is not an easy task.

> In the context of responsible government, the most telling questions turn around the problem of establishing a balance between the autonomy that the Crown corporation requires as an organizational form to perform the task it has been given, on the one hand, and the government's need to control and direct the corporation and Parliament's need to oversee or scrutinize it, on the other. This problem of balance runs through every aspect of the complex interrelationships between Parliament, government . . . , and the Crown corporations.[76]

This problem engenders a number of difficulties. It is sometimes suggested that the managers of Crown corporations engage in activities contrary to the desires of politicians, or without consulting politicians, which later cause political embarrassment. This situation is frustrating to politicians who must bear criticism, even though they feel that they have very little control over these corporations in some cases. The managers of Crown corporations are also placed in a difficult position, because they are frequently ridiculed in the media for their inability to make a profit or to operate more efficiently. However, the problem is sometimes that profit and efficiency have been sacrificed to political concerns.

Accountability to Whom?

Not only is there this division between a concern for profits and public purpose, but there is also some concern that accountability is divided among a confusing number of different organizations.

---

[74]This controversy is described in Allan Tupper, *Bill S-31 and the Federalism of State Capitalism* (Kingston, Ont.: Queen's University, Institute of Intergovernmental Relations, 1983). For a general discussion of the Caisse, see Claude Forget, ed., *La Caisse de dépôt et placement du Québec: Sa mission, son impact et sa performance* (Montreal: Institut C. D. Howe, 1984).
[75]Stephen Brooks and A. Brian Tanguay, "Quebec's Caisse de dépôt et placement: Tool of Nationalism?" *Canadian Public Administration*, vol. 28 (Spring 1985), pp. 99–119.
[76]Langford, "Crown Corporations as Instruments of Policy," p. 240.

Democratic theory would hold that all governmental entities are ultimately accountable to Parliament, and this is reiterated in section 98.1 of the Financial Administration Act: "Each Crown corporation is ultimately accountable, through the appropriate Minister, to Parliament for the conduct of its affairs." Earlier in this chapter, it was suggested that Parliament has a number of ways of exerting its control, but a sober assessment of the role of Parliament would have to admit that its control is rather weak and sporadic.

More effective control resides with the government, but even here there is significant division. Legally, the shares of a Crown corporation are held by the minister in trust for the Crown, but that does not mean that the minister can make unilateral decisions about Crown corporations. Members of the Board of Directors and the chief executive officer can be appointed by the minister only after consultation with Cabinet. Then the roles are reversed, so that directives can only be given by Cabinet after consultation with the appropriate minister.

Different aspects of the financial affairs of the corporation could come under the scrutiny of the President of the Treasury Board or the Minister of Finance. Of course, the Prime Minister's Office and the Privy Council Office might become involved in the affairs of the corporation in certain cases, and some corporations are subject to the decisions of regulatory agencies.

All of these complicated relationships add up to a proliferation of actual or potential accountability relationships. Unfortunately, this situation was not improved in any way by the 1984 amendments to the Financial Administration Act. It is notable that a recent report prepared for the Ontario government suggests that the Management Board (the Ontario equivalent to the federal Treasury Board) should be a focal point for the accountability of Crown corporations.[77]

Problems of Mandate and Reporting

A part of the problem of ensuring accountability is the difficulty of specifying a mandate for the corporation. Cabinet and legislature are frequently reluctant to specify a corporation's mandate in such a narrow fashion that it could not engage in innovative behaviour and take advantage of a changing environment. After all, one reason for choosing the corporate form is to allow it to be more flexible and innovative. However, there have been allegations that some corporations have used this broad mandate to move into areas of activity which were not envisaged for them when they were created. Langford uses the phrase "mandate creep" to describe this phenomenon.[78]

This problem has been exacerbated by the uneven quality of reports which corporations provide to the government and legislature. These reports ought to make it possible to determine that the corporation actually followed the plan that was approved at the beginning of the year, but in some cases it is difficult to do this. At any rate, the precise penalties for deviating from the approved plan are unclear. For example, the Auditor General pointed out that the budgets of

---

[77]Ontario, Agencies, Boards and Commissions Project, *First Report* (July 1985), pp. 46–49.
[78]Langford, "Crown Corporations as Instruments of Policy," p. 256.

approximately 25 per cent of Crown corporations were not approved in 1982, yet this seems to have no impact on their operations.[79]

PROPOSALS FOR REFORM

The problems mentioned above cover a very wide range, but the most serious problems have been identified in the area of accountability. Thus most of the reforms discussed below will be geared to improving accountability. Patrice Garant, for one, applauds this trend, but he also sounds a note of caution:

> This awakening [to the need for better accountability] was necessary because Crown corporations are neither private companies nor "states within the state." But beware the pendulum! Some reform proposals, while well intended, are dangerous because they contradict both the raison d'être of the Crown corporation network and certain objectives inherent in this choice of instrument designed to ensure adequate intervention by the public authority.[80]

There are no simple solutions to the difficulties caused by the large and diverse agglomeration of Crown corporations. One of the more thoughtful students of the corporate form has suggested that a major rethinking of the whole sector is necessary:

> What is needed is a rethinking of Crown corporations' purpose and role that would result in a major reorganization of the Crown corporation sector. This would include the "de-incorporation" of many organizations and better organizational forms found or devised, the wind-up of several Crown corporations and the amalgamation of their activities with departments, and the privatization of all or parts of some corporations or their activities.[81]

Privatization

One of the most persistent recent proposals for reform has been the suggestion that certain Crown corporations ought to be privatized, i.e., returned to the private sector in some form. There have been some examples of this. The shares which the British Columbia government held in the British Columbia Resources Investment Corporation were distributed free to all residents of the province on the grounds that their taxes had paid for the development of the company.[82] There are also cases where corporations have been sold to other private sector corporations, e.g., the sale of de Havilland to Boeing in 1986.[83]

---

[79] *Annual Report of the Auditor General of Canada to the House of Commons for the Fiscal Year Ending March 31, 1982* (Ottawa: Minister of Supply and Services Canada, 1982), pp. 75-76.
[80] Garant, "Crown Corporations," pp. 39-40. (Footnote omitted.)
[81] Gracey, "The Real Issues in the Crown Corporations Debate," p. 132.
[82] Theodore M. Ohasi, "Privatization in Practice: The Story of the British Columbia Resources Investment Corporation," in Theodore M. Ohasi, et al., *Privatization: Theory & Practice* (Vancouver: The Fraser Institute, 1980), pp. 16, 28-50.
[83] An excellent consideration of the issues and guide to how to go about privatization is contained in Ontario, Agencies, Boards and Commissions Project, *Second Report: Privatization of Ontario*

One of the problems with privatization is that "if the Crown corporation is very profitable and hence marketable, then the government is reluctant to lose this source of revenue. If the agency is only modestly profitable or a losing proposition, then no one will want to buy it."[84] For example, Air Canada could probably be sold relatively easily, but since it is a money-making operation, the government would be foregoing its potential future profits. On the other hand, few, if any, purchasers would be interested in Canada Post Corporation.

Compensation Principle

One of the major irritants to managers of Crown corporations is that they are frequently criticized for failure to make a profit when this failure comes about not as a result of their mismanagement, but because the government demands that the corporation do something which is in the broader national interest, but *not* in the corporation's economic interest. It has sometimes been suggested that when a corporation incurs expenses in this situation, it should be compensated out of general tax funds. This would allow the corporation to act in the national interest without suffering financially as a result.

A good example of this principle is in passenger rail service. For years, Canadian National Railways argued that passenger rail traffic was not economically viable and that it would look much better financially if it confined itself to carrying freight. In 1978, VIA Rail was created as a separate entity to take over the passenger rail service portion of Canadian National Railways and CP Rail operations. It did this by renting crews, equipment and track from the established companies. Now, CN Rail is no longer saddled with the financial difficulties of passenger rail and earns a profit on the economically viable portion of its operation. The government provides a subsidy to operate VIA Rail because it is felt to be in the national interest to have a passenger rail service, and the amount of that subsidy is no longer hidden.

A great deal of analysis and thought went into the 1984 amendments to the federal Financial Administration Act. The fact that the preceding list of possible reforms is much shorter now than it would have been before those revisions is testimony to the improvement it represented in the accountability regime for Crown corporations. However, it is clear that the role of Crown corporations is still a subject of heated debate. That debate can become particularly heated around the role of a relatively new form of public enterprise called mixed enterprise.

MIXED ENTERPRISE

At the beginning of this chapter a *mixed enterprise* was defined as a Crown agency "in which the federal government has taken a direct equity position in

---

Crown Corporations (Report prepared for the Ministry of Treasury and Economics and the Management Board of Cabinet, n.d., 1985?).
[84]Allan Tupper and G. Bruce Doern, "Public Corporations and Public Policy in Canada," in Tupper and Doern, eds., *Public Corporations and Public Policy in Canada*, p. 42.

common with other participants for the purposes of implementing a public policy or satisfying a public need."[85] It was mentioned earlier that there is some difficulty in deciding exactly which organizations fall within the definition of a Crown corporation; this task is even more difficult for mixed enterprise. However, there have been a number of listings[86] of these entities, and there is some similarity in them. Using the more extensive listing of Langford and Huffman, it is possible to identify four general groupings of these enterprises.

International Development Funds. The Canadian government participates in a number of international organizations, such as the Asian Development Bank whose mandate is "to lend funds, promote investments and provide technical assistance to developing countries, and generally, to foster economic growth in the Asian Region."[87] These agencies usually require some financial contribution from Canada, but besides fulfilling some altruistic objectives, they provide the opportunity for Canadians to sell goods and services in the other member countries.

Domestic Development Activities. The federal government participates in a number of joint ventures with provincial governments and private groups, such as native peoples' organizations, to stimulate employment and economic development within Canada. For example, the Newfoundland and Labrador Development Corporation was established "to complement the regional development incentives program as a source of venture capital for manufacturing and resource development in the province."[88] Funding is provided jointly by the federal and Newfoundland governments.

Bridge Authorities. The federal government also is involved in joint ventures in bridge construction both domestically, e.g., Saint John Bridge Authority, and internationally, e.g., Thousand Islands Bridge Authority. There are not many of these ventures, but they are important in the areas in which they are located.

Commercial Ventures. The mixed enterprises with the highest profiles are the commercial ventures, most notably the Canada Development Corporation (CDC) and Telesat.[89]

The idea for something like the CDC came in the nationalistic times of the 1960s with the idea of a corporate vehicle to buy back Canada from foreign investors. However, when it was formed in 1971, its role was considerably more

---

[85]Canada, Royal Commission on Financial Management and Accountability, *Final Report*, pp. 358–359.

[86]Treasury Board of Canada Secretariat, *Crown Corporations and Other Canadian Government Corporate Interests*, p. 13 and pp. 36–39; Langford and Huffman, "The Uncharted Universe of Federal Public Corporations," pp. 258–269.

[87]Treasury Board of Canada Secretariat, *Crown Corporations and Other Canadian Government Corporate Interests*, p. 36.

[88]Canada, Department of Regional Economic Expansion, *Annual Report, 1981–1982* (Minister of Supply and Services Canada, 1983), p. 9.

[89]Only the former company will be discussed here. A good overview of the activities of Telesat is contained in G. Bruce Doern and James A. R. Brothers, "Telesat Canada," in Tupper and Doern, eds., *Public Corporations and Public Policy in Canada*, pp. 221–249.

limited. Its major early purchases were in the energy and mining fields, although it has also invested in pharmaceutical, soft drink, and electronics companies. Originally, all of the company's shares were held by the government, but beginning in 1975 share offerings were made to the public. The short history of the CDC illustrates one of the major problems with mixed enterprise — accountability.

Problems of Accountability and Control

Earlier in this chapter, the problems of accountability of fully owned Crown corporations were discussed. Those problems are magnified considerably with regard to mixed enterprise because the government has a less dominant position. Wholly owned Crown corporations face the dilemma of whether they will be engines of profit or instruments of public policy, but this dilemma is considerably exacerbated when the company's shares are publicly traded. Even a hint that the government will force a corporation to act as an instrument of public policy, and so not maximize profit, could result in a sharp decline in the value of the company's shares.[90] In this situation, management will resist the blandishments of the government with a concern for the rights of other shareholders who could see the price of their shares drop if the corporation became involved in some unprofitable policy initiative. In such cases, there is some concern that management can have almost complete autonomy because of divisions of power on the Board of Directors and the inability of the minister to provide directives or other controls.[91] Stephen Brooks's analysis of the CDC situation leads him to the conclusion that a Crown corporation can function as *either* an engine for profit *or* an instrument of public policy, *but not both*.[92]

This chapter has focussed on the Crown corporation as an organizational form. Its main value is in carrying on commercial and financial operations at arm's length from the government of the day. The next chapter considers another organizational form that is also at arm's length — the regulatory agency.

---

[90]This is exactly what happened in May 1981. Stephen Brooks, "The State as Entrepreneur: From CDC to CDIC," *Canadian Public Administration*, vol. 26 (Winter 1983), p. 534.

[91]For a catalogue of cases in which management has not followed the obvious desires of government, see Stephen Brooks, "The Mixed Ownership Corporation as an Instrument of Public Policy," *Comparative Politics* (forthcoming).

[92]"The State as Entrepreneur: From CDC to CDIC," pp. 541–543.

BIBLIOGRAPHY

Ashley, C. A., and R. G. H. Smails. *Canadian Crown Corporations: Some Aspects of their Administration and Control.* Toronto: Macmillan of Canada, 1965.

Auditor General of Canada. *Report of the Auditor General of Canada to the House of Commons for the Fiscal Year Ended March 31, 1976.* Ottawa: Minister of Supply and Services Canada, 1976.

Auditor General of Canada. *Annual Report of the Auditor General of Canada to the House of Commons for the Fiscal Year Ending March 31, 1982.* Ottawa: Minister of Supply and Services Canada, 1982.

Baetz, Mark, and Donald Thain. *Canadian Cases in Business-Government Relations.* Toronto: Methuen, 1985.

Borins, Sandford F. "World War Two Crown Corporations: Their Wartime Role and Peacetime Privatization." *Canadian Public Administration*, vol. 25 (Fall 1982): 380–404.

Brazeau, Jean, and Cathy Schutz. "Crown Corporations and Competition Policy." In *Government Enterprise: Roles and Rationale.* Papers presented at a symposium sponsored by the Economic Council of Canada in Ottawa (September 1984): 424–446.

Brooks, Stephen. "The Mixed Ownership Corporation as an Instrument of Public Policy." *Comparative Politics* (forthcoming).

Brooks, Stephen. "The State as Entrepreneur: From CDC to CDIC." *Canadian Public Administration*, vol. 26 (Winter 1983): 525–543.

Brooks, Stephen, and A. Brian Tanguay. "Quebec's Caisse de dépôt et placement: Tool of Nationalism?" *Canadian Public Administration*, vol. 28 (Spring 1985): 99–119.

Canada. House of Commons. Standing Committee on Public Accounts. *Minutes of Proceedings and Evidence*, no. 22, April 11, 1978.

Canada. Office of the Comptroller General. "Corporations in Which the Government Has an Interest." Photocopy, 1980.

Canada. Privy Council Office. *Crown Corporations: Direction — Control — Accountability.* Minister of Supply and Services Canada, 1977.

Canada. Royal Commission on Financial Management and Accountability. *Final Report.* Hull: Minister of Supply and Services Canada, 1979.

Carter, Richard. "Les enterprises publiques: pourquoi et pour qui?" *Canadian Public Administration*, vol. 26 (Summer 1983): 239–254.

Chandler, Marsha A. "State Enterprise and Partisanship in Provincial Politics." *Canadian Journal of Political Science*, vol. 15 (December 1982): 711–740.

Eichmanis, John, and Graham White. "Government by Other Means: Agencies, Boards and Commissions." In *The Government and Politics of Ontario*, 3rd ed., edited by Donald C. MacDonald. Scarborough, Ont.: Nelson Canada, 1985, pp. 82–99.

Elford, E. Craig, and W. T. Stanbury. "Mixed Enterprises in Canada." In *Economics of Industrial Structure*, edited by D. G. McFetridge. Research study for the Royal Commission on the Economic Union and Development Prospects for Canada. Toronto: University of Toronto Press, forthcoming.

Forget, Claude, ed. *La Caisse de dépôt et placement du Quebec: Sa mission, son impact et sa performance*. Montreal: Institut C. D. Howe, 1984.

Garant, Patrice. "Crown Corporations: Instruments of Economic Intervention — Legal Aspects." In *Regulations, Crown Corporations and Administrative Tribunals*, edited by Ivan Bernier and Andrée Lajoie. Research study for the Royal Commission on the Economic Union and Development Prospects for Canada, vol. 48. Toronto: University of Toronto Press, 1985, pp. 1–79.

Gélinas, André, ed. *Public Enterprise and the Public Interest*. Toronto: The Institute of Public Administration of Canada, 1978.

Gordon, Marsha. *Government in Business*. Montreal: C. D. Howe Institute, 1981.

Gracey, D. P. "The Real Issues in the Crown Corporations Debate." In *Public Administration in Canada: Selected Readings*, 5th ed., edited by Kenneth Kernaghan. Toronto: Methuen, 1985, pp. 122–140.

Hardin, Herschel. *A Nation Unaware: The Canadian Economic Culture*. Vancouver: J. J. Douglas, 1974.

Hodgetts, J. E. "The Public Corporation in Canada." In *Government Enterprise: A Comparative Study*, edited by W. Friedmann and J. F. Garner. London: Stevens & Sons, 1970, pp. 201–226.

Hogg, Peter W. *Constitutional Law of Canada*. Toronto: The Carswell Company, 1985.

Langford, John. "Crown Corporations as Instruments of Policy." In *Public Policy in Canada*, edited by G. Bruce Doern and Peter Aucoin. Toronto: Macmillan of Canada, 1979, pp. 239–274.

Langford, John. "The Identification and Classification of Federal Public Corporations: A Preface to Regime Building." *Canadian Public Administration*, vol. 23 (Spring 1980): 76–104.

Langford, John W., and Neil A. Swainson. "Public and Quasi-Public Corporations in British Columbia." In *The Administrative State in Canada*, edited by O. P. Dwivedi. Toronto: University of Toronto Press, 1982, pp. 63–87.

Nelles, H. V. *The Politics of Development: Forests, Mines & Hydro-electric Power in Ontario, 1849–1941*. Toronto: Macmillan of Canada, 1974.

Ohasi, Theodore M., T. P. Roth, Z. A. Spindler, M. L. McMillan, and K. H. Norrie. *Privatization: Theory & Practice*. Vancouver: The Fraser Institute, 1980.

Ontario. Agencies, Boards and Commissions Project. *First Report*. 1985.

Ontario. Agencies, Boards and Commissions Project. *Second Report: Privatization of Ontario Crown Corporations*. Report prepared for the Ministry of Treasury and Economics and the Management Board of Cabinet, n.d., 1985?

Prichard, J. Robert S., ed. *Crown Corporations in Canada: The Calculus of Instrument Choice*. Toronto: Butterworths, 1983.

Treasury Board of Canada Secretariat. *Crown Corporations and Other Canadian Government Corporate Interests*. Ottawa: Minister of Supply and Services Canada, 1984.

Tupper, Allan. *Bill S-31 and the Federalism of State Capitalism*. Kingston, Ont.: Queen's University, Institute of Intergovernmental Relations, 1983.

Tupper, Allan. "The Nation's Businesses: Canadian Concepts of Public Enterprise." Ph.D. diss., Queen's University, 1977.

Tupper, Allan, and G. Bruce Doern, eds. *Public Corporations and Public Policy in Canada*. Montreal: The Institute for Research on Public Policy, 1981.

Weaver, Robert Kent. "The Politics of State Enterprise: Railroad Nationalization in the United States and Canada." Ph.D. diss., Harvard University, 1982.

Wilson, V. Seymour. *Canadian Public Policy and Administration: Theory and Environment*. Toronto: McGraw-Hill Ryerson, 1981.

CASES

In *Case Program in Canadian Public Administration* (Toronto: Institute of Public Administration of Canada):

Canadian Cellulose Company, Limited, by Robert W. Sexty

Housing Corporation of British Columbia, by Robert W. Sexty

Saskatchewan Oil and Gas Corporation, by Robert W. Sexty

The Saskatchewan Government Insurance Office, by Robert W. Sexty

In Kenneth Kernaghan, *Canadian Cases in Public Administration* (Toronto: Methuen Publications):

This Hour Has Seven Days

8

Regulatory Agencies

This chapter will discuss the large and diverse group of governmental units commonly referred to as regulatory agencies. These units are probably the most misunderstood agencies of government because few ordinary citizens come into direct contact with a regulatory agency on a recurring basis. Compared to the Crown corporations discussed earlier, which deliver the mail, provide transportation, generate electrical power, and employ large numbers of people in fields such as fishing and mining, regulatory agencies have a much lower profile. However, this lack of *direct* contact between citizens and regulatory agencies masks the very great influence that these agencies have over our everyday lives. They influence the content of programs broadcast on radio and television through Canadian content and other regulations; they control the rates charged for transportation and telephone services, the rents charged for apartments in some provinces, and even the importation of hog-bristle paint brushes. The ongoing discussion about the proper form and scope of regulation is a reflection of the very significant, if indirect, impact that the actions of these agencies have on all of us and the very direct impact that they have on most businesses.

This chapter begins by establishing the definition of a regulatory agency. In keeping with the theme of this section of the book — the choice of organizational form — there will then be a discussion of some of the reasons why politicians choose regulatory agencies to accomplish particular objectives. This relates to the following section, which describes the powers of regulatory agencies. Next, the important aspects of political and judicial control of regulatory agencies will be discussed. Then, the operating procedures and organizational structure of a typical regulatory agency will be described. Finally, two very important policy issues concerning regulatory agencies will be addressed — the current problems associated with regulatory agencies and the solutions to these problems.

While this chapter deals with the general phenomenon of government regulation, it focusses specifically on regulation by regulatory agency rather than government department. A significant amount of regulation does emanate from government departments, and a lesser amount from other government organizations such as Crown corporations. Some obvious examples are the consumer protection regulations administered by the various federal and provincial departments responsible for consumer affairs and the regulation of technical aspects of aviation by the federal Ministry of Transport. This chapter focusses solely on regulatory agencies, not only because they perform extremely important regulatory functions, but also because they differ in structure and operation from operating departments.

DEFINITION OF A REGULATORY AGENCY

Defining the phrase "regulatory agency" is a bit like trying to describe the shape of an amoeba. Regulatory agencies come in so many sizes and shapes with such a variety of duties that it is difficult to generalize about them. In spite of this difficulty, one expert defined a regulatory agency as:

> A statutory body charged with responsibility to administer, to fix, to establish, to control, or to regulate an economic activity or market by regularized and established means in the public interest and in accordance with government policy.[1]

Two phrases in this definition — "regularized and established means" and "the public interest" — deserve special attention. First, regulatory agencies must set out specific rules of procedure and must follow those rules in working towards a decision. Although regulatory agencies are different from the ordinary law courts in ways that will be discussed later, these agencies do have certain judicial-like trappings, and the emphasis on "regularized and established means" of acting is one of them. This is one of the main characteristics which separates regulatory agencies from operating departments and Crown corporations. Of course, these latter two types of organization also have restrictions on their actions, but in general, they are able to make decisions in a manner which is considerably more flexible, and sometimes more secretive, than that of regulatory agencies.

Second, regulatory agencies are frequently directed to act in "the public interest," but it can be very difficult to define exactly what that means. When an agency is making a decision on rate setting, it must decide between the interests of consumers, who are members of the public, and shareholders of the company, who are also members of the public. In this situation, the strongest and most principled adherence to the public interest is not a very helpful guide to action. Still, a commitment to the public interest, however defined, is an important influence on the work of regulatory agencies.

Two improvements might be made in the definition given above. First, the emphasis on "economic activity or market" has more to do with traditional forms of regulation than with some of the newer forms of regulation in cultural, environmental, and social areas. A distinction is sometimes made between direct regulation and social regulation:

> *Direct regulation* refers to government interventions that directly prescribe such key determinants of economic performance as prices; entry into, and exit from, an industry or activity; standards of service; and rates of return. These are often administered by independent, quasi-judicial commissions that exercise authority over the regulated industry. In contrast, *social regulation* involves the setting of control standards or, alternatively, the provisions of incentives for producers to achieve specific social goals such as consumer health and safety or environmental protection. Unlike direct

---

[1]C. Lloyd Brown-John, *Canadian Regulatory Agencies* (Toronto: Butterworths, 1981), p. 35.

regulations, which are usually imposed on an industry-by-industry basis, social regulations frequently affect a wide range of industries.[2]

One of the major changes in the regulatory environment in recent years has been the movement towards more social regulation, e.g., regulation in areas of culture, such as more stringent rules on Canadian content in broadcasting, and environmental and social concerns such as pollution control, occupational health and safety, and consumer protection.

Second, the definition presented above does not take account of the fact that a regulatory agency is insulated from direct political intervention when it is making decisions in specific cases, although there is some political control over its general policy direction. The question of the appropriate role of the minister raises a conundrum. He or she is responsible for the policy outcomes of the activities of the agency, but cannot interfere in the making of individual decisions. The purpose of this apparent contradiction is to balance accountability to the minister and autonomy in the making of specific decisions. As will be seen later, this need for balance poses one of the more awkward dilemmas in regulatory reform.

These considerations bring about some changes in the definition presented above. The main advantage of this revised definition is its emphasis on the lack of direct ministerial control over individual decisions made by the regulatory agency. The legislature and the minister set the overall policy of the regulatory agency, but the concept of ministerial responsibility does not have the same meaning with regard to regulatory agencies as it does in the case of operating departments. In fact, it would be inappropriate for a minister to intervene when the agency is making a decision on a specific case.

A regulatory agency is a statutory body charged with responsibility to administer, to fix, to establish, to control, or to regulate an economic, cultural, environmental or social activity by regularized and established means in the public interest and in accordance with general policy guidelines specified by the government. This body is under the general direction of the legislature and a responsible minister with regard to policy matters, but possesses relative autonomy of action in making individual decisions within those policy guidelines.

FUNCTIONS OF REGULATORY AGENCIES

It is difficult to generalize about the functions of regulatory agencies because the powers and duties assigned to them by their enabling statutes vary widely. Richard Schultz has identified the five most common functions, each of which is examined below.

Adjudicative
This function is performed by all regulatory agencies. It involves:

[2]Economic Council of Canada, *Reforming Regulation* (Ottawa: Minister of Supply and Services Canada, 1981), p. 7. (Emphasis added.) See also, Economic Council of Canada, *Responsible Regulation: An Interim Report* (Hull: Minister of Supply and Services Canada, 1979), pp. 44–45.

the determination of outcomes in individual cases which typically deal with control over entry, the setting of prices or rates of return, and the setting of standards or rules of conduct by regulated enterprises.[3]

To understand the adjudication function properly, it is necessary to distinguish a regulatory agency from an ordinary court of law. The law courts are called upon to make a finding of fact and to relate that finding to a relatively precise piece of legislation. If the legislation is not precise in some area, there is usually some precedent set out in a decision on a similar case which can be used to assist in the application of the law.

In the case of a regulatory agency, the terms of the law which must be applied are considerably more vague. Statutes containing phrases such as "the public interest" or "public convenience and necessity" are very imprecise guides to action. Therefore, the regulatory agency must act much more on its own initiative in shaping policy than an ordinary court does.

> Granting that the [regulatory agency] which applies these legislative standards should maintain a judicial attitude, it cannot give a decision which is judicial in the narrow sense because there is no law for it to apply. If a decision is to be made at all, it must be made on grounds of policy and therefore the function in question is primarily legislative rather than judicial.[4]

There is a paradox here in that regulatory agencies are required to behave in a judicial-like manner in considering a case, but they actually make the decision based on policy considerations. This latter point explains why agencies are not bound by precedent. In the many cases in which agencies are allocating scarce resources, they simply could not follow precedent anyway. If all of the available slots on the radio dial have already been assigned, then the quality of the next application received is not relevant. The scarcity of slots on the dial precludes approval on the basis of precedent.

The adjudicative function tends to be the core activity of most regulatory agencies, but there are several other activities which are also a part of the responsibilities of many agencies.

Legislative

This function comprises "the ability to make general rules or regulations, in the form of delegated legislation, that have the force of law."[5] Most legislation which establishes regulatory agencies gives them some power to prescribe more

---

[3]"Regulatory Agencies and Accountability," a study prepared for the Royal Commission on Financial Management and Accountability, May 1978, unpublished manuscript, as referred to in Economic Council of Canada, *Responsible Regulation: An Interim Report*, p. 56. For a similar, but slightly different, list of functions, see Canada, Privy Council Office, *Submissions to the Royal Commission on Financial Management and Accountability* (Minister of Supply and Services Canada, 1978), pp. 2–77 to 2–93.

[4]J. A. Corry, "Introduction: The Genesis and Nature of Boards," in John Willis, ed., *Canadian Boards at Work* (Toronto: Macmillan of Canada, 1941), p. xxxvi.

[5]Economic Council of Canada, *Responsible Regulation: An Interim Report*, p. 56.

specific regulations within the guidelines set out in the legislation. These regulations are referred to as delegated legislation because they are made pursuant to powers delegated to the agency in the legislation. They could relate to either policy matters, i.e., specify the agency's approach to particular issues, or procedural matters, i.e., specify how applications are to be filed and hearings conducted.

Research

Most agencies employ some staff to conduct general research in the policy area which it is regulating. The purpose of this research is to allow members to remain conversant with recent trends in the field. For example, it could provide them with an early warning when there is a need for a shift in policy. The research staff is also sometimes used to evaluate applications and to provide advice to the members of the agency in making specific decisions.

Advisory

In many ways, this function follows from the research function. As a result of the research conducted and the findings flowing from hearings, the members and staff of the agency are frequently able to advise the minister and/or the operating department about the need for a fresh consideration of certain policy issues. The regulatory agencies are close to the regulated industry and its clientele, and therefore they have a good knowledge of emerging problems.

Administrative

Some agencies also have direct administrative responsibility for operating programs. For example, the Canadian Transport Commission provides subsidies to certain airlines and for railway grade crossing separations. This function is not found frequently in regulatory agencies because it could create a conflict situation for an agency when it must both operate a program affecting an industry and regulate that industry.

This listing of some of the duties of regulatory agencies provides an idea of the rather broad scope and diversity of this organizational form. Therefore, it should not be surprising that there are many varied reasons given for employing the regulatory agency form of organization.

THE RATIONALE FOR REGULATORY AGENCIES

The administrator, the economist, and the politician frequently see regulation in somewhat different lights.[6] The practising administrator frequently sees regulation as the easiest and cheapest method of attaining a particular objective. The economist is usually opposed to regulation, except in those relatively rare cases where it corrects some market imperfection. The politician must respond to the

---

[6]Roderick A. Macdonald, "Understanding Regulation by Regulations," in Ivan Bernier and Andrée Lajoie, eds., *Regulations, Crown Corporations and Administrative Tribunals* (Toronto: University of Toronto Press, 1985), pp. 84–89.

frequently conflicting demands of electors, and so sometimes views regulation as an easy method of farming out complex problems to independent agencies to be dealt with over the long term. It is not surprising, therefore, that there are many different reasons for the creation of regulatory agencies. Those discussed below constitute only a partial list.

Remove an Issue from "Politics"

The word politics is used here in the negative sense as relying too much on partisanship, compromise, and expediency, and not enough on fairness and hard economic facts.

Many of the decisions made by regulatory agencies are in rather delicate areas. In cases such as the regulation of broadcasting, there was a fear that one political party would attempt to use the media for partisan advantage. There are also cases in which regulatory agencies are rationing scarce resources. These resources could be slots on a radio or television dial or the right to develop a particular piece of land. Not only is there usually a large amount of money at stake in these cases, but they also frequently involve highly technical questions which require the attention of experts. For example, the question of whether an applicant has the engineering expertise and financial support to operate a radio station is a technical question best addressed by engineers and accountants. In this sense, it is sometimes reassuring to have decisions removed from the partisan political process so that they can be viewed more objectively.

However, this argument must be put in perspective. Most delicate issues of this kind consist of not only technical questions, but also contentious political ones. In the broadcasting case, the questions of engineering competence and financial support are predominantly technical ones, but questions of Canadian content, pornography, or appropriate programming mix are inherently political ones.

For this reason, the idea of using the vehicle of the regulatory agency to remove an issue from politics must be approached carefully. If it means providing experts with some scope to review technical problems outside the vagaries of the political process, then it is probably highly beneficial. If it implies that mixed technical and political questions can be resolved by technical experts, then it is not only naive, but dangerous, because it would suggest that politicians should not be held accountable for certain decisions simply because those decisions contain some technical element.

Provide an Impartial, Judicial-like Hearing

This reason is related to the previous one. It is the nature of parliamentary governments that Cabinet decisions are made in closed sessions and rely on information which is not necessarily available to the public. In this context, it is difficult for someone submitting an issue to Cabinet to know whether all important arguments have been considered before a Cabinet decision is made.

Thus, it is sometimes considered important to have a public forum in the form of a regulatory agency where all the facts in a case can be presented. The forum usually involves a relatively formal hearing in which petitioners can present their arguments and cross-examine one another. This process ensures that all parties have a fair opportunity to state their case as well as they can. Since the members of the agency presiding over the hearing and making the decision must be free from bias, it also ensures that a decision which takes account of the arguments of all sides will be rendered.

If the decisions were made in an overtly political arena, it might be difficult for politicians to escape at least the appearance of bias. Consider these examples. Since the Minister of Transport is responsible for the profitable operation of Air Canada, there might be a feeling that he or she would be partial with regard to the awarding of lucrative air routes. In the broadcasting field, some people who own companies which hold licences are prominently identified with a particular political party. Again, there could be an appearance of bias in either the renewal or the refusal to renew a licence depending on the political stripe of the government.

Apply Specialized Expertise

Many kinds of concerns assigned to regulatory agencies could be handled in the ordinary courts. After all, judges become very proficient at sorting through conflicting arguments, separating the important from the trivial, and rendering an impartial decision. These are all activities performed by members of regulatory agencies. However, while judges are learned in the law, they are not expected to have detailed knowledge of the activities of a particular industry. Also, one cannot expect different judges to apply an integrated, coherent policy in making decisions about an industry; judges decide individual cases based on the law. By way of contrast, the members of a regulatory agency develop specialized knowledge over the years and so are capable of making decisions reflecting consciously conceived policies. It is also important that these specialized decision makers can arrive at decisions more quickly than someone who must apply himself or herself to a new issue from the ground up, such as judges would be required to do.

Deal with Future Conditions which the Legislature Could Not Foresee

Frequently, technical and economic conditions are changing so rapidly that it is dysfunctional for the legislature to prescribe hard and fast rules in legislation which can only be changed by new legislation. It is preferable for the legislature to specify general principles and to allow the regulatory agency flexibility within those principles to respond to changing conditions.

Regulate a Natural Monopoly

A natural monopoly exists when the lowest costs are obtained by there being only one producer of a good or service,[7] i.e., certain technical aspects of the good or service mean that competition would increase its cost. For example, the delivery of electricity in a particular geographic area is a natural monopoly.

---

[7]Economic Council of Canada, *Responsible Regulation: An Interim Report*, p. 46.

The capital cost of installing two or more electrical service lines into every area of a city would be such that the costs could not possibly be lower than with one monopoly supplier. The problem with a natural monopoly is that the discipline of the market is not available to force the supplier to deal fairly with consumers. In the absence of that discipline, most economists argue that the situation of natural monopoly is one of the few cases in which government regulation is justified to ensure appropriate price and adequate service.

Smooth Market Instability

In recent years, there has been a trend towards the use of regulatory agencies for "supply management." The best examples are the marketing boards for such farm products as eggs, milk, and chickens. These agencies work by setting quotas on the overall quantity of the product that can be produced and allocating this quota among specific producers. The effect of this is to ensure that an excess of supply does not reduce prices paid to producers.

Marketing boards have been criticized on the grounds that they increase the price that must be paid by consumers. However, they also assure reasonable security of supply by preventing injurious competition which would force some suppliers from the market. In other words, consumers must pay a premium for eggs every time they buy them to ensure that there will always be some eggs available at a reasonable price. Whether the cost is worth the benefit is something that each voter must decide.

Prevent Discrimination where a Situation of Inequality Exists

This rationale bears some similarity to the natural monopoly argument in that there is some perceived inequality of bargaining power which government feels should be corrected. Most of the new kinds of social regulatory agencies in fields such as human rights, occupational health and safety, and rent control were created for this reason. The role of the regulatory agency in this case is to protect the weaker party by preventing the stronger party from taking unfair advantage of its position.

The agencies created as a result of this rationale have been the most controversial, because the existence of a perceived inequality which requires government intervention is frequently in the eye of the beholder. The controversy surrounding the need for rent control is one obvious example of an area in which not everyone is agreed on the need for protection.

Control Externalities or "Spill-overs"

A non-technical definition of an externality is a cost imposed by one person on another person or on society as a whole when the person imposing the cost has no market incentive to minimize or control the cost. The most common example is pollution. The obvious market incentive is for polluters to minimize their expenditure on pollution control equipment so that the entire cost of pollution will be borne by society as a whole. In this situation, a regulatory agency with the power to enforce particular standards is the obvious solution.

Low-cost Option from the Standpoint of Government

If a government wants to have an impact on a particular kind of behaviour, it has a number of options, ranging from exhortation, through tax incentives and grants, to coercive legislation. The lowest-cost option from the standpoint of the government is simply to say: Thou shalt not. There is a cost to the government of establishing and operating a regulatory agency, but the impact per dollar spent of a regulatory agency is usually greater than that of an operating department or Crown corporation because of its coercive powers.

A classic example of the use of this rationale is the treatment of the Niagara escarpment in southern Ontario. The escarpment is a unique geological formation and prime recreation area for people living in the area. In the 1960s, there was considerable pressure on the Ontario government to control development in this area. A number of options were considered, including buying the entire escarpment or strategic portions of it. Not surprisingly, the Ontario government decided to establish a regulatory agency, the Niagara Escarpment Commission, and give it the power to say: Thou shalt not develop here without prior permission. This was clearly the low-cost option from the standpoint of the government.

Regulation is the low-cost option *only* from the standpoint of the government. As will be discussed in more detail later, regulation can impose significant costs on others. In the Niagara escarpment example, many people saw the value of their land plummet when it became unlikely that it could be used for subdivisions or resorts. It has been suggested that the low cost of regulation makes it particularly attractive to governments facing simultaneous demands for decisive action and financial restraint.[8]

The reasons noted above constitute only a partial listing of the reasons for establishing and preserving regulatory agencies. This diversity of reasons demonstrates why these agencies have such a wide variety of roles. However, the main characteristics which cut across all agencies is their relative autonomy from direct political control and their judicial-like methods of operation. These characteristics will be examined in the next two sections.

POLITICAL CONTROL OF REGULATORY AGENCIES

A central feature of parliamentary control of regulatory agencies is that the legislature, the Cabinet, and individual ministers set general policies and guidelines for their activities, but are kept at arm's length from their day-to-day operations. This section will discuss the method of accomplishing this balancing act.

---

[8]G. Bruce Doern, "Introduction," in G. Bruce Doern, ed., *The Regulatory Process in Canada* (Toronto: Macmillan of Canada, 1978), pp. 17–18.

Enabling Statutes and Other Legislation

Regulatory agencies are similar to operating departments and most Crown corporations in that they are formed as a result of enabling legislation, which specifies the structure of the agency, the procedures it must follow in considering cases, the limits of its authority, and the general policies it must apply in making decisions. In some instances, all of these components are specified in one statute; in others, they are divided among a number of pieces of legislation. For example, the Canadian Transport Commission was created by the National Transportation Act,[9] but it draws most of its powers from the Aeronautics Act,[10] the Railway Act,[11] and the Canada Shipping Act,[12] among others.

Legislative committees also check the work of regulatory agencies. They scrutinize the operation of regulatory agencies in the same manner as that of operating departments and Crown corporations. Thus, the committee members can question the minister responsible for an agency and/or the members of the agency about its implementation of policies or its operating procedures.

Committee on Regulations and Other Statutory Instruments

In addition to the policy-oriented legislative committees which oversee the activities of regulatory agencies, there can be specialized committees which review *all* regulations and delegated legislation.[13] This was first employed in Saskatchewan in the early 1960s and came to the federal government in 1971 in the form of the Senate and House of Commons Standing Joint Committee on Regulations and Other Statutory Instruments.[14] All regulations made under delegated legislation by either operating departments or regulatory agencies are referred to this committee. It has a very detailed mandate, which includes determining that the regulation is in line with the authorizing legislation, that it does not violate the Charter of Rights and Freedoms, and that it does not intrude into an area which is the prerogative of Parliament.[15]

Appointment of Members

The decisions of regulatory agencies are made by a panel of members who are appointed by the Governor in Council, usually after consultation with the minister responsible for the agency. The minister will normally recommend the appointment of persons who share his or her views on the policy area.

This role in the appointment of members provides the minister with real power in setting the overall tone of the agency. However, when these appointments are for lengthy fixed terms of office and members can be removed only "for cause," the members have considerable autonomy. Therefore, the ability of anyone, including the minister, to interfere in a specific decision is limited.

---

[9]R.S.C. 1970, c. N-17.

[10]R.S.C. 1970, c. A-3.

[11]R.S.C. 1970, c. R-2.

[12]R.S.C. 1970, c. S-9.

[13]Canada, Senate and House of Commons, Standing Joint Committee on Regulations and Other Statutory Instruments, *Minutes and Proceedings*, February 16, 1984, pp. 1:4 and 1:5.

[14]Macdonald, "Understanding Regulation by Regulations," p. 96.

[15]The role of this committee will be discussed further in Chapter 15.

The allegation has often been made that this power of appointment has been used for patronage purposes. Clearly, there have been instances in which ministers have appointed people of their own political stripe, but allegations of patronage must be considered carefully. Evidence provided later in this chapter indicates that political appointments are not as common as popular opinion suggests.

Policy Statements and Directives

As noted above, it is inappropriate for a minister to intervene in specific cases before an agency. However, a minister, or the Cabinet collectively, can issue policy statements or directives to inform the regulatory agency of the government's desires in a particular area. For some agencies, it is not clear whether these are binding,[16] but for other agencies the legislation makes it clear that they are binding. These must be general policy statements and not directions concerning specific cases. Thus, it would be inappropriate for a minister to tell an agency: You must grant this broadcast licence to person A instead of person B. However, it would be appropriate for the minister to direct the agency that: The only applicants who should be considered for this broadcast licence are those who will agree to provide X per cent of Canadian content.

These policy statements or directives can be made secretly to the agency, but it is usually considered important that they should be made publicly. This gives all parties appearing before the agency the right to know what policy statements and directives have been made, and it acts as a constraint on any potential abuse of power by the minister.

Prior Approval of Decisions

In some instances, the decision of a regulatory agency does not become binding until it is approved either by the responsible minister or by the Cabinet collectively.[17] The role of the agency in this situation is to provide an impartial hearing to all concerned and to apply its specialized expertise in arriving at a recommendation for a decision. These recommendations are usually given publicly so that the Cabinet must consider very carefully both the recommendations and the supporting documentation. If this advice is ignored, allegations of inappropriate political influence can be made.[18]

Appeal

Some legislation dealing with regulation provides the right of appeal to the minister or to the Governor in Council, i.e., the Cabinet. Where this provision exists, the appellant usually has no right to appear personally before the minister or Cabinet, but must state in writing the reasons why the decision should be overturned. The minister or Cabinet considers these appeals carefully, but is somewhat reluctant to overturn a decision, partly to preserve the morale and integrity of the agency and partly to prevent a flood of similar appeals. It is

---

[16]Lucinda Vandervort, *Political Control of Independent Administrative Agencies* (Ottawa: Law Reform Commission of Canada, 1979), pp. 12–13.

[17]This is the case with certain decisions of the National Energy Board. R.S.C. 1970, c. N-6, s. 44.

[18]"PC Backers Win Review of TV-Station Licences," *The Globe and Mail*, November 13, 1985.

probably this reluctance to overturn decisions which explains the small number of appeals that are made to Cabinet.

However, this appeal mechanism is still a valuable safety valve. At the extreme, it prevents the members of the agency from behaving in some entirely inappropriate manner, because they know that their decision could be appealed to a higher level. In a less extreme vein, the minister or Cabinet can use the selective acceptance of certain appeals to signal changes in policy at the political level.[19] Members of regulatory agencies are usually sensitive to this sort of signal.

Political control of regulatory agencies is geared to ensuring that the agencies follow the policy guidelines set out by the government. Judicial control of regulatory agencies, which is discussed in the next section, is geared to ensuring fairness in the handling of cases.

JUDICIAL CONTROL OF REGULATORY AGENCIES

Chapter 16 contains a full treatment of judicial control of administrative actions in general, and of regulatory decision making in particular. It is useful to note here that there is usually much discussion about which type of redress is more effective — political or judicial. The answer depends on a number of factors. First, a court rarely *changes* the decision of a regulatory agency. The court considers only the *process* followed by the agency, not the *merits* of its decision. A court can find that an agency followed an improper procedure, and so overturn the decision. At this point, the agency is free to reconsider the matter, follow the proper procedure, and arrive at exactly the same decision. The court would then be satisfied. Of course, there is also the possibility that a different procedure will produce a different result.

If it is clear that the agency has followed the proper procedure, but there is still dissatisfaction with the decision reached, then the most likely source of redress lies at the political level. It is usually only the minister or Cabinet who can consider the *merits* of the decision and substitute another final and binding decision.

These two sections have considered the unique methods of political and judicial control exercised with regard to regulatory agencies. The organization and operation of regulatory agencies are also unique, as will be seen in the next section.

STRUCTURE AND OPERATION OF REGULATORY AGENCIES

It is very difficult to generalize about the structure and operation of regulatory agencies, because each agency is somewhat different. However, this section will describe some of the usual structures and procedures of regulatory agencies.

---

[19]Vandervort, *Political Control of Independent Administrative Agencies*, p. 35 and pp. 59-60.

Organizational Structure

Regulatory agencies are virtually always headed by a panel of members. The panel usually consists of five to ten members, but the number can vary quite widely. In 1984, the Ontario Municipal Board was composed of thirty-nine members.[20] Panel members are collectively responsible for the agency's operation.

The method of appointment and removal of panel members obviously has an impact on the independence of the agency from political control. To maximize independence, members should be appointed for relatively lengthy terms, and should be removable only for cause. This is the situation that exists for most federal agencies, but Brown-John found that many members of regulatory agencies do not have the security of tenure needed for independence.[21]

One member of the panel is designated as the chairperson or president of the agency. This individual is considered the administrative head of the agency and usually has the responsibility for assigning fellow panel members to cases, as well as supervising the public servants who work for the agency.

The fact that the agency is headed by a panel means that there is scope for the representation of diverse interests on the panel, e.g., geographic regions, special interest groups. Members of the Canadian Radio-television and Telecommunications Commission are traditionally appointed from different regions of the country, and labour relations boards contain a roughly equal balance between members sympathetic to the union and employer sides.

The background of panel members obviously has some impact on agency decisions. The specialized knowledge possessed by former employees of the regulated industry makes them choice candidates for appointment to the agency. It has sometimes been suggested that a preponderance of these people as panel members will make the agency "soft" on the industry.

However, a recent Canadian survey indicates that members of regulatory agencies are more likely to be former public servants than former employees of the regulated industry.[22] This same survey found that there were not large numbers of former politicians serving as members of regulatory agencies, thus negating somewhat the image of these agencies as repositories of patronage appointees. However, a recent report of the Law Reform Commission of Canada suggests that the highly political nature of the appointments to these agencies can have a detrimental effect on their operations.[23] The commission recommends that the process be opened up considerably by advertising for interested candidates for open positions and by consulting with interested groups about potential members.

The members preside over hearings and make decisions, but it is unusual for all members to be present at any one hearing. Thus, several hearings can be held at the same time, and the work of the agency can be speeded up. Members can be assigned to cases by the chairperson on a random basis, or there can be a

---

[20]The Ontario Municipal Board, *79th Annual Report* (1985), p. 15.

[21]*Canadian Regulatory Agencies*, p. 118.

[22]Caroline Andrew and Rejean Pelletier, "The Regulators," in Doern, ed., *The Regulatory Process in Canada*, pp. 150–152; Brown-John, *Canadian Regulatory Agencies*, pp. 114–116.

[23]*Report on Independent Administrative Agencies: A Framework For Decision Making*, Report 26 (Ottawa: Law Reform Commission of Canada, 1985), p. 77.

committee system that allows members to specialize. The committees of the Canadian Transport Commission are organized along modal lines, i.e., air, rail, and commodity pipelines with some overlapping membership to facilitate communication between them. In some agencies, there is also a special committee to hear appeals concerning decisions of other committees.

All regulatory agencies have a fairly extensive staff of experts in law, economics, accounting, engineering, and whatever other specialty is required. The main functions of this staff involve supporting the work of the members in arranging hearings, conducting both general research and specific investigations concerning individual applications, and advising members on legal and/or technical aspects of their work.

Operating Procedures

This review of the operating procedures of regulatory agencies will focus on the legislative and adjudicative functions; these are the most important and visible of the five functions discussed earlier.

Legislative Function. The enabling legislation usually gives the agency some discretion in establishing specific regulations within the guidelines set out in the Act. After new legislation (or a major amendment to existing legislation) is passed, the agency begins to consider the specific rules and regulations it needs to adopt to give effect to this legislation. The agency also periodically reconsiders its substantive policy in a particular area. These are very important opportunities for the regulated industry and consumer interest groups to affect the agency's policies.

When the agency is making or amending its policy or regulations, it usually notifies all interested parties through such measures as formal letters, advertisements in newspapers or trade publications, and news announcements in the media. In some cases, this notice is an open-ended request for any comments which interested parties want to tender. In other cases, the staff of the agency prepares some tentative working documents on which comments are invited.

Interested parties are usually requested to submit written comments first. On the basis of these comments, some people will be invited to attend a hearing to present their views and be questioned by the members of the agency. In some cases, these hearings are held at the home base of the agency, but in others, the members travel to major cities across the country or province to obtain a wide cross-section of views. Then, the members prepare a formal set of regulations or a formal policy statement which will be binding in all future cases.

Adjudicative Function. The adjudication process — the consideration of individual cases — can begin in a number of ways. Usually, an individual case begins when an application is submitted to the agency requesting, for example, a rate increase or a change in service level. The process can also be initiated by the agency or some third party where, for example, there is concern that a regulated company is not meeting some obligation.

In accordance with the requirements of natural justice,[24] there is usually a

---

[24]Natural justice is described in more detail in Chapter 16.

requirement that *notice* be provided to all interested parties that an application is under review. Any party who comes forward at this time is called an *intervener*. An intervener can prepare a submission supporting or opposing the application or proposing some middle ground. Typically, the interveners will be consumers, consumers' groups, or companies in the industry affected by the application. However, even government departments or other governments can intervene before a regulatory agency.

As interventions are received, the public servants who work for the regulatory agency will begin to analyse both the original application and the comments provided by interveners. They will then prepare a summary of the relevant issues for the panel, and possibly even a recommendation concerning the final disposition of the application.

Whether a full hearing will then be held depends on the requirements in the legislation and regulations and the importance of the case. When there is a full formal hearing, the process begins with a presentation explaining the applicant's position. Then, the agency will usually invite some of the interveners to explain their positions. The hearings of some agencies are very formal, almost judicial procedures held in settings which resemble a courtroom and involve the presence of lawyers, formal presentation of evidence, and cross-examination of witnesses. Other agencies strive to keep their proceedings as simple and informal as possible. In this situation, the members might only leave the room for a few minutes and return to present their decision verbally. In more complex cases, several months could be required for members to deliver a lengthy written decision with reasons.

These procedures are carefully worked out to ensure fairness to all sides and a thorough consideration of the issue. A survey has indicated that most of those involved in the regulatory process are quite satisfied with the process,[25] but some commentators have identified flaws in the system.

PROBLEMS IDENTIFIED WITH REGULATION

The role of regulation and regulatory agencies in society is currently the subject of much debate. Agencies are attacked on one side for being too assertive and intrusive, and on the other for being "captive" of the interests which they were established to regulate. In this section, some of the main criticisms of regulatory agencies will be considered, and in the next section some of the possible reforms will be discussed.[26]

Cost of Regulation
Although regulation is usually seen as the low-cost option from the standpoint of government, it can impose sizeable costs on other parties. The most obvious examples are the direct costs incurred by the regulated industry and by other affected parties. The firms in the regulated industry must maintain extensive

---

[25]Brown-John, *Canadian Regulatory Agencies*, p. 143.
[26]An excellent recent review of problems and reforms is contained in David J. Mullan, "Administrative Tribunals: Their Evolution in Canada from 1945 to 1984," in Bernier and Lajoie, eds., *Regulations, Crown Corporations and Administrative Tribunals*, pp. 155-201.

records in a format specified by the regulatory agency. All parties affected by
regulatory agencies incur substantial information costs to keep themselves abreast
of initiatives by the agency and by other groups affected by the agency. Then,
there are legal and other costs involved in preparing a case and actually appearing before the regulatory agency.

However, these direct costs might be only the tip of the iceberg.[27] The major
costs of regulation could come from a slowdown in the introduction of innovations as a result of the need for clearance from a regulatory agency. The pharmaceutical industry has long made this claim, but there are numerous other
examples.

It is important to emphasize that benefits as well as costs arise from regulation.
The record keeping required of regulated industries allows the regulatory agency
to consider intelligently requests for rate increases. The slowness in the introduction of new innovations sometimes keeps dangerous products off the market.
This is not to suggest that all forms of regulation are justified. Clearly, there are
cases in which legislators or regulators have become over-zealous.

There are also *hidden* costs of regulation. Economists argue that the optimum competitive situation occurs when barriers to entering an industry are
low. Easy entry for new firms forces existing firms to be competitive in both
price and quality of product. Regulatory agencies virtually always raise barriers
to entry in the regulated industry. Barriers can be direct, such as the need for
prior approval from the regulatory agency, or indirect, but equally effective,
such as residence or minimum capitalization requirements. Still other barriers
can be psychological in that entrepreneurs will simply choose not to enter an
industry in which the regulations are seen as intrusive, particularly if the barriers are felt to be unfair or unreasonable.

The Empty Consumers' Chair

It is sometimes said that the purpose of a regulatory agency is to protect the
consumer. While some legislators might intend this, it is not, strictly speaking,
legally correct. The members of a regulatory agency listen to the arguments
presented by the various parties and attempt to arrive at an optimum decision
based on those arguments. They are clearly restrained from favouring one side
or the other; they must decide on the basis of the arguments presented. If one
side is able to present its arguments more persuasively or more forcefully, then,
other things being equal, it is likely to win.

This premium on the ability to make one's case well is significant, because it
has been suggested that producers have an advantage over consumers in the
regulatory process.[28] There are usually a relatively small number of producers
(sometimes, only one), and in actions such as rate increase applications, each

---

[27]A good discussion of the nature of some of these costs is contained in Economic Council of
Canada, *Responsible Regulation: An Interim Report*, pp. 34-38.

[28]Anthony Downs, *An Economic Theory of Democracy* (New York: Harper & Row, 1957), ch. 13,
esp. p. 254ff; Michael J. Trebilcock, et al., *The Choice of Governing Instrument* (Ottawa: Minister of Supply and Services Canada, 1982), pp. 7-10.

producer has a large amount at stake. This makes it easy for producers to work together and spend large sums of money to defend their claims. On the other hand, there are a large number of consumers, each of whom has a fairly small amount at stake in any given rate increase. Therefore, it is difficult for consumers to band together to fight rate increases. To put it directly: How much would you be willing to spend to prevent your telephone bill from increasing by fifty cents per month? Probably considerably less than a telephone company would be willing to spend to gain the several million dollars which it has at stake in the same application.

Captive Agency Theory

The captive agency theory is in many ways complementary to the above arguments about the lack of consumer power in the regulatory process. The captive agency theory suggests that, over time, the agency is captured by the industry which it was set up to regulate, and so becomes supportive of that industry. This is a gradual process in which the agency develops a concern for the orderly development of the industry; this concern gradually comes to mean the protection of the companies currently in the industry from any disruptive forces such as excessive competition from new entrants.

Marver H. Bernstein has developed a life cycle theory of regulatory agencies which explains this capture.[29] An agency is usually born as the result of political activism by groups concerned about some perceived problem. These groups work long and hard against difficult odds to encourage legislators to introduce some regulatory legislation. However, when the necessary legislation is passed, these groups run out of steam, partly because it is innately difficult to hold such large and diverse groups together, and partly because people drift away when they feel that the battle is over. Paradoxically, it is at precisely this time, when the fledgling agency is just beginning its operations and drafting its regulations, that it needs public input the most.

The people staffing the new agency are unlikely to be knowledgeable about the industry, since it has never been regulated before. Where should they turn for assistance and advice? The groups which agitated for the legislation in the first place are no longer strong and active. The only other source of knowledge about the industry is the industry itself. Therefore, the new regulators seek the advice of the regulated industry about how it wants to be regulated. This close contact allows the regulated industry to have a subtle, but effective, impact on the regulatory agency at its crucial formative stage. Once the pattern of close consultation between regulator and regulatee — with limited public involvement — is established, then it simply continues and becomes closer over the years.

At the same time, politicians tend to lose interest in the agency. They feel that the problem has been solved by the mere creation of the agency and would rather not become involved in the sometimes very antagonistic atmosphere that exists when specific decisions are made. This is more likely to happen in the

---

[29]*Regulating Business by Independent Commission* (Princeton, N.J.: Princeton University Press, 1955), ch. 3.

American situation, in which agencies are truly independent of executive control, than in the Canadian situation, where there is some element of ministerial responsibility. However, there is some evidence that this occurs in Canada as well.[30]

According to Bernstein's theory, over time the agency becomes highly judicialized and totally unwilling to take any policy initiatives. When people making budgeting decisions see the organization in this state, they are likely to decrease the agency's budgetary allocation, thus driving away good employees and worsening the downward spiral. The organization can continue in this spiral almost indefinitely unless some crisis snaps it out of its lethargy. It simply no longer possesses the drive and initiative to regulate the industry effectively.

Most discussion of the captive agency theory has been anecdotal, rather than more rigorous, because of the problems involved in testing it seriously. For example, how does one determine that agency decisions are favouring the industry? One serious consideration of the theory for a Canadian regulatory agency suggests that the capture hypothesis does not hold and that the process is much more complex than the hypothesis suggests.[31]

The Accountability-Autonomy Conundrum

A major characteristic of a regulatory agency is that it operates at arm's length from direct political control. This creates a conundrum in that the agency must be accountable to the minister and the legislature, but at the same time it must have autonomy in making individual decisions. Some of the problems that this raises were identified by a report of the Economic Council of Canada:

> This form of compromise between regulatory independence and political control has led in recent years to a great deal of tension, confusion and compromise. The record of both the federal and provincial governments' relationships with their regulatory agencies raises a number of challenging questions. Who should make regulatory policy? How should such policy be made — through open, participatory hearings in advance of specific cases or as a result of appeals to the cabinet following a specific case? Should [regulatory agencies] perform *both* adjudicative functions, for which they appear to be well suited, as well as policy advisory, research, and administrative functions, for which they may be less well suited. In particular, if a policy advisory role is retained, should the agency's advice to the government be confidential or made only in public documents? Finally, is it realistic to expect a government to be able to clearly articulate its policy positions, except in rather general terms, in advance of specific choices that embody the means of implementing them?[32]

---

[30]W. H. N. Hull, "Captive or Victim: The Board of Broadcast Governors and Bernstein's Law, 1958-68," *Canadian Public Administration*, vol. 26 (Winter 1983), p. 560.

[31]Ibid.

[32]Economic Council of Canada, *Responsible Regulation: An Interim Report*, p. 57. (Emphasis in original. Footnote omitted.)

Weak political control of the agency might allow it to act at cross-purposes with other government agencies, or to make decisions which are not in the overall public interest. However, excessive political control deflates the morale of the agency and could lead to dominance by powerful interest groups. The conundrum of accountability and autonomy is one of the most difficult problems to handle in discussing regulatory reform.[33]

Regulatory Agencies and Federalism

In recent years regulatory agencies have made decisions with a substantial impact on federal-provincial relations.[34] In some cases, decisions by federal regulatory agencies have allowed the federal government to intervene in provincial areas in a manner which ignored the concerns of provincial governments about both the content of decisions and the process by which the decisions were made.

One example of the difficult interaction between the regulatory process and federalism is in the field of airline regulation. Ordinarily, a provincial government can purchase assets it wants without obtaining prior approval from the federal government. However, if the asset which the province wishes to purchase is an airline, then it might have to obtain prior approval of the Canadian Transport Commission. This was the position in which the Alberta government found itself when it wanted to acquire Pacific Western Airlines. Ultimately, the matter was resolved, but the process did little to further good relations between Edmonton and Ottawa.[35]

Schultz has described this sort of situation as being characterized by regulatory agency independence and federal-provincial interdependence.[36] Federal and provincial governments frequently enter into agreements to share authority in particular policy areas. However, regulatory agencies, asserting their independence of executive control, can take the position that they are not bound by such agreements. This is exactly what the CRTC did with regard to an agreement between the federal and Manitoba governments regarding cable television.[37]

Sometimes the conflict is less direct, but no less significant. Both energy-producing and energy-consuming provinces have a real stake in certain decisions of the National Energy Board. Provincial governments feel that they should have some sort of special status in board hearings because they are the legitimate government representing the people of their province. However, most regulatory

---

[33]Richard Schultz, "Regulatory Agencies and the Canadian Political System," in Kenneth Kernaghan, ed., *Public Administration in Canada: Selected Readings*, 4th ed. (Toronto: Methuen, 1982), pp. 70-80.

[34]One of the most thorough writers in this field is Richard J. Schultz. He has addressed the general question in *Federalism and the Regulatory Process* (Montreal: Institute for Research on Public Policy, 1979) and a more specific policy area in *Federalism, Bureaucracy, and Public Policy. The Politics of Highway Transportation Regulation* (Montreal: McGill-Queen's University Press, 1980).

[35]A good description of this controversy can be found in: Allan Tupper, "Pacific Western Airlines," in Allan Tupper and G. Bruce Doern, eds., *Public Corporations and Public Policy in Canada* (Montreal: The Institute for Research on Public Policy, 1981), pp. 293-299.

[36]Richard Schultz, "The Regulatory Process and Federal-Provincial Relations," in Doern, ed., *The Regulatory Process in Canada*, pp. 128-131 and passim.

[37]Vandervort, *Political Control of Independent Administrative Agencies*, pp. 40-42.

agencies adopt the position that provincial governments have the same status as any other intervener.

Compliance

Traditionally, it has been assumed that regulatees will automatically comply with the rulings of regulatory agencies; agencies have a number of mechanisms such as the imposition of fines or the lifting of licences that tend to ensure compliance. For this reason, the question of compliance has received little study. However, there is a growing understanding that ensuring compliance can be a real problem because regulatees can circumvent rulings in both subtle and overt ways.

Some of the best examples of subtle evasion are in the area of broadcasting regulation. The CRTC usually issues a licence to a broadcasting company with the condition that it provide a certain level of Canadian content. After a period of operation, the licensee sometimes argues that it has not quite fulfilled its obligation for economic or practical reasons. The CRTC is then confronted with a difficult dilemma. It can either lift the licence of the company and leave an area with reduced or, in some cases, no service, or it can slap the company on the wrist and ask it to do better in the future. So far, the CRTC has usually pursued the latter course and been subjected to some criticism for being too weak. It would likely be subjected to equal criticism from other quarters if it pursued the firmer course. Thus, in the real world, compliance is not as automatic as some assume.

There are also examples of more overt refusals to comply with agency directives. Some of the most awkward examples of overt refusals have occurred as a result of federal-provincial disputes,[38] but the most colourful incidents occurred in the mid-1970s when the dish-type satellite-receiving antennas were illegal. On numerous occasions when RCMP officers attempted to seize these devices at remote mining or lumber camps, they were simply chased away by the irate residents, thus prompting one commentator to suggest that while the Mounties may always get their man, they don't always get their dish.[39]

PROPOSALS FOR REFORM

These perceived problems with regulation have generated many proposals for changes in the regulatory process. The most important of these are discussed below.

Deregulation

As its name suggests, this is not a proposal to reform regulation, but rather a proposal to eliminate it. The basic thrust of this proposal is that regulation is now too heavy-handed, and that the "invisible hand" of the market place is a better means of checking excesses than the heavy hand of government.

---

[38]Richard Schultz, "Regulation and Public Administration," in Kenneth Kernaghan, ed., *Canadian Public Administration: Discipline and Profession* (Toronto: Butterworths, 1983), p. 209.
[39]Ibid.

The first major example of deregulation was in the airline industry in the United States under President Carter. At this point, the jury is still out on the success of this initiative because its consequences are so far-reaching and complex. Fares have definitely been reduced between major cities, and more smaller towns now have air service provided by new, small companies operating energy-efficient propeller equipment. Some major airlines have gone out of business, thus supporting the hypothesis that weak performers are protected by regulation. However, there is some concern that as competition becomes more intense, the large companies that are better able to withstand short-term losses will drive out other companies and an oligopoly will develop.

Steps towards deregulation in Canada have been rather tentative.[40] There has been some discussion of this possibility in both the airline and trucking industries, but there is concern that the Canadian situation might not lend itself to deregulation as readily as that in the United States. The sparse population and smaller capital markets in Canada mean that new competitors might find it more difficult to enter the market. Thus, deregulation in Canada might simply amount to removing the controls which now prevent oligopoly industries from exploiting consumers without adding any other type of protection.

The most vocal critics of deregulation have been the regulated industries themselves. The fact that these companies feel relatively comfortable with the current regime of regulation could provide support for the captive agency theory, which suggests that regulatory agencies act to protect the interests of existing companies and limit excessive competition.

Deregulation might work better in some policy sectors than in others. In some fields, such as air travel and trucking, competition could replace economic regulation. However, if current regulatory mechanisms in the cultural, environmental, and social fields were dismantled, it is difficult to see what mechanisms would replace them. It is noteworthy that the Economic Council of Canada recommended less regulation in many areas, but advocated *more* regulation in areas such as environmental pollution and occupational health and safety.[41]

In sum, deregulation could do much to lighten the burdens which governments sometimes impose on industry. However, because it could unleash some very complex phenomena, its use must be considered very carefully in each policy area before it is attempted.

Sunset Legislation

Sunset legislation has some of the same characteristics as deregulation. The basic idea is that regulatory agencies would be established for a certain finite period of time, and if they were unable to prove their worth over that period, they would be allowed to die.[42] This is a remedy for the frequently discussed phenomenon that a government agency seldom dies, even when its raison d'être seems to

[40]Gil Reschenthaler, Bill Stanbury, and Fred Thompson, "Whatever Happened to Deregulation?" *Policy Options*, May-June 1982, pp. 36-42.
[41]*Reforming Regulation*, esp. chs. 8 and 9. For a good discussion of the balance of issues to consider in deregulation, see pp. 136-138.
[42]Economic Council of Canada, *Responsible Regulation: An Interim Report*, pp. 78-81.

have passed. Under sunset legislation, the onus would be on the agency to prove its continued value.

Statement of Cost Impacts

Another method of making governments more sensitive to the impact of regulatory agencies on society in general is the proposal that all new regulatory initiatives be accompanied by a Regulatory Impact Analysis Statement (RIAS).[43] This statement would contain a quantified listing of the costs and benefits of the proposal that would accrue to both the government and the *private sector*. The significance of the RIAS is that it would for the first time attempt to set out the *total costs* of a particular regulation.

The federal government established a policy of requiring the preparation of *Socio-Economic Impact Analyses* (SEIA) for any major new regulatory initiatives in health, safety and fairness regulation, but not in the area of economic regulation, e.g., rate setting.[44] The SEIA is a statement of costs and benefits considered by Cabinet before a decision is made about adopting new regulations. SEIAs have been prepared in such diverse areas as safety of 1.5 litre soft drink bottles, transportation of dangerous goods, and automotive lead emissions.

One companion recommendation which has not been implemented is a regulatory budget. "A *regulatory budget* . . . identifies and sets limits on the regulatory compliance costs that a department or agency can impose on the private sector."[45] The problem was identified earlier that regulation is the low-cost option for government, but it could impose significant costs on the private sector. This proposal would allocate a regulatory budget to each department and agency that would include both agency and private sector costs. Programs would then have to be juggled in such a manner that this budget would not be exceeded. This would impose an additional discipline on agencies and force them to consider the costs which they impose on the private sector when they are regulating.

More Consumer Involvement

The significance of greater consumer involvement in the regulatory process is clear, but there are so many specific proposals to accomplish this that it is impossible to cover more than a few of them here. They are all designed to put the consumer on a more even footing with the producer.

Consumers' Associations. Among the associations representing Canadian consumers are the broad-based Consumers' Association of Canada and specific associations representing such groups as automobile owners and airline travellers. For reasons discussed earlier, it is usually felt that these associations are somewhat weaker than the producers and producers' associations with which they must do battle. Therefore, it is sometimes suggested that the strength of these consumers' groups ought to be bolstered. The usual suggestion is an infusion of

[43]Ibid., pp. 76–77.

[44]*Report on Regulatory Reform* (A review published periodically by the Office of Regulatory Reform), Issue No. 3 (March 1982).

[45]Canada, House of Commons, Special Committee on Regulatory Reform, *Report* (Ottawa: Minister of Supply and Services Canada, 1981), p. 13. (Emphasis added.)

government funding, tax incentives, or some payments from the regulated industry.

Funding for Interveners. Another proposal is that the regulated industry and/or its association should provide funding to all legitimate interveners in regulatory proceedings. Regulated industries point to the difficulties of controlling costs and of distinguishing legitimate from nuisance interveners.

The Agency as Advocate. The current legal situation of the agency is that it is an impartial referee between the various interests before it. It has been proposed that the agency should instead be charged with defending the interests of the consumer. This proposal would weight the regulatory process in favour of the consumer, and so place the onus on the industry to prove the efficacy of its claim for higher rates or different service levels.

Consultation and Advance Notice

Another way of involving both consumers and regulatees in the regulatory process is to require agencies to consult with affected groups to identify and define problems even before definite action is contemplated. The Economic Council of Canada has recommended that this general consultation procedure be supplemented by a two-step Advance Notice System.[46] The first step would be to provide a formal notice of intent to modify regulations, either through a notice in the *Canada Gazette*, or through an annual regulatory calendar that would list major regulations (and significant background information) which the government plans to issue in the following eighteen to twenty-four months. This would provide an opportunity for those affected to argue their cases. Then, the proposed regulations, accompanied by the Regulatory Impact Analysis Statement, would be published, followed by a ninety-day comment period before the regulations became official.

One of the current major complaints of businesses and consumer groups is that regulations are imposed without prior notice and without an understanding of the difficulties of compliance. The purpose of these procedures is to allow for input into the regulatory process by all those affected by it *before regulations are established.*

The federal government responded to this concern by publishing a semi-annual "Regulatory Agenda" beginning in 1983.[47] These agendas include information about possible changes in regulations administered by some federal departments and agencies. This procedure provides those affected with an opportunity to make their views known in advance of the full development of regulations by departments.

Resolving the Accountability-Autonomy Conundrum

A number of different proposals have been made to resolve the apparent conflict between the need for both accountability to political forces and some autonomy from the vagaries of partisan politics.

---

[46] Economic Council of Canada, *Responsible Regulation: An Interim Report*, pp. 74-76.
[47] See, for example, Supplement to the *Canada Gazette*, Part I, May 25, 1985.

Douglas G. Hartle has recommended that all agencies be designated as either *advisory agencies* or *decision-making agencies*.[48] The *advisory agencies* would emphasize accountability in that they would conduct research in their policy field and *advise* the government concerning new policy initiatives. These agencies would differ from operating departments in that they would have an element of independence in the manner in which they gathered evidence and prepared recommendations. They could hold public hearings and present their advice to the minister publicly. However, accountability would be emphasized with these kinds of agencies because the minister would be able to accept or reject the advice offered.

Decision-making agencies would emphasize autonomy. These agencies would be guided by government policy directives in making decisions on individual cases, but their decisions could not be overturned by politicians, except in exceptional circumstances. This is similar in some ways to a proposal made earlier by the Ontario Committee on Government Productivity, which would also have had the effect of classifying agencies according to their major function and assigning different amounts of independence to them accordingly.[49]

Classification schemes such as these possess the virtues of simplicity and clarity. However, they might be too abstracted from the real world to be very useful. The accountability-autonomy conundrum simply reflects the love-hate relationship which many Canadians have with politicians. On the one hand, we mistrust politicians and fear that they will act for improper, self-serving motives. On the other hand, we sometimes see appeal to politicians as a way of escaping the tyranny of the bureaucracy. It might well be that there is no simple way out of this accountability-autonomy dilemma. The ideal arrangement might involve a continued balancing of the two to ensure both are present in appropriate levels in the decision-making process.

Policy Directives

One recommendation which would modify the current accountability regime suggests that Cabinet should be able to issue policy directives to regulatory agencies.[50] Through this means the government could convey its desires with regard to particular policy areas to the regulatory agency before the agency made any specific decisions. This would allow the regulated industry, consumers, and other interested parties to know what the rules of the game were before they started to play. It would also improve accountability, because it would make it clear when the agency was acting at the request of the government and when the agency was making its own policy.

Better Accountability to Parliament

There is also a perceived need for better accountability to Parliament, which is the ultimate source of the authority of all regulatory agencies. The House of

[48]*Public Policy Decision Making and Regulation* (Toronto: Institute for Research on Public Policy, 1979), pp. 131–133.
[49]*Report Number Nine* (1973), pp. 40–45.
[50]Canada, House of Commons, Special Committee on Regulatory Reform, *Report*, pp. 15–17.

Commons Special Committee on Regulatory Reform has pointed out that:

> The Standing Joint Committee on Regulations and other Statutory Instruments reviews regulations and other published statutory instruments using criteria that relate to the legality and propriety of the measures examined. There is, however, no analogous arrangement facilitating parliamentary examination of subordinate legislation from the point of view of policy or merit.[51]

The committee went on to recommend a considerably enhanced parliamentary committee system in which each of the standing committees would review the activities of regulatory agencies in its substantive area. Specifically, the committees would monitor the regulatory process in general, review the merits of specific regulations, and review regulatory activities using the program evaluations prepared under the auspices of the Office of the Comptroller General. These and other recommendations of the committee were all geared to improving the accountability of regulatory agencies to Parliament.

The Provincial Role in the Federal Regulatory Process

As mentioned earlier, one of the sore points with provincial governments is that their interests are sometimes very directly affected by the actions of federal regulatory agencies, yet they have no special status with regard to those agencies. The federal government also experiences embarrassment in this area because it is sometimes unable to issue directives to its regulatory agencies, even in areas in which it has entered into an agreement with a province.[52]

One of the most radical remedies suggested is that there should be some "regulatory sharing" between the federal and provincial governments.[53] This would involve a mixture of federal and provincial supervision of an industry. This might mean that certain aspects of the licensing process which are of great concern to the provinces could be delegated to them. This proposal is by its nature unclear because the precise arrangements would have to vary in different policy areas. There is currently an example of this kind of sharing in the cable television field in Manitoba and Saskatchewan.[54]

Another proposal is that provincial governments should have some role in the appointment of members of federal regulatory agencies. There are constitutional reasons why provincial governments could not directly make these appointments, but provincial governments could be allowed some input in appointments made by the federal government through such mechanisms as recommending a slate of acceptable people or commenting on people proposed by the federal government.

Another proposal for change would allow the federal government to issue directives to any federal regulatory agency in an area in which a federal-provincial agreement existed. This would require the agency to make decisions based on the terms of the agreement.

---

[51]Ibid., p. 24.
[52]Vandervort, *Political Control of Independent Administrative Agencies*, pp. 91–92.
[53]Schultz, *Federalism and the Regulatory Process*, pp. 89–91.
[54]Vandervort, *Political Control of Independent Administrative Agencies*, pp. 90–94.

The impact of regulatory agencies on federalism (and vice versa) is a general area that bears watching over the next few years, because federal-provincial relations could become extremely tense if federal regulatory agencies do not deal with provincial concerns in a sensitive manner.

More Co-participation and Fewer Binding Decisions

Traditionally, the economic kinds of regulatory agencies have borrowed some trappings from the courts in that they hear arguments concerning an issue, go away to discuss it, and return from on high with a decision which is binding on all parties. There is no room for negotiation or compromise between the parties after the process has started.

The newer cultural, environmental, and social agencies sometimes behave a bit differently. The Foreign Investment Review Agency, in its original form, was a classic example of this. The main part of the application process involved detailed negotiations between the agency and the investor to determine what benefits the investor would be willing to provide to Canada in exchange for the right to do business in the country. Thus, rather than presenting an all-or-nothing decision, the agency was free to discuss the overall situation with the applicant and work out an arrangement that was beneficial to all. It is sometimes argued that this co-participative style is likely to be the style of the future.

Office of Regulatory Reform

In 1979 the federal government established the Office of the Coordinator, Regulatory Reform (later renamed the Office of Regulatory Reform) within the Treasury Board. The role of the office is to provide advice about regulatory matters to Cabinet, regulatory agencies, and other agencies of the federal government.[55] In particular, the office has been concerned with the publication of the Regulatory Agendas, the preparation of Socio-Economic Impact Analyses, and the simplification of records retention requirements for businesses.

The office was originally established as a short-term project, but has since become a permanent program. This indicates the commitment of the federal government to a serious attempt at regulatory reform.

Similar initiatives have been undertaken in some provinces. Saskatchewan initiated a Regulatory Reform Project in 1982, the major strategies of which are to:

1. REFINE existing regulatory programs to make them more efficient;
2. REMOVE those regulatory requirements that may be excessive, repetitious, obsolete or questionable;
3. REPLACE direct regulation with new streamlined and cost-effective methods of government support and/or indirect intervention.[56]

In the first three years of the program, 1,354 regulations and eight statutes were repealed as obsolete. Departments proposing new regulations are now required

[55]*Report on Regulatory Reform*, Issue No. 1 (September 1981).
[56]Saskatchewan, *General Framework for Regulatory Reform* (photocopy).

to prepare an impact assessment, which is reviewed first by a Regulatory Review Committee composed of government members of the legislature, and then by Cabinet, before new regulations can be put into effect.

CONCLUSION

The most common organizational forms used by governments are the operating department, the Crown corporation, and the regulatory agency. In this and the previous two chapters these forms have been discussed and the reasons for choosing one to accomplish a particular objective have been considered. However, the story is not quite complete yet. There are a number of other organizational forms which are used less frequently, but are still important for an overall understanding of the operations of government. The next chapter will consider some of these other forms such as Royal commissions, task forces, and advisory councils.

BIBLIOGRAPHY

Bernier, Ivan, and Andrée Lajoie, eds. *Regulations, Crown Corporations and Administrative Tribunals*. Research study for the Royal Commission on the Economic Union and Development Prospects for Canada, vol. 48. Toronto: University of Toronto Press, 1985.

Bernstein, Marver H. *Regulating Business by Independent Commission*. Princeton, N.J.: Princeton University Press, 1955.

Brown-John, C. Lloyd. *Canadian Regulatory Agencies*. Toronto: Butterworths, 1981.

Canada. House of Commons. Special Committee on Regulatory Reform. *Report*. Ottawa: Minister of Supply and Services Canada, 1981.

Canada. Office of Regulatory Reform. *Report on Regulatory Reform*. Various issues.

Canada. Privy Council Office. *Submissions to the Royal Commission on Financial Management and Accountability*. Minister of Supply and Services Canada, 1978.

Canada. Senate and House of Commons. Standing Joint Committee on Regulations and Other Statutory Instruments. *Minutes and Proceedings*, no. 1, February 16, 1984.

Doern, G. Bruce, ed. *The Regulatory Process in Canada*. Toronto: Macmillan of Canada, 1978.

Economic Council of Canada. *Reforming Regulation*. Ottawa: Minister of Supply and Services Canada, 1981.

Economic Council of Canada. *Responsible Regulation: An Interim Report*. Hull: Minister of Supply and Services Canada, 1979.

Hartle, Douglas G. *Public Policy Decision Making and Regulation*. Toronto: Institute for Research on Public Policy, 1979.

Hull, W. H. N. "Captive or Victim: The Board of Broadcast Governors and Bernstein's Law, 1958-68." *Canadian Public Administration*, vol. 26 (Winter 1983): 544-562.

Law Reform Commission of Canada. *Report on Independent Administrative Agencies: A Framework For Decision Making*, Report 26. Ottawa: Law Reform Commission of Canada, 1985.

Ontario. Committee on Government Productivity. *Report Number Nine* (1973).

Reschenthaler, Gil, Bill Stanbury, and Fred Thompson. "Whatever Happened to Deregulation?" *Policy Options* (May–June 1982): 36–42.

Saskatchewan. *General Framework for Regulatory Reform*. Photocopy.

Schultz, Richard J. *Federalism and the Regulatory Process*. Montreal: Institute for Research on Public Policy, 1979.

Schultz, Richard J. *Federalism, Bureaucracy, and Public Policy: The Politics of Highway Transportation Regulation*. Montreal: McGill-Queen's University Press, 1980.

Schultz, Richard J. "Regulatory Agencies and the Canadian Political System." In *Public Administration in Canada: Selected Readings*, 4th ed., edited by Kenneth Kernaghan. Toronto: Methuen, 1982, pp. 70–80.

Schultz, Richard J. "Regulation and Public Administration." In *Canadian Public Administration: Discipline and Profession*, edited by Kenneth Kernaghan. Toronto: Butterworths, 1983, pp. 196–210.

Trebilcock, Michael J., Douglas G. Hartle, J. Robert Pritchard, and Donald N. Dewees. *The Choice of Governing Instrument*. Ottawa: Minister of Supply and Services Canada, 1982.

Tupper, Allan. "Pacific Western Airlines." In *Public Corporations and Public Policy in Canada*, edited by Allan Tupper and G. Bruce Doern. Montreal: The Institute for Research on Public Policy, 1981, pp. 285–317.

Vandervort, Lucinda. *Political Control of Independent Administrative Agencies*. Ottawa: Law Reform Commission of Canada, 1979.

Willis, John, ed. *Canadian Boards at Work*. Toronto: Macmillan of Canada, 1941.

CASES

In *Case Program in Canadian Public Administration* (Toronto: Institute of Public Administration of Canada):

The Grain Dust Case: Public Policy Analysis and Regulation, by G. Bruce Doern and John Kowalski

Regulatory Decision: Airlines, by Peter Clancy

9

Other Non-departmental Organizations

The most commonly used forms of government organization are the operating department, the regulatory agency, and the Crown corporation discussed in detail in the previous chapters. However, a number of other organizations and instruments which are less widely used are still very important. These include Royal commissions, task forces, and advisory councils. These forms of organization provide the Cabinet and individual ministers with alternative sources of policy advice beyond that provided by public servants. This chapter also discusses a non-organizational means of obtaining such advice — the mechanism of coloured papers. Some other important types of organization, such as interdepartmental task forces and intergovernmental committees, are dealt with in Chapters 14 and 17, respectively.

The dominant theme of Part II of this book is the choice of organizational form — why governments choose particular organizational forms to respond to particular problems. A common characteristic of all of the forms discussed in this chapter is that they are more involved in *consulting* or *researching* than in *implementing* or *doing*. Frequently, the problems faced by a government are so severe and far-reaching that the government must study the situation carefully and seek policy advice widely before it acts, so that it does not act unwisely. Cynics would likely argue that some of the instruments discussed below are really "non-responses" geared to distracting people's attention and making it appear that government is interested, when in fact the desire is simply to defer consideration of something until later, possibly after the next election.

> Even where such comment has been perceptive, its implied criticism may have been misplaced. Institutionalized delay may have its merits where no adequate consensus for action exists. Grasping a nettle firmly is a fairly reliable formula for experiencing pain, but not necessarily for making progress. In any event, it is clear that in the case of a large majority of Royal commissions and task forces of recent years the object has been enlightenment, not evasion. Their aim has been to achieve more wide-spread public understanding of questions at issue and a more informed basis for policy choices by the decision-makers.[1]

---

[1]Ronald S. Ritchie, *An Institute for Research on Public Policy* (Ottawa: Information Canada, 1971), p. 8.

ROYAL COMMISSIONS AND TASK FORCES

The federal Inquiries Act provides for three types of inquiries. Part II of the Act allows a departmental minister to appoint a commissioner or commissioners for the purposes of a departmental investigation. These kinds of commissions are more limited in scope and less formal and public than the Royal commissions and task forces discussed in this chapter. Part IV of the Act empowers the Governor in Council to allow an international commission to carry on a portion of its work in Canada. This is a very specialized kind of arrangement and will not be discussed in this chapter.

Part I of the Inquiries Act governs those commissions with a much higher profile, such as the Royal commissions and task forces. It stipulates that the Governor in Council, i.e., Cabinet, may "cause inquiry to be made into and concerning any matter connected with the good government of Canada or the conduct of any part of the public business thereof."[2]

Royal commissions and *task forces* are temporary organizations constituted to investigate either specific incidents or general policy concerns and report to government. They usually go out of business after the delivery of their report, and so are not involved in the implementation of any of their recommendations.

There are more similarities than differences between task forces and Royal commissions. The Law Reform Commission of Canada has suggested that there is little reason to make a distinction between the two. "The adjective 'royal' is much abused, with some commissions technically entitled to its use not employing it, and others appropriating it when they have no business doing so. In our view, the term is best ignored."[3] In this section, the advice of the commission will be followed, and there will a discussion of commissions appointed under Part I of the Inquiries Act without regard to the term used to describe any particular commission. However, there are some distinctions which are sometimes drawn between the two forms.[4]

Royal commissions are more formal in their organization. For example, the members of the commission are appointed, and its mandate is assigned by an order in council. A task force might receive its mandate by a letter from the Prime Minister or another minister. Royal commissions are used for major tasks requiring lengthy analysis; task forces emphasize speed of reply. Royal commissions conduct most of their proceedings in public and produce *public* reports containing recommendations to the government. Task forces can report publicly, but are frequently asked to report privately. Public reports are harder for the government to ignore than private ones. As noted above, one should not make too much of these differences; there is wide variance in individual cases, and the statements of tendency mentioned above do not always apply.

---

[2]R.S.C. 1970, c. I-13, s. 2.

[3]*Commissions of Inquiry* (Ottawa: Minister of Supply and Services Canada, 1977), p. 5.

[4]These differences in form and tone are discussed in M. J. Trebilcock, et al., *The Choice of Governing Instrument* (Ottawa: Minister of Supply and Services Canada, 1982), p. 40; and V. Seymour Wilson, "The Role of Royal Commissions and Task Forces," in G. Bruce Doern and Peter Aucoin, eds., *The Structures of Policy-Making in Canada* (Toronto: Macmillan of Canada, 1971), pp. 115, 121–126.

Commissions appointed under the Inquiries Act have been a very popular device in Canada; between 1867 and 1979, 425 of them were established.[5] In the Trudeau era, the task force appointed under Part I or Part II of the Inquiries Act became more popular than the full-blown Royal commission in terms of numbers, but Trudeau is responsible for the largest Royal commission by almost any measure — the Royal Commission on the Economic Union and the Development Prospects for Canada (Macdonald Commission).

Commissions can be appointed to delve into any area the government desires, but Hodgetts has identified four major areas in which commissions have been active.[6]

- Catastrophic incidents — train wrecks, air disasters, bridge collapses;
- Social or cultural problems of national importance — broadcasting, arts and sciences, bilingualism and biculturalism;
- Economic matters — transportation, banking and finance, corporate concentration, economic future of the country; and
- Government organization — financial and personnel management, morale in the foreign service.

The purposes for which commissions have been used have changed over time. Writing in 1964, John Courtney identified a trend which continues to this day:

> The trend, therefore, of recent royal (sic) commissions has been away from investigations important only to a limited number of people or a restricted geographic area and toward examinations of importance to the Canadian people as a whole. The changing pattern may be characterized as one away from "intensive" inquiries, of only limited significance, to one of "extensive" inquiries, of national significance. The effect of the changing pattern has been to turn the royal commission of inquiry into an investigatory technique suitable for publicizing group sentiments on a national basis and for formulating national objectives. The modern royal commission has become, in effect, a vehicle by which individuals, groups and governments are permitted to state their views on matters of concern to the nation as a whole.[7]

Reasons for Use

Several reasons why governments would use the Royal commission or task force form of organization rather than some of the more permanent structures dis-

---

[5]George Fletcher Henderson, *Federal Royal Commissions in Canada, 1867–1966: A Checklist* (Toronto: University of Toronto Press, 1967). This has been updated by Denise Ledoux, *Commissions of Inquiry Under the Inquiries Act, Part I: 1967 to date* (Ottawa: Library of Parliament, 1980). These figures are reasonably accurate, but exact numbers are virtually impossible to confirm. Law Reform Commission of Canada, *Commissions of Inquiry*, p. 10.

[6]J. E. Hodgetts, "The Role of Royal Commissions in Canadian Government," in *Proceedings of the Third Annual Conference of the Institute of Public Administration of Canada* (1951), pp. 354–355.

[7]John Childs Courtney, "Canadian Royal Commissions of Inquiry, 1946 to 1962: An Investigation of an Executive Instrument of Inquiry" (Ph.D. diss., Duke University, 1964), p. 121. J. E. Hodgetts makes a similar distinction in "Public Power and Ivory Tower," in Trevor Lloyd and Jack McLeod, eds., *Agenda 1970: Proposals for a Creative Politics* (Toronto: University of Toronto Press, 1968), pp. 271–278.

cussed in earlier chapters are discussed below. All of the organizations and instruments discussed in this chapter have in common a concern with study and consultation rather than implementation. As will be discussed later, this is both the strong and the weak point of the commission form.

Identify Innovative Approaches. Commissions usually employ people from outside the public service. It is hoped that they will be able to take a fresh look at some problem and propose an innovative solution. The Royal Commission on Financial Management and Accountability (Lambert Commission) was composed of a bank president, a political scientist, a former public servant, and an accountant with both business and public sector experience. In this case, the combination of members with public service experience and outsiders with a fresh view produced some innovative ideas about changes in government structures.

This positive point highlights a potential problem for the government. Governments do not have as much control over the activities or final conclusions of Part I commissions as they have over departmental or Part II task forces. Independent commissions report publicly, and their recommendations cannot be ignored by the government. Politicians are aware that they are unleashing a potentially very powerful force by creating an independent commission, and so are reluctant to use this device in circumstances where they feel a need to control or at least influence the outcome.

On the other hand, where governments can make a valid case against the proposals of a commission, they are somewhat freer to reject advice from an independent commission than they would be from a body more closely related to the government.

> This lack of accountability then preserves flexibility for the politician at the conclusion of the inquiry, in that at that point he is free either to embrace warmly the results or to indicate that he is not bound to accept the inquiry results. In contrast to this, in those situations where the inquiry is directly accountable to the politician, he is less able to disown the results.[8]

Fact-finding. Royal commissions and task forces are frequently established to investigate disasters or questionable activities to determine exactly what happened and recommend measures to prevent their recurrence. The Foisy Commission inquiry into the serious train accident outside Edmonton in 1986 is an example of an investigation of a disaster; the McDonald Commission[9] of the late 1970s, which investigated certain alleged wrongdoings of the Royal Canadian Mounted Police, is an example of an investigation of questionable activity.

Postpone an Embarrassing Problem. It is sometimes suggested that governments have established commissions merely to ensure that a problem is temporarily placed on the back burner, and that, with luck, the problem might go away altogether. The Royal Commission on Corporate Concentration was

[8]Trebilcock, *The Choice of Governing Instrument*, p. 45.
[9]Canada, Commission of Inquiry Concerning Certain Activities of the Royal Canadian Mounted Police, *Report* (Ottawa: Minister of Supply and Services Canada, 1981).

appointed when Paul Desmarais of Power Corporation was attempting to take over the giant Argus Corporation. The takeover bid was unsuccessful, and no action was taken on the recommendations of the Royal commission.

The delay caused by the use of the commission form is a frequent source of criticism:

> One can almost predict that nothing will be done without a Commission and in fact often not much is done with a Commission except to pass it on to the next Commission. It is a kind of commission chain letter process. Governments have been known to avoid a head-on collision with an issue for upwards of fifty years as was the case with the nationalization of wheat marketing.[10]

Stimulate Interaction with the Public. Royal commissions are frequently established as a two-way communications link — both obtaining the views of members of the public on an issue and communicating important facts to them. Some commissions invite the participation of the public through the presentation of written briefs or appearance before the commission.[11] The Task Force on National Unity (Pepin-Robarts Commission) travelled extensively and heard the views of many Canadians on this very emotional issue.

Commissions also arrange for research to be done on the problem at hand and prepare interim reports in an attempt to improve the level of discussion of the issue. These reports are frequently used to begin to sell the ultimate conclusions of the commission to the public and politicians.

Low-cost Way of Showing Concern. Governments are frequently under great pressure to prove that they recognize a particular problem and are striving to resolve it. A full-scale attempt to solve the problem will likely be expensive; commissions are often somewhat expensive, but the expense is almost certainly less than the expense of actually solving the problem.

> In sum, all public inquiries offer to politicians the opportunity to demonstrate concern about a policy issue and to indicate that action is being taken upon it, while deferring the need to expend substantial resources in response to a perceived policy concern.[12]

Operation

The order in council which establishes a commission sets out the mandate of the commission, the names of the commissioners, and, sometimes, the date by which it must report.

In the past, it was common for commissions to be headed by a single commissioner, frequently a judge. This reflects the investigatory nature of some com-

[10]Meyer Brownstone, "To Commission or not to Commission: As An Advisory Body," *Canadian Public Administration*, vol. 5 (Fall 1962), p. 261.

[11]For an analysis of the extent of this kind of participation, see Hugh Whalen, "Public Participation and, (sic) the Role of Canadian Royal Commissions and Task Forces: 1957-1969," Paper presented to the Annual Conference of the Institute of Public Administration of Canada (September 1981), p. 15.

[12]Trebilcock, *The Choice of Governing Instrument*, p. 44.

missions. Even today, commissions with an investigative role are frequently headed by a judge. The benefits of having someone with the expertise and prestige of a judge as a commissioner are fairly clear, particularly where the major role of the commission is investigative. However, where the commission is delving into political matters, the involvement of judges is more problematic. When Justice Willard Estey of the Supreme Court of Canada was appointed to investigate the collapse of the Canadian Commercial and Northland Banks, James Snell and Frederick Vaughan were strongly critical:

> The use of the judiciary, particularly members of the Supreme Court, to deal with political problems is a practice which should be ended for several reasons. First, it draws judges into political controversy. In taking advantage of the judicial reputation for non-partisanship, governments are actually maintaining a practice which tarnishes that reputation. The judiciary itself can be, and certainly has been, brought into disrepute through this process.
>
> Second, inquiries such as Judge Estey's are essentailly being asked to examine and comment upon the political judgment of a government. . . .
>
> . . . Why should judges be asked to assess political decisions? Surely that is the job of the electorate or of its elected representatives.[13]

The authors further mention the great work demands facing the court as a result of the large number of Charter cases coming up in the next few years. In recent years, the size of commissions has been expanding and there has been a tendency to appoint people with a diversity of backgrounds including, but not limited to, law.[14] The argument is sometimes made that the commissioners should be representative of the various interests affected by the commission, but this view has been criticized.

> The proper place for special interests is in the witness box, not on the Commission. The generous representation accorded various interests in Britain has, it seems to me, unfortunate consequences. Most members have firmly rooted convictions which no amount of evidence is likely to shake. Unanimous reports for that reason are seldom obtained. But, what is more serious to my mind, minority reports can be used as vehicles for carrying to the public the prejudices of special interests (at the public's expense of course).[15]

The actual activities of the commissions vary considerably depending on their mandate, but they usually involve both public input and academic research components.

The public input aspect also varies widely depending on the nature of the commission. Fact-finding commissions will usually focus on input from the people involved in the incident and experts in the field. Commissions appointed under Part I of the Inquiries Act even have the power to compel reluctant witnesses

---

[13]"Putting Judges in the Political Hot Seat," *The Globe and Mail*, October 10, 1985, p. A7.
[14]Henderson, *Federal Royal Commissions in Canada, 1867–1966* and Ledoux, *Commissions of Inquiry Under the Inquiries Act, Part I: 1967 to date*.
[15]Hodgetts, "The Role of Royal Commissions in Canadian Government," p. 358.

to attend.[16] Sometimes, commissions will cast their net considerably wider to seek the views of a cross-section of the public. The Pepin-Robarts Commission, mentioned above, was one of the clearest examples of this.

Commissioners also usually arrange for academic research to provide them with some background on the issue under review, e.g., the history of the issue, how is it handled in other countries. This usually involves hiring academics or consultants to produce background papers, which may or may not be published and made available to the public. The Macdonald Royal Commission on the Economic Union and Development Prospects for Canada employed several study teams that produced almost three hundred studies, ultimately published in seventy-two volumes.[17]

Some commissions produce interim reports to advise the public of the direction in which their thinking is going; this could incite some additional public participation. The commission always produces a final report containing its analysis of the situation and some recommendations. The commission's final report can sometimes be accompanied by a minority report, or a dissent from some part of the majority report if all commissioners are not in full agreement.

The Provincial Scene

This section has focussed mainly on federal Royal commissions and task forces, partly because these are the most widely known and partly because there has been little systematic study of provincial commissions.[18] However, provincial governments have legislation similar to the federal Inquiries Act which provides for the establishment of these kinds of bodies. Some of the areas investigated by provincial bodies seem very similar to those investigated by federal bodies, for example, the Nova Scotia Royal Commission on Pensions (reported 1983) and Manitoba's Task Force on Government Organization and Economy (reported 1978).

Criticisms

The most common criticisms of the commission form of organization relate to cost, delay, and the lack of any implementation mechanism. For a device which was supposed to provide an ad hoc review of a specific problem, modern-day commissions can appear incredibly bureaucratic. Large numbers of people are hired and masses of literature are produced over the several-year life of the commission. When the commissioner is a high-profile person receiving a large per diem payment, the criticism can be even stronger.[19]

---

[16]R.S.C. 1970, c. I-13, s. 4.

[17]For a list of the published reports, see Canada, Royal Commission on the Economic Union and Development Prospects for Canada, *Report: Volume Three* (Ottawa: Minister of Supply and Services Canada, 1985), pp. 679–690.

[18]There is a listing of provincial Royal commissions. Lise Maillet, *Provincial Royal Commissions and Commissions of Inquiry* (Ottawa: Minister of Supply and Services Canada, 1986).

[19]Editorial, "A Royal Waste," *Vancouver Sun*, September 9, 1983; "Macdonald Commission Members Get $350 a Day," *Toronto Star*, May 3, 1983; "Macdonald Commission: Chairman Eager to Demonstrate He's Worth His Wages," *Calgary Herald*, November 10, 1983.

Delay can also be a problem in a situation in which people want some change quickly. They become very frustrated with another study and more paper about an issue that they regard as urgent.

These criticisms must be weighed against the quality of the recommendations and other output of the commission. Even the largest commissions cost considerably less than ordinary operating departments. Commissions have the further benefit of being finite; the costs incurred will continue for only a limited period. Even the delay caused by commissions is frequently beneficial. Commissions are sometimes used to show a government's concern, while simultaneously marking time to see how a situation will develop. The Task Force on National Unity appointed shortly after the election of the Parti Québécois in 1976 is one example of this. Commissions are sometimes used to delay decisions, but it is better to delay and adopt a good solution than to act quickly and do the wrong thing.

The fact that there is usually no mechanism to ensure implementation of commission recommendations is a cause for some concern. This lack of responsibility for implementation could cause commissions to propose utopian recommendations which are effectively useless. On the other hand, it is sometimes argued that entrenched bureaucracies resist implementation of even reasonable recommendations.[20] In any event, with no continuing organization responsible for implementing these recommendations, the likelihood of their adoption is considerably reduced.

However, this criticism must also be considered carefully. Some people have a scoreboard mentality about commission recommendations, in that they record the number of recommendations implemented versus the total number of recommendations. By this measure, few commissions look good. However, a more thoughtful analysis of the *general tone* of commission recommendations suggests that governments have usually taken the recommendations very seriously and implemented at least some portion of them.[21] Also, certain commissions have set a tone for change that goes far beyond any specific recommendation.[22] The classic example of this is the Royal Commission on Bilingualism and Biculturalism, which operated in the late 1960s. There is no question that the status of the French language was considerably enhanced as a result of the attention devoted to the activities of the commission. Counting recommendations in this situation is meaningless.

One criticism of the commission form of organization that has been made in the past is less relevant today. J. E. Hodgetts, among others, has lamented the fact that the commission route was taken too frequently and this prevented the establishment of more permanent research bodies either within departments or as semi-autonomous institutions.[23] This criticism is less apt today than when

---

[20]Wilson, "The Role of Royal Commissions and Task Forces," pp. 119–120.

[21]Courtney, "Canadian Royal Commissions of Inquiry," pp. 140–155, 158.

[22]G. Bruce Doern and Richard W. Phidd, *Canadian Public Policy: Ideas, Structure, Process* (Toronto: Methuen, 1983), pp. 543–544.

[23]"Should Canada Be De-Commissioned? A Commoner's View of Royal Commissions," *Queen's Quarterly*, vol. 70 (Winter 1964), p. 489–490.

Hodgetts made it over twenty years ago. Governments now have a significant research capacity both within the ordinary bureaucracy and in semi-autonomous agencies, such as advisory councils.

ADVISORY COUNCILS

Advisory councils come in such a wide variety that it is very difficult to generalize about them. This section will first discuss some of their general characteristics and then illustrate their activities and functions by a more detailed discussion of two councils.

An advisory council is an organization composed of private citizens created by the government to provide an independent source of advice to a minister. It is established outside the normal departmental bureaucracy and does not ordinarily have responsibility for administering programs.[24]

The members of these councils are private citizens; neither politicians nor public servants ordinarily serve as members. This ensures the council's independence. Another assurance of independence comes from the fact that the council ordinarily provides its advice to the minister publicly, free of any potential laundering by the public service. However, the independence of these advisory councils is limited by the fact that they obtain most, if not all, of their funding from government.

The people who serve on these bodies are sometimes representatives of particular interest groups in that they are asked to serve by the minister after consultation with certain relevant groups. Members are also chosen because of their personal status and expertise. There seems to be no recent study of the characteristics of members of advisory councils, but a somewhat dated study suggested that members of these councils do not exactly constitute a cross-section of society. Managerial and professional types each accounted for about 30 per cent of the membership of the large number of councils surveyed, while "homemakers" accounted for 8 per cent and "factory/industrial workers" accounted for 5 per cent.[25]

Audrey D. Doerr has identified four broad categories of councils:
• central advisory bodies, e.g., Economic Council of Canada;
• functional advisory councils, e.g., Fisheries and Oceans Research Advisory Council;
• granting councils, e.g., Social Science and Humanities Research Council; and
• consultative bodies, e.g., Canadian Advisory Council on the Status of Women.[26]
She goes on to suggest that this diversity means that advisory councils can combine a number of different functions.

As bodies composed of representatives from the private sector, they serve as vehicles for channelling public opinion on particular issues. Conversely,

[24]A few advisory councils do have program responsibilities which can pose some difficulties for them; see Peter Aucoin, "The Role of Functional Advisory Councils," in Doern and Aucoin, eds., *The Structures of Policy-Making in Canada*, pp. 154–178.
[25]C. Lloyd Brown-John, "Advisory Agencies in Canada: An Introduction," *Canadian Public Administration*, vol. 22 (Spring 1979), p. 87.
[26]*The Machinery of Government in Canada* (Toronto: Methuen, 1981), p. 121.

they assist the government in this capacity by generating support for the latter's policies. As independent research centres, they can serve as counterweights to bureaucratic expertise in the departments. Thus, they can serve as critics and consensus builders in the policy process. In providing a link between governmental and private interests, advisory councils can become engaged in the reciprocal exchange of information and opinions. In the case of granting councils, such bodies also serve to define and focus policy issues in applied research and provide technical knowledge in pure research undertakings.[27]

Advisory councils in some form have been around for a long time, but Prime Minister Trudeau established more of them than his predecessors. One of Trudeau's main concerns was to cultivate competing sources of information outside the normal government bureaucracy. Advisory councils are also an example of participatory democracy, which was one of the trappings of the Trudeau era.

Advisory councils are found along a continuum. At one end are the very formal, high-profile, well-staffed advisory councils, such as the Science Council of Canada, which sport many of the trappings of a bureaucracy. At the other end of the spectrum are the very small, low-profile organizations, such as the Canada Employment and Immigration Advisory Council, which have a very small staff frequently seconded from the department. It is easy to illustrate the role of advisory councils by focussing on one organization which fits at the highly organized extreme of the spectrum — the Economic Council of Canada — and one which fits closer to the opposite end — the Canadian Advisory Council on the Status of Women.

Economic Council of Canada

The Economic Council of Canada was founded in 1963 to function as a sort of "permanent Royal commission,"[28] with the objective of improving Canada's economic performance. It operates outside the regular government bureaucracy, with no administrative or program responsibilities. Its major roles are, first, to consider economic policies in the medium and long term and provide advice to the government and, second, to educate the general public about economic issues. It was originally intended to have a consensus-building role as well, but this has fallen on hard times, as will be discussed below.

The council is independent in that it sets its own research agenda and publishes anything it desires without the need to obtain prior government approval. However, it does sometimes receive requests from the Prime Minister to investigate particular areas. It has received such references in the areas of competition policy and regulation, among others. Even in these cases, the council publishes its findings without prior government approval.

The council's main activities involve conducting conferences and publishing various kinds of economic studies. In the period covered by the council's 1984–85

[27]Ibid.

[28]A good description of the rationales for the creation of the council and its early years of operation is contained in R. W. Phidd, "The Role of Central Advisory Councils: The Economic Council of Canada," in Doern and Aucoin, eds., *The Structures of Policy-Making in Canada*, pp. 204–245.

Annual Report, it was involved in symposia on the economic future of the western provinces, energy strategy, government enterprise, and the economic status of women in the labour market.

The council's publication program consists of an *Annual Economic Review*, some other research documents that reflect the views of the council, a large number of background research studies, and a magazine.

The council is composed of a full-time chairperson, two full-time directors, and up to twenty-five other directors all appointed by the Governor General in Council; the chairperson for seven years, the other members for three-year terms.[29]

The directors meets four or five times per year to decide on the general direction of the council's research and the specific content of its *Annual Review* and other publications. In 1985, the twenty-one part-time directors consisted of fourteen business people, four educators, two farmers, and one "former labour leader."[30] Some of the members of the council have backgrounds in economics, but many are chosen because of their general business knowledge and because of their links with other business or research organizations.[31] Politicians, public servants, or other government representatives have never been appointed to the council.

The council is not considered a part of the ordinary public service, but it is a large organization in its own right. In 1986, it employed 133 people plus a number of researchers involved in specific projects on a contract basis. In 1985–86 it had a total budget of just under nine million dollars.[32] The council also hires a number of researchers on a contract basis to carry out specific research projects.

When the council was created, it was hoped that it could engage in consensus building. This was to be done in general by educating the public about economic issues and more specifically by being a forum for *tripartitism* — discussion between business, government, and labour leaders to increase mutual understanding and improve productivity. In the past, the membership of the council included labour leaders, but in recent years they have refused to serve as a protest against various government policies. Thus, the council has not fulfilled its expectations as a consensus builder through no fault of the council.

Most assessments of the value of the council point out that its position outside the government bureaucracy with no program responsibilities is a double-edged sword.[33] On the one hand, the council has the freedom to examine government policy in an independent fashion and comment without prejudice. On the other hand, this very freedom means that the council has no levers to implement its recommendations.[34] The government does not usually comment on the coun-

---

[29]Economic Council of Canada Act, R.S.C. 1970, c. E-1, s. 4.

[30]Economic Council of Canada, *Strengthening Growth: Options and Constraints* (Ottawa: Minister of Supply and Services Canada, 1985), pp. ix–x.

[31]Phidd, "The Role of Central Advisory Councils," pp. 221–222.

[32]*1985–86 Estimates: Part III: Economic Council of Canada* (Ottawa: Minister of Supply and Services Canada, 1985), p. 4.

[33]Ritchie, *An Institute for Research on Public Policy*, pp. 10–12.

[34]Richard W. Phidd and G. Bruce Doern, *The Politics and Management of Canadian Economic Policy* (Toronto: Macmillan of Canada, 1978), pp. 478–480.

cil's publications, but there have been occasions when council publications have "received widespread attention at the political and administrative level (sic)."[35] There are clearly cases where the government has seemed to be pursuing policies championed by the council, although whether that is coincidence is obviously impossible to determine.

Canadian Advisory Council on the Status of Women (CACSW)

The CACSW was formed in 1973 as a result of a recommendation of the Royal Commission on the Status of Women. The mandate of the council is

(a) to bring before the government and the public matters of interest and concern to women; and

(b) to advise the Minister [responsible for the status of women] on such matters relating to the status of women as the Minister may refer to the Council for its consideration or as the Council may deem appropriate.[36]

The council consists of thirty women appointed by order in council to serve three-year terms. Three members work full-time for the council; the other twenty-seven are part-time appointments. According to the *Annual Report*, they are chosen to represent "the regional, cultural, occupational and ethnic diversity of Canada" (p. 4). While the members of the council are not quite as elite as the members of male-dominated councils, they are not exactly a cross-section of Canadian society. Their backgrounds tend to be in small businesses, teaching, nursing, or social service agencies.

The CACSW is a much smaller organization than the Economic Council. It has forty-two permanent employees and a budget of just over two million dollars, all of which comes from the federal government.

The council attempts to influence government in a number of ways. For example, during 1983–84, it presented a brief to the Parliamentary Committee on Pension Reform, arguing that work done in the home should be recognized for pension purposes. It also held informal meetings with a number of government officials and representatives of task forces. For example, it discussed women's views on pornography, prostitution, and divorce law reform with officials of the Department of Justice.

The council produced a number of publications geared to showing the impact of laws and government policies on women. Some of these publications were: *Love, Marriage and Money*, *Prostitution in Canada*, and *Juggling a Family and a Job*. Like the Economic Council, the CACSW has an independent publication policy in that its does not consult with the government before publishing.

Also in 1983–84, the council held a three-day meeting attended by representatives of fifty women's groups. The meeting involved a number of workshops on such issues as the Canada Health Act, the Charter of Rights and Freedoms, and property law.

In a ten-year retrospective on its role, the CACSW argued that it has been instrumental in modifying the Canadian Charter of Rights and Freedoms,

---

[35]Doerr, *The Machinery of Government in Canada*, p. 122.
[36]Canadian Advisory Council on the Status of Women, *Annual Report, 1983–84*, p. 2.

changing laws on sexual assault, division of assets at dissolution of marriage, and citizenship. However, it is quick to note that more remains to be done.[37]

The Provincial and Local Government Scene

Advisory councils are also very widely used in other spheres of government. Some of the provincial councils mirror federal councils, such as the Manitoba Advisory Council on the Status of Women and the Ontario Law Reform Commission. Others are concerned with uniquely provincial concerns, such as Alberta's Irrigation Council and New Brunswick's Fisheries Development Board. Organizations such as heritage advisory councils and economic development councils play an important role in local governments; this will be discussed in more detail in Chapter 25.

Criticisms

One of the most difficult roles for these councils is to maintain their independence from government while at the same time maximizing their influence on government policy. The fact that appointments to these councils are made by government and most (if not all) funding comes from government means that a council that becomes too critical of government policy could jeopardize its existence. However, the government is not well served by a panel of sycophants; such a council would have no credibility with its community and so could not serve its purpose of being a two-way communications link.

This problem is well illustrated by a controversy which developed between the government and the Canadian Advisory Council on the Status of Women during the debate over the new constitution in the early 1980s. The CACSW wanted to hold a major national conference on the effect of the new constitution on women. It was likely that this would develop into a session that would be critical of the constitution and, by extension, of the Liberal government which proposed it. Lloyd Axworthy, the Minister Responsible for the Status of Women, asked the president of the council, Doris Anderson, to postpone the conference. She opposed this, but a majority vote of the council decided to delay it anyway. She then charged that the vote was influenced by inappropriate political interference by Axworthy and resigned from the council along with some other members. She was replaced as president by a women who had actively campaigned for Axworthy in the previous election.[38] This immediately caused a number of women's groups to suggest that this was inappropriate political meddling and destroyed the credibility of the council. *The Globe and Mail* editorialized that: "The effectiveness of the council appears to have been seriously undermined, if not fatally wounded."[39]

A related problem is that it can be very difficult to determine whether accommodative or assertive tactics will maximize a council's influence. Some constitu-

---

[37]The Canadian Advisory Council on the Status of Women, *Ten Years Later* (Ottawa: The Canadian Advisory Council on the Status of Women, 1979).

[38]Editorial, "And the Minister Will Sing My Way," *The Globe and Mail*, January 23, 1981, p. 6.

[39]Ibid.

ents of a council will argue that it should pursue a low-profile policy of influencing the government by friendly persuasion, while simultaneously other constituents will suggest that the best tactic is one of "going public" and bringing overt pressure to bear on the government. Members of councils suggest that the balancing of these two concerns is one of their most difficult tasks.

Advisory councils are also frequently criticized for being the captive of one part of its constituency, rather than speaking in the interests of all members of that constituency. The larger and more diverse the constituency group, the greater this problem becomes. The Canadian Advisory Council on the Status of Women has been attacked from both ends of the political spectrum on this issue.

Advisory councils clearly *can* serve a useful purpose, although they are in an innately difficult position. They must tread a middle course so that they retain credibility with the government, while not being captured by it. They must also be very skilful in balancing the interests of their constituents so that they are not captured by any one group. Maintaining these several different balancing acts is obviously a very difficult exercise.

COLOURED PAPERS

The commissions and councils discussed above are important organizations for fact-finding and consultation. Coloured papers are another set of instruments used for the same purposes.

Coloured papers are documents prepared by government departments to communicate current government thinking on a particular issue to interested individuals or groups and to stimulate public discussion on the issue. One of Canada's foremost students of the use of coloured papers argues that they have three basic purposes:
• to provide information to interested parties;
• to involve Parliament and the public in decision making; and
• to stimulate federal-provincial consultation.[40]

Coloured papers are not always a part of the policy-making process, although they have become more common since the Trudeau era.[41] When both kinds of coloured papers are used, a green paper would be followed by a white paper, although there is no set pattern, and sometimes one is used without the other.

A *green paper* is prepared fairly early in the policy-making process to stimulate discussion about the possibility of changing policy in a particular area. It is *not* a statement of government policy, but rather usually attempts to set out a list of the options which the government is considering and the advantages and disadvantages of each. This is a signal to those interested in a particular policy area that the government is contemplating modifying a policy, and that they should make their views known to the government at this time.

---

[40]Audrey D. Doerr, "The Role of Coloured Papers," *Canadian Public Administration*, vol. 25 (Fall 1982), pp. 370–376.
[41]For a good history of the process, see A. D. Doerr, "The Role of White Papers," in Doern and Aucoin, eds., *The Structures of Policy-Making in Canada*, pp. 180–187.

The phrase "green paper" is used generically to describe all government communications of this sort. The actual colours of the covers of the papers vary widely; it is becoming more common to refer to specific documents by their actual colours, such as the "blue paper" on Crown corporations[42] or the "orange paper" on social security[43] (sometimes irreverently called the "Halloween paper" after its rather garishly coloured cover).

A *white paper* is a statement of government policy. It usually provides a statement of policy in everyday, non-legislative language accompanied by an explanation and defence of the particular course of action chosen. It is the government's way of saying that it has reviewed the thinking in a particular area, possibly through the use of a green paper, and this is its decision about how to proceed. This is the government's opportunity for the "hard sell."

A white paper is less specific than draft legislation, and so groups still have an opportunity to effect some modifications in the government's approach to an issue. However, a white paper is meant to be government policy, and if the government is forced to make a major change after the white paper stage, the Opposition will use this opportunity to embarrass it.

Coloured papers have been prepared on such wide-ranging topics as energy, immigration, social security, and the constitution.[44] It is difficult to think of a major policy field that has not been the subject of a coloured paper.

Coloured papers are handled in a variety of ways after their release. They are frequently sent to parliamentary committees for formal discussion and review. This can sometimes lead to very wide-ranging participation in the policy making process:

> For example, the 1969 paper on tax reform was examined by two parliamentary committees. The Commons committee held a total of 146 meetings and heard 211 briefs presented by 820 individuals. Two sub-committees traveled across Canada and held 31 meetings to hear 68 briefs. In total, 524 briefs and 1,093 letters and other submissions were received by the Commons committee. The Senate committee received a total of 345 briefs from organized groups and individuals, of which it heard 118.[45]

This is an extreme case in terms of numbers of participants, but there is always great interest on the part of certain parties in the discussions on coloured papers.

Coloured papers play an important role in the policy development process because they encourage debate about a policy at a time when the government has that policy under review. Green papers provide a way for the government to gauge the depth and breadth of feelings about an issue without having to commit itself. White papers provide the government with the opportunity to state

---

[42]Canada, Privy Council Office, *Crown Corporations: Direction—Accountability—Control* (Minister of Supply and Services Canada, 1977).

[43]Marc Lalonde, Minister of National Health and Welfare, *Working Paper on Social Security in Canada*, 2nd ed. (1973).

[44]A more complete list of recent coloured papers is contained in Doerr, "The Role of Coloured Papers," pp. 378–379.

[45]Ibid., p. 372.

its case for a particular decision. Both devices encourage citizen participation in the policy-making process and help inform the public.

CONCLUSION

Part I of this book provided an introduction to some of the theories of organization and policy making. Part II built on that by providing a catalogue of some of the organizational forms and instruments employed by Canadian governments. The purpose of this part has been to provide a relatively straightforward description of these various organizations and instruments. Part III will do two things. First, it will breathe some life into the abstract organizational structures dealt with in Part II by discussing the values and characteristics of the people who populate those organizations. Second, it will discuss some of the interactions between and among these several organizations and between them and such parts of their environment as pressure groups and the media.

BIBLIOGRAPHY

Brown-John, C. Lloyd. "Advisory Agencies in Canada: An Introduction." *Canadian Public Administration*, vol. 22 (Spring 1979): 72–91.

Brownstone, Meyer. "To Commission or not to Commission: As An Advisory Body." *Canadian Public Administration*, vol. 5 (Fall 1962): 261–268.

Clokie, Hugh McDowell, and J. William Robinson. *Royal Commissions of Inquiry*. Stanford: Stanford University Press, 1937.

Courtney, John Childs. "Canadian Royal Commissions of Inquiry, 1946 to 1962: An Investigation of an Executive Instrument of Inquiry." Ph.D. diss., Duke University, 1964.

Courtney, John Childs. "In Defense of Royal Commissions." *Canadian Public Administration*, vol. 12 (Summer 1969): 198–212.

Doern, G. Bruce, and Peter Aucoin, eds. *The Structures of Policy-Making in Canada*. Toronto: Macmillan of Canada, 1971.

Doern, G. Bruce, and Richard W. Phidd. *Canadian Public Policy: Ideas, Structure, Process*. Toronto: Methuen, 1983.

Doerr, Audrey D. *The Machinery of Government in Canada*. Toronto: Methuen, 1981.

Doerr, Audrey D. "The Role of Coloured Papers." *Canadian Public Administration*, vol. 25 (Fall 1982): 366–379.

Hanson, Hugh. "Inside Royal Commissions." *Canadian Public Administration*, vol. 12 (Fall 1969): 356–364.

Henderson, George Fletcher. *Federal Royal Commissions in Canada, 1867–1966: A Checklist*. Toronto: University of Toronto Press, 1967.

Hodgetts, J. E. "Public Power and Ivory Tower." In *Agenda 1970: Proposals for a Creative Politics*, edited by Trevor Lloyd and Jack McLeod. Toronto: University of Toronto Press, 1968, pp. 256–280.

Hodgetts, J. E. "The Role of Royal Commissions in Canadian Government," in *Proceedings of the Third Annual Conference of the Institute of Public Administration of Canada* (1951): 351–367.

Hodgetts, J. E. "Should Canada Be De-Commissioned? A Commoner's View of Royal Commissions." *Queen's Quarterly*, vol. 70 (Winter 1964): 475–490.

Law Reform Commission of Canada. *Commissions of Inquiry*. Ottawa: Minister of Supply and Services Canada, 1977.

Ledoux, Denise. *Commissions of Inquiry Under the Inquiries Act, Part I: 1967 to date*. Ottawa: Library of Parliament, 1980.

Maillet, Lise. *Provincial Royal Commissions and Commissions of Inquiry*. Ottawa: Minister of Supply and Services Canada, 1986.

Phidd, Richard W. "The Economic Council of Canada: Its Establishment, Structure, and Role in the Canadian Policy Making System, 1963–74." *Canadian Public Administration*, vol. 18 (Fall 1975): 428–473.

Phidd, Richard W., and G. Bruce Doern. *The Politics and Management of Canadian Economic Policy*. Toronto: Macmillan of Canada, 1978.

Trebilcock, M. J., Douglas G. Hartle, J. Robert S. Prichard, and Donald N. Dewees. *The Choice of Governing Instrument*. Ottawa: Minister of Supply and Services Canada, 1982.

Whalen, Hugh. "Public Participation and, (sic) the Role of Canadian Royal Commissions and Task Forces: 1957–1969." Paper presented to the Annual Conference of the Institute of Public Administration of Canada, September 1981.

III

POLITICS, VALUES, AND PUBLIC ADMINISTRATION

10

Institutional and
Value Frameworks

Part II of this book described the forms of organization in the executive-
bureaucratic sphere of government. However, reading a description of the central components of the machinery of government is somewhat akin to visiting a
silent factory in the dead of night. You can see the machinery and be told how it
is supposed to operate, but you cannot understand how it really works until you
see it humming, whirring, clanking and, occasionally, breaking down. Moreover, you need to see how the operators use the machinery and how they relate
to one another.

Thus a primary purpose of Part III of this book is to explain the ways in which
the machinery of government operates in practice. This part focusses on the
role of the administrative bodies (departments, agencies, boards, and commissions) discussed in Part II and on the bureaucrats who manage them. It examines interaction in the executive-bureaucratic sphere among bureaucrats and
between bureaucrats and Cabinet ministers; it also examines interaction between
bureaucrats and actors outside this sphere, namely legislators, the courts, provincial governments, pressure groups, journalists, and the general public.

To facilitate a coherent treatment in this part of the book of the many interactions between bureaucrats and other political actors, this chapter sets out two
complementary frameworks — the institutional framework and the value framework. These frameworks are based on concepts and insights provided by scholarly writings in public administration, political science, and organization theory.
The final section of this chapter deals with the concept and practice of coordination, which is an extremely important and pervasive process in Canadian
governments.

THE INSTITUTIONAL FRAMEWORK

Such a large number of actors is involved in the public policy process that it is
essential to provide a means of identifying and classifying them. Moreover, since
this book is concerned with the role of *the bureaucracy* in the policy process, it is
necessary to devise a framework that permits a focus on administrative organizations.[1] Thus we have set out below an institutional framework that facilitates
an examination of interactions (1) within administrative organizations, (2)

---

[1] Although it is analytically convenient to speak of decisions being made by institutions and organizations, decisions are in reality made by individuals and groups within these institutions and
organizations.

between and among administrative organizations, and (3) between administrative organizations and actors outside the bureaucracy. The term administrative organization is used here to refer to either a department or a non-departmental body (e.g., Crown corporation, regulatory agency, advisory council).

The Concept of Power

The key concept underlying the institutional framework as well as the value framework discussed later is one that is central to scholarly writings in political science, organization theory, and public administration, namely the concept of *power*. The social science literature contains many varying and conflicting definitions and usages of the term power and the closely related concepts of influence, control, and authority.[2] It is generally agreed that power is a relational concept. It is, therefore, extremely useful for describing and explaining relations between and among organizations, groups, and individuals — and indeed, as we shall see, between and among governments. *Power* is defined here as "the capacity to secure the dominance of one's values or goals."[3] This definition is very similar to that of R. H. Tawney, who defined power as "the capacity of an individual, or group of individuals, to modify the conduct of other individuals or groups in the manner in which he desires, and to prevent his own being modified in a manner which he does not."[4]

Control and influence

There are two forms of power, namely control and influence. *Control* refers to that form of power in which A has authority to direct or command B to do something. For example, a deputy minister wields control over a subordinate when he or she exercises statutory or other authority to order the subordinate to act in a certain way. *Influence* is a more general and pervasive form of power than control. When B conforms to A's desires, values, or goals on such grounds as suggestion, persuasion, emulation, or anticipation, then A exercises influence over B. For example, a deputy minister may influence another deputy minister by persuading him or her to take a particular action. Influence can sometimes cause power to flow in unexpected directions when administrative subordinates who possess special expertise in some field can exercise influence over hierarchical superiors in the form of "authority of expertise" or "expert power." Bachrach and Lawler assert that influence "is the mode of power that both gives subordinates the capability of manipulating superiors and gives superiors the capability

---

[2]For example, some writers use the terms power and influence interchangeably; other writers distinguish power from influence by interpreting power as a force backed by coercive authority. Note that Max Weber "used *power* to refer to the ability to induce acceptance of orders; *legitimation* to refer to the acceptance of the exercise of power because it is in line with values held by the subjects; and *authority* to refer to the combination of the two — i.e., to power that is viewed as legitimate." Amitai Etzioni, *Modern Organizations* (Englewood Cliffs, N.J.: Prentice-Hall, 1964), p. 51.

[3]John F. Pfiffner and Frank P. Sherwood, *Administrative Organization* (Englewood Cliffs, N.J.: Prentice-Hall, 1960), p. 77.

[4]*Equality* (London: Allen and Unwin, 1931), p. 229.

of getting more from their subordinates than is specified in the formal role obligations."[5] They state also that "influence is two-directional in hierarchical relations, but it also applies to horizontal relations not lodged in an authority structure."[6] Thus, for example, influence is at work in interdepartmental and intergovernmental relations.

To exercise control, A must have authority in the sense of having access to the inducements, rewards, and sanctions necessary to back up commands. This is "authority of position" or "position power." A may also exercise influence over B through "authority of leadership" or "personal power," which involves the use of such means as persuasion, suggestion, and intimation rather than direction, supervision, and command. Moreover, authority of position puts A in a favourable position to exercise influence as a result of "the rule of anticipated reactions."[7] Application of this rule is evident in the innumerable instances in which administrative officials "anticipate the reactions" of those who have power to reward or constrain them. Officials tend to act in a fashion that would be applauded — or at least approved — by those whose favour they seek. Thus, those actors ordinarily perceived as exercising control (e.g., hierarchical superiors) can also exercise influence by affecting another actor's decisions in an informal, unofficial — even in an unintentional — way.[8] Heclo and Wildavsky's observation about the British government is equally applicable to Canada: "Most of the time on most issues, ministers, sitting alone at the top of their departmental empire, can exercise their political leadership only through civil servants' second-, third-, or fourth-hand anticipation of ministers' likely reactions."[9]

What distinguishes actors with the capacity to exercise both control and influence from those possessing only influence is that the former have at their disposal sanctions and inducements formalized by law and the organization chart. Influence over administrative organizations and over bureaucrats within these organizations can be exercised by those who do not have legally or formally sanctioned power to command or supervise. For example, pressure groups may seek favours from bureaucrats by offering inducements (e.g., gifts) or imposing penalties (e.g., criticism), but they have no legal or formal capacity to compel compliance to their wishes. This does not mean, however, that such influence cannot be as effective as control or, in some instances, even more effective. A bureaucrat may well grant special favours to pressure groups despite formal directions to the contrary from his or her administrative superior. Thus, influence can be exercised by those without either authority of position or authority of

---

[5]Samuel B. Bachrach and Edward J. Lawler, *Power and Politics in Organizations* (San Francisco: Jossey-Bass Publishers, 1980), p. 41.

[6]Ibid.

[7]The best single treatment of this concept may be found in Carl J. Friedrich, *Man and His Government* (New York: McGraw-Hill, 1963,) ch. 11.

[8]Some organizational theorists distinguish between "formal and informal" controls. In the context of our definition of control and influence, and throughout this book, all controls are of a formal nature; informal controls are subsumed under the broad definition of influences.

[9]Hugh Heclo and Aaron B. Wildavsky, *The Private Government of Public Money: Community and Policy Inside British Politics* (Berkeley: University of California Press, 1974), p. 376.

leadership through a variety of means, including persuasion, friendship, knowledge, and experience.

Internal and External Interactions

The preceding analysis provides the basis for the development of a framework showing the patterns of interaction both within administrative organizations and between these organizations and other participants in the public policy process. These interactions involve in large part the reciprocal exercise of power in the form of control and/or influence. From the perspective of any one organization, these interactions can be classified as internal, external-within government, and external-outside government. This classification is depicted both in Figures 10.1 and 10.2.

Figure 10.1 consists of five concentric circles, with the major actor — an administrative organization — at the centre. The order in which these circles are labelled from the centre outwards represents the organizational proximity of other actors to the organization. Proximity to the centre does not, however, indicate the extent of power exercised over the organization or over officials within the organization. For example, in some situations, a pressure group can exert more power over a department than a central agency can.

The innermost circle one depicts the internal pattern of interaction, that is, the administrative organization and its sub-units. For the sake of simplicity, the organization's administrative pyramid has been greatly compressed to indicate merely the major lines of interaction within the organization. Circles two and three portray the external-within government pattern of interactions, that is, it includes those actors outside the organization but within the particular government under consideration (i.e., other administrative organizations, political executives, legislators, the courts).

The outer limit of circle three is the boundary between actors within and outside government — the external-outside government pattern of interaction. Circle four includes actors in other governments, either in the same sphere or in different spheres of government . Finally, circle five contains the broad range of non-governmental actors (e.g., pressure groups, political parties, journalists). Each of these categories of interaction is covered in later chapters of this part of the book.

This framework for classifying interactions involving bureaucrats and other policy actors is explained in greater detail in Figure 10.2. Here the framework is specifically applied to the parliamentary-Cabinet form of government as it operates in Canada's federal and provincial governments. The framework can be modified slightly to apply to the municipal sphere of government as well. In addition, the framework can be used to examine systematically the vertical and horizontal relations of administrative organizations with other relevant actors and to identify the participants and their interactions in a particular policy field.[10]

---

[10]For an application of the framework to the policy field of aging, see Kenneth Kernaghan and Olivia Kuper, *Coordination in Canadian Governments: A Case Study of Aging Policy* (Toronto: Institute of Public Administration of Canada, 1983).

In Figure 10.2, the three broad patterns of interaction in the first column are subdivided to show the major categories of interaction in which an administrative organization may be involved, namely (1) intraorganizational (e.g., intradepartmental), (2) interdepartmental, (3) executive-bureaucratic, (4) legislative-bureaucratic, (5) judicial-bureaucratic, (6) intergovernmental, and (7) governmental–non-governmental. These various categories of interaction are discussed in Chapters 13 to 19. Thus the institutional framework provides the basis for organizing much of this part of the book.

Figure 10.1
INTERNAL AND EXTERNAL INTERACTIONS OF
ADMINISTRATIVE ORGANIZATIONS

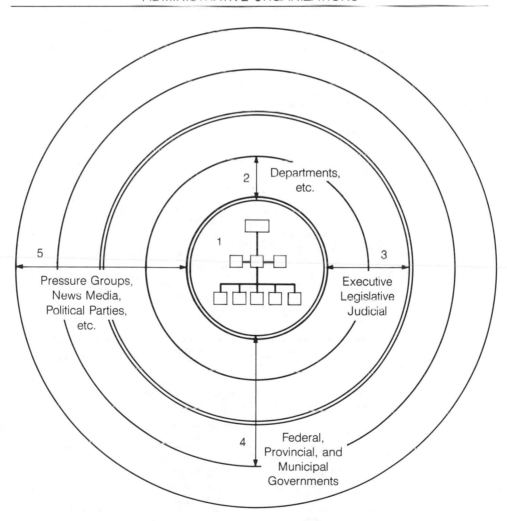

Figure 10.2
INTERNAL AND EXTERNAL INTERACTIONS OF ADMINISTRATIVE ORGANIZATIONS

1 Broad Patterns of Interaction	2 Major Categories of Interaction	3 Actors	4 Power Resources
Internal	Intradepartmental	Line units Staff units Field units	
External (within government)	Interdepartmental	Administrative organization Other administrative organizations	
	Executive- bureaucratic	Administrative organization	Expertise Experience Discretionary power Clientele support
		Prime Minister	Appointment/removal powers Information and advice from central agencies Chairmanship of Cabinet
		Cabinet Central Agencies	
	Legislative- bureaucratic	Administrative organization Parliament Auditor General	
	Judicial- bureaucratic	Administrative organization Federal courts Provincial courts	
External (outside government)	Intergovernmental	Administrative organization Institutions and organizations of other levels of government Intergovernmental bodies	
	Governmental- non-governmental	Administrative organization Non-governmental organizations	

Column three contains a further refinement of these categories into the potential actors in each category. Then column four lists the most significant means by which these actors can exercise control and influence (i.e., power) over one another. The interaction of these actors can be explained largely in terms of power relations, that is, relations between actors for the purpose of, or with the result of, affecting behaviour in a specific direction.

There is insufficient space in Figure 10.2 to provide a detailed list of the actors involved in the policy process and of their power resources (i.e., the means of control and influence available to them). It is evident, however, that column three could usefully be subdivided to show the sub-units of the various actors (e.g., departmental divisions and sections, Cabinet committees, legislative committees). Further, an even finer subdivision could be achieved by identifying individual roles associated with each of the organizations or groups listed in column three (e.g., bureaucrats, ministers, legislators). The effective application of the framework to a particular administrative organization in a specific policy field (e.g., Health and Welfare in aging policy) would require these more detailed subdivisions. In regard to power resources (column four), some elaboration is provided for illustrative purposes for interaction between the administrative organization and the Prime Minister or a provincial Premier.

Power relations between administrative organizations and other actors flow in two directions. Bureaucrats are not defenceless against pressures brought to bear on them by actors outside the bureaucracy. An examination of the real or potential impact of controls and influences over the bureaucracy must take account of the potent resources which bureaucrats can use to resist pressure and to exert power over others. Among the resources which bureaucrats possess to control and/or influence other actors are expertise, experience, budgetary allocations, confidential information, and discretionary powers to develop and implement policies and programs. These resources may be utilized in various ways. For example, bureaucrats may prevail over political superiors by virtue of special knowledge of a policy area (authority of expertise); they may feed selected bits of information to journalists to enhance support for a certain program; or they may disarm external critics by organizing them into advisory bodies.

In summary, the institutional framework can serve several purposes. First, it provides a means of examining interactions among participants in the public policy process and it places administrative organizations at the centre of these interactions. Second, it can be applied at any level of government and can focus attention on a specific administrative body or a specific policy field. Third, it is a heuristic device in that it portrays and suggests relationships that might otherwise be overlooked. Fourth, it is based on a concept in the social science literature that is central to understanding relations between and among governments, institutions, organizations, groups, and individuals, namely the concept of power. Fifth, it utilizes insights from conceptual and theoretical writings in organization theory and provides a linkage between intra- and interorganizational relations. Finally, it provides a systematic way of collecting, ordering, and analysing data.

THE VALUE FRAMEWORK

Values are enduring beliefs that influence the choices made by individuals, groups, or organizations from among available means or ends. Values are organized into value systems in which values are ranked in terms of their relative importance. Thus the bureaucrat has a value system or value framework in which various social, political, administrative, and personal values are ranked, admittedly very roughly, even unconsciously, in order of importance. The focus here is on *administrative* values. The interplay of administrative values with other categories of values will be discussed in Chapter 20.

Situational Considerations

The relative importance of administrative values varies according to "the situation," that is, according to the particular circumstances of time, place, and policy within which value choices are made. The bureaucrat seeking guidance as to the appropriate content of his or her administrative value system will find much advice, but little solace, in scholarly writings. Different authors single out different administrative values. There is, however, substantial overlapping in the values emphasized by various writers. Charles Gilbert, in his analysis of administrative responsibility in the United States, has distilled from the scholarly literature the administrative values of responsiveness, flexibility, consistency, stability, leadership, probity, candour, competence, efficacy, prudence, due process, and accountability.[11]

Since Gilbert's list is taken largely from American literature, it might be culture-bound in its application. The primary values affecting an official's decision tend to differ from one cultural setting and political system to another. A review of *Canadian* administrative history shows that among the most important administrative values are accountability, neutrality, efficiency, effectiveness, integrity, responsiveness, and representativeness. The dominant administrative values of a society, which will be reflected in administrative performance, depend on the complex of political, economic, and social conditions in that society. Moreover, the relative importance of these values alters with changes in these conditions. For example, the administrative values of representativeness and responsiveness may become predominant during a period when the general public or the government feels that the interests of certain disadvantaged minority groups must be better represented and their needs and demands better understood and satisfied. During such a period, considerations of efficiency and neutrality may be relegated to a secondary order of importance.

It is naive to suggest that a bureaucrat should in any given situation consider all the values noted above or rate them as equally important. An official will pay homage to a wide variety of values — but only in application to a number of different situations and at different times. Given the fact that some of these values are sometimes mutually incompatible, it would take considerable mental agility to demonstrate all or even most of these values in a single decision-making

---

[11]Charles Gilbert, "The Framework of Administrative Responsibility," *The Journal of Politics*, vol. 21 (August 1959), pp. 373–407.

situation. In any particular case, a bureaucrat will take into account a limited number of values.

Facts and Values

If an administrative issue is significant enough to require the formal or conscious preparation of alternative solutions and the evaluation of their possible consequences, each alternative will be an amalgam of what Herbert Simon refers to as the value and factual elements in any decision.[12] The mix of fact and value will, of course, vary greatly from one decision-making circumstance to another. Many decisions of a very routine and repetitive nature (programmed decisions) require little, if any, conscious value selection. Other decisions of a unique or novel nature (non-programmed decisions) may contain a substantial mix of value and factual elements. As Herbert Simon contends:

> Decisions are something more than factual propositions. To be sure, they are descriptive of a future state of affairs, and this description can be true or false in a strictly empirical sense; but they possess, in addition, an imperative quality — they select one future state of affairs in preference to another and direct behaviour toward the chosen alternative. In short, they have an *ethical* as well as a factual content.[13]

Sources of the Bureaucrat's Values

A focus on the bureaucrat's values is especially important in that bureaucratic behaviour may be explained or interpreted in terms of the interplay (1) among the individual bureaucrat's values, and (2) between the bureaucrat's values and the values of those with whom he or she interacts. Before an individual joins the public service, his or her general value system, as well as particular attitudes and orientations towards the public service, are moulded by powerful and enduring forces. This is accomplished through the process of socialization, i.e., "an individual's learning from others in his environment the social patterns and values of his culture."[14] The socializing "agencies" involved in this process include family, peer groups, schools, prior employment, and adult organizations. As a result of this socialization experience, an individual does not take up government employment with a *tabula rasa* so far as values relevant to bureaucratic decision making are concerned. In varying degrees, the several socializing agencies continue to affect the bureaucrat's values during his or her public service career. However, the bureaucratic organization which employs the individual is itself a powerful socializing agent. The individual's personal values and perceptions of the public service are altered by a process of *organizational socialization* which begins the very day he or she is recruited for a public service position. Organizational socialization refers to the process (a) through which the individual learns the expectations attached to the position he or she occupies in the organization,

---

[12]Herbert A. Simon, *Administrative Behaviour*, 2nd ed. (New York: The Free Press, 1957), pp. 45–60.
[13]Ibid., p. 46.
[14]Kenneth P. Langton, *Political Socialization* (New York: Oxford University Press, 1969), p. 3.

and (b) through which the individual selectively internalizes as values certain of the expectations of those with whom he or she interacts.

The bureaucrat is located at the focal position or core of a network of counter-positions occupied by such other policy actors as political executives, legislators, and administrative superiors. Each policy actor manifests certain expectations as to how the bureaucrat should behave in his or her official position. These expectations, in the form of commands, directions, guidelines, standards, and suggestions, express the values of the policy actor, and the bureaucrat is expected to reflect these values in his or her decisions.

The Crucial Link

It is precisely at this juncture that the theoretical link between the value framework and the institutional framework can be demonstrated. The bureaucrat is expected to be responsive to the values of the various policy participants as these values are expressed through the exercise of specific controls and influences. The policy participants shown in Figure 10.2 are then the primary sources of the official's administrative values.

Since various policy participants pursue different, and sometimes mutually exclusive, ends in their relations with bureaucrats, the official occupying a certain position will be the object of conflicting expectations and pressures as to his or her behaviour. The purpose of each participant's interaction with the bureaucrat will usually be the dominance of the participant's particular values and goals over those of both the bureaucrat and other participants. The problem for the bureaucrat is clearly posed — how can he or she be responsive to the multiplicity of values expressed?

The linkages between the institutional and the value frameworks help to explain the means by which the number and assortment of variables impinging on the bureaucrat may be reduced to more manageable proportions.

Over a considerable period of time, and in a variety of bureaucratic positions, an official might conceivably interact with virtually the whole range of policy participants and be subjected to a wide variety of controls and influences. As the incumbent of a specific position over a shorter period, an official will, however, only interact with, and be subjected to the power resources of, a limited number of actors. The range of these actors will be confined to those with a stake in either the activities of the official or the issue at hand. For example, a deputy minister of consumer and corporate affairs is the object of much greater pressure from outside the public service (e.g., interest groups and journalists) than a deputy minister of supply and services. More important, during the process of organizational socialization, the bureaucrat learns what kinds of behaviour will bring reward or punishment from various policy actors and what values they are seeking to realize. The bureaucrat's value system is usually most directly moulded by the values of those hierarchical associates on whom he or she relies most heavily for approval and reward, that is, political and administrative superiors and peers and subordinates. The bureaucrat is also expected, of course, to be responsive to the values of such other policy actors as legislators, interest group representatives, and the general public. Faced with complementary, conflicting, and contradictory expectations issuing from various sources, the bureaucrat can inculcate only some of the values manifested by those with whom he or she interacts.

This socialization experience can provide enormous practical and psychological benefits for the bureaucrat. Over time, the bureaucrat internalizes not only a commitment to certain administrative values, but also a commitment to the correctness of applying a value or a set of values to specific situations. He or she develops a value framework which facilitates the making of decisions because there is a point beyond which he or she will not go in contemplating, much less yielding to, pressures in his or her decision-making environment. The bureaucrat will refuse to examine the preset value system *a priori* in each decision situation and will be predisposed to accept or reject the exercise of power (i.e., control and influence) from certain directions.

The existence of this value framework for individual decision making relates also to the earlier discussion of the resources available to bureaucrats to withstand the exercise of power by other policy participants. The situation in which the official chooses to wield countervailing power and the resources he or she selects to control or influence others are in very large measure determined by this value system.

Value Conflict

Despite efforts to minimize the number of variables involved in any given decision-making situation, a condition of value conflict is a frequent one, especially for senior bureaucrats. Herbert Simon contends that at the lower levels of the organization, the framework for decision making is usually well established, in that "the factors to be evaluated have already been enumerated, and all that remains is to determine their values under the given circumstances."[15] At the senior levels of the organization, however, "the task is an inventive one. New values must be sought out and weighed; the possibilities of new administrative structures evaluated. The very framework of reference within which each decision is to take place must be constructed."[16]

The major categories of value conflicts which bureaucrats encounter are those: (1) between personal values and administrative values; (2) between and among administrative values; and (3) between administrative values and the values of other policy participants. The resolution of value conflicts involving personal and administrative values (e.g., ambition v. accountability or avarice v. integrity) depends on the personality and character of the particular bureaucrat. Anthony Downs contends that "most officials are significantly motivated by self-interest when their social function is to serve the public interest."[17] Downs provides a typology of public servants ranging from "purely self-interested officials" (i.e., climbers and conservers) through to "mixed-motive officials" (i.e., zealots, advocates and statesmen). Statesmen are the least self-seeking and most

---

[15]Herbert Simon, *Administrative Behaviour*, 2nd ed. (New York: The Free Press, 1957), p. 217.
[16]Ibid.
[17]Anthony Downs, *Inside Bureaucracy* (Boston: Little, Brown, 1967), p. 87.

public-oriented of bureaucrats. They are "motivated by loyalty to society as a whole and a desire to obtain the power necessary to have a significant influence upon national policies and actions. They are altruistic to a high degree because their loyalty is to the 'general welfare' as they see it."[18] The "statesman" type of public servant will have comparatively little difficulty reconciling personal and administrative values, but will occasionally be obliged to choose between and among administrative values he or she holds equally dear (e.g., accountability v. integrity or accountability v. responsiveness). Similarly, bureaucrats' values come into conflict with the values held by those with whom they interact (e.g., accountability v. responsiveness to an interest group's request or accountability v. efficiency expected by a professional colleague).

Bureaucrats may conceivably pass through one, two, or all three stages of value conflict. In practice, of course, these stages are not chronological; rather, they overlap and interact with one another. Thus, a choice between the administrative values of accountability and responsiveness is likely to be made in conjunction with, and to be affected by, controls and influences reflecting the values of other policy actors. We shall see in Chapter 12 that there is an intimate connection between the resolution of value conflicts and the concept of the public interest.

In summary, the role of the bureaucracy in the public policy process can be illuminated by using the institutional and value frameworks outlined above. The institutional framework may be used separately to examine relationships among bureaucratic actors and between these actors and other participants in the policy process. The value framework complements the institutional framework by showing that the values of individual bureaucrats are significantly affected by the values of those actors who exercise power over them. Thus, the frameworks facilitate the study of issues and concepts in public administration, where an essential basis for further analysis is knowledge of interactions within the bureaucracy and between the bureaucracy and other policy actors. The frameworks are especially useful for examining the nature and extent of coordination within and between governments.[19]

COORDINATION

The foregoing analysis provides a useful basis for examining the concept of *coordination*, which is critically important in the making and administration of public policy in Canada. The Prime Minister, at the centre of the machinery of government, looks out on a vast constellation of administrative organizations ranging from operating departments through central agencies, Crown corporations, and regulatory agencies to advisory councils and Royal commissions. Moreover, beyond the bounds of the federal government is an even larger number of administrative organizations in the provincial and municipal spheres of government with which the federal government must deal. Provincial Premiers face a similar but somewhat smaller array of organizations. It is evident that an

---

[18]Ibid., p. 88.
[19]See, for example, Kernaghan and Kuper, *Coordination in Canadian Governments*.

effort must be made to coordinate the activities of these organizations so as to avoid undue overlap and duplication.

Coordination of both the formulation and implementation of public policy is widely viewed as essential to efficient, effective, and responsive government and is considered especially desirable during periods of financial restraint. Also, public officials (whether politicians or bureaucrats) have become actively involved in coordination through consultative processes with persons and groups affected by official decisions. Consequently, greater attention has been paid in recent years to the coordination of the activities of administrative organizations and to coordination between governments and policy actors outside government. In addition, the challenge of managing intergovernmental relations, especially in federal states, requires increasingly vigorous efforts to coordinate the activities of organizations and officials in two or more orders of government.

Both the general public and public officials frequently bewail the absence or inadequacy of coordination in government. Coordination is often viewed as a means of ensuring that appropriate policy and program decisions are made, duplication and overlap are avoided, and effective and responsive services are provided. It is important, therefore, to dash false hopes and unrealistic expectations about the nature and utility of coordination. It is not a panacea for such government ills as inefficiency, ineffectiveness, and unresponsiveness. Nor is it a substitute for shared values and goals among participants in the policy process. It is evident that coordination can be used to achieve different and sometimes conflicting values and goals (for example, efficiency and responsiveness).

The Meaning of Coordination

Coordination is an extremely elusive and pervasive concept. There are formidable obstacles to seeking it, to achieving it, to recognizing it, and to evaluating its efficacy. Thus, working definitions of coordination and policy coordination will be helpful.

Coordination is a process in which two or more parties take one another into account for the purpose of bringing their decisions and/or activities into harmonious or reciprocal relation. Thus, policy coordination is a process in which two or more policy actors take one another into account for the purpose of bringing their decisions and/or activities with respect to policy development and implementation into harmonious or reciprocal relation. This process can be formal or informal. Note that throughout this book, unless otherwise specified, the term policy coordination encompasses coordination of both the development and implementation of policy. Note also that coordination is pursued both within administrative organizations and between these organizations and other policy actors.

Virtues and Limitations of Coordination

The curative effects of coordination can be impressive, but they are limited. Neither the process nor the outcome of all efforts at coordination is necessarily a good thing. Requirements that coordination be sought through time-consuming consultative techniques (for example, through extensive citizen participation) can lead to delay and indecision that may aggravate rather than remedy a problem. Also, the process of coordination can lead to an outcome of over-coordination. A convincing case can be made that redundancy in the form of duplication and overlap often serves a valuable purpose.[20] Landau contends that " 'streamlining an agency', 'consolidating similar functions', 'eliminating duplication', and 'commonality' are powerful slogans . . . . But it is just possible that their achievement would deprive an agency of the properties it needs most — those which allow rules to be broken and units to operate defectively without doing critical injury to the agency as a whole."[21]

Furthermore, the design and construction of formal structures for coordination do not ensure that coordination will be achieved. With respect to coordination *within* organizations, Andrew Dunsire notes that coordination is what we would expect if the activities of organizing, implementing, programming, and controlling "were all perfectly carried out." But "perfection is not just difficult, it is impossible." Thus the process of coordination involves remedial activity "to supplement basic design, to cope with disaster (or mere change), to bridge communication gaps, to integrate and reconcile different objectives and priorities." This remedial activity can be carried out through formal coordinating mechanisms, but Dunsire concludes that "coordinating activity and the responsibility for initiating it, is part of the bureaucrat's job."[22] In practice, however, unless the responsibility for coordination is specifically assigned as part of the bureaucrat's job description, many bureaucrats feel no burden to pursue it.

With respect to coordination *between* organizations, Andrew H. Van de Ven notes that researchers "have been more concerned with whether an actual flow of resources or activities occurred between agencies than whether a structural arrangement for coordination was established. This concern for the process of coordination is justified, because structural arrangements for coordination are often dismal failures in attaining tangible results."[23]

It is evident that coordination is sought and attained, not simply through formal structures and processes, but also through informal relations between and among policy actors. Moreover, we know that such informal interaction can either supplement and complement formal relations or impede and frustrate them.

Partisan Mutual Adjustment

The matter is further complicated by the difficulty of discerning when coordination is actually taking place. Charles Lindblom argues persuasively that through a process of "*partisan mutual adjustment*" a very large measure of coordination in government occurs without any deliberate, conscious attempt to coordinate. He contends that there are no coordinators in this process; rather, coordination comes about as "a by-product of ordinary decisions, that is, of decisions not

---

[20]See Martin Landau, "Redundancy, Rationality and the Problem of Duplication and Overlap," *Public Administration Review*, vol. 29 (July–August 1969), pp. 346–358.

[21]Ibid., p. 356.

[22]*Control in a Bureaucracy* (Oxford: Martin Robertson, 1978), p. 183.

[23]"On the Nature, Formation and Maintenance of Relations Among Organizations," *Academy of Management Review* (October 1976), p. 27.

specifically intended to coordinate."[24] He distinguishes this process from that of central coordination whereby for the most part "decision makers adapt to one another on instruction from a central decision maker."[25] He acknowledges also the existence of situations characterized by a mixture of central coordination and partisan mutual adjustment "where somebody can be both a central supervisor to a degree and a mutual adjuster."[26]

While central coordination is sought primarily through the exercise of control, partisan mutual adjustment is pursued through a broad range of techniques, most of which (e.g., negotiation, bargaining) require the exercise of influence. Lindblom's mixture of central coordination and mutual adjustment, which is found commonly within public organizations and frequently within government as a whole, involves the use of both control and influence. In a later work, Lindblom states that some political systems, such as the British, "rely more heavily on central coordination," whereas other systems, such as the American, depend "more heavily on mutual adjustment."[27] Canada's political system, like that of Britain, relies more on central coordination than mutual adjustment. His analysis, which has been greatly simplified here, indicates the large extent to which coordination is achieved as a result of the exercise of power for other purposes. Clearly, coordination through partisan mutual adjustment is difficult to recognize, much less evaluate.

These impediments to identifying and achieving coordination do not constitute grounds for pessimism regarding the value of formal structures and processes for coordination. These formal devices serve an essential purpose by harmonizing relations within and between organizations. This point is so well supported in scholarly writings and so manifest in practice that it requires little elaboration here.

Lindblom acknowledges the utility of central coordination and recognizes that governments cannot rely solely on partisan mutual adjustment. It is improbable that the interplay of free market forces in the political-administrative system will result in an appropriate measure of coordination. Perfect coordination — or a state close to it — is no more likely to be achieved in the polity and the bureaucracy than perfect competition in the economy. Thus, formal coordinating activities by governments are often needed to supplement coordination sought or attained through other means. Official rules or mechanisms are sometimes required to formalize coordinating relationships that have developed on an informal basis. In still other situations, beneficial informal coordination is stimulated by bringing together individuals, groups, and organizations in formal relationships. For example, in the sphere of intergovernmental relations, officials conduct much informal coordinating activity outside of and between formal meetings.

According to Lindblom, many interactions in the public policy process have the result, but not necessarily the purpose, of achieving coordination. Never-

---

[24] *The Intelligence of Democracy* (New York: The Free Press, 1965), p. 9.
[25] Ibid., p. 25.
[26] Ibid., p. 27.
[27] *The Policy-Making Process* (Englewood Cliffs, N.J.: Prentice-Hall, 1968), p. 82.

theless, the scholarly literature on both intraorganizational and interorganizational relations shows that many other interactions are specifically directed to promoting or improving coordination.

In the examination of interactions between the bureaucracy and other political actors provided in later chapters, special attention will be given to efforts and mechanisms designed to promote policy coordination.

BIBLIOGRAPHY

Aucoin, Peter. "Portfolio Structures and Policy Coordination." In G. Bruce Doern and Peter Aucoin, eds. *Public Policy in Canada*. Toronto: Macmillan, 1979.

Bachrach, Samuel B., and Edward J. Lawler. *Power and Politics in Organizations*. San Francisco: Jossey-Bass Publishers, 1980.

Downs, Anthony. *Inside Bureaucracy*. Boston: Little, Brown, 1967.

Dunsire, Andrew. *Control in a Bureaucracy*. Oxford: Martin Robertson, 1978.

Emerson, Richard M. "Power Dependence Relations." *American Sociological Review*, vol. 27 (February 1962): 31–41.

Friedrich, Carl J. *Man and His Government*. New York: McGraw-Hill, 1963.

Gilbert, Charles. "The Framework of Administrative Responsibility." *The Journal of Politics*, vol. 21 (August 1959): 373–407.

Kernaghan, Kenneth, and Olivia Kuper. *Coordination in Canadian Governments: A Case Study of Aging Policy*. Toronto: Institute of Public Administration of Canada, 1983.

Landau, Martin. "Redundancy, Rationality and the Problem of Duplication and Overlap." *Public Administration Review*, vol. 29 (July–August 1969): 346–358.

Lindblom, Charles E. *The Intelligence of Democracy*. New York: The Free Press, 1965.

Lindblom, Charles E. *The Policy-Making Process*. Englewood Cliffs, N.J.: Prentice-Hall, 1968.

Litwak, Eugene, and Lydia F. Hylton. "Interorganizational Analysis: A Hypothesis on Co-ordinating Agencies." *Administrative Science Quarterly*, vol. 6 (1962): 395–420.

Marrett, Cora Bagley. "On the Specification of Interorganizational Dimensions." *Sociology and Social Research*, vol. 56 (1971): 39–97.

Pfiffner, John. F., and Frank P. Sherwood. *Administrative Organization*. Englewood Cliffs, N.J.: Prentice-Hall, 1960.

Self, Peter. *Administrative Theories and Politics*. 2nd ed. London: Allen and Unwin, 1977.

Simon, Herbert A. *Administrative Behaviour*. 2nd ed. New York: The Free Press, 1957.

Van de Ven, Andrew H., Dennis C. Emmett, and Richard Koenig Jr. "Frameworks for Interorganizational Analysis." In Anant R. Negandhi, ed. *Interorganization Theory*. Kent, Ohio: Kent State University Press, 1975.

Wamsley, Gary L., and Mayer N. Zald. *The Political Economy of Public Organizations*. Bloomington, Indiana: Indiana University Press, 1976.

11

Power, Politics, and Bureaucracy

BUREAUCRATIC POWER

Power was defined in the previous chapter as "the capacity to secure the dominance of one's values or goals." In this sense, public servants wield substantial power by virtue of their role in policy development and execution. If the machinery of government could be so arranged that bureaucrats simply implemented laws spelled out in very specific terms by the legislature, enforced judicial decisions interpreting these laws, and administered policies and programs under the close supervision of political executives, few value problems would exist for most bureaucrats. The realm of politics and policy would belong to elected representatives and would be sharply delineated from the administrative sphere. The value issues in any situation would be worked out by others so that the bureaucrat's primary concern would be to adhere to those values emerging from the legislative, executive, and judicial spheres of government.

The historical record shows that an era of such bureaucratic innocence has never existed in modern democratic states. There is in reality much room for the injection of public servants' values into decisions and recommendations. It is generally acknowledged that public servants exercise significant power in both the development and execution of policy. In a lecture on the threat to parliamentary responsible government, Robert Stanfield, a former leader of the federal Progressive Conservative Party, stated that, "while the House of Commons has been losing control, so also has the Government. The ministers just do not have the time to run such a vast show and make such a vast range of decisions. Consequently, more and more is for all practical purposes being decided by and implemented by the bureaucracy."[1] And in a reminiscence on thirty years as a senior public servant and a minister, Mitchell Sharp observed that "top public servants are powerful persons in the machinery of government at the federal level. They wield great influence. They do so because they are, in the main, professionals who have been selected for their proven administrative ability and who devote their full time to government. In many cases, they have a greater influence upon the course of events than have Ministers, particularly the weaker and less competent."[2] The extent of this bureaucratic power clearly varies in accordance with such factors as the government's view of the proper

---

[1]The George C. Nowlan Lecture, Acadia University, February 7, 1977. Reprinted in *The Globe and Mail*, February 8, 1977.

[2]Mitchell Sharp, "Reflections of a Former Minister of the Crown," address to the Toronto Regional Group of the Institute of Public Administration of Canada, November 29, 1976, pp. 6–7.

role of public servants in the political process, the policy or program under consideration, the department or agency involved, and the style and competence of ministers and their officials.

The Concept and Practice of Political Neutrality

A framework for examining the power of public servants may be devised by utilizing the concept of political neutrality. Political neutrality is a constitutional doctrine or convention according to which public servants should not engage in activities that are likely to impair — or appear to impair — their impartiality or the impartiality of the public service. The several interrelated ideas traditionally associated with the notion of political neutrality provide a useful model for examining the nature of interaction between public servants and other actors in the political system. The model also permits a consideration of the changing nature of bureaucratic power and of the role of public servants in the policy process. The major elements of the traditional model may be summarized as follows:

1. politics and policy are separated from administration: thus politicians make policy decisions; public servants execute these decisions;
2. public servants are appointed and promoted on the basis of merit rather than of party affiliation or contributions;
3. public servants do not engage in partisan political activities;
4. public servants do not express publicly their personal views on government policies or administration;
5. public servants provide forthright and objective advice to their political masters in private and in confidence; in return, political executives protect the anonymity of public servants by publicly accepting responsibility for departmental decisions; and
6. public servants execute policy decisions loyally irrespective of the philosophy and programs of the party in power and regardless of their personal opinions; as a result, public servants enjoy security of tenure during good behaviour and satisfactory performance.

As a means of explaining the nature and extent of bureaucratic power in the Canadian political system, each of these six elements of political neutrality will be examined separately below. Special attention is centred on the degree to which actual practice has departed from the requirements of the traditional model.

(1) Politics and Administration

The politics-administration dichotomy. The political neutrality of public servants has traditionally rested on the possibility of a separation between politics and administration and on a related distinction between policy and administration. Frequently, the two dichotomies are treated as synonymous — as if the terms politics and policy are interchangeable. The scope of activity covered by the term politics is, however, much broader than that embraced by the term policy. "*Politics* is concerned, throughout the sphere of government, with the whole business of deciding what to do and getting it done. *Policy* is the decision as to what to do; *administration* is getting it done."[3] According to the politics-administration dichotomy, political executives and legislators are concerned with the formation of policy and public servants are concerned with its implementation. Policy decisions are political; administrative decisions are non-political. However, abundant evidence points to the important political and policy-advisory roles of public servants.

The distinction between politics and policy on the one hand, and administration on the other, has been central to the evolution of both the study and the practice of public administration. V. Seymour Wilson, who uses interchangeably the terms politics-administration dichotomy and policy-administration dichotomy, states that the dichotomy

> remains a powerful philosophy . . . . It has guided, and will continue to guide, many aspects of the actions and perceptions of politicians, public servants and the public . . . . The policy/administration dichotomy has a profound influence on just about every aspect of theory and practice in public policy and administration.[4]

From 1887 up to the end of the Second World War, most prominent writers on public administration wrote within a framework of a dichotomy between politics and administration. Woodrow Wilson's celebrated essay of 1887 on "The Study of Administration"[5] is usually taken as the point of departure for academic and theoretical writing on public administration in North America. In his essay, Wilson asserted that

> the field of administration is a field of business. It is removed from the hurry and strife of politics . . . administrative questions are not political questions . . . . "Policy does nothing without the aid of administration," but administration is not therefore politics.[6]

Wilson's distinction between politics and administration was accepted and perpetuated by such other pioneers as Frank Goodnow (1914), L. D. White (1926), and W. F. Willoughby (1927). In their writings, "the politics-administration dichotomy was assumed both as a self-evident truth and a desirable goal; administration was perceived as a self-contained world of its own, with its own separate values, rules and methods."[7] Set in proper historical perspective, these questionable views are more comprehensible.

During the late nineteenth and early twentieth centuries, administrative reform efforts in both the United States and Canada were devoted to eradicating patronage from the government service, with a view to promoting efficient adminis-

---

[3]R. J. S. Baker, *Administrative Theory and Public Administration* (London: Hutchinson, 1972), p. 13.

[4]*Canadian Public Policy and Administration* (Toronto: McGraw-Hill Ryerson, 1981), p. 99.

[5]Woodrow Wilson, "The Study of Administration." Reprinted in Peter Woll, ed., *Public Administration and Policy* (New York: Harper and Row, 1966), pp. 15–41.

[6]Ibid., pp. 28–29.

[7]Wallace S. Sayre, "Premises of Public Administration: Past and Emerging," *Public Administration Review*, vol. 18 (1958), p. 103.

tration. A separate, but overlapping, development which had its origins in industrial organization in the United States was the "scientific management" movement described in Chapter 2. This movement, which pursued efficiency in large-scale organizations by seeking the most rational means — the "one best way" — of performing any organizational task, had an enormous impact on the civil service reform movement in the United States. The tenets of the scientific management movement spread not only throughout the United States, but also to Canada and several European countries.

In both the United States and Canada, the two elements of the reform movement — efficiency through the elimination of patronage and efficiency through scientific management — reinforced one another and became integral components of the merit system. In Canada, the 1917–18 Report of the Civil Service Commission noted that the merit system in the Canadian civil service "consisted of two distinct parts: the first is concerned with the selection and appointment of individuals 'without regard to their politics, religion or influence'; the second is concerned with 'applying the methods of scientific employment to maintain the efficiency of these selected employees after they enter the service.' "[8] While the Civil Service Act of 1918 was a landmark event in establishing a merit system for the Canadian public service, political interference with the application of the system hindered efforts to eliminate patronage appointments.

Although there were no Canadian counterparts to American writers on public administration who articulated the notion of a separation between politics and administration, Canadian reformers operated within a similar framework. Implicit in their efforts to remove partisan political considerations from appointments to the public service was acceptance of the possibility and desirability of separating politics from administration — at least in so far as staffing the service was concerned. For example, the 1917–18 Report of the Civil Service Commission stated that the purpose of the 1918 Civil Service Act was to promote "efficiency and economy in the *non-political* Civil Service."[9]

Concurrent with this pursuit of impartial and efficient administration was a steady growth in the discretionary powers of public servants. While efficient staffing of the service required the separation of politics and administration, the need for effective development and execution of public policy drew administrative officials into the political maelstrom — not in the sense of partisan activity, but in the sense of involvement in the authoritative allocation of values for society. Public servants formulated rules and regulations to put flesh on the skeleton of vaguely worded statutes, enforced these rules and regulations, and adjudicated disputes arising from this enforcement. Moreover, the complicated and technical nature of public policy issues meant that political executives had to rely increasingly on public servants for policy advice and for the management of large-scale public organizations.

---

[8]Quoted in J. E. Hodgetts, et al., *The Biography of an Institution: The Civil Service Commission of Canada, 1908–1967* (Montreal: McGill-Queen's University Press, 1972), p. 56.
[9]Ibid. (Emphasis added.)

During the 1930s, writers on public administration who recognized the significant and growing political role of the bureaucracy lived uncomfortably with the textbook dichotomy between politics and administration.[10] The dichotomy came under increasing attack during the war years as many scholars gained practical administrative experience in government. Shortly after the war, a number of political scientists launched a devastating assault on the notion that politics and administration were or could be separated. Among this group of post-war authors, Paul Appleby stands out for his defence of the proposition that "public administration is policy making . . . . Public administration is one of a number of basic political processes."[11] In less celebrated and more broadly focussed works than those written by American authors, British and Canadian writers demonstrated during this same period a growing recognition of the blurring of the traditional constitutional line between politicians and bureaucrats in the parliamentary-Cabinet system of government.

By 1960, the interdependence of politics and administration had been enshrined in the theoretical literature on public administration and accepted by the major actors in the political system. By this time, however, recognition of the reality of bureaucratic power in the political process led to suggestions that public servants should assume the task and the orientation of "agents of social change." Public servants were encouraged to promote new and creative innovations and solutions in social policy by aggregating and articulating the needs of unorganized and disadvantaged groups (for example, consumers, the poor), and by stimulating groups and individuals to make demands on government for remedies to their social and economic ills. It was clear that public servants who undertook such activities were likely to clash on occasion with political and administrative superiors who did not perceive the proper role of a public servant to be an active initiator of social change. The basic question was the extent to which appointed public officials could or should share with elected representatives the responsibility for stimulating and responding to social change. Discussion of public servants as social change agents was intermingled with the movement for increased citizen participation in government decision making. This movement brought both politicians and public servants into more direct contact and confrontation with the general citizenry.

In the United States, these and other developments culminated in the late 1960s in a loose confederation of scholars and practitioners seeking a "new public administration."[12] Among the major concerns of the advocates of this movement were social equity, sensitivity to and representation of disadvantaged

---

[10]See for example, Luther Gulick, "Politics, Administration and the New Deal," *Annals of the American Academy of Political and Social Science* (1933), and Pendleton Herring, *Public Administration and the Public Interest*, 1936. (Reprinted in 1967 by Russell, New York.)

[11]Paul Appleby, *Policy and Administration* (University, Alabama: University of Alabama Press, 1949), p.170. See also Dwight Waldo, *The Administrative State* (New York: Ronald Press, 1948) and Harold Stein, *Public Administration and Policy Development: A Casebook* (New York: Harcourt, Brace, 1952).

[12]See Frank Marini, ed., *Toward a New Public Administration: The Minnowbrook Perspective* (Scranton, Pa.: Chandler, 1971).

minority groups, increased citizen participation in government decision making, and new forms of public organization.

The relevance of the new public administration movement for the relation between politics and administration is that some of its supporters called for a reformulation of the traditional roles of politicians and public servants.[13] It was argued that public servants, because of their expertise and experience and their close contacts with members of the public, are better qualified than political executives or legislators to determine the public interest. Public servants must, however, establish a value system with a focus on human dignity or administrative humanism; they should not simply reflect the values of their political masters. Implicit also was a resistance to political control over public administration. The new public administration movement drew attention to the actual and potential power of public servants and to the importance of their value system for decision making in government; however, it did not resolve — indeed, it complicated — the issue of finding an appropriate balance between the power of public servants and that of elected representatives.

Thus, the scholarly literature on public administration records an evolution since 1945 from a situation where only a few writers recognized the necessary involvement of public servants in politics to a situation where a few writers suggested that leadership in policy development rightly belongs to public servants rather than to politicians. The new public administration movement had little spillover effect on the study and practice of public administration in Canada. Nevertheless, scholars and practitioners in Canada are acutely aware that the line between politics and administration has become increasingly indistinct as both politicians and public servants participate actively in policy development. Moreover, the line is a fluctuating one, characterized by the expansion of bureaucratic power and the gradual politicization of the public service.

Policy development and policy implementation. Since the political role of public servants is attributed primarily to their contribution to policy development, much attention in the literature has focussed on the intermingling of policy and administration. The conventional view that a clear division may be made between policy and administration has always been a fiction, but has become increasingly untenable with the continuing growth of government activities and of bureaucratic power. The terms policy and administration are of limited use in distinguishing between the roles of political executives (i.e., Cabinet ministers) and public servants, because political executives and public servants are jointly involved in the administration of policy. Gordon Robertson, former clerk of the Privy Council, observed:

> I can hardly claim to be capable of complete objectivity. It would be easier to achieve such detachment if I could shelter behind the dictum so solemnly delivered from editorial pages and professorial podia that politicians, and not civil servants, make policy and civil servants, and not

---

[13]See especially Eugene P. Dvorin and Robert H. Simmons, *From Amoral to Humane Bureaucracy* (San Francisco: Canfield Press, 1972) and Louis C. Gawthrop, *Administrative Politics and Social Change* (New York: St. Martin's Press, 1971).

politicians, apply it. It is unfortunate that so clear and helpful a distinction should have so little truth about it.[14]

In the late 1970s, public administration scholars began to study more vigorously "the missing link" in the policy making process, namely policy implementation. It is now widely recognized that the power of bureaucrats is greatly enhanced by their dominant role in program implementation and service delivery. Subsequent discussion will, therefore, examine in turn the exercise of bureaucratic power in both policy formation and policy implementation.

Writers on bureaucratic power have long recognized the enormous influence of bureaucrats on policy *formation*. Senior public servants in particular make significant discretionary decisions as to the policy options to be set before their political masters. Moreover, in the development and presentation of policy proposals, these public servants are expected to be attuned to the *political* as well as the administrative, financial, and technical implications of their recommendations. By the late 1960s, the power of public servants in policy development was perceived to be so great that Prime Minister Trudeau endeavoured to place more policy-making power in the hands of politically accountable authorities, especially Cabinet ministers. To this end, the Cabinet committee system and the parliamentary committee system were reformed, the coordinating capacity of the Privy Council Office was strengthened, and the policy influence of the Prime Minister's Office was expanded. The use of such alternative sources of policy advice as task forces, white papers, and advisory councils provided a competing influence to departmental advice. The impact of these changes is discussed at various points throughout this book. However, it is notable here that these changes did increase the role of ministers in policy formation. Moreover, during the late 1960s, the power of the so-called "public service mandarins" (a small group of influential senior bureaucrats) was diffused among a broader range of political actors and among a greater number of senior public servants.[15]

Despite these reforms, certain public servants continue to exercise significant power by virtue of their central positions in the policy process (for example, the deputy minister of finance, the clerk of the Privy Council). Furthermore, despite the greater variety of available sources of policy advice, the very technical, complex and time-consuming nature of certain policy issues obliges ministers to continue to rely heavily on the advice of their officials. Robert Bryce, a former deputy minister of finance and clerk of the Privy Council, has observed that during the Trudeau years senior public servants had a great deal of influence on their ministers because they were "in day-to-day contact with them. It is this contact, the continued relationship, that develops into the kind of influence that is important and leads . . . to power."[16]

---

[14]"The Coming Crisis in the North," *Journal of Canadian Studies*, vol. 2 (February 1967), p. 3.
[15]See Kenneth Kernaghan and T. H. McLeod, "Mandarins and Ministers in the Canadian Administrative State," in O. P. Dwivedi, ed., *The Canadian Administrative State* (Toronto: University of Toronto Press, 1982), pp. 17–30.
[16]Quoted in Douglas Fisher, "A Mandarin Reflects on the Bureaucracy," *Executive*, December 1979, p. 90.

In the sphere of policy *implementation*, public servants also exercise substantial power. The extent of bureaucratic power in policy implementation depends largely on the specificity of the statute enacted by the legislature. In an early, but very perceptive, discussion of administrative discretion, the philosopher Wayne A. R. Leys developed a three-fold classification of discretion depending on the willingness and capacity of elected representatives to set down in statutes the criteria on which administrative decisions are to be based. Leys's classification of discretionary powers distinguishes among: (1) merely technical discretion, where the legislature has stated or assumed that the administrator knew the results which it desired; (2) discretion in social planning, where the legislature does not know exactly what it ultimately will want in the way of results; and (3) discretion in the work of reconciliation, where the legislature has, in effect, asked the administrator to break a political deadlock.[17] The first category, where discretionary judgement is limited, illustrates that care must be taken not to exaggerate the number of heavily value-laden issues confronting officials. A large percentage of the thousands of administrative decisions made each day present value problems of such minor significance that officials are scarcely aware of any value content in the decisions made. The second and third categories demonstrate the discretionary powers exercised by officials, either because of the complexity of the issue or of the inability of the executive or legislature to resolve the political conflicts involved. Both situations shift the burden of decision making from political executives, legislators, and judges to public servants. The making of decisions and recommendations on complex and technical matters of "social planning" requires the exercise of discretionary powers of a legislative and judicial nature. And the participation of officials in negotiation, bargaining, compromise, and reconciliation in order "to break a political deadlock" is undeniably *political* activity.

In the course of interpreting, clarifying, and applying policy, public servants can significantly influence the success of policy decisions taken by ministers and legislators. The care and enthusiasm with which public servants administer policy determines to a large extent the success of that policy. A series of individual, relatively minor decisions in a particular policy area can have a significant cumulative impact on the extent to which the original intent of Cabinet and Parliament is realized. Moreover, such decisions can help to determine the content of subsequent changes in existing policy. In wielding such discretionary powers, public servants are, of course, expected to ensure that their decisions are broadly attuned to the general policy of their minister and their department.

The discretionary powers of public servants in policy implementation are especially evident in the making and enforcement of regulations under authority delegated to them by Parliament or subdelegated to them by a minister or by Cabinet. The statutory provisions authorizing the making of regulations are often phrased in general or imprecise language which permits public servants to exercise significant discretion, both in the wording of the regulations and in the

---

[17]Wayne A. R. Leys, "Ethics and Administrative Discretion," *Public Administration Review*, vol. 3 (Winter 1943), p. 23.

application of their provisions to particular cases. Eric Hehner has repeatedly warned of the danger of "dispersed discretions." He argues:

> If regulations extend only to details of mechanical procedures, no real dis-
> cretionary powers are delegated. However, where the statutory provisions
> are only a skeleton and it is left to regulations to say "what, where, when,
> why, how and who," then we have created meaningful discretionary pow-
> ers . . . . When regulations are issued by the governor-in-council, or even
> by a minister of the Crown, there is at least a degree of accountability for
> this first step. Where the power is conferred upon a board or commission,
> review of its exercise becomes more difficult and remote. . . . If persons or
> bodies possessed of delegated powers redelegate them, we come to a state
> that may be described as "dispersed discretions."[18]

The delegation by Parliament of power to make regulations is now very common, and a large number of regulations has been made. The Special Committee on Statutory Instruments reported in 1969 that 420 of 601 statutes perused by the committee provided for delegated legislation, and that an annual average of 530 regulations had been passed between 1956 and 1968.[19] Then, in 1977, the Senate-House Committee on Regulations and Other Statutory Instruments, on the basis of its inquiry into "the subordinate law made by delegates of Parliament," provided examples not only of the substantial volume of subordinate law, but also of cases where public servants had exceeded the regulation-making authority granted to them by Parliament.[20] The committee recognized the need for subordinate legislation, but made a number of recommendations to ensure more effective parliamentary scrutiny of this legislation and more attention to the rights of individuals affected by it.

The exercise of discretionary powers is also pervasive in that these powers are dispersed to various levels of the hierarchy. Both the scope and importance of discretionary powers increase, however, as one moves up the administrative pyramid into the upper echelons of the bureaucracy. It is, therefore, among senior public servants that value problems and priorities are most crucial for the determination of public policy and the state of administrative responsibility. It is important, however, not to overestimate the value problems of the most senior bureaucrats and thereby to minimize the substantial, sometimes critical, significance of value choices made by professional, technical, and administrative personnel at lower levels of the hierarchy. The failure of such officials to act responsibly, particularly by making decisions that are efficient, effective, and responsive, may seriously jeopardize policies and programs determined at the top executive levels of the organization. Decisions judged to be irresponsible may be taken with the best of personal intentions; other irresponsible decisions

---

[18]Eric Hehner, "Growth of Discretions — Decline of Accountability," in Kenneth Kernaghan, ed., *Public Administration in Canada: Selected Readings*, 5th ed. (Toronto: Methuen, 1985), p. 342.
[19]House of Commons, *Special Committee on Statutory Instuments*, 3rd Report (Ottawa: Queen's Printer, 1969), p. 4.
[20]Senate and House of Commons, *Standing Joint Committee on Regulations and Other Statutory Instruments*, 2nd Report (Ottawa: Queen's Printer, 1977), esp. pp. 2–12.

may constitute deliberate efforts to obstruct or sabotage the implementation of government policies. Instances of this latter type of irresponsible administrative conduct are difficult to document, but there are numerous opportunities for such conduct. In a large organization — whether in the public or the private sector — the decision-making process may involve inputs and judgements by so many individuals that the person or persons guilty of irresponsible behaviour, whether unintentional or deliberate, are extremely difficult to pinpoint. This is the condition Robert Presthus describes as "organized irresponsibility."[21]

The role of provincial public servants in policy development and implementation is very similar to that of federal public servants. Kornberg, et al. have noted that "provincial bureaucracies exercise legislative powers in various ways. Some bureaucratic officials identify problem areas requiring the action of cabinets. They marshall the information ministers require to decide among competing priorities . . . and they either draft or assist in the drafting of legislation." In addition, these provincial public servants "formulate general and specific rules having the force of law as part of the process of implementing legislation which assemblies have enacted."[22] Clearly, policy implementation has a significant effect on the development and content of policy in all spheres of government.

Despite the fact that politics and policy cannot be easily separated from administration, the distinctions commonly made between politics and administration, policy and administration, and policy formation and implementation serve an extremely useful analytical and practical purpose. They enable political theorists to distinguish — not in an absolute sense, but as a matter of degree and emphasis — between the constitutional and legal functions of political executives and public servants. While the policy role of public servants has led some writers to refer to them as "permanent politicians" and "ruling servants," they remain, in fact and in democratic theory, subject to the overriding authority of elected representatives and the courts. It is useful then to refer to the *predominance* of ministers in policy formulation and the *predominance* of public servants in policy implementation, while acknowledging that both ministers and public servants are involved in both policy formation and implementation.

These dichotomies also serve a very practical end in that they enable politicians to preserve the appearance before the public that they, not the public servants, are the policy makers. Elected representatives have a stake in preserving the notion that public servants are neutral instruments of political masters. This notion in turn supports the doctrine that ministers must accept responsibility for the decisions of their administrative subordinates. Public servants also have an interest in preserving these convenient fictions so that they may retain their anonymity and be sheltered from public attack.

(2) Political Appointments

Merit and patronage. A second component of the traditional model of political neutrality is the practice whereby "public servants are appointed and promoted

---

[21]Robert Presthus, *The Organizational Society* (New York: Vintage Books, 1962), p. 53.
[22]Allan Kornberg, William Mishler, and Harold D. Clarke, *Representative Democracy in the Canadian Provinces* (Scarborough: Prentice-Hall, 1982), p. 184.

on the basis of merit rather than of party affiliation or contributions." *Political patronage* involves the appointment of persons to government service on the grounds of contributions, financial or otherwise, to the governing party; it is a blatant violation of the doctrine of political neutrality. Indeed, the appointment is made on the basis that the appointee is *not* politically neutral, but rather is politically partisan. Such appointments clash with the merit *principle* according to which

(1) Canadian citizens should have a reasonable opportunity to be considered for employment in the public service.

(2) selections must be based exclusively on merit, or fitness to do the job.[23]

The merit *system*, on the other hand, "is the mechanism in use at any time by which these goals are achieved." It is "an administrative device which can and should be adapted to changing circumstances."[24]

The merit system established by the Civil Service Act in 1918 greatly diminished, but by no means eliminated, patronage appointments. As late as 1944, H. M. Clokie claimed that Canada had not "fully emancipated herself from the laxness of appointment by favour which tends to paralyze all efforts to attain a sound merit system."[25] By 1945, however, the number of patronage appointments had been greatly reduced, and by 1962 the Glassco Commission was able to conclude that "for all practical purposes . . . the Civil Service Commission [now the Public Service Commission] has managed to eliminate political patronage appointments to those positions falling within its jurisdiction."[26]

Recipients and effects of patronage. Patronage appointments have certainly not disappeared altogether. A review of debates in the House of Commons in recent decades reveals numerous allegations and denials regarding the use of patronage in staffing the public service. Many of the alleged patronage appointments have been to lower-level or part-time positions, where the appointees are so far removed from policy development that their appointment has negligible effect on the status of political neutrality. Opposition parties, the news media, and the general public have shown greater interest in *senior* positions that are filled by patronage appointees rather than on a competitive basis by persons from within or outside the public service. The Cabinet has the authority to appoint deputy ministers, heads and members of agencies, boards and commissions, ambassadors, high commissioners, consuls general and certain other diplomatic representatives, and federal judges. Moreover, officials in the Prime Minister's Office are selected by the Prime Minister, and Cabinet ministers choose their assistants. All these appointments are exempt from the appointing power of the Public Service Commission.

---

[23]R. H. Dowdell, "Public Personnel Administration," in Kenneth Kernaghan, ed., *Public Administration in Canada*, 4th ed. (Toronto: Methuen, 1982), p. 196.
[24]Ibid.
[25]H. M. Clokie, *Canadian Government and Politics* (Toronto: Longmans, Green, 1944), p. 190.
[26]Canada, *Royal Commission on Government Organization*, vol. 1 (Ottawa: Queen's Printer, 1962), p. 371.

Among the persons who may be, and frequently are, appointed to exempt positions are retired legislators, defeated candidates of the governing party, and party supporters who have made significant financial or other contributions to the party's fortunes. For example, in the period following the 1972 general election, more than two-thirds of the thirty-eight retired or defeated Liberal politicians were appointed as heads or members of government agencies, contract employees in government departments, judges, or assistants to the Prime Minister or to ministers. An Opposition member was stimulated to propose a motion to the House of Commons "that this House request the government to table a list of all Liberal candidates defeated in the last election who have not yet been appointed to government positions, together with a list of the positions to which they will be appointed."[27] Defeated or retired Cabinet ministers have enjoyed particular success in finding a comfortable niche in government service.[28] Finally, the expansion of the personal staff of Cabinet ministers since 1960 has increased the importance of this group as a source of patronage appointments.[29]

Such appointments are often denounced on the grounds that they are made more on the basis of partisanship than merit. Nevertheless, the government has the authority to make these appointments on whatever basis it deems appropriate. A measure of merit is achieved with respect to the most senior posts because the government is not usually willing to bear the embarrassment that the appointment of an incompetent partisan may bring. Moreover, party supporters are more likely to find their reward in appointments to Crown agencies, boards, and commissions than to the regular departments of government. There are few partisan appointments to deputy ministerial posts.

The number of patronage appointments in each of the categories examined above is relatively small, but taking all the categories together, the number of *senior* positions filled by patronage appointees is substantial. The impact of these appointments on bureaucratic power is difficult to measure with any precision. Appointments to public service posts without competitive examination and on grounds of partisanship violate the merit principle, but not the merit system. Such appointments limit the influence of career public servants by blocking their access to some of the highest positions in government. Moreover, long-serving officials are obliged to share their influence in the policy process with newcomers who may have fresh ideas and unorthodox approaches, and who may not share the administrative values to which most public servants have become socialized.

Patronage in the provinces. The evolution of political patronage in Canada's provinces has been very similar to that of the federal government. Civil service acts were passed and civil service commissions or their equivalent were created to promote public service neutrality and efficiency through a merit system of

---

[27]Stanley Knowles, House of Commons, *Debates*, April 11, 1973, p. 3176.

[28]Between 1948 and 1972, 12.1 per cent of retiring or defeated ministers were appointed to patronage positions. See W. A. Matheson, *The Prime Minister and the Cabinet* (Toronto: Methuen, 1976), p. 121.

[29]See Chapter 14 for elaboration on the role of ministerial staff.

personnel management.[30] The timing of these reforms varied greatly from province to province, but in all cases effective reforms occurred more slowly than on the federal scene. Hodgetts and Dwivedi note that "until the early '60s, most provinces continued to present only the facade of a merit system, while combatting charges of patronage and personal favouritism in their public services." However, "by the mid-'60's nearly all provinces had made their central personnel agencies powerful enough to implement the merit principle."[31] Patronage appointments to agencies, boards, and commissions and to lower-level positions in certain operating departments remain a common practice in provincial governments. The Ontario government has available for political appointments more than three thousand full-time and part-time positions in agencies, boards, and commissions.[32] Some provinces (e.g., Saskatchewan)[33] are more inclined than others to make political appointments to senior posts in *departments* as well as in semi-independent bodies.

(3) Political Partisanship

Political sterilization. The traditional model of political neutrality requires that public servants not "engage in partisan political activities."[34] During the first fifty years of Canada's political history, the issues of political partisanship and political patronage were intimately linked. Patronage appointments were rewards for service to the governing party. Many of the appointees sought to enhance their progress within the service by continuing their partisan support of the governing party after their appointment. Thus, when a new party came into power, it replaced these persons with its own supporters.

In an effort to eliminate this practice, legislators provided in the 1918 Civil Service Act that no public servant could "engage in partisan work in connection with any . . . election, or contribute, receive or in any way deal with any money for any party funds." Violations were punishable by dismissal. The penalty was so severe and so clearly stated that, with the exception of the right to vote, the impact of the Act was the political sterilization of Canada's federal public servants. Despite this effective weakening of the link between patronage and political activity, the rigid restraints imposed in 1918 remained virtually unchanged

---

[30]See J. E. Hodgetts and O. P. Dwivedi, *Provincial Governments as Employers* (McGill-Queen's University Press, 1974), ch. 2.

[31]J. E. Hodgetts and O. P. Dwivedi, "Administration and Personnel," in David J. Bellamy, Jon H. Pammett, and Donald C. Rowat, eds., *The Provincial Political Systems: Comparative Essays* (Toronto: Methuen, 1976), p. 347.

[32]*The Globe and Mail*, August 6, 1985, p. 1.

[33]See S. M. Lipset, *Agrarian Socialism: The Cooperative Commonwealth Federation in Saskatchewan* (Berkeley: University of California Press, 1959); Evelyn Eager, *Saskatchewan Government* (Saskatoon: Western Producer Prairie Books, 1980), pp.164–167; and Hans J. Michelmann and Jeffrey S. Steeves, "The 1982 Transition in Power in Saskatchewan: The Progressive Conservatives and the Public Service," *Canadian Public Administration*, vol. 28 (Spring 1985), pp. 1–23.

[34]For a definition of political activity and an account of the arguments usually raised for and against the political activity of government employees, see Kenneth Kernaghan, *Ethical Conduct: Guidelines for Government Employees* (Toronto: Institute of Public Administration of Canada, 1975), pp. 26–28.

until l967. The primary explanation for those enduring restraints was the desire to ensure the political impartiality of public servants in the performance of their advisory and discretionary powers.

The Public Service Employment Act of l967 liberalized the long-standing restrictions on political activity. Section 32 of the Act provides that public servants, unless they are deputy heads, may stand for election to public office if the Public Service Commission believes that their usefulness would not be impaired by their candidacy. Employees who are elected must resign from the public service. The decisions of the Public Service Commission suggest that roughly 90 per cent of all public servants will be permitted to seek election if they wish. This liberalization of restraints on political candidacy has attracted a small number of public servants to the hustings for each federal election. Employees are not permitted to work for or against a candidate for election to a federal or provincial office, or for or against a political party; they are permitted, however, to attend political meetings and to make contributions to the funds of a political candidate or party.

Political activity in the provinces. In provincial governments, a common pattern has emerged with respect to public servants who wish to become candidates for public office. Although the number of senior and other officials who are prohibited from such activity varies from province to province, most public servants seeking candidacy and election may receive a leave of absence for a period preceding the date of the election. Employees who are elected must resign their public service position. In several provinces, however, an employee who is elected, but who ceases to be a representative within five years, will be reinstated to government service.

In regard to other forms of political activity (e.g., membership in political parties; attendance at political meetings, rallies, and conventions; making and soliciting financial contributions; canvassing for a political candidate), provincial governments vary greatly in their rules. In virtually every province, the right of public servants to support the party of their choice or no party at all is specifically protected by statute. For example, the Saskatchewan Public Service Act provides that no public servant (1) shall be obliged to contribute to a political party or to participate in political activities; (2) use his or her authority or influence to "control or modify" political action of another person; (3) engage in political activities at the workplace; or (4) participate in political activities likely to impair his or her usefulness in the public service.

The fact that most public servants may now stand for election and engage in a broader spectrum of political activities has heightened the general level of partisan activity and consciousness in Canada's public services, especially among younger employees. However, officials in senior and sensitive posts are usually required to refrain from partisan activity; thus those officials most actively involved in policy formation and in the discretionary application of policy retain their impartiality. Also, officials with many years of government experience seem to have difficulty overcoming their ingrained avoidance of political activity. Some public servants may justifiably perceive overt partisanship as an obstacle to promotion to the senior ranks of what is substantially a politically neutral public service. Moreover, one of the attractions of government employment at the senior levels is the opportunity to exercise influence in relative privacy and anonymity. While there have been some notable examples of public servants being transformed into Cabinet ministers, a Cabinet post is by no means a sure reward for a public servant who is elected to public office. Thus, the broadening of the permissible limits of political activity has modified the traditional doctrine and practice of political neutrality, but it has not had a significant effect on the exercise of bureaucratic power.

It is notable that the restrictions on the political partisanship of public servants, in both the federal and provincial spheres of government, have been challenged in the courts under the Canadian Charter of Rights and Freedoms. The issue is for the most part framed in terms of the need to strike the most appropriate balance between the political rights of public servants and the political neutrality of the public service. Section 2 of the Charter guarantees the fundamental freedoms of expression, peaceful assembly and association, and section 1 provides that the guarantees to rights and freedoms under the Charter are subject to "such reasonable limits prescribed by law as can be demonstrably justified in a free and democratic society." The issue before the courts then is whether the limits on the political partisanship of public servants can be demonstrably justified to be reasonable limits in contemporary Canadian society.

(4) Public Comment

Restrictions. The admonition that public servants "not express publicly their personal views on government policies or administration" is an integral component of the traditional model of political neutrality. The prime reason given by contemporary governments for restrictions on public comment is the need to preserve the confidence of the public and of political superiors in the impartiality of public servants.

Strict interpretation of this rule of official reticence requires that public servants not express personal opinions on government policies, whether they are attacking or supporting those policies. As explained below, this convention has been supplemented by statutory prohibitions relating to political partisanship and to the use of confidential information, by decisions of administrative tribunals, and by written guidelines.

Section 32 of the federal Public Service Employment Act restricts public comment by providing that "no employee shall engage in partisan work in connection with any . . . election." A few provincial governments accompany their regulations on political activities with guidance on partisan public comment. Section 14 of the Ontario Public Service Act, for example, states that "except during a leave of absence . . . a civil servant shall not at any time speak in public or express views in writing on any matter that forms part of the platform of a provincial or federal political party." Public servants on leave of absence to seek election are, of course, obliged to express personal and partisan views on campaign issues. Those who wish to return to government service if they are defeated may find it prudent to show discretion in their public statements, especially with respect to the policies and programs of the department to which they may wish to return.

Public servants, whether seeking election or not, are normally prohibited by an oath of office and secrecy and by the Official Secrets Act from disclosing or using for personal gain confidential information acquired by virtue of their government position. It is a serious offence to criticize publicly government policy or administration; the use of confidential information for this purpose would greatly compound the offence.

Formal written guidelines on public comment are so sparse that considerable uncertainty exists as to the rights of public servants in this area. It is well established in the civil service legislation of modern democratic states that the role of public servants in policy development and implementation requires that they enjoy fewer political rights than other citizens. In the area of public comment, the difficulty is to strike an appropriate balance between freedom of expression and political neutrality. The dilemma for a public servant who engages in public criticism of government is illustrated well by the celebrated Fraser case.

Mr. Fraser, an employee of the Department of National Revenue, began his public protest with attacks on the government's compulsory imposition of the metric system; he then extended his criticism to the proposed Charter of Rights. When Mr. Fraser's appeal against his subsequent dismissal was being heard by an adjudicator of the Public Service Staff Relations Board, Mr. Fraser said that if he discontinued his protests, he would be breaking "the common law that the citizen has a duty to speak out against a Government that lies to the people."[35] The adjudicator's decision that Mr. Fraser's dismissal was appropriate was upheld by the Supreme Court of Canada. The court stated that

> public servants have some freedom to criticize the government. But it is not an absolute freedom. . . . In some circumstances a public servant may actively and publicly express opposition to the policies of a government. This would be appropriate if, for example, the Government were engaged in illegal acts, or if its policies jeopardized the life, health or safety of the public servant or others, or if the public servant's criticism had no impact on his or her ability to perform effectively the duties of a public servant or on the public perception of that ability.[36]

Beyond public criticism. The decisions of the adjudicator and of the Supreme Court are of limited value in dealing with forms of public comment other than criticism of government. The issue of public comment is much more complex than the conventional rule suggests. This rule does not take adequate account of the extent to which public servants are inescapably involved in public comment in the regular performance of their duties. In speaking or writing for public consumption, public servants may serve such purposes as:

---

[35]*Neil A. Fraser, Grievor, v. Treasury Board (Department of National Revenue, Taxation), Employer*, Public Service Staff Relations Board Decision, May 31, 1982, p. 16.
[36]Supreme Court of Canada, *Neil Fraser and Public Service Staff Relations Board*, [1985] 2 S.C.R., pp. 468, 470.

1. providing information and analysis of a scientific or technical nature for consideration primarily by their professional colleagues within and outside government;
2. describing administrative processes and departmental organization and procedures;
3. explaining the content, implications, and administration of specific government policies and programs;
4. discussing, within the framework of governmental or departmental policy, the solution of problems through changes in existing programs or the development of new programs;
5. discussing issues on which governmental or departmental policy has not yet been determined;
6. explaining the nature of the political and policy process in government;
7. advocating reforms in the existing organization or procedures of government;
8. commenting in a constructively critical way on government policy or administration;
9. denouncing existing or potential government policies, programs, and operations; and
10. commenting in an overtly partisan way on public policy issues or on government policy or administration.[37]

This list moves from types of public comment which are generally expected, required, or permissible to those which are questionable, risky, or prohibited. Few public servants have ventured beyond the first four categories. The fourth category often involves public servants in bargaining, accommodation, and compromise on behalf of their political superiors. It is on these occasions that members of the public may see most clearly the nature and extent of bureaucratic power in the policy process. These meetings usually take place in private, but public servants are sometimes required to make presentations and answer questions in public forums where a larger measure of risk exists.

The extent to which public servants may venture beyond the first four categories of public comment was clarified in 1979 by the Clark government. To complement the government's freedom of information bill, Prime Minister Clark issued guidelines on communications between public servants and the public.[38] Public servants were advised that they "should be prepared to discuss frankly information within their areas of responsibility that describes or explains programs that have been announced or implemented by the government." Public servants were counselled not to "go beyond this discussion of factual information" and not "to discuss advice or recommendations tendered to Ministers, or to speculate about policy deliberations or future policy decisions." The guidelines stated that "it will be normal for public servants to be quoted by name, and to be interviewed" for both the electronic and print media. Finally, the guidelines prohibited the disclosure of information which was specifically pro-

---

[37]This classification is an expansion of that set out in Kernaghan, *Ethical Conduct*, p. 36.
[38]*Policy Guidelines for Public Servants: Communications with the Public*, November 23, 1979, reproduced in *Debates* (Commons), November 29, 1979, p. 1875.

hibited by law. However, public employees "*acting in good faith*"[39] under the guidelines were not to "be considered as having violated their oaths of secrecy." The new Trudeau government elected in 1980 retained these guidelines, but the Mulroney government elected in 1984 amended the guidelines by requiring that interviews with the public or the media "shall be on the record and for attribution by name."[40] While this amendment was made in the name of "open government," the view was widely expressed that it would have the effect of discouraging public servants from giving out even factual information.

As a result of the intimate links among politics, policy, and administration described earlier, public servants often enhance understanding of the political and policy process through their speeches and writings on the machinery of government and the administrative process. The major burden of explaining the political system to the public is, however, likely to remain with politicians and academic scholars.

Public advocacy of administrative reform and constructive criticism of government activities may complement the public servants' information and conciliation functions. However, the participation of public servants in these forms of public comment is restricted by their political superiors who bear public responsibility for the operations of government.

Denunciations and overtly partisan assessments of government policy or administration tend to be clearer than other forms of public comment in their manifestation and in the certainty of their punishment. Both the traditional admonition against public comment and recent decisions by administrative tribunals prohibit such activity unless public servants are on leave of absence to seek election.

The unwritten rule against public comment is subject to varying interpretations and applications in contemporary society. Public servants are now involved in forms of public comment not explicitly covered by the conventional rule, and the nature of this involvement constitutes a significant departure from a position of political neutrality. It appears that public servants will increasingly be required to attend public meetings to provide information about the substance and implementation of government policies and programs. As a result, the public will become more aware of the influence that public servants bring to deliberations on public policy matters. It is often difficult for public servants to discuss government policy without indicating, inadvertently or otherwise, some measure of the influence they have — or could have — over the content of policy.

(5) Anonymity and Ministerial Responsibility

The traditional model of political neutrality requires that "public servants provide forthright advice to their political superiors in private and in confidence. In return, political executives protect the anonymity of public servants by publicly accepting responsibility for departmental decisions." The anonymity of public

---

[39]Emphasis added.
[40]Office of the Prime Minister, *Policy Guidelines for Public Servants: Communications with the Public*, November 23, 1984.

servants depends in large measure on the vitality of the doctrine of individual ministerial responsibility according to which ministers are personally responsible to the legislature both for their own actions and for those of their administrative subordinates. Thus, public servants are not directly answerable to the legislature, and their minister protects their anonymity. Recent events have shown, however, that ministers will not invariably protect the anonymity of their officials by refusing to name or blame them publicly. This issue and the relationship of ministerial responsibility to political neutrality and anonymity are discussed in Chapter 15.

The decline of official anonymity. Public service anonymity depends significantly on factors other than the operation of ministerial responsibility. Departures from political neutrality in the areas of patronage and political activity also diminish official anonymity, but the greatest threat is probably the expansion of public comment described earlier. The increased interaction of public servants with both individual citizens and specific "publics" or clientele groups reveals the nature of official involvement in policy development. The cumulative impact of the growing information and conciliation functions performed by public servants is a gradual, but significant, decline in official anonymity.

The anonymity of public servants has been diminished also by their more frequent appearances before legislative committees. Their diplomatic skills are often severely taxed as they strive to describe and explain their department's program fully and frankly, while preserving their loyalty to their minister and their reputation for impartiality. On occasion, however, legislators, pressure groups, journalists, and others concerned with the committees' deliberations can discern the actual or potential power of public servants in the policy process. Elaboration on the interaction between public servants and legislators is contained in Chapter 15.

The pervasive role of the news media in contemporary society has been reflected in increased media coverage of the activities and identities of public servants. As explained in Chapter 19, the media and public servants share a mutual desire to inform the public about government programs. Public servants utilize the media for public relations and publicity — to tell their department's story and to sell their department's programs. The media serve as excellent channels of communication to the public for officials engaged in public comment requiring the description and explanation of government programs. The media in turn analyse the purposes and, whenever possible, identify the personalities involved in the development and administration of programs. This media coverage helps to limit bureaucratic power by exposing the activities of public servants to public questioning and criticism.

The extent to which public servants are exposed to the public's gaze through the news media depends largely on the position they occupy, on current interest in their department's activities, and on their personal views and their minister's views on anonymity. Certain public servants (for example, a deputy minister of finance) are better known because of the enduring importance of their position; others receive publicity during periods of public controversy in their sphere of responsibilities.

Although the tradition of anonymity remains strong among public servants, their visibility has been heightened by changes in political institutions and practices, and by the media's response to demands for more public information. This gradual decline in official anonymity is likely to continue and to reveal the expanding role of public servants in the political process.

(6) Permanency in Office

The case for security of tenure. The preservation of political neutrality requires that "public servants execute policy decisions loyally irrespective of the philosophy and programs of the party in power and regardless of their personal opinions. As a result, public servants enjoy security of tenure during good behaviour and satisfactory performance." Thus, in the event of a change of government, official neutrality helps to ensure continuity of administration by competent and experienced public servants, as well as the provision of impartial advice on policy options and the loyal implementation of policy decisions. Security of tenure enables a career public servant not only to establish and wield influence in the policy process, but also to continue to exercise such influence even if there is a change in the governing party. Long tenure in office enables public servants to acquire knowledge and experience both in specific policy fields and in the political-administrative system within which policy decisions are made. Permanence in office for public servants increases their power vis-à-vis politicians. Ministers cannot match the expertise of their senior officials, and the frequent rotation of ministers among departments prevents them from accumulating much experience in particular policy areas.

As public servants, especially at the senior levels, become more overtly or apparently political, the argument for political appointments to senior posts is strengthened. Thus, permanence in office depends largely on adherence to the elements of political neutrality already described. The merit system is designed to bring about a career public service by minimizing the number of patronage appointments and avoiding a turnover of personnel following a change of government. Senior public servants are not permitted to engage in partisan political activity or public criticism of government. Finally, the preservation of ministerial responsibility and public service anonymity helps to protect officials from public identification as supporters or opponents of particular policies.

Despite these efforts to achieve the fact and the appearance of administrative impartiality, Opposition party leaders have frequently promised, if elected, to turf out senior officials because of their assumed contribution to government policies to which these leaders are opposed. Public servants must be able to demonstrate, therefore, the capacity to adapt quickly and effectively to the requirements of a new governing party. Easily the best test of these adaptive qualities is the behaviour of public servants when a different political party comes into power.

When permanence in office for public servants has been combined with longevity in office by a particular political party, a change of government presents an especially difficult challenge to the capacity of public servants to serve impartially different political masters. It is understandable that senior officials who have worked closely with ministers in the development of existing policies should be apprehensive about the arrival of a new governing party. Shortly before Mr. Diefenbaker and the Progressive Conservatives ended the twenty-two-year reign of the Liberal Party in 1957, J. E. Hodgetts wondered about the effects of such a change: "Could we expect impartial service from the permanent servants or would we have to face some form of the American system of turning out the top ranking officials?"[41] During the Diefenbaker period, unhealthy tension often existed between senior public servants and the government. J. R. Mallory has observed, however, that "there were few resignations and few drastic changes in policy. The new ministers soon discovered that a good civil servant conceives it his duty to serve his political master to the best of his ability, and that the higher civil service was as effective at advising the new government as it had been the old."[42] In general, subsequent new governments have come to the same conclusion.

During the brief Clark period, few senior officials were invited or decided to resign. But ministers in the Clark government disagree as to whether they were well and faithfully served by senior bureaucrats. Flora MacDonald, the Secretary of State for External Affairs, stated[43] that her efforts to seek advice from persons outside government were resisted almost entirely by "those who really have their hands on the levers of power — the senior mandarins." She also complained about the use by senior bureaucrats of such "entrapment devices" as the many "crisis corridor decisions" with which she was faced, unduly lengthy and numerous memos, the late delivery of her submissions to Cabinet, and "the one-dimensional opinions put forward in memos." She noted that she "was expected to accept the unanimous recommendation of the Department" and that she was "seldom, if ever . . . given the luxury of multiple-choice options on matters of major import."

Miss MacDonald's experience was shared by Alan McKinnon, the Minister of National Defence and of Veterans Affairs.[44] He was especially critical of the "extraordinary influence" of the Prime Minister's Office and the Privy Council Office, sometimes in concert with departmental officials, on the "content" of Cabinet business. He asserted that the Clark government "met a form of passive, but inspired, resistance to change which proved highly effective, since it was presented with all the skill, and sometimes charm, that a group of highly intelligent men and women can muster when faced with a neophyte Cabinet, and a minority situation." He stated further that senior bureaucrats seemed

---

[41]J. E. Hodgetts, "The Liberal and the Bureaucrat," *Queen's Quarterly*, vol. 62, (1955), pp. 176-183. Following the 1957 election, John Meisel observed that the Liberal program "had, in the main, evolved gradually as the consequence of the continuous interaction of the cabinet and the leading experts in the civil service. . . . Much of what had, in the years immediately before the election, been called Liberal policies or the Liberal programme was actually the product of the intimate co-operation of leading civil servants and their ministers." John Meisel, *The Canadian General Election of 1957* (Toronto: University of Toronto Press, 1962), pp. 37-38.

[42]J. R. Mallory, *The Structure of Canadian Government* (Toronto: Macmillan, 1971), p. 116.

[43]See "The Ministers and the Mandarins," *Policy Options*, vol. 1 (September–October 1980), pp. 29-31.

[44]"An Address to the Rotary Club of Victoria," August 1980.

unable to believe that he "was interested in, or even capable of understanding the immense subtleties of the problems that they had to solve. It was clearly something of an eye opener to them that any minister should wish to originate policy himself." Mr. McKinnon was dismayed at the bureaucrats' "entrenched hostility to the concept of the minister actually having both the *power* as well as the *responsibility* . . . ."

The experience of other ministers was different.[45] One minister stated that his experience with officials in his own department and "indeed, generally, was not similar to Miss MacDonald's. I am not suggesting there might not have been some incidents where public servants with deep political or policy convictions which differ from mine, might have endeavoured to frustrate or mislead me. However, generally I found them to be hard-working, dedicated and professional."[46]

These differing views support the argument earlier in this chapter that the extent of bureaucratic power varies according to such factors as "the policy or program under consideration, the department or agency involved, and the style and competence of ministers and their officials." Prime Minister Clark stated that he and his government had no complaint regarding the treatment they received from the senior public service. He did ask, however, whether "a large and diverse country like ours can be as well served as Britain is by the exclusive reliance upon a professional Public Service, or whether we should be leaning more towards elements of the American system which allow a new government to bring in people who agree with its point of view."[47]

The case for politicization. There is some support in Canada for a system of political appointments similar to that in the United States. Supporters of a politicized public service usually cite the following benefits from political appointments to senior public service posts:
• a strong commitment to implementing the policies of the new government;
• a breath of fresh air in the form of new ideas and approaches towards government policies and processes;
• the restoration and preservation of political (ministerial) control over permanent officials and the decision-making processes of government;
• advice on policy issues that is more sensitive to their partisan political implications;
• greater trust by ministers in their policy advisors.

Under this system, the incumbents of the most senior public service positions would be replaced whenever a change in government occurred. Some senior appointments would thus be held on a temporary rather than a permanent basis. The power of career public servants would be reduced, because they would not normally be appointed to the highest administrative posts in government. How-

[45]Reported in confidential communications with Professor Kernaghan in October 1980.
[46]Ibid.
[47]Transcript of An Address (Including Question and Answer Period) to the 11th Annual Leadership Conference Sponsored by the Centre for the Study of the Presidency, Ottawa, October 19, 1980, p. 14.

ever, assuming regular changes in the governing party, the tenure in office of senior political appointees would be too brief to enable them to exercise as much power based on experience and expertise as career public servants do.

At present, a shift to a system of political appointments either in the federal government or in most provincial governments is unlikely. Career public servants in Canada can normally expect security of tenure during good conduct, adequate performance, and political neutrality. Note must be taken, however, of a gradual politicization of the senior bureaucracy in a few provinces, and of the fact that the Conservative government that came to power in Saskatchewan in 1982 dismissed about two hundred senior public servants. The Saskatchewan experience appears to be an aberration. Certainly the rationale for the sweeping nature of the dismissals is unclear; many of those dismissed were career public servants with no partisan affiliation.

Political Neutrality and Bureaucratic Power

The present operations of Canada's public services are not in accord with a strict interpretation of the traditional doctrine of political neutrality. Some of the requirements of the traditional doctrine remain substantially unchanged, but some have never been met, and others have been altered to keep pace with changing political, social, and technological circumstances. The elements of the doctrine may be updated and restated as follows:

1. Policy, politics and administration are intertwined.
2. Most public servants are selected and promoted on the basis of merit, but some positions are filled by partisans of the governing party.
3. Public servants may participate in a number of partisan political activities unless they occupy senior or sensitive positions.
4. Public servants are usually not permitted to criticize publicly their government's actions, but are involved in various other forms of public comment in the normal course of their duties.
5. Public servants provide confidential advice to ministers; ministers usually protect the anonymity of public servants, but this anonymity is gradually declining for other reasons.
6. Public servants usually execute policy decisions loyally regardless of their personal views and of the political complexion of the governing party.

Thus, public servants are actively involved in the political system both by necessity in the areas of policy development and execution, and by choice in the sphere of political partisanship. This involvement accounts in large part for the nature and extent of bureaucratic power in contemporary Canadian governments. The next chapter assesses the implications of this bureaucratic power for the concept and practice of administrative responsibility.

BIBLIOGRAPHY

Altshuler, Alan A., ed. *The Politics of the Federal Bureaucracy.* 2nd ed. New York: Harper and Row, 1977.

Appleby, Paul H. *Policy and Administration.* University, Ala.: University of Alabama Press, 1949.

Atkinson, Michael M., and William D. Coleman. "Bureaucrats and Politicians in Canada: An Examination of the Political Administration Model." *Comparative Political Studies*, vol. 18 (April 1985): 58–80.

Campbell, Colin. *Governments Under Stress: Political Executives and Key Bureaucrats in Washington, London and Ottawa.* Toronto: University of Toronto Press, 1983.

D'Aquino, Thomas. "The Public Service of Canada: The Case for Political Neutrality." *Canadian Public Administration*, vol. 27 (Spring 1984): 14–23.

Dawson, R. M. "The Civil Service of Canada." *Canadian Journal of Economics and Political Science*, vol. 2 (August 1936): 291.

Dvorin, Eugene P., and Robert H. Simmons. *From Amoral to Humane Bureaucracy.* San Francisco: Canfield, 1972.

Forget, Claude E. "L'administration publique: sujet ou objet du pouvoir politique." *Canadian Public Administration*, vol. 21 (Summer 1978): 234–242.

Hodgetts, J. E. "The Civil Service and Policy Formation." *Canadian Journal of Economics and Political Science*, vol. 23 (November 1957): 467–479.

Hodgetts, J. E., William McCloskey, Reginald Whitaker, and V. Seymour Wilson. *The Biography of an Institution: The Civil Service Commission of Canada, 1908–1967.* Montreal: McGill-Queen's University Press, 1972.

Kernaghan, Kenneth. "Changing Concepts of Power and Responsibility in the Canadian Public Service." *Canadian Public Administration*, vol. 21 (Fall 1978): 389–406.

Kernaghan, Kenneth. "Politics, Policy and Public Servants: Ministerial Responsibility Reexamined." *Canadian Public Administration*, vol. 19 (Fall 1976): 432–456.

Kernaghan, Kenneth. "Power, Parliament and Public Servants: Political Neutrality Revisited." *Canadian Public Policy*, vol. 5 (Autumn 1979): 383–396.

Kernaghan, Kenneth, and T. H. McLeod. "Mandarins and Ministers in the Canadian Administrative State." In O. P. Dwivedi, ed., *The Administrative State in Canada* (Toronto: University of Toronto Press, 1982).

MacDonald, Flora. "The Ministers and the Mandarins." *Policy Options*, vol. 1 (September–October, 1980): 29–31.

Meier, Kenneth J. *Politics and the Bureaucracy.* Belmont, Calif.: Duxbury Press, 1979.

Nakamura, Robert T., and Frank Smallwood. *The Politics of Policy Implementation.* New York: St. Martin's Press, 1980.

Peters, B. Guy. *The Politics of Bureaucracy.* 2nd ed. New York: Longman, 1984.

Pressman, Jeffrey L., and Aaron Wildavsky. *Implementation.* Berkeley: University of California Press, 1965.

Rourke, Francis E., ed. *Bureaucratic Power in National Politics.* 2nd ed. Boston: Little, Brown, 1972.

Santos, C. R. "Public Administration as Politics." *Canadian Public Adminis-
    tration*, vol. 12 (Summer 1969): 213–223.
Sharp, Mitchell. "The Bureaucratic Elite and Policy Formation." In W. D. K.
    Kernaghan, ed., *Bureaucracy in Canadian Government*. Toronto: Methuen,
    1973, pp. 82–87.
Wilson, V. Seymour. *Canadian Public Policy and Administration*. Toronto:
    McGraw-Hill Ryerson, 1981, ch. 4.
Wilson, Woodrow. "The Study of Administration." *Political Science Quarterly*,
    vol. 2 (June 1887): 197–222; reprinted in *Political Science Quarterly*, vol. 55
    (December 1941): 481–506.

CASES

In *Case Program in Canadian Public Administration* (Toronto: Institute of Public
Administration of Canada):
    The Draft Memorandum to Cabinet, by Douglas G. Hartle
In Kenneth Kernaghan, *Canadian Cases in Public Administration* (Toronto:
Methuen Publications):
    Public Interest or Collective Interest
    The Kroeker Case
    A Sensitive Position
    The Minister and the Doctor

12

Administrative Responsibility

THE IMPORTANCE OF ADMINISTRATIVE RESPONSIBILITY

In democratic states, it is not only the expansion of bureaucratic power which arouses concern; it is also the irresponsible exercise of that power. Thus, continuing attention centres on the means by which administrative power and administrative responsibility can be reconciled. This chapter examines the meaning and nature of administrative responsibility in contemporary democratic society, with particular reference to Canada. First, the importance of administrative responsibility is explained. Next, the conventional theories of administrative responsibility and challenges to these theories are described. Then, a distinction between objective and subjective responsibility is used to relate the concept of administrative responsibility to the institutional and value frameworks set out in Chapter 10 and to the concept of the public interest.

During the past twenty years in particular, public concern about responsibility in government has been stimulated in Western democratic states, including Canada, by events involving illegal or unethical activities by both politicians and bureaucrats. Discussion of incidents of political espionage, conflicts of interest, and disclosures of confidential information have revealed that both the general public and students of government disagree among themselves as to what constitutes irresponsible conduct, who should assume blame in particular cases, and what penalty should be paid.

The scope and complexity of government activities have become so great that it is often difficult to determine the actual — as opposed to the legal or constitutional — locus of responsibility for specific decisions. Although political executives (i.e., Cabinet ministers) are held responsible for personal wrongdoing, they are not expected to assume responsibility by way of resignation or demotion for acts of administrative subordinates about which they could not reasonably be expected to have knowledge. Yet, it is frequently impossible to assign individual responsibility to public servants for administrative transgressions because so many public servants have contributed to the decision-making process. The allocation of responsibility in government has been complicated even further by the interposition of political appointees or temporary officials between political executives and permanent public servants. Thus, the determination of where responsibility lies for certain government actions is often a difficult task.

While the involvement of political executives in dramatic and well-publicized events has drawn much public attention to the issue of *political* responsibility, the status of *administrative* responsibility has also become a matter of increasing anxiety. As noted in the previous chapter, elected officials make the final

292

decisions on major public policy issues, but public servants have significant influence on these decisions and have authority to make decisions on their own which affect the individual and collective rights of the citizenry.

As a consequence of all these factors, the long-standing concern of scholars and practitioners about the preservation of administrative responsibility has gradually become more acute. This concern is shared in varying degrees by all major actors in the political system — whether political executives, legislators, judges, interest group and mass media representatives, or members of the general public. In an effort by all these individuals to promote what they perceive to be responsible administrative conduct, the decisions of public servants are subject to an almost bewildering assortment of controls and influences. Indeed, while it is clear that political executives are responsible to the people through the legislature, public servants are often required to be responsible in several directions.

Differing perceptions of what constitutes responsible administrative behaviour may be explained in part by the difficulty of defining administrative reponsibility.[1] It is an elusive concept, which defies either brief or exact definition. In the large volume of literature on administrative responsibility, the concept has undergone a variety of interpretations of its content and approaches to its study. Despite confusion and disagreement about the meaning of the concept, however, its long and continuing usage attests to its importance in democratic thought. Academic scholars readily acknowledge the significance of administrative responsibility for the broad issue of democratic morality, and both politicians and bureaucrats show abiding interest in the practical means of eliciting and enforcing responsible administrative behaviour.

As a means of clarifying the meaning of administrative responsibility, and as a basis for subsequent discussion, it is useful to distinguish between administrative responsibility and administrative accountability. According to the widely accepted definition provided by Frederick Mosher,[2] administrative responsibility is a broad concept which includes administrative accountability. He distinguishes between *objective* responsibility (or accountability) and *subjective* or *psychological* responsibility. *Objective* responsibility "connotes the responsibility of a person or an organization *to* someone else, outside of self, *for* some thing or some kind of performance. It is closely akin to *accountability* or *answerability*. If one fails to carry out legitimate directives, he is judged *irresponsible*, and may be subjected to penalties."[3] *Subjective* or *psychological* responsibility, by way of contrast, focusses "not upon to whom and for what one *is* responsible (according to law and the organization chart) but to whom and for what one *feels* responsible and *behaves* responsibly. This meaning, which is sometimes described as *personal* responsibility, is more nearly synonymous with identifica-

---

[1]For an excellent discussion of the meaning of administrative responsibility and contending interpretations of the concept in the Canadian context, see V. Seymour Wilson, *Canadian Public Policy and Administration* (Toronto: McGraw-Hill Ryerson, 1981), ch. 7.

[2]Frederick C. Mosher, *Democracy in the Public Service* (New York: Oxford University Press, 1968), pp. 7–10.

[3]Ibid., p. 7. (Emphasis added.)

tion, loyalty and conscience than it is with accountability and answerability."[4] We shall return to these definitions later.

THEORIES OF ADMINISTRATIVE RESPONSIBILITY

The Conventional Theories

The traditional concepts of administrative responsibility may be explained by reference to the celebrated debate between Carl Friedrich and Herman Finer during the period 1935–1941.[5]

Both Friedrich and Finer correctly identified the source of burgeoning bureaucratic power as the rapid expansion of government's service and regulatory functions. They disagreed severely, however, on the most effective means of guarding against abuse of administrative discretion so as to maintain and promote responsible administrative conduct. Their disagreement was in large part an outgrowth of their differing conceptions of the capacity of political systems to adapt to change and of the proper role of public servants. To achieve administrative responsibility, Finer placed primary faith in controls and sanctions exercised over public servants by the legislature, the judiciary, and the administrative hierarchy. In his insistence on the predominant importance of political responsibility (that is, responsibility to elected officials), he claimed that "the political and administrative history of all ages" had shown that "sooner or later there is an abuse of power when external punitive controls are lacking."[6] Friedrich relied more heavily on the propensity of public servants to be self-directing and self-regulating in their responsiveness to the dual standard of technical knowledge and popular sentiment. While he admitted the continuing need for political responsibility, he argued that a policy was irresponsible if it was adopted

> without proper regard to the existing sum of human knowledge concerning the technical issues involved — [or] without proper regard for existing preferences in the community, and more particularly its prevailing majority. Consequently, the responsible administrator is one who is responsive to these two dominant factors: technical knowledge and popular sentiment.[7]

Friedrich asserted also that "parliamentary responsibility is largely inoperative and certainly ineffectual"[8] and that "the task of clear and consistent policy for-

---

[4]Ibid., p. 8. (Emphasis added.)

[5]Carl J. Friedrich, "Responsible Government Service Under the American Constitution," in *Problems of the American Public Service* (New York: McGraw-Hill, 1935), pp. 3–74 and "Public Policy and the Nature of Administrative Responsibility," in Carl J. Friedrich and Edward S. Mason, eds., *Public Policy* (Cambridge: Harvard University Press, 1940), pp. 3–24. Herman Finer, "Better Government Personnel," *Political Science Quarterly* (1936), pp. 569 ff. and "Administrative Responsibility in Democratic Government," *Public Administration Review*, vol. 1, no. 4 (1941), pp. 335–350. The most comprehensive statements of the opposing positions are found in the 1940–1941 exchange of articles.

[6]Finer, "Administrative Responsibility in Democratic Government," p. 337.

[7]Friedrich, "Public Policy and the Nature of Administrative Responsibility," p. 232.

[8]Ibid., p. 10.

mation has passed — into the hands of administrators and is bound to continue to do so."[9]

Finer admitted the difficulty, but stressed the necessity, of remedying the several deficiencies of political control over administrative officials. He believed that the means and modes of legislative control should be improved.[10] He argued further that officials should not determine their own course of action. Rather, the elected representatives of the people should "determine the course of action of public servants to the most minute degree that is technically feasible."[11]

Finer presented an excellent summary of his position and of his critique of Friedrich's stand in his explanation of "the two definitions" of administrative responsibility:

> First, responsibility may mean that X is accountable for Y *to* Z. Second, responsibility may mean an inward personal sense of moral obligation. In the first definition the essence is the externality of the agency or persons to whom an account is to be rendered; and it can mean very little without that agency having authority over X, determining the lines of X's obligation and the terms of its continuance or revocation. The second definition puts the emphasis on the conscience of the agent, and . . . if he commits an error it is an error only when recognized by his own conscience, and . . . the punishment of the agent will be merely the twinges thereof. The one implies public execution; the other hara-kiri.[12]

Finer described the sum of Friedrich's arguments as *moral* responsibility, as opposed to his own emphasis on *political* responsibility.

Friedrich's contention that administrative responsibility can be more effectively elicited than enforced raises a critical issue for contemporary discussion of administrative responsibility. He believed that responsible conduct depended to a large extent on "sound work rules and effective morale."[13] To this end, he suggested that the environment of government employment be changed. Public servants were to be granted the right to organize into staff associations and to bargain collectively with the government. Furthermore, responsibility to technical knowledge could not be assured unless public servants were permitted to discuss policy issues publicly. He noted that "in matters of vital importance the general public is entitled to the views of its permanent servants."[14] Finer argued for the preservation of the official's anonymity in order to avoid "bringing himself and his colleagues into partisan contempt"[15] and making him "the instrument of conflict between 'the general public' — and the legislature."[16]

An understanding of the Friedrich-Finer debate is an essential foundation on which to construct subsequent discussion in that it raises several of the major

---

[9]Ibid., p. 5.
[10]Finer, pp. 339–340.
[11]Ibid., p. 336.
[12]Ibid., p. 336. (Emphasis added.)
[13]Friedrich, p. 19.
[14]Ibid., p. 23.
[15]Finer, p. 349.
[16]Ibid.

issues of administrative responsibility still being debated by contemporary scholars, albeit in a vastly different social and political environment. These issues are
of enduring concern, and continue to challenge the capacity of scholars to appreci-
ate their dimensions and the ingenuity of practitioners to adopt institutional
and procedural innovations to meet their demands.

The strength of Finer's approach lay in his recognition of the continuing need
for political controls over the bureaucracy. Its primary weakness lay in his failure to anticipate the inadequacy of these controls to ensure administrative responsibility in a period of ever-accelerating political and social change. The strength of
Friedrich's argument rested on his awareness of the deficiency of solely political
controls. Its major weakness lay in the difficulty of reconciling conflicts between
the two criteria of technical knowledge and popular sentiment. Although the
Friedrich-Finer controversy preceded the post-war assault on traditional principles and tenets of public administration, the seeds of change had already borne
enough fruit for Friedrich to see the emerging trends. Among the developments
he foresaw were the rejection of the politics-administration dichotomy, with the
acceptance of the role of public servants in policy development; the increased
need to delegate to public servants powers of a legislative and judicial nature;
the strikingly rapid growth and significance of professionalism in the public
service; recognition of the effect of employee morale on work performance; agitation for the extension to public employees of the rights to bargain collectively
and to speak publicly on issues of public policy; and finally, demands for direct
citizen participation in the administrative process.

Criticisms of the Conventional Theories

During the past four decades, the Friedrich and Finer approaches have been
subject to a number of critiques, and alternative interpretations have been formulated.[17] Their approaches have remained the dominant contending ones,
however, and most writers on administrative responsibility have referred to the
Friedrich-Finer debate with a view to supporting, attacking, or updating one or
both sides of the argument. Thus, scholarly debate was carried on within the
context of these two conventional interpretations. In more recent years, these
traditional notions of administrative responsibility have come under attack.
Recent critiques have been less in the nature of frontal assaults on the theoretical underpinnings of administrative responsibility, and more in the nature of
integral parts of broader movements and larger issues in public administration
or political science.

An important element of intellectual ferment in the United States surrounding the reassessment of the theory, practice, and teaching of public administration "in a time of turbulence"[18] was reawakened interest in normative theory.[19]

---

[17]See, for example, the excellent summary and critique of five major interpretations in Arch
Dotson, "Approaches to Administrative Responsibility," *Western Political Quarterly*, vol. 10 (September 1957), pp. 701–727.

[18]The major published works on this reassessment include Frank Marini, ed., *Toward a New
Public Administration: The Minnowbrook Perspective* (Scranton: Chandler, 1971) and Dwight
Waldo, ed., *Public Administration in a Time of Turbulence* (Scranton: Chandler, 1971).

[19]Normative theory is a rationale of how some part of the world *should be*, rather than of how
it *is*.

Michael Harmon, for example, argues that both Finer and Friedrich, despite their differences, take a negative view of the nature of man, and of administrative man in particular, because they agree that "without the checks provided by either the law or the processes of professional socialization, the resultant behaviour of administrators would be both selfish and capricious."[20] Harmon looks to the existentialist's notion of self-development and self-actualization as a basis for a new theory of administrative responsibility. Officials are expected to become much more actively engaged in the initiation and promotion of policy. Harmon fails, however, to reconcile this increased participation with the conventional idea that administrators' decisions should be guided by the values and goals of elected politicians within the constraints of the law and the administrative hierarchy.[21]

Holtan Odegard, in his provocative work on administrative democracy,[22] looks beyond political and moral responsibility to a new kind of administrative responsibility, which he defines as intentional, mature, or "homonomous." It would be a responsibility "beyond both the heteronomy of constraining external authority and the autonomy of private independent conscience."[23] Odegard sees great promise for achieving this responsibility in the development of "professionlike attitudes" in the civil service. The elements of this development would include dedication to the public interest, refusal to take a stand on issues of partisan politics, identifying relevant publics and stimulating their organization and participation in policy formation, and professional commitment to fact, expertise, rationality, skill, and learning.[24]

Theodore Lowi's approach to administrative responsibility[25] contrasts sharply with the redefinitions by Harmon and Odegard. Among what Lowi describes as "proposals for radical reform" in the United States are suggestions which are reminiscent of the position articulated by Finer in the early 1940s. Lowi recommends that the Supreme Court declare "invalid and unconstitutional any delegation of powers to an administrative agency that is not accompanied by clear standards of implementation."[26] This call to the legislature to specify the course of action of public servants in more precise terms is complemented by a plea for "early and frequent *administrative rule making*."[27] Rather than relying primarily on case-by-case adjudication under a statute delegating broad powers in vague language, bureaucrats should formulate rules which provide standards for the adjudication of cases under that statute.

The views and proposals of Lowi on the one hand, and Harmon and Odegard on the other, offer a different, but related, version of the Finer-Friedrich debate.

---

[20]Michael M. Harmon, " Normative Theory and Public Administration: Some Suggestions for a Redefinition of Administrative Responsibility," in Marini, ed., *Toward a New Public Administration*, p. 173.

[21]See John Paynter, "Comment: On a Redefinition of Administrative Responsibility," ibid., p. 187.

[22]Holtan P. Odegard, *The Politics of Truth: Towards Reconstruction in Democracy* (University, Alabama: University of Alabama Press, 1971).

[23]Ibid., p. 284.

[24]Ibid., pp. 292–295.

[25]Theodore J. Lowi, *The End of Liberalism* (New York: Norton, 1969).

[26]Ibid., p. 298.

[27]Ibid., p. 299.

Accompanying such redefinitions of administrative responsibility is the argument that focussing on the traditional means of promoting responsible administrative behaviour has left us in a perilous position. Some scholars suggest that we lack imaginative and innovative proposals to cope with the issue of administrative responsibility in an era of uncertainty and rapid change. It is suggested also that the present and the anticipated effects of technological change on the structures and procedures of democratic government require that public administrative institutions keep the way open for rapid and perhaps radical reform.[28] The challenge is to find the means to reconcile administrative power and administrative responsibility in the complex decision-making milieu of the modern democratic state.

Objective and Subjective Responsibility

In the face of recent attacks and new perspectives on conventional notions and practices of administrative responsibility, it is appropriate to seek a broader, more inclusive classification than the Friedrich-Finer categories. The two meanings of administrative responsibility provided by Frederick Mosher, which were explained earlier in this chapter, meet this requirement admirably.

H. L. Laframboise has recently made a distinction between what he describes as dependent and independent accountability, which is similar to Mosher's distinction between objective and subjective responsibility.[29] Dependent accountability "is objective, responding to processes imposed by others, called to account by them and dependent on their judgment." Independent accountability "is subjective. Its base is personal integrity — the quality or state of sound moral principle — uprightness, honesty and sincerity coupled with a sense of wholeness derived from truth to one's inner self. One in effect calls one's self to account for one's actions."[30]

The presence of subjective or psychological responsibility is more difficult to discern than that of objective responsibility, but there is some evidence of its existence and its influence. The deputy ministers surveyed by the Lambert Commission were in complete agreement that they felt "personally responsible" for ensuring that they had good financial controls.[31] Moreover, when asked to what persons and organizations they considered themselves *most* responsible for spe-

---

[28]See the following articles in Waldo, ed., *Public Administration in a Time of Turbulence*: Edward I. Friedland, "Turbulence and Technology: Public Administration and the Role of Information-Processing Technology," pp. 134–150; Orion White, Jr., "Organization and Administration for New Technological and Social Imperatives," pp. 151–168; and Allen Schick, "Toward the Cybernetic State," pp. 214–233. See also Hubert Marshall, "Administrative Responsibility and the New Science of Management Decision," in C. S. Wallia, ed., *Toward Century 21: Technology, Society and Human Values* (New York: Basic Books, 1970), pp. 257–268 and Lewis C. Gawthrop, "Administrative Responsibility: The Systems State and Our Wilsonian Legacy," in H. George Frederickson and Charles R. Wise, eds., *Public Administration and Public Policy* (Lexington, Mass.: D. C. Heath, 1977), pp. 197–209.

[29]"Conscience and Conformity: The Uncomfortable Bedfellows of Accountability," *Canadian Public Administration*, vol. 26 (Fall 1983), pp. 325–343.

[30]Ibid., p. 326.

[31]Royal Commission on Financial Management and Accountability, *Final Report*, p. 458.

cific subjects, a large number of deputies answered "myself" in regard to per
forming the role of leader for the department's employees, managing their
executive team, and building their department's management capability.[32]

In addition to drawing a valuable theoretical distinction between the broad
concepts of objective responsibility and subjective responsibility, Mosher's
classification serves two other important purposes. First, it draws attention to
the *sources* from which one derives one's sense of responsibility, that is, the individuals to whom one *is* or *feels* responsible. The sources of administrative responsibility on which there is a substantial measure of agreement in scholarly writings
include political executives, legislators, judges, administrative superiors, members of the general public, interest group representatives, and journalists (see
Figure 10.2 in Chapter 10). Second, by distinguishing between such values as
accountability and answerability on the one hand, and identification, loyalty,
and conscience on the other, Mosher points to the significance for administrative responsibility of the official's value system.

In this context, it is significant that the administrative values noted in Chapter 10 are central not only to the evolution of Canadian public administration,
but also to the theoretical literature on administrative responsibility. The "responsible" bureaucrat is commonly perceived as the one who pursues such values as
accountability, neutrality, efficiency, effectiveness, responsiveness, representativeness, and integrity. Responsible bureaucratic behaviour is frequently assessed
in terms of the bureaucrat's ability to resolve conflicts among these values in the
light of the public interest.

THE PUBLIC INTEREST

The Meaning of the Public Interest
The concept of the public interest, like that of administrative responsibility, has
been interpreted in various ways.[33] It has been defined in terms of "the general
will," "the wisest and most foresighted interest," a moral imperative "resting on
natural law foundations," and "compromise — as the optimum reconciliation
of the competing claims of special and private interests."[34] Each of these definitions is to some extent partial or deficient. In the context of administrative deci-

---

[32]Ibid., p. 471.

[33]See especially Pendleton Herring, *Public Administration and the Public Interest* (New York:
McGraw-Hill, 1936); Frank Sorauf, "The Public Interest Reconsidered," *Journal of Politics*, vol.
19 (November 1957), pp. 616–639; Glendon Schubert, *The Public Interest: A Critique of a Political Concept* (Glencoe: The Free Press, 1960); Carl J. Friedrich, ed., *Nomos V: The Public
Interest* (New York: Atherton Press, 1962); Herbert J. Storing, "The Crucial Link: Public Administration, Responsibility and the Public Interest," *Public Administration Review*, vol. 24 (March
1964), pp. 39-46; and Richard E. Flathman, *The Public Interest* (New York: Wiley, 1966). For a
list of definitions of the public interest and a bibliography on this subject, see W. T. Stanbury,
"Definitions of the Public Interest," in Douglas G. Hartle, *Public Policy Decision Making and
Regulation* (Montreal: Institute for Research on Public Policy, 1979), pp. 213–218.

[34]Rowland Egger,"Responsibility and Administration: An Exploratory Essay," in Roscoe Martin,
ed., *Public Administration and Democracy: Essays in Honor of Paul H. Appleby* (Syracuse: Syracuse University Press, 1965), pp. 311–313.

sion making, for example, the first three definitions are too nebulous to provide sufficient guidance to the bureaucrat. However, the interpretation of the public interest as the best possible accommodation of conflicting particular interests provides an essential element of specificity.

The adjustment of the claims of special and private interests connotes a power struggle among competing groups, each possessing approximately equal access to the decision maker and devoting roughly equivalent resources to the struggle. In reality, as explained in Chapters 18 and 19, both access and resources in money, organization, supporters, and research capacity are uneven among various groups. Moreover, the interests of some segments of the population may not be represented because these segments are underprivileged, uneducated, uninformed, inarticulate, unorganized, underfunded, or simply uninterested. Even if the whole range of relevant special interests is taken into account, the definition is still incomplete. Public interest theorists commonly assert that the public interest is not the mere sum of special interests, no matter how evenly and equitably these interests are represented. Frequently, these special interests are too short-sighted or are unable on their own to reach an accommodation of their various interests. In these cases, the critical contribution to the determination of the public interest comes from the decision maker.

However, as explained in Chapter 10, the avenue to some decisions runs through a myriad of conflicting and complementary values. Among the obstacles along the road is the temptation to succumb to personal or narrow interests when a decision in the broader interest of the general public, or of substantial segments of the general public, is required. The extent to which bureaucrats are likely to suppress self-interest in a quest for the public interest is a matter for debate. Should the ultimate aim be the development of officials who, like Downs's *statesmen*, have a broad, altruistic, and idealistic devotion to government policies and programs? Or is the inculcation of loyalty to specific programs or administrative units, as in the case of Downs's *zealots* and *advocates*,[35] a sufficient and more realistic goal? Do those in academe or in public bureaucracies who envisage the eventual predominance of self-directing bureaucrats actively pursuing human dignity in every decision[36] have an unduly optimistic view of human nature? Downs contends that with rare exceptions "bureaucracies have few places for officials who are loyal to society as a whole" (i.e., for statesmen), and that "this is true even though all administrative textbooks and nearly all administrators at least verbally exhort all officials to exhibit such loyalty."[37]

---

[35]Downs, *Inside Bureaucracy* (Boston: Little, Brown, 1967), p. 88. "*Zealots* are loyal to relatively narrow policies or concepts, such as the development of nuclear submarines. They seek power both for its own sake and to effect the policies to which they are loyal . . . . *Advocates* are loyal to a broader set of functions or to a broader organization than zealots. They also seek power because they want to have a significant influence upon policies and actions concerning those functions or organizations."

[36]See especially Eugene P. Dvorin and Robert H. Simmons, *From Amoral to Humane Bureaucracy* (San Francisco: Canfield, 1972).

[37]Downs, *Inside Bureaucracy*, p. 111.

Determining the Public Interest

The resolution of value conflicts in the light of the public interest is sometimes a difficult challenge for public servants. This is demonstrated well by the following letter to the editor of the *Journal* of the Professional Institute of the Public Service:

> I have been concerned that too rigid an application of . . . "the Oath of Secrecy" conflicts with professional integrity. Now that environmental concerns, which are frequently matters of opinion, not fact, are being accorded increasing attention, the question becomes more urgent. Many . . . of Canada's professional biologists who are well-qualified to speak on environmental matters are muzzled because they are Civil Servants and so any environmental debate is frequently left to extremist and partisan voices.
>
> If one considers a hypothetical case where pressure is being applied, perhaps from ministerial level, to have a contract awarded to a firm which, for professional reasons, is deemed unsatisfactory, how far dare a Civil Servant go in opposing such seemingly unethical practices? What of an employee who is sufficiently troubled by such an incident to discuss it with a priest under "Seal of the Confessional?"
>
> . . . surely, our responsibility to Canada is greater than any duty we owe to our political masters of the day. We have standards of professional integrity to maintain and a moral position to uphold. The glib, cynical retort, "Well, you can always resign," is hopelessly inadequate . . . .
>
> (Name withheld by request)[38]

Clearly, bureaucrats seeking escape from a labyrinth of competing values and pressures need some guideposts to conflict resolution. They require "criteria of judgement," that is, standards against which they can measure conflicting alternatives. It has been suggested that the standards of *legitimacy*, *expediency*, and *morality* may provide these essential criteria.[39]

The standard of *legitimacy* stimulates bureaucrats to ask which of the various actors in the political system have the right to expect or demand certain decisions. Bureaucrats may interpret legitimacy formally as including only those with legal or hierarchical authority over them. Their perception of legitimacy may, however, be more subjective and embrace a broader range of political actors (e.g., representatives of special interests) whose status may not have been legitimized in any formal way.

The standard of *expediency* motivates bureaucrats to assess the relative strength of the negative sanctions which various political actors may impose for nonconformity to their desires. Decisions based primarily on expediency are not

---

[38]*Journal*, vol. 52 (November 1973), pp. 9–10.
[39]See Kenneth Kernaghan, "Responsible Public Bureaucracy: A Rationale and a Framework for Analysis," *Canadian Public Administration*, vol. 16 (Winter 1973), pp. 595–597. Similar dimensions have been suggested as a basis for *predicting* an individual's behaviour in situations of *role* conflict resolution. See N. Gross, W. S. Mason, and A. McEachern, *Explorations in Role Analysis* (New York: Wiley, 1958), ch. 17.

always self-seeking. Nor are they necessarily contrary to the public interest. If threatened by strong negative sanctions, bureaucrats may yield to narrow interests simply because the issue involved is comparatively unimportant. They may well be preserving and consolidating their resources to do battle against a more significant menace to the public interest. They will, therefore, evaluate the implications of their decisions for their short- and long-term survival.

The standard of *morality* encourages bureaucrats to resolve value conflicts according to their perception of the highest moral and ethical principles of contemporary society and their own sense of integrity. While morality is a highly personal and subjective standard, its application in the public service will be conditioned by the organizational socialization of bureaucrats and by the demands of the situation. Bureaucrats may receive valuable direction as to the morality of a decision if they ask themselves whether they would make the same choice if they had to explain their decision in public.

It is the bureaucrat's good fortune that there is likely to be a high correlation between the perceived legitimacy of a political actor's expectations and that actor's capacity to impose strong negative sanctions. Thus, the standards of legitimacy and expediency often combine to permit the bureaucrat an escape from value conflicts. Even when this happy coincidence exists, however, and especially when it does not exist, the standard of morality may be of comparable or even overriding importance to legitimacy and expediency in the reconciliation of conflicting values. Consider, for example, a situation where the public servant's superior desires one course of action (legitimacy); professional colleagues threaten strong negative sanctions if a second alternative is not followed (expediency); and his or her moral and ethical standards suggest that still a third course of action is preferable (morality). While a compromise solution may be worked out that will partially satisfy all three standards, the public servant will occasionally find "his back to the wall, where he must consult his conscience and consider the gods he worships."[40] A situation may well occur where the public servant's superior adopts a course of action which outrages his or her sense of morality. The public servant may resolve this clash between legitimacy and expediency on the one hand, and morality on the other, by accepting the superior's decision, requesting a transfer, or resigning.[41]

Except in situations where bureaucrats have been given complete discretionary authority, they may be able to shift the burden of choice among contending values to their hierarchical superior. *Hierarchy* in administration is a prime safeguard of administrative responsibility in that it forces "important decisions to higher levels of determination or at least higher levels of review where perspectives are necessarily broader, less technical and expert, more political."[42] At the highest policy-making levels of government, it may be argued that in the final analysis the determination of the public interest is the task of the elected repre-

---

[40]Egger, "Responsibility and Administration," p. 304.

[41]For elaboration on this point, see Kenneth Kernaghan, "The Conscience of the Bureaucrat: Accomplice or Constraint?" *Canadian Public Administration*, vol. 27, no. 4 (Winter 1984), pp. 576–591.

[42]Mosher, *Democracy and the Public Service*, p. 212.

sentatives. Bureaucrats cannot, however, escape the responsibility of providing their political masters with the best possible advice. Moreover, if only in the cause of personal survival, bureaucrats cannot evade the responsibility of pointing out the political, economic, and social costs and benefits of selecting one course of action over another.

Understanding of the major types of value conflict combined with criteria of judgement for their resolution may provide valuable guidance towards a decision in the public interest. The voluminous writings on the public interest demonstrate the difficulty of establishing specific and immutable criteria for its determination in any given situation. The public interest may fruitfully be viewed as a dynamic concept. Its content changes from one situation to another and depends in large part on the values of both the decision maker and the interests whose claims are considered. As noted above, the interplay of the standards of legitimacy, expediency, and morality in the resolution of value conflicts may provide valuable guidance in the determination of the public interest. Thus, for the bureaucrat, *the public interest* is what he or she deems it to be in the light of the values of the political actors involved as these values are measured against criteria of judgement for the resolution of value conflicts.

This definition does not set forth unchanging rules or prescriptions by which a substantive public interest may be determined. Rather, it is a procedural definition. The primary purpose in outlining the possible types of value conflict and the standards by which these might be resolved is to stimulate bureaucrats to recognize their biases, to suggest considerations they may unconsciously ignore, and to prompt them to ask the right questions of themselves and others before making a decision. No one expects bureaucrats to proceed through a detailed checklist of the great variety of pressures in their decision-making environment. Few will deny, however, the necessity for them to step back on occasion to examine the value premises on which they have been acting. "In general," the public interest "is a spur to conscience and to deliberation."[43]

An important distinction may be made between a *passive* as opposed to an *active* pursuit of the public interest. The public servant who considers the claims only of *organized* special interests and whose range of values is narrow and inflexible is passive in the search for the public interest. By way of contrast, the public servant who seeks the views of *all relevant interests* and whose value framework is comparatively broad and flexible is in active pursuit of the public interest. Each orientation has its virtues and drawbacks, depending on the issue at hand and the level of the organizational pyramid at which the decision is being made.

ADMINISTRATIVE RESPONSIBILITY AND THE PUBLIC INTEREST

The passive and active orientations towards the public interest may be linked with our earlier distinction between objective and subjective (psychological)

---

[43]J. Roland Pennock, "The One and the Many: A Note on the Concept of the Public Interest," in Friedrich, ed., *Nomos V: The Public Interest*, p. 182.

responsibility. In a brief and admittedly oversimplified fashion, the main characteristics of two hypothetically extreme types of bureaucrat — the objectively responsible and the subjectively responsible official — are suggested here.

Objectively responsible bureaucrats feel responsible primarily to the legal or formal locus of authority and take a passive approach to the determination of the public interest. Their most prominent characteristic and value is accountability to those who have the power to promote, displace, or replace them. The controls and influences which they internalize in the form of administrative values are those expressed by their hierarchical superiors. In making and recommending decisions, they anticipate and reflect the desires of their superiors. It is these superiors who have legitimate authority and who may most easily threaten or impose penalties to ensure compliance — a happy combination of legitimacy and expediency. Bureaucrats of this type do not actively seek the views of policy actors other than their superiors unless they are required to do so. For example, they consult parties with an interest in impending regulations only if such consultation is required by law or expected by their superiors. Their foremost administrative values include accountability and efficiency. They do not take initiatives or risks which may get them or their superiors into trouble. They are, for example, likely to err on the side of caution in their communications with the media. They also prefer, if possible, that their political and administrative superiors resolve any value dilemmas and determine the content of the public interest for them.

Objectively responsible bureaucrats perceive themselves as ultimately responsible to the general public through the administrative hierarchy, the political executive, and the legislature. Their behaviour is based on the possibility and the desirability of separating policy and administration — even at the senior levels of the public service. In Finer's terminology, they are, therefore, "politically" responsible.

Subjectively responsible bureaucrats are a striking contrast. They feel responsible to a broad range of policy participants and are active in the pursuit of the public interest. Their most outstanding characteristic and value is commitment to what they perceive to be the goals of their department or program. Since they view the expectations of a variety of policy actors as legitimate, the sources of their administrative values are numerous and diverse. Subjectively responsible public servants are frequently in conflict with their superiors, but they are not influenced much by the threat of negative sanctions. They seek the views of interests affected by their decisions and recommendations in the absence of, and even in violation of, any legal or formal obligation to do so. Their primary administrative values include responsiveness and effectiveness. They are innovative, take risks, and bend the rules to achieve their objectives. They urge their superiors to follow certain courses of action and are prepared to resolve by themselves the value dilemmas they encounter in their search for the public interest. Subjectively responsible bureaucrats are, for example, more likely than others to engage in "whistle blowing," that is, exposing actions of political and administrative superiors which are illegal, unethical, or unduly wasteful of public funds.

The subjectively responsible bureaucrat rejects the possibility and desirability of separating policy and administration — especially at the senior echelons of the bureaucracy. To use Finer's language again, officials of this type are "morally" responsible in that they look to their own conscience rather than to "external punitive controls" for guidance.

Neither the purely objective nor the purely subjective type is appropriate as a model of the responsible bureaucrat. Some characteristics of both types produce conduct which scholars and public officials generally view as undesirable. Undue emphasis on certain elements of objective responsibility may lead to behaviour that is unresponsive or ineffective. At the other extreme, too great emphasis on particular aspects of subjective responsibility may bring equally undesirable results in the form of behaviour that is unaccountable or inefficient.

If the public service was composed predominantly of either objectively or subjectively responsible bureaucrats, it would tend to manifest the same objectionable features. The "ideal" situation, then, would be a public service in which each public servant strikes that balance between the objective and subjective elements of responsibility which is appropriate to his or her responsibilities and level in the hierarchy. Subsequent chapters in this book will examine, among other things, the extent to which controls and influences over the exercise of bureaucratic power promote objective and subjective responsibility.

BIBLIOGRAPHY

Appleby, Paul. *Morality and Administration in Democratic Government*. Baton Rouge, Louisiana: Louisiana State University Press, 1952.

Bok, Sissela. *Lying*. New York: Panthcon, 1978.

Canada. Royal Commission on Financial Management and Accountability. *Final Report*. Ottawa: Supply and Services, 1979.

Canada. Privy Council Office. *Responsibility in the Constitution*. Submission to the Royal Commission on Financial Management and Accountability, March 1979.

Cameron, D. M. "Power and Responsibility in the Public Service: Summary of Discussions." *Canadian Public Administration*, vol. 21 (Fall 1978): 359–372.

Dotson, Arch. "Approaches to Administrative Responsibility." *Western Political Quarterly*, vol. 10 (September 1957): 701–727.

Dwivedi, O. P. "On Holding Public Servants Accountable." In O. P. Dwivedi, ed., *The Administrative State in Canada*. Toronto: University of Toronto Press, 1982, pp. 151–176.

Finer, Herman. "Administrative Responsibility in Democratic Government." *Public Administration Review*, vol. 1 (Summer 1941): 335–350.

Finer, Herman. "Better Government Personnel." *Political Science Quarterly* (1936): 569 ff.

Friedrich, Carl J. "Public Policy and the Nature of Administrative Responsibility." In Carl J. Friedrich and Edward S. Mason, eds., *Public Policy*. Cambridge: Harvard University Presss, 1940, pp. 3–24.

Friedrich, Carl J. "Responsible Government Service Under the American Constitution." In *Problems of the American Public Service*. New York: McGraw-Hill, 1935, pp. 3–74.

Friedrich, Carl J. *Nomos V: The Public Interest*. New York: Atherton Press, 1962.

Harmon, Michael M. "Normative Theory and Public Administration: Some Suggestions for a Redefinition of Administrative Responsibility." In Frank Marini, ed., *Toward A New Public Administration: The Minnowbrook Perspective*. Scranton, Pa.: Chandler, 1971, pp. 172–189.

Herring, Pendleton. *Public Administration and the Public Interest*. New York: McGraw-Hill, 1936.

Kernaghan, Kenneth. "The Conscience of the Bureaucrat: Accomplice or Constraint?" *Canadian Public Administration*, vol. 27 (Winter 1984): 576–591.

Kernaghan, Kenneth. "Responsible Public Bureaucracy: A Rationale and a Framework for Analysis." *Canadian Public Administration*, vol. 16 (Winter 1973): 572–603.

Laframboise, H. L. "Conscience and Conformity: The Uncomfortable Bedfellows of Accountability." *Canadian Public Administration*, vol. 26 (Fall 1983): 325–343.

Lowi, Theodore J. *The End of Liberalism*. New York: Norton, 1969.

Mallory, J. R. "Responsive and Responsible Government." Presidential Address, *Transactions of the Royal Society of Canada*, Series 1V, vol. 12 (1974).

Mosher, Frederick. *Democracy and the Public Service*. New York: Oxford University Press, 1968.

Odegard, Holtan P. *The Politics of Truth: Towards Reconstruction in Democracy*. University, Ala.: University of Alabama Press, 1971.

Schubert, Glendon. *The Public Interest: A Critique of a Political Concept*. Glencoe: The Free Press, 1960.

Spiro, Herbert. *Responsibility in Government: Theory and Practice*. New York: Van Nostrand Reinhold, 1969.

Thompson, Dennis F. "Moral Responsibility of Public Officials: The Problem of Many Hands." *The American Political Science Review*, vol. 74 (1980): 905–916.

CASES

In *Case Program in Canadian Public Administration* (Toronto: Institute of Public Administration of Canada):

A Conflict of Loyalties, by Kenneth Kernaghan

The Four Million Dollar Typo: A Case About Accountability, by Laurence E. St. Laurent and Sandford F. Borins

13

The Executive
and the Bureaucracy

In Canada, the executive part of government is composed of the *formal* executive (the Governor General, provincial Lieutenant Governors) and the *political* executive (the Prime Minister or provincial Premiers plus the Cabinet). The term *executive* is often used to encompass both the Cabinet and the bureaucracy, but a more descriptive term is the *executive-bureaucratic sphere* of government. This sphere includes three of the major categories of interaction shown in Figure 10.2, namely executive-bureaucratic, interdepartmental, and intradepartmental. The main actors involved in these categories are the Prime Minister (or Premier), Cabinet, Cabinet ministers, central agencies, departments, and other administrative units. The functions of these actors were outlined in Chapters 6 to 8. This chapter focusses on relations between the political executive and the bureaucracy; the next chapter deals with interdepartmental and intradepartmental relations. Two concepts of special utility in explaining these relations between and among political executives and bureaucrats are coordination and ministerial responsibility.

COORDINATION AND MINISTERIAL RESPONSIBILITY

Chapter 10 explained the importance and pervasiveness of coordination in Canadian governments. In this chapter, we will see that the Cabinet and the bureaucracy are the primary instruments for coordinating the development and implementation of public policy. Moreover, coordination is closely related to the principles of collective ministerial responsibility (or Cabinet responsibility) and individual ministerial responsibility which were discussed briefly in Chapter 6.

Ministerial Responsibility
According to the principle of *collective* ministerial responsibility, ministers are responsible as a group (that is, as members of the Cabinet) for the policies and management of the government as a whole. The Cabinet must resign if it loses the confidence of the legislature, that is, if it loses the support of the majority of the members of the House of Commons (or of a provincial legislature). Individual ministers must, in public, support the decisions of the Cabinet, acting as a collectivity, so as to maintain at least the appearance of Cabinet solidarity. More specifically, ministers are required, in private, to work out a consensus on the content of public policies and on the allocation of resources for the develop-

ment and implementation of these policies. Ministers who cannot support a
Cabinet decision in public are expected to resign from the Cabinet.

The principle of *individual* ministerial responsibility, which is explained at
length in Chapter 15, is subject to varying interpretations. In general, however,
it refers to the responsibility of the minister, as the political head of a department, to answer to the legislature and through the legislature to the public both
for his or her personal acts and for the acts of departmental subordinates.

Coordination and Hierarchy

The two principles of ministerial responsibility determine significantly the nature
of power relations not only between politicians and bureaucrats, but also among
the bureaucrats themselves. The principles have an especially important effect
on the organizational design of the executive sphere of government. Organization charts of the government of Canada typically depict this sphere as a hierarchical arrangement of offices (see chart included in this book). The Prime Minister
and the Cabinet stand at the pinnacle of the hierarchy from which lines of
authority flow down to departments headed by Cabinet ministers and to Crown
agencies reporting to Cabinet ministers. Those central agencies which have
departmental form and which report to a minister (e.g., Finance, Treasury Board
Secretariat) are normally portrayed as equal in status to the regular operating
departments and ministries of state strung horizontally across the chart. Other
central agencies (e.g., the Prime Minister's Office and the Privy Council Office)
are shown in a staff (advisory) relationship to the Prime Minister and the Cabinet.

However, the organization chart discloses little about the complex pattern of
power relations in the executive realm, especially in so far as these relations
involve the exercise of influence rather than control. The organization chart
exposes only the bare bones of political-bureaucratic interaction. This organizational skeleton reveals simply the formal lines of authority through which control
moves down the governmental pyramid and accountability moves up. The "informal organization" is hidden from view. Similarly, an organization chart of a
single department or agency that purports to describe the reality of administrative
life simply as a hierarchy of superior-subordinate relationships, or as a "chain of
command," is misleading.

The deficiencies or "pathologies" of bureaucracy in general, and of its hierarchical feature in particular, have been discussed at length elsewhere.[1] Hierarchy does, however, serve several important purposes. One of these is particularly
relevant to a discussion of ministerial responsibility, in that hierarchy provides
for unity of command and of direction, both at the top of the government (by
the Prime Minister or Premier and the Cabinet) and at the top of government
departments (by ministers). In other words, hierarchy promotes accountability.

---

[1]See, for example, J. March and H. Simon, *Organizations* (New York: Wiley, 1958); Victor A.
Thompson, *Modern Organization* (New York: Alfred A. Knopf, 1961); and Robert K. Merton,
"Bureaucratic Structure and Personality," in Robert K. Merton, ed., *Reader in Bureaucracy*
(New York: The Free Press, 1952).

Hierarchy also facilitates coordination. Beginning with the Cabinet as the central coordinating mechanism of government, various means of pursuing policy and administrative coordination permeate the executive-bureaucratic arena. We shall see that ministers, in fulfilling both their collective responsibility for coordinating government as a whole and their individual responsibility for coordinating their departments, are obliged to rely heavily on senior bureaucrats in central agencies and departments.

Aside from hierarchical control, power in the executive sphere is exercised in the form of influence. This fact is demonstrated well by the literature on the *bureaucratic politics* approach to policy making.[2] Allison and Halperin note that the bureaucratic politics approach focusses "primarily on the individuals within a government, and the interaction among them, as determinants of the actions of a government."[3] The interaction of these individuals, either within or between administrative units, may involve conflict, bargaining, compromise, and persuasion, rather than hierarchical control. However, in a parliamentary system, like that of Canada, bureaucratic politics tends to be *muted* "because (i) there is a conscious effort to coordinate policy; (ii) this coordination is made easier by the 'casual processes of intra-bureaucratic consultation and exchange'; and (iii) Cabinet is able, where necessary, to settle serious conflicts among departments with divergent interests and preferences."[4] Nevertheless, the bureaucratic politics model does indicate that, in executive-bureaucratic relations, power is exercised not only in the form of control through the governmental hierarchy, but also in the form of influence through bargaining and negotiation.

The Key Role of the Deputy Minister

Easily the most dominant *bureaucratic* actors in these relations are the deputy ministers (also called deputy heads) of government departments[5] and their central agency equivalents (e.g., the clerk of the Privy Council and secretary to the Cabinet, the secretary of the Treasury Board). Indeed, deputy ministers play such a pivotal role in the policy process that an effective means of understanding the place of the bureaucracy in the Canadian political system is to view the system from the perspective of a deputy minister.

Ministers play the leading roles in the political system as a whole, but they share centre stage with their deputies in the executive-bureaucratic theatre of government. The Royal Commission on Financial Management and Accountability treated the deputy as a critical link in the chain of accountability and concluded that "any defence of ministerial responsibility that did not take into account the real and independent role of the deputy in the administration of

---

[2]See the explanation of the bureaucratic politics approach in Chapter 5.

[3]Graham T. Allison and Morton H. Halperin, "Bureaucratic Politics: A Paradigm and Some Policy Implications," *World Politics*, vol. 24 (Supplement,1972), p. 43.

[4]Denis Stairs, "The Foreign Policy of Canada," in James N. Rosenau, Kenneth W. Thompson, and Gavin Boyd, eds., *World Politics: An Introduction* (New York: The Free Press, 1976), pp.185-186.

[5]See the discussion of deputy ministers in Chapter 14.

government would ultimately prove destructive to the doctrine itself."[6] Deputies yield the spotlight to ministers on ultimate policy decisions, but as supporting actors they perform onerous advisory and administrative roles. In carrying out these responsibilities, deputies must be sensitive not only to administrative, technical, and financial considerations, but also to the partisan political implications of their advice and actions. They are, in addition, entangled in the net of bureaucratic politics within their departments and between their departments and other administrative units. In short, deputies are challenged to perform the difficult feat of keeping their nose to the grindstone, their ear to the ground, and their back to the wall. Moreover, in the executive-bureaucratic sphere, deputies are required to look in three directions to find the audience for their performance. They must look upwards to their political superiors, laterally to their administrative peers, and downwards to their departmental subordinates. The pervasive role of deputy ministers will be evident in subsequent discussion of relations between and among bureaucrats, the Prime Minister, and the Cabinet.

THE PRIME MINISTER AND THE CABINET

The Prime Minister

In the Canadian political system, the Prime Minister (or a provincial Premier) and his or her Cabinet colleagues possess the foremost power and responsibility for making and implementing public policy. In very large part, they determine the political and policy parameters within which the many participants in the political system interact. In the executive realm of government, the Cabinet, acting primarily through Cabinet committees, provides the general framework of policies for which public servants must devise programs and for which resources must be allocated among the many departments and agencies.[7] Given their individual and collective responsibility for the performance of the public service, ministers must strive to control and influence bureaucratic behaviour. They are required to evaluate and coordinate policy and program proposals emanating from departments and to bring partisan political considerations to bear on these proposals. In their capacity as Cabinet members, federal ministers receive a great deal of political, policy, and administrative support from the central agencies described in Chapter 6 (the Prime Minister's Office, the Privy Council Office, the Treasury Board Secretariat, the Department of Finance); in their capacity as political heads of government departments, they receive this assistance from their deputy ministers and from the staff in their ministerial offices.

The federal Cabinet is located at the centre of a complicated network of political-bureaucratic relations, and the Prime Minister is the central figure in that network. It is generally acknowledged that the Prime Minister is much more

---

[6]Royal Commission on Financial Management and Accountability, *Final Report* (Ottawa: Supply and Services, 1979), p. 42.

[7]For an examination of the impact of the Mulroney government on the public service, see David Zussman, "Walking the Tightrope: The Mulroney Government and the Public Service," in Michael J. Prince, ed., *How Ottawa Spends, 1986–87: Tracking the Tories* (Toronto: Methuen, 1986), pp. 250–282.

than "first among equals" in relation to Cabinet colleagues. In fact, several scholars have argued in recent years that the Prime Minister's power has been aggrandized to the point where Canada has "prime ministerial" rather than Cabinet government. One author has even suggested that we "seem to have created in Canada a presidential system without its congressional advantages."[8] Similar arguments have *not* been made so strongly about the role of provincial Premiers. In any event, it is generally agreed that the claims about the expansion of prime ministerial power have some basis in reality, but have been overstated.

The power of the Prime Minister in the political system generally, and in relation to government departments specifically, is often exaggerated. Certainly the Prime Minister is a dominant figure by virtue of his or her responsibilities for leading the governing political party, chairing the Cabinet and key Cabinet committees, acting as chief spokesperson for the government, and appointing and removing both ministers and deputy ministers. Moreover, the Prime Minister can control and influence government departments (and individual bureaucrats), both indirectly through ministers and directly.

There are, however, severe constraints on the ability of the Prime Minister and, indeed, of most provincial Premiers to exercise their powers fully. Their time is so precious that they can afford to become actively involved only in those few policy areas or issues in which they have a personal interest, or which command attention on the grounds of urgency or partisan politics. Certainly, as chairman of Cabinet, the Prime Minister is the key actor in the central policy-making and coordinating institution of government, but he or she alone cannot direct or coordinate the activities of the vast number of bureaucratic actors in government. The Prime Minister must rely on the assistance of Cabinet colleagues and central agencies.

Over the past two decades, Canadian Prime Ministers as well as several provincial Premiers have made vigorous efforts to strengthen political control, especially Cabinet control, over the making and coordination of public policy. Among the primary means of pursuing this objective have been the reform of the Cabinet committee system and the expansion of the role of central agencies. The development and current status of each of these is discussed below. Table 13.1 provides a chronology of the evolution of Cabinet committees and central agencies from the beginning of the Diefenbaker government in 1957.

Cabinet Committees

The purpose of Cabinet committees is to make decisions and to make recommendations to full Cabinet on the content and, to a lesser extent, on the administration of public policies. To this end, the committees are concerned with the coordination of policies and programs, the allocation of human and financial resources for these activities, and ministerial control over the bureaucracy. Except

---

[8]Denis Smith, "President and Parliament: The Transformation of Parliamentary Government in Canada," in Thomas A. Hockin, ed., *Apex of Power*, 2nd ed. (Scarborough: Prentice-Hall, 1977), p. 323.

for the Treasury Board, which is a Cabinet committee provided for in the Financial Administration Act, the existence, responsibilities, and membership of Cabinet committees are determined by the Prime Minister.

The significance and sophistication of the Cabinet committee system in the federal government have increased greatly since the late 1930s, and especially

Table 13.1

EVOLUTION OF CABINET STRUCTURES AND CENTRAL AGENCIES

Prime Minister	Ministry Size	Cabinet and Central Agencies
Diefenbaker (1957–1963)	17–23	• infrequent meetings of committees • several Cabinet meetings weekly
Pearson (1963–1968)	25–26	• 9 standing committees (1968); issues generally to committee before Cabinet • Cabinet meetings weekly • Priorities and Planning (1968) • TBS split from Finance (1966) with separate minister
Trudeau (1968–1979)	27–33	• fewer committees with more authority • FPRO split from PCO (1975) • OCG split from TBS (1977) • MSED established (1979)
Clark (1979–1980)	30	• Inner Cabinet plus 12 committees • PEMS established • MSSD set up (proclamation 1980)
Trudeau (1980–1984)	32–37	• Priorities and Planning with authority to issue decisions • PEMS elaborated • MSERD with FEDCs (1982)
Turner (1984)	29	• Communications, Labour Relations, and Western Affairs commitees wound up • MSERD and MSSD wound up; FEDCs to DRIE • ''mirror committees'' wound up
Mulroney	38	• Foreign and Defence Policy wound up and then re-established • Communications Committee set up • Envelopes consolidated • PEMS rules simplified

Source: Abridged and slightly revised from Ian D. Clark, ''Recent Changes in the Cabinet Decision-Making System in Ottawa,'' *Canadian Public Administration*, vol. 28 (Summer 1985), pp. 188–189.

since the mid-1960s. Before the Second World War, there were only three Cabinet committees. In 1939, ten new committees were created to facilitate and coordinate Canada's war operations; by far the most important of these committees was the War Committee chaired by the Prime Minister. Between 1945 and 1964, Cabinet committees were largely of an ad hoc nature; they were usually created to consider specific issues referred to them by Cabinet, and they were abolished when their job was done.[9]

In 1968, however, Prime Minister Lester Pearson modified the Cabinet committee system by replacing the ad hoc committees with nine standing committees so as "to obtain, under the Prime Minister's leadership, thorough consideration of policies, co-ordination of government action, and timely decisions in a manner consistent with ministerial and Cabinet responsibility."[10] Special committeees and additional standing committees were subsequently established according to need. In 1968, Mr. Pearson created the Priorities and Planning Committee, which he chaired, to set overall government priorities as a framework for expenditure decisions. The practice of requiring that matters be considered by Cabinet committees before coming to the full Cabinet was initiated, and public servants were permitted to attend Cabinet committee meetings on a more regular and frequent basis.

The general configuration of the existing Cabinet system dates from the election of Pierre Elliott Trudeau as Prime Minister in 1968. In April of that year, Mr. Trudeau reorganized the Cabinet committee system "to permit a greater centralization of functions and the delegation of certain powers of decision to the committees."[11] The reduction in the number of standing committees to eight and the setting of regular times for the weekly meeting or meetings of each committee improved the attendance of ministers. An extremely important innovation was expanding the powers of the committees from making recommendations to Cabinet to allowing them to take certain "decisions" on their own. These decisions, called "committee recommendations" were annexed to the agenda for Cabinet meetings and were routinely ratified, unless a minister specifically requested that they be discussed in full Cabinet. As a result of these changes, the number of Cabinet meetings declined considerably, while the number of Cabinet committee meetings increased dramatically. The nature and responsibilities of Cabinet committees evolved over time, but by 1978, there were still eight committees; five of these dealt with major policy sectors (Economic Policy, Social Policy, Culture and Native Affairs, External Policy and Defence, and Government Operations), and three were coordinating committees (Priorities and Planning, Treasury Board, and Legislation and House Planning). Secretariat support for these committees (except for Treasury Board) was provided by the PCO. However, a special Cabinet committee called the Board of Economic Development Ministers (BED) was established in 1978 with a secretariat independent of the PCO.

---

[9]See W. A. Matheson, *The Prime Minister and the Cabinet* (Toronto: Methuen, 1976), pp. 83–91.

[10]Lester B. Pearson, Press Release, Office of the Prime Minister, January 20, 1964.

[11]Pierre Elliott Trudeau, Press Release, Office of the Prime Minister, "Statement by the Prime Minister on Cabinet Committee Structure," April 30, 1968.

Further changes in the Cabinet committee system were made by Prime Minister Clark in 1979. The Priorities and Planning Committee was replaced by an inner Cabinet of twelve ministers that had final decision-making authority; the full Cabinet, which met less frequently than under Mr. Trudeau, confined its deliberations primarily to coordination and to politically sensitive or controversial questions. (The inner Cabinet was abolished and the Planning and Priorities Committee was restored when Mr. Trudeau was returned to office in early 1980.) The secretariat for BED was enlarged and formalized in the form of a new central agency called the Ministry of State for Economic Development (MSED); still another central agency was created under the name of the Ministry of State for Social Development to provide staff support for the Cabinet Committee on Social and Native Affairs.

Easily the most important organizational initiative of the Clark government was the introduction of the Policy and Expenditure Management System (PEMS), also called the "envelope" system. This system is explained briefly later in this chapter and at some length in Chapter 23. The introduction of PEMS was integrally linked to the revision of the Cabinet committee system. Changes made by Mr. Clark and by subsequent Prime Ministers (Trudeau, Turner, and Mulroney) resulted in the Cabinet committee structure under Prime Minister Mulroney shown in Figure 13.1. It consists of six committees connected with PEMS, (Priorities and Planning, Treasury Board, Social Development, Economic and Regional Development, Foreign and Defence Policy, and Government Operations), and five other committees (Communications, Legislation and House Planning, Security and Intelligence, Public Service, and the Special Committee of Council).

Mr. Turner abolished three Cabinet committees; he dismantled the two "new" central agencies — the Ministries of State for Economic and Regional Development and for Social Development — so that public service support for Cabinet committees could be consolidated within the traditional central agencies — the PCO, the TBS, and the Department of Finance; and he eliminated the "mirror committees," which were composed of deputy ministers and were public service counterparts to the policy committees of Cabinet. Mr. Mulroney made several additional changes to the Cabinet decision-making system. These included the elimination of the Cabinet Committee on Foreign and Defence Policy[12]; the incorporation of its functions into the Priorities and Planning Committee; and the simplification of the procedures of PEMS.

It is worth emphasizing that the Priorities and Planning Committee is the lead Cabinet committee, both with respect to policy making in general and PEMS in particular. It is composed of the Prime Minister as chairman and about a dozen ministers, including the chairpersons of the other Cabinet committees and the Minister of Finance. A few additional ministers are chosen because of the Prime Minister's respect for their views, or to achieve regional representation. The committee is responsible for deciding upon the fiscal framework, for establishing overall government priorities, for detailed consideration of major policy issues, for federal-provincial matters of general import and for problems of a

---

[12]This Cabinet committee was reinstated in early July 1985.

cross-cutting nature that involve more than one Cabinet committee, and for managing the expenditure of public funds in several policy sectors. The authority given to the committee in 1980 has been retained through subsequent changes in government. Thus, the committee can now ratify decisions made by the various other Cabinet committees and can make final decisions on most other matters. In practice, "most items of general interest (e.g. Throne Speech preparation, major foreign policy initiatives) that are brought initially to Priorities and Plan-

Figure 13.1
CABINET COMMITTEES

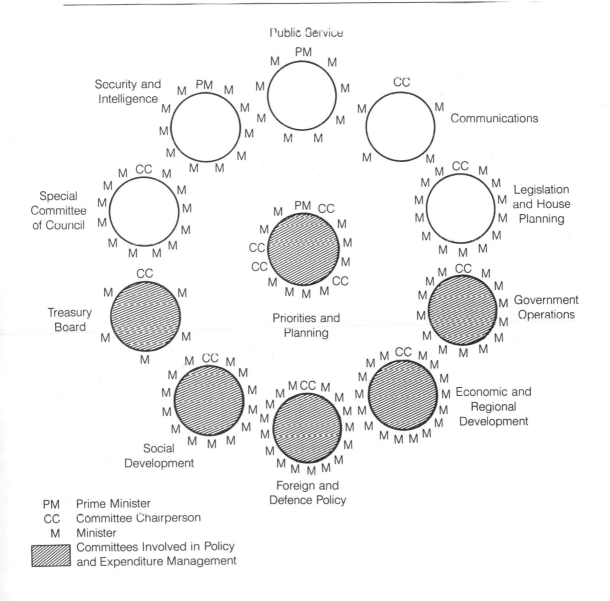

PM   Prime Minister
CC   Committee Chairperson
M   Minister
      Committees Involved in Policy
      and Expenditure Management

ning are subsequently taken to cabinet for discussion."[13] This ensures that "all ministers have a chance to express their views on virtually all matters of general interest."[14] Under the Mulroney government, the concentration of governmental power in the hands of the Prime Minister has been accompanied by an enhanced role for the Priorities and Planning Committee and the PMO.

As noted earlier, Cabinet committees, in performing their policy-making role, are concerned with the coordination of policies and programs, the allocation of financial and human resources, and control over the bureaucracy. The pursuit of these objectives is supported by the central agencies discussed in the next section, and is reflected in the purposes and procedures of PEMS and the Cabinet approval process discussed thereafter.

Central Agencies

The need for central agency support of the federal Cabinet and its committees can be vividly demonstrated by noting the volume of business handled by the Cabinet system. In 1983, the approximate annual workload of the system was 300 meetings of Cabinet and its committees, 900 memoranda to Cabinet examined, 750 records of decision produced, 75 government bills submitted to Parliament, 4,000 orders in council passed, and 6,000 Treasury Board decisions passed.[15]

As explained earlier, there is much debate as to which administrative units should be described as central agencies. In this chapter, the focus is on the Prime Minister's Office (PMO) and the so-called "traditional" central agencies, that is, the Department of Finance, the PCO, and the Treasury Board Secretariat (TBS). We shall see that these four agencies are important in the Cabinet decision-making process generally, and in PEMS in particular. The senior officials of these agencies together with those in the Federal-Provincial Relations Office (FPRO) have been described in a major study of federal central agencies as "super-bureaucrats" because they "are among the most powerful public servants in government," and because "in performing their duties they often cross the line between bureaucrat and policy maker."[16] The detailed description of the functions of these agencies provided in Chapter 6 will not be repeated here. This chapter is concerned with the interaction between central agencies and other actors in the executive-bureaucratic sphere of government.

Over the past two decades, the role of central agencies in assisting political executives to control and coordinate government policies and programs has expanded. In serving both the Prime Minister and the Cabinet, central agency officials control and influence departmental officials by affecting the allocation of human and financial resources, the organization of governmental and depart-

---

[13]Ian D. Clark, "Recent Changes in the Cabinet Decision-Making System in Ottawa," *Canadian Public Administration*, vol. 28 (Summer 1985), p. 199.
[14]Ibid.
[15]Information provided by Ian Clark, deputy secretary to the Cabinet, December 1, 1983.
[16]Colin Campbell and George J. Szablowski, *The Superbureaucrats: Structure and Behaviour in Central Agencies* (Toronto: Macmillan, 1979), p. 1.

mental machinery, and the coordination of intergovernmental relations. Central agencies thereby help to promote such administrative values as efficiency, effectiveness, and accountability.

During the early years of the first Trudeau government elected in 1968, the PMO and the PCO were reorganized and expanded so as to improve their advisory and coordinating functions. The growth in the size and expenditure of these offices led some commentators to compare them to the White House staff and the executive office of the president in the United States, and to suggest that the expansion of these offices was part of the Prime Minister's objective of "presidentializing" the Canadian political system and enhancing prime ministerial power. This suggestion now seems to have been greatly exaggerated. Moreover, there is wide recognition that "political executives require elaborate machinery and large staffs devoted to coordination and control just to get on with the job of governing."[17] The size of these offices has not been reduced by subsequent Prime Ministers.

The relative importance of the PMO and the traditional central agencies has shifted over the years since 1968, but all of them have continued to play a prominent role in supporting the Prime Minister and the Cabinet. The interaction and shifts in relative power among the central agencies themselves will be explained in the next chapter on interdepartmental and interagency relations. It is sufficient to note here that the balance of power among the agencies was altered as a result of the creation in 1979 of two new central agencies — the Ministry of State for Social Development (MSSD) and the Ministry of State for Economic Development, which in 1982 became the Ministry of State for Economic and Regional Development (MSERD). As noted above, these two agencies were abolished by Prime Minister Turner in 1984 as part of an effort to simplify the Cabinet decision-making system.

It is notable that the PMO is a central agency unlike the others in that it is primarily a partisan instrument of the Prime Minister. The overriding concern of PMO officials, who are political appointees rather than career public servants, is the political fortunes of the Prime Minister and the governing party. While they owe their first loyalty to the Prime Minister, these officials also serve the political interests of the Cabinet as a whole. Prime Minister Trudeau's stated aim was to have the PMO assist him "to exercise a greater degree of collective political control over a large and complex government apparatus" and "respond more effectively to the increased demands upon parliament, government and himself by a more active and interested public."[18] The PMO helps to ensure that the Prime Minister is knowledgeable about major policy issues, especially their political implications, and that he or she has an alternative source of policy advice to that provided by departmental ministers and officials.

---

[17]Colin Campbell, "Central Agencies in Canada," in Kenneth Kernaghan, ed., *Public Administration in Canada: Selected Readings* (Toronto: Methuen, 1985), p. 113.

[18]Marc Lalonde, "The Changing Role of the Prime Minister's Office," *Canadian Public Administration*, vol. 14 (Winter 1971), p. 521.

In contrast to the PMO, officials in the PCO are generally career public servants who are non-partisan; they are, however, highly sensitive to partisan considerations. The Department of Finance and TBS are also composed of career public servants. The Prime Minister and Cabinet rely heavily on the central agencies to control and influence the behaviour of departmental public servants. This is especially evident in the sphere of financial management, and specifically in the allocation and control of public funds through PEMS. Virtually all actors in the executive realm are significantly involved in the management and/or the expenditure of public funds, but we will see in Chapters 23 and 24 that the Department of Finance and the TBS are critical forces in influencing and facilitating Cabinet decisions on the management of financial resources.

The Prime Minister and, to a lesser extent, Cabinet ministers, with the assistance of central agencies, also exercise important functions in the sphere of human resource management, particularly in the staffing area. The Prime Minister and the Cabinet make what are called Governor in Council appointments to the senior levels of the bureaucracy. The choice of deputy ministers is, by convention, the prerogative of the Prime Minister, who receives advice from the secretary to the Cabinet and normally discusses possible candidates with the minister of the department in question. With respect to the several hundred senior positions in agencies, boards, and commissions, the prime minister usually consults with those ministers whose portfolio or region of the country is affected by an appointment. These appointments are made by the Governor in Council, that is, by the Cabinet, upon the recommendation of the Prime Minister. Under Prime Minister Mulroney, control over these appointments has been centralized in the PMO.

The Prime Minister wields substantial power not only in expenditure and human resource management, but also in the organization of the machinery of government. This function, for which staff support is provided by the PCO's Machinery of Government Directorate, involves the allocation of new policy and program responsibilities to specific departments, as well as major reallocations of existing responsibilities. The Prime Minister's control in this area is beneficial because it helps to avoid clashes among Cabinet ministers over the allocation of governmental responsibilities. In a formal sense, the creation of new departments is authorized by Parliament. However, since these major organizational initiatives involve public expenditures, they can only be put forward to Parliament by ministers after approval by Cabinet. Moreover, the Prime Minister and Cabinet have frequently made substantial modifications in existing government organizations under the authority of the Public Service Rearrangement and Transfer of Duties Act, which provides that the Governor in Council may

> (a) transfer any powers, duties or functions or the control or supervision of any part of the public service of Canada from one minister of the Crown to any other minister of the Crown, or from one department or portion of the public service to any other department or portion of the public service; or
> (b) amalgamate and combine any two or more departments under one minister of the Crown and under one deputy minister.[19]

---

[19]Canada, *Statutes*, 1918, c. 6, as amended in 1925, c. 23.

J. E. Hodgetts has noted that in a number of major reorganizations after 1966, Parliament was only able "to confirm belatedly decisions which were taken in considerable secrecy either by a small coterie of senior officials working with the prime minister or by the prime minister acting of his own accord."[20] Hodgetts concluded in the early 1970s that major reorganizational changes "seem to have become more and more the prerogative of the prime minister."[21] The Prime Minister is still the dominant decision maker with respect to the machinery of government.

The Policy and Expenditure Management System

The critical role of Cabinet committees and central agencies in the Cabinet decision-making system is evident in PEMS and in the Cabinet approval process, which is discussed in the next section. The overall aim of PEMS is to give Cabinet greater control over the management of both policies and expenditures. This objective is pursued by integrating the processes of policy making and of fiscal and expenditure planning within the Cabinet committee system. More specifically, PEMS is designed to ensure that the government's decisions on priorities and policies are integrated closely with the allocation of resources. Thus, policy decisions and related expenditure decisions are made by the same Cabinet committee and at the same time. PEMS decentralizes from Cabinet to Cabinet committees decision-making authority for both policies and expenditures with the intent of increasing ministerial direction and control. In addition, PEMS provides for the setting of priorities and expenditure *limits* before developing expenditure *plans*. This is intended to allow sufficient time in the planning process for ministers to review and change policies and to reallocate resources.

A central feature of this system is that specific expenditure limits, called resource envelopes, are set. Total expenditures covering a five-year period are divided into eight envelopes for eight policy sectors. Responsibility for managing the eight policy sectors within the expenditure limits is assigned to five Cabinet policy committees. For example, the social development envelope is assigned to the Cabinet Committee on Social Development, which allocates funds to various departments and agencies in that policy sector. The detailed consideration of PEMS in Chapter 23 will show that the prominent role played by central agencies in the Cabinet decision-making system since the late 1960s has been preserved under PEMS.

Cabinet Approval and Cabinet Documents

Figure 13.2 shows the process by which proposals from government departments for new policies are approved, amended, or rejected by Cabinet committees and by full Cabinet, and how the Cabinet's decision, in the form of a record of decision, serves as authority for the allocation of resources for the implementation of those policies. Also, it illustrates the formal and informal interaction among the major players in the executive-bureaucratic arena. Cabinet committees and central agencies clearly play an important role, but policy proposals are

---

[20]J. E. Hodgetts, *The Canadian Public Service* (Toronto: University of Toronto Press, 1973), pp. 61–62.
[21]Ibid., p. 63.

formally prepared by government departments and are presented by a minister to the appropriate Cabinet committee in the form of a document called a memorandum to Cabinet. Policy proposals can, of course, originate from a variety of sources, including political parties, interest groups, and individual citizens.

The two principles on which the Cabinet approval process is based are that "all ministers have the right to bring to their colleagues proposals for government action in their area of policy responsibility," and that "all ministers should have the opportunity to express an informed view within the cabinet process on

Figure 13.2
PROCESS OF CABINET APPROVAL

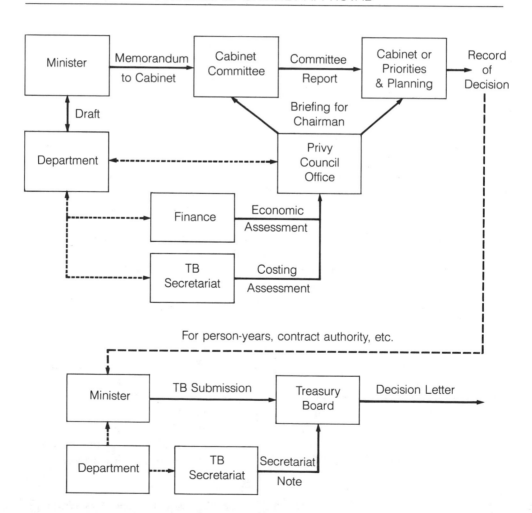

a proposal for which they will share collective responsibility."[22] The *Memorandum to Cabinet* is the key mechanism by which policy proposals are brought forward by ministers for consideration and approval by their Cabinet colleagues. It is also the formal means by which deputy ministers provide confidential policy advice to their ministers. The Cabinet memorandum is a more formal instrument than the frequently used *briefing notes* by which departments, through their deputies, provide policy information, analysis, and recommendations to their minister. Cabinet memoranda, which are normally based on extensive research and interdepartmental consultations, set out as briefly as possible the issues associated with a particular problem or proposal, alternatives for dealing with these issues, the implications of these various alternatives for such concerns as public relations, interdepartmental relations, federal-provincial relations and the party caucus, and recommendations for action. Another form of Cabinet document is called a *discussion paper*. It generally contains a much lengthier treatment of substantially the same matters covered in a Cabinet memorandum, with the exception of the recommendations and politically sensitive matters. Cabinet memoranda are kept secret, but discussion papers are released at the minister's discretion. Provincial Cabinet documents are broadly similar in content.

Following its consideration of a Cabinet memorandum, a Cabinet committee makes a recommendation, which is passed on to the Priorities and Planning Committee or to full Cabinet in the form of a committee report. Most committee recommendations are ratified without further discussion by the Priorities and Planning Committee or by the full Cabinet. Formal approval takes the form of a record of decision, which is circulated to all ministers for whatever follow-up is required. PCO officials play a very sensitive and influential role both in briefing committee chairpersons and in drafting committee reports and records of decision. Note the important role of the Department of Finance and the TBS in providing Cabinet committees, through the PCO, with an economic and a costing assessment of policy proposals contained in Cabinet memoranda.

The record of decision serves as a basis for ministers, on behalf of their departments, to request approval from Treasury Board and the TBS for the human and financial resources needed to implement approved policies. The source of funding, however, has already been identified by a Cabinet committee during discussion of the policy or program in question. Ministers seek Treasury Board approval through what is called a Treasury Board submission. In 1983, there were about 6,000 of these submissions, compared to about 900 memoranda to Cabinet. Under the Mulroney government, measures have been taken to reduce the number of Cabinet memoranda and Treasury Board submissions. Each submission is assessed by one of the several branches of the Treasury Board Secretariat (e.g., the Program Branch, the Administrative Policy Branch), and the secretariat recommends to the board whether submissions should be approved, rejected, or altered. The decision to approve or reject is provided in the form of a "decision letter." Figure 13.2 indicates by dotted lines the consultation between

---

[22]Clark, "Recent Changes in the Cabinet Decision-Making System in Ottawa," p. 198.

departments and central agencies that accompanies the preparation and pro-cessing of both Cabinet memoranda and Treasury Board submissions.

A primary purpose of the several reforms of the Cabinet decision-making system since the mid-1960s has been to enhance the power of political execu-tives over bureaucrats in the making of public policy. Yet, even after these changes, senior officials from departments and central agencies were permitted to attend Cabinet committee meetings to provide advice and support to their ministers or the Prime Minister. This participation provided an opportunity for bureaucrats to use their knowledge and experience to influence policy at a critical stage of its development. The Mulroney government decided in 1985 to limit strictly the attendance of bureaucrats at Cabinet committee meetings so as to help ensure the predominance of ministers in the making of policy decisions.

Reforms in the structures and processes of provincial Cabinet decision-making systems followed a pattern very similar to the federal reforms discussed above[23] and aimed to achieve the same objectives of Cabinet coordination and control of policy making. In most provinces, these objectives were pursued through an expanded Cabinet committee system dominated by planning and priorities com-mittees and treasury boards or management boards together with standing pol-icy committees. As on the federal scene, Cabinet secretariats and other central agencies were established or upgraded to support the Premier, the Cabinet, and Cabinet committees. An effort was also made in some provinces to link policy making with fiscal and expenditure planning along the lines of PEMS. The simi-larities between the federal reforms, for example, and the reforms in the prov-ince of New Brunswick are striking. Paul Leger observed in 1983 that the Cabinet committee system of decision making in that province

> is characterized by a sharing of power among ministers, aided by a system-atic "memorandum to cabinet" process which contributes better informa-tion and coordination to the decision-making process. Because policy committees also have budget decision-making responsibilities, the system is characterized by an integration of policy-making and financial planning. Its success depends heavily on a high level of coordination and cooperation among ministers and officials, together with mechanisms to link policy com-mittees on issues with government-wide implications.[24]

The emphasis in this chapter has been on interaction between the Prime Min-ister and the Cabinet on the one hand, and central agencies and departments on the other. We turn now to an examination of interaction between government departments, between departments and central agencies, and among the central agencies themselves.

---

[23]See Marsha A. Chandler and William M. Chandler, *Public Policy and Provincial Politics* (Toronto: McGraw-Hill Ryerson, 1979), ch. 4 and "Public Administration in Canada's Provinces," in Ken-neth Kernaghan, ed., *Canadian Public Administration: Practice and Profession* (Toronto: Butterworths, 1983), pp. 145–150. On the evolution of the Cabinet system in Ontario, see Richard A. Loreto, "The Cabinet," in Donald C. MacDonald, ed., *The Government and Politics of Ontario*, 2nd ed. (Toronto: Van Nostrand Reinhold, 1980), pp. 20–35.

[24]Paul C. Leger, "The Cabinet Committee System of Policy-Making and Resource Allocation in the Government of New Brunswick," *Canadian Public Administration*, vol. 26 (Spring 1983), p. 16.

BIBLIOGRAPHY

Aucoin, Peter. "Portfolio Structures and Policy Coordination." In G. Bruce Doern and Peter Aucoin, eds., *Public Policy in Canada*. Toronto: Macmillan, 1979.

Aucoin, Peter. "Organizational Change in the Machinery of Canadian Government: From Rational Management to Brokerage Politics." *Canadian Journal of Political Science*, vol. 19 (March 1986): 3-27.

Balls, Herbert R. "Decision-Making: The Role of the Deputy Minister." *Canadian Public Administration*, vol. 19 (Fall 1976): 417-431.

Campbell, Colin. *Governments Under Stress: Political Executives and Key Bureaucrats in Washington, London and Ottawa*. Toronto: University of Toronto Press, 1983.

Campbell, Colin, and George Szablowski. *The Superbureaucrats: Structure and Behaviour in Central Agencies*. Toronto: Macmillan, 1979.

Canada. Royal Commission on Financial Management and Accountability. *Final Report*. Ottawa: Supply and Services, 1979, ch. 4.

Chandler, Marsha A., and William M. Chandler. *Public Policy and Provincial Politics*. Toronto: McGraw-Hill Ryerson, 1979, ch. 4.

Clark, Ian. "Recent Changes in the Cabinet Decision-Making System in Ottawa." *Canadian Public Administration*, vol. 26 (Summer 1985): 185-201.

Doern, G. Bruce, and Richard W. Phidd. *Canadian Public Policy*. Toronto: Methuen, 1983, ch. 7.

Doerr, Audrey. *The Machinery of Government in Canada*. Toronto: Methuen, 1981, chs. 2-3.

French, Richard. *How Ottawa Decides: Planning and Industrial Policy Making, 1968–1984*. 2nd ed. Toronto: James Lorimer, 1984.

Johnson, A. W. "The Role of the Deputy Minister." *Canadian Public Administration*, vol. 4 (December 1961): 363-369.

Kernaghan, Kenneth, and Olivia Kuper. *Coordination in Canadian Governments: A Case Study of Aging Policy*. Toronto: Institute of Public Administration of Canada, 1983.

Lalonde, Marc. "The Changing Role of the Prime Minister's Office." *Canadian Public Administration*, vol. 14 (Winter 1971): 538-555.

Leger, Paul. "The Cabinet Committee System of Policy-Making and Resource Allocation in the Government of New Brunswick." *Canadian Public Administration*, vol. 25 (Spring 1983): 16-35.

Loreto, Richard. "The Structure of the Ontario Political System." In Donald C. MacDonald, ed., *The Government and Politics of Ontario*. 2nd ed. Toronto: Van Nostrand Reinhold, 1980, pp. 17-47.

Mallory, J. R. "The Lambert Report: Central Roles and Responsibilities." *Canadian Public Administration*, vol. 22 (Winter 1979): 517-529.

Matheson, William A. "The Cabinet and the Canadian Bureaucracy." In Kenneth Kernaghan, ed., *Public Administration in Canada: Selected Readings*. 5th ed. Toronto: Methuen, 1985, pp. 266-280.

Matheson, W. A. *The Prime Minister and the Cabinet*. Toronto: Methuen, 1976.

Nossal, Kim Richard. "Allison through the (Ottawa) Looking Glass: Bureaucratic Politics and Foreign Policy in a Parliamentary System." *Canadian Public Administration*, vol. 22 (Winter 1979): 610-626.

Robertson, Gordon. "The Changing Role of the Privy Council Office." *Canadian Public Administration*, vol. 14 (Spring 1971): 487–508.

Schultz, Richard. *Federalism, Bureaucracy and Public Policy*. Montreal: McGill-Queen's University Press, 1980.

Sharp, Mitchell. "Decision-Making in the Federal Cabinet." *Canadian Public Administration*, vol. 19 (Spring 1976): 1–7.

Smith, Denis. "President and Parliament: The Transformation of Parliamentary Government in Canada." In Thomas A. Hockin, ed., *Apex of Power*. 2nd ed. Scarborough: Prentice-Hall, 1977, pp. 308–325.

Van Loon, R. J. "The Policy and Expenditure Management System in the Federal Government: The First Three Years." *Canadian Public Administration*, vol. 26 (Summer 1983): 255–284.

Van Loon, R. J., and M. S. Whittington. *The Canadian Political System*. 3rd ed. Toronto: McGraw-Hill Ryerson, 1981.

Zussman, David. "Walking the Tightrope: The Mulroney Government and the Public Service." In Michael J. Prince, ed., *How Ottawa Spends, 1986–87: Tracking the Tories*. Toronto: Methuen, 1986, pp. 250–282.

CASES

In *Case Program in Canadian Public Administration* (Toronto: Institute of Public Administration of Canada):

The Draft Memorandum to Cabinet, by Douglas G. Hartle

Political Briefing Notes, by Michael J. Kirby and Sandford F. Borins

In Kenneth Kernaghan, *Canadian Cases in Public Administration* (Toronto: Methuen Publications):

This Hour Has Seven Days

14

Interdepartmental and Intradepartmental Relations

DEPARTMENTAL AND AGENCY INTERACTION

It is difficult to separate an analysis of interdepartmental relations from a consideration of the impact of central agencies on these relations. In our discussion of the Cabinet decision-making system in the previous chapter, we described the various means by which central agencies assist the Cabinet and its committees to control and coordinate the activities of departmental ministers and officials. Under PEMS and the Cabinet approval process, it is clear that a great deal of consultation between departments and central agencies is required. It makes little sense for a minister to bring forward Cabinet memoranda or Treasury Board submissions without ensuring that account has been taken of the views of central agencies which are in a position to advise Cabinet and Cabinet committees on the desirability of departmental proposals.

Interdepartmental Committees

Consultation between and among departments is, of course, essential in the development of policy and program proposals. Over the decade before the Turner government of 1984, sectoral deputy minister committees, often called "mirror committees," were established to facilitate interdepartmental consultation on matters that were to be considered by the policy committees of ministers. PCO officials promoted interdepartmental coordination by participating in the meetings of these committees. As part of an effort to shift some power in the direction of the departments, these committees were abolished by Prime Minister Turner. There was still a need, however, to ensure appropriate interdepartmental consultation. Therefore, the Mulroney government provided that the responsibility for ensuring that issues coming to Cabinet are the subject of adequate interdepartmental consultation lies with the sponsoring department.[1] For example, departments are expected to consult the Department of External Affairs when Canada's international relations might be affected, and the Federal-Provincial Relations Office when federal-provincial relations are involved. The Mulroney government required further that the interdepartmental consultation section of the executive summaries (now called "ministerial recommendations") of Cabinet memoranda should explain the consultations that have been undertaken by departments and highlight any interdepartmental disagreements

---

[1]Ian D. Clark, "Recent Changes in the Cabinet Decision-Making System in Ottawa," *Canadian Public Administration*, vol. 28 (Summer 1985), p. 195.

that still remain. The Privy Council Office and, where relevant, other central agencies were advised to continue to call meetings of deputy ministers for the purposes of coordination and exchange of information.

A valuable coordinating role continues to be played by the Coordinating Committee of Deputy Ministers, which is chaired by the secretary to the Cabinet and whose membership includes the deputy ministers from Finance, TBS, External Affairs, Justice, and the Federal-Provincial Relations Office. This committee provides an opportunity for an exchange of views between the secretary to the Cabinet and the administrative heads of central agencies on matters of general concern to the government. Other meetings, including a monthly deputy ministers' luncheon, are called by the secretary to the Cabinet for the purpose of informal discussion of matters of general interest. Still other interdepartmental committees at the deputy minister level (e.g., the Committee of Senior Officials on Executive Personnel), and at the assistant deputy minister level (e.g., the Interdepartmental Panel on Energy Research), serve a variety of purposes. Below these very senior levels, there are a large number of other committees involving public servants from two or more departments.

Types of Interdepartmental Committees

Audrey Doerr has provided a very useful classification of interdepartmental committees according to their major function.[2] *Committees to initiate* are created to mobilize departmental interest and support early on in the policy process. One of these committees might, for example, be created to review a Royal commission report and make recommendations on the appropriate governmental response to its proposals. Either a department or a central agency could chair and lead the committee in its work. *Committees to negotiate or arbitrate* are concerned with sorting out and reaching compromises on the appropriate allocation of roles and responsibilities for a particular matter. For example, the Interdepartmental Committee on Harbours involved two central agencies and three departments in determining responsibility for harbours. *Committees to advise* are concerned with providing advice to senior departmental officials and to ministers with respect to the substance of policy or the coordination of policy development. An example is the 1975 Senior Interdepartmental Committee on Labour Relations, which was chaired by the Privy Council Office and which focussed on improving labour relations and avoiding labour disruptions. *Committees to evaluate* are often created to assess policies or programs and to make appropriate recommendations for action. An example is the Committee of Senior Officials on Executive Personnel, chaired by the secretary to the Cabinet, which among other things evaluates the performance of senior officials. *Committees to monitor* "maintain a 'watching brief' on departmental activities in a particular policy or program area."[3] A well-known committee of this type was the so-called DM-10 Committee, established in 1975 and composed of ten deputy ministers, which monitored the economic and social policies of the government during the period of wage and price controls. Finally, *interdepartmental task forces* are

---

[2]Audrey Doerr, *The Machinery of Government in Canada* (Toronto: Methuen, 1981), pp. 138–142.
[3]Ibid., p. 141.

usually temporary bodies composed of public servants below the senior level who are loaned by departments and agencies for a particular task. An example is the 1974 Task Force on Decentralization in the Federal Public Service, which examined the rationale for decentralizing the public service on a regional basis.

The Effectiveness of Interdepartmental Committees

It is important to keep in mind that most of these interdepartmental bodies, whatever their primary function, are composed of representatives of both departments and central agencies. They can, therefore, not only help to coordinate policy development and implementation among departments, but they can also assist central agencies in their support of Cabinet and Cabinet committees.

Interdepartmental committees have been described as "the principal means of communication and deliberation in the federal bureaucratic establishment."[4] Attention has also been drawn to their value as "important means for central agencies to initiate or coordinate new undertakings. They support departmental policy making by bringing together a number of interested parties and resolving conflicts before recommendations are made to ministers. In each instance, consensus and support are sought through coordination."[5] Other observers have cautioned against expecting much effective coordination through interdepartmental committees. The committees have been damned by very faint praise as bodies whose existence "certainly cannot hurt."[6] In addition, "some participants have dubbed the interdepartmental committee system 'institutionalized discord' — the coordinate mechanism, in other words, has simply become in several respects one of the battlegrounds where interdepartmental combat occurs."[7] Richard Schultz has noted the enormous growth of what he calls "interdepartmentalism," which has resulted in more and more public servants being required "to negotiate . . . with officials in other departments. This negotiation process, bureaucratic politics, can only reinforce both the political role of members of the public service and correspondingly their influence in the system."[8] Similarly, H. L. Laframboise contends that "the blurring of departmental boundaries," together with such things as "the spread of collegial decision-making," and "the proliferation of watchdog agencies" has resulted in "an emphasis on interdepartmental negotiations, and this emphasis has been translated into a corps of interdepartmental diplomats of considerable dimensions."[9]

The effectiveness of interdepartmental committees varies from one committee to another, but in general they appear to serve a useful purpose in assisting

[4]Colin Campbell and George Szablowski, *The Superbureaucrats: Structure and Behaviour in Central Agencies* (Toronto: Macmillan, 1979), p. 24.

[5]Doerr, *The Machinery of Government in Canada*, pp. 138-139.

[6]R. J. Van Loon and M. S. Whittington, *The Canadian Political System*, 3rd ed. (Toronto: McGraw-Hill Ryerson, 1981), p. 511.

[7]Ibid.

[8]Richard J. Schultz, *Federalism, Bureaucracy and Public Policy: The Politics of Highway Regulation* (Montreal: McGill-Queen's University Press, 1980), p. 188.

[9]H. L. Laframboise, "The Future of Public Administration in Canada," *Canadian Public Administration*, vol. 24 (Winter 1982), p. 513.

Cabinet and central agencies to coordinate government activities. The number of interdepartmental committees declined over the period when the sectoral deputies committees were in operation. Now that these committees have been abolished and departments are required to ensure that they engage in adequate interdepartmental consultation, the number of committees is likely to increase.

Departments and Central Agencies

Central Agencies versus Departments

It is widely held that the expansion in the size and power of central agencies that occurred in the late 1960s and early 1970s reduced the power of both the ministers and senior officials of operating departments. The control and influence exercised by central agencies in the coordination of policy development and in the allocation of human and financial resources for departmental programs led to considerable tension in the relations between the agencies and line departments. The filtering of departmental policy and program proposals through Cabinet committees and central agencies helped to ensure that ministers and their senior officials understood the implications of their proposals for other departments and for the government as a whole; however, ministers and their officials expended a great deal of time and effort lobbying and bargaining with ministers and officials in other departments and in the central agencies. It was an extremely time-consuming process for ministers, and it tended to reduce their individual authority and influence in the Cabinet decision-making system. Richard French concluded that Prime Minister Trudeau's reforms of the Cabinet committee system "are generally understood to have instituted much needed structure and control after the helter-skelter confusion of the Pearson years."[10] However, he notes that "the sophisticated analytical demands and cumbersome procedures were seen as serious barriers to decisive action, resulting in the constant delay of 'analysis paralysis.' "[11] Similarly, "the advent of collegiality, the insistence on collective decision-making within the committee system, is believed to have frustrated some capable ministers, and the allegedly dominant role of certain senior PCO officials to have disheartened, even driven into early retirement, talented departmental officials."[12]

Richard Schultz, among others, has suggested that the role of central agencies in the decision-making process has been somewhat exaggerated. He contends that the line departments continue to possess powerful resources in any competition with central agencies. He notes that central agencies do not have the human resources or the expertise available to operating departments, that policy initiatives and policy implementation are primarily the responsibility of departments, that departments control the timing of their proposals and the information supporting them, and that departments may at times resist the coordinating efforts of central agencies.[13]

---

[10]Richard French, *How Ottawa Decides: Planning and Industrial Policy Making, 1968–1984*, 2nd ed. (Toronto: James Lorimer, 1984), p. 8.
[11]Ibid.
[12]Ibid.
[13]Schultz, *Federalism, Bureaucracy and Public Policy*, pp. 182–189.

The power of central agencies vis-à-vis departments may indeed be overstated. Nevertheless, the Turner and Mulroney governments, during 1984 and 1985, decided that the number and influence of central agencies, combined with the complexities of the Cabinet committee system and PEMS, made the decision-making system too complicated. Too much emphasis was being placed on the process of policy formulation as compared to policy content. Several reforms, some of which have already been mentioned, were introduced to bring about a simpler, more hierarchical model of Cabinet government. These reforms included the abolition of two central agencies (MSERD and MSSD), a reduction in the number of Cabinet committees, the abolition of the sectoral deputy ministers committees, the strengthening of staff support to ministers, and the simplification of the processes and procedures of Cabinet and its committees. These reforms were designed in large part to restore a greater measure of power in the decision-making process to the ministers of line departments.

Central Agencies

While these reforms, especially the elimination of two central agencies, will tend to reduce the power of central agencies in general, they will not necessarily diminish the power of the traditional central agencies, that is, the PCO, the TBS, and the Department of Finance. There will, however, be shifts in the relative power exercised by these agencies, both in their relations with departments and their relations with each other. Indeed, competition among the central agencies themselves helps to prevent the dominance of any one agency and, on occasion, helps departments to get their way by setting one agency against another.

The Treasury Board, which is a statutory Cabinet committee, was until 1967 chaired by the Minister of Finance and received its staff support from the Department of Finance. In 1967 the Treasury Board became a separate department of government under a Cabinet minister known as the President of the Treasury Board, who took over the chairmanship of Treasury Board from the Minister of Finance, who became an *ex officio* member of the committee. As noted in Chapter 6, the Treasury Board, with the assistance of its secretariat, carries out a very broad range of functions in the areas of expenditure management, human resource management, and government organization. There is an obvious need for cooperation and consultation between the TBS on the one hand, and the Department of Finance and the PCO on the other.

The Department of Finance lost some authority during the 1960s and 1970s not only to the Treasury Board, but also to the Privy Council Office and to other central agencies. For example, the department had to share its advisory role on economic policy with the Board of Economic Development Ministers, which was established in 1978 and which evolved into the Cabinet Committee on Economic and Regional Development with MSERD as its secretariat. The PCO strengthened its capability to advise on economic policy by recruiting its own economists, and the PCO and PMO together organized informal groups of economists from the universities and the private sector to advise the Prime Minister.

The nature of the competition among the three traditional central agencies is well illustrated by Richard French's argument that there were during the first Trudeau government three systems of planning, namely the Finance Planning

System, the Treasury Planning System, and the Cabinet Planning System.[14] In the competition among these three systems, the Cabinet Planning System, which had the support of the Prime Minister, prevailed over the other two systems promoted by the TBS and Finance. According to French, this system "placed substantial influence within the hands of a small group of senior planning personnel within the PCO . . . but this focus of influence, however visible within the bureaucracy and however common a target for disillusioned ministers and officials, was never strong enough to subsume the Finance and Treasury Planning Systems."[15]

Despite competing sources of advice and the adverse economic conditions of the 1970s, the Department of Finance continued to exercise strong influence on economic policy. Moreover, with the arrival of PEMS in 1979, the department's influence in the budgetary process was reaffirmed through its influence on the size of the overall budget and the level of the expenditure ceilings in the individual envelopes. While the PCO shared its role in economic and social policy with MSSD and MSERD, it continued to play a central role in the determination of government priorities and in the mangement of PEMS. The TBS lost some of its former influence on policy proposals to the sectoral policy committees of Cabinet and to MSSD and MSERD.

Then, the reforms in policy-making structures and processes made by Prime Ministers Turner and Mulroney altered once more the power relationships among the central agencies. The elimination of MSSD and MSERD means that the Department of Finance has greater responsibility for assessing the economic effectiveness of proposed policies and programs. The PCO has taken on those secretariat responsibilities for the policy committees which were previously performed by MSSD and MSERD, but the PMO has been playing a more active policy role. It is early yet to assess with any precision the impact of the recent reforms on the realignment of power among the central agencies.[16] The assessment must be made in the light of the effect on central agencies of the government's effort to place a greater measure of decision-making power in the hands of departments in general, and ministers in particular. In the next section, the relations within departments between ministers and public servants, and among the public servants themselves, are examined.

INTRADEPARTMENTAL RELATIONS

The internal structure of administrative organizations varies from one category of organization to another (e.g., from departments to Crown agencies to central agencies); it also varies from one organization to another within a single category (e.g., the Department of National Revenue, which is organized on the classical model, compared to the Ministry of Transport, organized on the

---

[14]French, *How Ottawa Decides*, pp. 18–58.

[15]Ibid., p. 58.

[16]For a useful preliminary assessment, see Peter Aucoin, "Organizational Change in the Machinery of Canadian Government: From Rational Management to Brokerage Politics," *Canadian Journal of Political Science*, vol. 19 (March 1986), especially pp. 17–27.

"ministry" model). In general, however, departments and those central agen
cies with departmental form are organized in a broadly uniform manner. They
are structured in a pyramidal fashion, with a minister as the political head and
a deputy minister as the administrative head of a formal organization with layers of
interlocking superior-subordinate relationships descending to the base of the
pyramid.

The Deputy Minister

The Deputy and the Minister

The individual responsibility of ministers as political heads of departments links
the Cabinet to the bureaucracy, and it establishes the minister as the locus of
formal authority in the departmental hierarchy for both policy formation and
execution. Ministers not only make the final decisions on policy questions; they
also bear constitutional and political responsibility for the proper administration of their departments. In practice, of course, ministers look for assistance to
their senior departmental officials, especially to their deputy minister who is the
administrative head of the department.

The deputy minister occupies a pivotal position at the border between the
political and bureaucratic spheres of government. Although the Prime Minister
has the power to appoint, transfer, and remove deputy ministers, their first loyalty is normally to their minister. This seemingly illogical arrangement reflects
the fact that ministers have both individual and collective responsibilities and
that deputies are expected to serve their ministers in both capacities. Deputies
not only serve their own minister, but through their support of the ministers'
collective responsibilities, also serve the government as a whole. Moreover,
deputies perform certain functions according to statute or on the authority of
the Cabinet, rather than of their minister. The Prime Minister's power to select
deputies helps to ensure continuity in departmental administration despite a
change of ministers, reminds deputies "of their need for a perspective encom-
passing the whole range of government" and "emphasizes the collective interest
of ministers, and the special interest of the prime minister in the effectiveness of
management in the public service."[17] The fact that the Prime Minister chooses
both ministers and deputy ministers enables him or her to seek a compatible
team in each department — both in terms of policy and management skills and
in terms of "personal chemistry." The Prime Minister is in a position to arbitrate
the occasional disputes that arise between deputies and their ministers and can
even refuse to shift deputies who are unacceptable to their ministers. For example, Joe Clark is reported to have granted a few ministers their request for a new
deputy, but to have refused the request of the Minister of External Affairs that
her deputy be dismissed or transferred.[18]

---

[17]Royal Commission on Government Organization, *Report*, vol. 1 (Ottawa: Queen's Printer, 1965),
p. 60.
[18]J. Simpson, *The Discipline of Power* (Toronto: Personal Library, 1980), p. 132.

The Deputy's Control and Influence

The authority of the deputy minister is based on both statutes and conventions. Many of the deputies' administrative responsibilities are spelled out in departmental Acts, the Interpretation Act, the Financial Administration Act, the Public Service Employment Act, and the Official Languages Act. Departmental Acts usually provide for the appointment by the Governor in Council of a deputy minister who is to hold office during pleasure, and some Acts actually delegate authority to the deputy for certain specified matters. The Interpretation Act is especially important, however, because it provides in section 23(a) that "words . . . empowering a Minister . . . to do an act or thing, . . . include . . . his . . . deputy." Thus, the minister can delegate a wide range of authority to the deputy. The Act states specifically, however, that the deputy cannot substitute for the minister in the making of regulations. Moreover, the deputy cannot answer to Parliament on behalf of the minister or sign Cabinet memoranda. The other Acts noted above delegate authority directly to the deputy, or provide for delegation to the deputy by the Treasury Board or the Public Service Commission. In contrast to the deputy's administrative responsibilities, his or her responsibilities to provide policy advice to the minister and to the government as a whole are based more on traditions and practices than on statutes.

In the realm of policy *development*, A. W. Johnson contends that the deputy minister's role as policy advisor entails the initiation of policy recommendations and policy studies without usurping the minister's initiative in these matters. He notes that "the cynics may suggest that this is power without responsibility; I suggest that it is more akin to responsibility without power."[19] The fact is that deputy ministers often do exercise power — in the form of influence — through policy initiatives in which their minister has had little involvement. In this connection, Mitchell Sharp has observed that

> the typical senior civil servant seems to be thought of as a quite intelligent but passive agent of government, waiting to be set in motion by his Minister and producing in time a memorandum of well-balanced pros and cons. There are occasions, of course, when the senior adviser has to perform exactly that function. But when I think back over my experience, I remember more occasions when civil servants by fruitful initiatives led the Government to adopt lines of policy which would have never occurred to them otherwise.[20]

The challenge, then, is to ensure that the deputy's role in policy formation combines power with responsibility. We shall see that deputies are either accountable to, or feel a sense of personal responsibility to, a wide variety of participants in the political system.

In the realm of policy *implementation*, Cabinet ministers may become involved in virtually any matter within the ambit of their departmental portfolio, including

---

[19]A. W. Johnson, "The Role of the Deputy Minister," in Kenneth Kernaghan, ed., *Public Administration in Canada: Selected Readings*, 5th ed. (Toronto: Methuen, 1985), p. 295.
[20]Mitchell Sharp, "The Bureaucratic Elite and Policy Formation," in Kenneth Kernaghan, ed., *Bureaucracy in Canadian Government*, 2nd ed. (Toronto: Methuen, 1973), p. 73.

the organization and management of the department. While ministers are responsible for the administration of their department, their burdensome duties oblige
them to leave most of the departmental administration to their deputy and other
senior officials. Moreover, deputies tend to be jealous of their managerial
responsibilities. They do not wish or expect ministers to intervene in administrative matters without their knowledge and consent. Ministers do on occasion
become involved in administrative matters, and senior officials are obliged to
accommodate them and obey their directions. Indeed, A. W. Johnson has asserted
that one of the important jobs of the deputy head is "to try to interpret to his
staff the rationale for ministerial forays into the day-to-day work of the civil
service."[21]

The extent to which ministers become involved in administration (and public
servants in policy formation) depends on individual personalities and capacities, as
well as on situational and time factors related to a department's particular
activities. Some ministers will by virtue of past experience and personal predisposition be very interested in administrative questions; others will prefer to leave
departmental administration almost solely in the hands of the public servants.
There appears to be no strong correlation between a minister's interest in administrative matters and his or her status as a strong or weak minister. The effective
minister appears to be the one who will intervene forcefully on important or
urgent matters of administration. Senior public servants may head off ministerial excursions into the administrative hierarchy not only by responding quickly
to ministerial requests, but by anticipating requests and providing suggestions
to deal with emerging problems which have not yet become a matter of ministerial concern.

Policy Advice or Management?

For reasons of partisan politics and personal advancement, both the Prime Minister and departmental ministers are primarily concerned with the formulation
rather than the implementation of policy. It is not surprising, therefore, that
many deputies perceive that their own careers will prosper if they focus on policy advice rather than on departmental management. It is notable also that
deputies are obliged to compete with other sources of advice for their minister's
attention on policy matters, whereas they have little competition in the sphere
of departmental administration. Although deputies reported to the Lambert
Commission that on average they spent two-thirds of their time on management,
a majority of them ranked the tasks of "supporting my minister" and "ensuring
that my department is responsive to the policy thrusts of government" as more
important than management responsibilities. This is a natural outcome of a
political system where ministers cannot be expected to be policy experts, and
of a reward system which seems to value policy contributions above sound
management.

Deputy ministers can, and do, become overloaded by the combined burden
of their policy and managerial duties. What has long been said about ministers

---

[21]Johnson, "The Role of the Deputy Minister," p. 292.

can now be said about many deputy ministers — that is, they have too much to do and they do too much. A persuasive argument could be made that deputies should be viewed more as experts in the machinery and process of government than as experts in the substance of public policy. The tendency to rotate deputies quickly among departments means that they cannot gain sufficient knowledge about the content and implications of departmental policy. They must, therefore, rely more heavily on the advice of their departmental specialists. The deputies' effective performance of their managerial duties is essential to their policy advisory responsibilities. The Lambert Commission observed that "deputy heads must be actively involved in the administration and operation of their departments if they are to be effective in offering policy advice and in developing programs that can be designed and carried out with value for money in mind."[22]

The Accountability of the Deputy Minister[23]

The deputies' job is complicated by the many authorities to whom they are accountable. Deputies are *directly* accountable only to political and administrative superiors, to the courts, and to any internal governmental authorities (e.g., central agencies) to which accountability is required by law or the administrative hierarchy. They are not directly accountable to the legislature, pressure groups, the news media, or to the public. While it is agreed that in general deputies are accountable first of all to their minister, in practice they receive directions, rewards, and penalties from a variety of sources. These sources include the Prime Minister, their minister, the merit system as administered by the Public Service Commission, the Auditor General, and several central agencies, including TBS, the Comptroller General, the Department of Finance, the PCO, the FPRO, and so on. A former public servant, in a hypothetical letter from the secretary of the Cabinet to the Prime Minister, wrote that "we have been remarkably successful in multiplying the number of authorities to which deputy ministers are accountable, and it would be difficult, even for a hostile observer, to find a gap in the web we have spun."[24]

Despite the heavy burden of these existing accountability relationships, the Lambert Commission recommended that deputy ministers be required to account directly to the Public Accounts Committee of the House of Commons for the performance of specific or assigned duties, including those "relating to the probity and legality of expenditures, the economy and efficiency with which programs are run, and their effectiveness in achieving policy goals."[25] This proposal has been very widely discussed in Canada's public administration community.

Critics of the proposal argue that the administrative matters for which deputies would be accountable cannot easily be separated from the policy matters

---

[22]Royal Commission on Financial Management and Accountability, *Final Report* (Ottawa: Supply and Services 1979), p. 179.
[23]See the discussion of the concept of *accountability* in Chapter 20.
[24]H. L. Laframboise, "A Note on Accountability," *Optimum*, vol. 13-14 (1982), p. 84.
[25]Royal Commission on Financial Management and Accountability, pp. 374-375.

for which ministers would be accountable; that holding deputies accountable for "their effectiveness in achieving policy goals" suggests, incorrectly, that ministers can usually provide clear policy objectives; that a formal, written division of responsibilities between a minister and his or her deputy is not in keeping with the traditional, informal pattern of relations between them; and that if public servants are held accountable to parliamentary committees their anonymity will suffer.

Supporters of the proposal contend that the direct accountability of deputies would stimulate them to pay greater heed to their management tasks and to seek from those in authority over them clear statements of their responsibilities. Moreover, while at first glance the proposal seems to threaten the doctrine and practice of ministerial responsibility, it is similar to the "accounting officer" mechanism in Britain whereby a senior departmental official, usually the equivalent of our deputy minister, accounts directly to the Public Accounts Committee for the expenditure of public funds. There has been no suggestion that this British practice encroaches to any significant extent on ministerial responsibility. It is argued further that deputies already appear before parliamentary committees to explain departmental policy and its administration; the responsibility for the defence of policy and for administrative matters that are not delegated or assigned to deputies would remain with ministers. The anonymity of deputy ministers would decline somewhat, but the anonymity of their advice on policy matters would be preserved.

Ministerial Staff

The Expansion of Staff Assistance to Ministers

Relationships between ministers and deputy ministers are complicated further by the role of the minister's office staff. Ministerial assistants are appointed by the minister and are usually described as "exempt staff" because they are not subject to the provisions of the Public Service Employment Act. Since the tenure of ministerial assistants is tied directly to that of the minister, they are subject to the vicissitudes of partisan politics. A measure of employment protection is assured, however, by section 37(4) of the Public Service Employment Act, which provides that a person who has served at least three years as an executive assistant, a special assistant, or a private secretary to a minister is entitled to a position in the public service for which he or she is qualified at a level at least equivalent to that of private secretary to a deputy minister. Ministerial assistants frequently take advantage of this opportunity.

Since the early 1960s, the size of the minister's office staff has gradually increased; however, the influence of ministerial staff has not only waxed and waned over that period, but has also varied from one minister and one department to another. Until the Mulroney government of 1984, ministers were usually authorized under Treasury Board guidelines to hire an executive assistant, a policy advisor, as many special assistants as funds permitted, one private secretary, and support staff. Some ministers supplemented this staff by seconding departmental public servants and/or using departmental funds to hire people on a contract basis. When he came into office, Prime Minister Mulroney decided to upgrade the quality of ministerial staff by authorizing each minister to hire a chief of staff to be paid $80,000 (or more) per year. The chief of staff is intended to function, not as a senior policy advisor to the minister, but as the minister's chief political advisor and as the manager of the minister's office.[26] The PMO has been given a significant role in the selection of the chiefs of staff so as to ensure that they are sensitive to the Prime Minister's wishes and concerns.

The Functions of Ministerial Assistants

The role of the ministerial assistant is meant to be complementary to, rather than competitive with, the deputy head and other senior public servants. The functions of the minister's staff relate to the management of the minister's office and the enhancing of his or her political fortunes, rather than to the day-to-day administration of the department or to the development of substantive policy. Blair Williams has identified four major categories of work performed by ministerial assistants in support of their minister's onerous responsibilities.[27] The *planning, organization, and administration* function includes handling the minister's itinerary and managing his or her office; the *liaison* function involves facilitating effective relations between the minister on the one hand, and the department, other ministers, the party, members of Parliament, and the minister's constituency on the other. It should be noted that ministerial staff increasingly deal with the concerns of pressure groups on behalf of their ministers. The *public relations* function requires interaction with the department's information services unit and with the news media to advance the minister's political and policy objectives. The *research* function involves the collection of data and information to support the various other functions performed for the minister. Williams did not specifically mention the function of assisting the minister to control the bureaucracy, perhaps because ministers' offices do not have adequate staff to perform this function well. Donald Savoie has argued that the policy advisory capacity of the offices should be strengthened so that ministerial staff can assist ministers to give policy directions to their departments and can evaluate the policy advice coming from the departments.[28]

Ministerial Staff and Departmental Officials

Harmonious relations between the minister's staff and departmental officials require a clear understanding of their respective spheres of action. Tension and conflict have resulted when ministerial assistants have tried to usurp the role of senior public servants by interfering in departmental administration, or by impeding contacts between the minister and departmental officials. Ministerial staff

---

[26]David Zussman, "Walking the Tightrope: The Mulroney Government and the Public Service," in Michael J. Prince, ed., *How Ottawa Spends, 1986–87: Tracking the Tories* (Toronto: Methuen, 1986), p. 265.

[27]Blair Williams, "The Para-political Bureaucracy in Ottawa," in H. D. Clarke, et al., *Parliament, Policy and Representation* (Toronto: Methuen, 1980), pp. 222–223.

[28]Donald J. Savoie, "The Minister's Staff: The Need for Reform," *Canadian Public Administration*, vol. 26 (Winter 1983), pp. 509–524.

must be careful also not to use their proximity to the minister for personal or private reasons. In the mid-1960s, following public revelations of questionable activities by ministerial assistants, J. R. Mallory warned of the potential danger of interposing political officials between the minister and the career public service. He argued that "they lack the training and professional standards of the civil service. . . . Not only do these functionaries wield great power because they control access to the Minister and can speak in his name, but they may wield this power with ludicrous ineptitude and in ways that are clearly tainted with political motives."[29] In part, no doubt, as a result of the adverse publicity of the 1960s, ministerial assistants tended to keep a low profile after that time, and they appear to have had little significant influence on the formulation of government policies and programs.[30] However, the influence of ministerial assistants is now on the rise as a result of the more active policy role being played by the chiefs of staff appointed under the Mulroney administration.

Departmental Management

There is no doubt that efficient and effective management of government departments is primarily the responsibility of deputy ministers. The Lambert Commission concluded that the deputy, as the manager of a government department,

> should focus critically on the policies, programs, and services that must be developed and implemented to fulfill the mandate of the department. Deputies must exercise their delegated authority over departmental organization, personnel, and operations to ensure that maximum value is obtained from resources. In managing existing programs, the deputy's concern must be with efficiency, doing better what is already being done. In implementing policy initiatives of the minister and the Government, when involved in the development of new programs, the deputy's concern must also be with effectiveness. The deputy must be concerned with changing current practices and directing resources to where they best serve the departmental mandate.[31]

The incentive for deputy ministers to pay more attention to the quality of their policy advice than of their departmental management was explained above. The relative importance of policy advisory and management skills does, of course, vary from one department to another. Some departments (e.g., Finance) are mainly policy oriented, whereas others (e.g., National Revenue) are mainly program oriented. In any event, sound departmental management is central to both the policy advisory and policy implementation responsibilities of the deputy minister. The quality of the deputy's performance depends greatly on the quality of the advice and assistance received from departmental subordinates. Thus, the success of the deputy, and indeed of the department and its minister,

---

[29]J. R. Mallory, "The Minister's Office Staff: An Unreformed Part of the Public Service," *Canadian Public Administration*, vol. 10 (March 1967), p. 27.
[30]Savoie, The Minister's Staff, p. 518.
[31]Royal Commission on Financial Management and Accountability, p. 185.

rests significantly on the extent to which the deputy is able to recruit, develop, and motivate competent departmental officials, especially senior managers.

In the federal public service, senior managers are members of the Management Category. The Public Service Commission has the authority to appoint public servants to this category, to promote them and to move them from one department to another, and to appoint persons to the category from outside the public service. However, the commission delegates to deputy ministers the authority to appoint or reassign members of the Management Category so long as there is no change in their occupational group or level. This arrangement gives deputy ministers some flexibility to deploy senior staff so as to meet their operational and career development needs.

In the management of their departments, deputies are constrained not only by the regulations and guidelines of the Public Service Commission, but by those of such central agencies as the PCO and the TBS. This chapter has already covered the diverse accountability mechanisms, including central agencies, to which deputy ministers are subject, and later chapters will examine the constraints on deputies and their departments in their management of human and financial resources. It is important to emphasize here that deputies are required to manage their departments in a political, legal, and bureaucratic environment which restricts considerably their freedom of action. This is one of the points of contrast between public and private sector management. The Cabinet, usually acting through central agencies, imposes various service-wide requirements on government departments with a view to achieving such objectives as efficiency and effectiveness, integrity and representativeness. For example, the Planning Programming Budgeting System (PPBS), the Operational Performance Measurement System (OPMS), and program evaluation were introduced to promote efficiency and effectiveness[32]; conflict of interest guidelines were formulated to stimulate a high level of integrity; and an affirmative action program was adopted to bring about a more representative public service. The job of deputy ministers and their senior managers is to fulfil their responsibilities to the best of their ability within the various constraints imposed by political executives and central agencies.

Deputy ministers play a critical role in pursuing not only interdepartmental coordination, but intradepartmental coordination as well. Most government departments are so large that deputies can only pursue coordination through regular, personal contacts with the most senior departmental officials. Deputies are required, therefore, to delegate authority for coordinating departmental activities to their subordinates and to create formal coordinating mechanisms. Many departments have a management committee or an executive committee composed of the deputy and his or her immediate subordinates. This committee determines the overall objectives and priorities of the department and deals with major managerial issues. Deputies, in concert with these senior managers, devise structures and processes to facilitate the coordination of policies and programs at all levels of the department. Formal mechanisms such as committees

---

[32]See the discussion of these matters in Chapters 23 and 24.

are supplemented by a broad range of informal means of seeking coordination (personal contacts, telephone calls, etc.).

Provincial governments, like the federal government, seek coordination through Cabinet committees and central agencies and through both interdepartmental and departmental committees. They have, as a result, experienced some of the same tensions between central agencies and line departments. In discussing problems associated with New Brunswick's Cabinet decision-making system compared to a highly centralized decision-making system, Paul Leger asks what authority and responsibility remain for the minister and deputy minister of a department "when almost every policy issue has interdepartmental implications." Moreover, "how can anyone be held accountable for policy, when everyone is? . . . The possibility always exists that creative and constructive departmental initiatives can be lost in the search for the 'common good.' "[33] It will be interesting to see if provincial governments follow the federal lead in a move away from the current decentralized decision-making system towards greater power for line departments, their ministers, and their senior officials.

CONCLUDING OBSERVATIONS

The story of interaction among the major players in the executive-bureaucratic arena is clearly a complicated one, but in essence, it is a tale of swings in the pendulum of power between political executives and bureaucrats and between departments and central agencies. Bureaucrats exercise a great deal of control and influence in the policy process, and political executives are not always successful in holding bureaucrats accountable for the exercise of this power. No matter what changes are made in the decision-making system, bureaucrats continue to play a pervasive and significant role. Control over the bureaucracy by the Prime Minister (or Premier) and the Cabinet is, however, only one means of holding bureaucrats accountable and responsible for their actions and decisions. The bureaucracy is far from a monolithic entity. We have seen in this chapter that bureaucrats compete with, and are constrained by, other bureaucrats. Subsequent chapters will show that other actors in the political system, namely legislators, judges, pressure groups, and the public, also check bureaucratic power.

---

[33]Leger, "The Cabinet Committee System of Policy-Making and Resource Allocation in the Government of New Brunswick," *Canadian Public Administration*, vol. 26 (Spring 1983), p. 33.

BIBLIOGRAPHY

Most of the items listed in the bibliography for Chapter 13 are also relevant to this chapter. See in addition the following items:

Canada. Royal Commission on Financial Management and Accountability. *Final Report*. Ottawa, Supply and Services, 1979, chs. 9–14.

Dobell, W. M. "Interdepartmental Management in External Affairs." *Canadian Public Administration*, vol. 21 (Spring 1978): 83–102.

Doern, G. Bruce. "The Cabinet and Central Agencies." In G. Bruce Doern and Peter Aucoin, eds., *Public Policy in Canada*. Toronto: Macmillan, 1979.

Doerr, Audrey. *The Machinery of Government in Canada*. Toronto: Methuen, 1981, chs. 4, 6.

Mallory, J. R. "The Minister's Office Staff: An Unreformed Part of the Public Service." *Canadian Public Administration*, vol. 10 (March 1967): 25–34.

Prince, Michael J., and John Chenier. "The Rise and Fall of Policy Planning and Research Units: An Organizational Perspective." *Canadian Public Administration*, vol. 23 (Winter 1980): 519–541.

Savoie, Donald J. "The Minister's Staff: The Need for Reform." *Canadian Public Administration*, vol. 26 (Winter 1983): 509–524.

Schultz, Richard J. "Prime Ministerial Government, Central Agencies and Operating Departments: Towards a More Realistic Analysis." In Thomas A. Hockin, ed., *Apex of Power*. 2nd ed. Scarborough, Ont.: Prentice-Hall, 1977, pp. 229–236.

Sharp, Mitchell. "The Bureaucratic Elite and Policy Formation." In Kenneth Kernaghan, ed., *Bureaucracy in Canadian Government*. 2nd ed. Toronto: Methuen, 1973, pp. 69–73.

Williams, Blair. "The Para-political Bureaucracy in Ottawa." In H. D. Clarke, et al., eds., *Parliament, Policy and Representation*. Toronto: Methuen, 1980, pp. 215–230.

CASES

In *Case Program in Canadian Public Administration* (Toronto: Institute of Public Administration of Canada):

The Draft Memorandum to Cabinet, by Douglas G. Hartle

The Toronto Airport(s), by Sandford F. Borins

Bureaucratie, by Guy Demers

Policy Analysis: A Case Study, by David Zussman

All Things to All People: Government and Its Client Groups, by Sharon Bider and Peter McNaughton

15

The Legislature
and the Bureaucracy

The conventional wisdom among students of Canadian government and politics is that during this century there has been a decline in the power of the federal Parliament and the provincial legislatures and a rise in the power of the public service. The growth in the power of the public service, especially since the beginning of the Second World War, is generally acknowledged. Whether the overall power of the legislatures has actually declined has recently been shown to be a debatable and complex issue.[1] Nevertheless, it is widely recognized that at present the legislatures do not exercise effective power, in the sense of control and influence, over the executive in general and the public service in particular. The Royal Commission on Financial Management and Accountability argued:

> Under our system, Parliament must be the beginning and the end of the governmental process. It must scrutinize and approve all legislation and all proposals for the raising of revenues and the expenditure of funds, and must watch over the Government's implementation of the proposals to which it has assented. We think that Members of Parliament have not been adequately fulfilling their duty of forcing the Government to account for its administration.[2]

Neither the evolution nor the contemporary state of interaction between the legislatures and the public service has received much attention in the literature of Canadian political science and public administration. Yet relations between the legislatures and the public service affect significantly the exercise of power in the Canadian political system, especially by Cabinet ministers, legislators, and public servants.

The power of the legislature over the public service is wielded primarily in an indirect fashion through questioning and criticism of ministers responsible to the legislature for the administration of their departments. Since ministers are the formal constitutional intermediaries between legislators and public servants, the legislature's ability to affect the recommendations and decisions of public

---

[1]See Allan Kornberg and William Mishler, *Influence in Parliament: Canada* (Durham, N.C.: Duke University Press, 1976), pp. 52–57; Robert J. Jackson and Michael M. Atkinson, *The Canadian Legislative System* (Toronto: Macmillan, 1974), pp. 1–9; and John B. Stewart, *The Canadian House of Commons: Procedure and Reform* (Montreal: McGill-Queen's University Press, 1977), pp. 22–30.

[2]Royal Commission on Financial Management and Accountability, *Final Report* (Ottawa: Supply and Services, 1979), pp. 52–53.

servants rests heavily on the interpretation and application of the constitutional convention of *ministerial responsibility*. Ministerial responsibility is in turn tightly bound up with the conventions of *political neutrality* and *public service anonymity*. The definition and usage of these three constitutional conventions (often referred to as principles or doctrines) shape to a large extent the pattern of interaction between public servants on the one hand, and legislators and ministers on the other. For convenience, public service anonymity is included here under the broad heading of political neutrality.

MINISTERIAL RESPONSIBILITY AND POLITICAL NEUTRALITY

The meaning and relevance of ministerial responsibility have been the subject of continuing controversy in Canada in recent years. Some politicians, journalists, and academic scholars contend that the convention is a myth or that it is dead. But other commentators, who acknowledge the deficiencies of the traditional interpretation of ministerial responsibility, continue to treat it as a central feature of constitutional theory and practice. The Royal Commission on Financial Management and Accountability stated that the doctrine of ministerial responsibility is "a cornerstone" of the Canadian constitution in that "it identifies who has the final responsibility for decisions taken — the minister, and provides a forum in which he is publicly accountable — Parliament "[3] (or in the provinces — the legislature).

It is important to clarify the meaning of ministerial responsibility and its relation to the political neutrality of public servants as a foundation for informed discussion of its effects on the exercise of legislative and bureaucratic power. The following analysis focusses on the federal Parliament, but the experience in the provincial legislatures is very similar.

As explained in Chapter 13, collective and individual ministerial responsibility are separate, but interrelated, conventions. *Collective responsibility*, in its application to the government as a whole, prescribes that the Prime Minister and the Cabinet must resign or ask the Governor General for a dissolution of Parliament if the House of Commons passes a vote of no confidence in the government. In its application to individual ministers, collective responsibility prescribes that a minister must support government decisions in public, or at least suppress any public criticism of them. If ministers find a particular decision unacceptable, they must either stifle their objections or submit their resignation.

This chapter centres primarily on *individual* rather than collective responsibility. In the academic literature, several meanings and implications are given to individual ministerial responsibility, but there is widespread agreement that it has two major components.[4] The first is that the minister is answerable to

[3]Ibid., p. 371.

[4]See, for example, S. E. Finer, "The Individual Responsibility of Ministers," *Public Administration*, vol. 34 (1956), p. 379; A. H. Birch, *Representative and Responsible Government* (London: Allen and Unwin, 1964), pp. 139-140; R. M. Punnett, *British Government and Politics* (New York: Norton, 1968), p. 182; Jeffrey Stanyer and Brian Smith, *Administering Britain* (Glasgow: Fontana/Collins, 1976), pp. 180-181; Geoffrey Marshall and Graeme C. Moodie, *Some Problems of the Constitution*, 4th ed. (London: Hutchinson, 1967), pp. 67-74.

Parliament for all the administrative errors of his or her departmental subordinates in the sense that he or she must resign in the event of a serious error by these subordinates. This component of ministerial responsibility is often described as a myth. The second component of the convention is that the minister is answerable to Parliament in that he or she must explain and defend the actions of his or her department before Parliament. The importance of this component is ignored or minimized by some commentators on ministerial responsibility in Canada.

The convention of political neutrality, like that of ministerial responsibility, merits analysis in terms of the extent to which it reflects contemporary political and administrative practice.[5] Interpreted broadly, and including the convention of public service anonymity, political neutrality entails the separation of administration from politics and policy; the selection and promotion of public servants on the basis of merit rather than partisanship; the avoidance by public servants of partisan political activity and of the public expression of personal views on government actions; the provision by public servants of confidential advice to their ministers; ministerial protection of public service anonymity; and the loyal implementation of government decisions by public servants regardless of their personal views.

The Resignation of Ministers

The first component of ministerial responsibility requires that a minister must resign if a serious administrative error committed by his or her department is exposed. Despite frequent calls by Opposition parties for ministerial resignations on the grounds of actual or alleged departmental mismanagement, in practice ministers do not resign as penance for administrative bungling in their department. It is now almost universally accepted that it is unreasonable to hold ministers personally responsible in the form of resignation for the administrative failings of their subordinates. Ministers cannot hope to have personal knowledge of more than a small percentage of the administrative actions taken by their officials. Moreover, they must restrict their attention to those administrative matters which are especially important or politically sensitive. Former Prime Minister Trudeau stated that a minister "can't possibly know everything which is done in the Department by every last Civil Servant and therefore it would be folly to try and pretend that the Minister will be held accountable and must resign when somewhere down the line at the end of a corridor the ten thousandth person committed something illegal or contrary to Government standards or norms."[6]

These factors of size and complexity, together with the burden of the ministers' political obligations, compel them to rely on their senior officials for advice on the administrative, technical, and political implications of policy proposals and decisions. The power of public servants to make discretionary decisions in the implementation of policies further enhances their policy role in that the

---

[5]For an analysis of the evolution and present status of the convention of political neutrality, see Chapter 11.
[6]Office of the Prime Minister, Transcript of Press Conference, November 18, 1977.

implementation process has a substantial impact on the success of policy decisions and on the content of future policies. Thus public servants are actively
involved in politics in the sense of determining or influencing the allocation of
public resources among competing forces. It is clear that the first element of the
doctrine of political neutrality outlined earlier, namely that administration is
separated from politics and policy, is a fiction. In a formal sense, ministers do
make decisions and public servants execute those decisions, but public servants
exercise enormous influence on both policy development and implementation.
It is, therefore, unrealistic to expect ministers to accept personal responsibility
for all the acts of their departmental officials. Why should ministers "carry the
can" when they have little or no knowledge of its contents?

Thus the vicarious responsibility of a minister for departmental actions is
limited and is tied to the particular circumstances of the case at hand. This view
has been supported recently by a committee of senior public servants who asserted
that

> a Minister is subject to various degrees of responsibility. He must certainly
> accept full responsibility for matters done properly under his instructions
> or in accordance with his policy. However, in the case of a problem not
> affecting an important question of policy, he is generally thought to have
> met his responsibility if he takes the matter in hand. Where the matter is
> essentially between a complainant and a particular official, the Minister
> can hardly be expected to have had prior knowledge of the case or to have
> had an opportunity to influence it personally. He cannot be acquainted
> with, or personally criticized for, every detail of administration in his
> department.[7]

This statement implicitly raises the often ignored issue of distinguishing the
minister's personal mistakes from those of his or her officials. It is usually a
formidable task for Parliament and the public to discover whether specific administrative acts were "done properly under his [the minister's] instructions or in
accordance with his policy." Ministers are understandably reluctant even to admit
that an administrative error has been made by their department. And when
confronted with proof of error, they will usually deny personal knowledge of, or
involvement in, the events in question. On this basis, they then contend that
they should not have to accept full responsibility in the form of resignation, or
indeed to assume any personal blame. If departmental failures are admitted or
apparent, ministers are inclined to blame their officials, rather than to accept
personal or vicarious responsibility. The usual practice is that ministers inform
Parliament that the fault lies with departmental officials and promise that the
offenders will be disciplined and their mistakes corrected.

Cases do arise where the personal culpability of a minister is evident or where
the magnitude of the error causes the government considerable embarrassment.
Even if the minister "accepts full responsibility" in such situations, the practical
effects on his or her career depend largely on personal, partisan, and situational

---

[7]Government of Canada, *Report of the Committee on the Concept of the Ombudsman*, Ottawa,
July 1977, p. 16.

factors. If the minister under attack is an unpopular member of Cabinet, if the electorate is unusually outraged, or if the government is in a minority position in Parliament, the Prime Minister might be tempted to seek or accept the minister's resignation. The long-standing practice in Canada, however, is to enfold the offending minister in the Cabinet's protective cloak, so that a matter of individual ministerial responsibility becomes one of collective responsibility. Nevertheless, a minister's reputation suffers from the unfavourable publicity accompanying demands for his or her resignation, so that after the next Cabinet shuffle or the next election, he or she may be heading a less prestigious department or sitting on a government backbench.

Two other aspects of ministerial resignation deserve brief mention. First, a number of recent cases in Canada show that ministers will almost invariably be compelled to resign if personal misconduct in the form of unethical, immoral, or illegal activities is revealed. For example, a federal minister resigned when it was revealed that he had forged the signature of his ladyfriend's husband so that she could obtain an abortion, and a provincial minister resigned when he was charged with having arranged the murder of his wife. Second, incumbent ministers cannot be held responsible, especially by way of resignation, for administrative sins allegedly committed within their departments during the tenure of their predecessors.

It is clear that in practice ministers do not resign to atone for either serious mismanagement by their officials or personal administrative mistakes. Indeed, if ministerial protestations of innocence are accepted at face value, ministers rarely make mistakes. Thus, the demand for ministerial resignations on the grounds of maladministration may appear to be a feeble weapon in the parliamentary arsenal of Opposition parties. Yet, this component of ministerial responsibility has important consequences for both ministers and public servants. Parliamentary and public calls for one's resignation, like the probability of being hanged the next morning, effectively concentrate one's attention. A minister's efforts to refute or defuse the allegations are vigorously supported by his or her senior officials, whose duty it is to keep their minister out of trouble. The reputation and career prospects of public servants tend to prosper or suffer along with those of their minister.

In the event of maladministration by departmental officials, the conventions of both ministerial responsibility and political neutrality require that ministers protect the anonymity of the wrongdoers by declining to identify them publicly. Since public servants are expected to serve their minister loyally by supporting departmental policy in public, even if they oppose it vigorously within the confines of the department, ministers are expected to shield them from public criticism. However, in recent years there have been some notable departures from conventional practice by ministers who have named and blamed officials in public. For example, in 1978, Jean-Pierre Goyer, then the federal Minister of Supply and Services, was sued for libel by a public servant whom he had criticized both inside and outside the House of Commons. Mr. Justice Lieff of the Ontario High Court, who awarded damages to the official for Mr. Goyer's statement outside the House, observed:

It is a long standing convention of parliamentary democracy and the doctrine of ministerial responsibility which it encompasses that civil servants
are to remain faceless to the public. Civil servants are responsible to their
ministers. Ministers, as elected officials, are responsible to the public . . . .
Furthermore, . . . no matter how advanced the state of erosion of public
service anonymity . . . a minister should not be able to blame or castigate
personally a civil servant of a department under his control in public and
then fall back on the legal defence of qualified privilege. If that were the
case and the civil servant were defamed he would be in the peculiar position of being prevented from obtaining vindication for spurious allegations
by the minister.[8]

Although the instances in which ministers have publicly criticized their officials are exceptional, officials cannot invariably rely on their ministers to protect their anonymity. Moreover, in return for ministerial protection, public
servants must not abandon the shelter of ministerial responsibility by engaging
in unapproved forms of partisan political activity or in public criticism of government policies. Also, public servants must moderate their public praise of
government actions and avoid public identification with specific policies, decisions, or views so that they may retain their office in the event of a change in the
governing party. Ministers have a corresponding responsibility not to praise public
servants in a manner that identifies them publicly with specific policy initiatives. Yet, at a press conference on December 22, 1969, Prime Minister Trudeau
announced the move of a deputy minister from one department to another and
observed that when the official was deputy minister of Indian affairs and northern development, "he did a first-class job in developing the north . . . one of his
brain children, I suppose, was the Pan-Arctic which he developed with Mr. Laing,
who was minister there . . . and the whole Indian policy, I think, was largely the
result of [the deputy] and his team."[9]

All these considerations point to the strong links between political neutrality
and ministerial responsibility. It is notable, however, that some advocates of
legislative reform believe that a weakening of these conventions is justifiable to
achieve the greater good of increased administrative accountability. For example, the Special Committee on Reform of the House of Commons concluded
that "the doctrine of ministerial accountability undermines the potential for
genuine accountability on the part of the person that ought to be accountable
— the senior officer of the department [the deputy minister]."[10]

The Answerability of Ministers
The second component of ministerial responsibility corresponds closely to its
current practice. Ministers do explain and defend their department's policies

[8]*Stopforth v. Goyer*, 20 *Ontario Reports* (2d) 1978, p. 273. This decision was overturned in the
Ontario Court of Appeal on the grounds that the occasion of Goyer's comments outside Parliament "was one of qualified privilege." 23 *Ontario Reports* (2d) 1979, p. 700.
[9]Office of the Prime Minister, Transcript of Press Conference, December 22, 1969.
[10]House of Commons, Special Committee on Reform of the House of Commons, *3rd Report*, June
1985.

and administration before Parliament, especially during question period. Opposition members and, on occasion, government backbenchers utilize a variety of other opportunities (for example, motions, opposition days) to seek information and explanations from ministers. But an inordinate amount of parliamentary, media and public attention centres on the daily oral question period. It is notable that ministers almost always respond to questions in their sphere of responsibility, despite the fact that they can neither be obligated to answer nor to give reasons for refusing to answer.[11] A strong impetus to answer to Parliament is that a minister may suffer adverse political consequences for declining to answer. The Speaker of the House of Commons has observed that he "is not in a position to compel an answer — it is public opinion which compels an answer."[12] Certainly, a minister who refuses to answer questions on an important issue, especially if he does not provide a reasonable explanation for his position, receives severe criticism from Opposition members and the news media. There is, therefore, both constitutional and political pressure on ministers to justify their department's actions to Parliament.

The willingness of ministers to answer questions in the legislature does not ensure that all their replies are informative, plausible, or even comprehensible. Experienced ministers tend to be artful dodgers who often bob and weave to avoid direct hits from Opposition inquiries and allegations. Brian Chapman admits that ministerial responsibility "may be a useful tag for harrying ministers in Parliament," but he notes that "even then it smacks rather of a verbal game of cowboys and Indians."[13] Nevertheless, on the premise that ministerial evasion and circumlocution on a serious matter may be motivated by a desire to conceal politically embarrassing information, not only Opposition members but also journalists may be prompted to investigate the matter more vigorously.

The fact that a single identifiable minister is answerable for the activities of a specific department assists backbench members of the legislature in their handling of constituents' inquiries or complaints about government administration. A question in the legislature is sometimes the last recourse of a member who has been unable to obtain a satisfactory answer through private correspondence with a minister.

Although, as noted earlier, ministers are not expected to resign for departmental errors made during the term of office of their predecessors, they must answer to Parliament for those errors. This rule ensures a focus of continuing responsibility for government administration, despite changes in the political heads of departments or in the governing party itself. Parliament's capacity to control and influence public servants is enhanced because one minister is required to answer for administrative actions, no matter when these actions took place. Incumbent ministers will usually be obliged to rely heavily on their departmental officials for knowledge of what occurred during the tenure of their predecessors. In such situations, the ability of ministers to answer to Parliament for their

---

[11]Arthur Beauchesne, *Rules and Forms of the House of Commons of Canada*, 4th ed. (Toronto: Carswell, 1958), section 181 (3), p. 153.

[12]House of Commons, *Debates*, February 6, 1978, p. 567.

[13]Brian Chapman, *British Government Observed* (London: Allen and Unwin, 1963), p. 38.

department rests largely on the continuity of administration provided by their permanent public servants. Thus, the operation of ministerial responsibility is closely tied to the permanency in office of public servants. Permanency in turn depends on the preservation of several of the other elements of political neutrality described earlier.

An important corollary of the answerability of ministers for the administration of their departments is that public servants do not answer directly to Parliament for their decisions and recommendations. In the words of S. E. Finer, "the minister alone speaks for his Civil Servants to the House and to his Civil Servants for the House."[14] The application of this principle protects the anonymity of public servants, since it provides that the minister and only the minister is answerable to Parliament. The willingness of a few ministers occasionally to name and blame their officials has had no significant effect on the status of official anonymity. The impact of allegations made against public servants by members of Parliament has in general also been minimal.

Nevertheless, a combination of factors related to the growth of bureaucratic power is bringing about a gradual decline in public service anonymity. These factors are the heightened visibility arising from the increasing extent to which officials are required to explain government policies in public forums, the expanded coverage by journalists of the activities and identities of specific officials, and the more frequent appearances of public servants before legislative committees.

The traditional interpretation of ministerial responsibility not only precludes public servants from answering directly to Parliament; it also prevents them from responding publicly to parliamentary criticism of their administrative actions. The minister replies to public accusations against his or her officials. In the face of allegations of serious administrative error, however, public servants, with the permission of their minister, have appeared before parliamentary committees to explain and defend their actions. The practice of official reticence and ministerial defence which normally prevails extends to attacks on public servants by persons outside Parliament, notably journalists. As a result, responsibility for departmental administration is focussed on the minister, and public servants try to preserve official anonymity by avoiding involvement in public or political controversy.

The preceding analysis indicates that the resignation component of the convention of ministerial responsibility may be restated as follows: A minister is not answerable to Parliament for all the administrative errors of his or her department in the sense that he or she must resign in the event of a serious error by the department. The second component of the convention, namely that the minister is answerable to Parliament in that he or she must explain and defend the actions of the department before Parliament, is unchanged.

Reports of the death of individual ministerial responsibility are greatly exaggerated. If the life of the convention depended on ministerial resignations for the misdeeds of departmental subordinates, it would be mortally wounded. But

---

[14]Finer, "The Individual Responsibility of Ministers," p. 394.

because of the vitality of its answerability component, ministerial responsibility remains a central, operative convention of the Canadian constitution. Indeed, parliamentary debate on ministerial responsibility has centred on its interpretation and application, not on its existence. The concept of ministerial responsibility helps to define and determine how power is and should be exercised in the Canadian political system, and who is or should be held responsible for the exercise of that power. It provides a major frame of reference for the allocation of power and responsibility among ministers, legislators, and public servants. The fact that the practice of ministerial responsibility does not correspond in full to its theory does not justify denial of the existence or importance of the convention — especially in the absence of a viable alternative. V. Seymour Wilson, in his insightful analysis of ministerial responsibility and bureaucratic accountability, concludes that "Canadian discourse on administrative power continues to be dominated by the doctrine of ministerial responsibility,"[15] and that "ministerial responsibility and all its trappings will continue to be around for a long time."[16]

LEGISLATIVE CONTROL AND INFLUENCE

An essential condition for a complete and comprehensible system of responsibility in government is that elected or appointed officials, or both, bear responsibility for all government actions. In a parliamentary democracy, if officials waste public funds, break the law, or violate citizens' rights, the public expects that someone will be held accountable for these misdeeds. If ministers do not accept responsibility for departmental transgressions, the focus of blame shifts to public servants. But the conventions of ministerial responsibility and political neutrality still protect the anonymity of public servants and restrict their answerability to Parliament. As a result, some commentators claim that these conventions permit public servants to exercise power without publicity or responsibility.[17] On those exceptional occasions when blame is publicly attributed to specific officials, disciplinary action is handled as an internal administrative matter, with the result that the public rarely learns what penalties, if any, are imposed. Consequently, it appears to the public that on some occasions, neither ministers nor public servants are held accountable for maladministration.

Can the federal and provincial legislatures help to ensure responsibility in government by controlling or influencing bureaucratic action?[18] There are three major means by which this can be done. These are: (1) debates, questions, and other procedures in the legislature; (2) reliance on certain "watchdog" agencies

---

[15]*Canadian Public Policy and Administration* (Toronto: McGraw-Hill Ryerson, 1981), p. 197.
[16]Ibid., p. 220.
[17]See, for example, J. R. Mallory, "Responsive and Responsible Government," Presidential Address, section II, *Transactions of the Royal Society of Canada*, series IV, 12 (1974), p. 221; and Claude E. Forget, "L'administration publique: subject ou objet du pouvoir politique?" *Canadian Public Administration*, vol. 21 (1978), pp. 234–242.
[18]For a general discussion of bureaucratic power and administrative responsibility respectively, see Chapters 11 and 12.

which report directly or indirectly to the legislature; and (3) the use of legislative committees. The first means, which involves influencing the bureaucracy indirectly by influencing ministers, has been discussed at length above.

Watchdog Agencies

The second means involves the use of such agencies as ombudsmen and auditors to assist legislators to affect bureaucratic behaviour. The Office of the Ombudsman, which is an extremely important watchdog agency in the provincial sphere of government, does not exist in the federal government. There are, however, a number of important federal agencies which are often described as "specialized ombudsmen" or "mini-ombudsmen." These are the offices of the Correctional Investigator, the Official Languages Commissioner, the Canadian Human Rights Commissioner, the Privacy Commissioner, and the Information Commissioner. The most prominent watchdog agencies in the federal sphere of government are the Public Service Commission and the Office of the Auditor General.

The Ombudsman

Among the most popular of the various institutional and procedural safeguards designed to check bureaucratic power is the ombudsman. The Office of the Ombudsman originated in Sweden in 1809 and was adopted by Finland in 1919. No other countries appointed an ombudsman until after the Second World War. Then, a large number of countries around the world adopted the institution to help deal with the problem of ensuring that citizens' rights were protected in the face of rapidly growing bureaucracies in virtually every governmental jurisdiction.[19] An ombudsman has now been appointed in every Canadian province except Prince Edward Island, which because of its small size has less need for the institution. The first Office of the Ombudsman in Canada, indeed the first in North America, was established in Alberta in September 1967. The Office of the Ombudsman has also been widely adapted for use in non-governmental organizations, notably in universities.

The major function of an ombudsman is to investigate citizens' complaints about improper, unfair, or discriminatory administrative treatment. An ombudsman is usually authorized by statute to obtain access to the government documents and to call the witnesses necessary to investigate these complaints. If he or she believes that certain complaints are justified, the public servants involved will be requested to remedy the mistakes. The ombudsman is responsible to the legislature and presents an annual report to that body describing the cases that have been dealt with by his or her office and the progress that has been made in redressing any administrative injustices. It is important to emphasize that

> ombudsmen possess influence rather than control. They cannot alter administrative decisions. But they are well placed to cause those who have this power to review and change decisions which, after careful examination,

---

[19]For an account of the evolution of the Office of the Ombudsman, both in Canada and other countries, see Donald C. Rowat, *The Ombudsman Plan: The Worldwide Spread of an Idea*, 2nd ed. (Lanham, Maryland: University Press of America, 1986).

appear to be unreasonable, oppressive or simply wrong in the circumstances. This influence, like that of auditors general, derives from their authority to investigate matters in depth and, as a last resort, to report their findings publicly to the legislature.[20]

There are, of course, other means of recourse available to citizens who believe they have suffered injustice at the hands of the bureaucracy. These include direct appeals to the public servant responsible for the action at issue and/or to the public servant's superiors, to members of Parliament, to administrative tribunals such as the Tax Review Board, and to the courts. However, the hearing of appeals by officials in the same department or agency responsible for the original decision may not result in the fact or the appearance of impartiality; members of Parliament have neither time nor resources equivalent to those of an ombudsman; the jurisdiction of appeal tribunals is limited; and court action can be both costly and time consuming. Citizens are usually required to exhaust all the legal remedies available to them before complaining to the ombudsman. Thus, ombudsmen deal with complaints about unfair, rather than illegal, administrative action. The simple and inexpensive process of bringing grievances to an ombudsman has great appeal for the average citizen.

A study by a group of federal senior public servants noted that a federal ombudsman "would increase the awareness of ministers and officials of the need to deal promptly and equitably with individuals who perceive that they are victims of an administrative injustice," and concluded that an ombudsman "would be a desirable adjunct to the existing system of complaint handling in the departments and agencies of the federal government."[21] Despite considerable discussion over the years of the desirability of creating a federal ombudsman,[22] including the introduction of a bill for that purpose,[23] there is little current interest in the proposal.

Mini-ombudsmen

Part of the explanation for the absence of a federal ombudsman is that the federal government has several "specialized ombudsmen" who serve a purpose similar to, but considerably narrower than, that of a general-purpose ombudsman. These include (1) the Office of the Correctional Investigator, established in 1973 to investigate complaints made against prison authorities by or on behalf of inmates; (2) the Office of the Official Languages Commissioner, which was created in 1970 to administer the Official Languages Act by protecting the lan-

---

[20]Committee on the Concept of the Ombudsman, "The Ombudsman," in Kenneth Kernaghan, ed., *Public Administration in Canada: Selected Readings*, 5th ed. (Toronto: Methuen, 1985), pp. 374–375.

[21]Ibid., p. 379.

[22]See Henry J. Llambias, "Canada: Introduction," in Gerald E. Caiden, ed., *International Handbook of the Ombudsman. Country Surveys* (Westport, Conn.: Greenwood Press, 1983), pp. 27–28, 34, and Rowat, *The Ombudsman Plan*, ch. 13.

[23]In April 1978, the Liberal government introduced Bill C-43, entitled the Ombudsman Act. For a critical analysis of the bill, see K. A. Friedmann and A. G. Milne, "The Federal Ombudsman Legislation: A Critique of Bill C-43," *Canadian Public Policy*, vol. 6 (Winter 1980), pp. 63–67.

guage rights of individuals, monitoring all federal agencies to ensure proper application of the Act, and making recommendations for improved adherence to the spirit and the letter of the Act; (3) the Canadian Human Rights Commission, which was established to implement the Canadian Human Rights Act (1976–77) and is responsible for investigating complaints of discrimination, trying to resolve or settle these complaints, and using research and public education to reduce discriminatory attitudes and behaviour; (4) the Office of the Information Commissioner, set up in 1983 to administer the Access to Information Act by investigating complaints against denial of access to government information; and (5) the Office of the Privacy Commissioner, established in 1983 to implement the Privacy Act and, specifically, to inquire into complaints from persons who believe that their privacy rights have been abridged.[24] The Correctional Investigator reports to Parliament through the Solicitor General, whereas the Human Rights, Information, and Privacy Commissioners report to Parliament through the Department of Justice. The Office of the Official Languages Commissioner is more independent of the executive in that its reports go directly to Parliament, where its work is scrutinized by the Joint Committee of the House and the Senate on Official Languages Policy and Programs and its estimates are examined by the Commons Standing Committee on Miscellaneous Estimates.

The Public Service Commission

The federal Public Service Commission is an independent agency which serves Parliament as the guardian of the merit principle in public personnel management.[25] The promotion of merit through the elimination of patronage has traditionally been a dominant concern of the commission. In this regard, J. E. Hodgetts has observed that the commission, "from its neutral vantage point, represents the institutionalized conscience of legislators, warding off the demon patronage rather like Alcoholics Anonymous wards off the demon rum on behalf of its membership."[26] The commission's annual report is tabled in Parliament by the secretary of state for consideration by the Miscellaneous Estimates Committee.

The Auditor General

Aside from the Office of the Official Languages Commissioner, the only federal watchdog agency that reports to Parliament directly rather than through a minister is the Office of the Auditor General, which is discussed at length in Chapter 24. The Auditor General reports annually to Parliament on whether departments have kept proper financial records and whether public funds have been spent as appropriated by Parliament. Moreover, the Auditor General is authorized to report cases where "money has been expended without due regard for economy

---

[24]For additional information on the offices of the Information Commissioner and the Privacy Commissioner, see Chapter 19.

[25]For elaboration on the commission's functions and its relationship with the Treasury Board Secretariat, see Chapter 21.

[26]J. E. Hodgetts, *The Canadian Public Service* (Toronto: University of Toronto Press, 1973), p. 264.

and efficiency; or . . . satisfactory procedures have not been established to measure and report the effectiveness of programs."[27]

The Auditor General enjoys considerable autonomy from executive control and can, therefore, influence significantly relations betweeen Parliament and the executive. Ministers and public servants are fearful that the annual report of the Auditor General will single out their department or programs for criticism. Traditionally, the annual reports have provided powerful ammunition for the guns of the parliamentary Opposition by describing instances of inappropriate, questionable, and illegal government spending, which are widely publicized in the media. Provincial auditors play a role similar to, but less publicized than, that of the Auditor General.

Legislative Committees

Legislative committees are the third major means by which the legislature can exercise control or influence over the bureaucracy. The federal Parliament usually has about twenty standing (permanent) committees, a small number of special committees, and a few joint committees of the Senate and the House of Commons. Each standing committee covers several departments and agencies. For example, the Committee on Agriculture deals with the Department of Agriculture, the Canadian Dairy Commission, the Canadian Livestock Feed Board, the Farm Credit Corporation, and the National Farm Products Marketing Council.

The functions of parliamentary committees may be divided into policy development (involving primarily evaluation of the purpose and content of proposed legislation), review of existing policies, and scrutiny of departmental administration (especially through examination of the estimates). In practice, these functions often overlap, and committee members vary in the emphasis they place on each function. Kornberg and Mishler estimate that standing committees as a whole "spend about 50% of their time considering the estimates of the departments and divide the remainder of their time between scrutinizing current legislation and conducting investigations, collecting information on particular problems and preparing reports for the consideration of the House."[28]

The Public Accounts Committee and the Standing Joint Committee (i.e., of the Senate and the House of Commons) on Regulations and Other Statutory Instruments deserve special attention. They enjoy a greater measure of independence from Cabinet control because, unlike other committees, they are chaired by a member of the Opposition. In a majority government situation, however, the majority of the committees' members are from the government party.

The Public Accounts Committee examines both the *Public Accounts* (i.e., the government's year-end financial statements) and the Auditor General's report as a basis for making recommendations to the House of Commons. With the assistance of the Auditor General, the committee has uncovered, investigated, and

---

[27]The Auditor General Act, Canada, *Statutes*, 1977, c. 34, s. 7 (2).
[28]Kornberg and Mishler, *Influence in Parliament: Canada*, p. 33.

reported on several scandals involving the expenditure of public funds and has recommended corrective action in many other instances where public money has been improperly spent.

The Standing Joint Committee on Regulations and Other Statutory Instruments was established by the Statutory Instruments Act, which came into force in January 1972.[29] The primary function of the committee is to scrutinize the use of delegated legislative authority by Cabinet, ministers, and public servants. The term *statutory instruments* refers to the rules, regulations, orders, etc. made by the executive under delegated legislative authority. As noted in Chapter 11, the contemporary power of the bureaucracy rests in part on authority delegated to the executive by Parliament, whose members do not have the time or the expertise to provide in legislation for every contingency. The committee examines statutory instruments in the light of fifteen criteria, including, for example, whether a regulation "trespasses unduly on the rights and liberties of the subject" or "appears for any reason to infringe the rule of law or the rules of natural justice." The committee has severely criticized the government for lack of cooperation and inadequate responses to the committee's recommendations. In 1980, for example, the committee noted:

> There are also traditions in the Public Service, most notably in the drafting of statutes and subordinate legislation, which are more in keeping with administrative ease than accountability to Parliament and observance of the law. The absence of a clearly articulated philosophy of respect for liberty and propriety in the activities of the executive government of Canada is a serious problem.[30]

Eric Hehner has suggested that if ministers and government departments have no respect for this parliamentary committee, nobody else can be expected to take it seriously. Moreover, he worries that unless members of Parliament provide an effective mechanism for reviewing the exercise of delegated legislation, "Parliament as we have known it will become relatively impotent."[31] The committee's warnings that the executive often does not exercise delegated authority in keeping with the intent of Parliament have received surprisingly little media attention.

Among the most common proposals for parliamentary reform are measures which will enhance the effectiveness of committees in evaluating the policies and scrutinizing the administrative actions of the executive. The reform of the parliamentary committee system in the 1960s shifted to the committees much of Parliament's capacity to scrutinize the administration of government departments.[32] Current proposals for change include a more vigorous investigative

[29]Gary Levy, "Delegated Legislation and the Standing Joint Committee on Regulations and Other Statutory Instruments," *Canadian Public Administration*, vol. 22 (Fall 1979), pp. 349–365.
[30]*Fourth Report*, July 1980.
[31]Ibid., pp. 349, 350. See also J. R. Mallory, "Curtailing 'Divine Right': The Control of Delegated Legislation in Canada," in O. P. Dwivedi, ed., *The Administrative State in Canada* (Toronto: University of Toronto Press, 1982), pp. 131–149.
[32]See T. A. Hockin, "The Advance of Standing Committees in Canada's House of Commons: 1965 to 1970," *Canadian Public Administration*, vol. 13 (Summer 1970), pp. 105–202 and C. E. S. Franks, "The Dilemma of the Standing Committees of the Canadian House of Commons," *Canadian Journal of Political Science*, vol. 4 (September1971), pp. 461–476.

role for committees, specialization by committee members in specific policy fields, and improved support facilities in the form of research staff and funds.[33] The feasibility of such proposals depends to some extent on what objectives parliamentarians wish to pursue through parliamentary committees, but it depends primarily on whether the government will permit changes in the nature and operations of these committees.

Public servants already answer to parliamentary committees by explaining the administrative and technical implications of existing and proposed policies. An increase in the investigative work, specialization, and expertise of committee members would enable them to engage in better informed and more penetrating questioning of officials. This would encourage public servants to perform their administrative tasks more economically, efficiently, and effectively, especially if committee members focussed their attention on the scrutiny of departmental administration. If members devoted a substantial portion of their efforts to policy development and policy review, officials would continue to refer to their minister those inquiries involving policy matters. But the enhanced competence of committee members combined with the difficulty of separating policy and administrative considerations would cause public servants to reveal more frequently and clearly their influence on policy formation. The effect on ministerial responsibility would be negligible because ministers would continue to deal with questions on the substance and direction of government policy.

The reinforcement and extension of the activities and expertise of parliamentary committees would improve Parliament's capacity to hold public servants accountable for the *administration* — but not for the *content* — of government policies. Thus, these reforms would not satisfy those who contend that the responsibility of public servants should be commensurate with their power in the political process. They claim that for Parliament to play a significantly greater role in promoting administrative responsibility, there must be some shift in answerability for *policy* from ministers to public servants. The implementation of this proposal would have very important implications for Canada's parliamentary institutions and practices, in both the federal and provincial spheres of government.

Relations between ministers and public servants would be complicated by the difficulty of distinguishing their respective contributions to the development of specific policies. The answerability of public servants to Parliament would compete with their accountability and loyalty to their minister. The remaining healthy component of ministerial responsibility — the answerability of ministers — would be severely weakened. Even the convenient fiction of a separation between policy and administration would be extremely difficult to maintain. There would be a dramatic decline in public service anonymity, and the senior echelons of the service would be politicized. Public servants would be compelled to defend their policy recommendations before parliamentary committees and the public. Officials would become personally associated with particular policies and would, therefore, become involved in political controversy. Security of tenure

---

[33]See Special Committee on Reform of the House of Commons, *3rd Report*, June 1985 and Government of Canada, Royal Commission on Financial Management and Accountability, *Final Report* (Ottawa: Supply and Services, 1979), ch. 22.

for senior officials would be replaced by a system of political appointments, and a consequent turnover of public servants with a change of government.

This hypothetical pattern of relations between politicians and public servants indicates that public servants cannot be held answerable to Parliament for *policy* matters without major modifications in the present practice of ministerial responsibility and political neutrality. It also demonstrates the comparatively small extent to which the conventions have evolved towards this pattern of behaviour from their traditional interpretation. Current trends suggest that the conventions will continue to evolve, or will be altered, in the direction of greater administrative answerability to Parliament, but that ministers will retain formal responsibility for the defence of government policy. Thus Parliament has the potential to increase its power over the public service, especially in the sphere of overseeing administration, without breaching those constitutional conventions affecting most directly the conduct of the public service.

The power of Parliament over the public service rests largely on its ability and inclination to control and influence the executive as a whole. But Parliament's success in checking the executive hinges on such factors as the devotion of committee members to their work, the creation of a non-partisan atmosphere in committee deliberations, the government's willingness to take committee reports seriously, and improved access to much government information now treated as confidential. Reforms in the structures and processes of Parliament would help to augment Parliament's power over both ministers and public servants. In particular, several measures could be adopted to increase the answerability of public servants for departmental administration. The Royal Commission on Financial Management and Accountability (the Lambert Commission)[34] made several useful recommendations for reforms to enhance the accountability of both ministers and senior bureaucrats to Parliament.[35]

The commission's recommendations involve a much more active role for parliamentary committees. The commissioners suggested that the deputy minister be designated the chief administrative officer of the department and be held directly accountable to Parliament through the Public Accounts Committee for specified administrative duties.[36] Ministers would remain accountable for policy objectives and decisions. Several years later, the Special Parliamentary Committee on Reform of the House of Commons discussed the possibility of an even broader measure of deputy ministerial responsibility:

> We have heard many arguments that a new doctrine of deputy ministerial responsibility relating exclusively to matters of administration should be established. . . . Such a doctrine would set out the obligations of senior public servants and include the obligation to testify before parliamentary committees on matters of administration. Under this system, the testimony

---

[34]*Final Report*, chs. 21, 22.
[35]See also Special Committee on Reform of the House of Commons, *3rd Report*, June 1985 and the recommendations in Thomas D'Aquino, G. Bruce Doern, and Cassandra Blair, *Parliamentary Democracy in Canada: Issues for Reform* (Toronto: Methuen, 1983).
[36]See the discussion of this proposal in Chapter 14.

of deputy ministers before committees would be an everyday occurrence. Furthermore, regular open contact between the senior public service and Members of Parliament should lead to a more realistic understanding of administrative practices and more precise pinpointing of accountability.[37]

The Lambert commissioners also proposed that the number and size of standing committees in the House of Commons be reduced, and that these committees be allowed to recommend the partial reduction of proposed government expenditures and to submit substantive reports on the estimates to the House. Also, each committee would have a chairperson elected for the life of a Parliament and a budget to engage staff assistance.

The commissioners did not believe that their proposed reforms would erode the doctrine of ministerial responsibility. Indeed, they argued that "the concept of direct accountability of officials before Parliament through one of its committees would reinforce the minister's and the Cabinet's ability to be responsible for the conduct of the affairs of government."[38] The commissioners do acknowledge, however, that the success of efforts to increase government's accountability to Parliament on administrative matters depends largely on the determination of ministers and parliamentarians to achieve this end. J. R. Mallory notes that in trying to improve the operations of the House of Commons we must remember that "it is a political body made up of political parties whose *raison d'être* is to win the electoral battle and become the government. No activity, no matter how worthy, which does not accord with this primary objective is likely to be embraced by the House."[39]

The report of the Special Parliamentary Committee on Reform of the House of Commons contained many of the same proposed reforms as the Lambert report mentioned above. The Mulroney government agreed to implement some of the committee's recommendations, including those which will reduce the size of parliamentary committees, give the committees more permanent membership so as to encourage the development of special expertise among their members, and provide committees with their own budgets for research staff and legal counsel. The government also agreed to permit a parliamentary committee to review senior bureaucratic appointments, including those of deputy ministers and heads of Crown agencies. It is too early to assess the success of these changes in achieving more effective parliamentary control and influence over the executive in general, and the bureaucracy in particular.

In addition to the three major forms of interaction between legislators and public servants described above, senior bureaucrats, with the consent of the minister concerned, provide occasional briefings to parliamentary caucuses on such matters as departmental structures and functions and the operation and content of new programs. "The briefings are to provide factual and background material necessary to allow informed discussion of the subject under discussion,

---

[37] *3rd Report*, p. 21.
[38] Ibid., p. 375.
[39] J. R. Mallory, "Parliament in the Eighties," in R. Carty and W. Ward, eds., *Entering the Eighties: Canada in Crisis* (Toronto: Oxford University Press, 1980), p. 132.

consistent with preserving the necessary confidences of government and with maintaining the traditional impartiality of public servants."[40] Finally, there are various informal contacts between legislators and public servants at social events and through oral or written requests for information about such matters as programs, budgets, and constituents' complaints.

A number of provincial governments have also taken some modest measures to enhance the accountability of ministers and public servants to the legislature, especially for financial administration. For example, in Ontario, the Public Accounts Committee has been chaired by an Opposition member since 1968, and in 1977 the provincial auditor was authorized not only to report on the economy and efficiency of government operations, but also to verify that departments have appropriate procedures to enable them to report on the effectiveness of these operations.

Many students of the federal Parliament and provincial legislatures are pessimistic that the changes in government machinery and attitudes needed for a significant increase in legislative power over the bureaucracy will be made. Nevertheless, as noted above, some important reforms have recently been made. It was explained in Chapters 6 and 7 that the difficulty which legislatures have in exercising control and influence over departments is compounded with respect to Crown corporations and regulatory agencies, which enjoy a greater measure of autonomy than departments from executive as well as legislative control. In any event, even a more powerful legislature would be an insufficient instrument to ensure responsible public bureaucracy. The role of the legislature must be supplemented by controls and influences exercised by other actors in the political system, including the judiciary, which is discussed in the next chapter.

---

[40]Office of the Prime Minister, *Cabinet Procedures and Ministerial Guidelines*, September 18, 1984, Annex A — Briefings by Officials to Parliamentary Caucuses, dated June 1981.

BIBLIOGRAPHY

Atkinson, Michael M. "Parliamentary Government in Canada." In Michael S. Whittington and Glen Williams, eds., *Canadian Politics in the 1980s*. 2nd ed. Toronto: Methuen, 1984, pp. 331-350.

Canada. House of Commons. Special Committee on Reform of the House of Commons. *3rd Report*. June 1985.

Canada. Royal Commission on Financial Management and Accountability. *Final Report*. Ottawa: Supply and Services, 1979, chs. 21-22.

Clarke, Harold D., Colin Campbell, F.Q. Quo, and Arthur Goddard, eds. *Parliament, Policy and Representation*. Toronto: Methuen, 1980.

Committee on the Concept of the Ombudsman. "The Ombudsman." In Kenneth Kernaghan, ed., *Public Administration in Canada: Selected Readings*. 5th ed. Toronto: Methuen, 1985, pp. 374-379.

Denton, T. M. "Ministerial Responsibility: A Contemporary Perspective." In R. Schultz, et al., eds., *The Canadian Political Process*. Toronto: Holt, Rinehart and Winston, 1979, pp. 344–362.

Doerr, Audrey. "Parliamentary Accountability and Legislative Potential." In Harold D. Clarke, et al., eds. *Parliament, Policy and Representation*. Toronto: Methuen, 1980, pp. 144–159.

Gélinas, André. *Les parlementaires et l'administration au Québec*. Québec: Les Presses de l'Université Laval, 1969.

Jackson, Robert J., and Michael M. Atkinson. *The Canadian Legislative System: Politicians and Policymaking*. 2nd ed. Toronto: Macmillan, 1980.

Kersell, J. E. *Parliamentary Supervision of Delegated Legislation: The United Kingdom, Australia, New Zealand and Canada*. London: Stevens, 1960.

Kersell, J. E. "Statutory and Judicial Control of Administrative Behavior." *Canadian Public Administration*, vol. 19 (Summer 1976): 295–307.

Kornberg, Allan. *Canadian Legislative Behaviour*. Toronto: Holt, Rinehart and Winston, 1967.

Mallory, J. R. "Curtailing 'Divine Right': The Control of Delegated Legislation in Canada." In O. P. Dwivedi, ed., *The Administrative State in Canada*. Toronto: University of Toronto Press, 1982, pp. 131–150.

Rowat, Donald C. *The Ombudsman*. 2nd ed. Toronto: University of Toronto Press, 1968.

Rowat, Donald C. *The Ombudsman Plan*. Toronto: McClelland and Stewart, 1973.

Slatter, Frans F. *Parliament and Administrative Agencies*. Study paper for the Law Reform Commission of Canada. Ottawa: Supply and Services, 1982.

Stewart, John B. *The Canadian House of Commons: Procedure and Reform*. Montreal: McGill-Queen's University Press, 1977.

Vandervort, Lucinda. *Political Control of Independent Administrative Agencies*. Study paper for the Law Reform Commission of Canada. Ottawa: Supply and Services, 1979.

CASES

In Kenneth Kernaghan, *Canadian Cases in Public Administration* (Toronto: Methuen Publications):
  A "Miner" Problem
  The Foot and Mouth Disease Epidemic

16

The Judiciary
and the Bureaucracy

The last three chapters have examined the bureaucracy's relations with the executive and legislative branches of government. This chapter is concerned with the impact on the bureaucracy of the third branch of government — the judiciary. More specifically, it is concerned with the major concepts, issues, and developments in the sphere of judicial review of administrative action. It describes the grounds for judicial review, the remedies or forms of relief available, the use of privative clauses, and the utility of judicial review. The main focus of the chapter is the federal sphere of government and the Federal Court of Canada in particular, but attention is paid also to noteworthy developments in the provinces. The chapter begins by explaining briefly the judicial system within which judicial review of administrative action takes place.

THE CANADIAN JUDICIARY

Unlike the executive and legislative branches of government, which are integrally linked to one another, the judiciary is independent from the other branches of government. The independence of judges is considered crucial to the impartial administration of justice and is guaranteed by various measures, including tenure in office for judges during good behaviour.

The structure of the courts in Canada is shown in Figure 16.1. This structure is determined by the Constitution Act, 1867, which provides for separate federal and provincial courts, but permits cases to be appealed from provincial to federal courts, including the Supreme Court of Canada, which stands at the apex of the judicial hierarchy. Section 101 of the Act authorizes Parliament to establish a court of appeal for Canada and any other courts required for "the better administration" of federal laws. Section 92(14) grants to the provinces exclusive jurisdiction over the administration of justice in the provinces, "including the Constitution, Maintenance, and Organization of Provincial Courts, both of Civil and Criminal Jurisdiction, and including procedure in Civil Matters in those Courts." However, section 91(27) confers on the federal Parliament exclusive jurisdiction over criminal procedure, and sections 96, 99, and 100 give the federal government power over the appointment, salaries, and removal of all superior, county, and district judges in the provinces. Since the provinces are authorized to create and operate certain courts for which the federal govern-

Figure 16.1
THE HIERARCHY OF CANADIAN COURTS

1. Federal Courts—established by *federal* statutes with judges appointed by the *federal* government.

Supreme Court of Canada

Federal Court of Canada	
Trial Division	Court of Appeal

2. Provincial Courts—established by *provincial* statutes with judges appointed by the *federal* government.

Supreme Court or Superior Court of a Province	
Trial Division	Appellate Division

County or District Courts

Surrogate Courts

3. Provincial Courts—established by *provincial* statutes with judges appointed by *provincial* governments.

Provincial Court (criminal cases)	Juvenile Court	Family Court	Small Claims Court

ment is authorized to appoint and pay the judges, federal and provincial governments are required to cooperate in the administration of justice.[1]

The structure of courts in the *provinces* is similar from one province to another. At the top of the court system in each province is a court, which, depending on the province, is called the Supreme Court or the Superior Court. The superior courts in some provinces have two divisions — the trial and appellate divisions — whereas other provinces have two separate courts, each with its own enabling statute. The Supreme Court of Ontario, however, has three divisions — the High Court of Justice, the Court of Appeal, and the Divisional Court. The superior courts have jurisdiction in both criminal and civil cases, and they hear appeals from decisions of the lower courts. The next level down is composed of county or district courts, which have original jurisdiction over a certain geographical area in criminal cases and in civil cases in which the amount of money at stake is less than a certain amount. Remember that judges of the superior, county, and district courts are appointed and paid by the federal government. Surrogate courts responsible for the settlement of estates are also at this level. County court judges normally preside over these courts. Below the county or district courts are the provincial courts, which deal with such matters as criminal acts, juvenile offences, family problems, and small claims. In some provinces, these various matters are handled by separate courts, whereas in other provinces they are handled by divisions of the provincial court. The judges of these courts are appointed and paid by the provincial government.

The two major *federal* courts are the Federal Court of Canada, which is the primary court with which we are concerned in this chapter, and the Supreme Court of Canada. The Supreme Court is the highest court in the land and is a general court of appeal for both civil and criminal cases. It hears appeals from the Federal Court of Canada and from the provincial appeal courts. It also deals with questions of law or fact referred to it by the federal Cabinet (e.g., on such matters as interpretation of the Constitution Acts and the validity of federal or provincial legislation).

The Federal Court of Canada is composed of the Trial Division, which is a court of original jurisdiction, and the Federal Court of Appeal. The Trial Division has original jurisdiction to hear and grant relief in cases involving claims against the Crown and exclusive jurisdiction to hear and grant relief in cases involving appeals against the decisions of federal boards, commissions, and other tribunals, except where the Federal Court of Appeal has jurisdiction to review a decision or order of such a tribunal. The Trial Division also has jurisdiction in federal-provincial and interprovincial disputes and in such areas as income tax appeals,[2] estate tax appeals, and citizenship appeals. The Appeals Division has jurisdiction to hear appeals from the Trial Division and to review and set aside

---

[1]Perry S. Millar and Carl Baar, *Judicial Administration in Canada* (Kingston and Montreal: McGill-Queen's University Press, 1981), ch. 4.

[2]Note that in 1983 the Tax Court of Canada replaced the Tax Review Board. This court hears appeals on matters arising under statutes relating to taxation (e.g., the Income Tax Act); its decisions can be reviewed by the Federal Court.

decisions of federal boards, commissions, and tribunals in cases where these decisions are required by law to be made on a judicial or quasi-judicial basis, or where a federal tribunal failed to observe a principle of natural justice, exceeded its jurisdiction, made an error in law, or based its decisions on an erroneous finding of fact.

Before the Federal Court Act[3] came into force on June 1, 1971, judicial supervision of federal administrative authorities was exercised by the provincial superior courts, by the Exchequer Court of Canada, and by the Supreme Court of Canada. The newly established Federal Court took over judicial review jurisdiction from the provincial superior courts, replaced the Exchequer Court, and assumed some appeals against administrative authorities that previously had gone to the Supreme Court. The objective of the transfer of jurisdiction to the Federal Court from the provincial superior courts was basically to provide uniformity of judicial review of the actions and decisions of federal administrative authorities.

Sections 18 and 28 of the Act provide for the Federal Court's review of the decisions of any "federal board, commission or other tribunal." And section 2(g) defines these words as "any body or any person or persons having, exercising or purporting to exercise jurisdiction or powers conferred by or under an Act of the Parliament of Canada." The judicial review jurisdiction conferred on the Federal Court has been interpreted to embrace a broad range of decision makers in the federal government.[4]

JUDICIAL REVIEW OF ADMINISTRATIVE ACTION

The Focus on Agencies

The public administration community, in its examination of the means by which responsible administrative behaviour may be pursued in Canada, has devoted relatively little attention to the utility of judicial review of administrative action. However, since the early 1970s, a substantial volume of publications has resulted from the increased interest of the legal community in administrative law[5] in

---

[3]*Revised Statutes of Canada*, 1970, 2nd Supp., ch. 10.

[4]Among the bodies held to be "federal boards, commissions or other tribunals" are the Tariff Board; the Hamilton Harbour Commissioners; the Minister of Consumer and Corporate Affairs, acting under the Bankruptcy Act; the Canadian Radio and Television Commission; the National Parole Board; the Commissioner of Penitentiaries; the Commissioner of Patents; and the chairman of a board of referees constituted under the Unemployment Insurance Act. Among the bodies held *not* to fall within the phrase are the Crown; the Liquor Control Board of the Northwest Territories; a District Supervisor under the Indian Act; and the Canadian Broadcasting Corporation. Robert F. Reid and David Hillel, *Administrative Law and Practice*, 2d ed. (Toronto: Butterworths, 1978), pp. 474–475.

[5]Administrative law is that branch of public law which "deals with the legal limitations on the actions of governmental officials, and on the remedies which are available to anyone affected by a transgression of these limits. The subject invariably involves the question of the lawful authority of an official to do a particular act which, in the absence of such authority, might well be illegal (or *ultra vires*) and give rise to an actionable wrong." David Phillip Jones and Anne S. de Villars, *Principles of Administrative Law* (Toronto: Carswell, 1985), p. 1. The other two branches of public law are constitutional law and criminal law.

general and judicial review in particular. This development was partly a recognition of the extensive regulatory and adjudicative powers now exercised by administrative officials, especially those in semi-independent agencies. But the major stimulant was the creation in 1970 of the Federal Court of Canada and the court's subsequent review of the decisions of public authorities.

Like Britain, Canada has a large number of conventional government departments organized in hierarchical form and headed by ministers. But unlike Britain and like the United States, many government activities in Canada are conducted by agencies enjoying a measure of independence from government. John Willis has noted that in the field of administrative law Canadians "have inherited from England the principle of ministerial responsibility and the common law of judicial review, but have borrowed the institution of the 'independent regulatory commission' and many of the matters regulated from the United States and have modified them to suit our own peculiar conditions."[6] In particular, regulatory agencies in Canada are not as "independent" of the political executive as the independent regulatory commissions in the United States.

Nevertheless, as explained in Chapter 8, Crown agencies in Canada are less accountable than conventional departments to Cabinet, to ministers, and to Parliament. Thus, in the search for responsible administrative behaviour, judicial control is relatively more important with respect to agencies (boards, commissions, and tribunals) than to regular departments. Indeed, the primary focus of scholarly writings is on judicial review of decisions of federal (and provincial) agencies; comparatively little attention has been paid to judicial control of the decisions and actions of conventional departments.

From among the confusing assortment of Crown agencies, a category of agencies described as "independent deciding and advisory bodies" has been singled out on the grounds that these agencies possess regulatory, adjudicative and/or advisory powers.[7] Within this category, two subcategories are of special relevance to the subject of this chapter. The first subcategory, composed of fourteen agencies, is that of *regulatory agencies* "whose primary functions are licensing, making rules and orders, and supervising activities in a particular industry or sector of the economy, all of which have profound impact on, and control over the behaviour of individuals and corporations."[8] This category contains such centrally important and politically sensitive agencies as the National Energy Board, the Canadian Transport Commission, the Atomic Energy Control Board, and the Canadian Radio-television and Telecommunications Commission. The second subcategory, composed of six agencies, is that of *deciding tribunals* "that perform a specialized adjudicative function affecting individual rights."[9] Agencies in this group include the Immigration Appeal Board and the Pension Appeal Board.

---

[6]"Administrative Law in Canada," *Canadian Bar Review*, vol. 39 (1961), p. 254.
[7]Royal Commission on Financial Management and Accountability, *Final Report* (Ottawa: Supply and Services, 1979), pp. 309–325, 435–437.
[8]Ibid., p. 309.
[9]Ibid., p. 310.

The reason for drawing attention to these regulatory agencies and deciding tribunals is not to suggest that conventional government departments and other Crown agencies do not exercise important discretionary powers that may be reviewed by the courts; rather, the purpose is to highlight those bodies that are most visible to the public, that have a significant measure of independence from political direction and control, and that exercise administrative and quasi-judicial functions.

Discretionary Powers

The importance of judicial review and of other means of control over administrative action arises in large part from the exercise of discretionary powers by public officials. Discretionary powers "are those which involve an element of judgment or choice by the person exercising them and comprise all government functions from fact finding to setting standards."[10] As noted in Chapters 11 and 15, bureaucrats exercise a striking number and variety of discretionary powers under delegated legislative authority. In 1977 the Law Reform Commission of Canada depicted a catalogue of almost 15,000 discretionary powers as "only the tip of the iceberg."[11] Most of these discretionary powers are delegated to the Governor in Council (that is, the Cabinet), but they are also conferred on ministers and individual officials and on agencies, boards, commissions, and tribunals. (Unless otherwise specified, throughout the rest of this chapter, the term "tribunal" will be used to encompass all of these individual officials or groups of officials.)

Some statutes delegate discretionary powers to more than one authority. For example, under the Clean Air Act[12] much is left to be "prescribed" by the Cabinet; authority to determine standards and to determine who should be required to conform to them is delegated to the minister; and inspectors are given powers of enforcement to be applied in accordance with what the inspector "reasonably believes" to be the facts or with what he or she "deems necessary." Rules made under delegated legislative authority are described by a variety of names, including regulations, statutory instruments, and orders in council. These rules constitute "subordinate" or "delegated" legislation. Although the courts do review the exercise of legislative functions, notably to determine whether the exercise is *ultra vires* (beyond the powers of) the organization exercising them, the major concern of the courts, and thus of this chapter, is the review of judicial and quasi-judicial functions. Neither the Cabinet nor individual ministers can be expected to exercise their delegated powers solely on their own. For example, a minister could not find time to decide upon every application for a licence. Thus statutes often permit the Cabinet and ministers, either expressly or by "necessary intendment," to subdelegate authority. David Mullan states that there is a rule that ministers "are generally entitled to exercise their statutory powers through

---

[10]Law Reform Commission of Canada, *A Catalogue of Discretionary Powers in the Revised Statutes of Canada* (Ottawa: Information Canada, 1975), p. 2.
[11]Ibid., p. 23.
[12]*Statutes of Canada*, 1970–72, ch. 47.

responsible persons in their departments and that in such circumstances ministerial decisions cannot be questioned on the basis that they were not made by
the Minister personally."[13] He notes further that "this rule is founded on the
doctrine of ministerial responsibility. The Minister is accountable to the Legislature but not to the courts for actions of his subordinates."[14] The subdelegation
of discretionary powers has led to a condition of what has been described as
"dispersed discretions" and a consequent decline in the accountability of public
authorities to the legislature, and through the legislature to the public. It is
notable also that bureaucrats, on the basis of their experience and expertise,
influence ministers by advising them as to the appropriate exercise of powers
within ministerial discretion.

Appeal and Review

Judicial control over the decisions of tribunals may be founded either on statutory provisions for appeal or review (known as statutory or direct remedies), or
on the courts' inherent supervisory jurisdiction over inferior tribunals. No right
of appeal against a tribunal's decision exists unless that right is expressly conferred by statute. Statutory provision may be made for appeals to the courts, to
the Cabinet, to ministers, to deputy ministers, or to an administrative body
either within a government department (for example, the Determinations and
Appeals Section of the Source Deductions Division, Department of National
Revenue [Taxation]), or outside of it (for example, the Immigration Appeal
Board). The legislature often provides for statutory *review* as well as statutory
appeal, but when neither is provided, the courts may exercise their inherent
supervisory authority to review the decisions of inferior tribunals.

Classification of Function

A central issue in respect to judicial review of administrative discretion is the
classification of the function (that is, administrative, judicial, quasi-judicial)
performed by the tribunal. The nature of the function being exercised may well
determine whether, and on what grounds, the courts will grant relief. The courts
usually review the exercise of a judicial or quasi-judicial function, but not of an
administrative function. It is painfully evident from a study of administrative
law that the courts have had great difficulty in distinguishing precisely and consistently between these various functions.

René Dussault notes that "the main distinction between judicial and quasi-
judicial functions is based on the complete absence of discretion in the former
as contrasted with the existence of some discretion in the latter. When an administrative officer exercises judicial functions he is governed by a statutory direction
to apply the law; his decision must be inferred from the law. But when he exercises quasi-judicial functions he has a statutory permission to use his own discretion and to be guided by considerations of public policy."[15] Despite this distinction,

---

[13]David J. Mullan, *Administrative Law*, 2nd ed. (Toronto: Carswell, 1979), p. 92.
[14]Ibid.
[15]René Dussault, "Relationship between the Nature of the Acts of the Administration and Judicial Review: Quebec and Canada," *Canadian Public Administration*, vol. 10 (September 1967),
p. 316.

in administrative law the courts normally use the terms judicial and quasi-judicial interchangeably.

An equally elusive, but much more important, distinction is that between an administrative function and a quasi-judicial function. Reid and Hillel note that, in classifying functions, courts consider whether the exercise of the power will affect existing rights; "if it has an effect, the classification will be quasi-judicial; if none it will be administrative. If the decision is based on policy, not law, or made in pursuance of an unfettered discretion, the classification will be 'administrative.' On the other hand, if law, or objective standards, limit the exercise of discretion, it will be classified as quasi-judicial."[16] They assert also that their general impression is that "classifying functions is less a logical system than a method by which the courts signal their intention to supervise tribunals or to abstain. Thus, a classification as quasi-judicial will signal an intention to exert a close supervision, whereas a classification as administrative will indicate an intention to supervise slightly, if at all."[17] In the area of licensing, for example, the functions of licensing authorities are usually classified as quasi-judicial,[18] but the functions of several authorities have been held to be administrative.[19]

The confusion and frustration in the legal community stemming from the judicial-administrative dichotomy were not diminished by the Federal Court Act. Under section 28(1) of the Act, the Court of Appeal received jurisdiction in regard to decisions other than those "of an administrative nature not required by law to be made on a judicial or quasi-judicial basis." The Law Reform Commission of Canada has recommended that "future legislation providing for judicial review should avoid express use of the judicial/administrative classification of statutory powers to encourage the courts to avoid the tortuous rigours of this classification." The commission suggested further that the Federal Court be required or authorized "to review administrative, as well as judicial and quasi-judicial, decisions for conformity with natural justice unless the public interest that decisions conform with natural justice is outweighed by another public interest, such as efficiency in government, national security, confidentiality etc."[20] Among the objections to this suggestion is concern that by weighing one public interest against another, the court may become involved in "political controversies."[21] Thus, the nagging, perennial issue of the judicial-administrative dichotomy remains unresolved.

---

[16]Reid and Hillel, *Administrative Law and Practice*, p. 153.

[17]Ibid., p. 119.

[18]The following decisions have been classed as quasi-judicial: a public accountants council refusing to grant a licence; a highway traffic board revoking a licence because of a conviction for impaired driving; a superintendent of motor vehicles suspending an owner's licence; and the National Energy Board, in determining whether to issue a certificate for a pipeline. Ibid., p. 148.

[19]Decisions held to be administrative include a public utilities commission quashing a licence to operate a bus service; a motor carrier board considering an application for a licence to operate a public service vehicle; the (former) Board of Broadcast Governors hearing an application for a broadcasting licence; and the revocation of a driver's licence. Ibid., pp. 137-138.

[20]Law Reform Commission of Canada, *Federal Court—Judicial Review*, Working Paper 18 (Ottawa: Supply and Services, 1977), p. 38.

[21]Norman M. Fera, "LRC's Proposals for Reform of the Federal Judicial Review System — A Critical Examination and Counterpoise," *Manitoba Law Journal*, vol. 8 (1977), p. 535.

Grounds for Review

The courts, unless otherwise instructed by statute, may review the exercise of administrative discretion if a tribunal has (1) breached the rules of "natural justice"; (2) violated the doctrine of *ultra vires*, that is, acted outside the jurisdiction conferred on it by statute by exceeding its powers, abusing its powers, or committing errors of procedure; or (3) made errors of law. Each of these grounds for judicial review will be examined briefly in turn.[22]

Natural Justice

The two fundamental principles of natural justice are *audi alteram partem* (hear the other side) and *nemo judex in sua causa debet esse* (no one should be a judge in his or her own cause.) The *audi alteram partem* principle encompasses the notions that a party whose rights might be affected should have (1) adequate notice of the allegations against him or her and of the tribunal's intention to make a decision; (2) the right to be heard, specifically to present proofs and arguments; (3) the right to cross-examine witnesses and sometimes the right to legal representation; and (4) the right to an adjournment for a reasonable period of time to allow for preparation of his or her case. In the case of *Blais v. Basford*,[23] the Minister of Consumer and Corporate Affairs terminated Blais's business licence on the basis of a report by the superintendent of bankruptcy. The Federal Court ordered the reinstatement of the licence on the grounds that "the Minister must act fairly and impartially and in this case should have offered Blais an opportunity to answer material in the report of the Superintendent." However, the application of the *audi alteram partem* principle depends on the circumstances of the case. Mr. Justice Mahoney of the Federal Court has observed that "what is reasonable in a particular case may run the gamut from merely giving the person to be affected written notice of the bold facts upon which it is proposed to act and inviting his written comments to a full dress oral hearing with witnesses and cross-examination all around. Those seeking certainty from precedents in this area will be disappointed."[24]

According to the *nemo judex in sua causa* principle, all forms of bias should be excluded from the proceedings and decisions of tribunals. The courts may intervene in the event of either "actual" bias or "a real likelihood" or "reasonable apprehension" of bias. The latter form of bias includes such factors as kinship, friendship, or business relations with a party to the proceedings, hearing appeals from one's own decisions, or manifesting undue hostility towards one of the parties.

---

[22]Many authorities in both Canada and Britain contend that infringements of "natural justice" and other justifications for judicial review may all be considered as "specialized applications of the *ultra vires* doctrine." J. F. Garner, *Administrative Law*, 4th ed. (London: Butterworths, 1974), p. 113. The Ontario Royal Commission of Inquiry into Civil Rights asserted that the principle of *ultra vires* comprehends "all powers of judicial review, except for review for error of law on the face of the record." *Report* (Toronto: Queen's Printer, 1968), vol. 1, no. 1, p. 247.

[23](1972) F.C. 151 (C.A.).

[24]"Hearings and Decisions: A Judge's Perspective," *Speakers' Remarks*, Seminar for Members of Federal Administrative Tribunals, April 5–7, 1978, Law Reform Commission of Canada, p. 105.

The two principles of natural justice explained above have traditionally applied only to tribunals exercising judicial or quasi-judicial functions, not to those exercising administrative functions. However, the Supreme Court of Canada has recently held that "even those exercising purely administrative or executive functions have a duty to act fairly and not arbitrarily and that, in certain instances, this will involve affording procedural protections to those affected by the decision."[25] This "duty to act fairly" requires that where the rights of an individual are affected a procedure should be followed which not only meets the minimum standards imposed by the statute, but also ensures that the case will be heard fairly.[26] The strongest affirmation of this duty came in a case in which the Supreme Court overturned the dismissal of a probationary police constable because he was not given reasons for his dismissal or an opportunity to respond to those reasons.[27] The significance of this decision is that the legislation did not require that reasons and an opportunity to respond be given; the court simply felt that "fairness" required it.

Ultra Vires

The courts will generally intervene and grant relief where a tribunal has acted outside the scope of authority bestowed on it by its governing statute. Where there has been an excess of powers, the courts have found *ultra vires* all types of decisions — whether judicial, quasi-judicial, or administrative. Indeed, excess of powers is the primary ground for judicial review. To take a hypothetical and extreme example, the action of an immigration tribunal in granting a licence to drive would be declared *ultra vires*. The determination as to whether there has been an excess of powers obliges the courts to examine the enabling statute very carefully to see if Parliament has empowered the tribunal to act in a certain situation. It is the authority of the tribunal to make a decision, not the merits of the decision itself, which is at issue.

Another ground for review, that of *errors of procedure*, also requires that the courts look to the enabling statute. Parliament may specify that a tribunal exercise its powers according to specific procedures. We have already seen that on grounds of natural justice the courts may require tribunals performing judicial or quasi-judicial functions to follow certain rules of procedure. Regardless of natural justice principles, however, the courts will insist that tribunals follow the procedural rules set out in the statute; otherwise the decision stemming from errors of procedure will be declared *ultra vires*.

An *abuse of power* occurs when a tribunal uses its power for a purpose not authorized by Parliament under the enabling statute. Thus, in considering whether there has been an abuse of power, and consequently whether a decision is *ultra vires*, the courts tend to look beyond the enabling statute to examine Parliament's intention. Abuse of power is usually expressed in terms of discre-

---

[25]David J. Mullan, *Administrative Law*, p. 98.
[26]Ibid.
[27]*Nicholson v. Haldimand–Norfolk Police Commrs. Bd.*, (1979) 1 S.C.R. 311.

tion exercised by a tribunal for improper purposes, in bad faith, or on irrelevant grounds.

In the celebrated Canadian case of *Roncarelli v. Duplessis*, the Supreme Court found abuse of power when the Attorney General (who was also the Premier) of the province of Quebec directed a licensing commission to cancel the liquor permit held by a tavern owner because he had acted as bondsman for persons accused of distributing allegedly seditious literature. The commission's decision was declared to be beyond its powers, and Justice Rand stated:

> In public regulation of this sort there is no such thing as untrammelled "discretion," that is, that action can be taken on any ground or for any reason that can be suggested to the mind of the administrator; no legislative act can, without express language, be taken to contemplate an unlimited arbitrary power exercisable for any person, however capricious or irrelevant, regardless of the nature or purpose of the statute . . . . "Discretion" necessarily implies good faith in discharging public duty; there is always a perspective within which a statute is intended to operate; any clear departure from its line or objects is just as objectionable as fraud or corruption.[28]

Errors of Law

The courts may review the decisions of tribunals for *errors of law on the face of the record*. The "record" for this purpose includes not only the formal decision, but also the reasons for the decision, documents initiating the proceedings, documents on which the decision is based, and documents cited in the reasons for decision. The words "on the face of the record" indicate that the courts will not review a decision unless the error is apparent.[29] The Federal Court Act, however, permits review by the Court of Appeal for errors of law, "whether or not the error appears on the face of the record."

Section 28(1) of the Federal Court Act provides for judicial review by the Court of Appeal on the grounds that a tribunal

(a) failed to observe a principle of natural justice or otherwise acted beyond or refused to exercise its jurisdiction;

(b) erred in law in making its decision or order, whether or not the error appears on the face of the record; or

(c) based its decision or order on an erroneous finding of fact that it made in a perverse or capricious manner or without regard for the material before it.

These grounds include all five of those common law grounds for review examined above and extend them in respect to error of law (b) and error of fact (c).

---

[28](1959) S.C.R. 121 at 140.

[29]Among the errors of law that have led to the quashing of the decisions of tribunals have been an error in the interpretation of a statute, the censuring of a manager of a pharmacy when only the pharmacy was charged; failure to make the necessary inquiry; and failure to observe a statutory condition. Reid and Hillel, *Administrative Law and Practice*, pp. 382–383.

Critics of the judicial review provisions of the Act have recommended that to avoid controversy over the scope of review set out in the Act, the grounds for review should be more clearly articulated. For example, the Law Reform Commission of Canada has proposed that the Federal Court should be empowered to review federal tribunals "for action contrary to law, including without limiting the generality of the foregoing:

- denial of natural justice
- failure to observe prescribed procedures
- *ultra vires* action
- error in law
- fraud
- failure to reach a decision or take action where there is a duty to do so
- unreasonable delay in reaching a decision or performing a duty
- lack of evidence to support a decision."[30]

Forms of Relief

The Law Reform Commission quotes with approval K. C. Davis's contention "that what is needed is 'a single, simple form of proceeding for all review of administrative action,' and one, moreover, that articulates the grounds of review and the forms of relief."[31] This reference to forms of relief brings us to a consideration of the common-law or ancillary remedies which the courts may use after the grounds for judicial review have been established. Statutory or direct remedies, namely appeal and review procedures provided by statute, were discussed above. The common law remedies are employed when no other form of relief is available, convenient, or effective. They include the prerogative remedies, namely *certiorari*, prohibition, *mandamus*, *habeas corpus*, and *quo warranto*, as well as the remedies of injunction, declaration, and damages.

The most frequently used writs in Canada are *certiorari* and prohibition. *Certiorari* is a writ issued by a superior court to quash a decision already taken by an inferior tribunal, whereas prohibition is a writ to restrain a tribunal from taking a certain action. Both writs are generally used against tribunals exercising judicial or quasi-judicial functions. Moreover, the grounds on which these writs are available are breach of the rules of natural justice; absence, excess, or abuse of jurisdiction; and error of law on the face of the record.

Mandamus is a writ used to compel an inferior tribunal to exercise the authority conferred on it by statute. Unlike *certiorari* and prohibition, this writ is not restricted to tribunals exercising a judicial or quasi-judicial function. To obtain the writ of *mandamus*, an affected party must show that the tribunal is authorized or required to perform a certain duty, that the tribunal has been asked to perform that duty, and that refusal of the tribunal to perform the duty can be proved or implied.

---

[30]*Federal Court—Judicial Review*, p. 30. See also David J. Mullan, *The Federal Court Act: Administrative Law Jurisdiction*, prepared for the Law Reform Commission of Canada (Ottawa: Supply and Services , 1977), pp. 64–74, and Fera, "LRC's Proposals for Reform," pp. 529–547.
[31]*Federal Court—Judicial Review*, p. 27.

An injunction is a remedy which requires an inferior tribunal to take a particular action or, more commonly, to refrain from taking some specified action beyond its powers. An injunction is generally available only if an equally effective alternative remedy is not available. It can be used against tribunals exercising administrative as well as judicial or quasi-judicial functions.

An action for declaration (or declaratory judgement) asks the court to declare and define whether some act taken or proposed by a tribunal is beyond its powers. Like an injunction, a declaration is available for administrative as well as judicial or quasi-judicial decisions. Actions for declaration are infrequent. Moreover, they are normally combined with requests for other forms of relief, notably injunctions.

Damages is a remedy which requires that a certain amount of money be paid to compensate for an injury or wrong done to an individual. Tribunals, like ordinary citizens, are liable to an action for damages. Obviously, the remedy of damages is most useful in situations where the tribunal has already taken some action or decision. A remedy like *certiorari* that simply quashes the original decision would be of little help once the harm has been done. The remedy of damages is available in respect to administrative as well as judicial and quasi-judicial functions. Damages were awarded against the Attorney General (and Premier) of Quebec in the case of *Roncarelli v. Duplessis* mentioned earlier.

Habeas corpus is a writ used to require that a person who has been detained be brought before a court for the purpose of determining whether or not the detention is legal. This writ is not used very much in the sphere of administrative law. It is normally restricted to immigration cases where it is often used to challenge orders for custody or deportation.

Quo warranto is a writ used to inquire into whether an appointment to a public office established by statute is legal. The use of this writ has in large measure been made unnecessary by statutory provisions relating to appointments to public office.

Under section 18 of the Federal Court Act, the Trial Division of the Federal Court has exclusive original jurisdiction to issue to federal tribunals "an injunction, writ of *certiorari*, writ of prohibition, writ of *mandamus* or writ of *quo warranto*, or grant declaratory relief.[32] But the jurisdiction of the Trial Court can be exercised only when the Court of Appeal does not have jurisdiction. And, as we have already seen, the Appeal Court has broad jurisdiction under section 28 to review the decisions of tribunals on several grounds. Despite the Federal Court's efforts to clarify the jurisdiction belonging to each of its two divisions, considerable confusion and debate remain. The Law Reform Commission has recommended that judicial review of federal administrative action "should originate in the Trial Division . . . from which there would be an appeal, with leave, to the Court of Appeal."[33] It is notable also that no consensus has emerged among legal writers on the desirability and content of changes in the forms of relief set out in the Act.[34]

---

[32]For a review of the court's use of these remedies, see Mullan, *Administrative Law*, pp. 197–240.
[33]*Federal Court—Judicial Review*, p. 19.
[34]See, for example, ibid.; see also Mullan, *The Federal Court Act*, pp. 71–72; and Fera, "LRC's Proposals for Reform," pp. 539–544.

Privative Clauses

With a view to allowing administrative tribunals to operate efficiently and quickly, Parliament and the provincial legislatures frequently use "privative clauses," that is, statutory provisions designed to prevent judicial review of administrative action. These clauses differ in the strength of their wording, but the standard privative clauses are typically worded as follows: No decision, order, direction, declaration or ruling of the tribunal shall be questioned or reviewed in any court and no order shall be made or proceedings taken in any court, whether by way of injunction, declaratory judgement, *certiorari*, *mandamus*, prohibition, *quo warranto*, or otherwise to question, review, prohibit or restrain the tribunal or any of its proceedings.

Despite the clear intention of the legislators to exclude judicial review through the use of privative clauses, Canadian courts have generally given little or no effect to these clauses. A major reason for the courts' dislike of privative clauses is that these clauses aim to interfere with the court's inherent supervisory jurisdiction over inferior tribunals, and thereby to free the tribunals from the traditional restraint of judicial review. Moreover, the courts presume that Parliament and the provincial legislatures did not intend, through the use of privative clauses, to permit tribunals to do anything they wish. There is at present a division of opinion among legal scholars as to the likely outcome of this dispute between the legislatures and the courts; however, the emerging doctrine of "a duty to act fairly" as well as certain provisions of the Canadian Charter of Rights and Freedoms will likely reduce the impact of privative clauses.

Innovations in the Provinces

A Judicial Review Procedure Act was enacted by Ontario[35] in 1971 and by British Columbia[36] in 1976. The Ontario Act introduced a new means of applying for judicial review of administrative action called an "application for judicial review." This new remedy was one of the reforms proposed by the Royal Commission of Inquiry on Civil Rights in Ontario (the McRuer Commission), which explained the purpose of the remedy as follows:

> Instead of a multiplicity of forms of applications to compel, prohibit or set aside the exercise of statutory powers, there should be a single application to the court in which all the relief obtainable under any of the existing remedies would be available without the technical complexities, provoking much legalistic debate, which often obstruct, delay and sometimes defeat a decision on its merits.[37]

Among other things, the Act authorizes the court to treat applications for *certiorari*, prohibition, and *mandamus* as if they were applications for judicial review.

At the same time as this new remedy was created, the Judicature Act was amended to establish a division of the Ontario High Court called the Divisional Court. This court was given the primary responsibility for cases involving judi-

---

[35]*Revised Statutes of Ontario*, 1980, c. 484.
[36]*Revised Statutes of British Columbia*, 1979, c. 209.
[37]*Report*, vol. 1, p. 325.

cial review and statutory appeals. Most High Court judges serve on the Divisional Court on a rotating basis.

The British Columbia Judicial Review Procedure Act is very similar to the Ontario Act, but there are some important differences. For example, in British Columbia, the Act was not accompanied by the establishment of a new division of the Supreme Court; as a result, a single judge of the Supreme Court hears applications for judicial review.

In Ontario, the Judicial Review Procedure Act of 1971 was accompanied by the enactment of the Statutory Powers Procedure Act,[38] which set forth minimum rules for the proceedings of certain tribunals exercising statutory powers of decision. Among the procedures imposed on the tribunals are reasonable notice of hearing to the parties involved, hearings open to the public except under specified conditions, the right to representation by counsel, and the right to cross-examination. The province of Alberta has a similar statute entitled the Administrative Procedures Act.[39]

THE UTILITY OF JUDICIAL REVIEW

There is a division of opinion, primarily between academic legal scholars and lawyers, over the desirability of the current trend towards the expansion of judicial review of administrative action. Several academic authors have regretted the increased willingness of the courts to question the exercise of administrative discretion.[40] These writers are in general agreement that judicial review is not intrinsically a good thing.

Indeed, judicial review has in practice a number of deficiencies as a means of preventing and remedying abuses of bureaucratic power and thereby helping to promote responsible administrative behaviour.[41] The courts review only a minuscule number of the millions of decisions made annually by administrative authorities. Thus, "although the spectre of judicial intervention may be an inhibiting factor for administrative agencies, . . . it is a remote possibility in reality."[42] The success rate of litigants in respect to both judicial review and reconsideration by inferior tribunals is not high. Judicial review is uneconomic in that usually neither the amount of money nor the issue involved is significant enough to justify the high cost of the proceedings. Indeed, in a substantial proportion of cases, the litigants clearly have the financial resources to bear the cost; moreover, there are few cases of the social welfare type where the cost would tend to discourage aggrieved persons from seeking judicial review. Finally,

---

[38]*Revised Statutes of Ontario*, 1980, c. 484.

[39]*Revised Statutes of Alberta*, 1980, c. A-2.

[40]See, for example, P. H. Hogg, "Judicial Review: How Much Do We Need?" *McGill Law Journal* 20 (1974), pp. 157–176; William H. Angus, "Judicial Review: Do We Need It?" in Daniel J. Baum, ed., *The Individual and the Bureaucracy* (Toronto: Carswell, 1975), pp. 101–135; and Paul Weiler, *In the Last Resort: A Critical Study of the Supreme Court of Canada* (Toronto: Carswell, 1974), pp. 131–154.

[41]See especially Angus, "Judicial Review," pp. 101–114.

[42]Ibid., p. 105.

judicial review tends to focus on certain areas of public administration (for example, land-use zoning and building permits, labour relations, tax assessment, and licensing) so that many areas of administrative action are relatively untouched by judicial review.

Those academic scholars favouring a narrow scope for judicial review point to the benefits of having decisions made by tribunals possessing expertise and experience in various areas of administrative activity and providing more expeditious and inexpensive proceedings than the courts. They acknowledge, however, that judicial review is the best form of control when values fundamental to the legal order as a whole (for example, civil liberties values and constitutional issues) are in question. In Professor Hogg's words, "judicial review is rarely needed, but when it is needed nothing else will do."[43]

THE CANADIAN CHARTER OF RIGHTS AND FREEDOMS

The Charter is likely to have a significant effect on administrative law in general and judicial review of administrative action in particular.[44] It only came into full force in 1985, and there have not yet been enough judicial decisions to provide an adequate basis for predicting its long-run impact on administrative law. However, one legal scholar has noted that "the imposition of the *Charter* as the supreme law of the land does mean that the sources of Canadian administrative law have been substantially increased. The legality of bureaucratic conduct is now decided not only in accordance with fidelity to legislation, but also by the normative concepts contained in the *Charter*."[45] Moreover:

> The *Charter* must be taken seriously by administrators who, to date, may have had little, if any experience with the judicial process. It must be regarded as a limitation upon every administrative action and every statutory instrument. It has "constitutionalized" administrative law, procedure and practice.
>
> There is no point being irritated about it because it reduces administrative efficiency: that was precisely what it was intended to do. If the administration thinks that something is "reasonably justified", it must be prepared not merely to assert it, but to prove it. Gone are the days when one can simply say, "Trust us, we are the public service."[46]

It is likely that the courts will use the Charter to assert strongly the rights of individuals. Sections 7 and 15 of the Charter will have an especially important effect on administrative law, and therefore on the conduct of public administration. Section 7, on legal rights, provides in part, "Everyone has the right to life, liberty and security of the person and the right not to be deprived thereof

---

[43]Angus, "Judicial Review," p. 99.
[44]See G. J. Smith, *Charter of Rights and Administrative Law* (Toronto: Carswell, 1983).
[45]Andrew J. Roman, "The Possible Impact of the Canadian Charter of Rights and Freedoms on Administrative Law," *Les Cahiers de Droit*, vol. 26 (June 1985), p. 341.
[46]Ibid., p. 358.

except in accordance with the principles of fundamental justice." In the *Singh* case,[47] for example, the Supreme Court held that it was a breach of "the principles of fundamental justice" not to provide an oral hearing to refugee claimants. Legal scholars have observed that the wording of section 7 "constitutionalizes" the procedural aspects of natural justice (or the duty to be fair), and that the reference to *principles of natural justice* "may ripen into a substantive (as opposed to a procedural) limitation on . . . the content of parent legislation which can be enacted [and] . . . provide a method to scrutinize the merits of a delegate's decision."[48] Section 15 provides in part, "Every individual is equal before the law and has the right to the equal protection of the law without discrimination and, in particular, without discrimination based on race, national or ethnic origin, colour, religion, sex, age, or mental or physical disability." This section, which deals with equality rights, only came into effect in 1985, but has already spawned a large number of cases in the lower courts.

The trend towards greater judicial activism in the review of administrative discretion, which existed before the Charter came into force, is highly likely to continue. But even if the importance of judicial review increases substantially, judicial control will remain as only one weapon in the arsenal of controls and influences available to preserve and stimulate responsible administrative behaviour. While there are occasions when only judicial review will do, administrative responsibility may usually be pursued by other means.

---

[47]*Singh v. Minister of Employment and Immigration*, (1985) 17 D.L.R. (4th), 422.
[48]Jones and de Villars, pp. 39–40.

BIBLIOGRAPHY

Angus, W. H. "Judicial Review: Do We Need It?" *McGill Law Journal*, vol. 20 (1974): 177–212. Also printed in Daniel J. Baum, ed., *The Individual and the Bureaucracy*. Toronto: Carswell, 1975, pp. 101–135.

Canada. Law Reform Commission. *Federal Court—Judicial Review*. Working Paper 18. Ottawa: Supply and Services, 1977.

Canada. Law Reform Commission. *Judicial Review and the Federal Court*. Report no. 14. Ottawa: Supply and Services, 1980.

de Smith, S. A. *Judicial Review of Administrative Action*. London: Stevens and Sons, 1959.

Dussault, René. "Relationship between the Nature of the Acts of the Administration and Judicial Review: Quebec and Canada." *Canadian Public Administration*, vol. 10 (September 1967): 298–322.

Dussault, René, and Lois Borgeat. "Le droit administratif: une réalité omniprésente pour l'administrateur public." *Canadian Public Administration*, vol. 24 (Winter 1982): 653–673.

Hogg, Peter. "Judicial Review: How Much Do We Need?" *McGill Law Journal*, vol. 20 (1974): 157–176.

Jones, David Phillip, and Anne S. de Villars. *Principles of Administrative Law*. Toronto: Carswell, 1985.

Kersell, J. E. "Statutory and Judicial Control of Administrative Behaviour." *Canadian Public Administration*, vol. 19 (Summer 1976): 295–307.

Millar, Perry S., and Carl Baar. *Judicial Administration in Canada*. Kingston and Montreal: McGill-Queen's University Press, 1981.

Mullan, David J. *Administrative Law*. 2nd ed. Toronto: Carswell, 1979.

Mullan, David J. *The Federal Court Act: Administrative Law Jurisdiction*. Prepared for the Law Reform Commission of Canada. Ottawa: Supply and Services, 1977.

Morton, F. L., and Leslie A. Pal. "The Impact of the Charter of Rights on Public Administration: A Case Study of Sex Discrimination in the Unemployment Insurance Act." *Canadian Public Administration*, vol. 28 (Summer 1985): 221–244.

Reid, Robert F., and David Hillel. *Administrative Law and Practice*. 2nd ed. Toronto: Butterworths, 1978.

Roman, Andrew J. "Regulatory Law and Procedure." In G. Bruce Doern, ed., *The Regulatory Process in Canada*. Toronto: Macmillan, 1978, pp. 68–93.

Roman, Andrew J. "The Possible Impact of the Canadian Charter of Rights and Freedoms on Administrative Law." *Les Cahiers de Droit*, vol. 26 (June 1985): 339–359.

Smith, G. J. *Charter of Rights and Administrative Law*. Toronto: Carswell, 1983.

CASES

In *Case Program in Canadian Public Administration* (Toronto: Institute of Public Administration of Canada):

The Ben Fisher Case, by Nancy LePitre, Salim Mansur, and Wilbur Grasham

17

Intergovernmental
Administrative Relations

Intergovernmental relations are critically important in the Canadian political system. Discussion of the processes and outcomes of interaction among federal, provincial, and municipal governments pervades both scholarly and popular writings on Canadian politics. One author has observed that Canada may be "the only country where you can buy a book about federal-provincial relations at an airport."[1] Intergovernmental relations affect virtually every policy field and have significant political, economic, social, and cultural consequences; they affect the day-to-day lives of Canadians by helping to determine such things as the cost of gasoline and oil, the quality of hospital care, and the availability of television programs.

This chapter contains basic information on the political, constitutional, and financial aspects of intergovernmental relations, but is primarily concerned with the administrative dimension of these relations. The focus is on the role of intergovernmental officials and their interaction with each other and with Cabinet ministers and legislators. This chapter examines (1) the meaning and evolution of federalism and intergovernmental relations; (2) the striking growth since the early 1960s in the machinery for intergovernmental liaison; (3) models of intergovernmental relations which help to explain the functions of intergovernmental officials; and (4) the power and responsibility of these officials. The impact of intergovernmental relations on government regulation was examined in Chapter 8.

FEDERALISM AND INTERGOVERNMENTAL RELATIONS

Meaning and Evolution

Federalism may be defined as a political system in which the powers of the state are formally divided between central and regional governments by a written constitution, but in which these governments are linked in a mutually interdependent political relationship.[2] In the Canadian context, this definition captures the enduring legal and constitutional elements of Canadian federalism, the politics which pervade the federal system, and the necessity for intergovernmental interaction. Federalism and intergovernmental relations are not the same

---

[1]Peter C. Newman, *Maclean's Magazine*, October 1, 1979, p. 3.
[2]Adapted from M. J. C. Vile, *The Structure of American Federalism* (London: Oxford University Press, 1961), p. 199.

thing; rather, federalism provides the structural framework within which inter-governmental relations are conducted. The federal form of government ensures that there are at least two orders (or levels) of government (e.g., federal and provincial governments in Canada). In modern federal states these orders of government tend to be highly interdependent and interactive. Broadly inter-preted, the term *intergovernmental relations* embraces not only federal-provincial relations, but also interprovincial, federal-municipal, and provincial-municipal relations. The main emphasis in this chapter is on federal-provincial liaison, but specific reference is made to the activities of officials involved in interpro-vincial relations. Provincial-municipal and federal-municipal relations are dis-cussed in Chapter 25.

A recent book provided a dictionary of almost five hundred words and phrases that have been used to describe and explain concepts of federalism.[3] While sev-eral of Canada's many contributions to concepts of federalism were not acknowl-edged, Canada was mentioned in more than twenty entries on the list. In Canada, as elsewhere, both the meaning and evolution of federalism have frequently been explained by adding adjectives to the word federalism. For example, James R. Mallory[4] and Edwin R. Black[5] have each used five different labels to classify and explain concepts of Canadian federalism.

In Mallory's classification, *quasi*-federalism characterized the early decades of the Canadian federation during which the federal government dominated the provincial governments, in part by making frequent use of the federal con-stitutional powers to disallow and reserve provincial legislation. The next stage was *classical* federalism, which approached K. C. Wheare's celebrated "federal principle" according to which the powers of government are divided "so that the general and regional governments are each, within a sphere, co-ordinate and independent."[6] Between the late 1800s and 1930, except for the First World War, provincial powers increased as a result of strong political leadership in certain provinces and judicial decisions favouring the provinces in constitutional disputes with the federal government. Both the federal and provincial govern-ments enjoyed exclusive jurisdiction in certain policy fields, and jurisdictional conflicts were resolved by the courts. Increased federal-provincial consultation was formally recognized by the first federal-provincial conference of first minis-ters (the Prime Minister of Canada and the provincial Premiers) held in 1906, and federal assistance for the financing of provincial responsibilities began in such areas as transportation and agriculture. The growing importance and expense of the provinces' responsibilities for health, education, and welfare required not only federal subsidies, but also a provincial search for new reve-nues through the use of such forms of taxation as personal and corporate income taxes.

---

[3] William H. Stewart, *Concepts of Federalism* (Lanham: University Press of America, 1984).
[4] James R. Mallory, "The Five Faces of Federalism," in P.-A. Crépeau and C. B. Macpherson, eds., *The Future of Canadian Federalism* (Toronto: University of Toronto Press, 1965), pp. 3–15.
[5] Edwin R. Black, *Divided Loyalties: Canadian Concepts of Federalism* (Montreal: McGill-Queen's University Press, 1975).
[6] K. C. Wheare, *Federal Government*, 4th ed. (London: Oxford University Press, 1963), p. 10.

This period of classical federalism was interrupted by the first phase of *emergency* federalism — the First World War — and was ended by the second phase — the Depression and the Second World War. During both wars, the courts supported the federal government's exercise of broad powers over the economy and over matters of property and civil rights, which in peacetime were clearly within provincial jurisdiction. During the Depression, the federal government provided financial assistance to the provinces through a variety of intergovernmental arrangements, and during the Second World War, the provinces withdrew from the fields of personal and corporate income tax in return for "rental" payments from the federal government.

It is difficult to pinpoint the precise date when *cooperative* federalism emerged, but Donald Smiley noted in the early 1960s that the development of Canadian federalism since 1945 had been "a process of continuous and piecemeal adjustment between the two levels of government," and that these adjustments had overwhelmingly been made through "interaction between federal and provincial executives" rather than through formal constitutional amendment or judicial interpretation.[7] Under cooperative federalism, the constitutional division of powers was preserved, but federal and provincial ministers and public servants engaged in consultation and coordination to reach joint decisions on policies and programs of mutual concern.

During the late 1940s and the 1950s, the federal government dominated federal-provincial relations, but in the 1960s provincial governments gradually acquired the expertise and influence to deal with the federal government on a more equal basis. Gradually also, *executive* federalism, a term first used by Donald Smiley, began to be applied more often than cooperative federalism to describe the nature of federal-provincial relations. Garth Stevenson has explained that the main features of cooperative federalism were "the fragmentation of authority within each level of government, the absence of linkages between different issues and functional domains, the forging of specific intergovernmental links by different groups of specialized officials, and the lack of publicity or public awareness of what was happening." Executive federalism, by way of contrast, involved "the concentration and centralization of authority at the top of each participating government, the control and supervision of intergovernmental relations by politicians and officials with a wide range of functional interests, and the highly formalized and well-publicized proceedings of federal-provincial conference diplomacy."[8]

By the latter half of the 1960s, the term cooperative federalism had become a misnomer because intergovernmental relations were characterized by a great deal of conflict and confrontation, as well as consultation and collaboration. It is notable also that both cooperative federalism and executive federalism have coexisted with another centrally important variant of federalism described by Mallory as *double-image* federalism; this form combines interaction between

---

[7]Donald V. Smiley, "The Rowell-Sirois Report, Provincial Autonomy, and Post-War Canadian Federalism," *Canadian Journal of Economics and Political Science*, vol. 28 (February 1962), p. 54.

[8]Garth Stevenson, *Unfulfilled Union*, rev. ed. (Toronto: Gage, 1982), pp. 190–191.

the central government and the provinces with a special relationship between French- and English-speaking Canadians. Certainly, French-English relations have been a critical and persistent factor in intergovernmental relations, especially since the early 1960s.

Garth Stevenson contends that there are basically two concepts of Canadian federalism and that they can be depicted as opposite ends of a continuum, with unity (centripetal federalism) at one pole and diversity (centrifugal federalism) at the other. "Centripetal federalists prefer to strengthen the federal government's power at the expense of the provincial governments; centrifugal federalists prefer to do the reverse."[9] Perhaps the most popular image in discussions of federal-provincial relations, however, is that of a pendulum swinging between the centralization of powers in federal hands and the decentralization of powers to the provinces.

Interstate and Intrastate Federalism

Since the late 1970s, increased interest has been shown in the *intrastate* dimension of Canadian federalism as opposed to the traditional *interstate* dimension. *Interstate* federalism refers to "the distribution of powers and financial resources between the federal and provincial governments as well as the relations between those two orders of government," whereas *intrastate* federalism refers to "arrangements whereby the interests of regional units — the interests either of the government or of the residents of these units — are channelled through and protected by the structures and operations of the central government."[10] These arrangements could include reform of the electoral system to make each party in the House of Commons more representative of the various regions of the country, reform or replacement of the Senate so that it could provide more effective representation in Parliament of regional and provincial interests, and reform of the Supreme Court to make its members more sensitive to regional and provincial concerns. Among the proposed arrangments affecting the public service specifically are a bureaucracy which is more representative in its composition of the regions of the country and formal representation of provincial governments in federal agencies, boards, and commissions.

Alan Cairns has distinguished between *centralist* and *provincial* intrastate federalism. The centralist version "is an attempt to weaken provincial governments by increasing the attractiveness of Ottawa to that complex regional/provincial network of interests, values, identities, and socio-economic power whose support is a crucial resource in intergovernmental competition." The provincial version is an attempt to provide direct representation of the provincial governments in the institutions and decision-making processes of the federal government.[11]

---

[9]Ibid., pp. 41–42.
[10]Donald V. Smiley and Ronald L. Watts, *Intrastate Federalism in Canada*, Research Study for the Royal Commission on the Economic Union and Development Prospects for Canada, vol. 39 (Toronto: University of Toronto Press, 1985), p. 4.
[11]Alan C. Cairns, *From Interstate to Intrastate Federalism in Canada* (Kingston: Queen's University, Institute of Intergovernmental Relations, 1979), pp. 11–12.

Much of the discussion of the instrastate perspective has centred on the federal Cabinet, the Senate, the Supreme Court, and the electoral system, rather than on bureaucratic institutions and processes.[12] However, it has been suggested that the federal bureaucracy would be more sensitive to regional needs and aspirations if its composition was more representative of the regions (e.g., more senior public servants in Ottawa who were born in the Atlantic provinces), and if it was restructured with more emphasis on regional considerations (e.g., decentralization of power to federal field units in the regions).[13]

FEDERAL-PROVINCIAL FISCAL RELATIONS

While federal financial assistance to provincial governments dates back to Confederation and was especially important during the Depression, federal-provincial fiscal relations have been an especially prominent theme in Canadian federalism since the Second World War. The subject is extremely complex and has been examined at length elsewhere.[14] However, a brief explanation of its development and characteristics is essential to understanding contemporary intergovernmental relations.

The federal-provincial financial relationship is based on four elements: shared cost programs or conditional grants, tax collection agreements, established programs financing, and equalization. Each of these will be considered in turn.[15]

Shared cost programs or *conditional grants* involve payments by the federal government to provincial governments which choose to undertake programs according to conditions specified by the federal government. The largest such program is the Canada Assistance Plan. The general thrust of this plan is that the federal government will pay one-half of the cost of provincial social assistance programs. In turn, the provincial programs must meet certain conditions, e.g., no discrimination against applicants from another province.[16]

The *tax collection agreement* is an agreement between the federal government and nine provinces which allows the federal government to collect both

---

[12]See generally Smiley and Watts, *Intrastate Federalism*.

[13]For an examination of the value of these suggestions, see Kenneth Kernaghan, "Representative and Responsive Bureaucracy: Implications for Canadian Regionalism," in Peter Aucoin, ed., *Regional Responsiveness and the National Administrative State*, Research Study for the Royal Commission on the Economic Union and on Development Prospects, vol. 37 (Toronto: University of Toronto Press, 1985).

[14]See A. Milton Moore, J. Harvey Perry, and Donald I. Beach, *The Financing of Canadian Federation: The First Hundred Years* (Toronto: Canadian Tax Foundation, 1966) and D. V. Smiley, *Canada In Question: Federalism in the Eighties*, 3rd ed. (Toronto: McGraw-Hill Ryerson, 1980), ch. 6.

[15]A good overview of the history and current state of the federal-provincial fiscal relationship is provided in Richard M. Bird, *Financing Canadian Government: A Quantitative Overview* (Toronto: Canadian Tax Foundation, 1979), ch. 5 and Canada, House of Commons, Parliamentary Task Force on Federal-Provincial Fiscal Arrangements, *Fiscal Federalism in Canada* (Ottawa: Supply and Services Canada, 1981).

[16]A good summary of the provisions of most federal-provincial transfer payment programs is found in Canadian Tax Foundation, *The National Finances* (annual publication of the Canadian Tax Foundation, Toronto).

federal and provincial personal taxes (except for Quebec) and corporate taxes (except for Alberta, Ontario, and Quebec) and to remit the provincial portion of the taxes to the provinces. The purpose of this agreement is to provide an administrative convenience to provincial governments and to limit tax competition between provinces by establishing some uniformity in the method of calculation.

Established Programs Financing (EPF) is an innovative transfer payment program begun in 1977.[17] In that year, the federal government terminated three very large conditional grants to the provinces — for medicare, hospital care, and post-secondary education — and replaced them with a combination of cash payments and tax room. *Tax room* means that the federal government agrees to reduce its income tax rate by a certain number of "tax points" so that provincial governments can increase their tax rates accordingly. Because of the tax collection agreement discussed above, this type of shift is not evident to the taxpayer.

One of the characteristics of EPF was that the provincial governments were not obliged to spend the money on medical or hospital care or post-secondary education; they could use the funds generated for purposes of their own choosing. However, there were still some conditions attached to the receipt of the cash payments. For example, this is the mechanism which the federal government used to pass the Canada Health Act, which reduces the cash payments to any province that allows physicians to "extra-bill."

Equalization is a program through which the federal government makes unconditional grants to those provinces that have a weak tax base.[18] An *unconditional grant* is a payment which can be used for any purpose that the province desires; the federal government requires no accounting for how the money is spent. The purpose of the equalization program is to allow the so-called "have-not" provinces to provide adequate public services to their citizens without imposing excessively high taxes.

The current complex system of transfer payments could well weaken the accountability of the provincial governments for the expenditure of public funds. A strict concept of accountability would suggest that the government which gets the credit for spending funds should be the same government which must take the blame for raising taxes. The ability to spend someone else's money does little to encourage thrift or accountability. However, there are a number of valid reasons for transfer payments, including the need to redistribute wealth between provinces and the desire to have national programs with uniform national standards.[19]

One of the major controversies surrounding intergovernmental fiscal relations in recent years has been the use of conditional versus unconditional grants.

---

[17]Thomas J. Courchene, *Refinancing the Canadian Federation: A Survey of the 1977 Fiscal Arrangements Act* (Montreal: C. D. Howe Research Institute, 1979).

[18]The details of the current equalization formula are given in Canadian Tax Foundation, *The National Finances: 1984–1985* (Toronto: Canadian Tax Foundation, 1985), pp. 309–312. See also Thomas J. Courchene, *Equalization Payments: Past, Present and Future* (Toronto: Economic Council of Canada, 1984), ch. 2.

[19]A general discussion of the rationale for intergovernmental transfers is provided in Robin W. Boadway, *Intergovernmental Transfers in Canada* (Toronto: Canadian Tax Foundation, 1980), ch. 3.

The government providing the grant frequently favours conditional grants because they can be directed to specific purposes and accountability can be ensured through the use of specific regulations or audits. On the negative side, recipient governments sometimes feel that the conditions attached to grants are insensitive to local conditions, and that the record keeping and other administrative requirements imposed are excessive. Therefore, recipient governments tend to favour unconditional grants because this type of grant maximizes their freedom. Governments providing grants are concerned about unconditional grants because they could be used in ways that were deemed inappropriate by the providing government, and because the government ultimately supplying the funds frequently does not receive the credit when the money is spent. This has brought about the federal government's recent concern about the inadequate "visibility" it has received for services paid for by federal funds, but provided by provincial governments.

The general trend in the 1950s and 1960s was that the federal government introduced a number of shared cost programs that encouraged provincial governments to embark on new programs. However, in the 1980s, faced with a weak economy and rising deficits, the federal government has begun to take unilateral action to reduce its transfer payments to provinces. This has incited the ire of provinces, which feel that the federal government pushed them into beginning these programs and is now leaving them "holding the bag." The federal government's tough stance on fiscal relations coincided with its tough stance on constitutional issues.

FEDERAL-PROVINCIAL CONSTITUTIONAL RELATIONS

The impact of federal-provincial relations on the evolution of Canada's constitution is a long and intricate story in which many of the constitutional issues have been primarily financial ones. There have, however, been a number of constitutional developments with special relevance for contemporary federal-provincial relations and, consequently, for the officials involved in these relations. As noted above, quasi-federalism and classical federalism gave way to cooperative, executive, and double-image federalism. Dissatisfaction with judicial interpretation of the division of powers contained in the British North America Act, the lack of a formula for amending the Act without the consent of the British Parliament, and the expansion in the scope and cost of government activities led to increasing use of extra-constitutional arrangements negotiated by the two orders of government.

Then, a series of federal-provincial conferences, which began in 1968, sought agreement on constitutional reform. These efforts were given enormous impetus by the election of the separatist Parti Québécois government in Quebec in 1976 and the 1980 referendum campaign on "sovereignty-association," at which time the federal government promised constitutional change. Also, during the 1970s and early 1980s, intergovernmental tensions were severely exacerbated by sharp disgreements over the ownership of natural resources, especially petroleum, and over the allocation of the revenues flowing from the exploitation of these resources. The dispute raged not only between the federal government and the energy-producing provinces (especially Alberta), but also between these provinces and the energy consuming provinces (especially Ontario).

For the 1980-1981 constitutional meetings, the first ministers agreed upon an agenda containing twelve contentious items — a statement of principles as a preamble to the constitution, a charter of human rights (including language rights), equalization, the nature of the economic union, a formula for amending the constitution in Canada (referred to as patriation of the constitution), a reformed upper house with regional representation, reform of the Supreme Court, the ownership of natural resources and related issues of trade and taxation, offshore resources, fisheries, communications (including broadcasting), and family law. Following the failure of the September 1980 meeting of first ministers, however, the federal government decided to proceed unilaterally to resolve the issue of constitutional amendment. After lengthy debate in the federal Parliament, the provinces were presented in November 1981 with a federal proposal for constitutional change, which all provinces, except Quebec, finally accepted. Agreements were reached on only a few of the agenda items, and these agreements were enshrined in the Constitution Act, 1982, which was approved formally by the British Parliament. This Act provided, among other things, an amending formula ensuring that all changes to the constitution would henceforth be made in Canada, a charter of rights and freedoms, a commitment to the principle of equalization, confirmation of provincial ownership of resources, and affirmation of the existing rights of aboriginal peoples.

Federal action during this period supported Prime Minister Trudeau's assertion in 1982 that cooperative federalism was dead. Moreover, there was little evidence of executive federalism at work, in that federal-provincial conference diplomacy was replaced by unilateral federal decision making. It is significant that in 1985 Prime Minister Mulroney found it desirable to announce the rebirth of cooperative federalism as a signal of a renewed federal commitment to consultation and collaboration with the provinces. Nevertheless, federal-provincial disagreements continue, especially over fiscal arrangements and the management of the economy.

Intergovernmental officials were major players in the extensive federal-provincial bargaining leading up to the Constitution Act and are centrally involved in implementing the constitutional accord and in bargaining over unresolved issues in federal-provincial relations. The active participation of these officials in intergovernmental relations has, especially over the last three decades, resulted in an impressive array of intergovernmental administrative structures.

MACHINERY FOR INTERGOVERNMENTAL RELATIONS

The network of intergovernmental structures includes separate departments or other administrative units within governments,[20] administrative units within indi-

---

[20]For an examination of the evolution of these intergovernmental bodies, see Timothy B. Woolstencroft, *Organizing Intergovernmental Relations* (Kingston: Institute of Intergovernmental Rela-

vidual departments, intergovernmental secretariats, and a large number of intergovernmental committees. The creation of these structures has both resulted from, and stimulated the proliferation of, intergovernmental conferences and meetings. The major reasons for the development of this complicated web of intergovernmental contacts, especially between federal and provincial governments, are the expansion of the activities of all governments, the increased interdependence of federal and provincial responsibilities, and the consequent need to design and operate machinery to manage these contacts.

As early as 1972, there were 482 federal-provincial liaison bodies, ranging in scope and importance from the First Ministers' Conference to such specialized federal-provincial committees as those on meteorites and pest control.[21] There are now more than 1,000 federal-provincial *committees* of varying degrees of importance. Some of these committees meet more than once, and some do not meet at all during a particular year. The number of federal-provincial *meetings* more than doubled between 1967 and 1977, and continued to increase until the early 1980s when fewer meetings were held because of the reduced importance of constitutional matters and the economic recession.[22] The number of federal-provincial meetings increased again following the election in September 1984 of the Mulroney government with its emphasis on the renewal of cooperative federalism. During the next twelve months, a total of 438 federal-provincial meetings were held. They involved first ministers (13 meetings), ministers (353 meetings), and deputy ministers (72 meetings).[23] By 1977, 30 *interprovincial* liaison bodies had been established, of which 17 were at the ministerial level.[24] The government of Alberta reported that it participated in 47 interprovincial meetings in 1983. These included 2 First Ministers' meetings, 35 ministerial meetings, and 10 deputy ministerial meetings.[25]

The number of officials attending intergovernmental meetings varies greatly from one meeting to another, but it is notable that one of the largest gatherings, namely the First Ministers' Conference, attracted a total of 269 ministers and officials to Halifax in November 1985.[26] The number of intergovernmental offi-

---

tions, Queen's University, 1982); Bruce G. Pollard, *Managing the Interface: Intergovernmental Affairs Agencies in Canada* (Kingston: Institute of Intergovernmental Relations, Queen's University, 1986); and John Warhurst, "Canada's Intergovernmental Relations Specialists," *Australian Journal of Public Administration*, vol. 42 (Winter 1983), pp. 459–485.

[21]Gerard Veilleux, "L'évolution des mécanismes de liaison intergouvernemental," in Richard Simeon, ed., *Confrontation and Collaboration: Intergovernmental Relations in Canada Today* (Toronto: Institute of Public Administration of Canada, 1979), pp. 44–45.

[22]Bruce G. Pollard, *Managing the Interface: Intergovernmental Affairs Agencies in Canada*, pp. 70–71.

[23]Data provided by the Federal-Provincial Relations Office, June 1986. Some of the meetings were multilateral, involving all or most governments, but the majority of meetings were bilateral, involving the federal government and at least one provincial government. For example, only four of the thirteen First Ministers' meetings were multilateral.

[24]Veilleux, "L'évolution," p. 39.

[25]Alberta, Department of Federal and Intergovernmental Affairs, *Eleventh Annual Report* (Edmonton: Department of Federal and Intergovernmental Affairs, 1983), p. 13.

[26]Data provided by the Federal-Provincial Relations Office, June 1986.

cials attending such meetings does not, however, take account of the large number of officials who do not attend the meetings, but who are actively engaged in preparation for the participation of ministers and other officials. It is difficult to distinguish precisely between *intergovernmental officials* and other public servants. The term is normally used to refer only to so-called intergovernmental affairs specialists. These are senior administrative officials who are engaged solely or primarily in intergovernmental business. They are usually housed in central agencies and are responsible for the coordination of intergovernmental matters, both within their own government and with other governments. But, in varying degrees, many other officials are involved in intergovernmental relations. Thus, the term intergovernmental officials also refers to those officials whose formally designated responsibilities require them to spend the majority of their working hours on intergovernmental matters, but who are not normally described as intergovernmental affairs specialists. The most prominent among these officials are senior public servants in operating departments who look after intergovernmental issues affecting their department. In addition, there are officials, notably in senior positions, who devote relatively little time to intergovernmental issues, but whose occasional involvement has a major influence on the outcome of intergovernmental negotiations. It is evident that a large number of public servants are engaged in intergovernmental activities. The major focus of this chapter, however, is on the intergovernmental affairs specialists.

The critical importance of intergovernmental relations can be seen in the financial and human resources devoted to the conduct of these relations. The expansion since the 1960s in intergovernmental machinery and in the number and quality of the officials operating this machinery is striking. The development of administrative structures geared specifically to the management of intergovernmental relations was a response to the large and growing number of meetings and the desire of governments to coordinate and rationalize the efforts of their departments in various policy fields. There is virtually no policy field in which federal and provincial governments are not engaged in consultation and negotiation.[27] In 1961, the province of Quebec established a Department of Federal-Provincial Relations,[28] and gradually the federal government and other provincial governments have developed increasingly sophisticated mechanisms for handling intergovernmental business. In the federal government, the Federal-Provincial Relations Secretariat, which was established in the Privy Council Office in 1968, had by 1975 become the Federal-Provincial Relations Office (FPRO) with responsibility for coordinating federal-provincial relations both within the federal government and between the federal and provincial governments. The FPRO is headed by the secretary to the Cabinet for federal-provincial relations,

---

[27]See Table I in Kenneth Kernaghan, "Federal-Provincial Administrative Liaison in Canada," in Kenneth Kernaghan, ed., *Public Administration in Canada: Selected Readings*, 3rd ed. (Toronto: Methuen, 1977), p. 80. This table shows federal-provincial activity in seventeen specific policy areas and in a miscellaneous category.

[28]In 1967 this department was renamed the Department of Intergovernmental Affairs. It is notable that for a brief period in 1961, at the end of the Frost era, Ontario had a Department of Economics and Intergovernmental Relations.

who reports to the Prime Minister. In addition, eleven federal departments have formal federal-provincial units. All ten provincial governments established intergovernmental units either as separate departments, or as part of the Premier's Office or the Cabinet secretariat.[29]

Intergovernmental secretariats have also been established to provide support services for the meetings of the many liaison bodies. The major secretariat is the Canadian Intergovernmental Conference Secretariat which was set up in 1973 to serve the conferences of first ministers and all other intergovernmental bodies requesting its assistance.[30] It is jointly funded by the federal and provincial governments and provides such services as looking after conference arrangements and agendas, preparing conference transcripts and summary statements, and distributing documents. Some federal-provincial bodies (for example, the Canadian Council of Resource and Environment Ministers) have established their own secretariat.

Intergovernmental affairs specialists play a central role in government, both in the organizational sense and in the development and implementation of policy. They must be adept in *intra*governmental as well as *inter*governmental bargaining. Their influence is based to a large extent on their ability to wend their way skilfully through the labyrinth of intergovernmental affairs in search of agreement with officials in their own government and in other governments. An important element of their expertise is in the *process* of intergovernmental relations. They must also be more knowledgeable in a general way about the *substance* of a broad range of policy fields than senior officials in operating departments. Richard Schultz notes, however, that "central agencies are staffed by individuals who, while they may be specialists in the 'machinery of government' or in intergovernmental relations, are essentially amateurs and generalists when specific policy issues are discussed."[31]

A primary aim of intergovernmental affairs specialists is to ensure that operating departments in their own government will not weaken that government through the intergovernmental interactions in which they engage.[32] The extent to which these specialists perform primarily either a controlling or an advisory function to achieve this end varies from one government to another. There is a risk that intragovernmental conflict between the specialists on the one hand, and officials in operating departments on the other, will result from "overcoordination" of intergovernmental relations within a single government. Some intergovernmental units (e.g., Alberta's Department of Federal and Intergov-

---

[29]In 1983, the province of Nova Scotia disbanded its Office of Intergovernmental Affairs in the Executive Council Office and became the only government without a special unit for intergovernmental relations.

[30]This organization is the successor to the Constitutional Conference Secretariat established in 1968.

[31]Richard Schultz, "Prime Ministerial Government, Central Agencies, and Operating Departments: Towards a More Realistic Analysis," in Thomas A. Hockin, ed., *Apex of Power*, 2nd ed. (Scarborough: Prentice-Hall, 1977), p. 232.

[32]Donald V. Smiley, "An Outsider's Observations of Federal-Provincial Relations Among Consenting Adults," in Simeon, *Confrontation and Collaboration*, p. 110.

ernmental Affairs) have greater legal authority and more resources than other units to promote coordination of the intergovernmental activities of operating departments. Moreover, intergovernmental units, like other central agencies, play a staff role and are, therefore, subject to the normal line-staff problems which arise in large organizations.

A critical element in the intergovernmental policy process is the multitude of informal contacts, especially by telephone, which supplement the formal meetings of officials. The respect and trust among officials developed during formal contacts pave the way for frank and productive discussions outside of, and between, formal meetings. During these discussions, officials exchange a great deal of information about their government's position on matters of continuing concern and negotiation. An essential attribute of intergovernmental officials is their ability to obtain current information about the perceptions and positions of other governments. This information is a crucial input in determining the officials' advice to their political and administrative superiors. The ability of officials to gather such information enables them to exercise influence in the policy process apart from that which flows from their hierarchical position.

In the 1950s and early 1960s, the undeveloped state of formal machinery for intergovernmental liaison meant that informal contacts among officials were essential to the effective conduct of federal-provincial relations. Despite the sophisticated infrastructure that has been built since that time, the increased magnitude and complexity of intergovernmental relations has meant that informal communications are still important to the smooth operation of the formal machinery. Indeed, this informal interaction has increased substantially since the mid-1960s.[33]

INTERPROVINCIAL ADMINISTRATIVE RELATIONS

Interprovincial relations are broadly similar to federal-provincial relations in their organization and participants. Interprovincial interactions occur on both a formal and informal basis; they involve both political executives (Premiers and ministers) and public servants, and they cover virtually all provincial policy fields. Most of the intergovernmental bodies created during the formalization of federal-provincial relations are also used to coordinate interprovincial relations.

Provincial political leaders and bureaucrats meet to discuss problems of mutual concern and, when appropriate, to work out joint or common solutions to these problems. Among the formal interprovincial mechanisms for collaboration is the Conference of Premiers, which is the provincial version of the First Ministers' Conference. The premiers' conference is held annually and is attended by all ten provincial Premiers and their senior advisors. The federal government is invited to send observers to the conference, and normally a few officials from the Privy Council Office and/or the Department of Finance will attend.

Below the level of the Premiers, ministers of most provincial departments meet regularly with their counterparts in other provinces not only to exchange

[33]Veilleux, "L'évolution," p. 36.

information and ideas, but also to seek interprovincial coordination. For example, the Canadian Council of Resource and Environment Ministers aims to bring about integrated comprehensive resource-use planning for social and economic development. Probably the most effective interprovincial interactions for seeking coordination are the meetings of public servants from both the senior administrative and the professional/technical levels of various departments. These meetings are more numerous than those at the political level.

There are also important interprovincial meetings organized on a regional basis, notably meetings of the Western Premiers' Conference and of the Council of Maritime Premiers. The latter body is composed of the Premiers of New Brunswick, Nova Scotia, and Prince Edward Island and is served by a permanent secretariat. The council was established in 1971 "to promote unity of purpose, ensure maximum coordination of activities and establish the framework for joint actions and undertakings among the three governments."[34]

Despite the expansion of formal interprovincial relations, especially during the past decade, the number of interprovincial committees and meetings is considerably smaller than that in the federal-provincial realm. Accurate data on the number and type of formal relations involving the provinces are difficult to obtain, but the province of Alberta participated in 60 interprovincial meetings in 1975 and 47 interprovincial meetings in 1983. Even more difficult to document are the many informal contacts involving both provincial ministers and bureaucrats. Aside from the interprovincial meetings, the many federal-provincial meetings provide opportunities for provincial officials to get together informally outside the meeting rooms. Moreover, many of the same political and bureaucratic officials participate in both types of meeting. These personal contacts are subsequently utilized, via telephone, telex, and letter, to seek interprovincial policy coordination.

It is clear that the participation of officials in formal federal-provincial and interprovincial meetings is only the tip of a sizeable iceberg. Below the waterline is a complex network of formal and informal interactions which affect significantly the outcome of intergovernmental negotiations. This network includes interaction between officials and other political actors, among officials in a single department or agency, between officials in different departments and agencies, and among officials in different orders of government.

MODELS OF INTERGOVERNMENTAL ADMINISTRATIVE INTERACTION

Three distinct, but complementary, models can be used to explain the role and the power of officials in the processes and outcomes of intergovernmental relations in Canada. These are the *cooperation*, *bargaining*, and *bureaucratic politics* models.

---

[34]Council of Maritime Premiers, *Annual Report, 1984–85* (Halifax: Council of Maritime Premiers, 1985), p. 6.

The *cooperation* model refers to intergovernmental relations involving to a very large extent program specialists from each order of government. Harmonious and productive interaction is facilitated because these program specialists share a body of knowledge and skills and possess a common set of professional attitudes and values relating to their particular policy fields (for example, welfare officials, foresters).[35] In this model, program specialists are permitted to exercise a large measure of autonomy from control by political and administrative superiors, especially those in intergovernmental relations units, treasury boards, and finance departments. The value of this model for explaining policy development and implementation in certain areas of federal-provincial relations has been demonstrated well in respect to the Canada Assistance Plan.[36]

This type of interaction was characteristic of the cooperative federalism period and was more prevalent in the post war years up to the early 1960s than it is now. Gradually during the 1960s and increasingly during the 1970s, the influence of program specialists suffered a relative decline as a result of the growing ascendancy in intergovernmental relations of central agency officials who pursued broader public policy goals than officials from program departments.[37] Donald Smiley anticipated that these central agencies would not develop "the kind of allegiance to common procedures and values which so much facilitates intergovernmental relations among program specialists" because "the concerns of the former relate to fundamental political choices about which consensus is more difficult to establish than in respect to more technical matters."[38]

The reduction in the importance of horizontal relations among program specialists resulting from the increased influence of central agencies was accompanied by the creation and growth of new structures and arrangements for the coordination of intergovernmental relations within each government. As a consequence of the institutional centralization of intergovernmental relations under what has been called executive federalism, fewer matters were handled at the lower levels of the governmental pyramid; rather, intergovernmental conflicts gravitated towards the political and senior administrative levels. Since ministers and senior administrators tended not to share values, attitudes, and skills to the same extent that program specialists did, the level of intergovernmental conflict increased. In this milieu, the *bargaining* model explains the processes and outcomes of intergovernmental relations better than the cooperation model.[39]

---

[35]This model is elaborated in Donald V. Smiley, "Public Administration and Canadian Federalism," *Canadian Public Administration*, vol. 7 (September 1964), pp. 371–388, and *Constitutional Adaptation and Canadian Federalism Since 1945* (Ottawa: Information Canada, 1970), ch. 7.

[36]Rand Dyck, "The Canada Assistance Plan: The Ultimate in Cooperative Federalism," *Canadian Public Administration*, vol. 19 (Winter 1976), pp. 587–602. Professor Dyck acknowledges some limited relevance for the bargaining model, but notes that "the policy development involved in the Canada Assistance Plan can best be understood in terms of Smiley's discussion of shared norms among program administrators" (p. 598).

[37]See Simon McInnes, *Federal-Provincial Negotiation: Family Allowances, 1970–1976* (Ph.D. thesis, Carleton University, April 1978).

[38]Smiley, "Public Administration and Canadian Federalism," p. 387.

[39]For an explanation and application of what we call the bargaining model, see Richard Simeon,

The bargaining model refers to intergovernmental relations involving primarily ministers and senior administrators from each order of government. Interaction takes the form of a bargaining process in which these ministers and officials present and defend their government's position on specific public policy issues. The focus of attention is on the political resources, strategies, and tactics used by participants in the process. Richard Simeon, on the basis of his study of federal-provincial negotiation over three broad policy issues, concluded that the participants in federal-provincial relations "are not scattered throughout the system in the form of federal cabinet members, members of Parliament, bureaucrats and party leaders; rather they are concentrated and limited largely to provincial premiers, senior cabinet members, and senior officials on the one hand, and their federal counterparts on the other."[40]

A third model, which complements both the cooperation and bargaining models, is the *bureaucratic politics* model. This model, which has been used most often to study foreign policy, has also been applied recently to the study of intergovernmental relations in Canada.[41] The model refers to bargaining over intergovernmental matters among ministers and officials in departments and agencies *within* each order of government. It is *intra*governmental rather than *inter*governmental bargaining that is involved. Despite use of the term *bureaucratic* politics, the model is concerned with interaction among both ministers and officials.

Richard Schultz and Simon McInnes, in their case studies of federal-provincial negotiations, focus on the impact of *intra*governmental bargaining on *inter*governmental bargaining. Schultz contends that

> the bureaucratic politics model. . . attempts to answer questions such as why the negotiators adopted the objectives, strategies and tactics they did . . . . Interactions between governments may not . . . explain, by themselves, the outcomes of intergovernmental negotiations. From the bureaucratic politics perspective, the complex intergovernmental process cannot be separated from the direct relations between governments.[42]

Schultz also offers the bureaucratic politics model as a complement to what he describes as Simeon's "government-as-unitary-actor" model. Simeon states that the "perceptions, attitudes and behaviour" of political leaders and officials are his main concern, but that in his book, "Canada's eleven governments are the actors" and that "for most purposes each will be considered as a single unit."[43]

Federal-Provincial Diplomacy: The Making of Recent Policy in Canada (Toronto: University of Toronto Press, 1972), especially chs. 2 and 13.

[40]Ibid.

[41]See Richard Schultz, *Federalism, Bureaucracy and Public Policy* (Montreal: McGill-Queen's University Press, 1980); Simon McInnes, *Federal-Provincial Negotiation: Family Allowances, 1970–1976*; and Kim Richard Nossal, "Bureaucratic Politics in Canadian Government," *Canadian Public Administration*, vol. 22 (Winter 1979), p. 298.

[42]Schultz, *Federalism, Bureaucracy and Public Policy*, pp. 434–435.

[43]Simeon, *Federal-Provincial Diplomacy*, p. 13.

The bureaucratic politics approach suggests that it might be more productive to consider *each* government as a loose coalition of organizations and the negotiating positions of the governments as *outcomes* of an internal negotiating process.

In the field of intergovernmental relations, governments are often treated as single actors because they normally present a united front in negotiations with other governments. This united front may, however, be a mask that conceals conflict among ministers and officials *within* governments. Neither departments and agencies nor whole governments are homogeneous entities. The process of intragovernmental bargaining, which is intertwined with that of intergovernmental bargaining, has been ignored or unduly minimized by many students of Canadian federalism. Intragovernmental bargaining over intergovernmental matters involves both elected and appointed officials, but much of this bargaining takes the form of internal administrative politics. Intragovernmental bargaining occurs not only over the substance of intergovernmental policy, but also over the distribution of resources between intergovernmental affairs and other government activities. Thus officials who are not significantly engaged in intergovernmental relations indirectly affect the success of these relations by influencing the resources devoted to intergovernmental activities, both in the government as a whole and in individual departments and agencies.

THE POWER AND RESPONSIBILITY OF INTERGOVERNMENTAL OFFICIALS

The Power of Intergovernmental Officials

It has been suggested that there has been a politicization of intergovernmental affairs specialists. Politicization refers here to the process by which officials become increasingly involved in politics, either in the partisan sense or in the broader sense of the authoritative allocation of values for society. As explained in Chapter 11, public servants in general have become more politicized as a result of departures from some aspects of the traditional doctrine of political neutrality. Have intergovernmental officials become politicized, and if so, has this politicization taken different forms and emphases from that of other officials?

The overriding objective of intergovernmental relations is the determination of policy; and officials are centrally involved in the intergovernmental policy process. Like other public servants, intergovernmental officials use their knowledge, experience, and discretionary authority to exercise power in the formation and administration of public policy; they engage in consultation and bargaining with other political actors; and their ministers rely heavily on them for advice on complex issues. Thus, in the intergovernmental field, as in other areas of government, the line between the policy contributions of ministers and officials is blurred.

However, the role of intergovernmental officials in the policy process can be distinguished from that of other officials in two significant ways. Intergovernmental officials cannot exercise control, in the sense of authority, over their counterparts in other governments; rather, they must exercise influence through a process of bargaining. Compared to bargaining with pressure groups, for example, where government officials retain ultimate authority to decide or recommend a course of action, bargaining between governments requires give and take among negotiators of roughly equal status.

Second, intergovernmental officials, especially those who participate in formal meetings, enjoy more discretionary power in the bargaining process than most other officials. They are, therefore, more involved in politics in the broad sense than many of their colleagues. In the intergovernmental policy process, usually several governments, and often all eleven governments, are involved in a complicated bargaining process. The outcome of negotiations is frequently a tentative agreement representing a delicate balancing and accommodation of numerous and diverse interests. The federal and provincial Cabinets, individual ministers, and even legislatures are sometimes reluctant to force a renewal of these intricate negotiations unless their objection to the agreement worked out by their officials is substantial.

Donald Smiley claims that the federal-provincial relations specialist, "in his stance toward other governments . . . has a single-minded devotion to the power of his jurisdiction. And because his counterparts in other governments have the same motivations, conflict is inevitable."[44] But the extent of concern over jurisdiction varies from government to government and from official to official. Some governments, such as Quebec, and some officials, such as Alberta's officials during the energy negotiations, have been primarily disposed towards protection of jurisdiction. Other governments have sought to minimize future intergovernmental conflict by seeking to rationalize the distribution of powers through disentanglement and the clarification of accountability. Resistance to such rationalization, in so far as it involves the movement of a power to another order of government, has often come from the department currently exercising that power, rather than from intergovernmental affairs specialists.

Both scholars and practitioners of intergovernmental relations have perceived a tendency among intergovernmental officials to become somewhat more politicized than other bureaucrats. A distinguishing feature of the doctrine of political neutrality is that public servants explain policy and ministers defend it. But in the course of intergovernmental negotiations, the line between explanation and defence of policy becomes clouded. As a result, intergovernmental officials tend to be more involved in "politics" in the broad sense of that term.

Moreover, some intergovernmental officials (for example, in such provinces as Quebec and Alberta) occasionally develop an especially intense commitment to the objectives of their own government or their own minister that goes somewhat beyond the loyalty expected from public servants. This strong sense of loyalty appears primarily among senior intergovernmental specialists whose working environment is often highly political in the partisan sense and whose duties

---

[44] Smiley, "An Outsider's Observations," p. 110. See also Veilleux, "L'évolution," p. 45, and Roy E. Lloyd, "The Effects of the Changing Nature of Federal-Provincial Relations on the Role of the Bureaucracy" (Paper presented to the Annual Conference of the Institute of Public Administration of Canada, Victoria, September 1977), p. 9.

require the management of conflict with other governments. They may be moti
vated both by pressure "not to let the minister down" and by personal commitment to government policies. It is natural for such loyalty and commitment to
result from the obligation continually to explain and defend those policies. Vigorous defence by intergovernmental officials of the policies of the government
of the day is not usually prompted by partisan support for the governing party,
but it does on occasion have that appearance.

The Responsibility of Intergovernmental Officials

In the sphere of intergovernmental relations, pinpointing those who are actually, rather than formally, responsible for government decisions is difficult because
an important locus of decision making is an intergovernmental body of ministers or officials. There is not space here to examine the broad range of controls
and influences which may promote responsible behaviour by intergovernmental officials. Attention will, therefore, focus on relations between intergovernmental officials in different jurisdictions, and between these officials on the one
hand and Cabinet members and legislators on the other.

The increased influence of the provinces in federal-provincial relations rests
on several factors, including the constitutional distribution of responsibilities,
the relative wealth of a province, and the electoral success of its political leaders. However, a major reason for the growth of provincial power has been the
heightened expertise of provincial intergovernmental officials. The expertise of
federal officials, which explained to a large extent the federal government's
dominant influence in intergovernmental relations during the 1950s and early
1960s, is now more closely matched by the expertise of provincial officials.

In the intergovernmental policy process, officials exercise significant power,
in the sense of influence, over Cabinet members and legislators. Gordon Robertson, former secretary to the Cabinet for federal-provincial relations, has
asserted that "intergovernmental business in Canada . . . is conducted by Cabinet members, notably by First Ministers. . . . Interministerial conferences are
thus an adjunct to executive power, a demonstration of where power actually
resides, and the centrepiece of what Donald Smiley has called 'executive federalism.' "[45] This assertion does not take adequate account of the fact that executive federalism involves relations between both ministers *and officials* and that
officials exercise significant influence over policy development before, during,
and after interministerial conferences. Moreover, as noted earlier, officials exert
much policy influence in connection with the very large number of intergovernmental meetings below the ministerial level. The influence of intergovernmental officials arises not only from their expertise, but also from the formal and
informal bargaining, often on a multilateral basis, in which they engage on
behalf of their ministers.

But the influence of intergovernmental officials in relation to ministers should
not be exaggerated. Cabinet members, either individually or collectively, pos-

---

[45]Gordon Robertson, "The Role of Interministerial Conferences in the Decision-Making Process,"
in Simeon, *Confrontation and Collaboration*, p. 80.

sess ultimate control over the government's stance on all intergovernmental matters. Officials must be highly sensitive to the desires of the Cabinet as a whole and of individual ministers in regard to both the substance and strategy of negotiations. Moreover, Cabinet members are the central actors in making decisions on major and politically sensitive intergovernmental issues and in much of the negotiation leading to those decisions.

Compared to Cabinet members, legislators have little control or influence over intergovernmental activities. Indeed, legislators do not exercise much power over the executive in general, or officials in particular, in any area of government activity.[46] There is general agreement with the observation that intergovernmental business in Canada "is conducted by governments . . . not by legislatures," and that "this works because a Cabinet in our parliamentary system can normally 'deliver' legislative support on virtually any matter, save possibly in minority situations."[47]

According to the principle of collective ministerial responsibility, the Cabinet is responsible to the legislature. Yet, there is normally much more discussion of intergovernmental matters in conferences than in the federal Parliament or provincial legislatures. There are few opportunities for legislators to examine intergovernmental policy issues before legislation incorporating agreements reached at conferences is presented to the legislature. Since this legislation is often the outcome of complicated and protracted negotiations among governments, ministers are understandably reluctant to make changes at the legislative stage with which other governments may disagree. Robert Stanfield, former leader of the federal Progressive Conservative Party, has noted that "the frustrations of Members of Parliament are increased by federal-provincial deals, agreements and resulting legislation which confront Parliament as *faits accomplis*."[48] In a comment on Mr. Stanfield's remarks, Gordon Gibson, former leader of the Liberal Party in British Columbia, said that "federal-provincial agreements are so cast in stone from the time of the agreement that even if the opposition were able to convince the government that amendments should be made it would be too late to change things in any significant respect."[49] It is notable also that the federal Parliament and the provincial legislatures have not developed intergovernmental machinery, for example, standing committees, to parallel the sophisticated mechanisms established by the executive.

Despite the claims of some journalists and politicians to the contrary, informed observers of the Canadian federal system deny that federal-provincial conferences constitute an additional order of government. There are differences of opinion, however, about the effect of intergovernmental meetings on the accountability of governments to Parliament and the provincial legislatures. Gordon

[46]See Kenneth Kernaghan, "Power, Parliament and Public Servants: Ministerial Responsibility Reexamined," *Canadian Public Policy*, vol. 5 (Summer 1979), pp. 383–396.
[47]Robertson, "Role of Interministerial Conferences," p. 80.
[48]"The Present State of the Legislative Process in Canada: Myths and Realities," in W. A. W. Neilson and J. C. MacPherson, eds., *The Legislative Process in Canada: The Need for Reform* (Institute for Research on Public Policy; distributed by Butterworths, Toronto, 1978), p. 44.
[49]Ibid., p. 52.

Robertson has stated that "federal-provincial conferences do not in fact reduce the accountability as such of governments to Parliament and to legislatures. Parliament is the locus of responsibility and accountability for our national government but, because of the nature of our system, it is not the public and apparent locus of regional argument and compromise."[50] In a formal sense, this statement is accurate, but the weight of opinion supports Donald Smiley's contention that "to the extent that the actual locus of decision-making in respect to an increasing number of public matters has shifted from individual governments to intergovernmental groupings, the effective accountability of executives both to their respective legislatures and to those whom they govern is weakened."[51]

The accountability of intergovernmental officials is a serious concern, but accountability is only one of several values associated with the broad concept of administrative responsibility. Responsible intergovernmental officials must also be concerned with such values as responsiveness and effectiveness. It is important to determine not only whether these officials are accountable to ministers and legislators, but also whether they are sensitive to the needs and desires of other political actors and whether they are successful in achieving their government's objectives. Thus, in addition to intergovernmental and intragovernmental conflicts, officials face conflicts between administrative values (for example, accountability versus responsiveness, or responsiveness versus effectiveness).

Intergovernmental management involves to a very large extent the management of conflict and complexity. Alan Cairns has observed that "contemporary intergovernmental coordination is not a simple matter of agreement between a handful of political leaders and their staff advisers. It requires . . . the containment of ineradicable tendencies to conflict between the federal vision of a society and economy, and ten competing provincial visions."[52] The key role of intergovernmental officials in seeking to harmonize these diverse perspectives ensures that the management of intergovernmental relations will remain a dominant concern of students and practitioners of Canadian public administration.

[50]Robertson, "Role of Interministerial Conferences," p. 83.

[51]Smiley, "An Outsider's Observations," p. 107.

[52]Alan Cairns, "The Governments and Societies of Canadian Federalism," *Canadian Journal of Political Science*, vol. 10 (December 1977), p. 722.

BIBLIOGRAPHY

Aucoin, Peter, and Herman Bakvis. "Regional Responsiveness and Government Organization: The Case of Regional Economic Policy in Canada." In Peter Aucoin, ed., *Regional Responsiveness and the National Administrative State*. Research study for the Royal Commission on the Economic Union and Development Prospects for Canada, vol. 37. Toronto: University of Toronto Press, 1985, pp. 51–118.

Black, E. R. *Divided Loyalties: Canadian Concepts of Federalism*. Montreal: McGill-Queen's University Press, 1975.

Cairns, Alan. "The Governments and Societies of Canadian Federalism." *Canadian Journal of Political Science*, vol. 10 (December 1977): 695–725.

Cairns, Alan. "The Other Crisis of Canadian Federalism." *Canadian Public Administration*, vol. 22 (Summer 1979): 175–195.

Careless, Anthony G. S. *Initiative and Response: The Adaptation of Canadian Federalism to Regional Development*. Montreal: McGill-Queen's University Press, 1977.

Doerr, Audrey. "Public Administration: Federalism and Intergovernmental Relations." *Canadian Public Administration*, vol. 25 (Winter 1982): 564–579.

Dupré, J. Stefan, et al. *Federalism and Policy Development: The Case of Adult Occupational Training in Ontario*. Toronto: University of Toronto Press, 1973.

Dyck, R. "The Canada Assistance Plan: The Ultimate in Cooperative Federalism." *Canadian Public Administration*, vol. 19 (Winter 1976): 587–602.

Kernaghan, Kenneth. "Representative and Responsive Bureaucracy: Implications for Canadian Regionalism." In Peter Aucoin, ed., *Regional Responsiveness and the National Administrative State*. Research study for the Royal Commission on the Economic Union and Development Prospects for Canada, vol 37. Toronto: University of Toronto Press, 1985, pp. 1–50.

Robertson, Gordon. "The Role of Interministerial Conferences in the Decision-Making Process." In Richard Simeon, ed., *Confrontation and Collaboration — Intergovernmental Relations in Canada Today*. Toronto: Institute of Public Administration of Canada, 1979, pp. 77–88.

Savoie, Donald J. *Federal-Provincial Collaboration*. Montreal: McGill-Queen's University Press, 1972.

Schultz, Richard J. *Federalism, Bureaucracy and Public Policy: The Politics of Highway Transport Regulation*. Montreal: McGill-Queen's University Press, 1980.

Schultz, Richard J. *Federalism and the Regulatory Process*. Montreal: Institute for Research on Public Policy, 1980.

Simeon, Richard, ed. *Confrontation and Collaboration: Intergovermental Relations in Canada Today*. Toronto: Institute of Public Administration of Canada, 1979.

Simeon, Richard, ed. *Intergovernmental Relations*. Research study for the Royal Commission on the Economic Union and Development Prospects for Canada, vol. 63. Toronto: University of Toronto Press, 1985.

Simeon, Richard. "Intergovernmental Relations and the Challenges to Canadian Federalism." *Canadian Public Administration*, vol. 23 (Spring 1980): 14–32.

Smiley, D. V. *Canada In Question: Federalism in the Eighties*. 3rd ed. Toronto: McGraw-Hill Ryerson, 1980.

Smiley, D. V. *Constitutional Adaptation and Canadian Federalism Since 1945*. Ottawa: Information Canada, 1970.

Smiley, Donald V., and Ronald L. Watts. *Intrastate Federalism in Canada*. Research study for the Royal Commission on the Economic Union and Development Prospects for Canada, vol. 39. Toronto: University of Toronto Press, 1985.

Stevenson, Don. "The Role of Intergovernmental Conferences in the Decision-Making Process." In Richard Simeon, ed., *Confrontation and Collaboration — Intergovernmental Relations in Canada Today*. Toronto: Institute of Public Administration of Canada, 1979, pp. 89–98.

Veilleux, Gerard. "Intergovernmental Canada: Government by Conference? A Fiscal and Economic Perspective." *Canadian Public Administration*, vol. 23 (Spring 1980): 33–53.

Wilson, V. Seymour. "Federal-Provincial Relations and Federal Policy Processes." In G. Bruce Doern and Peter Aucoin, eds., *Public Policy in Canada*. Toronto: Macmillan, 1979, pp. 190–214.

Woolstencroft, Timothy B. *Organizing Intergovernmental Relations*. Kingston: Institute of Intergovernmental Relations, Queen's University, 1982.

CASES

In *Case Program in Canadian Public Administration* (Toronto: Institute of Public Administration of Canada):

L'Affaire "Caloil," by Michel Paquin

Federal-Provincial Diplomacy: Re-Negotiating EPF, by David Siegel

Oil Spill in the Bay of Fundy: A Case Study in Crisis Management, by J.W.F. Pullen

The Allocation of a National Housing Budget, by Barbara Carroll

18

Pressure Groups, Political Parties, and the Bureaucracy

The political actors who influence administrative organizations from outside government include not only other governments, but also a number of non-governmental actors. The most prominent of these are pressure groups, political parties, the general public, and the news media. This chapter discusses the interaction of pressure groups and political parties with the bureaucracy; the next chapter discusses the bureaucracy's relations with the public and the media and includes an examination of the issues of freedom of information and individual privacy.

PRESSURE GROUPS

Definition and Classification

Pressure groups (or interest groups)[1] are organizations composed of persons who have joined together to seek their mutual interest by influencing public policy. These groups do not have hierarchical or legal authority over government officials. They do, however, exercise *influence* over both the development and implementation of public policy. Their efforts are commonly described as lobbying. To many Canadians, the term lobbying has unsavoury connotations of illegal, immoral or inappropriate means of influencing government decision makers.[2] This perception has its origins in the practice of lobbying in the United States during much of the nineteenth century when "lobbyists" would frequent the lobbies and corridors of legislative buildings to influence legislators, sometimes with offers of bribes in the form of money, women, and so on. *Lobbying* refers here simply to a legitimate means of influencing government decisions through individual or collective action.

---

[1] For our purposes, these two terms can be used interchangeably. It is notable, however, that often the term interest group is used when the broad range of functions performed by these groups is under consideration, whereas the term pressure group is used when the focus of discussion is primarily on the exercise of political pressure.

[2] Professor William Stanbury has observed that "our attitude toward lobbying can be likened to that toward sex. At one and the same time they are perceived as healthy and natural acts, but they are also seen as embarrassing, slightly taboo, even 'dirty' activities to be removed from polite conversation." "Lobbying and Interest Group Representation in the Legislative Process," in W. A. W. Neilson and James C. MacPherson, eds., *The Legislative Process in Canada* (Montreal: Institute for Research on Public Policy, 1978), p. 175.

Every policy field and every policy issue attract the attention of one or more pressure groups. These groups are, therefore, extremely numerous and pervasive in the Canadian political system. They represent to government the interests of business, labour, agricultural, professional, social, welfare, religious, and public interest organizations. Examples of each of these types of organization are the Canadian Manufacturers' Association, the Canadian Labour Congress, the Canadian Federation of Agriculture, the Canadian Bar Association, the Canadian Council on Social Development, the Canadian Welfare Council, the Presbyterian Church in Canada, and the Canadian Arctic Resources Committee. Some pressure groups have been established solely for the purpose of lobbying government, whereas for other groups lobbying is a very small, incidental part of their activities. Few groups have been organized solely to lobby government; most groups perform such other functions as exchanging information among their members and representing the members to the public.

The number of lobbyists and the extent of lobbying activity in Ottawa and the provincial capitals are difficult to measure with any precision. In mid-1980, it was estimated that there were 300 trade and professional associations in Ottawa alone and that they employed more than 2,000 people and spent over $122 million annually.[3] In 1978 a survey of 703 Canadian companies showed that slightly more than 50 per cent of them engaged in communications with political leaders or public servants in the federal government.[4] Moreover, lobbying is carried on not just by pressure group executives, but also by professional lobbyists, lawyers, legislators (notably senators), and individual citizens. James Gillies notes that lobbying by business people involves the public affairs departments of business firms, permanent staff members located in Ottawa, trade associations, public affairs consulting companies (which publish newsletters and assist clients to approach the appropriate government officials), and one-on-one contacts between senior business executives and public officials.[5]

Pressure groups have been classified into a variety of types according to such criteria as their objectives, activities, and structure. But a broad and useful distinction can be made between *institutional* groups and *issue-oriented* groups.[6]

Institutional groups are characterized by organizational continuity and cohesion; they are highly knowledgeable about the policy-making process and about how to get access to public officials, in part because they usually employ a professional staff; their membership is stable; they have concrete and immediate

---

[3]Estimate of Ken Clements, president of the Ontario Chapter of the Institute of Association Executives, as reported by Robert Stevens, "Lobbyists a Big Cog in Ottawa Economy," *Ottawa Journal*, May 8, 1980, p. 29. I. A. Litvak estimated that there were 700 national trade associations in *Canada* in 1981 compared to 3,200 in the United States. "National Trade Associations: Business-Government Intermediaries," *Business Quarterly*, vol. 47 (Summer 1982), p. 35.

[4]Institute for Political Involvement, *A Report on the Prospects for Increased Involvement of Business People in the Canadian Political System* (Etobicoke, Ont.: 1978), p. 5.

[5]James Gillies, *Where Business Fails* (Montreal: Institute for Research on Public Policy, 1981), pp. 60–76.

[6]See A. Paul Pross, "Pressure Groups: Adaptive Instruments of Political Communication," in A. Paul Pross, ed., *Pressure Group Behaviour in Canadian Politics* (Toronto: McGraw-Hill Ryerson, 1975), pp. 10–18.

operational objectives, but their ultimate aims are sufficiently broad that they can bargain with government over achieving particular concessions; and their long-run credibility with government decision makers is more important than any single issue or objective. Examples of institutional groups are the Canadian Medical Association and the Canadian Chamber of Commerce. Issue-oriented groups, however, tend to be poorly organized; they have little knowledge of government and of how to contact public officials; there is a constant turnover in their membership; they normally focus on only one or two issues; and they are not usually concerned about their long-run credibility with public officials. Examples of issue-oriented groups are those concerned about a particular threat to the environment and those opposed to specific projects of land developers.

In reality, virtually all pressure groups fall on a continuum between these two extreme types and can be discussed in terms of the extent to which they possess the characteristics primarily of one or the other type. Most groups can be described as either mature or fledgling groups depending on the extent to which their characteristics conform to the institutional or issue-oriented ends of the continuum.[7] A good example of a group that has gradually moved along this continuum from fledgling to mature is Greenpeace.

Another distinction is often made between *special interest* groups and *public interest* groups. The vast majority of pressure groups fall into the special interest category on the grounds that they are primarily motivated by particular interests that affect their members directly (for example, the British Columbia Home Owners' Association or the Canadian Council of Furniture Manufacturers). *Public interest* groups, by way of contrast, are said to be concerned with the broader, more general interests of the public (for example, the Consumers Association of Canada, the Canadian Arctic Resources Committee). As in the case of institutional and issue-oriented groups, special interest and public interest groups can best be depicted on a continuum because most groups are motivated by a mixture of self-interest and public interest. For tactical reasons, all groups tend to emphasize the extent to which their activities serve the public interest.

Functions of Pressure Groups

Communication

Given that the overriding objective of pressure groups is to influence the development and execution of public policies, it is not surprising that their main function is two-way communication between their members and public officials. The *content* of this communication ranges from detailed, technical data on existing or proposed policies, programs and regulations, to irate demands for government action on particular issues (for example, environmental pollu-

---

[7]William D. Coleman distinguishes between the "policy advocacy" (lobbying) role of pressure groups and their growing "policy participation" role (their active participation in the formulation or implementation of public policy, or both). "Analyzing the Associative Action of Business: Policy Advocacy and Policy Participation," *Canadian Public Administration*, vol. 28 (Fall 1985), pp. 413–433.

tion). The *form* of the communication depends to some extent on its content, but it is determined also by the *type* of pressure group. Institutional groups tend to benefit more than issue-oriented groups from the fact that government–pressure group relations involve a two-way flow of communication and influence. Public officials rely, sometimes very heavily, on the expertise and experience of pressure groups for information on the efficacy of existing policies and on the implications of new proposals. Institutional-type groups, in large part because of the information they are able to provide to governments, have greater access to government officials, especially to Cabinet ministers and senior bureaucrats.

Bureaucrats and, to a lesser extent, Cabinet ministers also utilize pressure group contacts to communicate with the groups' members. Many pressure groups regularly pass along to their members, through newsletters and other internal means of communication, information about government policies and programs. This practice is mutually beneficial in that the group provides a service to its members and the bureaucrats get their message to the group's membership.

Legitimation

The communication function of pressure groups is closely related to another important function that groups perform in the political system — legitimation. Through consultation with pressure groups whose members will be affected by proposed policies, government officials can assess the probable effects of adopting these policies and can seek support for them. Such consultation gives these policies a measure of legitimacy in that those groups representing persons likely to be affected by the policies have had their views heard and ostensibly taken into account by government decision makers. Certainly, government officials are well advised to consult any group whose opposition to policies could weaken the legitimacy of the policies in the eyes of the public.

Thus, bureaucrats routinely consult certain pressure groups in the development and implementation of policies. Indeed, in a major survey of pressure group behaviour, Robert Presthus found that 50 per cent of federal bureaucrats and 68 per cent of provincial bureaucrats in Canada described their departments' relations with lobbyists as either "almost an integral part of our day-to-day activity" or "usually taken into account during policy making."[8] The importance of the legitimation function is evident in the efforts of bureaucrats to promote the creation and maintenance of particular pressure groups. Presthus reported that 45 per cent of federal bureaucrats and 50 per cent of provincial bureaucrats answered yes to the question: "Has your own or any other Department ever created an interest group in order to facilitate the implementation of a policy or program?"[9] This activity not only ensures a complementary source of outside knowledge and experience; it also serves the legitimation function by

---

[8]Robert Presthus and William Monopoli, "Bureaucracy in the United States and Canada: Social, Attitudinal and Behavioral Variables," *International Journal of Comparative Sociology*, vol. 18 (March/June 1977), p. 186.

[9]Ibid., p. 187.

ensuring outside support for the government's policies, facilitating group input into the policy process that might not otherwise take place, and promoting the representation of disadvantaged groups. For example, a former senior bureaucrat has acknowledged bureaucratic initiatives in "presenting for ministerial approval measures designed to assist members of disadvantaged sectors of society in forming groups and organizations and otherwise gaining some power in matters affecting their social and economic needs.[10]

Targets of Pressure Group Activity

It is critically important to the success of pressure groups that, in their interactions with government, they identify and aim at the right targets. They must decide first of all whether to direct their efforts to the federal, provincial, or local spheres of government — or to all of them.[11] The federal nature of Canada has important effects on the organization and operations of pressure groups. Many Canadian pressure groups are federations; that is, they are composed of provincial bodies that lobby the provincial governments and a national organization that focusses its efforts on Ottawa. Many other groups are not large enough to have provincial components or affiliates of a national organization, and are obliged therefore to channel their limited resources to those governments where they will do the most good. Another impact of federalism on pressure group activity is that to be effective on issues that involve more than one level of government, groups may be required to lobby simultaneously federal, provincial, and local governments.

Whether pressure groups are lobbying federal or provincial governments, the usual targets of their activity are Cabinet ministers, bureaucrats, and legislators, all of whom play important roles in the public policy process. This process may be divided into pre-legislative, legislative and post-legislative stages. Bureaucrats are especially powerful in the post-legislative stage through their implementation of policy decisions.

As a result of their policy advisory responsibilities and the sheer volume of decisions they make, bureaucrats are the most frequent targets of pressure group activity. Table 18.1 shows that Canadian bureaucrats are a more common focus of attention by pressure group leaders than either Cabinet ministers and legislators in Canada or bureaucrats in the United States. Moreover, close observers of the Canadian political scene have attested to the prominent role of bureaucrats in government–pressure group interaction:

> . . . the greatest leverage lies not with the politicians but with the bureaucrats.[12]

---

[10]Richard Splane, "Social Policy-Making in the Government of Canada: Reflections of a Reformed Bureaucrat," in S. A. Yelaja, ed., *Canadian Social Policy* (Waterloo: Wilfrid Laurier University Press, 1978), p. 215.

[11]For a discussion of the impact of federalism on pressure group activity in Canada, see Helen Jones Dawson, "National Pressure Groups and the Federal Government," in Pross, ed., *Pressure Group Behaviour*, pp. 30–35.

[12]Jim Bennett of the Canadian Federation of Independent Business, quoted in *The Globe and Mail*, October 25, 1980, p. 11.

Table 18.1

PROPORTION OF INTEREST GROUPS RANKING EACH TARGET FIRST

Target	Canada	United States
	%	%
Bureaucracy	40	21
Legislators	20	41
Cabinet	19	4
Legislative Committees	7	19
Executive Assistants	5	3
Judiciary	3	3
Others	6	9
	(393)	(604)

Source: Adapted from Robert Presthus, *Elites in the Policy Process* (London: Cambridge University Press, 1974), p. 255.

> . . . civil servants are obviously of key importance and they are a target group that most successful interest groups understand has to be dealt with.[13]

> Any lobbyist . . . will tell you that the real levers of power lie with the bureaucracy, among the mandarins whose own concerns and perceptions are the main source of policy.[14]

Most policy initiatives originate in the bureaucracy. One Ottawa lobbyist has noted that "most new ideas begin deep in the civil service machine. The man in charge of some special office . . . writes a memo suggesting a new policy on this or that. It works its way slowly up and up. At that stage civil servants are delighted . . . to talk quietly to people like us, people representing this or that corporation or industry directly involved. This is the time to slip in good ideas."[15] It is especially important for pressure groups to influence a policy before it becomes enshrined in a Cabinet memorandum, which is very difficult to have changed. It makes sense for pressure groups to lobby at the level, or levels, of the bureaucracy where a decision or recommendation affecting their interests can be made. Thus, lobbying will often be aimed at professional and technical personnel, rather than at senior executives and managers.

Lobbyists are frequently advised to "leave no stone unturned" in their efforts to influence those government officials who can help them to achieve their objectives. An Ottawa lobbyist has advised that "the effective lobbyist will maintain contact with the project as it goes up through the department, making sure he

---

[13]J. Hugh Faulkner, "Pressuring the Executive," *Canadian Public Administration*, vol. 25 (Summer 1982), p. 244.

[14]John Gray, "Insiders Go to Mandarins before Ministers," *The Globe and Mail*, October 27, 1980, p. 1.

[15]Quoted in Clive Baxter, "Familiars in the Corridors of Power," *Financial Post*, July 12, 1975, p. 6.

talks to every rung on the ladder. If you forget to talk to someone, he or she may be offended, and may influence the policy to your detriment."[16] Pressure groups must, however, choose their targets very carefully so as not to spread their limited resources too thinly and end up having little influence anywhere.

The power of bureaucrats does not, of course, give them the final say on major public policy issues; that authority belongs to Cabinet ministers. Pressure groups are frequently obliged, therefore, to lobby ministers to influence not only the decisions of individual departments, but also those of Cabinet as a whole and Cabinet committees. Moreover, ministers are often the ultimate target of lobbying aimed at bureaucrats and legislators by pressure groups that are striving to influence those who can influence ministers. Cabinet ministers have enormous power in all three stages of the policy process — if they decide to exercise that power. In practice, they have neither time nor inclination to participate actively in the post-legislative stage; rather, they tend to leave policy implementation to the bureaucrats.

Thus, it is tempting for group representatives to aim their *initial* lobbying efforts at Cabinet ministers. But, since ministers are busy people, it is usually inadvisable to approach them before other appropriate avenues of influence have been exhausted. There is little to be gained and something to be lost by expending a minister's time and goodwill when a bureaucrat or a legislator will serve just as well or even better. Admittedly, if a group gets Cabinet approval for a proposal, it has won its case. However, if a group loses at Cabinet level, there is no higher body with which it can lodge an appeal. Moreover, access to ministers is generally harder to obtain than to bureaucrats and legislators. For reasons outlined earlier, institutional-type pressure groups tend to receive readier access to ministers than do other pressure groups. Ministers, like bureaucrats, need contacts with experienced, knowledgeable, and influential groups not only to assess better the merits and costs of policy proposals, but also to increase political support for the government as a whole or for their own departments. They also use pressure groups as an alternative source of information and advice to that provided by the bureaucracy. A former Cabinet minister has asserted that "deputy ministers and their supporting policy advisors have no particular monopoly on wisdom and they can as easily become victims of myopia or tunnel vision as anyone else."[17]

We shall see later that the nature of the Cabinet committee system and other policy-making structures has a very significant impact on lobbying targets and tactics. It is sufficient to note here that, to be effective, pressure groups need to be knowledgeable about the operations of the machinery of government and to realize that even the enthusiastic support of the minister most directly involved with their concerns may not be sufficient to ensure success.

It has already been noted that, compared to Cabinet ministers and bureaucrats, legislators and legislative committees are a secondary target of pressure

---

[16]Andrew Roman, "Comments on Lobbying," in W. A. W. Neilson and J. C. MacPherson, eds., *The Legislative Process in Canada* (Montreal: Institute for Research on Public Policy, 1978), pp. 214–215.
[17]Faulkner, "Pressuring the Executive," p. 241.

group activity. Nevertheless, legislative support for pressure groups can be extremely important, especially on issues of widespread public concern, and can complement a group's efforts to influence officials in the executive-bureaucratic arena. Government backbenchers have opportunities to influence government decisions in party caucus meetings and in formal and informal meetings with ministers and bureaucrats. Opposition members are anxious to receive representations from pressure groups so as to understand better the groups' problems and to obtain ammunition to be used against the government. If individual legislators and legislative committees had more influence on the formulation and implementation of public policy, pressure groups could usefully spend more time and effort lobbying the legislature. At present, it is understandable that knowledgeable pressure groups will spend comparatively little time trying to influence public policy during the legislative stage of the policy process.

After identifying and selecting their targets from among ministers, bureaucrats, and legislators, pressure groups have to narrow in on more specific targets, that is, on the most appropriate minister(s), department(s), legislator(s), and legislative committee(s). Pressure groups must know not only whom to lobby, but as we shall see, what tactics will best ensure success. Above all, groups need to get access to government decision makers; otherwise they are obliged to influence public policy indirectly by influencing the news media and public opinion. This latter method of persuasion can be effective, but in general it is less successful, especially over time.

Recognition of Pressure Groups

Pressure group access to public officials, particularly to bureaucrats, depends largely on the extent to which the group has earned official recognition, that is, on the extent to which officials perceive the group as useful, credible, and legitimate. Professor David Kwavnick has noted:

> One of the major prizes in the struggle between competing interest groups
> . . . is tangible *recognition* by government of the status and representative
> capacity claimed by interest group leaders for their respective organizations. Such recognition is conferred when government canvasses interest group leaders for nominations to official bodies and when government calls a group's leader into consultation on legislative or administrative matters.[18]

Clearly, recognition facilitates both access and influence for pressure groups. Those groups that are regularly consulted by government have an early-warning system that alerts them to governmental initiatives affecting their interests. They are in a better position than other groups, therefore, to anticipate or react to these initiatives. Once groups have achieved this level of recognition, they are wise to ensure that they preserve it by cultivating their contacts in government and continuing to do whatever brought them recognition in the first place.

---

[18]David Kwavnick, "Pressure Group Demands and the Struggle for Organizational Status: The Case of Organized Labour in Canada," *Canadian Journal of Political Science*, vol. 3 (March 1970), p. 58. (Emphasis added.)

What are the bases of recognition? The first basis is the *expertise* and *experience* which underlie the information that pressure groups are able to provide to government officials. Bureaucrats naturally tend to consult and to grant readier access to those groups on whom they can rely for accurate data required for informed policy making. A former Cabinet minister has attributed the success of an especially effective pressure group to the fact that "their information is as good as the government's . . . . They do not appear before the executive or . . . agencies of government with half-baked information."[19]

Certain pressure groups gain and maintain recognition more easily than other groups because they constitute *the sole clientele* or a large part of the clientele of a specific department (for example, farmers' organizations vis-à-vis the Department of Agriculture, or labour organizations vis-à-vis the Department of Labour). This clientele relationship involves reciprocal costs and benefits. A department can rely on a clientele group as a source of information and as a channel of communication to the group's members. It can also use the group to get support for its policies from other departments, and indeed from the general public, by claiming to speak for the interests of the major group affected by the department's policies. To do this, the department must maintain good relations with the group and take special pains to avoid open conflict with it. Similarly, the group can benefit in the way of access and influence by receiving such departmental recognition. But if a group is tied too closely to a single department, it may have nowhere else to go, with the result that the department may be able to influence unduly its activities. So far as possible, therefore, a group will normally cultivate support in other departments so that not all its lobbying eggs are in a single basket.

Another important basis of pressure group recognition is the group's *political clout*. Not only ministers and legislators, but also bureaucrats are interested in the political impact of pressure group activity on the next election. While bureaucrats are expected to be non-partisan, they are at the same time expected to be politically sensitive. They should be able to advise the minister as to the likely effects of proposed policies on various segments of society, including those segments represented by influential pressure groups. Thus, bureaucrats should strive to be aware of the possible effects of government decisions on the voting behaviour of a pressure group's membership. Moreover, bureaucrats need to know what the likely implications of policy proposals will be on the bureaucratic or organizational politics within the government itself. A former Cabinet minister has stated that "most civil servants are professionally disposed to push or recommend policy that is likely to achieve political support both at the cabinet level and within the public service."[20] Thus, bureaucrats are more likely to grant official recognition to groups that have the resources to influence the political fortunes of their minister or of the government as a whole. Moreover, they will be more favourably disposed towards groups that can help them to help the minister.

---

[19]Faulkner, "Pressuring the Executive," p. 246.
[20]Ibid., p. 242.

A final notable source of recognition is the use by pressure groups of lobbying tactics that are approved by, or at least acceptable to, government decision makers. These tactics are discussed in the next section.

Pressure Group Tactics

Before deciding on the tactics to be employed, effective pressure groups take special pains to identify the appropriate targets of their lobbying activities (for example, federal, provincial, and local governments; ministers, bureaucrats, and legislators). They then progressively home in on the organizations and individuals within government most likely to be of assistance to them. It is evident that groups require up-to-date and accurate knowledge of the machinery of government to find their way through the labyrinth of government to the correct targets. Once this has been done, lobbying tactics can be geared to the needs and biases of these targets.

Ideally, an excellent tactic for pressure groups is to lobby all those government officials who can influence or actually make a decision affecting their interests. Realistically, however, most groups are obliged to utilize their limited financial and staff resources to lobby carefully selected officials. It is important, therefore, that groups lobby at the most appropriate level of the governmental hierarchy. Effective lobbying, both in the short and the long run, requires groups to provide officials with well-researched and relevant data. Thus, once access has been granted, pressure groups must ensure that their arguments are based on very thorough homework so as to enhance their success in influencing a specific policy as well as increasing their long-run credibility and legitimacy.

Groups are also well advised to attempt to influence policy at the earliest possible stage of its development and to follow the progress of that policy all the way through the policy-making process, including the post-legislative or implementation stage. "Any organization seeking to influence public policy must be prepared to come back again and again at whatever level of government is dealing with an issue. In other words, the group must have tenacity."[21] Groups will be able to perform this task more successfully if their contacts with government officials are sufficiently cordial and continuous to allow them to anticipate or learn quickly about policy initiatives. Thus, once again, a group's tactics are determined significantly by the extent of its recognition.

In general, pressure groups seek to influence public officials, especially bureaucrats, through quiet, behind-the-scenes consultations, rather than through media campaigns and public demonstrations that are designed to influence decision makers indirectly. Institutional-type pressure groups are more likely to use the former tactic because they are interested in influencing government decisions on a number of issues over a period of time, whereas issue-oriented groups tend to focus on a single problem or have fewer of the resources discussed earlier that encourage government officials to grant them recognition and access. In the face of limited opportunities to make their case directly to public officials, they hope to influence public policy indirectly by mobilizing public support for their

---

[21]Ibid., p. 247.

cause through the news media and even public demonstrations. Institutional groups are more likely to absorb defeat on a particular issue without "going public" because they know that there are other battles to be fought and that mounting public and media campaigns to win their point is unlikely to be to their long-run advantage. They are inclined to minimize publicity and confrontation and to avoid the adversarial approach. The head of the Grocery Products Manufacturers Association has stated that "we're not prepared to go on Parliament Hill and slaughter a pig to have our representations heard — unless we're absolutely forced to."[22] And the president of the Retail Council of Canada has observed that "the marshalling of public support through the media is sometimes the right recipe for tackling a particular issue, but not often. Only the most simplistic of issues is likely to be well understood by the public."[23] Pressure groups need to remember that official recognition is hard to win, but relatively easy to lose. This consideration determines significantly the tactics used by many groups.

The discreet approach to lobbying is more acceptable to bureaucrats because they want to keep their minister out of trouble and keep themselves out of the public spotlight. Neither they nor the department as a whole wish to be the object of public attack, because this is likely to affect detrimentally their own and possibly their minister's career prospects. Moreover, when government officials and group representatives meet in private and in confidence, where they are removed from the immediate pressure of public and media opinion, it is easier for them to work out an accommodation of their differences.

Certainly, some pressure groups, especially those of the issue-oriented variety, have had great impact on specific policy decisions by mobilizing public opinion on their side. It is possible also for groups to influence decisions without enjoying much in the way of access based on official recognition and without going to the media or the public. This usually will require the pushing of several pressure points at the same time (that is, ministers, bureaucrats, and legislators). On some occasions, even institutional groups resort to media campaigns or join with issue groups to pressure the government. These are exceptional situations, however, and the aim of most groups, including those concerned about a single issue of lasting importance, is to use those tactics most likely to achieve their objectives while preserving or enhancing their official recognition.

Representatives of well-recognized pressure groups are more likely to be invited to become members of one or more of the many advisory councils or committees established by the government or by individual departments to advise ministers or bureaucrats on policy. Appointment to such bodies as the Economic Council of Canada, the National Advisory Council on Aging, and the Canadian Advisory Council on the Status of Women gives group members an opportunity to advance the interests of the groups or clientele they were appointed to represent.

---

[22]David Morley, quoted in Julianne Labreche, "The Quiet Persuaders of Parliament Hill," *Financial Post*, November 29, 1980, p. 34.

[23]Alasdair J. McKichan, "Comments on Lobbying," in Neilson and MacPherson, eds., *The Legislative Process in Canada*, p. 223.

Well-recognized groups tend to adhere to the "rules of the game" for government-pressure group relations. These rules are not spelled out in any document; rather, they are composed of understandings based on experience as to what kind of behaviour is expected on both sides. With respect to bureaucracy-group relations, perhaps the most important of these informal rules is that private exchanges of information and opinion are to be kept confidential. Bureaucrats do not expect that the content of their private discussions with group representatives will be reported publicly or used as a basis for criticism of themselves or their department in other parts of the government. Similarly, pressure groups do not expect that the substance of their submissions to government will be shared with competing pressure groups or, without their consent, with other interested parties in the policy process.

Both common sense and the present nature of the policy process suggest that pressure group representations to government should, where feasible, be framed in terms of the public interest. The requests of pressure groups are more likely to be met if they are attuned to the priorities and plans of the government than if they amount to blatant, self-interested special pleading. For example, in a time of high inflation and high unemployment, officials are likely to look favourably on proposals that may reduce inflation and unemployment. Similarly, proposals that require the expenditure of substantial public funds during a time of severe economic restraint are unlikely to receive a sympathetic hearing. In short, pressure groups can advance their own interests by demonstrating that these interests enhance or at least complement the broader public interest.

One effective and frequently used tactic to demonstrate the public interest — or at least a broad interest — in a group's submission is to engage in cooperative lobbying. This requires that groups create formal or informal alliances with other groups who share their views on a particular policy issue. Cooperative lobbying enables several groups to present a united front to government as an indication of widespread concern. At the same time, the groups profit from this cooperative arrangement by sharing information and contacts. Even competing pressure groups may benefit from consultation with one another because they can learn the content and strength of their opponents' arguments, even if they cannot work out a common position to present to government. But "the lobbyists will be better received if they have reached an accommodation with the other interested protagonists — be they labour, other industries, consumers, etc."[24]

Effects of Changes in the Policy Process

As noted earlier, pressure groups need to be knowledgeable about the policy process in general and about the organization and operations of the specific departments and agencies they wish to influence. Groups must be especially vigilant to keep up to date on changes in structures and procedures in both the executive-bureaucratic and the legislative spheres of government.[25] Such changes

[24]Ibid., p. 220.
[25]See Peter Aucoin, "Pressure Groups and Recent Changes in the Policy-Making Process," in Pross, ed., *Pressure Group Behaviour in Canadian Politics*, pp. 174–192.

often signal shifts in the distribution of power within government and can therefore affect significantly the appropriate targets and tactics of pressure group activity.

Among the most important changes are those that affect the relative power of ministers and bureaucrats, departments and central agencies, and ministers and backbenchers. For example, during the Trudeau years, it was widely argued that the expansion of the Cabinet committee system and the growth in the size and responsibilities of the Prime Minister's Office and the Privy Council Office resulted in a greater concentration of power in the hands of ministers and central agency officials relative to departmental officials. The priorities set by ministers with the advice of central agency officials provided the policy framework within which government decisions were made. It became important, therefore, that pressure groups influence not only the policy and program decisions of individual departments and agencies, but also the general priorities of government. They were encouraged to frame their proposals so as to take account of the broader public interest, rather than simply to appeal to the narrower interests of individual departments. They had to be sensitive also to the central agencies' concern for coordination among the policies and programs of various departments. As a result of these changes, pressure groups often had to seek greater access to ministers and central agency officials. This proved to be a difficult task, because ministers were busy and central agency officials tended to minimize contacts with pressure groups on the grounds that central agencies had much less influence on public policy than was generally perceived.

Changes in the budgetary process are especially important for pressure group activity. Groups need to be familiar with the major actors and stages in the budgetary process so that they know when and where to exert influence if their proposals require the expenditure of public funds. The introduction in the early 1980s of the policy and expenditure management system — or the envelope system as it is commonly known — has had important repercussions for pressure group activity. There are a great many actors in this system, with the result that pressure groups are advised to touch as many bases as they can with the resources at their disposal. Moreover, since policy and expenditure management decisions are tied together in the system, the expenditure implications of policy decisions are made clearer, so that the competing requests of pressure groups for government funds are more evident. Given the power of Cabinet ministers in policy committees to make decisions affecting other departments, it is important that groups influence as many of the ministers as possible on the relevant committees. One effective way of influencing these ministers is to influence the bureaucrats who give them advice, but again, it is not usually sufficient to get support from the senior officials of a single department because there is now an institutionalized competition for funds among departments.

An additional challenge for pressure groups arises from their need to detect actual as opposed to apparent shifts in power. For example, it is generally agreed in retrospect that during the 1970s the power of the central agencies vis-à-vis operating departments was somewhat exaggerated and that departments still had considerable expertise that enabled them to influence the decisions of ministers and central agency officials.

Legislative changes can also have substantial impact on the targets and tactics of pressure groups. For example, changes in the mid- and late 1960s in the standing committee system of the federal Parliament gave that body a more significant role in the examination of policy proposals and in the scrutiny of government administration. Parliamentary committee meetings provide a formal opportunity for pressure groups to present their views on the content and implementation of policies and programs. As a result, pressure groups now spend more time lobbying individual legislators and making formal submissions to committees. Groups cannot realistically expect these lobbying efforts to result in changes to the general thrust of legislation introduced into Parliament by Cabinet ministers. Pressure groups can, however, educate legislators on their purposes and problems in the hope of bringing about minor changes in legislation and promoting their interests in party caucus and in parliamentary discussions. If legislative reform results in greater clout for legislative committees in the development and oversight of policy, pressure groups will have a much greater incentive to lobby legislators.

The impact of changes in policy-making structures and procedures will vary according to the type of pressure group. Institutional groups are likely to be able to adapt more quickly and effectively to changes affecting the channels of access and influence in the executive-bureaucratic arena. But legislative reforms that give more control or influence to committees will tend to force institutional groups more into the open so that they will be obliged to compete on a more equal footing with issue-oriented groups, which are more visible and which tend to make more use of the media and of public opinion campaigns.

POLITICAL PARTIES AND IDEOLOGIES

Public administration scholars have paid very little attention to interaction between political parties and the bureaucracy. The functions of political parties are usually described as interest aggregation and articulation, the recruitment and training of political leaders, and the education and socialization of the public on political matters; control or influence over the bureaucracy is rarely mentioned. In brief, *political parties* are organizations which seek to get their members elected to political office and to gain and maintain control of the government. They pursue this objective both from inside and from outside the government. The internal and external components of political parties are often referred to as the parliamentary and the extra-parliamentary party. Earlier chapters discussed relations between the bureaucracy and the parliamentary party, that is, the parties' elected members in the legislature and in party caucus. The brief treatment of political parties provided here is concerned with the impact on the bureaucracy of the extra-parliamentary party, that is, the parties' national and provincial executives and offices and the constituency associations.

Political parties, whether acting through an executive elected by party members or through party meetings and conventions, are generally perceived to be quite remote from the operations of the bureaucracy. The influence of political parties on bureaucratic decisions and recommendations tends to be indirect and often intangible. This influence is, however, greater than it is popularly perceived.

There are two general types of interaction between political parties and bureaucrats. The first involves the bureaucrat as citizen; the second involves the bureaucrat as government employee.

The most direct contacts between bureaucrats and political parties take the form of participation by public servants in the activities of political parties. As noted in Chapter 11, significant restrictions have been placed on the partisan political activities of public servants so as to preserve political neutrality. Within the bounds of these restrictions, public servants do seek nomination and election to public office and provide various forms of support for individual candidates and political parties. The right of public servants to participate in partisan political activities has gradually been extended over the past twenty years, and there are strong pressures for further relaxation of the constraints on such activities. Through the limited opportunities to contribute directly to political parties, bureaucrats can have some direct influence on the policy positions adopted by political parties, but their participation usually has to be very circumspect. The most senior public servants and those in sensitive positions are usually excluded from any kind of partisan political activity. As noted in Chapter 11, however, some senior public servants are political appointees, that is, their appointment by the governing party is based on the fact that they have been involved in partisan politics.

The influence of the extra-parliamentary wing of political parties on the bureaucrat as government employee is very indirect and difficult to assess. This influence is exercised in the form of policies, proposals, and promises which have implications for the bureaucracy as a whole or particular parts of it, and which are made during party meetings, leadership conventions, and election campaigns. Political candidates and political parties, especially if they are in Opposition, frequently join in the bureaucrat bashing that falls on such fertile ground among the electorate generally. Charges of inefficient, ineffective, and unresponsive bureaucratic behaviour are usually accompanied by promises of cutbacks in the number of public servants and in the amount of money they spend. It is understandable that political parties that have been in Opposition for a long time, for example the Conservatives in Ottawa, should become antagonistic towards the bureaucracy and view some bureaucrats as being too close to the governing party. This leads to threats that many senior bureaucrats will be turfed out with a change of government and to unhappiness among many of the party faithful when these threats are not carried out.

Aside from attacks on the general performance of the bureaucracy, political parties and their leaders adopt party platforms which have implications for public servants working in particular policy fields, and which can range from broad promises to reduce expenditure on social policy to specific promises to abolish certain programs or agencies. While experience has shown that once in office political leaders often deviate substantially from their party's platform, policies set by political parties can be very influential, especially through the publicity received in the news media.

There are often significant differences between political parties with respect to their views on the bureaucracy. For example, in the federal sphere, the argument is often made that the two major political parties are simply two sides of the same coin. Nevertheless, the Progressive Conservative Party tends to be more inclined than the Liberal Party to lament the size and expenditures of government and to propose such solutions as privatization of Crown corporations and deregulation. The New Democratic Party, which favours policies likely to require a larger governmental apparatus and is affiliated with the trade union movement, generally avoids broad attacks on the bureaucracy and vigorously supports collective bargaining in the public sector.

It is difficult for bureaucrats to separate completely their role as citizen or voter from that of government employee, and it is, therefore, reasonable to assume that on occasion sympathy for a political party will carry over into decisions or recommendations on the job. Equally problematic is assessing the effect of the ideological commitments of bureaucrats. These commitments do not have to be manifested by a formal or emotional attachment to a particular political party; the bureaucrat who is politically neutral in the partisan sense still has many opportunities to inject personal ideological preferences into the policy-making process. These preferences will obviously affect the bureaucrat's views on major policy issues involving such social values as the redistribution of income and the protection of human rights.

There are well-documented cases in Canada where the ideological preferences of bureaucrats appear to have had a significant influence on policy development. There was substantial and successful resistance by senior bureaucrats to the social values and goals of the CCF government which defeated the Liberals in Saskatchewan in 1944.[26] Another example is provided by Richard Splane, who has described the important influence of federal bureaucrats, notably social workers in the Department of National Health and Welfare, on the reform of social policy in Canada.[27] Within the framework of support for such reform by successive ministers, the credo of these bureaucrats "consisted almost wholly of a belief that in the interests of all Canadians, and particularly of those least-advantaged, a high priority should be given to the development of a comprehensive nation-wide social security system."[28]

CONCLUDING OBSERVATIONS

The growth in the number and apparent influence of pressure groups has raised concern that they rival and even threaten to supplant political parties as the

---

[26]S. M. Lipset, *Agrarian Socialism: The Cooperative Commonwealth Federation in Saskatchewan* (Berkeley: University of California Press, 1959), ch. 12.
[27]"Social Policy-Making in the Government of Canada: Reflections of a Reformed Bureaucrat," in Yelaja, ed., *Canadian Social Policy*, pp. 209–226.
[28]Ibid., p. 211.

primary channel of communication between citizens and their governments. Unlike political parties, however, pressure groups do not seek, through the electoral process, overall control of government and thereby of policy making and implementation; rather, pressure groups attempt to affect particular government decisions. Moreover, political parties aggregate the needs and wishes of a vast number of interests in society, whereas pressure groups aggregate the views of a much narrower range of interests. While such large pressure groups as the Canadian Labour Congress and the Canadian Manufacturers' Association are concerned about a wide range of policy issues, at the other extreme there are pressure groups with a very small membership who are concerned about a single issue (for example, a group opposed to a halfway house in their neighbourhood).

Collectively, pressure groups have in fact diminished to some extent the role of political parties as intermediaries between the citizen and the state. But the increasing attraction of pressure group activity is in large part a response to the decline of political parties in the political system for reasons other than the proliferation and influence of pressure groups. Members of political parties who become backbench members of the legislature exercise little power in the political system compared to Cabinet ministers and senior bureaucrats. Furthermore, lobbyists are usually better able than individual legislators to deal with technical matters. "If a plant manufacturing railway box cars is threatened with closure and the loss of two thousand jobs, that would be an appropriate area of concern for the local Member of Parliament. [However], if . . . that same plant had a problem with the Department of Transport on the safety aspects of the design of a journal box, that would be more appropriate for solution by that company's management or the industry's trade association."[29] It is natural that citizens should pursue their self-interest by using whatever channel of communication best enables them to influence public policy.

The bureaucracy is influenced not only by pressure groups and political parties, but also, as explained in the next chapter, by the news media and the public.

---

[29]Alasdair J. McKichan, "Comments on Lobbying," in Neilson and MacPherson, eds., *The Legislative Process in Canada*, p. 221.

BIBLIOGRAPHY

Aucoin, Peter. "Pressure Groups and Recent Changes in the Policy-Making Process." In A. Paul Pross, ed., *Pressure Group Behaviour in Canadian Politics*. Toronto: McGraw-Hill Ryerson, 1975, pp. 174–191.

Coleman, William D. "Analyzing the Associative Action of Business: Policy Advocacy and Policy Participation." *Canadian Public Administration*, vol. 28 (Fall 1985): 413–433.

Dawson, Helen Jones. "Consumers Association of Canada." *Canadian Public Administration*, vol. 6 (March 1963): 92–118.

Dawson, Helen Jones. "Interest Group: The Canadian Federation of Agriculture." *Canadian Public Administration*, vol. 3 (June 1960): 134–149.

Dawson, Helen Jones. "National Pressure Groups and the Federal Government." In A. Paul Pross, ed., *Pressure Group Behaviour in Canadian Politics*. Toronto: McGraw-Hill Ryerson, 1975, pp. 30–35.

Dawson, Helen Jones. "Relations between Farm Organizations and the Civil Service in Canada and Great Britain." *Canadian Public Administration*, vol. 10 (December 1967): 450–470.

Faulkner, J. Hugh. "Pressuring the Executive." *Canadian Public Administration*, vol. 25 (Summer 1982): 240–253.

Gillies, James, and Jean Piggott. "Participation in the Legislative Process." *Canadian Public Administration*, vol. 25 (Summer 1982): 254–264.

Kwavnik, D. *Organized Labour and Pressure Politics: The Canadian Labour Congress, 1956–1968*. Montreal: McGill-Queen's University Press, 1972.

Lipset, S. M. *Agrarian Socialism: The Cooperative Commonwealth Federation in Saskatchewan*. Berkeley: University of California Press, 1959.

Paltiel, Khayyam Z. "The Changing Environment and Role of Special Interest Groups." *Canadian Public Administration*, vol. 25 (Summer 1982): 198–210.

Presthus, R. *Elite Accommodation in Canadian Politics*. Toronto: Macmillan, 1973.

Presthus, R. *Elites in the Policy Process*. Cambridge: Cambridge University Press, 1974.

Pross, A. Paul. *Group Politics and Public Policy*. Toronto: Oxford University Press, 1985.

Pross, A. Paul. "Input Versus Withinput: Pressure Group Demands and Administrative Survival." In A. Paul Pross, ed., *Pressure Group Behaviour in Canadian Politics*. Toronto: McGraw-Hill Ryerson, 1975.

Pross, A. Paul, ed. *Pressure Group Behaviour in Canadian Politics*. Toronto: McGraw-Hill Ryerson, 1975.

Pross, A. Paul. "Pressure Groups: Talking Chameleons." In Michael S. Whittington and Glen Williams, eds., *Canadian Politics in the 1980s*. 2nd ed. Toronto: Methuen, 1984, pp. 287–311.

Stanbury, W. T. *Business Interests and the Reform of Canadian Competition Policy*. Toronto: Methuen, 1977.

Stanbury, W. T. "Lobbying and Interest Group Representation in the Legislative Process." In W. A. W. Neilson and J. C. MacPherson, eds., *The Legisla-*

tive Process in Canada. Montreal: The Institute for Research on Public Policy, 1978, pp. 167–207.

Taylor, Malcom G. "The Role of the Medical Profession in the Formulation and Execution of Public Policy." *Canadian Public Administration*, vol. 3 (Fall 1970): 233–255.

Thorburn, Hugh G. *Interest Groups in the Canadian Federal System*. Special Study for the Royal Commission on the Economic Union and Development Prospects for Canada. Vol. 69. Toronto: University of Toronto Press, 1985.

Thorburn, Hugh G., ed. *Party Politics in Canada*. 5th ed. Scarborough: Prentice-Hall, 1979.

Winn, C., and J. McMenemy. *Political Parties in Canada*. Toronto: McGraw-Hill Ryerson, 1976.

CASES

In *Case Program in Canadian Public Administration* (Toronto: Institute of Public Administration of Canada):

Closing the Baldwin Hospital, by Harold B. Wodinsky, Marsha Barnes, and Raisa B. Deber

Screening the Boat People? Case Studies in Health Policies, by Peter Owen, Peggy Purvis and Raisa B. Deber

All Things to All People: Government and Its Client Groups, by Sharon Bider and Peter McNaughton

La politique du transport urbain dans la région de Québec, by Louise Quenel-Ouellet and Gilles Bouchard

L'Affaire "Caloil," by Michel Paquin

The Grain Dust Case: Public Policy Analysis and Regulation, by G. B. Doern and John Kowalski

Suncor Inc., by J. R. D'Cruz

We'll Take You On, Mr. Toyota: A Case on Japanese Imports and the Future of the Canadian Automobile Industry, by Sandford F. Borins, John M. Curtis, R. Moroz, and Tony R. Washington

Regulatory Decision: Airlines, by Peter Clancy

In Mark C. Baetz and Donald H. Thain, *Canadian Cases in Business-Government Relations* (Toronto: Methuen, 1985):

#17 – The Canadian Federation of Independent Business and the MacEachen Budget

#18 – Imperial Oil and the "Bertrand Report"

19

The Public, the Media, and the Bureaucracy

It is widely acknowledged that "Canada combines the British tradition of a strong executive and centralized leadership with a *relative* freedom from mass pressure and popular constraint."[1] Nevertheless, Canadian politicians pay much lip service to the importance of public input into the policy-making process, and in a democratic society a persuasive argument can be made for encouraging such input.

The discussion in the previous two chapters of relations between the bureaucracy and non-governmental actors is supplemented in this chapter by an examination of bureaucratic interaction with the public and the media. The nature of this interaction is significantly influenced by the pressures for freedom of information and individual privacy, which are examined in the latter half of this chapter.

THE PUBLIC AND PUBLIC OPINION

In practice, politicians and bureaucrats face formidable obstacles in eliciting and assessing public input. It is difficult even to define the *public* and so to discern the public's *opinion* on political and administrative issues. The term public is variously defined as the total population, the total adult population, the electorate, an aggregation of pressure groups, the most influential organized interest, and so on. A useful distinction is often made between the public as a whole and the multiple *publics* or segments of the public that make up the total population. The public is clearly not a homogeneous entity whose collective view can easily be obtained; rather, it is fragmented into a large variety of organized and unorganized groups and individuals whose opinions on many issues conflict. Public opinion, then, is an aggregate of individual and group opinions.

The public and public servants have strong incentives to interact with one another. Public servants actively seek the public's views as at least a partial basis for making both recommendations and decisions. They not only want to inform the public about government activities and to seek the public's reaction to existing and proposed policies and programs; they also want to stimulate widespread support among the population at large for their departments' undertakings. For the public, the extent of the bureaucracy's power provides good reason for efforts to enhance public influence on government decision making. J. A. Corry

---

[1]Richard E. B. Simeon, "The 'Overload Thesis' and Canadian Government," *Canadian Public Policy*, vol. 2 (Autumn 1976), p. 550. (Emphasis in original.)

has observed that "the clamour for citizen involvement" arises in part from the suspicion among citizens "that decisions that impinge solely on them are actually being made, not by their representatives in the legislatures or by ministers directly responsible to their representatives," but rather "on high by persons nameless and faceless to them."[2] Certainly members of the public, in their capacity as voters, are far removed from the most important official decision makers —Cabinet ministers and senior bureaucrats.

The traditional mechanisms for interaction between government and society, namely the electoral system, political parties, legislators, pressure groups, and the mass media, permit the public to exercise little direct influence over politicians and bureaucrats. The electorate obviously constitutes an extremely large and important segment of the public, but election results are a very inexact measure of public attitudes on any specific public policy issue. Similarly, political parties in Canada reflect a wide range of opinion on policy issues. Neither the electoral system nor parties are an effective means by which the public can influence bureaucratic decisions. Furthermore, legislators have insufficient capacity and inclination to hold ministers responsible for their administration of departments and agencies. Yet bureaucrats, to whom ministers delegate substantial powers, are even further removed from legislative control and influence. Thus, the public, acting through its elected representatives, has relatively little influence over the bureaucracy.

Pressure groups are another extremely important segment of the public, but despite their professed concern for the broad public interest, their primary concern is usually their self-interest. Moreover, these groups are often in conflict with one another. Even so-called public interest groups (for example, the Consumers' Association of Canada) can legitimately claim to speak for only a portion of the public. The mass media provide other channels of communication between the public and the bureaucracy by reflecting and, to some extent, shaping public opinion. But, like pressure groups, various media organizations disagree on public policy issues and therefore send conflicting signals to government officials as to the content of public opinion.

PUBLIC PARTICIPATION

During the 1960s there was an upsurge of public concern that these traditional mechanisms provided inadequate opportunities for public input into the policy process. The institutions and processes of representative democracy were complemented by a vigorous emphasis on what was popularly described in Canada and elsewhere as participatory democracy. During the 1968 federal election campaign, Pierre Elliott Trudeau frequently used this term to sum up his commitment "to make government more accessible to people, to give citizens a sense of full participation in the affairs of government, and full control over their repre-

---

[2]J. A. Corry, "Sovereign People or Sovereign Governments," in H. V. Kroeker, ed., *Sovereign People or Sovereign Governments* (Montreal: Institute for Research on Public Policy, 1981), p. 11.

sentatives."[3] To achieve these ends, demands were made both for improvements in the representative system (that is, public input through popularly elected representatives and political parties) and for instruments to permit more *direct* public participation in the policy process (for example, task forces and advisory bodies).

Public participation is a broader concept than that of citizen participation — although the two terms are often used interchangeably. *Public participation* refers to a broad range of direct and indirect forms of participation, including citizen participation. *Citizen participation* connotes direct participation of individual citizens and citizens' groups in government decision making. It is notable that the purpose of citizen participation is more to stimulate decision makers to take account of a wider range of considerations at an earlier stage in the policy process than to enable citizens to scrutinize the administration of government programs.

Sherry Arnstein has provided a helpful means of conceptualizing the gradations of citizen participation by identifying eight rungs on "a ladder to citizen participation."[4] The ascending rungs on the ladder depict a progression of citizen involvement from forms of "non-participation" to participation involving the actual exercise of citizen power. The eight rungs make up three major levels. The first and lowest level is labelled *non-participation* and includes (1) manipulation by the power structure and (2) therapy for the organization. The second level is described as *token participation* and includes (3) communication with the groups, (4) consultation with the groups, and (5) placation of the groups. The third and highest level, that of *real citizen power*, contains the rungs of (6) partnership, (7) delegated power, and (8) citizen control. We shall see that much of what passes for citizen participation in Canada is, in Arnstein's terms, a form of tokenism.

Virtues and Limitations of Public Participation

Advocates of increased public participation in general and citizen participation in particular contend that participation benefits both members of the public and government officials. It is argued that the overriding benefit to the public is greater *responsiveness* of government decisions, programs, and services to the public's needs and desires. Participation facilitates a valuable exchange of information between the government and citizens who are directly — and often acutely — affected by government activities. Politicians and public servants thereby become more knowledgeable about the impact of their decisions, especially on individuals and groups whose views and concerns might otherwise be overlooked. Easier and more equal access to official decision makers stimulates participation by individual citizens and by such groups as the poor and native peoples; it thereby helps to reduce the influence of well-organized and well-connected interests which usually enjoy good access to government officials.

---

[3]Pierre Elliott Trudeau, *Campaign Speech: Ottawa* (Ottawa: The Liberal Party of Canada, 1968).
[4]Sherry R. Arnstein, "A Ladder to Citizen Participation," *Journal of the American Institute of Planners*, vol. 35 (July 1969), pp. 216–224.

In addition, individual participants can receive substantial educational and social returns from participation. Exposure to new ideas and to people with different values develops greater tolerance and sensitivity towards the views of others. Moreover, working with other people for common objectives promotes a sense of belonging and can enhance one's self-image. It is notable that these benefits can accrue to participants even when the government's commitment to meaningful participation is not genuine.

For government officials, public participation not only helps to ensure that their decisions will be more responsive to public wants and needs; it also enhances the legitimacy of these decisions in the eyes of those who have made a direct or indirect input into the policy process. Participating individuals and groups are more likely to accept decisions when they see — or perceive — that their views have been heard and taken into account. The argument is frequently made that public participation enhances the *effectiveness* as well as the responsiveness of public decisions by sensitizing government officials to the likely consequences of their decisions.

Critics of increased participation express, with varying degrees of intensity, one or more of the following concerns. Improving opportunities for indirect public input into the policy process through legislatures and political parties is praiseworthy, but Canadians in general are not inclined to participate actively and directly in the policy process. Thus, the creation or reform of institutions and procedures to promote direct citizen interaction with government officials is not worth the effort. Moreover, the benefits that may result from the heightened responsiveness of public officials and especially of bureaucrats, who make the bulk of government decisions, have offsetting disadvantages. Consultation with citizens, citizens' groups, and advisory bodies can be extremely time consuming and, therefore, an inefficient use of the time and energy of public officials. Such consultation can also lead to less efficient and effective government by causing delays in the making of decisions and the delivery of programs. Efficiency and effectiveness can be further reduced if "expert" public servants are obliged to take undue account of the views of "amateur" citizens. Alan Altshuler has asserted that "groups of laymen — and especially groups of poorly educated laymen with little or no administrative experience — have particular handicaps as decision-makers. They have little time to devote to consideration of the issues; their concerns are selfish and immediate; they lack technical competence."[5]

Another concern about the development of participative mechanisms is that they may create a mere facade of increased involvement by traditionally under-represented groups. For example, the poor and the uneducated may participate more actively, but on balance enjoy no greater influence than they had before. Organized interests that are already influential often utilize participative mechanisms to obtain even better access to government officials and thereby to exercise even greater influence on government decisions — sometimes at the expense of less well-organized but more deserving citizens. Public servants can also use citizen participation to their advantage. They can blur the lines of

---

[5]Alan Altshuler, *Community Control* (Washington, D.C.: Urban Institute, 1970), p. 45.

accountability by delegating decision making powers to citizens' groups or sharing these powers. They can encourage participation so as to co-opt or pacify citizens who might otherwise publicly criticize government policies and programs. Finally, public servants can build support for — or reduce opposition to — their activities by involving affected interests in the decision-making process.

Mechanisms for Public Participation

Despite these concerns, efforts to facilitate public participation have since the 1960s been undertaken by all levels of government in Canada.

Both political parties and pressure groups have been affected by the trend towards greater public participation. The inner workings of Canada's major political parties have been democratized to allow increased participation by their members in shaping the parties' stance on policy issues. New pressure groups have sprung up to exert influence on behalf of previously unrepresented or underrepresented segments of the population. Government officials have encouraged the participation of groups representing such interests as consumers, environmentalists, and the poor by assisting them with public funds. Citizens' groups (for example, residents' and ratepayers' associations) concerned with such issues as housing, zoning, and transportation have been especially active in the sphere of local government.

The parliamentary system has been reformed to provide more opportunities for testimony on policy issues by members of the public, including individual citizens, and more appearances by public servants before legislative committees to explain government policies and programs. Parliamentary committees have travelled to various parts of the country to consult individuals and groups on policy questions, and effective use has recently been made of parliamentary task forces, now described as special committees. These are composed of backbench members of all political parties who, acting largely on a non-partisan basis, consult members of the public and make recommendations to government on such policy matters as regulatory reform, North-South relations, and federal-provincial fiscal arrangements.

Legislative committees have also enhanced public participation by holding hearings to examine the *coloured papers*,[6] especially white papers and green papers, issued by government. The publication of these papers provides the public with information about existing and proposed policies (for example, in the areas of tax reform, immigration, public access to information) as well as an invitation to comment on these policies. The extent and impact of public participation resulting from the issuing of these papers vary greatly depending on both citizen and legislative interest in the subject matter. The number of submissions from the public can be impressive. For example, the House of Commons committee examining the White Paper on Tax Reform (1969) received 524 briefs and 1,093 letters and other submissions from groups and individu-

---

[6]For a more detailed discussion of coloured papers, Royal commissions, task forces, and advisory councils, see Chapter 9.

als.[7] However, the federal government has not yet developed systematic mechanisms to provide for parliamentary and public participation in the consideration of coloured papers.[8]

Even Royal commissions — a traditional source of policy advice to the executive — responded to the public participation movement by seeking the public's views more frequently and systematically (for example, the federal Royal Commission on Bilingualism and Biculturalism, the Ontario Royal Commission on Electric Power Planning). But task forces of various kinds have been used much more often than Royal commissions to obtain information and ideas from the public and to assess public opinion (for example, the 1966 Task Force on Housing, the 1977 Task Force on National Unity, and the many departmental task forces on a broad range of topics).

Both Royal commissions and task forces use public opinion surveys (often called social surveys) to assess the public's views on current and proposed government activities. The extensive use of such surveys by Cabinets, political parties, and individual politicians is well known. The public is less knowledgeable, however, about the existence and the results of the many public opinion surveys, of varying degrees of sophistication and reliability, that are conducted by or for government departments. The results of these surveys are not routinely disclosed to the public, but many are now available under the Access to Information Act. In general, the data from social surveys are a useful input into the government's assessment of public opinion. An advantage of these surveys is that they can provide information on the needs and desires of all segments of the public, including those who are disadvantaged, unorganized, or uneducated. A survey carried out for the 1969 Task Force on Government Information showed that a very large number of Canadians could not participate effectively because they knew so little about government and the services it provides.[9]

Another means by which public participation can be pursued is through the use of advisory bodies to government. The creation of advisory boards and councils is in keeping with the desire for more *direct* citizen participation in government decision making. Unlike most of the mechanisms discussed above, advisory bodies can be used for direct interaction between citizens and public officials, especially bureaucrats. A large number of advisory bodies has in fact been established at all levels of Canadian government to provide advice to politicians and bureaucrats (for example, the Economic Council of Canada advises the federal Cabinet; various provincial councils on the status of women, the elderly, the handicapped, etc., advise the relevant government departments). Many advisory bodies containing representatives of citizens' groups have been established as non-governmental organizations supported by public funds.[10] It is very diffi-

---

[7]Audrey Doerr, "The Role of Coloured Papers," *Canadian Public Administration*, vol. 25 (Fall 1982), p. 372.

[8]Ibid., p. 370.

[9]Government of Canada, *To Know and Be Known*, Report of the Task Force on Government Information (Ottawa: Queen's Printer, 1969), vol. 1, p. 3.

[10]For an account and an evaluation of efforts to encourage citizen participation in Winnipeg, see Phil H. Wichern, *Evaluating Winnipeg's Unicity: Resident Advisory Groups, 1971–1984*, Research and Working Papers, no. 11 (Winnipeg: Institute of Urban Studies, University of Winnipeg, 1984).

cult to find genuine cases of an actual delegation of authority over decision making, program administration, and/or the expenditure of public funds to groups of citizens at the community level.

A more controversial response to the public participation movement has been the provision of government funding for groups which otherwise would be unable to afford to participate effectively in the policy process. Some observers of the political scene find it strange that a government would provide funds for groups which are likely to use those funds to make life more difficult for the government. There is no doubt, however, that such funding widens the range of groups which are able to participate effectively in government decision making and increases the range of viewpoints to which public officials are exposed. In the federal sphere of government, for example, consumers' and native peoples' groups have been the main beneficiaries of this kind of government funding. It is no easy task for government to decide which groups should be funded, how much money they should receive, and which departments or agencies should provide it. Despite the problems of administering government funding of such groups, the practice seems likely to expand.

Despite these advances in the level and means of public participation since the late 1960s, there remains a gap between promise and performance. Perceptions of the size of this gap vary according to individual views about the appropriate extent of participation. Few instances of public participation in Canada have been found above the "tokenism" rungs of Arnstein's ladder of citizen participation. Kenneth Bryden contends that public participation in Canada has been largely of an "instrumental" rather than a "consummative" nature. He notes that "participation as instrumental action is based on the idea of *taking part* in political life in order to protect and advance one's individual interests in a competitive situation." However, consummative participation refers to participation as an end in itself and "involves *sharing* in a community by cooperating for a common good, thereby fostering the participant's development and self-realization."[11] To enhance public participation in general, Bryden recommends the establishment of an information network, devolution of authority in large organizations, and direct participation in decision making in the neighbourhood and in the workplace.[12]

The fundamental means of public participation in the Canadian political system remains the process of nominating and electing public officials. But the various mechanisms discussed above have provided a vital complementary means of involving members of the public in the policy process. In particular, they have stimulated a greater sense of responsiveness to the public among politicians and bureaucrats. Elected officials, notably Cabinet ministers, have neither the time nor the expertise to handle all the representations made by members of the public. Certainly, in the municipal sphere, the result of efforts to facilitate citizen participation has largely been to increase citizen interaction with public employees rather than with councillors. Thus, participation has affected bureau-

---

[11]Kenneth Bryden, "Public Input into Policy-Making and Administration," *Canadian Public Administration*, vol. 25 (Spring 1982), p. 94. (Emphasis in original.)
[12]Ibid., pp. 100–105.

crats not only indirectly through their political superiors, but also directly through increased interaction with individual citizens and citizens' groups.

THE MEDIA

Like pressure groups, the media of mass communication, commonly known as the mass media or the news media, act as intermediaries between the government and the public. The term mass media includes radio, television, newspapers, and magazines. Unlike pressure groups, the mass media transmit much information for the sake of transmitting information, rather than for the purpose of influencing public policy. Moreover, compared to pressure groups, which tend to represent well-defined interests to carefully identified officials, the media's audience, both within government and among the public, tends to be broader and more diffuse.

The Media and the Government

A key function of the media is to provide information to the public. Similarly, a major responsibility of government in a democratic society is to inform the public about the institutions and processes of government and about the programs and services offered by departments and agencies. In varying degrees, all government departments generate news and information. For some departments, like Statistics Canada, performing the service of gathering and disseminating information to the public is their main raison d'être. Other departments provide information of importance to the public at large (e.g., the Department of Energy, Mines and Resources on energy conservation), or to more specialized groups (e.g., the Department of National Health and Welfare on income security for the elderly and several other departments on scientific and technological advances). In addition, as a basis for policy development and implementation, government officials require information on the needs and demands of the citizens they serve. In contrast to their relations with many pressure groups, government officials do not usually look to, or depend on, the media for information of a technical nature; rather, they are interested in media coverage of a political or policy nature bearing on the activities of other governments or the attitudes of the general public — or particular sections of the public.

In the sphere of government-media interaction, the major participants on the government side are ministers, members of Parliament, and public servants, especially senior public servants and information officers in government departments and agencies. On the media side, the primary participants are journalists, editorial executives, and the owners of print and broadcast organizations. The media and the government pursue different objectives through their provision of information. In very general terms, government officials want to get their message to the public without stirring up the political waters. In some cases, this is useful to the media because it provides them with a ready source of up-to-date news at minimal cost; however, the media's objective of attracting a large audience can often be best achieved by rocking the boat. It is notable that the media are by no means a homogeneous entity; thus the government can occasionally achieve its objectives in communicating with the public by taking advantage of competition and conflict between and among various media organizations.

The media play a critical role as two-way channels of communication between the governors and the governed. Newspapers, magazines, television, and radio carry information from the public to politicians and bureaucrats and from these officials to the public. The media not only serve as "filters" for this information; they aim also to influence the attitudes and behaviour of both government officials and members of the public. Thus, the media both reflect and influence public opinion.

Governments cannot and do not rely solely on the media to communicate with the public. Much information is exchanged through correspondence and telephone calls between officials and citizens and through government publications and direct mailings aimed at the general public or particular groups. But government information appears to be transmitted most effectively through the media. Indeed, a survey for the federal Task Force on Government Information found that Canadians learn about government programs primarily through the mass media. In order of priority, the reported sources of federal information were "television, newspapers and magazines, radio, friends and relatives, government publications, public servants and Members of Parliament, and associations and clubs."[13] It is noteworthy also that a substantial portion of government information that is transmitted through the media takes the form of advertising paid for by public funds. This is an aspect of the relationship between government and the media which could potentially compromise the integrity of the media.

A broad and admittedly oversimplified distinction can be made between two categories of government-media interaction. The first category involves the exchange of information largely of a factual nature on the content and administration of government programs. The second category involves an exchange of news and views primarily on political and policy issues. The main actors in the first category are public servants at various levels of the administrative hierarchy, whereas the most important actors in the second category are politicians and senior public servants.

The Media and Public Servants

Most government contacts with the media are handled by public servants who strive to utilize the media to support their political superiors, to publicize their department's activities, to obtain favourable comment on these activities, and to seek public reaction to proposed policies and programs (sometimes in the form of "trial balloons"). Public servants also attempt to keep secret from the media any information that would affect adversely their departments or themselves; and if damaging information is uncovered by the media, public servants usually work to minimize its negative impact. Moreover, the amount and type of information provided by public servants are significantly affected by rules

---

[13] *To Know and Be Known*, vol. 2, p. 50.

and conventions on the confidentiality of government documents and on the bounds of permissible public comment. Public servants must be especially careful not to stray too far over the nebulous line between politics and administration by performing the minister's role of defending or speculating upon public policy.

The media do not perceive their primary function vis-à-vis government as publicizing government activities in a manner designed to please public officials. The media do transmit a great deal of factual material from government to the public, but they serve several other functions in their interactions with government. The media see themselves more as watchdogs of the public interest than as purveyors of government information. They help to set the public agenda by selecting from among the enormous volume of available information those items to which they will give special prominence or continuing attention. They contribute to the development of public policy by subjecting events and personalities to critical analysis through such means as newspaper editorials and television documentaries. They stimulate reform in government by exposing mismanagement, corruption, and illegality. And they make a judgement as to what government-provided information is publicity that merits dissemination and what appears to be propaganda that may be disregarded.

Our earlier discussion of relations between politicians and bureaucrats suggested that media coverage of bureaucratic activities and personalities has diminished somewhat the anonymity of public servants. In addition to assessing the regular activities of public servants, the media have a strong incentive to break through the barriers of government secrecy to get a controversial, dramatic, or exciting story that may involve public servants. The media are, however, subject to such legal restraints on their activities as the Official Secrets Act, the laws of libel, and requirements regarding the revealing of sources of information. Moreover, in Canada, there is not much of a tradition or practice of investigative journalism, especially of the type whereby "crusading" journalists expose and publicize government scandals or mismanagement.

Given the intermediary role of the media between the government and the public, government officials are well advised to develop and preserve cordial relations with both the print and electronic media. They can accomplish this in part by providing material in an appropriate form and at the proper time. Similarly, media representatives can gain the trust and confidence of public officials by "responsible" use of government information. The development of informal relationships based on friendship and long association are also mutually beneficial to the exchange of information. Where political and policy issues are involved, the desire of politicians and bureaucrats to "tell the department's story" may well conflict with the media's desire to tell the whole story. Certain "friendly" journalists may receive preferential treatment in the form of advance notice of upcoming developments, access to public officials, or confidential information. They must be careful, however, that they are not thereby captured and manipulated by public servants.

Much of the impact of the media on public servants is, of course, indirect. Although, as noted earlier, the news media do on occasion focus on the activities of individual public servants, bureaucratic anonymity is still basically intact. Public servants can be greatly affected, however, by news stories dealing in a critical or erroneous way with their departments, or with policies or programs for which they have some responsibility. Care should be taken not to exaggerate the overall influence of the media on the bureaucracy; but the potential influence of the media and its actual influence in particular circumstances help to constrain the exercise of bureaucratic power.

There are few research studies on which to base an assessment of the media's impact on the attitudes and decisions of public servants. The nature and importance of interaction with the media depends on such factors as the public servants' responsibilities, their level in the hierarchy, and their department. Information officers seek to enhance the reputation of their departments through such public relations efforts as providing briefings for journalists and churning out press releases. Senior public servants are anxious to ensure that media coverage of departmental activities does not embarrass their political superiors. Thus, senior bureaucrats who brief ministers for questions in the legislature or from the media monitor news stories so as to anticipate questions that might be asked. For example, news stories in *The Globe and Mail*, *The Financial Post*, and *Le Devoir* are often the basis for questions to ministers in the House of Commons.

FREEDOM OF INFORMATION AND INDIVIDUAL PRIVACY

Freedom of Information

It is widely argued that open access to government information enables the public and the media to make a more informed contribution to government decision making. This issue of access to information is discussed separately here not only because of its importance for relations between the bureaucracy and both the public and the media, but also because of its implications for ministerial responsibility and political neutrality.

The government of Canada has traditionally operated on the principle that all government information is secret unless the government decides to release it. Many proponents of freedom of information legislation contend that this principle should be reversed so that all government information will be released unless the government can make a good case for keeping it secret. Under this latter approach, the burden on the public of justifying requests for the disclosure of information is lifted, and the burden of justifying non-disclosure of information is imposed on the government, specifically on ministers and public servants. The federal Access to Information Act (the ATI Act)[14] permits the government to keep a great deal of information confidential, but in general, the Act follows the second approach. Its stated purpose is

> to provide a right of access to information in records under the control of a
> government in accordance with the principles that government informa-

---

[14]Canada, *Statutes*, 1980–81–82–83, c. 111, Schedule I.

tion should be available to the public, that necessary exceptions to the right of access should be limited and specific and that decisions on the disclosure of government information should be reviewed independently of government.[15]

An important development in the movement towards more openness in Canadian government was the publication in June 1977 of the Liberal government's green paper entitled *Legislation on Public Access to Government Documents*.[16] This green paper contains a brief but quite comprehensive examination of the possible consequences for government of freedom of information legislation. On October 24, 1979, the newly elected Progressive Conservative government introduced Bill C-15 — the Freedom of Information Act. Then, on July 17, 1980, the re-elected Liberal government introduced Bill C-43 — the Access to Information Act, which was passed on July 7, 1982, and came into effect on July 1, 1983.

Ministerial Responsibility and Political Neutrality

Much discussion of freedom of information legislation in both the federal and provincial spheres of government has centred on the issue of whether such legislation would encroach unduly on ministerial responsibility. Somewhat less concern focussed on the possible reduction in the political neutrality and anonymity of public servants.

It is easy to understand why ministers and senior public servants do not share the enthusiasm of persons outside government for freedom of information legislation in general and for access to material on the decision-making process in particular. The release of information revealing ministerial and public service contributions to, and debates over, policy has important consequences for both ministerial responsibility and political neutrality. Documents which disclose disagreement among ministers or between ministers and public servants could be exploited by the government's opponents to the political disadvantage of the ministers. It is natural that ministers should not want to answer to the legislature and the public for the content of documents which are likely to be controversial and which could be kept secret. Ministers do not deliberately seek trouble.

Similarly, senior public servants generally resist the expansion of public access to official documents which lay bare their personal views and values on policy issues. If public servants are drawn into public debate over their contributions to policy development, their anonymity will decline. Moreover, to the extent that the public servants' written advice is at odds with their minister's decision, both ministers and public servants may be publicly embarrassed. Ministers may strive to avoid such situations by surrounding themselves with political appointees or with "yes-men." This will threaten both the frankness and the completeness of departmental advice and also undermine the security of tenure associated with a career in the public service.

---

[15]Ibid.

[16]Honourable John Roberts, Secretary of State, *Legislation on Public Access to Government Documents* (Ottawa: Supply and Services, 1977).

The impact of more open government on the doctrines of ministerial responsibility and political neutrality should not, however, be exaggerated. The evolution of these doctrines that has already occurred has been explained in Chapters 11 and 15. The implementation of freedom of information legislation requires further evolution of these doctrines, but it does not require their drastic alteration or abandonment. The importance of the doctrine of ministerial responsibility in particular will be evident in the following sections on exemptions and the review process. Exemptions refer to classes of information that may or must be kept secret; the review process refers to mechanisms for reconsidering and/or overruling decisions by ministers or public servants not to disclose information.

Exemptions

The subjects of exemptions and review mechanisms are closely related. Judgements on the number and nature of exemptions considered desirable depend to a large extent on the method adopted to review complaints about non-disclosure. If ministers have the final authority to determine whether a particular document falls into an exempted category, they will be inclined to approve legislation providing for a small number of specific exemptions. But if a person or body independent of ministers makes the final determination on exemptions, ministers will likely favour legislation which contains a large number of specific exemptions or a smaller number of very broad exemptions. Thus decisions on the exemptions to be included in the legislation are usually taken in relation to the review mechanisms that will be adopted.

There is much agreement from one government to another that certain types of information should be kept secret, such as documents relating to national defence and security, personal information on individual citizens, financial or commercial information collected by government on a confidential basis, and records on criminal investigations. There is, however, considerable variation among governments in the comprehensiveness of the exclusions within the different classes of information.

In Canada, the exemptions (and exclusions) set out in the ATI Act are substantial. The Act provides, subject to a number of exemptions, that a Canadian citizen, a permanent resident, or a Canadian corporation "has a right to and shall, on request, be given access to any record under the control of a government institution" (section 4). However, records containing information obtained in confidence from a foreign government, an international organization, or a provincial, municipal, or regional government in Canada are exempted from disclosure unless the government or the organization in question agrees to release or permit the release of the records (section 13).

The confidentiality of records may be retained if they "could reasonably be expected to be injurious to the conduct . . . of federal-provincial affairs, including information (a) on federal-provincial consultations or deliberations; or information (b) on strategy or tactics" of the Canadian government bearing on the conduct of federal-provincial affairs (section 14). Very broad exemption is provided also for information which, if disclosed, "could reasonably be expected to be injurious to the conduct of international affairs, the defence of Canada or any state allied or associated with Canada or the detection, prevention or suppression of subversive or hostile activities" (section 15).

In addition, records may be exempted from disclosure if they contain information relating to law enforcement and investigation (section 16), or if their release might threaten the safety of individuals (section 17), or affect adversely the financial interests of Canada (section 18). Records are also exempted if they contain personal information (section 19), or if they contain trade secrets, financial, commercial, scientific, or technical information which if disclosed could harm a third party (that is, firms and corporations) (section 20).

Some exemptions and some specific *exclusions* in the Act reflect the concern of ministers and public servants about the preservation of ministerial responsibility and public service anonymity. Exemptions include advice developed by or for a government institution or Cabinet minister, an account of consultations involving public servants and a Cabinet minister (or a Cabinet minister's staff), plans developed for negotiations conducted by the government, and plans bearing on personnel management or the administration of a government institution that have not yet been put into operation (section 21). *Exclusions* from disclosure relate to "confidences of the Queen's Privy Council for Canada" (that is, the Cabinet). The excluded documents include Cabinet memoranda; discussion papers prepared for Cabinet; Cabinet agendas or records of Cabinet deliberations or decisions; records relating to consultation among ministers in respect of government decisions and policies; records used to brief ministers on these decisions and policies; and draft legislation (section 69). These exclusions do not apply to "confidences" more than twenty years old; discussion papers relating to decisions which have been made public; and all other discussion papers more that four years old (section 69).

The length and breadth of the exemptions and exclusions in the Act have been severely criticized by many segments of the Canadian public. Thus, the review mechanism established to make the final decision on the exemptions is a critically important component of the ATI Act. Before examining the review process, however, it is an enlightening experience to play the party game called "Airplane." This game has been utilized by Canada's Information Commissioner to explain to students that, although in the abstract they may strongly favour unlimited access to government information, they may in practice see some virtue in the Act's exemptions. The scenario for the game is as follows:

> An airplane skidded off the runway; the passengers were unhurt save for one who died, apparently from a heart attack. For some unknown reason the passengers were left incommunicado at the airport under police protection.
>
> Students are assigned to play the following roles: an arms dealer who holds a new patent on a weapon sought by many governments; a diplomat known to be engaged in high level peace negotiations; an aging actress and her lover, a well-known sex symbol; an RCMP officer who is escorting a prisoner-informer being taken to protective custody in another penitentiary; a student who was supposed to be at class; a Minister of Transport; a

Solicitor General; a commissioner of the RCMP; the Information Commissioner; and a representative of the estate of the dead person. Finally, someone plays the journalist who is assigned to the story and must obtain the passenger list under the Access to Information Act.[17]

The Information Commissioner notes that "it is amazing how quickly [students] become protective of their characters," and that "it soon becomes clear that freedom of information invariably involves disclosure of information, collected by someone else, affecting yet another person's interests."[18] This game demonstrates well the need to balance the public's right to know with the individual's right to privacy. In addition to the provisions in the ATI Act exempting personal information from disclosure, individual privacy is protected by the Privacy Act, discussed later in this chapter.

The Review Process

Initially, the task of applying the exemption provisions to requests for access to government documents is performed by public servants. However, instances arise where citizens wish to appeal to a higher authority against a public servant's decision to deny access to all or part of certain documents. Thus, freedom of information legislation must provide a review process which specifies the person or persons with authority to review the decisions of public servants.

Experience in Canada suggests that ministers and public servants tend to favour a review process in which ministers have ultimate authority to decide whether a particular document will be released. However, persons outside government tend to prefer a review mechanism which allows ministerial decisions on access to be overruled. The green paper noted that the ideal review process would be characterized not only by speed, efficiency, and minimal cost, but also by public credibility and consistency with ministerial responsibility. The difficulty facing the drafters of public access legislation is that the latter two attributes may be incompatible. The challenge in drafting freedom of information legislation is to devise a mechanism which will satisfy the public in terms of credibility, but which will not infringe unduly on ministerial responsibility. The major choice is between two categories of review mechanism:

1. those which confer final authority on a minister; and
2. those which bestow final authority on a person, body, or institution other than a minister.

Among the review mechanisms proposed for the federal government were Parliament, an information auditor, an ombudsman, an information commissioner with advisory powers, an information commissioner with powers to order disclosure, and judicial review.[19] The latter two mechanisms received the most serious consideration because, unlike the other options, they allowed for minis-

---

[17]See Office of the Information Commissioner, *Annual Report, 1983–1984* (Ottawa: Supply and Services, 1984), p. 3.
[18]Ibid.
[19]For an explanation of these, see ibid.

terial decisions to be overruled. Most persons who were willing to have ministerial decisions reversed by an independent review mechanism favoured judicial review. This preference can be explained in part by the experience of Sweden and the United States with review by the courts. An equally important consideration was a widespread lack of confidence in the willingness of ministers to permit adequate access to official information. It is evident also that a freedom of information act that permits citizens to appeal to the courts tends to inspire a higher measure of public confidence in the Act. However, a system of judicial review alone removes all control from the minister. Therefore, it is not surprising that a hybrid system was adopted.

The system adopted for the ATI Act is a *two-tier* review mechanism involving an Information Commissioner *and* judicial review. Under the Act, the Information Commissioner, who describes herself as "a statutory ombudsman,"[20] is authorized to receive and investigate complaints when access to a record is refused; when unreasonable fees are imposed for searching for or producing a record; where a public official unreasonably extends the time limit for producing a record; when a record is not provided in the official language requested; and "in respect of any other matter relating to requesting or obtaining access to records" under the Act. The commissioner may also initiate a complaint on "reasonable grounds." After investigating a complaint, the commissioner recommends whether or not a record should be released; he or she cannot require that a record be disclosed. Following the commissioner's investigation, the complainant, or the commissioner with the complainant's consent, may apply to the Federal Court for review of any refusal to disclose a record. The court may then order the head of a government institution to disclose — or not to disclose — all or part of a record.

Implementation of the Access to Information Act

Persons seeking information under the Act must write to the appropriate department and must identify as precisely as possible the information they require. Assistance in this regard is available in the *Access Register*, which contains a description of the records held by each department. Copies of the register and of access request forms can be obtained in public libraries and government information offices in major population centres, as well as in about 2,000 postal stations in rural areas. Each department has an access coordinator to assist applicants to identify the records required. The department has thirty days either to produce the information requested or to provide reasons why a request has been denied. If the request is for a large number of records or is complicated, the department can extend the time limit, but must inform the applicant of the situation. The role of the Information Commissioner and the Federal Court in cases where access to information is denied was described earlier. An application fee of five dollars must accompany each request for information. Applicants must also pay for any time in excess of five hours spent in processing a request and for copying and computer-processing time.

---

[20]Office of the Information Commissioner, *Annual Report, 1984–1985* (Ottawa: Supply and Services, 1985).

During the first nine months of the Act's operation, government institutions received 1,520 requests for information. Twenty-one institutions received 81 per cent of the requests. The number of requests made to these institutions ranged from 141 for the RCMP, 112 for the Department of National Revenue, and 106 for the Department of National Health and Welfare, down to 29 for the Department of Finance, 28 for the Department of Agriculture, and 27 for the Department of Public Works.[21]

In the cases where applicants received none or only part of the information they requested, by far the most frequent reasons for denying access were that the records contained confidential business information, information about another person, or "advice or recommendations, accounts of consultations or deliberations, plans of positions for negotiations or unimplemented management plans."[22]

During the same nine-month period, the Office of the Information Commissioner received 150 complaints[23] (about 8.5 per cent of the requests processed by government institutions). More than half of the 46 complaints investigated by the end of the period arose from a refusal to disclose all or some of the information requested. The commissioner found that about a third of these complaints were well founded and resulted in remedial action by the government institution involved. The remainder were dismissed by the commissioner, abandoned or taken care of without any action on the part of the commissioner or any government institution.[24]

A widely held view among proponents of freedom of information legislation is that it will gradually change the attitude of ministers and public servants towards public access to official information. It has been suggested also that government officials will become more supportive of open government when they realize that it has more benefits and fewer disadvantages than they anticipated.

The Leaking of Confidential Information

The exemption or exclusion from disclosure of certain classes of information provides both opportunity and motivation for the unauthorized disclosure (commonly called "leaking") of confidential information. Such disclosure normally involves leaks of government documents, often enclosed in plain brown envelopes, to the media or to Opposition members of the legislature. Beginning in the early 1970s, there has been a seemingly unprecedented number of leaks, especially from the federal government. Since 1983, these leaks have, of course, been largely confined to material that remains confidential under the Access to Information Act. Confidential information is sometimes leaked by public servants who believe that they are acting in the public interest, but information is

---

[21]Information Policy Section, Administrative Policy Branch, Treasury Board Secretariat, August 1, 1984.

[22]Ibid., p. 3.

[23]Office of the Information Commissioner, *Annual Report, 1983–1984* (Ottawa: Supply and Services, 1984).

[24]The pattern and disposition of complaints received during the following reporting year were roughly similar. See Office of the Information Commissioner, *Annual Report, 1984–1985*.

also leaked for reasons unrelated to a search for the public interest (e.g., vindictiveness, partisan politics). Moreover, some of this information is leaked not by bureaucrats, but by Cabinet ministers trying to float trial balloons on policy issues.

The unauthorized disclosure of confidential information is constrained by a variety of statutes and regulations. The most severe instrument is the Official Secrets Act, which is intended to combat espionage by providing up to fourteen years in prison for persons who disclose secret information to foreign powers. Offences under this Act are rare, and its penalties are too harsh for comparatively minor offences in the sphere of confidentiality. However, employees are required to take an oath of office and secrecy by which they swear (or affirm) that they will not, without proper authorization, make known any confidential matter that comes to their knowledge. In situations where the duties of a position involve the handling of classified material or access to it, a security clearance may be required for all candidates seeking that position.

Provincial public servants are also subject to the Official Secrets Act and are required to take an oath of office and secrecy. Moreover, certain departments in both orders of government are specifically required by statute to preserve the confidentiality of certain information. For example, provincial taxing and assessment statutes generally provide penalties for the disclosure of confidential information to persons not legally entitled to receive it.

In practice, it is very difficult to pinpoint and discipline public servants who have surreptitiously disclosed confidential information, and the practice is therefore an effective and usually risk-free method by which bureaucrats can oppose government policy or expose what they believe to be government abuse, negligence, or corruption. The penalty for those who are caught is uncertain, but it can be severe. For example, in 1985, a senior employee of the federal Department of Indian Affairs and Northern Development, who allegedly leaked a confidential document describing the Conservative government's plans to cut costs on Indian programs, was dismissed and charged with breach of trust under the Criminal Code — an offence that carries a maximum sentence of five years' imprisonment. The criminal charge was subsequently withdrawn, but the dismissal was not.[25]

Individual Privacy

Concern for individual privacy is the other side of the coin from concern about access to information. Indeed, the Privacy Act[26] and the Access to Information Act came into effect on the same day — July 1, 1983. The Privacy Act replaces and expands on the protection to individual privacy previously provided in the Canadian Human Rights Act. Individual privacy is protected by restricting access to personal information held by the federal government on Canadian citizens and permanent residents. The Act contains principles of fair information practices which direct government institutions to limit their collection of informa-

---

[25]See *The Globe and Mail*, September 7, 1985, p. 5.
[26]Canada, *Statutes*, 1980-81-82-83, c. 111, Schedule II.

tion to what is needed to do their work; if possible, to gather the information directly from the individuals concerned; and to inform the individuals what use is to be made of the information. In addition, individuals have the right to see all information which the government has on them in its roughly 2,200 federal personal information banks. Copies of the Personal Information Index, which describes the activities of each department, what kind of information it collects, and whom to contact for access, are available in public libraries and post offices across Canada.

A Privacy Commissioner is appointed under the Act to initiate complaints on his or her own initiative and to investigate complaints from individuals who believe that their privacy rights have been denied. Grounds for complaint include denial of some or all of the information requested, denial of the right to correct or annotate some of the information on one's file, and use of information which contravenes the Act. The commissioner describes himself both as "a specialized ombudsman for privacy, the single voice in the federal government with a mandate to speak on behalf of privacy rights," and as an auditor responsible for determining "whether personal information is collected, held by, and disposed of by federal government institutions" according to the Act.[27]

During the period from April 1, 1985, to March 31, 1986, government agencies received about 36,000 applications regarding access to personal information. During the same twelve-month period, the Office of the Privacy Commissioner completed work on 401 complaints regarding the denial of privacy rights; 221 of these complaints were found to be justified.[28]

Two major criticisms of the Act have been made. First, 19 of the approximately 2,200 personal information banks are "exempt" in that individuals cannot have access to their files, if any, in these banks. Among these closed files are the RCMP's criminal operational intelligence records and Revenue Canada's customs intelligence records. Second, some provinces have made very broad claims for confidentiality under the provision of the Act that exempts from disclosure information that was obtained in confidence from a provincial government. The challenge is to "strike an appropriate balance between the individual's right to know and the state's right to withhold information in the national interest."[29]

Information and Privacy Legislation in the Provinces

Several provincial governments have enacted freedom of information or privacy acts, or both.[30] The government of Nova Scotia, with the enactment of its Freedom of Information Act[31] in 1977, was the first government in the Com-

---

[27] Office of the Privacy Commissioner, *Annual Report, 1983–1984* (Ottawa: Supply and Services, 1984), pp. 2, 7.

[28] Office of the Privacy Commissioner, *Annual Report, 1985–1986* (Ottawa: Supply and Services, 1986), p. 26.

[29] Ibid., p. 10.

[30] The Ontario Government's Freedom of Information and Protection of Privacy Act (Bill 34) received second reading in the legislature in the spring of 1986.

[31] *Statutes*, Nova Scotia, 1977, c. 10.

monwealth to make access to information a legal right. This Act also makes provision for the protection of privacy. The New Brunswick Right to Information Act,[32] which was adopted in 1978 and came into force in 1980, is especially notable for its review mechanism. An individual who has been denied access to information by a minister may appeal the minister's decision either to the provincial ombudsman or to a judge of the Supreme Court. The ombudsman can only *recommend* to the minister that the information be released, whereas the judge can *order* its release. Moreover, if an individual is not satisfied with the minister's response to the ombudsman's recommendation, he or she can still appeal the minister's decision to a Supreme Court judge.

The most comprehensive provincial statute in this area is the Quebec Act on Access to Documents held by Public Bodies and the Protection of Personal Privacy,[33] which was enacted in 1982 and came into effect in stages between 1982 and 1984. An Access to Information Commission, headed by a chairperson and two other commissioners, was created to enforce the Act and to serve as a court to settle disputes between the government and the citizens on matters of access to information and individual privacy. The Act applies to more than 3,500 government administrative units, including departments, agencies, Crown corporations, *municipalities, and private and public educational institutions.*

CONCLUDING OBSERVATIONS

Although participative mechanisms are still at a rudimentary stage in Canada, advocates of public participation have grounds for optimism. The opportunities for participation incorporated into many of the formal mechanisms for government decision making are unlikely to be withdrawn. There is, therefore, reasonable promise that participative mechanisms will be expanded and refined and that public input into the policy process will be further enhanced.

In addition, the gradual movement towards greater openness at all levels of Canadian government through the enactment of freedom of information legislation helps to ensure that *public* participation is *informed* participation. At the same time, legislative measures are being taken to maintain the privacy of information held by the government on individual citizens. In the Canadian context, legislation on these two matters is very recent; we can, therefore, expect that this legislation will be modified and refined on the basis of experience with its implementation and new advances in information technology.

---

[32]New Brunswick, *Statutes*, 1978, c. R-10.3.
[33]Quebec, *Statutes*, 1982, c. 30.

BIBLIOGRAPHY

Altshuler, Alan. *Community Control*. Washington, D.C.: Urban Institute, 1970.

Arnstein, Sherry R. "A Ladder to Citizen Participation." *Journal of the American Institute of Planners*, vol. 35 (July 1969): 216-224.

Black, E. R. *Politics and the News*. Toronto: Butterworths, 1982.

Bryden, Kenneth. "Public Input into Policy-Making and Administration." *Canadian Public Administration*, vol. 25 (Spring 1982): 81-107.

Canada. Hon. John Roberts, Secretary of State. *Legislation on Public Access to Government Documents*. Ottawa: Supply and Services, June 1977.

Canada. *To Know and Be Known*. Report of the Task Force on Government Information. Ottawa: Queen's Printer, 1969.

Doerr, Audrey. "The Role of Coloured Papers." *Canadian Public Administration*, vol. 25 (Fall 1982): 366-379.

Draper, James A., ed. *Citizen Participation: Canada*. Toronto: New Press, 1971.

Fletcher, Frederick J. *The Newspaper and Public Affairs*. Research Study no. 7 for the Royal Commission on Newspapers. Ottawa: 1981.

Fox, David. *Public Participation in the Administrative Process*. Study paper for the Law Reform Commission of Canada. Ottawa: Supply and Services, 1979.

Fox, Larry. *Freedom of Information and the Administrative Process*. Toronto: Ontario Royal Commission on Freedom of Information and Individual Privacy, Research Study no. 10, 1979.

Galnoor, I., ed. *Government Secrecy in Democracies*. New York: Harper and Row, 1977.

Government of Ontario. *Citizen Participation: A Working Paper*. Toronto: Committee on Government Productivity, 1971.

Kernaghan, Kenneth. *Freedom of Information and Ministerial Responsibility*. Toronto: Ontario Royal Commission on Freedom of Information and Individual Privacy, Research Study no. 2, 1978.

Knight, K. W. "Administrative Secrecy and Ministerial Responsibility." *Canadian Journal of Economics and Political Science*, vol. 32 (February 1966): 77-84.

Kroeker, H. V. *Sovereign People or Sovereign Governments*. Montreal: Institute for Research on Public Policy, 1981.

Lotz, Jim. "Citizen Participation: Myths and Realities." *Optimum*, vol. 5 (1974): 53-60.

Lotz, Jim. "Public Hearings — For Confrontation or Dialogue?" *Optimum*, vol. 9 (1978): 5-12.

McDonald, Virginia. "Participation in the Canadian Context." *Queen's Quarterly*, vol. 84 (1977): 457-475.

McNiven, J. D. "Bureaucratic Imperatives and Citizen Access: Some Theoretical Possibilities." *Optimum*, vol. 7 (1976): 22-32.

Meisel, John. "Citizen Demands and Government Response." *Canadian Public Policy*, vol. 11 (Autumn 1976): 564-576.

Mishler, William. *Political Participation in Canada*. Toronto: Macmillan, 1979.

Rankin, T. Murray. *Freedom of Information in Canada: Will the Doors Stay Shut?* Ottawa: Canadian Bar Association, 1979.

Robertson, Gordon. "Confidentiality in Government." *Archivaria*, no. 6 (Summer 1978): 3–15.

Rowat, Donald C., ed. *Administrative Secrecy in Developed Countries*. New York: Columbia University Press, 1979.

Rowat, Donald C. "How Much Administrative Secrecy?" *Canadian Journal of Economics and Political Science*, vol. 31 (November 1965): 479–498.

Rowat, Donald C. "The Right of Public Access to Official Documents." In O. P. Dwivedi, ed. *The Administrative State in Canada*. Toronto: University of Toronto Press, 1982, pp. 177–192.

Siegel, Arthur. *Politics and the Mass Media in Canada*. Toronto: McGraw-Hill Ryerson, 1983.

Smiley, D. V. *The Freedom of Information Issue: A Political Analysis*. Toronto: Ontario Royal Commission on Freedom of Information and Individual Privacy, Research Study no. 1, 1978.

Sproule-Jones, Mark. "A Description and Explanation of Citizen Participation in a Canadian Municipality." *Public Choice*, vol. 17 (Spring 1974): 73–83.

Thayer, Frederick C. *Participation and Liberal Democratic Government*. Toronto: Committee on Government Productivity, 1971.

Wronski, W. "The Public Servant and Protest Groups." *Canadian Public Administration*, vol. 14 (Spring 1971): 65–72.

CASES

In *Case Program in Canadian Public Administration* (Toronto: Institute of Public Administration of Canada):

Closing the Baldwin Hospital, by Harold B. Wodinsky, Marsha Barnes, and Raisa B. Deber

Screening the Boat People? Case Studies in Health Policies, by Peter Owen, Peggy Purvis, and Raisa B. Deber

All Things to All People: Government and Its Client Groups, by Sharon Bider and Peter McNaughton

La politique du transport urbain dans la région de Québec, by Louise Quenel-Ouellet and Gilles Bouchard

The Development Dilemma: The Case of Quinpool Road, by Katherine A. Graham in conjunction with E. Grant MacDonald and T. J. Plunkett

20

Administrative
Values and Ethics

The value framework in Chapter 10 singled out certain administrative values as central to the evolution of public administration in Canada. The primary administrative values were identified as neutrality, accountability, efficiency, effectiveness, responsiveness, representativeness, and integrity. In this chapter, each value is discussed separately, but representativeness and integrity are given lengthier treatment because they receive comparatively little consideration elsewhere in the book.

ADMINISTRATIVE VALUES

Neutrality
The value system of the individual bureaucrat is central to an analysis of bureaucratic behaviour because bureaucrats cannot be completely value neutral in making important decisions. As noted in Chapter 11, bureaucrats usually abstain from partisan conflicts. They are, however, actively involved in politics in the broad sense of participation in the authoritative allocation of values for society. The role of bureaucrats in the contemporary political process is important in large part because they are not value neutral. They possess power both to make and to influence decisions with significant consequences for individual and corporate citizens. Bureaucrats are not neutral instruments of political masters. They may feel responsible to a variety of political actors other than those to whom they are accountable in the legal or hierarchical sense. Bureaucrats have never been value neutral, and they have become less so as their discretionary powers have increased.

In the exercise of their advisory and decision-making powers, bureaucrats are, of course, expected to act within a policy context determined by their political superiors. Where they have full discretion to make decisions, they are expected to anticipate the reactions of their ministers by making decisions which they believe the ministers would like them to make. The difficulty of ensuring such bureaucratic behaviour helps to explain the importance of accountability.

Accountability
The quest for administrative accountability, then, arises largely from the fact that bureaucrats are not value neutral. As discussed earlier, accountability involves concern for the legal, institutional, and procedural means by which bureaucrats can be obliged to answer for their actions. It has been a recurring theme throughout this book, both because it has been one of the major values

441

in the development of Canadian public administration and because of its current importance.[1] Indeed, the present emphasis on accountability threatens to minimize unduly the significance of such other administrative values as effectiveness and responsiveness.

This emphasis is a result not only of the need to strengthen accountability in government; it is also a result of the very broad interpretations which the word accountability has gradually acquired. For example, the Royal Commission on Financial Management and Accountability (the Lambert Commission) viewed accountability as "the activating, but fragile, element permeating a complex network connecting the government upward to Parliament and downward and outward to a geographically dispersed bureaucracy grouped in a bewildering array of departments, corporations, boards and commissions."[2] This definition portrays well the breadth of meaning currently given to the notion of accountability in government. It is, however, too sweeping a definition to be very useful in operational terms; moreover, it covers the accountability of both politicians and bureaucrats, whereas our primary concern is with public service accountability. A more narrow and, for our purposes, a more useful definition of accountability is "the obligation of public servants to be answerable for fulfilling responsibilities that flow from the authority given them . . . . Internal accountability holds public servants answerable to their line superiors for their own actions and the actions of their subordinates . . . . External accountability holds public servants answerable to the public as well. The normal channel through which this requirement is satisfied is the minister."[3]

This definition draws attention to the critical fact that public servants in the federal and provincial governments are directly accountable only to a limited number of political actors, and that to hold public servants accountable, one must be able to exercise authority over them. Indeed, a more useful distinction than that between internal and external accountability is that between direct and indirect accountability. Public servants are directly accountable only to political and administrative superiors, to the courts, and to any internal governmental authorities (e.g., central agencies) to which accountability is required by law or the administrative hierarchy. They are not directly accountable to the legislature, to pressure groups, to the news media, or the general public. However, they are generally required to explain their decisions and actions to these entities, and they may feel a sense of psychological or personal responsibility towards them.

It bears repeating that accountability has long been associated with the notion of administrative responsibility. In fact, there is substantial agreement in the

---

[1]For an account of efforts and problems connected with the pursuit of administrative accountability in the Canadian context, see O. P. Dwivedi, "On Holding Public Servants Accountable," and R. W. Phidd, "The Administrative State and the Limits of Rationality," in O. P. Dwivedi, ed., *The Administrative State in Canada* (Toronto: University of Toronto Press, 1982), pp. 151-176 and pp. 233-250 respectively.

[2]Government of Canada, Royal Commission on Financial Management and Accountability, *Report* (Ottawa: Supply and Services, 1979), p. 9.

[3]Adapted from Government of Ontario, Management Board of Cabinet, *Accountability*, OPS Management Series (Toronto: Queen's Printer, 1982).

public administration literature that accountability is very similar in meaning to the notion of *objective* responsibility, which is one of the two major types of administrative responsibility discussed in Chapter 12. Objective responsibility is the responsibility which public servants have to political and/or administrative superiors who can penalize them for failing to fulfil legitimate directives. The other type of administrative responsibility, which is variously described as subjective, psychological, or personal responsibility, is the responsibility which public servants *feel* towards other participants in the political system.

Enforcing accountability for the exercise of bureaucratic power has become increasingly difficult as our public services have continued to grow in size and as their responsibilities have grown in complexity. The decision-making process in government is often so lengthy and complicated that it is difficult to single out those public servants who should be held accountable for specific recommendations and decisions. Moreover, as explained in Chapter 15, the present application of the doctrine of ministerial responsibility does not ensure that ministers will be held responsible for maladministration in their departments.

Another obstacle on the road to accountability is the wide range of authorities to which public servants are deemed to be accountable. While, in general, it is agreed that public servants are accountable first of all to their minister, in practice public servants receive directions, rewards, and penalties from a variety of sources. This is one of the major differences between public and private sector administration.

Federal and provincial governments have an impressive array of mechanisms to promote administrative accountability.[4] Reforms over the past two decades have included the restructuring of the Cabinet committee system (e.g., the use of policy committees with substantial decision-making powers); an expansion in the number and size of central agencies (e.g., Cabinet secretariats, treasury and management boards, and intergovernmental relations units); changes in the legislative committee system (e.g., new committees and revised procedures); strengthening the role of auditors and adopting a comprehensive auditing system; establishing the Federal Court to hear appeals against administrative decisions; and changing the structures and operations of regulatory agencies and Crown corporations.

Efficiency and Effectiveness

Despite the current concern with accountability, the most consistently dominant value in Canadian public administration over the broad sweep of the twentieth century has been efficiency. Moreover, much of the emphasis on accountability has really been directed to holding public bureaucrats accountable for the efficient and effective use of public funds. The values of efficiency and effectiveness are interdependent, but distinct in meaning. *Efficiency* is a measure of performance which may be expressed as a ratio between input and output. Effectiveness is a measure of the extent to which an activity achieves the organiza-

---

[4]See Audrey D. Doerr, *The Machinery of Government in Canada* (Toronto: Methuen, 1981), and Marsha A. Chandler and William M. Chandler, *Public Policy and Provincial Politics* (Toronto: McGraw-Hill Ryerson, 1979).

tion's objectives. Thus, efficiency and effectiveness may complement one another but they may also conflict. For example, the construction of a thousand houses for native people at an appropriate cost and quality and on schedule may be an efficient and effective operation. The completion of these houses long after they are needed is efficient, but ineffective. The timely construction of adequate homes at very high cost is effective, but inefficient.

There has been increasing emphasis, especially since the late 1960s, on the so-called three E's — economy, efficiency, and effectiveness. During this period, however, effectiveness has gradually superceded economy as the major companion value of efficiency. Treasury Board has been the prime mover since the late 1960s in promoting efficiency and effectiveness throughout the public service. The board has supported the introduction of more sophisticated techniques of achieving and assessing efficiency and effectiveness, including the planning-programming-budgeting system, cost-benefit analysis, the operational performance measurement system, management by objectives and program evaluation. The Office of the Comptroller General, which was established in 1978, has the responsibility of developing systems to stimulate the efficiency and effectiveness of government operations, in part by designing and promoting procedures for program evaluation. Moreover, the Auditor General's Act of 1977[5] broadens the Auditor General's powers to include reporting on instances where money has been spent without "due regard to economy or efficiency," or where "satisfactory procedures have not been established to measure and report the effectiveness of programs, where such procedures could appropriately and reasonably be implemented." Elaboration on the role of these various managerial techniques and administrative organizations in relation to the pursuit of efficiency and effectiveness is provided in Chapter 24 on the management of financial resources.

Responsiveness

Administrative responsiveness refers to the inclination and the capacity of public servants to respond to the needs and demands of political institutions and of the public. Thus, public servants are expected to be responsive to two major sets of participants in the political system. The first set includes political executives and legislators; the second set includes the general public as well as various "publics," that is, groups and individuals affected by the decisions and recommendations of public servants.

Administrative responsiveness is usually discussed in relation to the second set of participants. The Royal Commission on Government Organization (the Glassco Commission) concluded that "the importance to the public of efficiency and integrity in the machinery of government . . . is unquestionably great. . . . But even greater is the importance of a service responsive to public wants and expectations."[6] As noted in Chapter 19, a major purpose of the movement for increased

---

[5]Canada, *Statutes*, 1976–1977, c. 34.
[6]Canada, Royal Commission on Government Organization, *Report* (Ottawa: Queen's Printer, 1962), vol. 1, p. 63.

public participation is greater government responsiveness, especially by public servants, to the public's wants and needs. However, the public service acts as an intermediary between elected representatives, particularly Cabinet ministers, and the public. Public servants are required to respond to the demands of political superiors, rather than those of the public. Thus, apparent unresponsiveness to citizens' demands may stem from a need to be responsive to politicians' demands. Public servants may be required to reconcile responsiveness with such other values as accountability and efficiency. For example, the emphasis on these latter two values during times of financial restraint in government is usually to the detriment of administrative responsiveness to the public.

The responsiveness of public servants depends significantly on the strength of the commitment of political leaders and public servants to open government. Easy access to information enables the public to make a more informed contribution to government decision making. Moreover, public access to such information encourages public servants to consider policy in terms of its impact on the citizenry, and thereby tends to stimulate them to be more responsive to public needs and expectations. Thus, administrative responsiveness can be considerably enhanced by freedom of information acts and by an overall government commitment to open communications with the news media and the public at large.

The new and modified participative mechanisms discussed in Chapter 19 have improved the capacity of public servants to respond to popular sentiments. However, administrative responsiveness depends not only on the public servants' capacity to respond through formal mechanisms; it also depends on their inclination to respond, whether through formal or informal means. A genuine dedication to responsiveness, complemented by more open government, can help to increase public confidence in government and to improve the public's image of the public service.

Representativeness

The Meaning of Representative Bureaucracy

The values of responsiveness and representativeness are closely related in that the argument is frequently made that a more representative public service is a more responsive public service. This argument will be explored here in the context of a discussion of representative bureaucracy.

Representative bureaucracy is a tricky concept, and it has been interpreted in a variety of ways.[7] A strict interpretation of representative bureaucracy would

---

[7]For an examination of the theory of representative bureaucracy and of its inadequacies, see V. Subramaniam, "Representative Bureaucracy: A Reassessment," *American Political Science Review*, vol. 61 (December, 1967), pp. 1010–1019; Arthur D. Larson, "Representative Bureaucracy and Administrative Responsibility: A Reassessment," *Midwest Review of Public Administration*, vol. 7 (April 1973), pp. 78–89; Kenneth John Meier, "Representative Bureaucracy: An Empirical Analysis," *American Political Science Review*, vol. 69 (June 1965), pp. 526–542; and V. Seymour Wilson and Willard A. Mullins, "Representative Bureaucracy: Linguistic/Ethnic Aspects in Canadian Public Policy," *Canadian Public Administration*, vol. 21 (Winter 1978), pp. 513–538.

require that the public service be a microcosm of the total society in terms of a wide range of variables, including race, religion, education, social class, and region of origin. However, there is disagreement in academic writings as to what purposes representative bureaucracy serves, what degree of representativeness is desirable, and what variables should be included. Proponents of representative bureaucracy recommend its adoption on the following grounds:

1. Public servants exercise significant power in the political system.
2. External controls over public servants by the political executive, the legislature, and the courts are inadequate to check administrative power and so to ensure administrative responsibility.
3. A public service which is representative of the total population will be responsive to the needs and interests of the general public and will therefore be more responsible. This central proposition of the theory of representative bureaucracy is based on several subpropositions:
   (a) If the values of the public service as a whole are similar to those of the total population, then the public service will tend to make the kind of decisions which the public would make if it were involved in the decision making.
   (b) The values of public servants are moulded by the pattern of socialization they experience before they enter the public service, that is, by such socializing forces as education, social class, occupational background, race, family and group associations.
   (c) The values arising from this socialization will not be modified by prolonged exposure to bureaucratic values.
   (d) The values arising from socialization will be reflected in the behaviour of public servants and therefore in their recommendations and decisions.
   (e) Thus, the various groups in the population should be represented in the public service in approximate demographic proportion so that public servants will be responsive to their interests both in policy development and program delivery.

Critics of representative bureaucracy acknowledge the extensive power of public servants and the consequent need to provide controls to preserve and promote administrative responsibility. They contend, however, that the assertion that external controls are inadequate to ensure responsible administrative conduct requires more investigation. These critics also point to the logical and empirical failings of the theory of representative bureaucracy.

They contend first of all that in a representative public service the values of the public service *as a whole* will not be similar to those of the general population; rather, the values of *individual* public servants *may* be similar to the values of those groups in the population they are supposed to represent. Moreover, the public service as a whole does not make decisions; rather, decisions are made by individual public servants who, by acting on behalf of groups whom they represent, would serve the interests of particular segments of the public rather than the total population. Also, it is not sufficient for the public service as a whole to be broadly representative of the total population; for all interests to be represented in the decision-making process, each major administrative unit must be representative of the total population, especially at its senior levels where the most important recommendations and decisions are made.

Opponents of representative bureaucracy observe further that a public servant with certain social and educational origins will not necessarily share the values of persons outside the public service who have similar origins. The life-long process of socialization continues after entry to the public service, in the form of resocialization to the values of the service as a whole or of particular administrative units. Moreover, representatives of a specific group in the population, particularly if they achieve high office in the public service, are likely to be upwardly mobile and may well share the socio-economic and other values of those with whom they work, rather than of the group from which they came. In this regard, Peta Sheriff regrets the lack of research on the strength of pre-occupational and post-occupational experience, and concludes that although "the very cornerstone of the representative bureaucracy thesis has no direct evidence to support it . . . the suspicion that pre-occupational socialization must have some influence is sufficient to maintain the thesis."[8] However, even if public servants continue to share the values of certain groups despite organizational socialization, these values may not be significantly reflected in the public servants' behaviour.

Thus, it is logically possible to have a representative public service which is not responsive, and a responsive public service which is not representative. Indeed, Meier and Nigro conclude that the most senior levels in the United States public service "are an unrepresentative demographic group holding quite representative attitudes."[9]

Canadian Writings

The major points of contention in a thought-provoking debate on representative bureaucracy in Canada[10] involve the extent to which the values of efficiency, effectiveness, neutrality, and responsiveness conflict with that of representativeness. In this debate, Donald Rowat objects to John Porter's sacrifice of representativeness for the sake of efficiency and suggests that both values can be achieved. He argues that representativeness "is essential to the efficiency of the bureaucracy, in the sense of the latter's effectiveness in a democratic, pluralistic society."[11] Porter asserts that persons of various social origins will be found in the bureaucracy in roughly the same proportion as in the population as a whole *if* government recruitment and promotion policies do not discriminate against particular groups, *if* educational facilities to qualify persons for public service appointments are equal as between these groups, and *if* these groups are equally motivated to join the public service. He contends that "in the theoretically ideal

---

[8]Peta E. Sheriff, "Unrepresentative Bureaucracy," *Sociology*, vol. 8 (1974), p. 449.

[9]Kenneth John Meier and Lloyd C. Nigro, "Representative Bureaucracy and Policy Preferences: A Study in the Attitudes of Federal Executives," *Public Administration Review*, vol. 36 (July–August 1976), p. 467.

[10]John Porter, "Higher Public Servants and the Bureaucratic Elite in Canada," *Canadian Journal of Economics and Political Science*, vol. 24 (November 1958), pp. 483–501; Donald C. Rowat, "On John Porter's Bureaucratic Elite in Canada," ibid., vol. 25 (May 1959), pp. 204–207; and John Porter, "The Bureaucratic Elite: A Reply to Professor Rowat," ibid., vol. 25 (May 1959), pp. 207–209.

[11]Rowat, p. 204.

bureaucracy, the candidate for office neither gains nor loses as a result of eth-nic, religious or regional origins."[12]

Rowat, who is more concerned with what can be realized in practice than with a search for a theoretically ideal bureaucracy, observes that Porter's condi-tions of equality do not exist and cannot be easily achieved. He contends that representativeness must be actively sought — even at the expense of technical effi-ciency and neutrality. Intelligent persons with the potential to rise to higher levels in the service could be recruited and provided with the required in-service education and training. Moreover, competent members of underrepresented groups could be brought into the public service from outside. Porter opposes the recruitment of outsiders on the grounds that this practice threatens the neu-trality of the service and the concept of the bureaucratic career. He states that "since the basis of power associations are frequently ethnic, regional or reli-gious, the idea that these groups should be represented in the bureaucracy con-tradicts the notion of the official as the servant of the state."[13] Rowat does not agree that the appointment of "bureaucratic outsiders" would endanger politi-cal neutrality, and he argues that a public service which complemented career public servants with outsiders would be more responsive, since a career bureau-cracy tends to "lose contact with and lack understanding of the changing feel-ings, needs and desires of the great variety of people and groups found in our dynamic, pluralistic society."[14]

Rowat does not suggest that underrepresented groups should be represented in *precise* proportion to their presence in the total population, and he rejects the use of quotas for recruitment and promotion as unworkable. He does sug-gest, however, that recruitment to the public service should be guided by the principle of representation.

Porter objects on several grounds to Rowat's plea for representativeness. He first poses the basic question as to which of the many and varied groups in soci-ety should be represented in the public service. He then contends that Rowat's proposals for recruiting members of underrepresented groups and providing them with in-service training serve the principle of equal opportunity rather than representativeness. He states also that "in a society of classes, the upwardly mobile are seldom representative of the social interests from which they origi-nated."[15] Finally, he notes the assumption in the theory of representative bureau-cracy that political institutions are inadequate to cope with modern demands and questions the view that "ways can be found for governmental bureaucracy to make up for the deficiencies in our representative political institutions."[16]

Two decades after the Porter-Rowat debate, Wilson and Mullins expressed doubt "that members of a bureaucracy chosen from various relevant groups will be likely to act as agents or spokesmen for their groups and group inter-

---

[12]Porter, "Higher Public Servants," pp. 490–491.
[13]Ibid., p. 490.
[14]Rowat, p. 207.
[15]Porter, "The Bureaucratic Elite," p. 208.
[16]Ibid., p. 209.

ests."[17] Moreover, they concluded that support for representative bureaucracy "on the assumption that it would be politically representative in any meaningful sense is not only bogus, but also dangerous."[18] Like Rowat, Wilson and Mullins assert that technical efficiency should not be stressed at the expense of representativeness.

Another perspective on the issue of representative bureaucracy in Canada has been provided by Dennis Olsen,[19] who updated to 1973 the study of the bureaucratic elite conducted by John Porter in 1953. On the basis of an examination of data on the social background, career, and education of federal and provincial bureaucrats, Olsen concluded that, compared with the 1953 bureaucratic elite, the 1973 group is "more open, more heterogeneous, and probably more meritocratic." However, these changes have taken place very slowly, and he envisages for the future that the overall pattern will be characterized by a "marked persistence of both social class and ethnic preferences in recruitment."[20]

The Representativeness of the Canadian Bureaucracy

Data on the composition of the Canadian public service in relation to the total population show that the service is not a microcosm of Canadian society. A number of important groups are underrepresented in the service, and both the senior and middle echelons are unrepresentative of the general population. The middle ranks are more representative than the senior level, however, and are representative of the total population on the criterion of region of origin. Beattie, et al. concluded that compared to the senior bureaucracy the middle level was "quite open and heterogeneous." It drew "amply from a wide range of significant social categories in the Canadian mosaic — new and old-stock Canadians, the several regions of Canada, rural and urban areas, the various social class levels — all sectors, in fact, except the Francophone population of Canada."[21] By way of contrast, the senior level of the bureaucracy contained an overrepresentation of males, anglophones, the middle and upper classes, Ontarians, and the well educated. But Dennis Olsen, after comparing data from 1953 and 1973, concluded that the senior ranks have gradually become more representative of the general population. He asserts that "the new elite is drawn from a little lower in the class system, ethnic representation is a little more balanced, the new elite is more highly educated than the old, and . . . a greater proportion of the new elite is made up of *career* civil servants."[22] Nevertheless, the senior level is not very representative of the total population. For example, 92 per cent of the bureaucratic elite had university degrees compared to 8 per cent of the male labour force; only 3 per cent were women; and persons of British ethnic origin were substantially overrepresented, persons of French origin were slightly under-

---

[17]Wilson and Mullins, Representative Bureaucracy," p. 533.

[18]Ibid., p. 534.

[19]*The State Elite* (Toronto: McClelland and Stewart, 1980).

[20]Ibid., p. 82.

[21]Christopher Beattie, Jacques Desy, and Stephen Longstaff, *Bureaucratic Careers: Anglophones and Francophones in the Canadian Public Service*, Research study no. 11 for the Royal Commission on Bilingualism and Biculturalism (Ottawa: Information Canada, 1972), p. 87.

[22]Olsen, p. 82. (Emphasis in original.)

represented, and all other ethnic groups were heavily underrepresented.[23] In terms of social class, the bureaucratic elite was primarily of middle-class origin and "only 15% of the bureaucratic elite . . . could be described as possibly of working class origin."[24]

It is not the policy of the federal government to establish in the public service a microcosm of the Canadian mosaic by pursuing exact demographic representation of all groups in society; rather, the government's aim is to achieve a more proportionate representation of a limited number of politically significant, but underrepresented, groups. In this regard, the Public Service Commission has stated that the underrepresentation of francophones, women, native peoples, and the handicapped "may have the effect of reducing the sensitivity of the Public Service to the needs of particular elements of the population."[25] Thus, a prime motivation underlying present efforts to represent these groups more adequately is to make the public service more responsive, both in the provision of policy advice and the delivery of services. As explained above, the assumption that representativeness will promote responsiveness is central to the theory of representative bureaucracy. The government also presumes that members of underrepresented groups who join the public service will remain sensitive to the needs and claims of these groups. In view of the deficiencies of the theory of representative bureaucracy outlined earlier, the benefits of representation in terms of increased responsiveness are likely to be less than anticipated. However, we know very little about the extent to which the expanded representation of francophones, women, and native peoples has had a policy impact by advancing the substantive interests of these groups.

Increased representation has effects which are not covered by the theory of representative bureaucracy. Representation has a symbolic impact, which explains in part its appeal to government officials and which helps to promote quiescence and stability in the Canadian political system. The statutes, regulations, and administrative units designed to increase the representation of francophones, women, and native peoples evoke symbols of equality of opportunity and upward mobility for members of these groups. In the name of equal opportunity, the government has instituted programs to recruit and train group members who have not enjoyed equal access to the public service. Also, recruitment to senior posts from outside the service and post-entry training geared to promotion to the higher ranks of the service demonstrate the opportunities for group members to attain senior policy-making posts.

These measures serve a partisan political purpose in that they help to sustain or increase electoral support for the governing party. Evidence of partisan motivation can be seen in the fact that, except for handicapped persons, the groups for whom increased representation has been sought have mobilized for political action and are highly visible and vocal in their demands for greater participa-

---

[23]Ibid., pp. 71–78.
[24]Ibid., p. 79.
[25]Public Service Commission, *Annual Report 1976* (Ottawa: Minister of Supply and Services, 1977), p. 15.

tion in the political and administrative systems. The government's efforts on behalf of francophones, women, and native peoples have brought about a more representative public service. It is not practicable, however, to attempt to represent proportionately all the myriad groups which make up the Canadian mosaic. Experience to date suggests that future government measures towards a more representative public service will be directed primarily to underrepresented groups which become politically influential.

The policies, practices and achievements of the federal government in respect of representative bureaucracy, equal opportunity, and affirmative action are explained further in Chapter 21.

Integrity

In the practice of public administration, the concept of integrity can be interpreted to cover a broad range of bureaucratic behaviour, including truthfulness in dealings with superiors, colleagues, and other policy actors, probity in the expenditure of public funds, and so on. The concept is used here, however, to refer to *public service ethics*, that is, to principles and standards of right conduct for public servants. The concept of integrity and the related concern about administrative ethics have been so significant in recent years that the remainder of this chapter will be devoted to these matters. The ethical problem areas which have received most attention, and which are explained below, are conflicts of interest, confidentiality, political activity, and public comment.

ADMINISTRATIVE ETHICS

Opportunities for public servants to become involved in unethical conduct arise from the power they exercise in the development and administration of public policy. In particular, their discretionary decision-making powers and their access to confidential information provide considerable scope for unethical conduct. Ethical rules[26] are designed to ensure that public servants conduct the public's business without using their government position for personal, private, pecuniary, or partisan gain.

Historically, the public's interest in the ethical conduct of government officials, whether politicians or public servants, has waxed and waned as instances of wrongdoing have been exposed, publicized, debated, punished, and then forgotten. But since the early 1970s, there has been continuing anxiety among the public and within governments about the ethical standards of public officials.[27]

The *public's* concern about public service ethics has been prompted in large part by the knowledge of ethical offences actually or allegedly committed by public servants. In some countries, certain instances of official misconduct have been especially shocking or controversial (e.g., the Watergate affair and the

---

[26]The term "ethical rules" refers to statutes, regulations, or guidelines on ethical conduct, or to any combination of these instruments.

[27]See Kenneth Kernaghan, "The Ethical Conduct of Canadian Public Servants," *Optimum*, vol. 4, no. 3 (1973), pp. 5-18.

Pentagon Papers in the United States); in other countries, the cumulative impact of offences of smaller magnitude has stimulated public agitation for higher standards of ethical performance. The news media have played a key role in exposing unethical conduct and in maintaining the public's interest in the nature of the offences and the fate of the offenders. In part as a result of this publicity, there is a widespread public perception that ethical standards are too low and a suspicion that many ethical infractions are never uncovered. These views are reinforced by sporadic but continuing revelations of ethical misconduct. Furthermore, the public's view as to what constitutes unethical behaviour has changed over time. For example, political activity by public servants has gradually become more acceptable, while conflicts of interest, especially in the area of public servants' subsequent employment in the private sector, have become less tolerable.

The concern of *governments* about public service ethics has been based on both administrative and partisan political considerations. It is difficult, however, to discover to what extent the adoption of ethical rules is a response to actual or anticipated ethical problems, and to what extent it is intended to assure the public of the government's commitment to high ethical standards. The public's unhappiness about ethical transgressions, together with confusion inside and outside government as to what constitutes unethical conduct, demonstrate the need to clarify and specify ethical standards. Elaboration of ethical rules is also required as a result of the efforts of public service unions to extend the rights of their members (e.g., in regard to political activity or outside employment). Finally, the political fortunes of the governing party tend to be enhanced by minimizing the number of ethical infractions committed by either elected or appointed officials.

The remainder of this section examines, in turn, Canadian developments affecting the ethical conduct of public servants; the form, content and administration of codes of ethics; the costs and benefits of these codes for public servants and for those whom they serve; and the implications of codes of ethics for administrative responsibility.

The Ethics of Canada's Public Servants

Disclosures of unethical conduct by government officials during the early 1970s prompted several governments to assess the desirability of providing or improving ethical rules. In 1973, the federal government promulgated a code of ethics with major emphasis on the conflict of interest area.[28] During the same year, the Ontario and Newfoundland governments adopted measures regulating conflicts of interest.[29] These initiatives, together with continuing public criticism and cynicism regarding the ethical standards of public officials, had a snowballing effect. By the end of the decade, most provincial governments had adopted

---

[28]The Privy Council, *Guidelines to be Observed by Public Servants Concerning Conflict of Interest Situations*, P.C. 1973-4065, December 18, 1973, and Treasury Board, *Standard of Conduct for Public Service Employees*, Circular no.1973-183, December 31, 1973.

[29]Ontario, *The Public Service Act*, Regulation 603/73, October 1, 1973. Newfoundland, Statutes, 1973, no. 113.

written rules to regulate the ethical behaviour of public servants. Developments in the municipal sphere of government have been much slower.

The rules adopted differ greatly from one government to another in their form (i.e., statutes, regulations, guidelines, or a combination of these measures); in their content; in the types of government officials covered; in the provisions for administration; and in the penalties for violations. All governments focus primarily on the several variants of conflict of interest; some give attention, usually in separate statutes or regulations, to the areas of political activity, public comment, and confidentiality. Public servants in regular government departments are usually covered separately from politicians and often separately from other public employees, but the conflict of interest statute in British Columbia applies to provincial and municipal elected and appointed officials, including employees in agencies, boards, and commissions.[30] Some conflict of interest rules require disclosure of assets, whereas others simply require a declaration that the public servant has no conflicts of interest. Sanctions for ethical offences range from the specific — "a fine of not more than $10,000"[31] — to the more general — "dismissal or other disciplinary action pursuant to . . . the Public Service Act."[32]

Governments provide little or no data on the number and nature of ethical offences committed, but it appears that the percentage of public servants involved in unethical conduct is very small. Ethical rules are, however, not designed simply to catch offenders, but to provide guidance to public servants who are uncertain as to what activities are permissible and what activities are prohibited.

The Style and Substance of Ethical Rules

Although Canadian governments have taken varying approaches to the form, content, and administration of their ethical rules, it is widely acknowledged that the best approach is a code of ethics that contains comprehensive coverage of the major ethical problem areas and effective means for the code's administration. It is useful to codify existing rules by bringing them together in a single document (e.g., Alberta's code), or at least incorporating in that document reference to service-wide rules already existing in statutes and regulations (e.g., the 1973 federal code).

Safeguards against unethical conduct can take the form of statutes providing for prosecution and punishment by the regular courts (e.g., Criminal Code provisions on bribery and corruption), or of statutes, regulations, or guidelines administered within the government itself. Prosecution by the courts (for example under the Criminal Code) is too blunt an instrument to apply to most unethical practices. Many instances of unethical conduct fall into a "grey zone" in that they are unacceptable, but cannot be effectively handled by the courts. In other cases, it is debatable whether an offence has actually been committed, since many ethical issues are very complex and the offence may be more apparent

---

[30]British Columbia, *Public Officials and Employees Disclosure Act, Statutes,* 1974, c. 73.
[31]Ibid.
[32]Alberta, *A Code of Conduct and Ethics for the Public Service of Alberta,* 1978.

than real. In such circumstances, governments are required to exercise judgement as to what penalty, if any, is appropriate. Penalties can range from a reprimand to dismissal.

Codes of ethics may be depicted on a continuum from "the Ten Commandments" approach to "the Justinian Code" approach, depending on the general and limited or the specific and comprehensive nature of their content. The 1973 federal code of conduct fell between these two extremes. The eight clauses of the federal conflict of interest guidelines were broadly worded principles, but the code of conduct explicitly recognized this. It stated:

> Any attempt to identify the totality of potential areas of conflict . . . could never be totally comprehensive and would require constant review and interpretation. Instead, a more workable approach has been taken to identify certain principles, the violation of which would clearly establish a situation of conflict of interest. With these published principles, the overall intent is established and actual situations can be scrutinized to determine whether the principles are respected.

The code suggested also that individual departments and agencies should "supplement these guidelines with more specific provisions pertaining to their own operations." These departmental provisions helped compensate for the generality of the service-wide guidelines.

The *content* of a government's ethical rules reflects the ethical problems that have been encountered. In such countries as Canada, the United States, and Britain, ethical rules have focussed primarily on conflicts of interest and, to a lesser extent, on confidentiality, political partisanship, and public comment. Senior public servants with discretionary authority and confidential information have the greatest opportunities to benefit from unethical conduct. But temptations to engage in unethical behaviour exist at all levels of the administrative hierarchy and at all levels of government (e.g., a senior official with contracting authority in a federal department, or a secretary in a municipal government with access to confidential development plans). It is useful, therefore, to describe briefly each of the four problem areas.

Conflicts of interest constitute the most pervasive and problematic area of unethical activities not only because of the prospect of financial gain from such activities, but also because of the many varieties of the offence. *A conflict of interest* may be defined as a situation in which a public employee has a private or personal interest sufficient to influence, or appear to influence, the objective exercise of his or her official duties. The varieties of conflict of interest include bribery and corruption, gifts and entertainment, influence peddling, self-dealing, the use of confidential information for private gain, outside employment, and subsequent employment.[33]

The Criminal Code provides severe penalties for public servants in all spheres of Canadian government who engage in *bribery and corruption*. The receipt of

---

[33]For elaboration on these types of conflict of interest, see Kenneth Kernaghan, *Ethical Conduct: Guidelines for Government Employees* (Toronto: Institute of Public Administration of Canada, 1975), pp. 13–16.

gifts and entertainment of significant value from individuals, groups, or firms with whom the employee has official dealings sometimes borders on bribery and corruption. However, the propriety of accepting gifts or hospitality is usually judged on the basis of whether the benefit to the employee is of sufficient value to be likely to influence, or appear to influence, the objective discharge of that person's responsibilities. In 1974, twenty-five employees of the Ontario Housing Corporation were charged under the Criminal Code with having accepted gifts from developers. The gifts included colour television sets, Caribbean trips, and amounts of money ranging from $200 to over $12,000.[34] However, employees of the Central Mortgage and Housing Corporation who accepted developers' gifts in the form of liquor, cheese, chocolates, and lunches were simply reprimanded.[35]

Influence peddling is the use of one's official position to influence government decisions to the benefit of persons or firms in whose activities one has a financial or other personal interest. For example, in 1973, a public servant in the federal Department of Regional Economic Expansion who had authority to award grants was dismissed for, among other things, buying shares in a company that was seeking a grant from the department. Another form of influence peddling, which involves influencing the appointment of friends or relatives to government jobs, is commonly described as nepotism.

Self-dealing refers to a situation in which employees take some action in an official capacity which involves dealing with themselves in their private capacity. This situation arises most commonly where an employee influences the awarding of a contract to a company which he or she owns in whole or in part. For example, in 1977, a former chief of security services for the Department of the Secretary of State admitted in court that while working for the government he had rented equipment from a firm in which he was a partner.[36]

The *use of confidential information for private gain* constitutes a conflict of interest. For example, in 1985 senior municipal employees in Regina were dismissed because they took advantage of advance, confidential information to take property options on city-owned building lots.[37]

Outside employment, or "moonlighting," constitutes a conflict of interest when that employment reduces significantly the time and effort which public servants devote to their official duties, or when that employment is incompatible with their duties. Thus, a public servant who slept all day on the job after driving a taxi all night would be in a conflict of interest situation; so would a public servant responsible for regulating marine safety who worked for a company selling marine safety equipment.

The *subsequent employment* or *post-employment* problem arises when a public servant resigns or retires from government to join a firm with which he or she has had official dealings, or which could benefit unduly from information that the public servant acquired while in government. There is often concern that

---

[34] *The Globe and Mail*, October 2, 1974.
[35] *The Globe and Mail*, May 4, 1979.
[36] *The Globe and Mail*, July 15, 1977.
[37] *The Globe and Mail*, September 23, 1985.

this person may have conferred benefits on the firm in the hope of future employment, or that the firm might gain a competitive advantage by gaining access to confidential information, including even trade secrets.

Another ethical problem area is that of *confidentiality* of government information. It has been suggested that some documents have deliberately been leaked by political leaders for partisan political purposes, but most leaks appear to be the work of public servants who wish to embarrass the government of the day or to protect what they perceive to be the public interest. Some proponents of freedom of information legislation contend that if members of the public had broader access to government information, the motivation for unauthorized disclosure would be significantly reduced. However, under freedom of information acts many of the documents most eagerly sought by journalists, scholars, and others are excluded from disclosure (e.g., Cabinet papers, information on security matters).

Rules on the *political activity* of public servants vary considerably from one government to another. As explained in Chapter 11, constraints on political activity are justified primarily by the desire that public employees both serve and appear to serve the public and their political superiors in an objective, non-partisan manner.

The same rationale is given for restricting *public comment* by public servants. Few Canadian governments provide service-wide rules on this ethical problem area. Some governments have rules forbidding public statements which make use of confidential information, but for guidance on what types of public comment are permissible, most public servants have to rely on unwritten rules based on traditional practices and understandings.

The effective *administration* of ethical rules in these several problem areas is critical to their success in promoting high ethical standards. Provisions for administration of the rules ideally should include publicity, enforcement, and grievance procedures.[38] In governments with a large number of employees and administrative units, it is usually necessary to delegate to individual departments and agencies responsibility not only for elaborating on service-wide rules, but also for administering the rules for their own employees. Alberta's Code of Conduct includes explicit provision for such departmental responsibility and is accompanied by administrative instructions in support of the code which are designed, among other things, to ensure the consistency of departmental instructions with the code.

Benefits and Costs of Codes of Ethics

Whether or not ethical rules take the form of a code, they confer benefits and costs on public servants and on their political and administrative superiors.

Both the drafting and administration of codes of ethics require a balancing of political, administrative, and legal considerations. A central and pervasive concern is balancing the desire for high ethical standards with the preservation of the individual rights of public servants. A major principle guiding the adminis-

---

[38]See Kernaghan, *Ethical Conduct*, pp. 50–52.

tration of the Alberta government's code is that public servants "should enjoy the same rights in their private dealings as any other citizen unless it can be demonstrated that a restriction is essential to the public interest." Although some governments have paid little attention to the impact of codes of ethics on their employees' rights, most governments have been sensitive to this problem.

Perhaps the single greatest advantage of a code of ethics is the measure of certainty it provides as to the ethical conduct expected from public servants. Unwritten rules in the form of understandings and practices leave much room for argument as to what the content of the rules actually is and what penalties must be paid for violating them. Written rules can reduce disagreement over permissible activities and provide a mechanism for resolving disputes where disagreement remains. The existence of a common set of ethical standards helps ensure that no public servants are exploiting their public office for private gain. It also ensures that all public servants have the same — or, at the very least, clearly differentiated — rights and restrictions in respect of activities outside government.

It is often convenient for public servants to be able to cite chapter and verse of written rules that forbid their involvement in certain activities (e.g., the receipt of gifts and entertainment from members of the public). Also, the development of a code of ethics may prompt governments to reassess their existing written or unwritten rules so that the rights and participation of public servants in regard to certain activities (e.g., political partisanship, outside employment) may be enhanced. Both public servants and their political superiors benefit from the increased public trust in government that tends to result from the careful drafting and effective administration of a code of ethics. A code provides one means by which political leaders and senior managers can hold public servants accountable for their activities. Moreover, if ethical standards are raised by the existence of a code, the possibility that the government of the day may suffer political embarrassment from the ethical misconduct of its employees is reduced. Members of the public receive both psychological and practical benefits from high ethical performance by public servants. Taxpayers are assured that employees on the public payroll are less likely to use their position for personal gain. Moreover, citizens can expect — indeed they can demand — that public employees serve them in an equitable and impartial manner.

The existence and administration of codes of ethics or of ethical rules in any form impose some costs, especially on public servants. Since ethical rules are designed in large part to prevent and penalize ethical offences, they should not impose unduly heavy burdens on public servants who are neither involved nor likely to become involved in unethical practices. The need to control offenders and to provide clear guidance for all public servants sometimes results in restrictions that public servants find repugnant, or even unacceptable. For example, restrictions in the conflict of interest sphere are particularly irritating to public servants whose right to personal privacy may be infringed by requirements that they disclose their assets or whose participation in financial activities outside government may be curtailed. As a consequence of strict measures to ensure that ethical standards are not only high, but also appear to be high, governments may lose some of their employees and fail to attract new, well-qualified recruits, who find the measures unduly constraining on their private lives and individual rights. This problem complicates the already difficult task of those authorities responsible for administering ethical rules. For these authorities, the administration of the rules can often be a difficult, time-consuming, and frustrating task.

A central question for governments is whether the tasks of drafting and administering a code of ethics are worth the effort. In the absence of firm evidence over time on the nature and number of ethical offences, it is difficult to conduct a cost-benefit analysis. Nevertheless, a comparatively large cost in time and effort may be justified by the benefit of increased public confidence in government and in the responsibility of public servants.

Ethical Rules and Administrative Responsibility

Written rules can be very effective in promoting ethical conduct in certain problem areas and in informing actual or potential offenders of the standards to which they are expected to adhere. However, not all ethical problems can be handled by statutory or administrative prohibitions; nor can these prohibitions guarantee ethical behaviour by those who are determined to abuse their public office. It is necessary to complement formal rules and sanctions by relying on the self-discipline of public servants. Self-discipline, in the sphere of ethical conduct as in other spheres of administrative activity, is developed during the socialization of the individual that precedes and follows entry into the public service. The challenge is to instil in public servants a code of behaviour which will reduce the likelihood of their involvement in unethical conduct.

The critical components of the socialization process are education and training and the model of behaviour provided by one's fellow citizens and administrative colleagues. A major emphasis on ethical issues during the pre-employment and in-service education and training of public servants would help to heighten their sensitivity to, and understanding of, ethical considerations. When the service was much smaller and less complex, the high ethical performance of senior public servants tended to have a pervasive influence on the public service. Senior officials now have personal contact with a relatively small percentage of their employees, and there is no assurance that their influence on ethical matters will flow down the administrative pyramid. This fact helps explain why many senior public servants support the codification of ethical standards as a means of promoting responsible administrative conduct.

The Task Force on Conflict of Interest

This federal task force, which reported in mid-1984,[39] focussed primarily on conflict of interest problems in the public sector, but it also examined partisan activity and public comment. The task force lamented the disorder of the existing system for regulating ethical conduct and provided evidence that the system is unduly complicated and often unfair and unreasonable. The task force concluded that unwritten rules are no longer adequate to ensure an appropriate

[39]Government of Canada, Task Force on Conflict of Interest, *Ethical Conduct in the Public Sector* (Ottawa: Supply and Services, 1984).

level of ethical behaviour and proposed that the current rules and procedures be replaced by a code of ethical conduct combined with procedural rules to minimize conflicts of interest. The proposed code would take the form of a set of principles which would be binding on all Cabinet ministers and public servants and would be enshrined in a statute to be entitled the Ethics in Government Act. Supplemental codes of rules and procedures would be devised to meet the unique needs of particular departments and agencies.

The centrepiece of the task force report is the recommendation that an Office of Public Sector Ethics be established and that an ethics counsellor be appointed to administer it. The counsellor would exercise four major classes of functions, namely advisory, administrative, investigative, and educational.

The counsellor would provide advice to the Prime Minister, ministers, deputy ministers, and agency heads regarding the rules and procedures applicable to those officials who report to them or who are appointed by them. To promote uniform treatment of ethical issues in all parts and at all levels of the public sector, departments and agencies would consult the counsellor on their procedures to minimize conflicts of interest and on their supplemental codes. The counsellor's administrative role would involve ensuring that procedures are followed and acting as trustee for certain kinds of trusts. The investigative function would be performed only at the request of the Prime Minister, ministers, or heads of departments and agencies, and would involve looking into allegations that there has been an infringement of the code or the procedures. Finally, the counsellor would perform an educational role to ensure that all public office holders in the federal government are knowledgeable about the rules and procedures affecting ethical conduct.

The New Federal Code

The Mulroney government did not establish the office of ethics counsellor; nor did it enshrine a code of ethical conduct in an Ethics in Government Act. However, in September 1985, Mr. Mulroney announced a new *Conflict of Interest Code*[40] for public office holders. The term "public office holders" includes Cabinet ministers, their exempt staff, and public servants. (Members of Parliament and judges are excluded.) Provision is made for the compliance of these officials with the code, and special attention is paid to the post-employment problem in the form of compliance measures for "former public office holders and public office holders anticipating departure from public office." On the basis of Mr. Mulroney's code, Treasury Board promulgated *The Conflict of Interest and Post-Employment Code for the Public Service*.[41] The principles of the code,[42] which cover the various areas of conflict of interest explained above, are as follows:

Every employee shall conform to the following principles:
(a) employees shall perform their official duties and so arrange their pri-

---

[40]Office of the Prime Minister, *Conflict of Interest and Post-Employment Code for Public Office Holders*, September 1985.
[41](Ottawa: Supply and Services, 1985).
[42]Ibid., sec. 7.

vate affairs in such a manner that public confidence and trust in the integrity, objectivity and impartiality of government are conserved and enhanced;

(b) employees have an obligation to act in a manner that will bear the closest public scrutiny, an obligation that is not fully discharged by simply acting within the law;

(c) employees shall not have private interests, other than those permitted pursuant to this Code, that would be affected particularly or significantly by government actions in which they participate;

(d) on appointment to office, and thereafter, employees shall arrange their private affairs in a manner that will prevent real, potential or apparent conflicts of interest from arising but if such a conflict does arise between the private interests of a public office holder and the official duties and responsibilities of that employee, the conflict shall be resolved in favour of the public interest;

(e) employees shall not solicit or accept transfers of economic benefit, other than incidental gifts, customary hospitality, or other benefits of nominal value, unless the transfer is pursuant to an enforceable contract or property right of the public office holder;

(f) employees shall not step out of their official roles to assist private entities or persons in their dealings with the government where this would result in preferential treatment to any person;

(g) employees shall not knowingly take advantage of, or benefit from, information that is obtained in the course of their official duties and responsibilities and that is not generally available to the public;

(h) employees shall not directly or indirectly use, or allow the use of, government property of any kind, including property leased to the government, for anything other than officially approved activities; and

(i) employees shall not act, after they leave public office, in such a manner as to take improper advantage of their previous office.

Both new and current employees are required to sign a document certifying that they have read and understood the code and that they will observe it as a condition of appointment and employment.

It is too early to assess the impact of the new code, but there appears to be an increased determination in government to ensure that ministers and public servants adhere to — and are perceived to adhere to — high ethical standards.

CONCLUSIONS

The administrative values discussed above are certainly not the only important values in the evolution of Canadian public administration. The concept of equity, for example, has become increasingly significant during the past two decades.

Equity has been a central theme in the new public administration movement discussed in Chapter 11, and in the specifically Canadian context it is included in many discussions of government regulation and is one of the major values to be balanced in determining merit. However, the values discussed above remain the most prominent ones.

The need for public servants to balance various administrative values which complement or clash with one another has been a major theme both in this chapter and throughout the book. It is important to remember, however, that a bureaucrat's value system contains not only administrative values, but also personal, political, and social values. Some values fall into more than one of these categories. For example, efficiency is generally considered to be an administrative value, but representativeness and responsiveness can be viewed both as administrative and political values. In any event, what is significant is not the category to which particular values belong, but their relative ranking in the bureaucrat's value system. This ranking is, of course, largely determined by the control and influence over the bureaucrat exercised by the political actors discussed in this part of the book.

BIBLIOGRAPHY

In addition to the items shown below, see relevant items in the bibliography of Chapter 11 (on neutrality), Chapter 12 (on accountability), Chapter 21 (on representativeness), and Chapters 23 and 24 (on efficiency and effectiveness).

Baker, Walter A. "Accountability, Responsiveness and Public Sector Productivity." *Canadian Public Administration*, vol. 23 (Winter 1980): 542–547.

Canada, Royal Commission on Financial Management and Accountability. *Final Report*. Ottawa: Supply and Services, 1979.

Dwivedi, O. P. "On Holding Public Servants Accountable." In O. P. Dwivedi, ed., *The Administrative State in Canada*. Toronto: University of Toronto Press, 1982, pp. 151–176.

Hodgetts, J. E. "Government Responsiveness to the Public Interest: Has Progress Been Made?" *Canadian Public Administration*, vol. 24 (Summer 1981): 216–231.

Hodgetts, J. E. "Implicit Values in the Administration of Public Affairs." *Canadian Public Administration*, vol. 25 (Winter 1982): 471–483.

Kernaghan, Kenneth. "Codes of Ethics and Administrative Responsibility." *Canadian Public Administration*, vol. 17 (Winter 1974): 527–541.

Kernaghan, Kenneth. "Codes of Ethics and Public Administration: Progress, Problems and Prospects." *Public Administration*, vol. 58 (Summer 1980): 207–224.

Kernaghan, Kenneth. *Ethical Conduct: Guidelines for Government Employees*. Toronto: Institute of Public Administration of Canada, 1975.

Kernaghan, Kenneth. "Representative Bureaucracy: The Canadian Perspective." *Canadian Public Administration*, vol. 21 (Winter 1978): 489–512.

Kingsley, J. Donald. *Representative Bureaucracy: An Interpretation of the British Civil Service*. Yellow Springs, Ohio: Antioch Press, 1944.

Krantz, Harry. *The Participatory Bureaucracy*. Lexington: Lexington Books, 1976.

Krislov, Samuel. *Representative Bureaucracy*. Englewood Cliffs, N.J.: Prentice-Hall, 1974.

Larson, Arthur D. "Representative Bureaucracy and Administrative Responsibility: A Reassessment." *Midwest Review of Public Administration*, vol. 7 (April 1973): 79–89.

Porter, John. "Higher Public Servants and the Bureaucratic Elite in Canada." *Canadian Journal of Economics and Political Science*, vol. 24 (November 1958): 483–501.

Porter, John. "The Bureaucratic Elite: A Reply to Professor Rowat." *Canadian Journal of Economics and Political Science*, vol. 25 (May 1959): 207–209.

Rowat, Donald C. "On John Porter's Bureaucratic Elite in Canada." *Canadian Journal of Economics and Political Science*, vol. 25 (May 1959): 204–207.

Smith, Bruce L. R., and D. C. Hague, eds. *The Dilemma of Accountability in Modern Government*. New York: St. Martin's Press, 1971.

CASES

In *Case Program in Canadian Public Administration* (Toronto: Institute of Public Administration of Canada):

    A Conflict of Loyalties, by Kenneth Kernaghan

    The Alan Jeffrey Affair, by Kenneth Kernaghan

In Kenneth Kernaghan, *Canadian Cases in Public Administration* (Toronto: Methuen Publications):

    Mr. Smith's Expense Account

    Reality or Appearance?

    The Resigning Engineer

IV

THE MANAGEMENT OF ORGANIZATIONAL RESOURCES

21

The Management
of Human Resources

While it is true in government as elsewhere in Canadian society that "money talks," the Lambert Commission asserted that "the *management of personnel* in all its aspects is as important as, if not more important than, *financial management* in achieving effective overall management of government activities."[1] Certainly the competence and performance of public employees are key determinants of successful policy formation and execution. This chapter examines the management of human resources in Canadian government by explaining the concept of merit, the evolution of public personnel management, the legislative and organizational environment in which personnel management is set, the major personnel processes, and the issues of equal opportunity and affirmative action.[2]

THE CONCEPT OF MERIT

Merit is the most pervasive and enduring theme in public personnel management. To understand the concept of merit, one must distinguish between the merit *principle* and the merit *system*. As explained in Chapter 11, the merit *principle* requires that "1. Canadian citizens should have a reasonable opportunity to be considered for employment in the public service," and "2. Selections must be based exclusively on merit, or fitness to do the job."[3] The merit *system* "is the mechanism in use at any time by which these goals are achieved . . . . A merit system is an administrative device *which can and should be adapted to changing circumstances*."[4] The federal Public Service Commission has argued that "the policies of merit . . . should continue to provide for appointment to, and career advancement within the Public Service to be based on the merit of each individual but taking into account the requirements of . . . other principles."[5]

---

[1] Canada, Royal Commission on Financial Management and Accountability, *Final Report* (Ottawa: Supply and Services, 1979), p. 25. (Emphasis added.)

[2] For an examination of the evolution and issues of personnel management in the provinces, see J. E. Hodgetts and O. P. Dwivedi, *Provincial Governments as Employers* (Montreal: McGill-Queen's University Press, 1974). See also, by the same authors, "Administration and Personnel" in David J. Bellamy, Jon H. Pammett, and Donald C. Rowat, eds., *The Provincial Political Systems: Comparative Essays* (Toronto: Methuen 1976), pp. 341–356.

[3] R. H. Dowdell, "Public Personnel Administration," in Kenneth Kernaghan, ed., *Public Administration in Canada*, 4th ed. (Toronto: Methuen, 1982), p. 196.

[4] Ibid. (Emphasis added.)

[5] Public Service Commission, *Public Service and Public Interest* (Ottawa: Supply and Services, 1978), p. 12.

These other principles are efficiency and effectiveness, sensitivity and responsiveness, equality of opportunity, and equity. Similarly, the Committee on Personnel Management and the Merit Principle (known as the D'Avignon Committee) concluded that "if the public service is to attract the talent it needs, legislation must permit selection on the basis of . . . the individual's ability to meet . . . more than the requirements of a specific set of duties."[6]

It is notable that despite the advances in organizational theory during this century, organizational practice in the public personnel field continues to be based to a large extent on the scientific management school of thought, which emerged in the early decades of this century and which is described in Chapter 2. But "current organizational theory, which views organizations more in terms of social systems, suggests that individuals should know the results expected of them [and] have some influence over the work they perform and over the possible application and development of their own abilities to varying tasks in support of those results."[7] In brief, it is argued that a less rigid interpretation of merit should be complemented by enhanced concern about some of the influences on motivation considered in Chapters 3 and 4.

The personnel policies of our public services do not always reflect what we have learned from organizational theorists about the behaviour of people in organizations. The objective of public personnel administration should be to supply a sufficient number of well-qualified and well-motivated persons at the appropriate time to ensure successful development and implementation of government policies and programs. Greater emphasis has traditionally been placed on providing well-qualified, rather than well-motivated, public employees. Given the evolution of public personnel administration in the unique Canadian environment and the recency of important insights into organizational behaviour, this emphasis is understandable. The long-standing concern about the quality of employees' preparation and performance can now, however, be joined by increased attention to the quality of their working life and its effects on their performance.

There have been few significant events, developments, and reforms in the public service that have not affected public personnel management in general and merit in particular. Merit has been pursued within the broader context of the administrative values discussed in Chapters 10 and 20. The priority which public servants assign to each of these values at any given time is a reflection of the desires and expectations of the various actors in the political system who control or influence public servants. Among the most important of these actors are political superiors. The uniqueness of personnel management in the public, as opposed to the private, sector can be explained in large part by the political environment within which public servants work.[8] Evidence of the importance of the politics of public personnel management has been provided in earlier discussion of such matters as political appointments, political partisanship, public comment, anonymity, permanency in office, ministerial responsibility, and representative bureaucracy. Additional evidence is set forth in this chapter.

---

[6]*Report* (Ottawa: Supply and Services, 1979), p. 78.
[7]Ibid.
[8]See Dowdell, pp. 194–196.

EVOLUTION OF THE PUBLIC PERSONNEL SYSTEM

The development of public personnel management in Canada may fruitfully be viewed in terms of the effect on merit, and to a lesser degree, on motivation of the shifting but abiding importance of the dominant administrative values. In the federal sphere of government, this evolution may for analytical purposes be divided chronologically into five periods — pre-1918, 1918–1945, 1946–1966, 1967–1978, and 1979 to the present. In each of these periods, public personnel management has been affected by a different mix of administrative values as the priority of the various values has risen and declined.

The Patronage Era

The pre-1918 period was dominated by efforts to promote political neutrality by eliminating, or at least minimizing, political patronage in the appointment of public servants.[9] Indeed, between 1867 and 1918, as many as five Royal commissions and a judicial inquiry on the federal public service devoted considerable attention to the evils of patronage. The first major step towards the abolition of patronage was the Civil Service Amendment Act of 1908, which established the Civil Service Commission. The Act also provided for appointment on the basis of merit and for heavy penalties for partisan political activities by public servants. However, the Act applied only to the "inside service," that is, those public servants working in Ottawa.

From Patronage to Merit

The second period (1918–1945) began with the passage of the Civil Service Act in 1918. The search for political neutrality was supplemented by concern for efficiency. The major objective of the Act was the "promotion of economy and efficiency in the non-political public service." Merit was to be achieved through "selection and appointment without regard to politics, religion or influence" and through "the application of methods of scientific employment to maintain the efficiency of these selected employees after they enter the service." The Act applied to both the "inside" and "outside" services. Severe restrictions in this Act on partisan political activities remained virtually unchanged until 1967.

Continued pursuit of political neutrality and efficiency had important effects on personnel administration. The emphasis during the 1920s on eradicating patronage rather than on improving efficiency led to a very significant decline in patronage appointments and partisan political activities by 1930. In the 1930s, the Civil Service Commission, with its persistent focus on merit in terms of selection of the best qualified candidates, lost ground to the Treasury Board, which emphasized economy and efficiency not only in the personnel area, but through-

---

[9]Valuable information and analysis on the nature and extent of patronage from the pre-Confederation period to the mid-1930s are provided by R. McGregor Dawson in *The Principle of Official Independence* (London: P. S. King and Son, 1922), ch. 3; *The Civil Service of Canada* (London: Oxford University Press, 1929); and "The Canadian Civil Service," *Canadian Journal of Economics and Political Science*, vol. 2, August 1936. For a detailed treatment of the evolution of merit in the Canadian federal public service, see J. E. Hodgetts, William McCloskey, Reginald Whitaker, and V. Seymour Wilson, *The Biography of an Institution: The Civil Service of Canada: 1908–1967* (Montreal: McGill-Queen's University Press, 1974).

out government. This emphasis continued during the war years as the government's concern for effective management was manifested in part by executive control over personnel administration.

The Roots of Reform

The post-war period (1945–1966) provided a strikingly different environment for public personnel management. The rapid expansion of government activities in an increasingly complex and technological society required not only a much larger number of employees, but also a greater proportion of employees with professional, technical, and managerial skills. By the end of this period, public service unions had won the right to bargain collectively and to strike. Efficiency remained the paramount administrative value as the Royal Commission on Government Organization (the Glassco Commission)[10] examined personnel management as part of its task to recommend changes to "promote efficiency, economy and improved service in the dispatch of public business." Political neutrality was a continuing but secondary concern. As explained in Chapter 20, representativeness emerged as a primary administrative value, specifically in regard to remedying the long-standing discrimination in the public service against French-speaking Canadians.

The Fruits of Reform

The 1967–1978 period was an especially momentous one in the evolution of public personnel administration. Public service managers in general, and personnel administrators in particular, felt the full effects of reforms generated in the previous period. Among the most important reforms were collective bargaining, language training, new management techniques, and departmental reorganizations.

A larger number of administrative values contended for precedence during the 1967–1978 period. The former emphasis on economy and efficiency was supplemented by vigorous concern for effectiveness. Disclosures of mismanagement and of inefficient and ineffective use of public funds led to widespread anxiety about the accountability of public servants. Revelations of numerous ethical offences involving government officials aroused unprecedented concern about the integrity of these officials. The representativeness of the public service became a major issue as the claims of women, native peoples, and the handicapped were added to those of French-speaking Canadians. The Trudeau government's promises of participatory democracy gave responsiveness a higher place among the bureaucrats' value priorities. Finally, the importance of political neutrality was renewed with the increased recognition of the changing role of bureaucrats in the political system.

The Present Discontents

In 1979, the Special Committee on Personnel Management and the Merit Principle[11] (the D'Avignon Committee) reported that the basic personnel problems

---

[10]*Report* (Ottawa: Queen's Printer, 1962–63), 5 volumes.
[11]*Report*, p. 5.

were a lack of leadership, excessive and inflexible regulation, managers who were ill-equipped for managing, and an absence of accountability for the proper management of human resources. As will be explained later, the government has taken several initiatives during the 1980s to seek remedies to these problems. It was evident by the end of the 1970s that the traditional concept of merit would have to be reevaluated and reinterpreted to take account of other governmental concerns and objectives affecting personnel management. Indeed, in recent years, the Public Service Commission has repeatedly proposed, and the Treasury Board has accepted, the argument that the principles of the merit system noted near the beginning of this chapter should govern all aspects of personnel management. These principles overlap significantly with the primary administrative values discussed in earlier chapters. We shall see that during the 1980s the values of efficiency, accountability, and representativeness have had an especially important impact on personnel management.

THE LEGISLATIVE AND ORGANIZATIONAL FRAMEWORK

The performance of the personnel function pervades government but the development and administration of personnel policy in the federal government are determined largely by a small number of key statutes and organizations. The scope and objectives of public personnel activities and their allocation among these organizations are set out in three major statutes. The Financial Administration Act (FAA) (1951) states that the Treasury Board is charged, among other things, with broad responsibility for "personnel management in the public service, including the determination of terms and conditions of employment of persons therein." The Public Service Employment Act (PSEA) of 1967 grants the Public Service Commission (PSC) exclusive authority to appoint persons to and within the public service according to merit, and to manage such matters as appeals, lay-offs and dismissals, and political partisanship. The Public Service Staff Relations Act, also passed in 1967, sets out the responsibilities of the Public Service Staff Relations Board and provides for the structure and operation of the collective bargaining process and for the resolution of disputes and grievances.

Other notable statutes affecting personnel management are the Official Languages Act (1969), which designates French and English as Canada's official languages, provides for their use in the federal government, and authorizes an official languages commissioner to report on this usage; the Canadian Human Rights Act, which covers such matters as discriminatory employment practices and the privacy of personal information; and the Public Service Superannuation Act, which is concerned with pension and death benefits.

The major authority for the formulation and implementation of personnel policy is vested in the Treasury Board and the Public Service Commission. The Treasury Board is a Cabinet committee composed of six ministers, including the President of the Treasury Board as chairperson. It is supported by the Treasury Board Secretariat, which is headed by a secretary with the rank of deputy minister and is in effect the central management agency of government. Its very broad responsibilities in the personnel field include the development and interpretation of policies, programs, and procedures in regard to the organization of the public service, positions, compensation, training and development, official languages, discipline, working conditions, human resource needs and their utilization, classification of employees and employee benefits, and other terms and conditions of employment necessary for effective personnel management. In addition, the secretariat represents the government as employer in the collective bargaining process. Although most of the secretariat's several branches are involved to some extent in personnel management, the leading role is played by the Personnel Policy Branch headed by a deputy secretary.

The Public Service Commission's overriding objective is "to ensure that appointments to and within the Public Service are based on merit; that they meet the needs of the Public Service; and that they are free from discrimination on the basis of sex, race, national origin, religion, colour, marital status, or age.[12] To pursue this objective, the commission has authority to recruit, select, promote, transfer, demote and dismiss public servants; to provide staff development and training, including language training, within the framework of Treasury Board policies; to hear and decide appeals relating to appointments or to demotions and dismissals for incompetence or incapacity; to investigate allegations of discrimination in public service employment practices; and to administer regulations on political activities by public servants, including decisions on requests for leave of absence to seek political office. The commission, unlike the Treasury Board, does not report to a Cabinet minister; rather, under the Public Service Employment Act, the commission is a politically independent agency which is accountable to Parliament for the administration of the Act. The commission is headed by a chairperson of deputy minister rank and two commissioners.

There has been much controversy over the appropriate allocation of roles and responsibilities in the sphere of personnel management between the secretariat and the commission. Debate reached the boiling point in the late 1970s as a result of recommendations from the Lambert Commission and the D'Avignon Committee that the staffing and training responsibilities of the Public Service Commission be transferred to a reconstituted Treasury Board (to be called the Board of Management). The Lambert Commission wanted to leave the Public Service Commission with responsibility for reporting to Parliament "those instances where personnel policies, procedures, and actions fail to support the merit principle,"[13] whereas the D'Avignon Committee suggested that the commission exercise the broader responsibility of providing "an independent parliamentary audit of the overall system of personnel administration and management of human resources."[14]

These recommendations were designed to eliminate confusion and tension arising from the Public Service Commission's management role in staffing the public service and its role in monitoring the staffing system on Parliament's behalf. Both D'Avignon and Lambert argued that all operational responsibili-

---

[12]Public Service Commission, *Strategy Document for 1982–1987*, p. 4.
[13]*Final Report*, p. 125.
[14]*Report*, p. 71.

ties for personnel management should be exercised by the government's central management agency (the proposed new Board of Management) so as to ensure unified direction and clear accountability and to reduce the need for constant collaboration between the commission and the Treasury Board. The commission and other opponents of the proposed reforms argued that if staffing came under the authority of a minister heading a management board rather than of the politically independent commission, the likelihood of political intervention in appointments would be increased. Moreover, the commission's audit of merit or of personnel management more generally would likely lead to confrontation between the commission and the proposed Board of Management.

The outcome of the debate was that the federal government rejected the recommendations for a restructuring of the Treasury Board and the Public Service Commission and for a realignment of their roles. Instead, the government approved a formal agreement worked out by the two organizations on the allocation of their roles and responsibilities in key areas of public personnel management. Statutory authority for personnel management clearly belongs to the board, except in the areas of appointment and appeals, which are the sole responsibility of the commission. The two bodies share a number of responsibilities in such areas as human resource planning programs for special groups, and looking after the most senior level of managers.

Both the board and the commission delegate much of their operational authority for various personnel activities to departments under the direction of deputy ministers and have created mechanisms and procedures to help ensure that deputy ministers and other departmental officials are accountable for their exercise of that delegated authority. These mechanisms include general statements of procedures to be followed and after-the-fact monitoring mechanisms to ensure that they have been followed.

A few provincial governments have taken the general approach recommended for the federal government by the Lambert and D'Avignon reports. For example, under the new Civil Service Act (1984) in New Brunswick, the Civil Service Commission's staffing and appointment functions were transferred to the Board of Management, which henceforth will exercise the authority for personnel management. The responsibility of the commission is now to safeguard the merit principle in the areas of staffing and appointment and to exercise its powers of audit and investigation as a basis for reporting to the legislature on government practices in these areas. The commission noted that this change would mean that it "will no longer be in a perceived conflict of interest situation imposed by the former Act, where it was responsible for conducting audits and hearing appeals on its own appointments."[15]

In addition to the Treasury Board and the Public Service Commission, federal organizations with important roles in personnel management are the Public Service Staff Relations Board (PSSRB) (discussed under collective bargaining in the next chapter), the Privy Council Office (PCO), the Committee of Senior Officers on Executive Personnel (COSO), and the Advisory Committee on Executive Compensation.

---

[15]New Brunswick, *Report of the Civil Service Commission for the Period Ended December 31, 1984* (Fredericton: 1985), p. E4.

The PCO's personnel functions are limited in their scope, but are critical in their impact, because the PCO exercises the major influence on personnel policy and appointments for the most senior ranks of the public service. It is the Prime Minister's prerogative to make a large number of order in council appointments, including deputy ministers, heads of Crown agencies, and federal judges. The clerk of the Privy Council and secretary to the Cabinet advises the Prime Minister on the qualifications of existing and prospective order in council appointees. In this capacity as advisor on senior appointments, the clerk is assisted by the Senior Personnel Secretariat in the PCO, which in turn provides advice on career planning and on senior personnel policy. In addition, this secretariat provides staff support to the Committee of Senior Officials (COSO), established in 1968, and to the Advisory Group on Executive Compensation, also established in 1968. COSO undertakes an annual evaluation of the performance of order in council appointees and makes salary recommendations for them to the government. It is composed of three permanent members (the clerk of the Privy Council and secretary to the Cabinet as chairperson, the secretary of the Treasury Board, and the chairperson of the Public Service Commission) and four other senior deputy ministers appointed on a rotating basis. The Advisory Group on Executive Compensation is composed of seven leading private sector executives who make recommendations to the government on rates of pay and conditions of employment for public service managers.

THE MAJOR PERSONNEL PROCESSES

In practice, the distribution of responsibilities for personnel management among the key organizations discussed above and the many other administrative bodies within government is very complex. A comprehensive examination of the entire field of human resource management in Canadian government cannot be provided here, but we have set out below an explanation of the major personnel processes, namely, classification, human resource planning, staffing, training and development, and performance evaluation. The issue of political neutrality, which has important implications for personnel management, was discussed in Chapter 11.

Job Classification

Job classification is the process by which jobs are assigned to an occupational group within an occupational category and to a level within that group. Both logically and chronologically, classification normally precedes the other main personnel processes. It supplies an essential basis for effective human resource management in general, and appropriate wage and salary administration in particular.

An *occupational category* includes a broad range of occupations of the same type, distinguished by the nature of the duties performed and the education required. The six occupational categories in the federal public service and the approximate number of employees in each category at the end of 1985 were as follows: Management (4,400), Scientific and Professional (23,220), Administrative and Foreign Service (57,978), Technical (27,184), Administrative Support (68,437), and Operational (41,813). An occupational *group* within a category includes occupations which require similar types of work involving similar skills (e.g., the actuarial science group within the Scientific and Professional Category) and which are often related to the labour market outside the public service. There are 71 occupational groups in the federal public service.

The primary task in classification is *job evaluation*, which consists of (1) the analysis of a job in terms of its duties and responsibilities, its physical and mental demands, the knowledge and skills it requires and the conditions under which it is performed; (2) the writing of a job description which explains the duties, working conditions, and other aspects of the job; and (3) the assessment of these job characteristics against the classification standard established for the relevant occupational group. Each group has a *classification standard*, which contains a definition of the category within which the group falls, the groups within each category, the job evaluation plan, and the descriptions of benchmark positions[16] to be used as guides for assessing jobs and rating them according to their level in the group. Jobs at the same level are assigned the same salary range. Since classification is essentially a matter of judgement, it is common practice to obtain more than one person's judgement by having jobs evaluated and rated by committees who advise the official responsible for the final decision. This work is usually done within departments, but is subject to review by Treasury Board.

Classification Creep

A problem that has plagued the classification system in recent years is called *classification creep*. This phenomenon results from the reclassification of positions so that the persons holding them receive higher pay and sometimes fancier titles for doing the same job. Among the many reasons for reclassifying positions upward is to keep an employee who is being wooed by another department, or to raise salaries during a period of government salary restraint. Treasury Board classification audits in 1978 and 1983 revealed essentially the same thing, namely that more than 20 per cent of positions in the public service were misclassified and that over 80 per cent of these were overclassified and the rest underclassified.[17] The Auditor General confirmed the Treasury Board's estimate that in 1983 classification error cost taxpayers 125 million dollars.[18] Governments at all levels have found it difficult to resist or reverse this creative classification practice.[19] Certainly the phenomenon illustrates well the close link between classification and compensation.

---

[16]A benchmark description is "the description of illustrative work performed in a job which exemplifies the degrees of the factors and/or the classification levels in an evaluation plan." It is usually made up of "the identification of information, a summary of the duties stating the function and purpose of the job, a list of duties, the percentage of time devoted to each duty, and specifications written in terms of factors used in the rating plan." Government of Canada, Treasury Board Secretariat, *Personnel: A Manager's Handbook* (Ottawa: Supply and Services, 1982), p. 82.

[17]*The Globe and Mail*, April 27, 1984, p. 8.

[18]Office of the Auditor General, *Report for the Fiscal Year Ended March 31, 1984* (Ottawa: Supply and Services, 1984), pp. 8-15.

[19]On May 16, 1986, the Treasury Board announced a program to crack down on job misclassification. *The Globe and Mail*, May 17, 1985.

The Management Category

An extremely important reform in human resources management in the early 1980s placed virtually all of the federal government's top executives and managers in a newly created Management Category, which contains about 4,400 employees. Previously, the only distinct management group was the Senior Executive Category, which consisted of almost 1,400 executives. The other managers were spread over 55 different occupational groups. The Management Category consists of the Executive (EX) and Senior Management (SM) groups. The category includes senior public servants who have responsibility for policy development; program formulation and delivery; the design and operation of management machinery; and the management of personnel, finances, and public affairs. The EX Group is composed of five levels up to and including most assistant deputy ministers, and the SM Group is made up of a single level immediately below the EX Group.

The primary objectives of the formation of the category were (1) to establish a simplified staffing system designed to attract, develop, and retain management talent; (2) to establish a single classification system for all senior managerial personnel; (3) to replace appointment-to-position by appointment-to-level so as to enable deputy ministers to redeploy senior managers in response to changing needs; (4) to increase the accountability of managers by specifying accountabilities in job descriptions; (5) to provide training and development programs to give managers the knowledge and skills required to manage in a context of increased accountability; (6) to establish a new compensation system that will ensure fair and equitable compensation both within the public service and in relation to the private sector; and (7) to set up a pay system clearly linked to performance, including rewards for outstanding achievement.

Pay Equity

Pay equity — or *equal pay for work of equal value* — is an issue of considerable current importance in the management of human resources in both the public and private sectors of the economy. It is one component of the broader concept of *employment equity*, which is a management strategy to identify and remove attitudinal and systemic barriers so as to ensure that women and minority groups are equitably represented and remunerated at all levels of an organization.[20] Employment equity is integrally related to the issue of affirmative action, which is discussed later in this chapter.

Pay equity is a short-hand term for *equal pay for work of equal value*. This concept must be distinguished from that of equal pay for equal work, which requires that men and women of the same employer be paid the same for doing the same job, or for a job that is very similar. The concept of equal pay for work of equal value permits comparisons to be made between different jobs performed for the same employer. For example, if one job classification, such as a public

---

[20]See Royal Commission on Equality of Employment, *Report* (Ottawa: Supply and Services, 1985), pp. 193–194.

health nurse, is of equal value to another, such as a public health inspector, then employees in these two categories should receive the same base pay.

A primary purpose of pay equity programs is to ensure that women receive equal pay for doing work that has the same value as that done by men. Historically, women have been segregated into certain low-paying jobs (for example, clerical, sales, and service jobs); these jobs have received lower rates of pay than jobs of equivalent value that are traditionally performed by men. Pay equity programs strive to devise a job evaluation method that removes sex bias from job classifications. If the requirements of a female dominated job category, such as secretary, were found to be equivalent in terms of skill, effort, responsibility, and working conditions to those of a higher-paid job category in which males predominated, then a pay adjustment would be made for the female-dominated category.

Among the concerns about pay equity programs is the argument that the value of dissimilar jobs cannot be easily compared. In particular, it is argued that, in addition to the usual components of job evaluation described earlier in this chapter, account must be taken of such factors as market considerations, that is, the supply of and demand for persons able to perform certain jobs, and the collective bargaining process.[21] Despite these and other concerns about pay equity, several governments in Canada are convinced that the benefits of pay equity outweigh the disadvantages. For example, the federal government is exploring with public service unions the ways in which pay equity could be implemented; the government of Manitoba has passed legislation providing for the allocation of 1 per cent of the public service payroll over four years for pay-equity adjustments; and the government of Ontario proposes to introduce legislation to increase the wages of female public servants to the level of their male counterparts.

Human Resources Planning

Human resources planning is the process through which a government strives to ensure that it has — and will continue to have — the appropriate number and quality of employees to carry out its responsibilities. This process aims to eliminate the gap between the existing supply of qualified employees and the current and anticipated demand for them. There is a very close relationship between this planning and virtually all other areas of public personnel management. In the government of Ontario, for example, the process of human resources planning is considered to be composed of supply and demand forecasting, career planning, employee appraisal and assessment, training and development, and recruitment.[22]

In the areas of staffing and of training and development in particular, human resources planning requires that an appropriate balance be struck between the

[21]For a discussion of the issues involved in the implementation of pay equity, see Government of Ontario, *Green Paper on Pay Equity*, 1985.

[22]Management Board of Cabinet, *Human Resources Planning*, OPS Management Series Process 22-3 (Toronto: Queen's Printer, 1982), p. 7.

government's desire for human resources of specific kinds and the career aspirations of individual employees. Human resources planning would be a much simpler task if governments could treat current and future employees as automatons. Individuals could then be inserted in the appropriate slots in the administrative hierarchy as they completed prescribed forms of management experience and training. However, career development does not always conform to organizational needs. Individuals have career goals, job preferences, and personal idiosyncrasies which often run counter to the government's need for employees with particular qualifications. Individuals may not want to accept positions for which they have the required skills and experience, or they may not wish to engage in training, or in particular forms of it.

It is useful to distinguish between human resource planning *by* managers and *for* managers. Planning *by* managers "must include consideration of the number and kinds of people who will be needed to carry out departmental programs; when, where and how they will be obtained; what training or development they will need; how much they will cost; and the implications for program plans of inability to obtain the people required."[23] Thus, human resources planning is an essential part of both financial and program planning. In the mid-1970s, this fact was recognized by a new Treasury Board policy on personnel management planning; this policy gave managers in departments and agencies a larger role in human resources planning with a view to achieving program goals more efficiently and effectively. The eventual realization that planning for human resource requirements must be integrated with strategic planning led to the introduction within the federal government in 1985 of a service-wide Human Resource Management System. Individual departments and agencies feed into this service-wide system by identifying the human resource implications of their long-term and short-term plans.

Human resource planning *for* managers takes place within the context of managing the Management Category described above. Indeed, a major reason for creating the category was to facilitate planning for human resource needs that would produce highly qualified executives and senior managers. These senior public servants now receive formal management training to enable them to conduct appropriate human resource planning for the rest of the public service.

Staffing

The integral link between attracting capable employees and attaining program objectives suggests that staffing may well be the key element of public personnel management. We have already seen that determining staffing needs and the means of meeting these needs is a central feature of human resource planning.

Staffing is a complex process, especially in government where account must be taken of policy and procedural considerations that are absent in most private sector organizations (for example, language requirements). However, the staffing process in Canadian governments is normally characterized, and to some extent simplified, by a number of policy and program components (for exam-

---

[23]*Personnel: A Managers Handbook*, p. 24.

ple, delegation of staffing authority, open and closed competitions) and of sequential and interrelated steps (for example, written tests, interviews). Moreover, these policies, programs, and procedures are usually spelled out in considerable detail in a personnel management manual.

The central activities in staffing are recruitment and selection. *Recruitment*[24] involves identifying candidates for public service positions by such methods as inviting job applications from within and from outside the public service and using a human resource inventory system. *Selection* involves the screening of these candidates through such means as application forms, written examinations, and interviews. The activities of recruitment and selection are followed by appointment to a specific position or level in the public service.

The Public Service Commission has statutory authority over staffing. It establishes and enforces selection standards, and it appoints the more than four thousand members of the Executive (EX) and Senior Management (SM) groups within the Management Category. Most other appointments are made by individual departments under authority delegated by the commission.

It is difficult to design and operate a staffing system that will satisfy fully all the parties affected by it. The D'Avignon Committee noted that the staffing system in the federal government was "viewed by managers as slow, inflexible and inefficient; by bargaining agents as misguided and inequitable; and by employees as frequently failing to ensure that their qualifications are fairly and objectively assessed."[25]

The obstacles to achieving a statisfactory staffing system can be easily demonstrated by reference to certain problem areas. Consider first the area of delegated staffing authority. By 1967, the Public Service Commission had not formally delegated any staffing authority to federal departments; but by 1985 delegated staffing authority covered about 98 per cent of public service appointments. The stated aim of the Public Service Commission in this area is to protect employees' rights while providing managers with the flexibility they need "to be accountable for their actions and to provide effective and efficient management."[26] To this end, the commission establishes basic staffing policies and guidelines and then audits departmental compliance with them. Among the staffing deficiencies revealed by the audits have been insufficient or non-existent documentation with respect to statements of qualifications, lists of interview questions, rating guides, and selection board reports; inadequate training of managers in staffing; imprecise allocation of staffing responsibilities between managers and staffing officers; and departures from established rules and regulations in making acting appointments.

The delegation of staffing authority was a partial response to a second staffing problem, namely long delays and procedural rigidities in recruitment and selection. A 1981 study showed that, compared to three large Canadian corpo-

---

[24]See P. K. Kuruvilla, "Public Service Recruitment in Canada: Some Perspectives and Problems," *Indian Journal of Public Administration*, vol. 26 (January–March 1980), pp. 62–90.

[25]*Report*, p. 183.

[26]Public Service Commission, *Annual Report: 1981*, p. 4.

rations, the federal government's selection processes "generally took 34 working days longer to complete a promotional competition, largely because of statutory notice requirements (20 days) and subsequent rights of appeal (a further 14 days)."[27]

Data Stream, another mechanism designed in part to speed up the staffing process, has been renamed the Management Resources Inventory System (MRIS) to reflect recent changes in its coverage. Data Stream was introduced in 1970 as an up-to-date computerized inventory of skills, knowledge, experience, and other relevant data on about 110,000 public servants. For a variety of technical and psychological reasons, this mechanism was widely distrusted as a means of identifying potential candidates for vacancies. Its successor, MRIS, contains more complete data on about 25,000 employees at the senior levels of the service. Most positions are now filled as a result of distributing "posters" describing job openings and inviting applications.

A third problem in the staffing area is the perception of many employees that selection board procedures do not necessarily result in the choice of the most meritorious candidate. There is unhappiness about the relative weighting given to the factors of knowledge, abilities, sensitivity, potential for advancement, and seniority. There is concern also about the inadequate training of board members in selection techniques, about the inadequacy of the interview technique for predicting probable success and assessing the relative merits of candidates with roughly the same qualifications, and about bureaucratic patronage resulting from the bias of board members towards certain candidates. A former public service commissioner has stated that despite efforts to adhere to the merit principle, "we know . . . [that] managers are understandably inclined to favour their immediate staff, whose work they have already seen, over other candidates"; that "managers tend to select in their own image"; that "interviews, even if structured, are an imperfect predictor of success in a job"; that "written examinations, while undoubtedly more objective, may in fact be no more reliable a predictor"; and that "the criteria for certain jobs tend to be overblown or to be of questionable relevance to successful job performance."[28]

A fourth staffing problem is the scarcity of personnel of requisite quality in certain occupational groups (e.g., computer science programmers and systems analysts, engineers, and auditors). The difficulty of recruiting qualified personnel in these fields is attributable to a variety of factors, including competition with industry, universities, and other governments. It has become very difficult to make public service employment sufficiently attractive, especially at the senior levels of the service. A parity of salary scales between the public and private sectors is necessary to attract qualified people to government service, to discourage able public servants from leaving government, and to promote mobility between the public and private sectors. Equally important, however, is improved human resource planning in the public sector which will enable and encourage

---

[27]Ibid., p. 13.
[28]John Edwards, "Equal Opportunity in the Public Service," *Dialogue*, vol. 6 (February 1982), p. 4.

government to convey to post-secondary institutions its future personnel needs.

A final problem in the staffing area is reconciling the merit principle with the desire for a *representative* public service. This matter was discussed in Chapter 20 in connection with representative bureaucracy and is discussed separately in the final section of this chapter on equal opportunity and affirmative action.

Training and Development[29]

In some governments, the terms *training* and *development* are used interchangeably, whereas in other governments a distinction is made between training, which prepares people to perform their present jobs, and development, which prepares them for future jobs. Still other governments include development as part of training. For example, the federal government defines training as "any learning activity that contributes to the acquisition by employees of knowledge, skills and experience that helps them to do their present jobs efficiently or prepares them to assume other responsibilities."[30] This latter definition will be used here.

In the federal government, while the Treasury Board is responsible for overall policy direction, the Public Service Commission conducts central training courses and programs and provides advice and assistance to departments; in addition, individual departments provide programs to meet their own needs. Governments have recently placed greater emphasis on the training of managers, who are in turn encouraged to ensure that their subordinates are adequately trained. This emphasis is reflected in the importance attributed to the training of the federal Management Category and its counterpart in other governments.

A great variety of objectives and approaches are involved in the training of government employees. Among the objectives are making sure that employees can perform their current responsibilities adequately, retraining employees who have become surplus, orienting employees who have taken on a new job, and ensuring through developmental training that qualified employees will be available to meet future needs. The three main approaches to the process are (1) formal classroom training within government; (2) formal classroom training by universities, colleges, or consulting firms; and (3) on-the-job training and experience. The programs available range all the way from intensive one-day or weekend sessions, through residential sessions lasting several days or as long as two months, to funded educational leave for as long as a year for senior managers.

Despite the large investment of time and money which some governments make in training and developing their employees, it is widely acknowledged that virtually every government needs to do more. It is also generally recognized that there are formidable obstacles to increasing substantially the current level of investment.

First, elected politicians in general are not very sympathetic to calls for more training and development. Many politicians are reluctant to allocate resources for this purpose because the benefits are not immediately evident or easily eval-

---

[29]See P. K. Kuruvilla, "Training and Development in Public Service: The Canadian Experience," *Indian Journal of Public Administration*, vol. 27 (July–September 1980), pp. 814–826.

[30]*Personnel: A Manager's Handbook*, p. 51.

uated and/or the political pay-off is not apparent. Second, even among some senior appointed officials there is insufficient recognition of the necessity for adequate training. In some governments, especially at the municipal level, there appears to be little concern about the adequacy of personnel to meet the demands of existing positions, much less about planning for those employees required in the 1990s and beyond. The "hope and a prayer" approach to training and development, according to which governments trust that qualified personnel will somehow emerge when needed, is woefully inadequate.

The scarcity of financial resources is another major obstacle to developing and preserving a body of highly skilled and knowledgeable employees, even among those governments where the importance of training and development is readily acknowledged. Training and development programs are costly, not only in terms of the infrastructure required to make opportunities available, but also in terms of the time lost from substantive work while employees are taking courses. Financial support for training and development is related also to what is sometimes described as "the great training robbery." It is often difficult to show that those who have completed certain programs are better able to perform their present duties or to take on new and more challenging tasks. It is reasonable for politicians to ask whether a good case can be made for investing in this area. More attention needs to be paid, therefore, to evaluating the wide assortment of available programs.

The importance of training and development to efficient and effective government is frequently underrated. The D'Avignon Committee asked how the deadwood, diminished productivity, reduced service to the public, and poor public image that result from failure to provide adequate training for public servants can be justified.[31] The committee viewed training as an essential cost of doing business and described the Catch 22 situation which arises when training expenditures are treated as the first budgetary item to be cut in time of governmental or departmental restraint:

> . . . having failed to provide adequate training so that people can perform at an effective level, we (the public, the government, Treasury Board, the PSC, senior managers in relation to junior managers . . .) castigate these people for not performing adequately.[32]

Performance Evaluation

Performance evaluation (often called employee appraisal) is a process involving the systematic collection and analysis of information about the performance of employees over time. It is integrally linked to the other personnel processes discussed above. Employees must not only be recruited, selected, trained and paid; they must also be evaluated in terms of their overall performance. Effective employee appraisal must be preceded by the process of *performance review*, which is "a continuous process in which a supervisor and an employee consider the duties to be performed by the employee, the achievements expected, the

---

[31] *Working Paper*, p. 176.
[32] *Report*, p. 213.

evaluation criteria and the results actually achieved."[33] *Employee appraisal*, which is based on this performance review, "identifies an employee's various qualifications, estimates potential, identifies and proposes responses to training and development needs, and indicates future assignments."[34] This employee appraisal is contained in a formal written report, which often includes a summary of the performance review.

The overriding purpose of performance evaluation is to improve the contribution and motivation of each employee. More specifically, it provides a means of assessing the advisability of pay increases and promotion, the strengths and weaknesses of an employee's present performance, and his or her potential for advancement and need for training and development. In addition, performance evaluation gives supervisors a regular opportunity to communicate with and motivate their employees and to check the effectiveness of such other personnel processes as selection and training.

A formal appraisal report is typically prepared once each year for permanent employees and more frequently, usually quarterly, for probationary employees. To facilitate comparison of employees within a single department and with employees in other departments, a common set of evaluation categories are normally used across the government as a whole. For example, the federal government uses the five categories of outstanding, superior, fully satisfactory, satisfactory, and unsatisfactory. It is notable that the supervisor's own evaluation is affected by his or her effectiveness in evaluating subordinates.

Performance evaluation, like job classification, is a difficult undertaking because it involves a substantial measure of personal judgement. It is widely recognized that the objectivity, validity, and reliability of rating systems are often questionable. The former public service commissioner quoted earlier noted that "performance appraisal information, although improving in quality, is still not as reliable a yardstick of performance and potential as we would like it to be."[35] The fact that one supervisor's "superior" is another supervisor's "satisfactory" raises questions about the fairness of the process.

Performance evaluation, which is supposed to assist employees to enhance their contribution and motivation, can often have the opposite effect. Employees are aware of the impact of performance evaluations on their compensation and career prospects; thus they frequently view evaluations with fear and trepidation. If the process and the outcome of evaluation are not seen as fair, they may actually reduce the employees' motivation to perform at their current level. The matter of fairness is complicated by the fact that many employees have an inflated perception of their performance and may well resent even a "satisfactory" rating. Supervisors, in turn, are sensitive to these high expectations and to the career impact of evaluation decisions; they are, therefore, reluctant to assign low ratings, which they then have to explain and defend in face-to-face meetings with employees. Supervisors are especially reluctant to assign ratings which

---

[33]*Personnel*, p. 49.
[34]Ibid.
[35]John Edwards, "Equal Opportunity in the Public Service," p. 4.

may get them involved in the time-consuming process of grievances and appeals. Consequently, supervisors are understandably tempted to rate each employee as at least satisfactory. The annual employee appraisal tends to be easier when supervisors provide employees with an informal, ongoing assessment of their performance, rather than storing up the good and bad points of an employee's performance for discussion at a single time during the year.

EQUAL OPPORTUNITY AND AFFIRMATIVE ACTION

The federal and provincial governments have adopted programs to promote equal opportunity for segments of the population that historically have been underrepresented in the public service. As explained in Chapter 20, the federal government is committed to improving the representation of certain "target groups," namely women, francophones, native people, the handicapped, and visible minorities. Among the provinces, there is some variation as to the particular groups considered to be inadequately represented. The underrepresentation of women is an important concern in all provinces, whereas concern about the participation of such groups as francophones and native peoples is limited to provinces where these groups make up a significant proportion of the population. The issues of representative bureaucracy and equal opportunity are closely linked in that the attainment of a representative public service depends largely on the extent to which equality of opportunity actually exists for various groups in society. Appropriate representation of these groups can be achieved most successfully when group members have equal access to the education and training required to equip them for government service, equal interest in working for government, equal knowledge of job vacancies in the public service, and protection from discrimination. Each of the target groups has been inequitably treated in more than one of these respects.

In the federal government, the Treasury Board Secretariat and the Public Service Commission have played the leading roles in developing, implementing and monitoring equal opportunity programs. The stated purpose of the programs is to ensure that all Canadians have equal access to employment in the public service and to redress historical imbalances in the representation of certain groups in the public service. To this end, the two agencies devised programs for francophones and women in the 1960s which were strengthened and supplemented by programs for indigenous people, visible minorities, and the disabled during the 1970s and 1980s.

These programs may be grouped into three categories, namely training and development, new or modified administrative units and practices, and vigorous recruitment. In the sphere of training and development, programs have included training opportunities to upgrade women in the Administrative Support Category for promotion to management posts; language training; and the Northern Careers Program for native people. Among new administrative structures in the Public Service Commission are the Office of Equal Opportunities for Women, the Office of Native Employment, and the Coordinators of Services to Handicapped People. Special efforts have been made through a variety of programs to recruit qualified persons from all the target groups. There has, for example, been a black persons employment program in Nova Scotia since 1973.

These programs to overcome artificial institutional barriers to public service employment are of limited use in overcoming attitudinal barriers, notably prejudice against the target groups, which exist not only in the public service, but in Canadian society as a whole. There is, however, an ongoing effort in government to "sensitize" public service managers to the importance of removing obstacles to equal access to public service employment. To ensure that managers are sensitive to this effort, success in enhancing the participation of these groups is now deemed to be one element of the managers' performance evaluation. The Public Service Commission has observed that "an important positive re-enforcement to managerial sensitization is the evaluation of managers vis-à-vis their utilization of human resources . . . specifically with respect to the participation of under-represented groups."[36]

There have been complaints from public servants and from their unions that equal opportunity programs violate the merit principle and discriminate against candidates for appointment and promotion outside the target groups. The commission has responded by explaining that merit is a dynamic principle whose application requires the reconciliation of the values of efficiency and effectiveness, sensitivity and responsiveness, equality of access to public service employment, and equity. Moreover, according to the commission, the equal opportunity programs do not amount to reverse discrimination because individual abilities rather than group characteristics are emphasized in appointments and promotions.

The commission has opposed the setting of *quotas* for the employment of underrepresented groups on the grounds that (1) it is very difficult to decide which groups or interests in society should be represented, and (2) quotas clash with the merit principle by creating two classes of public servants — those who received their jobs because they were meritorious and those who received them because they were members of an underrepresented group. The commission has, however, supported the Treasury Board requirements that departments set realistic *targets* for increasing the representation of the target groups. The commission asserts that these targets are not quotas; rather, they are described as yardsticks by which the government's success in attracting qualified candidates from underrepresented groups can be measured.

To assess the extent to which the federal government's equal opportunity programs have been successful, it is useful to examine briefly the experience of the three major target groups — francophones, women, and native people.

Francophone Representation

Barriers to equal opportunity for French-speaking persons have existed both in the government and in the francophone community itself for most of this century. During the post-Confederation period before the 1918 Civil Service Act,

---

[36]Public Service Commission, *Equality of Access: Equal Opportunity Programs and the Merit Principle* (Ottawa: Public Service Commission, 1982), p. 3.

francophones were numerically well represented in the public service. They were not, however, as well represented as anglophones at the senior levels. Moreover, many of the francophone appointments rested on patronage, whereas the 1918 Act emphasized merit and efficiency. Especially after 1918, the public service was pervaded by an anglophone linguistic and cultural bias. Merit and efficiency were linked to formal education and technical qualifications. French-language or bilingual competence was not considered a component of merit or likely to enhance efficiency. Furthermore, written examinations and interviews for recruitment and promotion reflected anglophone values and the anglophone educational system to the disadvantage of francophones. Finally, the view was widely held that the Quebec educational system was a significant barrier to francophone representation because it emphasized education for such occupations as law, medicine, and the priesthood and did not therefore provide its graduates with the technical, scientific, and commercial skills required for appointment to the public service.

All these factors combined to reduce the motivation of francophones to seek or retain positions in the federal administration. The result was a decline in the proportion of francophones in the public service from 21.58 per cent in 1918 to 12.25 per cent in 1946 and a decline at the deputy minister level during the same period from 14.28 per cent to zero.[37]

During the early 1960s, the so-called Quiet Revolution in Quebec focussed national attention on francophone grievances about their inadequate participation in the public service. And the Glassco Commission reported in 1963 that francophones were badly underrepresented in the service. The commissioners noted that public confidence in the public service will depend on "how representative it is of the public it serves," and to achieve representativeness "a career at the centre of government should be as attractive and congenial to French-speaking as to English-speaking Canadians."[38]

Then, in 1966, Prime Minister Pearson made his landmark statement on bilingualism in the public service in which he promised that the "linguistic and cultural values of the English-speaking and French-speaking Canadians will be reflected through civil service recruitment and training."[39] The Royal Commission on Bilingualism and Biculturalism, which reported in 1967, gave enormous impetus to this objective. Prime Minister Trudeau, in accepting in principle the broad objectives proposed for the public service in the commission's report, stated that "the atmosphere of the public service should represent the linguistic and cultural duality of Canadian society, and that Canadians whose mother tongue is French should be adequately represented in the public service — both in terms of numbers and in levels of responsibility."[40] Then, in keeping with the

[37]V. Seymour Wilson and Willard A. Mullins, "Representative Bureaucracy: Linguistic/Ethnic Aspects in Canadian Public Policy," *Canadian Public Administration*, vol. 21 (Winter 1978), p. 520.

[38]Royal Commission on Government Organization, *Report* (Queen's Printer, 1963), vol. 1, pp. 27–29.

[39]House of Commons, *Debates*, April 6, 1966, p. 3915.

[40]Ibid., June 23, 1970, p. 8487.

aim of the Official Languages Act passed in 1969, the Treasury Board established the Official Languages Program with three major objectives — providing
services to, and communicating with, the public in both official languages, enabling public servants to work in the official language of their choice, and achieving
the full participation in the service of members of both the anglophone and
francophone communities.

In a concerted effort since the late 1960s to increase francophone representation in the public service, the major strategies adopted by the government have
included more active recruitment of francophones, the designation of language
requirements for public service positions, the establishment of French-language
units in the service, and the development of an extensive language training system.[41] Individual public servants and public service unions have severely attacked
these measures on the grounds that the measures violate the merit principle
and amount to reverse discrimination against anglophones. The government's
response to these charges is that bilingual competence is an element of merit,
and that by increasing the number of positions requiring bilingual competence
the government would "increase the opportunities for qualified francophones
and thus at one and the same time preserve the merit principle and achieve the
goal of a more representative Public Service."[42] These strategies have helped to
reduce institutional barriers in the government to francophone representation.
Attitudinal change is more difficult to measure, but there appears to be less
overt resistance to government programs in this area than there was initially,
and the public service milieu is now a much more bilingual one. In addition, a
significant perceived barrier in the francophone community has been largely
overcome in that, since 1960, the Quebec educational system has produced large
numbers of university and college graduates with the requisite qualifications
for public service appointments.

A tangible indicator of progress is the fact that francophones are now represented in the public service in almost exact proportion to their numbers in the
total population — an increase from 12.25 per cent of the service in 1946 to 27.8
per cent in 1985. However, only 20.3 per cent of the Management Category is
composed of francophones. The Public Service Commission concluded in 1977
that "the proportion of francophones in the federal Public Service has not yet
reached that 'critical mass' that would allow the two language communities to
survive, to be self-sustaining and to come into their own, yet this is one of the
preconditions for efficient and high-quality service to all Canadians."[43] The evi-

[41]For information on the implementation and effectiveness of these strategies, see the annual
reports of the Commissioner of Official Languages. On the history of language-training pro-
grams and the Office of the Commissioner of Official Languages, see the twelve-volume work by
Gilles Bibeau, *Report of the Independent Study on the Language Training Programmes of the
Public Service of Canada*, 1975. On the issue of language of work, see the special report of the
Commissioner of Official Languages entitled *Language of Work in the Federal Public Service*,
December 1982.

[42]C. M. Drury, *Minutes of Proceedings and Evidence of the Standing Committee on Miscellaneous Estimates*, March 9, 1971, Issue no. 11:8.

[43]Public Service Commission, *Annual Report 1977* (Ottawa: Minister of Supply and Services,
1978), p. 27.

dence provided in subsequent annual reports of the commission — and of the Commissioner of Official Languages as well — reaffirms this conclusion. In 1985, the Official Languages Commissioner reported that "in spite of general progress, the underlying problems are practically the same as those pointed out in every Annual Report since 1980: Anglophones are under-represented in Quebec and in the Administrative Support category; Francophones are under-represented in management generally . . . , in the Scientific and Professional category and in bilingual regions outside Quebec."[44]

Female Representation

The underrepresentation of women in Canada's public services has existed from Confederation to the present day because of obstacles to equal opportunity both in the government and in society generally.

By 1885, only 23 of 4,280 public servants were women, and more than one-third of these were junior clerks in the Post Office Department. The proportion of women in the service rose gradually to 14 per cent in 1928 and to 18.7 per cent in 1937. It accelerated during the war years and reached 35 per cent in 1943, but declined after the war and remained at about 27 per cent during the 1960s.[45] Since, by 1970, women constituted about 30 per cent of the total labour force, they were not badly underrepresented in the public service in relation to the private sector. However, they were — and remain — poorly represented at the senior levels of the service. In 1971, only 14.1 per cent of officer positions in the service were held by women, whereas women made up 29.3 per cent of the service as a whole.[46]

Before 1970, the government took little action to promote female representation in the public service. It was not until 1955 that the restriction against hiring married women for government employment was abolished. The Royal Commission on Government Organization (the Glassco Commission) noted in 1963 that the government had not fully implemented equality of treatment for women and called upon the government to show "creative leadership in providing equal opportunities for women."[47] In the 1967 Public Service Employment Act, sex was included along with race, national origin, colour, and religion as a basis on which it was forbidden to discriminate. Then, the Royal Commission on the Status of Women reported in 1970 that women do not enjoy equal opportunity to "enter and advance in Government Service, and that their skills and abilities are not being fully used there. Attitudes and practices seem to be at fault."[48] The commissioners made numerous recommendations to ensure equality of

---

[44]Commissioner of Official Languages, *Annual Report* 1985 (Ottawa: Supply and Services, 1986), p. 41.

[45]Stanislaw Judek, *Women in the Public Service* (Ottawa: Queen's Printer, 1968), pp. 7–9, and Kathleen Archibald, *Sex and the Public Service* (Ottawa: Queen's Printer, 1970), p. 106.

[46]Calculations based on Public Service Commission, *Annual Report 1971* (Ottawa: Information Canada, 1972), pp. 44–45.

[47]Vol. 1, p. 275.

[48]Royal Commission on the Status of Women, *Report* (Ottawa: Information Canada, 1970), p. 138.

opportunity for women in the public service, and the government implemented most of these recommendations.

Barriers to equal opportunity for women have been similar in the public and private sectors of society. The under-utilization of women has generally been attributed to differences in formal education and work experience between men and women and to low career expectations, high absenteeism, and high turnover among female employees. Studies on the role of women in the public service conclude that these factors are not sufficient to explain fully the lower salaries and subordinate positions received by women. The attitude that women do not perform as well as men in managerial and supervisory positions helps to explain the underrepresentation of females at the senior levels of the service.

As with francophones, the government used a variety of strategies to remove barriers to female representation, including new administrative structures, active recruitment, and training. To date, the success of these government strategies to increase female representation has been modest, but progress is being made. Between 1975 and 1985, the percentage of women in the public service rose from 35.6 per cent to 41.6 per cent. At the end of 1985, women made up 82.7 per cent of the Administrative Support Category and 7.8 per cent of the Management Category.

The Representation of Native People

The underrepresentation of native people[49] in the public service is much more striking than that of francophones and women. The federal government estimates that native people constitute as much as 4 per cent of the Canadian population, but as of December 1981, they made up less than 1.5 per cent of the public service. Of these employees, 54 per cent worked for the Department of Indian Affairs and Northern Development, and the majority of the rest worked in five other departments. Less than 0.5 per cent of positions in the Management Category were occupied by native people.

This underrepresentation of native people reflects the lack of effective native participation in the Canadian labour force as a whole, and results from a formidable array of instititional and attitudinal barriers to representation both in the government and in the native community. Native people have been isolated culturally and geographically from the mainstream of Canadian society. Inadequate educational facilities and opportunities have made it difficult for them to obtain the academic qualifications required for entry into the public service, especially at the senior levels. As a result of the small number of native people in the public service and of their concentration in the lower ranks, native people are not sufficiently aware of career opportunities in the more senior echelons. There is no visible cadre of native public servants whose achievements they are motivated to emulate. Furthermore, the government's recruitment practices tend to emphasize formal academic qualifications rather than practical experience, and to stress competence in the French or English languages rather than in a

---

[49]The term "native people" refers to status Indians, Inuit, Metis, and non-status Indians.

native language. Discriminatory attitudes towards native people, which are wide-spread in Canadian society, are found also in the public service.[50]

These various governmental and societal factors have combined to discourage native people from seeking positions in the service and to confine those who do enter primarily to lower-level positions. To overcome these obstacles, the federal government has adopted strategies similar to those used to increase the representation of francophones and women. New administrative units have engaged in active recruitment and training of native people.[51]

Affirmative Action

Despite its efforts to increase the representation of the target groups, the federal government is not satisfied that sufficient progress has been made. In June 1983, the government announced its continued commitment to a bureaucracy "that is representative of and responsive to the people it serves,"[52] and introduced an affirmative action program to accelerate the participation in the public service of the target groups. *Affirmative action* was defined as "a comprehensive systems-based approach to the identification and elimination of discrimination in employment. It makes use of detailed analyses to identify and systematically remove employment policies, practices and procedures which may exclude or place at a disadvantage the three target groups"[53] (women, indigenous people, and handicapped people). The government stressed that the merit principle is to be preserved, and that the numerical goals being set were not quotas, but rather, "an estimate of what can be achieved when systemic barriers are eliminated and some temporary special measures are put in place to accelerate training and development experience."[54] The President of the Treasury Board announced that implementation of the affirmative action program would be viewed as a major consideration in the performance of deputy ministers. While this affirmative action program does not establish quotas, its use of temporary special measures, numerical goals, and pressure on senior bureaucrats to achieve these goals is likely to result in greater emphasis on the reponsiveness/sensitivity components than on the efficiency/effectiveness components of public service merit.

The legal basis for affirmative action programs in the federal sphere of government was laid in 1977 by the Canadian Human Rights Act. This Act established the Canadian Human Rights Commission to investigate complaints about discrimination by federal departments, Crown corporations, and businesses under federal jurisdiction, to work out settlements in individual cases, and to promote the reduction of discriminatory practices through publicity and research. The wording of section 15(1) of the Act suggests that measures taken to redress his-

---

[50]See *Native People and Employment in the Public Service of Canada*. A report prepared by Impact Research for the Public Service Commission, October 1976, pp. 40–44.
[51]See Public Service Commission, *Annual Report* 1985 (Ottawa: Supply and Services, 1986), pp. 27–28.
[52]Treasury Board, *Affirmative Action in the Public Service, News Release*, June 27, 1983.
[53]Ibid.
[54]Ibid.

torical imbalances in the participation of certain groups does not amount to "reverse discrimination."

More recently, the recommendations of the Royal Commission on Equality in Employment[55] and the coming into force of section 15 — the equality rights section — of the Canadian Charter of Rights and Freedoms prompted the federal government to promote employment equity as part of its affirmative action program. It is especially important to note that affirmative action programs are protected under the Charter. Section 15 guarantees "equal protection and equal benefit of the law without discrimination" and then goes on to say that this guarantee "does not preclude any law, program or activity that has as its object the amelioration of conditions of disadvantaged individuals or groups includ ing those that are disadvantaged because of race, national or ethnic origin, colour, religion, sex, age or mental or physical disability." In other words, preferential treatment for groups which have historically suffered from discrimination does not constitute reverse discrimination.

As explained earlier in this chapter, employment equity seeks to eliminate attitudinal and systemic barriers in public and private sector organizations to the equitable representation and remuneration of women and minority groups. The term *systemic barriers* (or systemic discrimination) refers to an employment policy, practice, procedure, or system that excludes or has a negative effect on women or minority groups, whether or not that effect was intended, and which cannot be justified as being job-related. For example, if 15 per cent of the geologists in Canada are women, but only 6 per cent of the geologists in the Department of Energy, Mines and Resources are women, the burden is on the department to show that this is not the result of discrimination. The explanation could be that the department requires that all the geologists it hires have ten years of working experience and that relatively few female geologists have that experience. Consideration would be given to removing this requirement because its impact is to penalize women more than men, even though no discrimination was intended by the requirement. The federal Employment Equity Act (Bill C-62), which was passed by the House of Commons in March 1986, requires employers who employ "one hundred or more employees on or in connection with a federal work, undertaking or business" to report annually to the government on the extent to which they have achieved results in promoting employment equity.

In September 1985, the federal government expanded its affirmative action program by announcing special measures to promote employment equity in the federal public service for members of *visible minority groups*.[56] These initiatives were in part a response to the recommendations of the House of Commons Special Committee on Participation of Visible Minorities in Canadian Society.[57] A

[55]*Report* (Ottawa: Supply and Services, 1984).

[56]Treasury Board, *Special Employment Measures for Members of Visible Minority Groups, News Release*, September 9, 1985. These measures were expanded in mid-1986. See Treasury Board, *Enhanced Employment Opportunities to Help Visible Minority Persons and Other Affirmative Action Target Groups, News Release*, June 26, 1986.

[57]Canada, House of Commons, *Equality Now! Report of the Special Committee on Visible Minorities in Canadian Society*, Issue no. 4, March 8, 1984.

government survey showed that members of visible minority groups are under-represented in the public service in that they make up about 1.7 per cent of the service compared to more than 4 per cent of the labour force. The new measures to be introduced included revising employment application forms to allow members of visible minority groups to so identify themselves, providing estimates of the availability of qualified members of these groups in the labour market to help public service managers establish targets for hiring members of these groups, and incorporating a special section on visible minorities in training courses for public service managers.

CONCLUDING OBSERVATIONS

The management of human resources is a centrally important function of government which is closely related to several of the subjects examined in earlier chapters. Many of the issues discussed in this chapter are of an enduring nature; despite continuing efforts, they have not yet been resolved to the satisfaction of the government or its employees. Other issues have emerged more recently. One of these — equal opportunity — has such important political and administrative ramifications that it promises to have a continuing impact on public administration at all levels of Canadian government. Another issue — collective bargaining — is of such pervasive and enduring significance in human resource management that it merits the separate treatment it receives in the next chapter.

BIBLIOGRAPHY

Archibald, Kathleen. *Sex and the Public Service*. Ottawa: Queen's Printer, 1970.

Baker, Walter. "Executive Manpower Requirements of the Canadian Public Services in the 1980's." In Kenneth Kernaghan, ed., *Executive Manpower in the Public Service: Make or Buy?* Toronto: Institute of Public Administration of Canada, 1975, pp. 39-62.

Beattie, Christopher. *Minority Men in a Majority Setting*. Toronto: McClelland and Stewart, 1975.

Bird, Richard M. *The Growth of Public Employment in Canada*. Toronto: Butterworths, 1979.

Borins, Sandford F. *The Language of the Skies: The Bilingual Air Traffic Control Conflict in Canada*. Montreal: McGill-Queen's University Press, 1983.

Campbell, Colin, and George Szablowski. *The Superbureaucrats: Structure and Behaviour in Central Agencies*. Toronto: Macmillan, 1979.

Canada. *Report of the Special Committee on the Review of Personnel Management and the Merit Principle*. Ottawa: Supply and Services, 1979.

Canada. Royal Commission on Administrative Classification in the Public Service. *Report*. Ottawa: King's Printer, 1946.

Canada. Royal Commission on Bilingualism and Biculturalism. *Report*. Vol. 3. Ottawa: Queen's Printer, 1965.

Canada. Royal Commission on Financial Management and Accountability. *Final Report*. Ottawa: Supply and Services, 1979.

Canada. Royal Commission on Government Organization. *Report*. 5 vols. Ottawa: Queen's Printer, 1962.

Canada. Civil Service Commission. *Personnel Administration in the Public Service*. Ottawa: Queen's Printer, 1958.

Chartrand, P. J., and K. L. Pond. *A Study of Executive Career Paths in the Public Service of Canada*. Chicago: Public Personnel Association, 1970.

Cloutier, Sylvain. "Senior Public Servants in a Bicultural Society." *Canadian Public Administration*, vol. 11 (Winter 1968): 397-398.

Dowdell, R. H. "Public Personnel Administration." In Kenneth Kernaghan, ed., *Public Administration in Canada: Selected Readings*. 4th ed. Toronto: Methuen, 1982.

Hodgetts, J. E. *Pioneer Public Service: An Administrative History of the United Canadas*. Toronto: University of Toronto Press, 1955.

Hodgetts, J. E., and O. P. Dwivedi. *Provincial Governments as Employers*. Montreal: McGill-Queen's University Press, 1974.

Hodgetts, J. E., William McCloskey, Reginald Whitaker, and V. Seymour Wilson. *The Biography of an Institution: The Civil Service of Canada: 1908–1967*. Montreal: McGill-Queen's University Press, 1972.

Judek, Stanislaw. *Women in the Public Service*. Ottawa: Queen's Printer, 1968.

Kernaghan, Kenneth. "Representative Bureaucracy: The Canadian Experience." *Canadian Public Administration*, vol. 21 (Winter 1978): 489-512.

Kernaghan, Kenneth, ed. *Executive Manpower in the Public Service: Make or Buy*. Toronto: Institute of Public Administration of Canada, 1975.

Kuruvilla, P. K. "Public Service Recruitment in Canada: Some Perspectives and Problems." *Indian Journal of Public Administration*, vol. 26 (January–March 1980): 62-90.

Kuruvilla, P. K. "Training and Development in Public Service: The Canadian Experience." *Indian Journal of Public Administration*, vol. 26 (July–September 1980): 814-826.

Laframboise, H. L. "Administrative Reform in the Federal Public Service: Signs of a Saturation Psychosis." *Canadian Public Administration*, vol. 14 (Fall 1971): 303-325.

Love, J. D. "Personnel Reorganization in the Canadian Public Service: Some Observations on the Past." *Canadian Public Administration*, vol. 22 (Fall 1979): 401-404.

Olsen, Dennis. *The State Elite*. Toronto: McClelland and Stewart, 1980.

Pollard, Bruce G. *Managing the Interface: Intergovernmental Affairs Agencies in Canada*. Kingston: Institute of Intergovernmental Relations, Queen's University, 1986.

Stahl, O. Glenn. *Public Personnel Administration*. 8th ed. New York: Harper and Row, 1983.

Wilson, V. Seymour, and Willard A. Mullins. "Representative Bureaucracy: Linguistic/Ethnic Aspects in Canadian Public Policy." *Canadian Public Administration*, vol. 21 (Winter 1978): 513-538.

CASES

In *Case Program in Canadian Public Administration* (Toronto: Institute of Public Administration of Canada):

The Problem Program, by L. S. Wong

Implementing Bilingual Air Traffic Control in Quebec, by Sandford F. Borins

The Ben Fisher Case, by Nancy LePitre, Salim Mansur, and Wilbur Grasham

Trying to Fire the Medical Officer of Health: A Case Study, by Alison McGear, Ted Darby, and Raisa B. Deber

In Kenneth Kernaghan, *Canadian Cases in Public Administration* (Toronto: Methuen Publications):

B and B or Not

Fear of Flying

The Difficult Supervisor

Friends and Lovers

Robbery or Delusion?

22

Collective Bargaining

Public sector collective bargaining is a continuing source of concern and controversy in Canadian society. Among the many important issues in public personnel management, the issue of collective bargaining has received the most attention from both scholars and the general public. A recent book begins by asserting that "in the past fifteen years, no change *in Canadian public administration* has had greater impact than the advent of collective bargaining for public sector employees."[1] Another recent book begins by stating that "among the leading developments *in Canadian industrial relations* since the mid-1960's have been the extension of collective bargaining rights, frequently including the right to strike, to employees of senior levels of government, and the rapid expansion of bargaining in this sector as well as in the parapublic sector, such as hospitals and schools."[2] The primary reason for the focus on public sector collective bargaining in both the public administration and industrial relations communities is that its processes and outcomes have significant effects beyond our governments as well as within them. For example, public sector strikes disrupt the provision of such important government services as mail delivery, air traffic control, and police protection. Moreover, collective bargaining agreements in the public sector on wages, fringe benefits, and working conditions influence settlements in the private sector.

Compared to the private sector, the emergence of collective bargaining in the public sector is very recent. It was during the period from the early 1960s to the mid-1970s that the federal government and most provincial governments granted their employees the statutory right to bargain collectively. The growth of public service unionism over the past two decades has, however, been extremely rapid.[3] Public sector employees constitute slightly less than one-quarter of the total labour force, but they make up almost one half of all union members. Moreover, the three largest unions in Canada are public service unions — the Canadian Union of Public Employees (mostly municipal government employees), the National Union of Provincial Government Employees, and the Public Service Alliance of Canada (federal government employees).

[1]Mark Thompson and Gene Swimmer, eds., *Conflict or Compromise: The Future of Public Sector Industrial Relations* (Montreal: The Institute for Research on Public Policy, 1984), p. xvii. (Emphasis added.)

[2]Jacob Finkelman and Shirley B. Goldenberg, *Collective Bargaining in the Public Service: The Federal Experience in Canada* (Montreal: Institute for Research on Public Policy, 1983), vol. 1, p. 1. (Emphasis added.) This two-volume work contains an excellent comprehensive examination of the evolution and present status of the federal collective bargaining regime.

[3]For a succinct account of the growth of public sector unionism in the federal, provincial, and municipal spheres of government, see Joseph B. Rose, "Growth Patterns of Public Sector Unions," in Thompson and Swimmer, *Conflict or Compromise*, pp. 97–108.

This chapter examines the evolution, the legal and administrative framework, and the operation of collective bargaining in the public sector. While this examination reflects the fact that most of the scholarly and public attention given to collective bargaining has centred on the federal sphere of government, reference is made also to developments in the provincial and municipal realms.

THE EVOLUTION OF PUBLIC SECTOR COLLECTIVE BARGAINING

Municipal government employees received the right to bargain collectively earlier than their federal and provincial counterparts. Collective bargaining in the municipal sphere of government has developed rapidly since the Second World War, so that now almost all municipal corporations with more than fifty employees and a population exceeding ten thousand bargain collectively with at least some of their employees.[4] Aside from police and fire fighters, nearly all of whom are prohibited from taking strike action and for whom special legislation is usually provided, municipal employees have long had the same rights under provincial labour legislation as private sector employees. The majority of municipal employees who have the right to bargain collectively belong to the Canadian Union of Public Employees, which is affiliated with the Canadian Labour Congress. (The congress is a central union body with which more than two million trade unionists are affiliated through ninety national and international unions.)

Many other public sector employees, in both the federal and provincial spheres of government, have long enjoyed the right to bargain collectively under general labour legislation. Included in this group are employees of various government boards and agencies, for example, Air Canada and the CNR in the federal sphere and hydro-electric commissions and liquor control boards in the provinces. In addition, in the health and education sectors, many employees have, under general labour legislation, the right to bargain collectively, including the right to strike; for other employees in this sector, the right to strike is denied or restricted in some way.

For federal and provincial employees in regular government departments, the right to bargain collectively was slow in coming — except in the province of Saskatchewan. As early as 1944, the CCF government in that province included its employees under the general provincial labour legislation (the Trade Union Act). Other provincial governments, including Ontario in 1962, gradually gave their employees the right to bargain collectively, but it was not until 1965 that a second provincial government — the government of Quebec — granted its employees the right to strike. The federal government granted collective bargaining with the right to strike in 1967, and several provincial governments (New Bruns-

---

[4]See T. J. Plunkett, "Municipal Collective Bargaining," in *Collective Bargaining in the Public Service* (Toronto: Institute of Public Administration of Canada, 1973), p. 4, and Shirley B. Goldenberg, "Public Sector Labour Relations in Canada," in *Public Sector Bargaining*, Industrial Relations Research Association Series (Washington: Bureau of National Affairs, 1979), p. 254.

wick, British Columbia, and Newfoundland) did the same shortly thereafter. The other provinces have adopted collective bargaining for government employees, but have substituted third-party arbitration (to be explained later) for the right to strike.

The Evolution of the Federal System

The development of the federal regime for collective bargaining in the public service merits special attention because it is generally perceived to be a unique and imaginative approach to labour relations in the public sector, and because its operation has been the focus of so much controversy. Although public service staff associations did not receive legal recognition until the Civil Service Act of 1961, one of the first associations — the Civil Service Rifle Association — was created exactly a century earlier. Postal workers organized into staff associations as early as 1889 when the Railway Mail Clerks Association was established. This was followed by the Federated Association of Letter Carriers in 1891 and the Canadian Postal Employees Association in 1911. Other categories of employees organized into such associations as the Civil Service Association of Ottawa (1907), the Civil Service Federation (1909), the Professional Institute of the Public Service of Canada (1920), and the Amalgamated Civil Service of Canada (1920).[5]

The efforts of the staff associations to persuade the government to adopt some mechanism for consulting with them finally led in 1944 to the creation of the National Joint Council of the Public Service of Canada, which was closely modelled on the National Whitley Council in the United Kingdom.[6] The National Joint Council was an *advisory* body with an official side composed of senior public servants and a staff side composed of persons chosen from the staff associations according to the size of their membership. According to the government, the purpose of the council was

> to provide machinery for regular and systematic consultation and discussion between the employer and employee sides of the public service in regard to grievances and conditions of employment, and thereby to promote increased efficiency and better morale in the public service.[7]

The duties of the council were to make recommendations to the Cabinet, the Treasury Board and/or the Civil Service Commission on such matters as recruitment, training, hours of work, promotion, discipline, health, welfare, and seniority.

---

[5]See J. E. Hodgetts, *The Canadian Public Service* (Toronto: University of Toronto Press, 1973), pp. 323–325, and J. E. Hodgetts, William McCloskey, Reginald Whitaker, and V. Seymour Wilson, *Biography of an Institution: The Civil Service Commission of Canada, 1908–1967* (Montreal: McGill-Queen's University Press for the Institute of Public Administration of Canada, 1972).

[6]For an account of the evolution of the council, see L. W. C. S. Barnes, *Consult and Advise: A History of the National Joint Council of the Public Service of Canada, 1944–1974* (Kingston: Queen's University, Industrial Relations Centre, 1975).

[7]J. L. Ilsley, Minister of Finance, as quoted by P. K. Kuruvilla in "Collective Bargaining in the Canadian Federal Public Service," in Kenneth Kernaghan, ed., *Public Administration in Canada: Selected Readings*, 5th ed. (Toronto: Methuen, 1985), p. 224.

The council was successful in improving communication and general relations between the government and its employees and in enhancing employee morale. However, by the early 1950s, the staff associations were sufficiently disillusioned with their ability to influence government policy through the consultative mechanism of the council that they began to agitate for the right to bargain collectively. The Civil Service Act of 1961 granted legal recognition to the staff associations for the first time and gave them the right to be consulted on remuneration, as well as on terms and conditions of employment. However, the consultative procedures proved unsatisfactory to the staff associations, who renewed their agitation for collective bargaining. Then, during the 1963 federal election campaign, the Liberal Party promised, if elected, to introduce collective bargaining. Following their return to office as a minority government, the Liberals, with the strong support of the New Democratic Party, appointed the Preparatory Committee on Collective Bargaining, which was composed entirely of senior public servants and chaired by A. D. P. Heeney. The committee's terms of reference were "to make preparations for the introduction into the Public Service of an appropriate form of collective bargaining and arbitration, and to examine the need for reforms in the systems of classification and pay applying to civil servants and prevailing rate employees."[8]

In addition to proposing the system of collective bargaining discussed below, the committee recommended that the National Joint Council be preserved "as a forum for the systematic study and discussion of problems that transcend those of particular bargaining units."[9] The government accepted this recommendation, and the council continues to exist as an effective mechanism for promoting the efficiency of the public service and the well-being of public servants by providing for consultation between the government and employee organizations.[10] The council deals with such matters as relocation policy, travel policy, and disability insurance. These are matters for which it is appropriate to have the same policy across the entire public service, and which could not be easily and quickly negotiated separately by over eighty different bargaining units.

The resistance of the federal and provincial governments to public sector collective bargaining had been founded in part on the principle of *the sovereignty of the state*. The application of this principle to public sector labour relations meant that the government could not adopt a system, such as collective bargaining or compulsory arbitration, which required it to give up its final decision-making authority in order that terms and conditions of employment could be determined jointly. As late as 1964, Jean Lesage, the Premier of Quebec, proclaimed that "the Queen does not negotiate."[11] Governments were willing to downplay this argument somewhat when collective bargaining was established,

[8]The Preparatory Committee on Collective Bargaining in the Public Service, *Report* (Ottawa: Queen's Printer, 1965), p. 1.

[9]Ibid., p. 40.

[10]See Finkelman and Goldenberg, vol. 1, ch. 5.

[11]Shirley B. Goldenberg, "Collective Bargaining in the Provincial Public Services." In *Collective Bargaining in the Public Service* (Toronto: Institute of Public Administration of Canada, 1973), p. 11.

but we shall see that some remnants of the principle of sovereignty remain in that the system of collective bargaining in federal and provincial governments is somewhat more restrictive than that found in the private sector.

THE LEGAL AND ADMINISTRATIVE FRAMEWORK OF THE FEDERAL SYSTEM

The Preparatory Committee's recommendations led to the enactment of a statutory framework for collective bargaining[12] made up of two new statutes — the Public Service Staff Relations Act[13] (PSSRA) and the Public Service Employment Act[14] (PSEA) — and an amended statute, the Financial Administration Act (FAA).[15] The PSSRA, which is discussed at length below, set out the structures and processes of the new collective bargaining system. The PSEA replaced the Civil Service Act and, among other things, abolished the Civil Service Commission's function of making recommendations to the Treasury Board on managerial matters such as pay determination. Amendments to the FAA specified the Treasury Board as employer for most of the public service and gave it the responsibility for negotiating collective agreements and determining other aspects of personnel policy.

The Public Service Staff Relations Act

This Act is administered by the Public Service Staff Relations Board, which is appointed by the federal Cabinet. The board is composed of a chairperson, a vice-chairperson, no fewer than three deputy chairpersons, and such other full-time and part-time members as the Cabinet deems necessary to fulfil the board's responsibilities. Subsequent discussion of the Act's provisions will show that the board plays an extremely important role in the collective bargaining system. It has responsibility for a broad range of matters, including the structure of bargaining units, the determination of exclusions from bargaining units, the settlement of interest disputes (that is, disputes arising from the renegotiation of a collective agreement), and the settlement of rights disputes (that is, disputes arising during the term of a collective agreement). In the collective bargaining process, the interests of the government as employer are represented by the Treasury Board, which is usually assisted by the relevant departmental representatives.

A Pay Research Bureau, which is administered by the PSSRB, prepares data on rates of pay, employee earnings, conditions of employment, and related practices prevailing both within and outside the public service. This information provides employers and bargaining agents with objective information and gives conciliators, conciliation boards, and arbitration boards access to material needed to fulfil their responsibilities.

---

[12]See Robert A. Vaison, "Collective Bargaining in the Federal Public Service: The Achievement of a Milestone in Personnel Relations," *Canadian Public Administration*, vol. 12 (Spring 1969), pp. 108–122.

[13]Canada, *Statutes*, 1966–67, c. 72.

[14]Canada, *Statutes*, 1966–67, c. 71.

[15]Canada, *Statutes*, 1966–67, c. 74.

The Structure of Bargaining Units

All employees belong to one of the seventy-one occupational groups in the public service, and these groups are classified into five occupational categories. These categories and some of the groups within them are shown below.

Occupational Category	*Occupational Group*
Scientific and Professional	Biological Sciences
	Law
	Scientific Regulation
Administrative and Foreign Service	Administrative Services
	Computer Systems
	Foreign Affairs
Technical	Aircraft Operations
	Electronics
	Primary Products Inspection
Administrative Support	Clerical and Regulatory
	Data Processing
	Office Equipment
Operational	Correctional
	Firefighters
	General Labour and Trades

Employee organizations (e.g., the Public Service Alliance of Canada, the Professional Institute of the Public Service) wishing to bargain with the government must be certified as *bargaining agents*. These employee organizations act as bargaining agents for *bargaining units*. A bargaining unit is a group of two or more employees that is determined under the PSSRA to constitute a unit of employees appropriate for collective bargaining. The bargaining units for which employee organizations act as bargaining agents must be based on the occupational groups into which the public service is divided by the Public Service Commission under the PSEA. Public service unions can act as the bargaining agent for more than one bargaining unit.

Exclusions from Collective Bargaining

The PSSRA provides for the exclusion of certain persons from collective bargaining. Those excluded are persons in managerial and confidential positions, as well as persons appointed to statutory positions (e.g., officers of Parliament, deputy heads), those who are locally engaged outside Canada, those who are paid fees of office, and those holding casual or part-time positions. In some cases, a whole group of employees is excluded (e.g., legal officers in the Department of Justice, personnel administrators). The rationale for the exclusion of most of these groups is that their membership in a bargaining unit would conflict with their responsibilities for negotiating or administering collective agreements.

The Scope of Bargaining

Under the PSSRA, certain subjects are excluded from collective bargaining. Subsection 56(2) states that no term or condition of employment may be included in a collective agreement if it requires legislative implementation (except for the appropriation of moneys), or if it is established under certain specified statutes. These statutes include the PSEA and the Public Service Superannuation Act.[16] This means that there can be no bargaining on matters falling within the jurisdiction of the Public Service Commission, namely, recruitment, promotions, transfers, lay-offs, discharge for incompetence or incapacity, rejection during the probationary period following recruitment, promotion or transfer, and superannuation (pension). Moreover, section 7 confirms the authority of the employer to determine the organization of the public service, to assign duties to positions, and to classify positions. This means that there can be no bargaining over such matters as job evaluation, the distribution of work, and the determination of duties.

Some of these limitations are specifically confirmed by subsections 86(3) and 70(3), which declare that "standards, procedures or processes governing the appointment, appraisal, promotion, demotion, transfer, lay-off or release of employees" may not be included in a concilation board report or an arbitral award (that is, a decision by an arbitration board). Moreover, subsection 70(4) provides that an arbitral award may not deal with any term or condition of employment that was not a subject of negotiation between the parties during the period before arbitration was requested. However, subsection 70(1) provides specifically that an arbitral award *may* "deal with rates of pay, hours of work, leave entitlements, standards of discipline and other terms and conditions of employment directly related thereto."

The Resolution of Interest Disputes

Interest disputes involve a renegotiation of an existing collective agreement. The PSSRA provides an innovative approach to resolving such disputes. At the beginning of each round of talks for a new agreement, the bargaining agent must specify which of two possible methods of impasse resolution it wishes to have applied during the bargaining process: (1) the referral of a dispute to binding arbitration, or (2) the referral of a dispute to a conciliation board followed, if necessary, by strike action. Thus, if the bargaining unit chooses the arbitration route, it has no right to strike. Once a choice has been made, it cannot be altered until the next round of negotiations.

No matter which option is chosen, if negotiations reach an impasse, either the bargaining agent or the employer may request that the chairperson of the PSSRB appoint a conciliator (also called a mediator) to help them to reach a settlement. The chairperson rarely refuses such a request. The conciliator must report to the chairperson within fourteen days or a longer period specified by

---

[16]The other statutes specified in the Act are the Government Employees [Workmen's] Compensation Act and the Government Vessels Discipline Act.

the chairperson on the probability of success or failure in reaching a settlement. As of September 1, 1981, conciliators had been appointed in just over 28 per cent of the sets of negotiations leading to the 871 collective agreements[17] reached under the PSSRA. If no agreement is reached as a result of conciliation, the next stage depends on whether the arbitration or conciliation-strike route has been chosen.

If the *arbitration route* of dispute resolution has been selected, the parties are expected to reach agreement on as many issues as possible before either party requests arbitration. If arbitration is requested with respect to the matters still in dispute, the PSSRB sets up a three-member body composed of one of its permanent members as an impartial presiding officer, and two other members; one of these two members is from a panel representing the employer's interests, and the other is from a panel representing the employees' interests.

Section 68 of the PSSRA sets out the following criteria upon which arbitral awards are to be made:

(a) the needs of the Public Service for qualified employees;
(b) the conditions of employment in similar occupations outside the Public Service, including such geographic, industrial or other variations as the Board may consider relevant;
(c) the need to maintain appropriate relationships in the conditions of employment as between different grade levels within an occupation and as between occupations in the Public Service;
(d) the need to establish terms and conditions of employment that are fair and reasonable in relation to the qualifications required, the work performed, the responsibility assumed and the nature of the services rendered; and
(e) any other factor that to it appears to be relevant to the matter in dispute.

The arbitration board will listen to the arguments presented on both sides and then produce a decision. The document containing the decision looks like, and has the same status as, a collective agreement, but it is technically referred to as an arbitral award. The award is final and binding on both parties.

If the *conciliation-strike route* of dispute resolution has been selected, and if the parties are unable to reach agreement on all or some of the matters on the bargaining table, either party may request that a conciliation board be established. Each party chooses one person for the conciliation board, and these two persons choose a third person to act as chairperson. The conciliation board is responsible for consulting the parties and reporting its findings and recommendations to the chairperson of the PSSRB within fourteen days or a longer period agreed upon by the parties or specified by the chairperson.

---

[17]A collective agreement is "an agreement in writing entered into between the Employer on the one hand, and a bargaining agent, on the other hand, containing provisions respecting terms and conditions of employment and related matters." The Treasury Board Secretariat and the Public Service Commission, *Personnel—A Manager's Handbook* (Ottawa: Supply and Services, 1982), p. 66.

A very important precondition to the establishment of a conciliation board is a determination of *designated employees*. These are employees who are members of a bargaining unit, but who are forbidden by subsection 79(1) of the PSSRA to take part in a lawful strike because their duties "consist in whole or in part of duties the performance of which at any particular time or after any specified period of time is or will be necessary in the interest of the safety or security of the public." The purpose of this provision is to ensure that the performance of certain essential services (e.g., by hospital workers, corrections officers) will not be disrupted by a public service strike. At the beginning of a round of bargaining, the employer provides a statement to the PSSRB and the relevant bargaining agent as to which employees or classes of employees are considered to be designated employees. If the bargaining agent files objections to the employer's statement, the determination as to designated employees is made by the PSSRB subject to an appeal to the courts.

If the recommendations of the conciliation board are unacceptable either to the employer or the union, the union has *the right to strike* seven days after the report is submitted to the chairperson of the PSSRB. Aside from designated employees, the right to strike is forbidden to employees in a bargaining unit for which a bargaining agent has not been certified by the PSSRB, and to employees in a bargaining unit for which arbitration has been chosen as the process of dispute settlement. Moreover, employees in a bargaining unit for which the conciliation-strike route has been chosen may not strike during the time that a collective agreement applicable to their bargaining unit is in force. Employee organizations are forbidden to declare or authorize a strike that would involve employees in an unlawful strike.

The Resolution of Rights Disputes

Federal public servants have a very broad right under subsection 90(1) of the PSSRA to present grievances not only in relation to the provisions of a collective agreement or an arbitral award, but also in relation to "a provision of a statute, or of a regulation, by-law, direction or other instrument made or issued by the employer, dealing with terms and conditions of employment." Moreover, the right to present a grievance extends to employees in managerial or confidential positions who are not permitted to belong to a bargaining unit, and even, on some matters, to former employees.

Employees with a grievance are normally required to begin by using the three or four levels of the grievance procedure in their department. However, grievances in the areas of classification and discharge are heard first at the final level of the department's grievance procedure. Grievances relating (1) to the interpretation or application of a collective agreement or arbitral award, and (2) to disciplinary action leading to discharge, suspension, or a financial penalty may be referred to third-party adjudication when the grievor is not satisfied with the results of the departmental grievance procedure. In such cases, the PSSRB selects an adjudicator from among its members. Employees may request that their grievance be heard by a board of adjudication. If the employer has no objection to this request, the board will consist of a member of the PSSRB as chairperson and one person selected by each of the parties.

Aside from the right to present grievances under the PSSRA, employees have the right under the PSEA to present appeals to the Public Service Commission in relation to appointments, release for incompetence or incapacity, violations of the rules on political partisanship, and fraudulent practices during an examination conducted by the commission.

THE OPERATION OF THE FEDERAL SYSTEM

This section examines the areas of disagreement between the federal government and the public service unions on each of the subjects discussed in the previous section. Several bodies of inquiry have examined these problem-areas and have recommended changes in the PSSRA to remedy them. Of particular importance are the reports by Jacob Finkelman,[18] the first chairperson of the PSSRB, by the parliamentary committee on employer-employee relations in the public service,[19] and by the D'Avignon Committee.[20] The recommendations in these reports have not yet led to significant changes in the PSSRA, but many of them are the subject of continuing discussions between the government and the public service unions. In general, the unions would prefer to have a collective bargaining system for the public sector which is based on the Canada Labour Code. Under the code, which regulates collective bargaining in the private sector, more matters are left to negotiation than under the PSSRA.

The Structure of Bargaining Units

A large number of bargaining units has resulted from the requirement that the units must correspond to the occupational groups into which the public service is divided. There are at present seventy-one occupational groups and eighty-one bargaining units (ten of the groups are divided into supervisory and non-supervisory units). This means that bargaining is virtually a constant process for the larger public service unions, which represent several bargaining units, and for the Treasury Board. In 1985, the Public Service Alliance of Canada represented as many as thirty-nine separate bargaining units. It has been argued that a reduction in the number of bargaining units would benefit the unions, the employer, and the public in that it would do away with the need to negotiate similar or identical provisions for inclusion in separate agreements and would reduce the number of interruptions of service to the public if negotiations break down. Finkelman and Goldenberg note some possible disadvantages from the consolidation of bargaining units,[21] but recommend that the PSSRB be given

---

[18]*Employer-Employee Relations in the Public Service of Canada: Proposals for Legislative Change* (The Finkelman Report) (Ottawa: Information Canada, 1974), Part I, 301 pp. and Part II, 82 pp.

[19]See Special Joint Committee of the House of Commons and the Senate on Employer-Employee Relations in the Public Service, *Report to Parliament*, Issue no. 47, February 26, 1976.

[20]Special Committee on the Review of Personnnel Management and the Merit Principle, *Report* (Ottawa: Supply and Services, 1979).

[21]Vol. 1, p. 116.

authority to bring about such consolidation where "it is shown in any particular case that it would be in the public interest to do so."[22]

Exclusions from Collective Bargaining

There has been a great deal of controversy between the government and public service unions over the exclusion from collective bargaining of persons employed "in a managerial or confidential capacity."[23] The unions have complained that some employees have been excluded not because of the duties they perform, but because the government wants to keep a certain number of persons on the job to run the operation in the event of a strike.

The Scope of Bargaining

Federal public service unions have been successful in achieving many of the terms and conditions of employment that are standard in private sector collective agreements. In addition, they are well ahead of the private sector in negotiating benefits in such areas as severance pay, maternity leave, and education leave. However, as noted earlier in this chapter, they are prohibited under the PSSRA from bargaining on such centrally important matters as classification, job security, staffing procedures, and superannuation. The unions continue to press strongly for a broadening of the scope of bargaining, especially in these areas.

The D'Avignon Committee[24] proposed that the scope of bargaining be broadened to include negotiation over certain staffing matters which are now under the PSEA, for example, guidelines regarding open and closed competitions, guidelines outlining the appropriate selection tools (i.e., written tests, oral interviews), and the rules governing order of lay-off and recall. The committee also recommended that a National Staffing Council be set up to bargain staffing and related matters. If the staffing council reached an impasse, the means of dispute settlement would be arbitration by the Public Service Commission. The government has not adopted these recommendations.

---

[22]Ibid., vol. 2, p. 697. On April 17, 1985, the President of the Treasury Board announced that the government had signed memoranda of understanding with the Public Service Alliance of Canada and the Professional Institute of the Public Service according to which it will be possible to negotiate master agreements covering approximately 80 per cent of the terms and conditions of employment found now in individual collective agreements. Impasses over the master agreements at the bargaining table will be resolved through binding conciliation; the right to strike will not apply to items included in the master agreements. Individual collective agreements will continue to be negotiated on matters not covered by the master agreements. Treasury Board, *News Release*, April 17, 1985. The signing of the first master agreement between the Treasury Board and the Professional Institute was announced on July 9, 1986. See Treasury Board, *Treasury Board and Professional Institute Sign Master Agreement, News Release*, July 9, 1986.
[23]See Finkelman and Goldenberg, vol. 1, pp. 31–45.
[24]Special Committee on the Review of Personnel Management and the Merit Principle, *Report,* pp. 125–137.

The Resolution of Interest Disputes

The issue of the scope of bargaining is closely related to that of the settlement of interest disputes in that the scope of matters which are arbitrable under the PSSRA is narrower than that of matters which are bargainable. As a result, if the bargaining agent chooses the arbitration route of dispute settlement, the employer can withdraw from any agreement reached to that point on non-arbitrable issues.

Initially, the public service unions selected the arbitration route rather than the conciliation-board route to the resolution of interest disputes. However, during subsequent negotiations there has been a gradual move in the other direction, so that a majority of the bargaining units has now chosen the conciliation-board option, with the right to strike. Finkelman and Goldenberg note that some of the reasons for this development are that "wages have been eroded by inflation, fears for job security have increased and, probably most important, more militant groups seem to have achieved better settlements."[25] Thompson and Swimmer conclude, however, that this development "seems more the result of constraints placed on arbitrators under that Act [the PSSRA] than of any general increase in militancy of pro-strike sentiments among federal workers."[26]

The unions object to being required to select either the arbitration or conciliation-board option before bargaining begins because the government can "manoeuvre by obliging unions to accept less in nonarbitrable areas to avoid going to arbitration in other areas. The employer can also force trade-offs in regard to nonarbitrable issues because, if nonarbitrable issues are in dispute, the unions have to accept trade-offs demanded by the employer or drop the issues entirely."[27] Thus, the unions would prefer that bargaining units be permitted to choose the dispute resolution mechanism at the time that a dispute arises in the bargaining process. Another approach would be to permit bargaining agents to change their choice from conciliation board to arbitration at any time during the bargaining process. This latter approach would be especially valuable for bargaining units that discovered that the number of "designated employees" was so large as to destroy the units' capacity to conduct an effective strike.

Despite considerable disgreement over the number of employees to be designated as performing essential services, the government and the bargaining agents had reached a generally acceptable working arrangement on the issue of designated employees. Then, in 1980 the Minister of Transport proposed to the PSSRB that in the event of a strike in the air-traffic-control unit, all operational traffic controllers should be designated. The PSSRB decided that it should designate only the number of employees necessary to maintain a level of service which would ensure the safety or security of the public. However, the Federal Court of

---

[25]Finkelman and Goldenberg, vol. 2, p. 699.

[26]Mark Thompson and Gene Swimmer, "The Future of Public Sector Industrial Relations," in Thompson and Swimmer, p. 462. See also in the same book Gene Swimmer, "Militancy in Public Sector Unions," pp. 147–195 and Douglas A. Smith, "Strikes in the Canadian Public Sector," pp. 197–228.

[27]Kuruvilla, p. 228.

Appeal,[28] in a decision upheld by the Supreme Court of Canada,[29] ruled, among other things, that the PSSRB could not discriminate between employees performing similar duties by designating only a few of them. Finkelman and Goldenberg assert that the impact of the court's decision is that reliance can no longer be placed on past agreements of the parties and past decisions of the board in respect of designation, that the decisions will affect designations in many other units than the air-traffic-control unit, and "the ability of employees in these units to conduct an effective strike will be severely hampered."[30]

Relations between the government and the unions were greatly aggravated by the enactment of the Public Sector Compensation Restraint Act (PSCRA), which was the cornerstone of the federal government's "6 and 5" program introduced in June 1982. This Act suspended for federal employees, including those employed by Crown corporations, the right to bargain collectively on monetary matters and the right to strike for a period of two years. Compensation increases were limited to specified percentages. Most provincial governments followed the federal lead by introducing similar restraints on employee compensation. Following the expiry of the PSCRA, normal collective bargaining has been restored, but public service unions are concerned that Parliament and provincial legislatures will be more inclined in the future to take legislative action to reduce "excessive" wage settlements or to end "disruptive" strikes. During the two decades since the enactment of the PSSRA, there has been considerable public pressure to reduce the rights of public servants to engage in collective bargaining and especially to take strike action. Yet, "by any measure, strikes in the public sector have not been numerous. The federal public service . . . has, with the exception of the Post Office, been especially peaceful. . . . public sector strikes have occurred most frequently in Quebec."[31] There have, however, been major public sector strikes in recent years in British Columbia, Saskatchewan, and Newfoundland.

The Resolution of Rights Disputes

The issue of the resolution of rights disputes[32] (disputes arising during the term of a collective agreement), like that of interest disputes, is related to the issue of the scope of bargaining. The extension of the scope of bargaining along the lines discussed above would oblige the government to expand its capacity for grievance adjudication because employees would have many more opportunities to present grievances. Moreover, there is some overlap between the PSSRA and the PSEA on the reasons for termination of employees. This has led to confusion among managers as to whether action for termination should be taken under the PSSRA provisions for discipline or under the PSEA provisions for in-

---

[28]*Re the Queen in Right of Canada and Canadian Air Traffic Control Association No. 2* (1982) 128 D.L.R. (3d) 685.

[29](1982) 1 S.C.R. 696.

[30]Vol. 2, pp. 509–510.

[31]Thompson and Swimmer, "The Future of Public Sector Industrial Relations," in Thompson and Swimmer, p. 458.

[32]See Katherine Swinton, "Grievance Arbitration in the Public Sector," in ibid., pp. 343–371.

competence or incapacity. To resolve this uncertainty, the D'Avignon Committee proposed that "all redress actions for termination, or demotion for cause, be taken through the grievance procedure under the PSSRA, whether it be for discipline or for incompetence or incapacity."[33] This solution is also favoured by the public service unions.

COLLECTIVE BARGAINING IN THE PROVINCES

The structure and operation of collective bargaining differ considerably from one province to another.[34] In the provinces, as in the federal sphere, it is the resolution of interest disputes that has attracted the most public and academic attention. This issue of interest dispute resolution is used here to illustrate the variety of approaches to the conduct of collective bargaining in the provinces.

A helpful means of explaining briefly the different approaches to interest dispute resolution in provincial governments is to discuss each province under one of four models of public sector collective bargaining. These are the private sector model, the hybrid (essential services) model, the public-private model, and the formal public sector model.[35]

The *private sector model* applies to Saskatchewan and Manitoba, where public sector employees are covered by the same legislation as private sector employees. Certain groups of employees in some provinces (for example, police and firefighters in Nova Scotia and New Brunswick) are subject to private-sector collective bargaining legislation and have the right to strike, while the rest of the public service is covered by separate legislation.

The *hybrid (essential services) model* applies to British Columbia and Quebec, where public employees are covered by the same legislation as private sector employees, but where both public and private sector employees are covered also by essential-services legislation. Thus, these provinces have characteristics of both the private sector model and the public-private model described below. Public sector employees have the statutory right to strike in these provinces, but there are exceptions (for example, teachers in British Columbia and public-safety employees in Quebec).

The *public-private model* applies to New Brunswick, Newfoundland, and to the federal regime, which has been examined above in detail. The labour relations regime in all three governments is similar to that for private sector employees, but the public and private sectors are covered by separate legislation. In New

---

[33]Special Committee on the Review of Personnel Management and the Merit Principle, *Report*, p. 141.

[34]For an account of the evolution of collective bargaining in the provinces, see J. E. Hodgetts and O. P. Dwivedi, *Provincial Governments as Employers* (Montreal: McGill-Queen's University Press, 1974), ch. 10.

[35]This classification is used in Kenneth P. Swan, "Differences Among Provinces in Public Sector Dispute Resolution," in David W. Conklin, Thomas C. Courchene, and William A. Jones, eds., *Public Sector Compensation* (Toronto: Ontario Economic Council, 1985), pp. 49–75; it is adapted from H. W. Arthurs, *Collective Bargaining by Public Employees in Canada: Five Models* (Ann Arbor: Institute of Labor and Industrial Relations, University of Michigan, 1971).

Brunswick and in the federal government, the public sector legislation is distinguished by its provisions for a choice of mechanisms for dispute resolution and for the designation of essential employees who are forbidden to participate in a strike. The legislation in Newfoundland is more restrictive with respect to such matters as the designation of employees and the availability of arbitration.

The *formal public sector model* applies to Alberta, Ontario, Prince Edward Island, and Nova Scotia, although the classes of employees covered by the legislation differ somewhat from one province to another. Among the important features of the legislation under this model are that the public sector is treated separately from the private sector, strikes are prohibited, and disputes are resolved through a conventional tripartite-arbitration system.

CONCLUSIONS

In all spheres of Canadian government, collective bargaining for public employees is probably the single most important issue in public personnel management. The introduction of public sector collective bargaining is very recent in the federal and provincial spheres, and a great deal of fine-tuning of the process remains to be done. The PSSRA, for example, does not provide a framework for employer-employee relations that is satisfactory to the government, the general public, or the public service unions. Yet, the continuing disagreements over the interpretation and application of the Act and the existence of well-considered proposals for its reform have not led to significant changes in its provisions. The government's hesitation in implementing proposed reforms is due in part to differences of opinion among members of the public regarding the desirability of permitting government employees to bargain collectively and to take strike action.

It seems unlikely that the right to strike will be withdrawn in those jurisdictions where it has been granted. However, in several provincial governments, public service unions and their supporters are still waging a campaign for the right to strike. In virtually all jurisdictions, including the federal government, there are strong pressures for reform of the existing collective bargaining regime. Moreover, employer-employee relations have been severely aggravated in recent years by legislation involving restraints on compensation, restraints on collective agreements, changes to the rules of the game, and direct legislative intervention,[36] as well as lay-offs, cutbacks, and the contracting out of services. The tensions arising from disagreements on these matters, and indeed from the nature of the collective bargaining process itself, will ensure that collective bargaining remains a dominant dimension of the study and practice of public administration.

---

[36]See Swan, pp. 65–71.

BIBLIOGRAPHY

Arthurs, H. W. *Collective Bargaining by Public Employees in Canada: Five Models*. Ann Arbor, Mich.: University of Michigan, Institute of Labor and Industrial Relations, 1971.

Barnes, L. W. C. S. *Consult and Advise: A History of the National Joint Council of the Public Service of Canada, 1944–1974*. Kingston: Queen's University, Industrial Relations Centre, 1975.

Barnes, L. W. C. S., and L. A. Kelly. *Interest Arbitration in the Federal Public Service of Canada*. Kingston: Queen's University, Industrial Relations Centre, 1975.

Canada. Preparatory Committee on Collective Bargaining in the Public Service. *Report*. Ottawa: Queen's Printer, 1965.

Canada. Special Committee on the Review of Personnel Management and the Merit Principle. *Report*. Ottawa: Supply and Services, 1979.

Christensen, Sandra. *Unions and the Public Interest*. Vancouver: The Fraser Institute, 1980.

Conklin, David W., Thomas C. Courchene, and William A. Jones, eds. *Public Sector Compensation*. Toronto: Ontario Economic Council, 1985.

Daniel, Mark J., and William E. A. Robinson. *Compensation in Canada: A Study of the Public and Private Sectors*. Ottawa: The Conference Board in Canada, 1980.

Finkelman, J. *Employer-Employee Relations in the Public Service of Canada: Proposals for Legislative Change*. Ottawa: Information Canada, 1974.

Finkelman, Jacob, and Shirley Goldenberg. *Collective Bargaining in the Public Service: The Federal Experience in Canada*. 2 vols. Montreal: Institute for Research on Public Policy, 1983.

Foot, David K., ed. *Public Employment and Compensation in Canada: Myths and Realities*. Toronto: Butterworths, for the Institute for Research on Public Policy, 1978.

Hodgetts, J. E., and O. P. Dwivedi. *Provincial Governments as Employers*. Montreal: McGill-Queen's University Press, 1974.

Institute of Public Administration of Canada. *Collective Bargaining in the Public Service*. Toronto: Institute of Public Administration of Canada, 1973.

Kuruvilla, P. K. "Collective Bargaining in the Canadian Federal Public Service." In Kenneth Kernaghan, ed., *Public Administration in Canada: Selected Readings*. 5th ed. Toronto: Methuen, 1985, pp. 224–235.

Love, J. D. "Personnel Reorganization in the Canadian Public Service: Some Observations on the Past." *Canadian Public Administration*, vol. 22 (Fall 1979): 402–414.

Maslove, Allan, and Gene Swimmer. *Wage Controls in Canada, 1975–1978*. Montreal: Institute for Research on Public Policy, 1980.

Swettenham, John, and David Kealy. *Serving the State: A History of the Professional Institute of the Public Service of Canada, 1920–1970*. Ottawa: The Professional Institute of the Public Service of Canada, 1970.

Thompson, Mark, and Gene Swimmer, eds. *Conflict or Compromise: The Future of Public Sector Industrial Relations*. Montreal: Institute for Research on Public Policy, 1984.

Vaison, Robert A. "Collective Bargaining in the Federal Public Service: The Achievement of a Milestone in Personnel Relations." *Canadian Public Administration*, vol. 12 (Spring 1969); 108–122.

CASES

In *Case Program in Canadian Public Administration* (Toronto: Institute of Public Administration of Canada):

M.T.I. Simulation: Public Sector Collective Bargaining, by Gene R. Swimmer and Claude P. Parent

Autorité et syndicalisme à Radio-Québec, by Kenneth Cabatoff

The Northville Simulation, by Gene R. Swimmer and Allan M. Maslove

The Ben Fisher Case, by Nancy LePitre, Salim Mansur, and Wilbur Grasham

Students or Doctors? The Emergence of Collective Bargaining Among Interns and Residents in Ontario, by Harold Wodinsky, Richard Nurse, and Raisa B. Deber

The Borough of York Strike, by D. Wayne Taylor

A Conflict of Loyalties, by Kenneth Kernaghan

23

The Budgetary Process

The previous two chapters considered the management of human resources. This chapter and the next will consider the management of financial resources. The establishment of the revenue and expenditure budgets will be discussed in this chapter. The next chapter will focus on financial operations during a fiscal year after the initial budget has been established. It is sometimes said that the budgetary process has three phases — preparation, adoption, and execution. This chapter will treat preparation; the next will deal with adoption and execution.

This chapter begins with a brief discussion of the preparation of the revenue budget, then proceeds to a discussion of various theories of the expenditure budget and a description of the preparation of the federal expenditure budget. The appendix at the end of this chapter explains the components of government financial statements in everyday language.

One of the great difficulties in preparing a government budget is that the budget typically has many objectives, not all of which are consistent with one another. In preparing a personal budget, one usually thinks in terms of the fairly unidimensional problem of adjusting expenditures to fit a relatively fixed income. The complicating factor in the preparation of government budgets is that they must address at least three objectives.

First is the setting of macro-economic policy, or at least that part of it which is influenced by fiscal instruments, i.e., levels of aggregate revenue, expenditure, and surplus or deficit. Governments set total revenue and expenditure targets so as to stimulate the economy or slow it down. The second objective involves influencing behaviour at a more micro level. Governments frequently use tax provisions, not just to raise revenue, but rather to encourage people to do, or refrain from doing, certain things. For example, customs duties raise a sizeable portion of government revenue, but their main objective is to protect domestic industry. Finally, a government budget must also raise the resources needed to fund expenditures.

The most difficult aspect of these three objectives is that not all of them point towards the same action at the same time. For example, in difficult economic times, government will need more revenue to fund unemployment insurance and social assistance plans. However, macro-economic principles suggest that it is desirable to reduce taxes to stimulate spending in hard economic times. The continuing adjustment of these seemingly irreconcilable factors makes government budgeting a most difficult task.

THE REVENUE BUDGET

It is an important principle of responsible government that no tax can be imposed without the approval of the legislature. At least once each year, the federal Minister of Finance or provincial Treasurer prepares a revenue budget which contains, among many other things, a request to the legislature to impose or change certain taxes. Actually, the government uses the revenue budget to:

(1) describe and interpret the major economic events of the recent past and the government's view of the economic outlook (frequently with the intent of altering private expectations);

(2) congratulate itself for any past improvement in the state of the economy and shift the blame for any past deterioration;

(3) announce changes (including no change) in fiscal policy (tax/expenditure/borrowing/lending) designed to stabilize the economy;

(4) propose changes in the tax/tariff structure designed to
   (a) implement social (income/wealth redistribution) policy,
   (b) implement economic (resource allocation) policy,
   (c) eliminate "technical" flaws or difficulties with existing tax/tariff structures; and

(5) deal with special measures such as incomes policy, federal-provincial fiscal relations, pensions, and special studies.[1]

The fiscal year of the federal and provincial governments begins on April 1 and ends the next March 31. There is a relatively short-lived tradition that the Minister of Finance presents the federal revenue budget close to the beginning of the fiscal year. Finance Minister Wilson has presented persuasive arguments that mid-January to mid-February is the ideal time.[2] There is no set rule for this timing; budgets are sometimes presented at other times of the year, and more than one budget can be presented in the same year. These deviations can stem from either political considerations, e.g., the desire to present an attractive budget on which to fight an election, or from volatile economic conditions such as changing international trade situations or energy prices.

The revenue budget is presented as a part of the minister's budget speech. There is no set format for this speech, but it usually contains most of the following elements:

(1) a review of economic conditions and problems based on information from a White Paper tabled a few days earlier [or at the same time as the budget];

---

[1]Douglas G. Hartle, *The Revenue Budget Process of the Government of Canada: Description, Appraisal, and Proposals*, Canadian Tax Paper No. 67 (Toronto: Canadian Tax Foundation, 1982), p. 6. (Footnotes omitted.)

[2]Michael H. Wilson, *The Canadian Budgetary Process: Proposals for Improvement* (Department of Finance, 1985), p. 8. A similar argument is made in Allan J. MacEachen, *The Budget Process: A Paper on Budget Secrecy and Proposals for Broader Consultation* (Department of Finance, 1982), p. 7.

(2) a statement of government revenues and expenditures over the past year and a comparison with the previous budget's estimation;

(3) an estimation of government expenditures and revenues for the upcoming year and the surplus or deficit; and

(4) notice of any ways and means motions — that is, motions to introduce bills to amend various tax acts.[3]

The third and fourth items are usually given the greatest attention. In recent years, when government deficits have been the rule, the level of the deficit and the attendant government borrowing requirements provide important signals to money markets. The notice of ways and means motions probably holds the greatest interest for most taxpayers because this is the announcement of changes in tax structure or rates, which means that new taxes will be introduced or new items taxed or tax loopholes opened or closed.

The minister's budget speech is given much more attention than other speeches in the legislature. Because it says so much about the government's financial situation, it can be regarded as a sort of "mini-throne speech." The date and time are set several weeks in advance, at an hour when stock markets are closed so that the contents of the speech will not affect stock prices precipitously. The media pays great attention to the event, and it is usually broadcast live on radio and/or television, followed by analysis by learned economists, representatives of interest groups, and the inevitable "man on the street." Several days of the legislature's time are set aside for what is euphemistically called debate on the budget speech. Actually, it is a time for the Opposition parties to criticize the minister for past mistakes and anticipated future mistakes.

After this debate, there is a vote of confidence concerning the overall budget. Since it is a vote of confidence, if it does not carry, then the government must, by convention, resign. This is what happened to the Trudeau government in 1974 and to the short-lived Clark government in 1979. Assuming that the government does survive the initial vote of confidence, the Minister of Finance will then introduce, over the next few months, a series of motions implementing the specific taxation measures first presented in the budget. Votes on these motions can be matters of confidence if the specific measure is central to the total budget package, but they are not ordinarily considered to be matters of confidence. However, defeat of a major tax measure can pose a serious problem for a government, because alternative sources of revenue will have to be found.

Budget Preparation

A later section of this chapter contains a lengthy discussion of the process involved in the preparation of the expenditure budget. It is difficult to discuss the preparation of the revenue budget in the same manner, because it is very much the personal work of the Minister of Finance or provincial Treasurer and his or her senior public servants.[4] The secrecy of the revenue budget is considered very

---

[3]Hartle, *The Revenue Budget Process*, p. 31. (Footnotes omitted.)

[4]One of the few to report on the revenue budget process is David A. Good, *The Politics of Anticipation: Making Canadian Federal Tax Policy* (Ottawa: Carleton University, School of Public Administration, n.d., 1980?), ch. 6.

important because, if some taxpayers had advance information about certain tax and other provisions of the budget, they could either profit unfairly or evade the intended effects of the provisions of the budget.

The minister is not totally isolated from public concerns in the preparation of the budget. While the budget is being prepared, the minister is kept constantly aware of the desires of other governments, business, labour, and other interest groups, and he or she usually consults in a general way with Cabinet colleagues. Shortly before public presentation of the budget, the minister will also consult with the Governor of the Bank of Canada.[5] Prime Minister Mulroney has been deeply involved in the preparation of the revenue budget, but previous Prime Ministers were not nearly so involved.[6] However, any breaches of secrecy which make information available to the general public are felt to be very serious.

The parliamentary tradition is that a Minister of Finance must resign if there is any leak of information about the budget. Resignations for this reason have occurred in Britain,[7] but there has never been a resignation in Canada. There have been several cases where Ministers of Finance or provincial Treasurers have suffered significant political embarrassment because of alleged violations of secrecy. In 1963, Walter Gordon was pressured to resign as federal Minister of Finance when it was discovered that he had employed certain non-civil servants, who had been sworn to an oath of secrecy, to assist him in the preparation of the budget.[8] In more recent times, a cameraman was able to take a picture of a page of the federal budget over Finance Minister Marc Lalonde's shoulder, a journalist found portions of an Ontario budget in the trash of a printing firm, and a Nova Scotia newspaper printed advance reports of the provincial budget which proved to be remarkably accurate.[9] In none of these cases did the minister resign.

One of the persistent proposals for reform of the revenue budget process is that the convention of secrecy should be relaxed somewhat. Business and other interest groups would like to know in advance what the minister's general thinking is and have an opportunity to influence that thinking. These interest groups can try to change the minister's recommendations to the legislature after they have been presented in the budget speech; but that is very difficult, because any change in the original proposals is taken as a sign of weakness. This lack of consultation could well be dysfunctional to the government, because it increases the possibility that some budget provisions could have unanticipated undesirable consequences. Moreover, this lack of consultation can be dysfunctional for the minister because it tends to make him or her a captive of the advice of departmental officials since outside consultation cannot occur.

[5]Hartle, *The Revenue Budget Process*, p. 8.

[6]Ibid., pp. 28-29.

[7]Robert J. Bertrand, Alice Desjardins, and René Hurtubise, *Legislation, Administration and Interpretation Processes in Federal Taxation*. Study for the Royal Commission on Taxation, no. 22 (Ottawa: Queen's Printer and Controller of Stationery, 1967), pp. 44-45.

[8]Walter L. Gordon, *A Political Man* (Toronto: McClelland and Stewart, 1977), ch. 8.

[9]Robert Martin, "Kerr Won't Quit Over Budget Leak," *The Globe and Mail*, April 19, 1986, p. A4.

There have been a number of specific proposals for reform.[10] They all recognize that secrecy is important for the announcement of certain kinds of tax changes, but most proposals suggest there should be a clear delineation of certain areas where secrecy is not important.

> The government believes that the fundamental rationale for budget secrecy now, as always, is to prevent the possibility of profit from advance knowledge about matters to be announced in a budget. Should this not be the sole context in which the government interprets and applies the concept of budget secrecy? If this were the accepted notion of budget secrecy, alleged budget "leaks" that do not relate in any way to the possibility of financial profit would not be considered the "stuff" of ministerial resignations. Indeed, such exaggerated reaction only serves to trivialize the concept of budget secrecy, perpetuate confusion and inhibit consultation.[11]

A usual suggestion for reform is that the minister should announce that changes are being considered in a particular field and then invite consultation with interested parties. The original announcement could be made either through a speech in the legislature, or by the use of the coloured paper process as discussed in Chapter 9.[12] Different proposals vary at this point, but the general idea is that members of the public could then make their views known to a legislative committee[13] and/or a permanent committee of experts established for this purpose.

In spite of considerable pressure to open up the system in some ways, governments of all stripes in both federal and provincial spheres have moved very haltingly in this direction. For example, in 1985 the federal Minister of Finance tabled some specific suggestions for improvements in the budgetary process in a number of areas, but his suggestions in the area of secrecy were very vague.[14] In 1985, the government of Ontario arranged for a "pre-budget consultation" which involved *in camera* presentations to the provincial Treasurer by 114 organizations.[15] Of course, secrecy required that this be a form of one-way consultation in that the groups could express their views to the Treasurer, but he could not respond to them in a meaningful fashion.

There are some disadvantages to opening up the budgetary process. One obvious disadvantage is that increased consultation usually leads to increased delay in implementation. A more serious problem could stem from the fact that consultation is always uneven; some groups are able to participate better than others:

> If governments invite public debate of tentative tax changes, it is probable that relatively concentrated, well-organized, and well-financed interests

---

[10]The major proposals are recounted in Hartle, *The Revenue Budget Process*, ch. 4.
[11]Wilson, *The Canadian Budgetary Process: Proposals for Improvement*, p. 27.
[12]D. J. Sherbaniuk, "Budget Secrecy," *Canadian Tax Journal*, vol. 24 (May–June 1976), p. 227.
[13]Ontario, Ministry of Treasury and Economics, *Reforming the Budget Process: A Discussion Paper* (Toronto: Queen's Printer for Ontario, 1985), pp. 5–8.
[14]Wilson, *The Canadian Budgetary Process: Proposals for Improvement*, pp. 25–27.
[15]Ontario, Ministry of Treasury and Economics, *Reforming the Budget Process: A Discussion Paper*, p. 1 and Appendix.

with much at stake will be the most intense and best prepared participants. Their views and assumptions will dominate in the policy arena. . . . Changes unfavorable to business or other well-organized interests will be strongly resisted, while passive citizens, each losing a little, will be " 'nickelled' and 'dimed' into economic oblivion."[16]

The continuing closed nature of the revenue budget process has had the effect of inhibiting comment about the process of budget preparation. However, a great deal of discussion has taken place about the preparation of the expenditure budget.

THEORIES OF THE EXPENDITURE BUDGET

The objective of a theory of the expenditure budget is to explain how governments decide what amounts will be spent on particular functions. Many competing theories have been developed by economists, political scientists, sociologists, and others. This section will review some of the major theories. Many readers will note a similarity between the general models of policy making discussed in Chapter 5 and the theories of budget making discussed below. This is because budget making is simply a specialized form of policy making.

Rational Economic Theory

Classical public finance economics suggests that government expenditure is justified on three different types of goods:[17]

- pure public goods — goods which when provided to anyone are enjoyed equally by all in society; the price mechanism cannot be used to exclude some, e.g., national defence;
- merit wants — goods which could be provided by the private sector, but which would not necessarily be provided in a quantity or at a price which would be deemed appropriate, e.g., education;
- group consumption goods — goods or services which each individual could buy, but which are more efficiently delivered if handled collectively, e.g., water supply, policing.

The demand for government services invariably far outstrips the funds available to pay for them. The question then becomes how government spending should be distributed so as to maximize its benefit. The standard maxim of economics is that dollars should be spent in areas where their marginal benefit is greatest.[18] This has led to the development of a series of rational techniques

---

[16]Robert A. Young, "Business and Budgeting: Recent Proposals for Reforming the Revenue Budgetary Process," *Canadian Public Policy*, vol. 9 (September 1983), p. 354. (Footnote omitted.)

[17]For a more detailed description of these categories, see D. A. L. Auld and F. C. Miller, *Principles of Public Finance: A Canadian Text* (Toronto: Methuen, 1977), ch. 2.

[18]This is actually a rather simplistic approach to an area of economic theory which is very complex. Students with the background and inclination are encouraged to consult a more detailed economics textbook for a fuller treatment of this area. For example, ibid., or Richard A. Musgrave, *The Theory of Public Finance* (New York: McGraw-Hill, 1959), chs. 1, 2, and passim.

such as operations research, systems analysis, and cost-benefit analysis to try to determine which government programs yield the greatest benefit.

The rational economic approach to the expenditure budget has the attraction of a certain intellectual rigour, internal consistency, and mathematical precision. The significance of this approach to budgeting can be seen from the fact that new proposals are almost invariably accompanied by a rational economic justification of their value.

However, many participants in the budgetary process question the practical relevance of some of this analysis. The manipulation of the numbers is always highly objective, but the validity of the numbers themselves is sometimes questioned. What is the value of one life saved? What is the ultimate value of a university versus a high school education? It is usually suggested that, in the tough pulling and hauling which is the real stuff of the budgetary process, these economic analyses are one, but only one, weapon used by the competing interests. Anyone involved in budgeting can cite many cases where political exigencies have carried far more weight in the budgetary process than careful, rational economic analysis.

Incrementalism

Incrementalism is the opposite end of the continuum from rationalism. Incrementalism recognizes that governments are frequently unable to make the comprehensive kinds of calculations required by rational economic theory and, in the face of this complexity, simply retreat into making budgetary calculations by considering last year's allocation plus or minus some minor revision. This is not just the result of despair about being able to make decisions, but stems also from the inability to stop and start programs quickly and from the existence of previous commitments.

> The largest determining factor of the size and content of this year's budget is last year's budget. Most of the budget is a product of previous decisions. As former [United States] Budget Director Stans put it, "There is very little flexibility in the budget because of the tremendous number of commitments that are made years ahead." The budget may be conceived of as an iceberg with by far the largest part below the surface, outside the control of anyone. Many items in the budget are standard and are simply reenacted every year unless there is a special reason to challenge them. Long-range commitments have been made and this year's share is scooped out of the total and included as part of the annual budget. There are mandatory programs . . . whose expenses must be met . . . . There are programs which appear to be satisfactory and which no one challenges any more. Powerful political support makes the inclusion of other activities inevitable.[19]

One effect of this is that the distribution of budgetary allocations does not change much from year to year. Each department's allocation increases by a certain percentage, so that there are seldom big winners or losers.

---

[19]Aaron Wildavsky, *The Politics of the Budgetary Process* (Boston: Little, Brown, 1964), p. 13.

Anyone who has been involved in the preparation of a budget appreciates this model. Budgets are frequently presented in two columns, with next year's request immediately adjacent to the previous year's actual and sometimes additional columns showing the increase or decrease in dollar and/or percentage terms. Politicians' questions usually focus on these *changes*, rather than on the absolute amount of the budget. A quick year-to-year comparison of budgetary allocations of most governments would confirm the presence of these incremental trends; there are seldom huge increases or decreases in expenditure allocations from one year to the next.

However, this theory also has its critics. Lance LeLoup has argued that one reason researchers find incremental patterns in budgets is that they focus on year-to-year changes rather than long-term trends.[20] For example, a year-to-year analysis of Canadian federal budgets of the 1970s would find that social expenditures increased only slightly more rapidly than defence expenditures in each year; this seems like incrementalism at work. However, the *cumulative* impact of these slight annual differences over a period of years amounts to a significant shift in government priorities. Incrementalism clearly has some explanatory value, but there are some changes which it cannot explain.

Another flaw in the incrementalism argument is that it is not so much a theory of how budgets are determined as it is a description of what the likely budget allocation levels will be. A theory which can be used to explain *how* budgets are determined is considered next.

Bureaucratic or Governmental Politics

The bureaucratic or governmental politics approach sees the expenditure budget as the outcome of a bargaining process involving various governmental and some non-governmental organizations. Governments are not monolithic entities; rather, they consist of, on the one hand, many departments and agencies which are in competition with one another for limited resources and, on the other hand, agencies which are responsible for deciding how to divide up these funds. The budget as ultimately determined is the product of the "to-ing and fro-ing" which takes place between and among these entities. In spite of its name, this approach is not limited to bureaucrats; politicians and even representatives of non-governmental organizations become involved.

One of the most common frameworks employed in parliamentary systems to discuss this model of budget making is "spenders" and "guardians."[21] Ministers in operating departments with large constituencies score points when they operate attractive, adequately funded programs. These ministers are "spenders" not just because they want to aggrandize their own positions (although that could be one motivation), but because they come to understand that their clientele has very real needs which can only be met by adequately funded programs. The

[20]"The Myth of Incrementalism: Analytic Choices in Budgetary Theory," in Robert T. Golembiewski and Jack Rabin, eds., *Public Budgeting and Finance: Behavioral, Theoretical, and Technical Perspectives* (New York: Marcel Dekker, 1983), pp. 69–70.
[21]These terms were popularized by Hugh Heclo and Aaron Wildavsky, *The Private Government of Public Money*, 2nd ed. (London: Macmillan Press, 1981), ch. 4.

"guardians" are the Minister of Finance and the President of the Treasury Board who score points for reducing deficits and holding the line on taxes. The overall size of the budget and its allocation among programs is an outcome of the "game" played by the "spenders" and "guardians."

Budgeting as an outcome of bureaucratic politics has been described fully in the United States, where it is easy to analyse because the budget-making process is very open.[22] The work in Canada is more fragmentary, but various players and former players have discussed some aspects of the game.[23]

It should be clear that this bureaucratic politics approach is consistent with the incremental approach discussed above; in fact, bureaucratic politics can explain the presence of incrementalism. In most organizations, neither the rules of the game nor the power relationships between organizations change rapidly. Given the stability of these factors, one would expect to find stability in budgetary allocations.[24]

Just like any game, each side has certain strategies and tactics which it employs to enhance its position. The spenders have the greatest array of potential tactics. They can begin with fairly obvious ones, such as padding their original requests. However, that alone seldom works, because guardians also understand the tactics of the game. Experienced spenders will supplement this basic strategy by a number of other tactics:

1. *Mobilize constituency interest groups.* A spending minister will encourage interest groups to make great demands on his or her department; this significantly increases the minister's bargaining power in Cabinet. Business groups have been very good at this.

2. *The thin edge of the wedge.* Start a program with a very small commitment of funds; when people become dependent on the program, the guardians cannot eliminate it, and in fact will probably be pressed to increase funding.

3. *Kill the Friendly Giant.* When pressed to make budget cuts, always cut the program which is most popular with the public, not least popular. This will bring public pressure to bear on the guardians who demanded the cuts in the first place. A few years ago, when CBC television faced severe budget restraint, it eliminated the popular program "Friendly Giant," which sparked great concern over the cuts.

4. *End run.* In the ordinary budget cycle, when many requests for funding are arrayed against one another, the competition for funds is very keen. A resource-

---

[22]There are so many of these studies that it is impossible to mention even the main ones, but some of the classics are: Wildavsky, *The Politics of the Budgetary Process*; Richard F. Fenno, Jr., *The Power of the Purse: Appropriation Politics in Congress* (Boston: Little, Brown, 1966); John P. Crecine, *Governmental Problem-Solving: A Computer Simulation Model of Municipal Budgeting* (Chicago: Rand McNally, 1969).

[23]Douglas G. Hartle, *The Expenditure Budget Process in the Government of Canada* (Toronto: Canadian Tax Foundation, 1978); Richard French, *How Ottawa Decides* (Toronto: James Lorimer & Company, 1980); Richard Van Loon, "The Policy and Expenditure Management System in the Federal Government: The First Three Years," *Canadian Public Administration*, vol. 26 (Summer 1983), pp. 255–285.

[24]Aaron Wildavsky is one of the analysts who presents this relationship very clearly. See *The Politics of the Budgetary Process*.

ful minister will propose a new program part way through the year and attempt to obtain a snap commitment from Cabinet, thus making an end run around the vicissitudes of the ordinary budget process.

5. *This program saves money.* It is surprisingly easy to argue that a program which costs a significant amount of money in the short run will actually result in a long-run saving. More money on fitness will reduce future health-care costs. Business development grants will generate future taxes. Of course, these relationships cannot be proven, but they sound good.

6. *Fire truck first.* There is an apocryphal story about one of the most audacious strategies of all. A fire chief wanted a new fire truck and a new fire station in the same year. When the city council told him that this was excessive in one year and that he could have either, but not both, he chose to buy the new fire truck. However, when the truck was delivered, it turned out that (you've probably already guessed) the existing fire hall was too small to accommodate the new truck.

Guardians also have tactics of their own, although it is possible that the rapid spending increases of the 1960s and 1970s were a result of an imbalance of power between spenders and guardians. Some of the responses to the above tactics are fairly obvious. For example, most recent budgetary systems have procedures to prevent "end runs," and the claims of program managers that "this program saves money" are usually met with requests to provide hard evidence. The one continuing tactic that guardians have is simply to underestimate revenue and so underestimate the amount available for expenditure. This allows them to paint the picture as being more bleak than it really is, and so increases their bargaining power.

Some people object to this "game" theory because they feel that it trivializes an important part of the governing process. However, the theory strikes a responsive note for anyone who has been involved in the process. "Game" theory should not be equated with deception or a lack of concern for the public interest, but rather it can be seen as a committed group of people interacting and being certain that all options are considered in arriving at an optimum decision.

Public Choice or Self-interest Theories

A variant of the game approach suggests that participants in the budgetary process — both politicians and public servants — attempt to influence budgetary decisions in their own self-interest, or in the interest of their political party or organization. Self-interest in this case should not be interpreted narrowly as income maximization; many people derive significant personal benefits from such things as seeing their personal ideological preferences implemented or assisting in the development of humanitarian social policies.

The working assumption of the public choice approach is that the ultimate goal of any politician or party currently in government is to retain office. This could stem from a venal desire to retain the power and privileges of office, or it could stem from a more upright belief that the ideology of your party is preferable to that of your competitors.

To retain office, politicians will engage in behaviour geared to maximizing the number of votes they can win in the next election. Anthony Downs suggests that this is one of the reasons why politicians are so disposed to redistribute from the rich to the poor, because there are more of the latter than the former.[25]

The refined approach is not simply to spend money hoping to buy votes, but rather to target funds so that they benefit undecided voters or voters in ridings where the results have been close in the past. Winn and Macnaughton found that in the period 1969–1974 a disproportionate share of federal regional development incentive funds went to Quebec ridings that had displayed volatile voting patterns and had elected a Créditiste member in the previous election.[26]

Bureaucrats can play the same sort of self-interest games, but their objective is different. Just like politicians, bureaucrats can have personal venal motivations stemming from the fact that a public servant's income and prestige are increased in line with increases in his or her budget and staff, or they can have more public-spirited ideas that expenditures on programs to which they are committed will further the public interest. Regardless of the underlying reasoning, public servants will use various strategies to increase the budgetary allocation to their program. The most prominent strategies suggested by Niskanen are to withhold information from, and control information available to, political decision makers and to ensure that the service of the bureau is provided on a monopoly basis so that comparisons of cost and quality of service cannot be made.[27]

One of the prescriptions proposed to overcome this strategy is to provide services through a number of different institutional arrangements, e.g., contracting out to other governments and private enterprise, so that comparisons are possible and competition drives prices down.[28] This is one of the major arguments usually made for contracting out public services.

Socio-economic Determinants

It is sometimes argued that political factors have little to do with budgetary outcomes, but rather that levels of public expenditure are influenced by certain socio-economic factors. For example, "Wagner's law" posits that "as per capita income rises in industrializing nations, their public sectors will grow in relative importance."[29] In general this means that as a country's per capita income increases, its level of public expenditure will increase even more rapidly. This has been confirmed in virtually every case in which it has been tested. Further proof of the weak explanatory power of political factors is provided by Frederic Pryor's study of capitalist and communist countries, which concluded that "in a

---

[25]*An Economic Theory of Democracy* (New York: Harper & Row, 1957), ch. 10.

[26]Bruce D. Macnaughton and Conrad J. Winn, "Economic Policy and Electoral Self Interest: The Allocations of the Department of Regional Economic Expansion," *Canadian Public Policy*, vol. 7 (Spring 1981), pp. 318–327.

[27]William A. Niskanen, Jr., *Bureaucracy and Representative Government* (Chicago: Aldine-Atherton, 1971), ch. 3 and passim.

[28]Ibid., chs. 18 and 19.

[29]Richard M. Bird, *The Growth of Government Spending in Canada* (Toronto: Canadian Tax Foundation, 1970), p. 70.

great many cases the degree of variation among nations with the same economic system is much greater than the variation between the two economic systems, even after the influence of other determinants has been removed."[30]

The importance of socio-economic variables can be explained from either the supply or the demand side. From the supply side, it might be argued that as societies become more affluent, their resistance to taxation is reduced, and so they are willing to provide more funding to government. On the demand side, it might be argued that as societies become more affluent and complex they demand more from government, first, in the area of social programs such as free education, and then in even broader areas, e.g., concert halls, domed stadiums, elaborate expositions.

There are a great many studies of the influence of socio-economic factors on budgetary allocations. Most studies suggest that there is a strong statistical relationship between increasing public expenditure and increasing per capita incomes, increasing urbanization, increasing levels of education of the population, and related socio-economic variables. One major test of this hypothesis in Canada, which covered the period from Confederation to the late 1960s, suggested that socio-economic variables explained a great deal of the pattern of expenditure, but that there was still a significant amount of change in expenditure that could not be explained by socio-economic variables.[31]

One of the major flaws of the socio-economic approach is that, while it confirms a statistical relationship between various variables, it does not *explain* how the socio-economic variables cause changes in expenditure. These socio-economic variables probably do impose constraints on decision makers, but one cannot ignore the fact that there are at least two groups of decision makers — politicians and public servants — who mediate between the socio-economic variables and the budget. Clearly, these people have some role in budget determination.

Political Factors

During election campaigns, political parties spend a great deal of time and money attempting to convince the public that voting for a particular party will produce significant policy changes. Most studies of budgeting indicate that this is simply not the case, at least with regard to levels of expenditure. It would be an overstatement to say that "politics doesn't matter," but most studies of expenditure patterns do not show major changes in budgetary allocations as a result of changes in the party in power.

There are a number of conventional wisdoms about other political factors which supposedly influence expenditure decisions. For example, minority governments spend more money, particularly in areas such as social services, in

---

[30]*Public Expenditures in Communist and Capitalist Nations* (London: Allen & Unwin, 1968), p. 285.

[31]David J. Falcone and Michael S. Whittington, "Output Change in Canada: A Preliminary Attempt to Open the 'Black Box' " (Paper presented to the Annual Meeting of the Canadian Political Science Association, Montreal, Quebec, June 4, 1972).

order to influence voting in the next election. The rise of "third parties" is some-times said to frighten governments into instituting policies which they would not otherwise adopt. The oft-cited Canadian example of this phenomenon is Mackenzie King's introduction of the "baby bonus" at a time of rising CCF fortunes.

Again, one should not overstate the case — it is clear that these conventional wisdoms accurately describe certain events — but the general evidence is that these political factors have fairly weak explanatory power.

The best explanation of expenditure patterns might be that there is no one simple explanation; rather, all of the above factors have *some* impact in deter-mining levels of expenditure. The relative importance of the different models might vary, depending on the policy area, the relative power of the government party, or other factors. Bruce Macnaughton conducted a major study of three areas of social policy and arrived at the conclusion that a combination of incrementalism and bureaucratic politics was

> important in all three policy areas and exerted the predominant influence on expenditure on unemployment insurance and old age pensions. Socio-economic variables were found to be the most important determinants of expenditures on family and youth allowances. Political variables, particu-larly support for the CCF/NDP, the presence of minority governments and elections and the level of electoral competition were found to have an inde-pendent effect in each policy area, although the exact variables differed. Overall, these findings suggest that socio-economic and organizational vari-ables restrict the discretion of policy-makers, but that, within this area of discretion, political variables enter into the decision-making process. This finding stands in contrast with most previous cross-sectional research stud-ies which have tended to conclude that political variables exert little or no influence on spending patterns.
>
> [This research] did not uncover any modes of explanation capable of accounting for the overall pattern of social security expenditure. Rather, [it] suggested that each explanatory mode, whether socio-economic, organi-zational, or political, focuses on a different aspect of reality. It is the inter-action among the three that determines expenditure outcomes. The basic question to be resolved, then, is not which is the single most useful expla-nation but rather how and in what manner these approaches can comple-ment one another.[32]

As Macnaughton's work indicates, it is unlikely that any one of these theories will precisely explain budgetary allocations. It is possible to find elements of each of them in real-world budgeting patterns, so that they each have some influence in the final process, although the level of their influence could well vary with the style of budgeting technique employed. The next section will dis-cuss those styles.

---

[32]"Public Finance for Political Profit: The Politics of Social Security in Canada, 1941-1977" (Ph.D. diss., Carleton University, 1980), pp. iii-iv.

STYLES OF THE EXPENDITURE BUDGET

There are many different styles of budgeting in use in different jurisdictions. There is no general consensus about the optimum approach to the expenditure budget; each organization seems to adopt a slightly different style. Regardless of the approach employed, it is usually argued that the ideal budgeting system has three factors: control; management; and planning and policy choice.[33]

"*Control* refers to the process of binding operating officials to the policies and plans set by their superiors."[34] A satisfactory budgeting system must have some method of ensuring that managers do not overspend their budgets and that they do not spend money on programs which have not been properly authorized.

A sound system of good *management* goes beyond simply ensuring that subordinates are following orders; it also ensures that work is organized so as to achieve efficiency and effectiveness.

When the problems of legal control were deemed to be solved, effective management was added to the purposes of budgeting. The budget was seen as a management tool to ensure the economical and efficient operation of departments and programs. The introduction of labour-saving equipment, the streamlining of paper processing, the careful determination of manpower needs, and the introduction of performance measurement procedures to relate results achieved to resources used are among the typical activities associated with management control.[35]

"*Planning* involves the determination of objectives, the evaluation of alternative courses of action and the authorization of select programs."[36] If planning is a part of the budgetary system, then the system can provide information about the future, which can be used in making trade-offs among policies. The ideal budgeting system will be able to deal with all three of these, but the search for that ideal has been somewhat elusive.

In searching for this ideal style, a number of innovations have been introduced over the years. It is sometimes difficult to find precise dividing lines between approaches, but it is possible to identify four major styles of budgeting that have been employed in recent years: line-item, performance, program, and zero-base. Some of the characteristics of these styles are illustrated in Table 23.1, and each style will be discussed in more detail below. However, it is important to understand that these different styles are not mutually exclusive. There are many examples of organizations creating hybrid systems by borrowing from different styles. For example, it will be argued that the current federal budgetary system contains elements of both program and zero-base budgeting.

---

[33]Donald Gow, *The Progress of Budgetary Reform in the Government of Canada* (Ottawa: Information Canada, 1973), p. 1.

[34]Allen Schick, "The Road to PPB: The Stages of Budget Reform," *Public Administration Review*, vol. 26 (December 1966), p. 244. (Emphasis in original.)

[35]Paul G. Thomas, "Public Administration and Expenditure Management," *Canadian Public Administration*, vol. 25 (Winter 1982), pp. 678–679.

[36]Schick, "The Road to PPB: The Stages of Budget Reform," p. 244. (Emphasis in original.)

Table 23.1
COMPARISON OF DIFFERENT STYLES OF BUDGETING

	Line-item	Performance	Program	ZBB
Building Block	Object of expenditure	Unit cost and units of service	Program	Decision package
Key Expert	Accountant	Cost accountant	Economist	Multi-disciplined program analyst
Time Horizon	Annual	Annual	Multi-year	Annual (some longer-term considerations)
Direction of Construction	Bottom-up	Bottom-up	Top-down	Bottom-up and top-down
Key Agency	Operating department	Operating department	Central agencies	Central agencies
Method of Evaluation of Manager	Does not overspend	Minimizes unit cost	Maximizes program performance	Maximizes program performance
Type of Decision Making	Decentralized	Decentralized	Centralized	Centralized
Dominant Philosophy of Decision Making	Incremental	Incremental	Rational	Rational
Strong Points	Emphasizes control Discourages conflict	More information for decision makers Emphasizes: –productivity improvement –cost minimization	Emphasizes rational process Emphasizes program and planning	Focus on priority setting Facilitates cost cutting Equal competition between established and new programs
Weak Points	Emphasizes status quo Little information for decision makers	No cross-program comparisons	High cost Dubious techniques	High cost Dubious techniques Morale problems

Line-item Budgeting

Line-item budgeting was chronologically the first style of budgeting employed in modern public administration and is usually considered to be the most rudimentary.[37] Figure 23.1 illustrates a page from a line-item budget. This page covers the entire budget of one department and shows how the requested funds will be spent by object of expenditure, e.g., salaries, rent, supplies. This illustrates the manner in which the line-item budget focusses on *inputs used* rather than *outputs achieved*.

Figure 23.1
EXAMPLE OF LINE-ITEM BUDGET

CITY OF ANYTOWN
FIRE DEPARTMENT
FISCAL YEAR ENDING DECEMBER 31, 1987

Object of Expenditure	1987 (Budget)	1986 (Actual)
Salaries—Regular	120,000	110,000
Salaries—Overtime	10,000	9,000
Casual Labour	9,000	8,000
Employee Benefits	12,000	11,000
Firefighting Equipment	11,000	10,000
Uniforms	6,000	5,000
Building Rent	24,000	22,000
Stationery	6,000	5,000
Cleaning Supplies	3,000	2,000
Travel	5,000	4,000
Vehicle Maintenance	4,000	3,000
Miscellaneous Expenses	3,000	3,000
TOTAL	213,000	192,000

The key person in the preparation of this type of budget is the accountant, because the process basically involves reviewing last year's budget and making revisions based on inflation and changes in the size of the population served. This process is usually carried out on an annual basis; there is ordinarily no attempt at long-range planning. The key agency is the operating department,

---

[37]A good general discussion of the chronological development of the different styles of budgeting is contained in James Cutt and Richard Ritter, *Public Non-Profit Budgeting: The Evolution and Application of Zero-Base Budgeting* (Toronto: The Institute of Public Administration of Canada, 1984), chs. 4–7. A specific description of how the evolution occurred in the Canadian federal government is given in Donald Gow, *The Progress of Budgetary Reform in the Government of Canada*.

and the budget is prepared on a "bottom-up" basis. This means that the process begins with the operating department preparing a request for funds, which it then passes upward to decision makers who, frankly, have a great deal of difficulty making any revisions in the original request because of the very detailed manner in which it is prepared. This leads to a decentralized style of decision making because decisions are made in operating departments with little opportunity for meaningful review by politicians.

The use of line-item budgeting makes it somewhat awkward to evaluate a manager's performance. The main sign of a good manager in this system is that he or she does not overspend the assigned budget; clearly, this is a minimal requirement for good management, but there is simply too little information available to make any other kind of judgement.

All of this adds up to a style of decision making on budgetary allocations which can only be incremental, i.e., this year's budgetary allocation is determined by making incremental changes in last year's allocation. This usually means uniform across-the-board increases in the allocations to all departments. Everyone involved in the process recognizes that this is inferior to a thoughtful process that seriously considers the needs of each department separately and provides more funding to agencies with greater needs. However, because of the dearth of meaningful information generated in a line-item budgeting system, there is no alternative to the incremental approach.

Line-item budgeting emphasizes the control aspect of the budget. It makes it very easy to prevent overspending or to determine who is responsible if it does occur. It also limits some of the conflict which is found in other styles of budgeting because it tends to compartmentalize spending, rather than emphasize trade-offs. This characteristic is a political defect in line-item budgeting. The limited information about output which is generated makes it very difficult for decision makers (politicians or senior managers) to make trade-offs about the quality of programs. Therefore, line-item budgeting does not lend itself to the management and planning and policy choice orientations which were discussed above.

Line-item budgeting is useful in the case of relatively small, simple organizations where all decision makers can grasp the roles of the different organizational units quickly and intuitively. The dearth of output information generated by it and its lack of a management or planning and policy choice orientation make it considerably less useful in large, dynamic organizations. Nonetheless, it is still used in some organizations, largely because of its simplicity of operation and because the accountants who frequently control the budgetary process feel comfortable with it.

The basic problem in line-item budgeting is its lack of an output orientation, i.e., the absence of any measuring technique to determine what is being accomplished by the expenditures. Therefore, it is not surprising that the next improvement in the budgetary process would address this concern for output measurement.

Performance Budgeting

The basic difference between line-item and performance budgeting was the output orientation of performance budgeting.[38] Line item budgeting measured only inputs used; performance budgeting established a relationship between inputs employed and outputs attained. The basic building block of performance budgeting was the unit cost of providing a service (inputs) and the number of units of service provided (outputs). Thus, a budgetary allocation was established by multiplying units of service (clients served, miles of road paved) by the unit cost of providing each service.

The key budgetary expert became the cost accountant because he or she possessed the esoteric skills needed to collect and calculate information about unit costs. The unit cost information created an additional method of evaluating a good manager, besides not overspending his or her budget. Managers performing similar duties could be evaluated by comparing the unit costs of their operations.

In making budgetary allocations, it was possible to escape from the incrementalism trap in a limited way. Reasonable estimates could usually be made about changes in the demand for the service, although even here incrementalism frequently had to be used as an aid in calculation. The unit cost side of the equation could be influenced somewhat by experience in other jurisdictions, but in the final analysis incrementalism was a frequent guide here as well.

The strong point of performance budgeting was that it added a management improvement focus to the control focus of line-item budgeting. It provided decision makers with enough information to consider management improvement and cost minimization techniques. However, performance budgeting did not provide any techniques for future planning; nor did it provide enough information to make trade-offs among programs. These techniques would come later.

Program Budgeting

In proceeding chronologically through the various budgetary styles, one can see a steady ascendancy in the basic building block from the object of expenditure, to the unit of service, to the entire program. But there were many more changes which came with program budgeting than just the emphasis on program.

In general, program budgeting was an attempt to adapt the rational decision-making techniques discussed in Chapter 5 to the budgetary process. A 1969 publication of the federal government described the concepts that were common to all program budgeting systems as:

(a) the setting of specific objectives;

(b) the systematic analysis to clarify objectives and to assess alternative ways of meeting them;

---

[38]A good description of the strengths and weaknesses of performance budgeting is contained in V. N. MacDonald and P. J. Lawton, *Improving Management Performance: The Contribution of Productivity and Performance Measurement* (Toronto: Ministry of Treasury, Economics and Intergovernmental Affairs, 1977), pp. 32–33.

(c) the framing of budgetary proposals in terms of programs directed toward the achievement of the objectives;

(d) the projection of the costs of these programs a number of years in the future;

(e) the formulation of plans of achievement year by year for each program; and

(f) an information system for each program to supply data for the monitoring of achievement of program goals and to supply data for the reassessment of the program objectives and the appropriateness of the program itself.[39]

Note the similarity between these steps and those mentioned in Chapter 5 under the general heading of rational techniques such as determining objectives, examining alternative methods of attaining objectives, implementing the optimum method, and installing feedback mechanisms to measure attainment of objectives.

In practice, the implementation of program budgeting, or Planning-Programming-Budgeting (PPB) as it was called in the federal sphere, involved the division of the activities of each department into discrete units called programs and the preparation of *multi-year* budgetary forecasts for each program. The purpose of the multi-year estimates was to alert decision makers to the full future costs of programs, particularly in cases in which programs started with a limited use of resources and expanded in future years.

Program budgeting is frequently described as a "top-down" system because it encourages a centralization of decision making by allowing decision makers to escape the excessive detail contained in line-item and performance budgets. Instead, the decision makers could communicate messages such as "we need to hold the line on social services," or "this is the year to provide a bit more to defence," by simply allowing smaller increases in social programs and greater increases in defence ones. This sort of movement of macro-levers is only possible because of the emphasis on broad programs instead of details of expenditure.

Program budgeting brought with it a large set of rational economic tools such as cost-benefit analysis, cost-effectiveness analysis, and systems analysis. These tools could maximize government performance by providing a rational, economic comparison of different methods of attaining goals, and even comparing the worth of trying to attain particular goals. The most extreme proponents of this kind of thinking argued that the ultimate purpose of government was to maximize human well-being—economic, physical, social, psychic, etc. —and that this well-being could be measured and rational techniques employed to determine which government programs would best attain this maximization of well-being. Others stopped somewhat short of these lengths, but all practitioners of program budgeting argued that there were rational, economic tools which could be used to make trade-offs between programs.

Since the economist was the primary person who employed these kinds of techniques, program budgeting caused the mantle of key expert to pass from

---

[39]Honourable C. M. Drury, *Planning-Programming-Budgeting Guide* (Ottawa: Queen's Printer, 1969), p. 8.

the accountant to the economist. The other structural change which occurred at the same time was the ascendancy of central agencies, in particular Treasury Board. If decision making is more centralized and trade-offs between departments are more important, then there is an obvious need for a central agency to deal with these various elements.

The strength of program budgeting is that it includes all three of the factors which are important for an ideal budgeting style — control, management, and planning and policy choice. In evaluating the worth of a manager, program budgeting emphasizes not just avoiding overspending or minimizing cost, but rather maximizing program performance. The multi-year focus allows for future planning, and the use of rational, economic techniques allows for effective, informed policy choice.

There have been a number of innovations in program budgeting and a number of other management techniques grafted on to it over the years.

In the federal government, management by objectives (described more fully in Chapter 3) was added to it in some departments.[40] It would seem that these two objectives-oriented approaches should meld together well, but the two innovations were developed separately by separate groups — PPB by financial officials and MBO by personnel officials — and were never really merged.[41] Whether it was for this or other reasons, MBO was adopted only in a small number of departments.

At roughly the same time as MBO was being imported, Treasury Board was developing its own system to supplement PPB and MBO. The key to the operation of both these systems is good measurement of the performance, or outputs, achieved by programs. The Operational Performance Measurement System (OPMS) was meant to be the performance measurement aspect of PPB and MBO.[42]

The concept of OPMS began with the idea that the ultimate goal of all government programs is to foster "individual and collective well-being," as evidenced by such things as national integrity, social justice, national wealth, and individual fulfilment. Of course, it is impossible to measure most of these things in a tangible way, and even if it were possible to measure overall change, measuring the impact of a *particular* program on national integrity would be most contentious.

Therefore, OPMS suggested the use of a hierarchy of proxy measures. It is, for example, impossible to measure the effect of industrial incentives on social justice. However, if we posit a series of means/ends relationships in which the use of industrial incentives begins a chain reaction which ultimately has an impact

---

[40]J. S. Hodgson, "Management by Objectives — The Experience of a Federal Government Department," *Canadian Public Administration*, vol. 16 (Fall 1973), pp. 422-431.

[41]H. L. Laframboise, "Administrative Reform in the Federal Public Service: Signs of a Saturation Psychosis," *Canadian Public Administration*, vol. 14 (Fall 1971), p. 312.

[42]Treasury Board, *Operational Performance Measurement, Vol. I: A Managerial Overview* and *Vol. II: Technical Manual* (Ottawa: Information Canada, 1974); D. G. Hartle, "Operational Performance Measurement in the Federal Government," *Optimum*, vol. 3, no. 4 (1972), pp. 5-18; Henning Frederiksen, "Is Operational Performance in Government Measurable?" *Optimum*, vol. 6, no. 4 (1975), pp. 23-41.

on social justice, then it is possible to measure some of these intermediate steps. For example, a certain amount of money (inputs, in OPMS terminology) is provided for industrial incentives; this is converted into a certain number of grants awarded to industries (operational outputs); these are converted into a certain number of new jobs (program outputs); and these, in turn, are converted into increased earned income (program effects), which results in improved social justice. The final step cannot be measured, but all the proxies leading to it can be. OPMS also prescribes the calculation of a number of ratios between the various proxies; for example, a measure of operational efficiency would be determined by dividing operational outputs by program inputs. These ratios could be used to measure changes in a program over time, or to compare programs.

As a result of implementation problems and bureaucratic resistance, OPMS was never widely adopted in the federal government. It now stands as an interesting possible approach to a recognized problem, but not an approach which has any support in the federal government.

However, a few other notable innovations in program budgeting have been more widely used. As a part of the PPB system, federal departments were required to prepare their budgets in three parts. The "A" budget represents the continuation of existing programs with adjustments made for inflation and changes in the population served. The "B" budget is the request for either the establishment of new programs or the enrichment and enhancement of existing programs. The "X" budget is a listing of the programs which a department would eliminate if it were forced to reduce its budget by a stated percentage. In other words, "X" budget items are the lowest priority programs ranked by the department. The idea was that "A" budget items would not be evaluated in depth because these programs were approved previously, but that there would be an in-depth review of the costs and benefits of new programs — the "B" budget items — before they were begun. As will be discussed in more detail later, the "A" and "B" budgets continue to play an important part in the federal budgetary process. The concept of the "X" budget is still discussed, but understandably, it has not been warmly welcomed by departments.

Another innovation in program budgeting has been most prevalent in municipal governments. For each program, the manager is required to estimate the effects on the program — in terms of levels of service — if it were to operate at three different levels of funding — the same budget as last year (adjusted by inflation and population served), and, say, 80 per cent and 120 per cent of last year's funding. This provides decision makers with a significant amount of knowledge which they can use in deciding on funding levels.

PPB was clearly the major budgeting innovation of the 1960s and the early 1970s. Virtually every government of any size in North America experimented with some form of program budgeting. The success of those experiments has been mixed. The Canadian federal government seems to be attaining a modicum of success with a revised program budgeting system called the Policy and Expenditure Management System (discussed in more detail below) after a long history of budget reform. First, there was PPB, which was supplemented by OPMS and experienced a failed marriage with MBO before finally becoming PEMS.

Other jurisdictions have been less successful. In the United States federal government, the death of PPB was reported as early as 1973.[43]

The reasons for the problems experienced with PPB are many and varied.[44] As noted above, it is an attempt to apply rational modes of decision making to the budget process. Therefore, many of the general criticisms of rational decision-making techniques are also applicable to PPB. The high cost in both dollars and time of implementing the system and the sheer complexity of some attempts were clearly problems. In some cases, the amount of time spent "getting ready to get ready" seriously weakened the credibility of those seeking to implement PPB. Also, the attempt to impose one system of evaluation on diverse programs led to some difficulties. Schick argues that the success of PPB in the United States Department of Defence stems in part from the fact that it was home-grown there; its failure in other departments stems from its status as a foreign intruder unable to adapt to the local customs.[45]

There is one outstanding reason for the problems of PPB that is too often overlooked. Changes in budgeting systems are not mere minor technical adjustments in procedures of import only to accountants. Certain changes in budgeting systems amount to vast shifts of power within organizations.[46] This was the case with PPB. PPB usually involved a shift from a decentralized form of budgeting, such as line-item or performance budgeting, to a highly centralized one. In the decentralized systems, individual departments present budget requests, but little information, to politicians. The politicians, in turn, do not have a group of qualified experts from whom they can seek advice. All of this means that the head of the department has fairly broad latitude to manage the department, with minimum scope for intrusion from either any other department or politicians.

PPB introduces a new actor to the scene — the strong central budget agency. If detailed documentation is to be prepared, cost-benefit analysis performed, and trade-offs made between various programs, there must be an organization to do these things. If the system is to function correctly, this organization must have the right to request significant amounts of information from departments and evaluate that information in order to make recommendations to politicians. This would allow the budget agency to have a clear "window" into the operation of departments and so provide the agency with the ability to exercise some degree of control over operating departments. Thus operating departments tend

[43]Allen Schick, "A Death in the Bureaucracy: The Demise of Federal PPB," *Public Administration Review*, vol. 33 (March–April 1973), pp. 146–156.

[44]The strongest critic of the system in Canada is one of its veterans, D. G. Hartle, "Techniques and Processes of Administration," *Canadian Public Administration*, vol. 19 (Spring 1976), pp. 24–29. One of the most prolific and perceptive critics of PPB in general has been Aaron Wildavsky, "The Political Economy of Efficiency: Cost-Benefit Analysis, Systems Analysis, and Program Budgeting," *Public Administration Review*, vol. 26 (December 1966), pp. 292–310, and "Rescuing Policy Analysis from PPB," *Public Administration Review*, vol. 29 (March–April 1969), pp 189–202.

[45]Schick, "A Death in the Bureaucracy," p. 147.

[46]This shift in power is described very well in A. Clayton, "Brother Could You Spare a Dime?" *Optimum*, vol. 12, no. 1 (1981), pp. 7–19.

to oppose the introduction of PPB because they fear the increased exposure which this window provides.

Additional difficulties with a rational system of budgeting surround the related problems of specifying goals, measuring benefits achieved, and predicting future conditions.[47] Government programs usually serve multiple goals, and many times people will disagree on the relative priority of those goals. Is the purpose of a youth employment program to have certain work activities carried out? To assist young people in developing good work habits? To provide funds to young people to continue their schooling? To buy votes? The likely answer is that it is all of these, but which one is seen as paramount will have an effect on how the program is designed and evaluated.

A related problem is the inability to measure in a rigorous, quantified fashion the benefits derived from government services. Everyone agrees that it is beneficial that the garbage is picked up, but how is this value determined objectively in dollars and cents so that costs and benefits can be compared? Arguably, *some* of the public health benefits could be measured, but what about the aesthetic, convenience and other benefits?

A final problem has to do with the difficulty of predicting the future. Many programs have a large initial cost, and a stream of benefits that flows far into the future. The value assigned to that stream of benefits can depend on the number of people who will enjoy them. For example, the total benefit derived from the construction of a second airport in Toronto is highly sensitive to whether one assumes that the level of usage remains steady, increases slightly, or increases significantly.[48] Yet, no one is able to predict with sufficient precision which situation will occur.

For these and other reasons, many have suggested that PPB has failed. It might well be that PPB has not failed, but rather that some people expected (and others promised) more than PPB could ever deliver. Stated baldly, some felt that PPB was a rational device which would enable us to remove politics from the budgetary process. Programs would be selected using various economic techniques. Politicians and interest groups would be so swayed by the clear and unequivocal answers provided by these techniques, and by the totally impartial rationality of the system, that they would immediately confirm the results. In retrospect, the kindest thing one can say is that this sort of thinking was naive. "One might wonder how a paper tiger such as PPB could possibly wreck the entrenched values defended by the armies of interest groups which patrol the budget scene."[49]

Zero-base Budgeting

In the 1970s, as the glamour of PPB waned, it began to be supplanted by the latest budgetary innovation — zero-base budgeting. Of course, PPB is still widely

[47]Peter Self, *Econocrats and the Policy Process: The Politics and Philosophy of Cost-Benefit Analysis* (London: Macmillan, 1975).

[48]Sandford F. Borins, *The Toronto Airport(s), Case Program in Canadian Public Administration* (Toronto: Institute of Public Administration of Canada, 1977).

[49]Schick, "A Death in the Bureaucracy," p. 149.

used, but the glamorous new technique of the late 1970s and early 1980s is ZBB. Charles Beard, writing in 1917, provided a rationale for this shift: "Budget reform bears the imprint of the age in which it originated."[50] PPB was one of the casualties of the economic downturn of the mid-1970s. PPB is a budgetary system for a dynamic, expanding government. It evaluates new programs and helps determine which to implement immediately and which must be put off until next year. It is more difficult to use in times of fiscal restraint. Enter zero-base budgeting.

Zero-base budgeting derives its name from the fact that conceptually managers are required to justify every dollar requested from zero up.[51] The implication is that if they cannot, their programs will be reduced or eliminated. The building block of ZBB is the decision package. The decision package is basically the program under program budgeting divided into several elements. One decision package could be 80 per cent of last year's funding for the program. A second package would be the increment from 80 per cent to 100 per cent; and the third could be an increment from 100 per cent to 120 per cent of last year's funding. A manager would then prepare a document for each decision package which provided a large amount of quantitative and other information about each package. Systems vary, but some of the usual components are:
- description of actions performed;
- achievements from actions (both a narrative and some quantitative measures might be required);
- consequences of not approving package;
- alternative methods of accomplishing the same objective; and
- calculation of a benefit-cost or similar ratio.

This provides decision makers with information not just about the total program, but about the outputs of various elements or levels of service of the program.

After preparation of these documents for each decision package, the ranking begins. It starts at the lowest level at which a manager has several decision packages under his or her control. This manager will rank these decision packages in order of priority and pass this ranking up to the next level in the hierarchy. The manager at this level will receive decision packages from a number of subordinates, which he or she in turn ranks in order of priority. This process continues up the hierarchy. In some organizations, as the process approaches the top levels of the hierarchy, committees are used to do the ranking. This frequently culminates in a final ranking done by committees of politicians (and sometimes administrators).

At the conclusion of this process, there exists a ranking of all decision packages from the most to the least attractive. At the same time that the ranking process is taking place, a decision is made concerning the level of total expenditure for the year. The final step is simply to start at the top of the list, add up proposed expenditures and accumulate until one arrives at the desired expenditure level. All programs above the line are accepted; all those below are rejected.

---

[50]As quoted in Schick, "The Road to PPB," p. 247.
[51]The definitive work about ZBB has been written by the man who developed it: Peter A. Pyhrr, *Zero-Base Budgeting* (Toronto: John Wiley, 1973).

Zero-base budgeting can be viewed as both a "bottom-up" and a "top-down" approach, because it allows lower level managers to participate in the ranking process, but saves final decisions for politicians and senior managers.

Zero-base budgeting has a number of features that aid in cost cutting and thus make it suitable for its time. In the first place, it evaluates *all* programs, not just new initiatives. The existence of the "A" and "B" budget systems in the federal government has meant that "A" items are usually not seriously reviewed for reductions. The attempt is to hold the line on new initiatives. Thus, this system does not provide any way to cut back. ZBB subjects existing programs to the same evaluation as new ones, and so at least raises the possibility that existing programs could be eliminated, and possibly even replaced by new, better ones.

Another important factor in ZBB that facilitates holding the line on spending is that the revenue constraint can be set first and the level of expenditure cut to fit it. This helps treasurers and other guardians of the public purse to withstand the onslaughts of spenders. This is likely one reason why ZBB has been most popular among municipal governments, which are not allowed to operate at a deficit.

Many of the criticisms of PPB are applicable also to ZBB. Both systems are attempts to achieve rationality in expenditure management. This is both their strength and their weakness. An additional flaw of ZBB is the effect on the morale of employees of this annual review to determine whether some programs will continue to exist. Presumably, large organizational units could be eliminated with great loss of jobs on the occasion of one of these reviews. If that is not really the case, then ZBB is not doing what it set out to do. This realization could well motivate managers to maximize their short-term successes, with possible poor consequences for the longer-term.

There have been some limited evaluations of ZBB systems in practice.[52] The usual conclusion is that the system has some real value, although sometimes not as much as had been hoped. It should be emphasized that most applications have been in existence such a short time that evaluation is problematic.

ZBB, like PPB, is a product of its times. PPB pointed the way to new programs; ZBB shows where to make cuts. The four styles of budgeting identified here are ideal types in that one seldom sees an example of a pure application of one type or the other. The more usual situation is a hybrid system which borrows the particular parts most suited to a particular environment and produces a new form of budgeting process. This is basically how the federal government's budgetary process has developed over time.

---

[52]James Cutt and Richard Ritter, *Public Non-Profit Budgeting*, chs. 8–11; Stephen L. Gould, Alan A. Oldall, and Fred Thompson, "Zero-Base Budgeting: Some Lessons From an Inconclusive Experiment," *Canadian Public Administration*, vol. 22 (Summer 1979), pp. 251–260.

THE FEDERAL POLICY AND EXPENDITURE MANAGEMENT SYSTEM

Systems such as PPB and ZBB are basically imports from the United States, although they were sometimes implemented with local variations. The Policy and Expenditure Management System (PEMS), or the "envelope" system, is a Canadian invention[53] which combines some elements of both PPB and ZBB. The development of PEMS arose from some of the same concerns which spurred ZBB. This section will discuss the early years of PEMS from 1979 to 1984 and the revisions made to it by the Mulroney government after that.

The major product of the budgetary process is a multi-volume set of documents entitled the *Estimates*, sometimes called the "Blue Book."[54] These volumes contain the detail of the expenditure budget and are tabled in the House of Commons by the President of the Treasury Board before the beginning of the fiscal year. Part II, which is called the *Main Estimates*, is debated in Parliament, and when it is passed it represents the formal legislation which provides authority for spending by the executive. After it is passed, it is referred to as the Appropriation Act for that year. The remainder of this chapter will describe the process involved in the preparation of the *Estimates*.

The Early Years: 1979–1984

The 1960s and 1970s saw government revenue rise rapidly. On the expenditure side, there were many new initiatives in health and social services to soak up the increase in revenue. As these buoyant revenues began to slow in the mid- to late 1970s, expenditures obviously had to follow, but this was not easily accomplished. A major part of the problem was that policies were frequently considered on a piecemeal basis, and a number of individual programs were begun without any understanding that their *cumulative* impact on the federal budget would be very serious. In essence, the problem was that *policy initiatives were being considered apart from their budgetary implications*.

One of the major culprits was the increasing use of tax expenditures in the 1970s. *Tax expenditures* are benefits enjoyed in the form of reduced taxes for individuals or corporations who do (or refrain from doing) certain things. For example, there have been programs which encouraged people to invest in scientific research or Canadian-made movies in exchange for a tax benefit. These tax expenditures were used in place of outright cash grants. Their attraction stemmed from the obviously mistaken notion that tax reductions did not really

---

[53]For a discussion of the origins of PEMS, see Sandford F. Borins, "Ottawa's Expenditure Envelopes: Workable Rationality at Last?" in G. Bruce Doern, ed., *How Ottawa Spends Your Tax Dollars: National Policy and Economic Development — 1982* (Toronto: James Lorimer & Company, 1982), pp. 64–66.

[54]The contents of the *Estimates* will be discussed in more detail in the appendix that follows this chapter.

"cost" anything because they did not show up as expenses.[55] Thus, departments could adopt particular policies through a tax expenditure with no idea of, or concern for, the amount of its cost to the treasury.

The Policy and Expenditure Management System was, as the name suggests, a marriage of the policy making and expenditure management systems. It was an attempt to force politicians to consider the budgetary implications of their actions. The system actually had a number of aims. These have been described by the then President of the Treasury Board as follows:

(a) to achieve closer integration of the government's priority setting, policy development and expenditure management decision-making processes;

(b) to decentralize decision-making authority, in recognition of the increasing range and complexity of government responsibilities and the interrelated policies and programs designed to discharge them;

(c) to increase Ministerial discretion and control over the policy, planning and expenditure decisions of the government; and

(d) to provide an adequate time frame in the planning process, so that Ministers can review existing policies and programs and bring about desirable changes in the use of resources to reflect changing priorities of the government.[56]

Prime Minister Trudeau's use of PEMS involved quite a lengthy and complex budget process. The Department of Finance prepared a five-year fiscal framework, which it updated each year. This was communicated to the Cabinet Committee on Priorities and Planning, which used the information to decide on the total level of government spending for a particular year, and then divided that pie into broad categories such as social development, external affairs, and defence. The "envelopes" which contained these allocations were then passed to the relevant Cabinet policy committee to further subdivide between departments and programs. Figure 23.2 illustrates the eight envelopes and the five Cabinet committees responsible for them in the 1986–87 fiscal year.

Sometimes, an envelope contained a "policy reserve." This was a pool of funds which the policy committee could use at its own discretion to launch new initiatives. Policy committees could create or add to their policy reserves by reducing expenditure on existing programs. There was also the possibility of a negative policy reserve which would force the committee to search for savings in its area.[57] One of the most significant innovations of this system was the power it gave to

---

[55]The illusions involved in tax expenditures are described in Kenneth Woodside, "The Political Economy of Policy Instruments: Tax Expenditures and Subsidies in Canada," in Michael M. Atkinson and Marsha A. Chandler, eds., *The Politics of Canadian Public Policy* (Toronto: University of Toronto Press, 1983), pp. 175–176 and passim.

[56]Donald J. Johnston, *Guide to the Policy & Expenditure Management System* (Minister of Supply and Services Canada, 1980), p. 14. This publication is currently (1986) being revised, but this passage is included to illustrate the thinking behind the creation of the system.

[57]Treasury Board of Canada, *Policy and Expenditure Management System Manual*, 2.2.

Figure 23.2
CABINET COMMITTEES AND EXPENDITURE ENVELOPES,
1986–87 ESTIMATES

Priorities and Planning	Foreign and Defence Policy	Economic and Regional Development	Social Development	Government Operations
Fiscal Arrangements $6.1 billion	External Affairs and Aid $3.1 billion	Economic and Regional Development $11.1 billion	Social Development $54.9 billion	Parliament $207 million
• Transfers to Provinces	• External Affairs • Foreign Aid	• Agriculture • Communications • Consumer and Corporate Affairs • Energy, Mines and Resources • Fisheries • Forestry • International Trade • Labour • Regional Industrial Expansion • Science and Technology • Transport	• Arts and Culture • CHMC • Employment and Immigration • Environment • Fitness and Amateur Sport • Indian Affairs and Northern Development • Justice • National Health and Welfare • Secretary of State • Solicitor General • Veterans' Affairs	• House of Commons • Library • Senate
Public Debt $27.4 billion	Defence $9.9 billion			Services to Government $3.4 billion
				• Canada Post • Central Agencies • National Revenue • Public Works • Supply and Services

Source: *1986–87 Estimates—Part I: The Government Expenditure Plan* (Ottawa: Minister of Supply and Services Canada, 1986), p. 9.

the policy sector Cabinet committees to make budgetary and policy decisions in their sectors as long as they stayed within their set expenditure limit.

Envelopes reflected not only cash expenditures, but also included new tax expenditures. Departments could still use tax expenditures instead of outright grants if they wished, but tax expenditures were no longer "free" to departments as they had been under the previous system; they showed up in their envelope as an expense.

An important aspect of the system in the Trudeau years was the presence of the Ministry of State for Social Development and the Ministry of State for Economic and Regional Development to provide support for two of the Cabinet committees with the greatest workloads. Among other things, these ministries prepared "assessment notes," which were comments about the various program proposals coming before the committees and provided ministers with a sectoral view (not just a departmental view) on how these new programs fit into existing programs. The ministries of state also had a general role in coordinating the programs and activities of the departments within their scope.

The effect of PEMS was to decentralize decision making in policy sectors to the Cabinet policy committee, so that the Cabinet ministers who were closest to the operational concerns of those policy areas made the decisions.

Another innovative aspect of this system was that there was no seemingly bottomless pot to which departments could keep returning to request additional funding for new policy initiatives. If individual departments or ministers wanted to embark on new programs, they would have to find the needed funds in their envelope. This might mean cancelling or rearranging existing programs, or making them operate more efficiently so that new money could be made available. Instead of the game discussed earlier in this chapter of spenders versus guardians, departmental ministers were now forced to be both spenders *and* guardians.

This is where the marriage of program and zero-base budgeting can be discerned. The basic building block of PEMS is the program, just as it was under traditional PPBS. What has been added is an absolute expenditure limit for each envelope, similar to the absolute spending limit found at the cut-off point in ZBB.

An Evaluation of PEMS: 1979–1984

PEMS is definitely an important innovation on the budgetary scene. It is based on some of the older building blocks, but it is sufficiently innovative that experts from many foreign countries have made pilgrimages to Ottawa to examine its workings. However, some problems have been identified with it.

The most basic problem that the Mulroney government identified with PEMS was, quite simply, that it had not been effective in limiting expenditure. In particular, ministers had never come to grips with "X" budgets, nor had they seriously considered statutory appropriations.[58] These appropriations are per-

---

[58]A more complete discussion of statutory appropriations is presented in the appendix to this chapter.

manent appropriations made under legislation other than the annual *Estimates* for such items as family allowances, veterans' benefits, and interest on the public debt. Expenditure on these items has been approved under other legislation, and so does not require annual approval. However, since statutory appropriations make up over 60 per cent of the total budget, it is clear that any attempt to reduce spending must examine these programs carefully.

Another potential weak point in the system was the "special allocation."[59] Usually, the policy reserves available to committees were either small or non-existent, so that they were clearly not designed to deal with major new initiatives or serious emergency situations. To deal with these areas, the Cabinet Committee on Priorities and Planning retained the right to make a special allocation. Some sort of safety valve was needed in extreme cases. However, if this mechanism was used too often, it could destroy the basic PEMS arrangements because it would provide a channel for an "end run" around the normal allocation process.

A related difficulty has been the creation of special envelopes. Some policy areas were deemed to be so important that they were set up as a single policy envelope. This special status obviously gave this policy area a preferred position and could invite the envy and wrath of other ministers.[60] In the late 1970s, energy was first given this status, then later folded back into the economic and regional development envelope. In the current arrangement, defence has its own envelope.

The increased responsibilities of the policy committees also caused some problems. Obviously, the expanded role of the committees led to more demands on the time of the ministers to manage the *envelopes*, rather than just their *departments*. This caused dissatisfaction on the part of ministers, because "ministers did not enter political life in order to undertake a career in management."[61] The changed role of the committees also introduced the double-edged sword of collegiality. "The benefits of collegiality can cut both ways; the more each minister can broaden his or her influence into another's portfolio, the more others can interfere in his or her mandate."[62] The Mulroney government attempted to limit this problem by providing individual ministers with more autonomy in the operation of their departments.[63]

An additional problem arose in dealing with reductions in "A" base items. The rule was straightforward: reductions stemming from policy changes went

[59]Richard Van Loon, "The Policy and Expenditure Management System in the Federal Government: The First Three Years," *Canadian Public Administration*, vol. 26 (Summer 1983), pp. 274–276; Borins, "Ottawa's Expenditure Envelopes: Workable Rationality at Last?" pp. 82–83.
[60]Van Loon, "The Policy and Expenditure Management System in the Federal Government: The First Three Years," pp. 276–277.
[61]An anonymous deputy minister quoted in Richard Van Loon, "Ottawa's Expenditure Process: Four Systems In Search of Coordination," in G. Bruce Doern, ed., *How Ottawa Spends: The Liberals, the Opposition & Federal Priorities—1983* (Toronto: James Lorimer & Company, 1983), p. 112.
[62]Ibid.
[63]Ian D. Clark, "Recent Changes in the Cabinet Decision-Making System in Ottawa," *Canadian Public Administration*, vol. 28 (Summer 1985), p. 197.

to the policy reserve (to be reallocated by the policy committee); reductions as a result of cost-saving innovations or greater efficiency were returned to Treasury Board to be reallocated by it.[64] Aside from the fact that this provided no incentive to ministers to encourage efficiency, it also led to disputes in contentious areas.[65]

In spite of these reservations, PEMS operated in the 1979–1984 period with few revisions. Richard Van Loon, one of the most perceptive and prolific analysts of the new system, has summed up his feelings in the following manner:

> The PEMS procedures are an improvement over their predecessors. They are an improvement because in spite of some ambiguities . . . they do impose a genuine discipline upon the development of most new proposals and because they do genuinely decentralize responsibility for a significant part of the policy management process to sectoral Cabinet committees.
>
> From these features a number of benefits derive. Policy proposals are much more carefully and widely analyzed than they were heretofore. Ministers and senior officials are much more aware of the initiatives and problems in other parts of the sector in which they work. The real priorities of the government emerge because new programs are chosen for funding on the basis of sometimes harsh trade-offs against one another in the context of a very limited policy reserve. The Prime Minister and Minister of Finance are not forced to deal with minor issues for these are devolved to Cabinet committees. The process is opened considerably (at least to those within the system) for policy proposals are widely discussed, major issues widely talked about and priorities made well known. The management system is far more corporate than it once was, although this has been achieved at some cost to individual autonomy and authority.[66]

As Van Loon goes on to argue, few people would suggest that PEMS is an ideal system, but on balance, it has proven to be highly satisfactory to the participants. However, budgeting styles are very much a product of the styles of governments. It should not be surprising that the style which fit the Trudeau government did not fit the Mulroney government.

The Mulroney Revisions to PEMS

Describing a dynamic process like a budgeting system can be like describing a cloud — by the time the description is finished, it has changed its shape so much that it is barely recognizable. No two budget years are the same. This is particularly true in the early years of a new government. With these caveats, this section will discuss the outline of the budgetary system as it seems to be shaping up under the Mulroney government.

One of the major concerns of the Mulroney government has been the reduction of the deficit. This goal has had a significant effect on both the substance

---

[64]Treasury Board of Canada, *Policy and Expenditure Management System Manual*, 2.10.

[65]Van Loon, "The Policy and Expenditure Management System in the Federal Government: The First Three Years," p. 270.

[66]"Ottawa's Expenditure Process: Four Systems In Search of Coordination," pp. 116–117.

and the process of the budget. The overriding concern with controlling expenditure has caused quite a bit of turmoil in the preparation of the budget. When Prime Minister Mulroney came to office, he appointed the so-called Nielsen task force to examine government programs and identify possibilities for expenditure reduction. Many changes in programs were held in abeyance pending this report; then when it was released in 1986, it had a significant impact on the budget process.

The general style of governing which Prime Minister Mulroney brought to office also had an impact on the budget process. This style had several elements. In terms of political ideology, he was concerned about streamlining government and reducing the size of the bureaucracy. He also wanted to emphasize political inputs into the policy-making process which would limit somewhat the role of public servants. These elements of political style were supplemented by a personal style which involved a brokerage, consultative approach to governing.[67]

The specific changes in tone in the budgetary process which have come about are:

- emphasis on a strategic plan geared to the government's *term of office* rather than a new five-year plan prepared each year by the bureaucracy;
- emphasis on ministers managing their own departments rather than collegial decision making in Cabinet committees;
- emphasis on greater political involvement in the departmental decision-making process and a more limited role for the permanent public service.

In keeping with these general ideas, the Mulroney government redefined PEMS somewhat immediately after coming to office:

> The principles and responsibilities underlying the system are:
> (a) the integration of policy and expenditure decision-making to ensure that policy decisions are taken in the context of expenditure limits with full consideration of the cost implications and that, in turn, expenditure decisions are taken in the context of the Government's priorities;
> (b) the establishment of expenditure limits (i.e., "envelopes") for broad policy areas consistent with the fiscal framework and the Government's priorities;
> (c) the responsibility of the Minister of Finance for macro-economic and tax policy, to recommend the fiscal framework and the annual envelope levels and to advise on the economic effectiveness of new proposals;
> (d) the responsibility of chairmen of policy committees to ensure that committees review existing expenditure priorities and, where appropriate, re-allocate resources within the envelope;
> (e) the responsibility of the Treasury Board for the overall integrity of the financial and other resource systems, the maintenance of the envelope accounts and provision of reports on the status of reserves, the accuracy of

---

[67]Peter Aucoin, "Organizational Change in the Machinery of Canadian Government: From Rational Management to Brokerage Politics," *Canadian Journal of Political Science*, vol. 19 (March 1986), pp. 17–23.

costing of present and proposed policies put before Ministers and Parliament, as well as for timely advice to Ministers on the efficient and effective management of public resources generally; and

(f) the discretion of individual Ministers to make expenditure decisions below certain thresholds without Cabinet approval where they judge that the policy or political implications of the decision are not sufficient to warrant collective Cabinet examination.[68]

In contrast with the Trudeau style, which emphasized collegial decision making, the Mulroney approach emphasizes the division of responsibilities for particular contributions to the overall budget picture.

However, there were many other differences in the two governments' approaches to PEMS. The traditional PEMS exercise involved the preparation of a five-year strategic plan each year, regardless of how many years were left in the government's mandate. In some cases this exercise was a case of just "going through the motions," because politicians were not very interested in five-year plans when they were going to be fighting an election in six months.

This kind of *pro forma* five-year strategic plan prepared by bureaucrats was replaced by a *political* strategic plan, which is found in the Prime Minister's initial throne speech[69] and the Minister of Finance's first major statement, *A New Direction for Canada*.[70] These documents set out the government's plan for its entire term of office.

Another important structural change by Mulroney has been the elimination of much of the formal documentation required as a part of the system under Trudeau. These formal planning documents have been replaced by less formal letters or memoranda, which each minister writes to the chairperson of his or her Cabinet committee. There is no specified format or timing for these documents; they could be submitted several times each year if a minister so desired. In general, they contain a discussion of overall departmental priorities and a request for funds for the upcoming year and some financial estimates for future years. These documents are used in the Cabinet policy sector committees to assist in setting priorities, which are then communicated to the Cabinet Committee on Priorities and Planning.

These letters or memoranda take the place of the "strategic overview," which was a very detailed, elaborate document required during the Trudeau years. The Mulroney government felt that the detail required in this document caused it to become a product of the public service rather than the minister, although it carried the minister's approval. Therefore, the Mulroney government opted in favour of a shorter, less detailed document which could be prepared by the minister and his or her political staff. This is another example of the manner in which Prime Minister Mulroney is emphasizing the need for ministers to control their departments.

---

[68]Canada, Privy Council Office, "Policy and Expenditure Management System: Principles and Procedures" (September 1984), pp. 1-2.
[69]Canada, House of Commons, *Debates*, November 5, 1984, pp. 5-8.
[70](Department of Finance, 1984).

Another structural change, which both streamlined the bureaucracy and emphasized political input, was made for Mulroney before he arrived in office. Immediately after Prime Minister Turner took office, he abolished the Ministries of State for Social Development and for Economic and Regional Development. Turner's avowed intention was to lessen bureaucratic influence in policy making. Clearly, Mulroney could have re-established these ministries when he came to office; his decision not to do so is further evidence of his desire to emphasize political control.

The problem discussed earlier of the "end run" by means of the special allocation has been obviated in recent years, because special allocations have been made in only a few highly exceptional circumstances; this is a reflection of the Conservative government's emphasis on expenditure reduction. However, unless one imagines the current restraint regime continuing indefinitely, the Conservatives will have to develop some mechanism to deal with requests for special allocations which could come up in response to some emergency, or as the time for the next election draws near.

These changes were all made because Mulroney wanted to emphasize political control of the bureaucracy, streamline government in general and the bureaucracy in particular, and reduce government expenditure. Gaining solid control of the budgetary process is one important way of accomplishing those goals.

The Current Budgetary Process

As discussed earlier, it can be very difficult to describe a budgetary process of a government, because it can change every year. However, Figure 23.3 provides a general outline of the budgetary process as it is developing in the Mulroney government.

The Department of Finance consults with the Treasury Board in recommending a fiscal framework. Treasury Board contributes information about "reference levels," i.e., the level of spending needed to continue existing programs at their current level. Finance then estimates the revenue likely to be generated in the coming year and provides some advice on the appropriate level of surplus or deficit needed to stimulate or slow down the economy. These recommendations are then conveyed to the Cabinet Committee on Priorities and Planning.

At the same time, individual ministers are considering their own departmental priorities and preparing some documentation that sets out those priorities and the rationale for them. Unlike the system under Trudeau, which emphasized uniform written documents to be prepared by all ministers, the Mulroney system emphasizes flexibility. Ministers decide on their format for this information, which is conveyed to the policy committees where the submissions of all ministers are considered and some recommendations are passed along to Priorities and Planning.

The Cabinet Committee on Priorities and Planning has the key role in the system. This committee decides on overall government priorities for the coming year. The committee then converts these general guidelines into more specific ideas in the form of major policy initiatives, the desired fiscal framework (overall taxation and expenditure levels), and levels of expenditure allocated to specific envelopes.

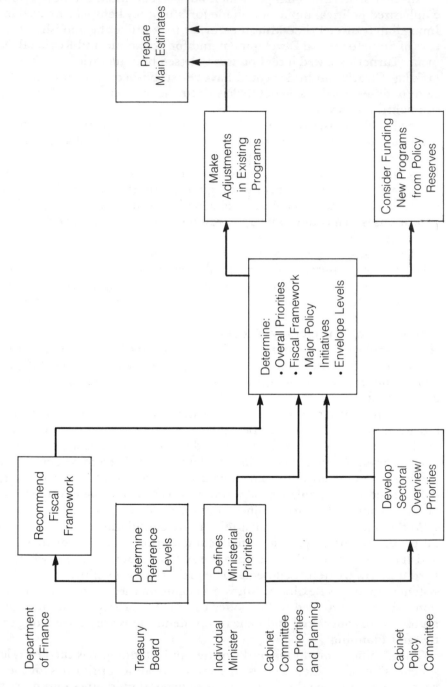

Figure 23.3
FEDERAL EXPENDITURE BUDGET PROCESS

Within these constraints, the expenditure budget is then prepared as a result of discussions involving Treasury Board, individual ministers, and the Cabinet policy committees. Individual ministers decide on details of expenditure within their departments. They can make minor program changes as long as they stay within their reference levels. Cabinet policy committees consider major new program initiatives and decide on the use of the policy reserve. Treasury Board is responsible for tying all of these threads together and preparing the *Main Estimates*. The preparation phase of the budgetary process ends when the President of Treasury Board tables the *Estimates* in the House of Commons in January or February shortly before the beginning of the new fiscal year on April 1.

CONCLUSION

This chapter has focussed on the preparation phase of the budget. This is a very important part of the total budget cycle, because it is so important in the determination of overall government priorities:

> The budget is the single most important policy statement of any government. The expenditure side of the budget tells us "who gets what" in public funds, and the revenue side of the budget tells us "who pays the cost." There are few government activities or programs which do not require an expenditure of funds, and no public funds may be spent without budgetary authorization. Deciding what goes into the budget (the budgetary process) provides a mechanism for reviewing government programs, assessing their cost, relating them to financial resources, making choices among alternative expenditures, and determining the financial effort that a government will expend on these programs. Budgets determine what programs and policies are to be increased, decreased, lapsed, initiated, or renewed. The budget lies at the heart of public policy.[71]

However, budget preparation is still only one-third of the total budget cycle. Adoption and execution are also important; these will be covered in the next chapter.

---

[71]Thomas Dye, *Understanding Public Policy* (Englewood Cliffs, N.J.: Prentice-Hall, 1972), p. 205.

APPENDIX: HOW TO READ GOVERNMENT FINANCIAL STATEMENTS

The various financial documents prepared by governments contain vast amounts of information that can be very useful for research. But many students, and even some more experienced researchers, shy away from the use of these documents because they imagine that they are much too difficult for the uninitiated to understand. It is very easy to be overwhelmed by the size, complexity, and esoteric terminology of some financial statements. In truth, there are some statements whose full import can only be comprehended by specialists, but even the uninitiated can learn quite a bit from some statements with just a rudimentary knowledge of terminology. This appendix will use normal, everyday language to introduce the wonders of government financial statements.

First, the neophyte should not be overwhelmed by the volume of information. There are two major government financial documents which are important to understand — *Estimates* and *Public Accounts*. These are the two main financial documents prepared by the federal and provincial governments. Municipal governments prepare similar types of documents, but they have different names. This appendix will focus on the federal documents, but it should provide assistance in reading provincial and local government financial documents as well, although certain changes will have to be made.

Estimates

The *Estimates*, or "Blue Book," is actually a multi-volume series of documents prepared before the beginning of the fiscal year as an output of the budgetary process described earlier in this chapter. These volumes contain the expenditure budget and represent the formal legislation which, when passed by the legislature, provides authority for spending by the executive. These documents focus entirely on the expenditure budget and so contain no information about revenue.

The format of the *Estimates* was revised significantly in the late 1970s so that more information is provided in a more easily understandable fashion. The *Estimates* is now presented in three parts, each geared to a different level of detail.

Part I of the *Estimates* consists of one volume called the *Government Expenditure Plan*. It contains a multi-year listing of expenditure by envelope, department, and major program within department. It also contains brief descriptions about the activities of each department and explanations of major increases or decreases in expenditures from previous years. This document is a good starting point to obtain a general understanding of how much of the total budget is consumed by a particular envelope/department/program, and what the trend is. However, it does not usually provide enough detail about these activities to be satisfactory for most researchers.

Part II also consists of one volume, referred to as the *Main Estimates*. It begins with a slightly more in-depth overview than was presented in Part I. Figure 23A.1 illustrates a page from the *Main Estimates* for the fiscal year 1985–86. On the left side of the page is a listing of the departments and agencies which have requested funds; on the right are the amounts requested under several headings.

The major headings distinguish between budgetary and non-budgetary transactions. *Non-budgetary transactions* are loans or advances made to organizations or investments in some entity.[72] These involve an outlay of cash, but it is expected that the funds will ultimately be repaid; therefore, they do not increase the government deficit. In accounting parlance, these involve the creation of an asset, rather than an expense. *Budgetary transactions* represent expenses, i.e., a once and for all outlay of funds for which no reimbursement is expected. To compare the two, the purchase of a Crown corporation or a loan to any organization is a non-budgetary transaction; the payment of salaries of government employees is a budgetary transaction. Both types of transactions are included in the *Estimates* because both require an outlay of cash. The difference between them is that a budgetary transaction affects the government's surplus/deficit position, while a non-budgetary transaction does not.

It is important to distinguish between these two types of transactions, but the distinction is sometimes abused because non-budgetary transactions do not increase the government's deficit, thereby making the government presenting the budget look more financially responsible. Governments sometimes consider transactions which ought to be budgetary as non-budgetary. For example, there is a temptation for a government to "loan" money to a Crown corporation, even though it realizes that there is little likelihood of it ever being repaid; this reduces the government deficit in the year the "loan" is made, but it creates a problem because these "loans" begin to pile up on the government's books. When the Liberal government took office in Ontario in 1985, it tackled this problem by making large one-time adjustments in the government's financial statements.[73]

The *Estimates* are further broken down between funds requested "under authorities to be voted" and "under previous authorities (statutory)." The latter category is usually referred to as statutory appropriations. *Statutory appropriations* are allocations of funds made under continuing legislation (not a part of the *Estimates*) that provides for a payment whenever a particular condition is met. Some examples of statutory appropriations are family allowances, veterans' benefits, or payments made to provincial governments as a result of intergovernmental agreements. Funds under this heading do not have to be approved each year because their expenditure is authorized under the original, enabling legislation. They are included in the *Estimates* for purposes of information and completeness. While some amount is stated for informational purposes, this amount could be exceeded because funds are paid to all claimants who meet the specified criteria, regardless of the amount shown in the *Estimates*.

---

[72]Greater elaboration is provided in: Treasury Board of Canada, *Guide on Financial Administration for Departments and Agencies of the Government of Canada,* 2nd ed. (Hull: Supply and Services Canada, 1979), 2.2.2; and Ontario, Ministry of Treasury and Economics, *Province of Ontario: Financial Report 1985*, p. 16.

[73]Robert F. Nixon, *1985 Ontario Budget* (Toronto: Ministry of Treasury and Economics, 1985), pp. 2-4, 39-44.

Figure 23A.1

Section	Department or agency	1985–86 Main Estimates Budgetary		
		Under authorities to be voted	Under previous authorities (statutory)	Total
	(thousands of dollars)			
9	External Affairs			
	External Affairs	753,389	25,613	779,002
	Canadian Commercial Corporation	15,826	. . . . .	15,826
	Canadian International Development Agency	1,355,008	6,792	1,361,800
	Export Development Corporation	. . . . .	. . . . .	. . . . .
	International Development Research Centre	86,000	. . . . .	86,000
	International Joint Commission	3,205	242	3,447
10	Finance			
	Finance	46,386	31,021,977	31,068,363
	Auditor General	39,045	3,923	42,968
	Insurance	12,262	1,244	13,506
	Tariff Board	2,430	268	2,698
11	Fisheries and Oceans	594,739	34,385	629,124
12	Governor General	5,449	686	6,135
13	Indian Affairs and Northern Development			
	Indian Affairs and Northern Development	2,250,650	34,431	2,285,081
	Northern Canada Power Commission	. . . . .	. . . . .	. . . . .
14	Justice			
	Justice	151,093	7,632	158,725
	Canadian Human Rights Commission	8,523	821	9,344
	Commissioner for Federal Judicial Affairs	3,253	103,438	106,691
	Federal Court of Canada	8,532	770	9,302
	Law Reform Commission of Canada	4,831	218	5,049
	Offices of the Information and Privacy Commissioners of Canada	2,938	294	3,232
	Supreme Court of Canada	4,143	1,951	6,094
	Tax Court of Canada	3,813	224	4,037
15	Labour			
	Labour	55,053	70,457	125,510
	Canada Labour Relations Board	5,419	562	5,981
	Canada Mortgage and Housing Corporation	1,466,566	660	1,467,226
	Canadian Centre for Occupational Health and Safety	7,687	. . . . .	7,687
16	National Defence	8,637,821	745,402	9,383,223
17	National Health and Welfare			
	National Health and Welfare	861,373	25,471,773	26,333,146
	Medical Research Council	130,308	275	130,583

Source: *Main Estimates 1985–86*, Part II, pp. 1-14, 1-15. Reproduced with permission of the Minister of Supply and Services Canada.

Non-budgetary (loans, investments and advances)			Total	1984–85 Main Estimates
Under authorities to be voted	Under previous authorities (statutory)	Total		
8	6,833	6,841	785,843	742,121
. . . . .	. . . . .	. . . . .	15,826	24,755
239,800	125,400	365,200	1,727,000	1,644,148
. . . . .	240,000	240,000	240,000	287,000
. . . . .	. . . . .	. . . . .	86,000	81,000
. . . . .	. . . . .	. . . . .	3,447	3,384
873	210,800	211,673	31,280,036	26,353,746
. . . . .	. . . . .	. . . . .	42,968	40,604
. . . . .	. . . . .	. . . . .	13,506	12,765
. . . . .	. . . . .	. . . . .	2,698	2,349
. . . . .	. . . . .	. . . . .	629,124	690,112
. . . . .	. . . . .	. . . . .	6,135	5,289
15,424	30,000	45,424	2,330,505	2,111,224
4,081	. . . . .	4,081	4,081	6,456
. . . . .	. . . . .	. . . . .	158,725	145,137
. . . . .	. . . . .	. . . . .	9,344	9,207
. . . . .	. . . . .	. . . . .	106,691	96,912
. . . . .	. . . . .	. . . . .	9,302	7,860
. . . . .	. . . . .	. . . . .	5,049	5,013
. . . . .	. . . . .	. . . . .	3,232	2,908
. . . . .	. . . . .	. . . . .	6,094	5,725
. . . . .	. . . . .	. . . . .	4,037	4,225
. . . . .	. . . . .	. . . . .	125,510	95,165
. . . . .	. . . . .	. . . . .	5,981	5,574
23,900	30,300	54,200	1,521,426	1,417,826
. . . . .	. . . . .	. . . . .	7,687	5,045
. . . . .	. . . . .	. . . . .	9,383,223	8,767,243
. . . . .	. . . . .	. . . . .	26,333,146	23,901,382
. . . . .	. . . . .	. . . . .	130,583	156,970

Figure 23A.2

National Health and Welfare
Ministry Summary

Vote	(thousands of dollars)	1985–86 Main Estimates	1984–85 Main Estimates
	National Health and Welfare		
	Departmental Administration Program		
1	Program expenditures	39,979	42,441
(S)	Minister of National Health and Welfare – Salary and motor car allowance	42	41
(S)	Contributions to employee benefit plans	4,135	3,911
	Total Program	*44,156*	*46,393*
	Health Services and Promotion Program		
5	Operating expenditures	21,873	21,865
10	Grants and contributions	26,725	24,969
(S)	Payments for insured health services and extended health care services	6,490,000	5,600,000
(S)	Contributions to employee benefit plans	1,475	1,341
	Total Program	*6,540,073*	*5,648,175*
	Social Services Program		
15	Operating expenditures	13,548	12,701
20	Grants and contributions	100,319	119,011
(S)	Canada Assistance Plan Payments	3,928,400	3,696,000
(S)	Contributions to employee benefit plans	1,397	1,203
	Total Program	*4,043,664*	*3,828,915*
	Medical Services Program		
25	Operating expenditures	348,259	329,149
30	Capital expenditures	27,794	31,120
(S)	Contributions to employee benefit plans	14,180	12,321
	Total Program	*390,233*	*372,590*
	Health Protection Program		
35	Operating expenditures	93,957	90,312
40	Capital expenditures	12,108	9,880
(S)	Contributions to employee benefit plans	9,518	8,389
	Total Program	*115,583*	*108,581*
	Income Security Program		
45	Program expenditures	65,234	60,632
(S)	Family Allowance payments	2,510,000	2,429,000
(S)	Old Age Security payments	8,874,000	8,286,000
(S)	Guaranteed Income Supplement payments	3,365,000	2,771,000
(S)	Spouse's Allowance payments	262,000	279,000
(S)	Contributions to employee benefit plans	10,876	9,472
	Total Program	*15,087,110*	*13,835,104*
	Fitness and Amateur Sport Program		
50	Operating expenditures	9,428	8,115
55	Contributions	52,351	52,925
(S)	Contributions to employee benefit plans	657	584
	Total Program	*62,436*	*61,624*

Vote	(thousands of dollars)	1985–86 Main Estimates	1984–85 Main Estimates
	XV Olympic Winter Games Program		
60	Operating expenditures	1,396	. . . . .
65	Capital expenditures	33,900	. . . . .
70	Contributions	14,502	. . . . .
(S)	Contributions to employee benefit plans	93	. . . . .
	Total Program	*49,891*	. . . . .
	Total Department	**26,333,146**	**23,901,382**
	Medical Research Council		
75	Operating expenditures	3,222	3,510
80	Grants and contributions	127,086	153,191
(S)	Contributions to employee benefit plans	275	269
	Total Program	**130,583**	**156,970**

Source: *Main Estimates 1985–86*, Part II, pp. 17-2, 17-3. Reproduced with permission of the Minister of Supply and Services Canada.

The appropriations "under authorities to be voted" are the annual appropriations that require the approval of the legislature each year. The only amount available to be spent on these programs is the amount specified in the *Estimates*; these limitations cannot be exceeded. Any funds allocated under annual appropriations that are not spent at the end of the year *lapse*, i.e., they cannot be carried over and spent in the following year.

As illustrated in Figure 23A.1, statutory appropriations are higher than annual appropriations in some departments, e.g., Finance and National Health and Welfare. For 1985–86, statutory appropriations amounted to 64 per cent of total funds requested. This raises some concern that the ability of the legislature to reduce expenditure is severely limited by the existence of these statutory expenditures. Although there is no restriction on the ability of the legislature to modify the underlying legislation, this can be politically awkward in some cases.

Close to the right margin, Figure 23A.1 lists the full amount of funds requested this year and the amount requested last year. This allows legislators to identify departments that are requesting significant increases in funding.

Figure 23A.2 illustrates a different grouping of information also found in Part II of the *Estimates*. This provides a breakdown of departmental allocations by vote. A vote is the appropriation approved by Parliament. Roughly speaking, there is one vote per program, although there could be more where a program involves a large capital expenditure or large amounts of grants and contributions (transfer payments to organizations or individuals).[74] Since Parliament has approved funds on the basis of votes, a department must obtain

[74]The general criteria to determine what constitutes a vote is set out in: Treasury Board, *Policy and Expenditure Management System Manual*, ch. 8; and, Canada, Treasury Board, *Report on the Study of the Accounts of Canada* (Ottawa: Minister of Supply and Services Canada, 1976), p. 140.

Figure 23A.3

National Health and Welfare
Department
Health Services and Promotion Program

Appropriation Authority

Authority is sought in these Estimates to spend
$48,598,000 for operating expenditures and grants and
contributions to operate the Health Services and
Promotion Program during the 1985–86 fiscal year.
Statutory authority exists for the Program's expenditures
on Health Care payments, which are estimated at
$6,490,000,000 for 1985–86. Additionally, contribu-
tions to employee benefit plans of $1,475,000 will be
made under existing statutory authority.

Objective

To develop, promote and support measures designed to
preserve and improve the health and well-being of
Canadians.

Activity Description

Health Insurance
Provides payments to provinces and territories in respect
of the cost of insured health services, and certain
extended health care services as provided under the
Federal-Provincial Fiscal Arrangements and Federal Post-
Secondary Education and Health Contributions Act,
1977; monitors compliance of provincial and territorial
health care insurance plans in accordance with the
program criteria and conditions of payment of the
Canada Health Act.

Health Services and Resources
Provides leadership and co-ordination and gives
technical and financial support to the provinces and
territories, professional associations, and international
organizations in the development and maintenance of
health services and facilities. Financial support and

consulting services are also provided to national
voluntary health organizations to assist their development and improve the efficiency and effectiveness of
health services. Information collection and dissemination in addition to collaborative efforts with the
provinces and territories play an important and integral
role in this activity.

Extramural Research
Fosters and supports public health research and related
scientific activities, through the National Health
Research and Development Program, which complement
departmental programs and hold the potential to
advance national health goals. Encompasses research
projects, studies and demonstrations, the training and
career development of research manpower in relevant
disciplines, and forums for the development of research
strategies and approaches and for the communication of
research outcomes.

Health Promotion
Develops and implements, in co-operation with
provincial and territorial governments and non-
governmental organizations, health promotion programs
directed to all Canadian residents and to special target
groups including those at high risk and those responsible
for the planning or provision of health and social
services.

Program Administration
Provides program direction, program planning, policy
development and financial and administrative services.

National Health and Welfare
Health Services and Promotion Program
Program by Activities

(thousands of dollars)	1985–86 Main Estimates					1984–85 Main Estimates
	Authorized person-years	Budgetary			Total	
		Operating	Capital	Transfer payments		
Health Insurance	13	768	.....	6,490,000	6,490,768	5,601,138
Health Services and Resources	73	6,519	.....	3,176	9,695	9,339
Extramural Research	19	1,132	.....	19,309	20,441	19,123
Health Promotion	113	12,249	.....	4,240	16,489	15,791
Program Administration	58	2,664	16	.....	2,680	2,784
	276	23,332	16	6,516,725	6,540,073	5,648,175

National Health and Welfare
Health Services and Promotion Program
Transfer Payments

(dollars)	1985–86 Main Estimates	1984–85 Main Estimates
Grants		
Health Services and Resources		
Grants to national voluntary health organizations to assist with the operating costs of national offices	3,176,000	3,072,000
Total grants	3,176,000	3,072,000
Contributions		
Health Insurance		
(S) Payments under the Federal-Provincial Fiscal Arrangements and Federal Post-Secondary Education and Health Contributions Act, 1977		
Insured Health Services Program	5,414,000,000	4,600,000,000
Extended Health Care Services Program	1,076,000,000	1,000,000,000
Extramural Research		
Contributions to persons and agencies to support activities of national importance for the improvement of health services and in support of research and demonstrations in the field of public health	19,309,000	18,077,000
Health Promotion		
Contributions to persons and agencies to support health promotion projects in the areas of community health, resource development, training and skill development, and research	4,240,000	3,640,000
Total contributions	6,513,549,000	5,621,717,000
Items not required		
Family Planning – Grants to assist in the development of provincial, municipal and voluntary services and for specific projects in this area	. . . . .	174,000
New Employment Expansion and Development (NEED) program	. . . . .	6,000
Total items not required	. . . . .	180,000
Total	6,516,725,000	5,624,969,000

Source: *Main Estimates 1985–86*, Part II, pp. 17-6, 17-7. Reproduced with permission of the Minister of Supply and Services Canada.

parliamentary approval to move funds between votes. This is the mechanism that Parliament uses to control the ways in which departments spend funds. The votes with numbers in the left margin are annual appropriations; those with "(S)" are statutory appropriations.

Also in Part II is some additional information about each program, as illustrated in Figure 23A.3. This provides a short description of the objectives and activities of each program, as well as some additional budgetary information.

Part II of the *Estimates* is very useful for research purposes. It provides both financial and some narrative background information on the activities of each department. It allows the researcher to locate the organizational unit responsible for a particular activity, and a review of previous years' *Estimates* allows some consideration of expenditure trends.

Part III of the *Estimates*, referred to as *Expenditure Plans*, contains one volume for each department and major government agency. These volumes contain a wealth of information about the activities of the various programs. Each volume takes a somewhat different approach, but the information provided involves details of departmental organizational structure, highlights of program performance in the previous year, new initiatives planned and updates on previous initiatives, and data on program effectiveness. Obviously, this provides a great deal of information for the legislator as well as the researcher. The data provided facilitate the identification of trends and the relating of expenditure information to output data.

All three parts of the *Estimates* are tabled in Parliament just before the beginning of the fiscal year. Part II, the *Main Estimates*, constitutes the initial request made by the government for funding. During the fiscal year, the government will usually present three or four sets of supplementary estimates to take account of changed conditions. *Supplementary estimates* are presented in roughly the same form as the *Main Estimates*, and could constitute a request for additional funds or involve a transfer of funds between votes not requiring any additional total funds. When the various sets of *Estimates* are passed, they are called the Appropriation Acts and become a part of the legislation passed in a particular Parliament, and can be located in the Statutes of Canada for that Parliament.

Public Accounts

The second major financial document is the *Public Accounts*. The *Public Accounts* is prepared after the government's year-end and contains the government's year-end financial statements. The federal *Public Accounts* is a three-volume document. The first volume contains most of the important information about government financial activities during the year. The second volume contains a large volume of detail about the transactions summarized in volume one. The third volume contains financial information about Crown corporations.

The first volume of *Public Accounts*, titled *Summary Report and Financial Statements*, contains information about all transactions which affect the Consolidated Revenue Fund. The *Consolidated Revenue Fund* is "the aggregate of all public moneys that are on deposit at the credit of the Receiver General."[75] This money is actually maintained in a number of separate accounts in a number of financial institutions, but it is viewed as one united fund. All funds collected by the government become a part of the Consolidated Revenue Fund, and all payments are made from the Consolidated Revenue Fund. The emphasis on "consolidated" stems from the fact that some governments maintain a number of separate accounts that are earmarked for specific purposes, such as highway expenditure or social services. The federal government feels that better cash management is obtained from accounting for only one fund, even though it is physically located in a number of different places and will be used for a number of different purposes.

---

[75]R.S.C. 1970, c. F-10, s. 2.

Figures 23A.4 to 23A.7 illustrate the statements contained in the *Public Accounts* which provide an overview of the transactions for the year. Figure 23A.4 provides details on revenue obtained in the current and several previous years. The information shown here can be used to identify major sources of government revenue and the trend of those sources.

Figure 23A.5 illustrates budgetary expenditures by department. This is the year-end listing of actual amounts spent, which is comparable to the budgetary transactions listed in the *Estimates* discussed earlier. Like the revenue side of the equation, this information can be used to compare major expenditure programs and the trend in those programs.

Figure 23A.4

COMPARATIVE STATEMENTS OF TRANSACTIONS

TABLE 1.2

GOVERNMENT OF CANADA
PUBLIC ACCOUNTS PRESENTATION (REVISED ACCOUNTING BASIS)
DETAILED STATEMENT OF TRANSACTIONS
(in millions of dollars)

	Year ended March 31				
	1980	1981	1982	1983	1984
I. Budgetary transactions					
A. REVENUE, Section 5					
Tax revenue—					
Income tax—					
Personal	16,808	19,837	24,046	26,330	26,967
Corporation	6,951	8,106	8,118	7,139	7,286
Non-resident	787	867	1,018	998	908
	24,546	28,810	33,182	34,467	35,161
Excise taxes and duties—					
Sales tax	4,698	5,429	6,185	5,894	6,660
Customs import duties	3,000	3,188	3,439	2,831	3,380
Excise duties	895	1,042	1,175	1,274	1,356
Other	502	573	564	685	755
	9,095	10,232	11,363	10,684	12,151
Energy taxes—					
Petroleum and gas revenue tax and incremental oil revenue tax		27	864	1,300	1,100
Natural gas and gas liquids tax		187	998	1,264	524
Excise tax—Gasoline	421	453	436	408	386
Oil export charges	750	842	519	392	215
Special petroleum compensation charge			473		
	1,171	1,509	3,290	4,024	3,231
	10,266	11,741	14,653	14,708	15,382
Other tax revenue	96	99	120	132	126
Total tax revenue	34,908	40,650	47,955	49,307	50,669
Non-tax revenue—					
Return on investments—					
Bank of Canada	1,084	1,459	1,853	1,879	1,744
Canada Mortgage and Housing Corporation	782	839	873	892	941
Exchange Fund Account	404	620	763	812	591
Farm Credit Corporation	210	243	285	346	408
Interest on bank deposits	244	318	701	433	395
Other return on investments	620	651	615	655	667
	3,344	4,130	5,090	5,017	4,746
Other non-tax revenue	684	618	1,023	799	911
Total non-tax revenue	4,028	4,748	6,113	5,816	5,657
Total revenue	38,936	45,398	54,068	55,123	56,326

Source: *Public Accounts of Canada 1984*, Vol. I, p. 1-7. Reproduced with permission of the Minister of Supply and Services Canada.

Figure 23A.5

COMPARATIVE STATEMENTS OF TRANSACTIONS   1·9

TABLE 1.3

GOVERNMENT OF CANADA
PUBLIC ACCOUNTS PRESENTATION (REVISED ACCOUNTING BASIS)
DETAILED STATEMENT OF TRANSACTIONS
(in millions of dollars)

	Year ended March 31				
	1980	1981	1982	1983	1984
I. Budgetary transactions					
B. EXPENDITURE, Section 6					
Agriculture	782	882	1,142	1,058	1,255
Communications—					
Canadian Broadcasting Corporation	522	783	665	745	816
Other	320	388	469	831	613
	842	*1,171*	*1,134*	*1,576*	*1,429*
Employment and Immigration—					
Unemployment insurance	1,167	946	1,047	2,148	2,854
Other	1,204	1,096	1,162	1,382	1,966
	2,371	*2,042*	*2,209*	*3,530*	*4,820*
Energy, Mines and Resources—					
Oil price stabilization	1,633	3,162	426	– 35	483
Petroleum incentive payments				1,809	1,729
Other	533	846	972	1,274	1,246
	2,166	*4,008*	*1,398*	*3,048*	*3,458*
Environment	457	530	678	817	900
External Affairs—					
Canadian International Development Agency	683	668	803	933	1,089
Other	520	588	775	867	883
	1,203	*1,256*	*1,578*	*1,800*	*1,972*
Finance—					
Public debt charges	8,524	10,687	15,168	16,971	18,146
Fiscal transfers	3,522	3,788	4,535	5,378	5,647
Other	209	129	121	140	125
	12,255	*14,604*	*19,824*	*22,489*	*23,918*
Fisheries and Oceans	314	368	441	483	609
Indian Affairs and Northern Development	1,127	1,417	1,507	1,681	2,052
Labour—					
Canada Post Corporation	293	486	672	290	483
Other	75	94	71	82	115
	368	*580*	*743*	*372*	*598*
National Defence	4,391	5,077	6,028	6,992	7,972
National Health and Welfare—					
Family and youth allowances	1,726	1,851	2,020	2,231	2,326
Insurance and medical care services	3,859	3,982	4,283	4,060	5,564
Canada Assistance Plan including contracting-out payments	1,653	1,941	2,298	2,832	3,288
Old age security benefits	6,319	7,418	8,585	9,643	10,406
Other	509	628	682	814	970
	14,066	*15,820*	*17,868*	*19,580*	*22,554*
National Revenue	581	677	816	900	982
Public Works—					
Canada Mortgage and Housing Corporation	896	1,058	968	1,574	1,605
Other	574	794	1,224	1,095	1,234
	1,470	*1,852*	*2,192*	*2,669*	*2,839*
Regional Industrial Expansion	1,049	1,194	1,334	1,157	1,222
Science and Technology	325	392	486	596	693
Secretary of State—					
Education support	1,608	1,693	1,730	1,677	2,252
Other	422	438	484	537	606
	2,030	*2,131*	*2,214*	*2,214*	*2,858*
Social Development		2	4	531	856
Solicitor General	907	1,038	1,184	1,319	1,496
Transport	1,636	1,851	2,292	2,908	3,259
Veterans Affairs	934	1,016	1,140	1,283	1,388
Other departmental expenditure	931	888	1,262	1,273	1,485
Total departmental expenditure	50,205	58,796	67,474	78,276	88,615
Provision for valuation of assets and liabilities	61	– 380	1,975	1,725	300
Total expenditure	50,266	58,416	69,449	80,001	88,915

Source: *Public Accounts of Canada 1984*, Vol. I, p. 1-9. Reproduced with permission of the Minister of Supply and Services Canada.

Figure 23A.6

COMPARATIVE STATEMENTS OF TRANSACTIONS   1·11

TABLE 1.4

GOVERNMENT OF CANADA
PUBLIC ACCOUNTS PRESENTATION (REVISED ACCOUNTING BASIS)
DETAILED STATEMENT OF TRANSACTIONS
(in millions of dollars)

	Year ended March 31				
	1980	1981	1982	1983	1984
II. Non-budgetary transactions[1]					
A. LOANS, INVESTMENTS AND ADVANCES, Section 7					
Crown corporations and agencies					
Lending institutions—					
Canada Deposit Insurance Corporation			− 200	60	140
Canada Mortgage and Housing Corporation	− 366	− 66	− 199	− 30	194
Export Development Corporation	155	124	52	− 40	− 5
Farm Credit Corporation	− 307	− 270	− 348	− 394	− 379
Federal Business Development Bank	− 245	101	125	145	172
	− 763	− 111	− 570	− 259	122
All other Crown corporations and agencies—					
Air Canada	16	13	14	16	17
Atomic Energy of Canada Limited	− 216	697	8	3	37
Canada Development Investment Corporation				− 396	
Canadian National Railways	108	− 8		− 41	− 62
Petro-Canada	80	− 440	− 129	− 457	− 612
Other	15	275	− 359	101	163
	− 373	537	− 466	− 774	− 457
	− 1,136	426	− 1,036	− 1,033	− 335
Other loans, investments and advances—					
Provincial and territorial governments	44	247	28	− 41	36
National governments including developing countries	− 384	− 309	− 276	− 273	− 167
International organizations (subscriptions less notes payable)	− 134	− 110	− 166	− 213	− 335
Veterans' Land Act Fund advances less allowance for conditional benefits	43	37	29	28	31
Government controlled corporations	4	− 2		88	− 29
Private sector enterprises	− 47	− 63	− 16	− 56	− 113
Miscellaneous	− 29	− 19	− 2	− 21	− 13
	− 503	− 219	− 403	− 488	− 590
Loans, investments and advances before allowance	− 1,639	207	− 1,439	− 1,521	− 925
Allowance for valuation of assets	311	− 630	350	1,650	300
Total loans, investments and advances after allowance for valuation of assets	− 1,328	− 423	− 1,089	129	− 625
B. SPECIFIED PURPOSE ACCOUNTS, Section 8					
Liability accounts—					
Canada Pension Plan Account	113	173	170	165	152
Superannuation accounts	1,966	2,307	3,014	3,483	3,862
Unemployment Insurance Account	− 150	− 682	− 15	− 3,289	− 459
Government Annuities Account	− 14	− 15	− 21	− 22	− 26
Canadian Ownership Account			75	− 8	757
Deposit and trust accounts	− 14	241	1,129	− 223	332
Provincial tax collection agreements account	118	728	− 56	− 384	277
Other	28	29	49	58	62
Total specified purpose accounts	2,047	2,781	4,345	− 220	5,157
C. OTHER TRANSACTIONS, Sections 9 and 12					
Cash in transit	− 130	− 693	16	− 736	689
Interest and matured debt less unamortized discount on Treasury bills	− 38	186	1,933	1,615	884
Accounts payable	91	772	178	549	866
Outstanding cheques and warrants	506	9	29	208	516
Miscellaneous	− 13	19	13	2	20
Total other transactions before allowance for valuation of liabilities	416	293	2,169	1,638	2,975
Allowance for valuation of liabilities	− 250	250	1,625	75	
Total other transactions after allowance for valuation of liabilities	166	543	3,794	1,713	2,975
Net non-budgetary transactions before allowances for valuation of assets and liabilities	824	3,281	5,075	− 103	7,207
Allowances for valuation of assets and liabilities	61	− 380	1,975	1,725	300
Net non-budgetary transactions after allowances for valuation of assets and liabilities	885	2,901	7,050	1,622	7,507

[1] Source/requirement (−).

Source: *Public Accounts of Canada 1984*, Vol. I, p. 1-11. Reproduced with permission of the Minister of Supply and Services Canada.

The government's *administrative budget* consists of all budgetary revenue and budgetary expenditure transactions. The surplus or deficit based on the administrative budget is the difference between budgetary revenue and budgetary expenditure. Computations from Figures 23A.4 and 23A.5 indicate a deficit in terms of the administrative budget for the year ended March 31, 1984, of $32,589 million (revenue of $56,326 and expenditure of $88,915). This administrative budget is not the same as the government's cash requirement, which will be discussed below.

Figure 23A.6 illustrates non-budgetary transactions. Again, this is a year-end reflection of the figures shown in the *Estimates*. They show the net inflow or outflow of funds for loans, advances and investments, i.e., the difference between loans and investments paid out and returns received in the form of loan repayments and sale of investments. For example, this statement shows that during 1983–84, the federal government received a repayment (net of any possible additional loans) from the Canada Deposit Insurance Corporation of $140 million. It also indicates that the federal government made a net loan to the Farm Credit Corporation of $379 million. The positive figures indicate net repayments of previous loans and investments, i.e., net inflows of funds. The negative figures reflect net pay-outs by the government.

The government's *cash budget* determines the total amount which the government will need to borrow in the upcoming fiscal year. The cash budget is determined by the budgetary and non-budgetary transactions already discussed. The result of these transactions is then adjusted by foreign exchange transactions, e.g., transactions which the government makes to adjust the value of the dollar on international markets. The net of these transactions determines the amount which the government needed to borrow in the past year.

Figure 23A.7 illustrates the calculation of the federal government's cash requirement for the fiscal year ended March 31, 1984. Budgetary expenditures exceeded budgetary revenue by $37,489 million, but for non-budgetary transactions, inflows exceeded outflows by $12,407 million, thus reducing the net cash requirement at that point to $25,082 million. The small inflow generated by foreign exchange transactions reduced the final requirement to $24,635 million. Government borrowing increased during the year by $26,468 million, so that its cash balance increased by $1,833 million.

The cash budget is important, since it has an impact on money markets because it is a signal of the demands which the government will be making on the market in future. A high cash requirement can drive up interest rates because it will place heavy demands on money markets. A low requirement might signal that there will be substantial amounts available for borrowing for business expansion.

There are other sections of the *Public Accounts* which break down each line of these three statements in considerably more detail by envelope, by department, and by specific non-budgetary transaction. Obviously, this information is very useful for research purposes.

The *Public Accounts* also contains the federal government's *Statement of Assets and Liabilities* as illustrated in Figure 23A.8. Assets are defined as anything of value owned by the government. In the case of the federal government, the

Figure 23A.7

COMPARATIVE STATEMENTS OF TRANSACTIONS 1·5

TABLE 1.1.1

GOVERNMENT OF CANADA
PUBLIC ACCOUNTS PRESENTATION[1]
SUMMARY STATEMENT OF TRANSACTIONS
(in millions of dollars)

		Year ended March 31				
		1980	1981	1982	1983	1984
I.	**Budgetary transactions**					
	A. Revenue	38,936	45,398	54,068	55,123	56,326
	B. Expenditure	− 51,724	− 58,066	− 67,674	− 79,776	− 88,615
	Deficit before extraordinary item	− 12,788	− 12,668	− 13,606	− 24,653	− 32,289
	Extraordinary item—Provision for valuation of certain assets, and for liabilities previously not recorded					− 5,200
	Deficit after extraordinary item	− 12,788	− 12,668	− 13,606	− 24,653	− 37,489
II.	**Non-budgetary transactions**					
	A. Loans, investments and advances[2]	− 119	− 493	1,239	21	925
	B. Specified purpose accounts[2]	2,047	2,781	4,345	− 220	5,157
	C. Other transactions	415	263	2,169	1,638	2,975
	Net source before extraordinary item	2,343	2,551	5,275	1,397	7,207
	Extraordinary item—Allowances for valuation of certain assets, and for liabilities previously not recorded					5,200
	Net source after extraordinary item	2,343	2,551	5,275	1,397	12,407
	Financial requirements (excluding foreign exchange transactions)	− 10,445	− 10,117	− 8,331	− 23,256	− 25,082
III.	**Foreign exchange transactions**[3]	− 128	1,157	− 347	− 1,177	447
	Total financial requirements[4]	− 10,573	− 8,960	− 8,678	− 24,433	− 24,635
IV.	**Unmatured debt transactions**[3]	7,878	11,153	9,367	22,392	26,468
	Change in cash[5]	− 2,695	2,193	689	− 2,041	1,833
V.	**Cash balance at end of year**	3,738	5,931	6,620	4,579	6,412

Details can be found in other sections of this volume.
[1] Consistent with the Statement of Transactions in Section 2 of this volume.
[2] For purposes of presenting the transactions of the Government,
  (a) loans, investments and advances, for the year 1980, include working capital advances to revolving funds, departments and agencies; and,
  (b) specified purpose accounts include advances made to the Unemployment Insurance Account.
[3] Unmatured debt payable in foreign currencies has been included as part of foreign exchange transactions.
[4] Cash requirements ( ).
[5] Cash decrease (−).

Source: *Public Accounts of Canada 1984*, Vol. I, p. 1-5. Reproduced with permission of the Minister of Supply and Services Canada.

assets consist of loans and advances made by the government to Crown corporations and other organizations, foreign exchange held, and cash. The federal government values all of its fixed assets (land, public buildings, equipment, vehicles, etc.) at one dollar. Also, on the left side of the balance sheet is the government deficit accumulated over the years, which amounted to $157,011 million as of March 31, 1984.

The right side of the statement lists all government liabilities, i.e., obligations on the part of the government to pay out funds in the future. These consist of accounts payable to suppliers, and Canada Savings Bonds and other long-term bonds.

Liabilities also include large amounts in "specified purpose accounts," or what might be generally called trust accounts. This is money paid to the government that is being held for some special purpose, sometimes on a long-term basis. For example, all funds contributed to the Canada Pension Plan are liabilities from

Figure 23A.8

GOVERNMENT OF CANADA

Statement of Assets and Liabilities
as at March 31, 1984
(in millions of dollars)

	1984	1983	Net increase or decrease (–)
ASSETS			
LOANS, INVESTMENTS AND ADVANCES, Table 7.1, Section 7—			
Crown corporations and agencies—			
Lending institutions—			
Canada Deposit Insurance Corporation		140	– 140
Canada Mortgage and Housing Corporation	10,224	10,418	– 194
Export Development Corporation	929	924	5
Farm Credit Corporation	4,500	4,121	379
Federal Business Development Bank	714	886	– 172
	16,367	*16,489*	*– 122*
All other Crown corporations and agencies—			
Air Canada	575	592	– 17
Atomic Energy of Canada Limited	833	870	– 37
Canada Development Investment Corporation	396	396	
Canadian National Railways	2,856	2,794	62
Petro-Canada	2,642	2,030	612
Other	1,530	1,693	– 163
	8,832	*8,375*	*457*
Total Crown corporations and agencies	*25,199*	*24,864*	*335*
Other loans, investments and advances—			
Provincial and territorial governments	1,213	1,249	– 36
National governments including developing countries, Table 7.6, Section 7	4,215	4,048	167
International organizations	3,306	2,917	389
Less: notes payable	1,153	1,099	54
	2,153	*1,818*	*335*
Veterans' Land Act Fund advances less allowance for conditional benefits	224	255	– 31
Government controlled corporations	429	400	29
Private sector enterprises	435	322	113
Miscellaneous	301	288	13
	8,970	*8,380*	*590*
	34,169	*33,244*	*925*
Less: allowance for valuation	5,700	4,000	1,700
TOTAL LOANS, INVESTMENTS AND ADVANCES	*28,469*	*29,244*	*– 775*
FOREIGN EXCHANGE ACCOUNTS, Table 10.1, Section 10—			
Exchange Fund Account—Advances, Table 10.2, Section 10	3,399	4,166	– 767
International Monetary Fund—Subscriptions	3,995	2,716	1,279
	7,394	*6,882*	*512*
Less: International Monetary Fund—Notes payable	3,244	2,283	961
Special Drawing Rights	1,058	1,040	18
	4,302	*3,323*	*979*
TOTAL FOREIGN EXCHANGE ACCOUNTS	*3,092*	*3,559*	*– 467*
CASH IN TRANSIT, Table 12.1, Section 12	*1,877*	*2,566*	*– 689*
CASH, Table 12.2, Section 12	*6,412*	*4,579*	*1,833*
FIXED ASSETS (valued at one dollar), Section 12			
NET RECORDED ASSETS	39,850	39,948	– 98
ACCUMULATED DEFICIT, Table 12.5, Section 12	*157,011*	*119,522*	*37,489*
TOTAL	**196,861**	**159,470**	**37,391**

Source: *Public Accounts of Canada 1984*, Vol. I, pp. 2-8, 2-9. Reproduced with permission of the Minister of Supply and Services Canada.

LIABILITIES

	1984	1983	Net increase or decrease (-)
SPECIFIED PURPOSE ACCOUNTS, Table 8.1, Section 8—			
Canada Pension Plan Account	26,612	24,108	2,504
Less: provincial government securities held by the Canada Pension Plan Investment Fund	25,116	22,764	2,352
	1,496	*1,344*	*152*
Superannuation accounts	33,791	30,672	3,119
Less: unamortized portion of actuarial deficiencies	1,103	1,846	- 743
	32,688	*28,826*	*3,862*
Unemployment Insurance Account	- 278	- 252	- 26
Less: interest-bearing loans	3,823	3,390	433
	- 4,101	*- 3,642*	*- 459*
Government Annuities Account	1,124	1,150	- 26
Canadian Ownership Account			
Canadian Ownership special charge	2,480	1,676	804
Less: investments	1,656	1,609	47
	824	*67*	*757*
Deposit and trust accounts	2,290	1,758	532
Provincial tax collection agreements account	1,308	1,031	277
Other	498	436	62
TOTAL SPECIFIED PURPOSE ACCOUNTS	*36,127*	*30,970*	*5,157*
OTHER LIABILITIES, Table 9.1, Section 9—			
Interest and matured debt	9,610	8,398	1,212
Less: unamortized discount on Treasury bills	1,016	688	328
	8,594	*7,710*	*884*
Accounts payable	4,307	2,991	1,316
Outstanding cheques and warrants	3,046	2,530	516
Allowance for employee vacation and termination benefits	1,900		1,900
Miscellaneous	134	114	20
TOTAL OTHER LIABILITIES	*17,981*	*13,345*	*4,636*
BORROWINGS OF AGENT CROWN CORPORATIONS, Table 7.4, Section 7	*11,825*		*11,825*
Less: borrowings expected to be repaid by these Crown corporations	10,675		10,675
ALLOWANCE FOR BORROWINGS EXPECTED TO BE REPAID BY THE GOVERNMENT	*1,150*		*1,150*
UNMATURED DEBT, Tables 11.1 and 11.9, Section 11—			
Payable in Canadian currency—			
Marketable bonds	56,811	48,304	8,507
Canada savings bonds	38,204	32,641	5,563
Special non-marketable bonds issued to the Canada Pension Plan Investment Fund	189	171	18
Treasury bills	41,700	29,125	12,575
	136,904	*110,241*	*26,663*
Less: Government's holdings of unmatured debt—			
Marketable bonds	164	(1)	164
Canada savings bonds held on account of employees	150	137	13
Special non-marketable bonds issued to the Canada Pension Plan Investment Fund	189	171	18
	503	*308*	*195*
	136,401	*109,933*	*26,468*
Payable in foreign currencies—			
Marketable bonds	2,183	3,409	- 1,226
Notes and loans payable in foreign currencies	3,039	1,825	1,214
	5,222	*5,234*	*- 12*
Less: Government's holdings of unmatured debt—			
Marketable bonds	20	12	8
	5,202	*5,222*	*- 20*
TOTAL UNMATURED DEBT	*141,603*	*115,155*	*26,448*
TOTAL	**196,861**	**159,470**	**37,391**

The accompanying notes are an integral part of this statement.
Details of assets and liabilities can be found in Sections 7 to 12 of this volume.
(1) Less than $500,000.

September 17, 1984.

WILLIAM B. BINDMAN,
Acting Comptroller General of Canada.

MARSHALL A. COHEN,
Deputy Minister of Finance.

PIERRE P. SICARD,
Deputy Receiver General for Canada.

the standpoint of the federal government because they must be repaid at some future time. Payments out of the account reduce the government's liability. The balance shown in the account of $26,612 million is the net amount held in trust to be paid out to contributors in the future. The $25,116 million figure represents the amount of CPP funds loaned to provincial governments. The difference of $1,496 million is the only portion of these funds that the federal government still has on hand.

It is interesting to note that one reason the accumulated government deficit seems so high is that all fixed assets owned by the government are valued at one dollar, yet the liabilities incurred to purchase those assets are shown at the amount needed to repay them. If the value of the fixed assets were changed to reflect their original purchase price or even current market value, the accumulated government deficit would automatically be reduced rather substantially.

Supplementary statements in the *Public Accounts* contain a large amount of detailed information about the various categories of items listed in the *Statement of Assets and Liabilities*. This includes details of transactions in the trust accounts, e.g., Canada Pension Plan, detailed lists of loans, advances, and investments, and details of unmatured debt. Again, this is an important source of information for anyone doing research on these trust funds, the financial situation of Crown corporations or agencies, and government indebtedness.

The *Public Accounts* also contains the opinion of the Auditor General of Canada on the accuracy of the statements presented by the government. Anyone using the *Public Accounts* should look at this section to determine how the Auditor General views the accuracy of these statements. In the last several years, the Auditor General of Canada has stated that, in his opinion, certain procedures followed by the federal government have the effect of misstating certain transactions reported in its statements. This is a technical accounting disagreement, rather than something that reflects on the credibility of the government; however, it can have an effect on how one uses the figures reported.

Volume II of the *Public Accounts*, referred to as *Details of Expenditure and Revenue*, contains a vast amount of information, mostly about the expenditure items contained in Volume I. Most of this book is devoted to a listing of the names of individuals and companies to whom government funds were paid during the year. Sometimes this information can be interesting in tracking down the nature of the relationship between a department and an individual or company, but this is useful only for a particular kind of research. Volume II of the *Public Accounts* is not ordinarily an important research tool.

Volume III of the *Public Accounts*, entitled *Financial Statements of Crown Corporations*, is frequently very useful, but the information is not always as complete or as helpful as that contained in the corporation's annual report. Also, the *Public Accounts* contains information about only some of the corporations in which the government has a financial interest.[76]

The *Public Accounts*, like the *Estimates*, contains a great deal of financial information. It is preferable to use financial information from the *Public Accounts*

---

[76]See Chapter 7 for a discussion of how this circumstance came about.

because it contains the audited figures prepared after the year-end, whereas the *Estimates* reflects amounts requested at the beginning of the year and so is subject to significant change during the year as a result of supplementary estimates or underspending. However, the advantage of the *Estimates* is that it tends to have more detail about the activities of departments. In practice, it is usually necessary to use some data from both reports, but the difference in the basis of the reports should not be forgotten.

All provincial governments prepare *Estimates* and *Public Accounts* documents, although in some cases the accounting assumptions and formats vary signifi cantly from the federal government. However, the variance is usually not so great that it is impossible to understand the statements after reading this section. It is always necessary to read the notes accompanying the statements carefully, and in some provinces there is a fair amount of supplementary information that is also helpful.

Municipalities also prepare budget requests at the beginning of the year and year-end statements, although these bear a myriad of different names. Because of certain technical aspects of municipal accounting, these statements can become very complicated. There are usually publications of the provincial Department of Municipal Affairs that can be helpful in unravelling the mysteries of these statements.

BIBLIOGRAPHY

Bertrand, Robert J., Alice Desjardins, and René Hurtubise. *Legislation, Administration and Interpretation Processes in Federal Taxation*. Study for the Royal Commission on Taxation, no. 22. Ottawa: Queen's Printer and Controller of Stationery, 1967.

Bird, Richard M. *The Growth of Government Spending in Canada*. Toronto: Canadian Tax Foundation, 1970.

Borins, Sandford F. "Ottawa's Expenditure Envelopes: Workable Rationality at Last?" In G. Bruce Doern, ed., *How Ottawa Spends Your Tax Dollars: National Policy and Economic Development — 1982*. Toronto: James Lorimer & Company, 1982, pp. 63-85.

Borins, Sandford F. *The Toronto Airport(s). Case Program in Canadian Public Administration*. Toronto: Institute of Public Administration of Canada, 1977.

Canada. Treasury Board. *Operational Performance Measurement, Vol. I: A Managerial Overview* and *Vol. II: Technical Manual*. Ottawa: Information Canada, 1974.

Canada. Treasury Board. *Report on the Study of the Accounts of Canada*. Ottawa: Minister of Supply and Services Canada, 1976.

Clark, Ian D. "Recent Changes in the Cabinet Decision-Making System in Ottawa." *Canadian Public Administration*, vol. 28 (Summer 1985): 185-201.

Clayton, A. "Brother Could You Spare a Dime?" *Optimum*, vol. 12, no. 1 (1981): 7-19.

Crecine, John P. *Governmental Problem-Solving: A Computer Simulation Model of Municipal Budgeting*. Chicago: Rand McNally, 1969.

Cutt, James, and Richard Ritter. *Public Non-Profit Budgeting: The Evolution and Application of Zero-Base Budgeting*. Toronto: The Institute of Public Administration of Canada, 1984.

Danziger, James N. *Making Budgets: Public Resource Allocation*. Beverly Hills, Ca.: Sage Publications, 1978.

Dobell, Rod. "Pressing the Envelopes." *Policy Options* (November–December 1981): 13–18.

Downs, Anthony. *An Economic Theory of Democracy*. New York: Harper & Row, 1957.

Drury, C. M. *Planning-Programming-Budgeting Guide*, rev. ed. Ottawa: Queen's Printer, 1969.

Dye, Thomas. *Understanding Public Policy*. Englewood Cliffs, N.J.: Prentice-Hall, 1972.

Falcone, David J., and Michael S. Whittington. "Output Change in Canada: A Preliminary Attempt to Open the 'Black Box.' " Paper presented to the Annual Meeting of the Canadian Political Science Association, Montreal, Quebec, June 4, 1972.

Fenno, Richard F., Jr. *The Power of the Purse: Appropriation Politics in Congress*. Boston: Little, Brown, 1966.

Frederiksen, Henning. "Is Operational Performance in Government Measurable?" *Optimum*, vol. 6, no. 4 (1975): 23–41.

French, Richard. *How Ottawa Decides*. Toronto: James Lorimer & Company, 1980.

Golembiewski, Robert T., and Jack Rabin, eds. *Public Budgeting and Finance: Behavioral, Theoretical, and Technical Perspectives*. New York: Marcel Dekker, 1983.

Good, David A. *The Politics of Anticipation: Making Canadian Federal Tax Policy*. Ottawa: Carleton University, School of Public Administration, n.d., 1980?

Gordon, Walter L. *A Political Man*. Toronto: McClelland and Stewart, 1977.

Gould, Stephen L., Alan A. Oldall, and Fred Thompson. "Zero-Base Budgeting: Some Lessons From an Inconclusive Experiment." *Canadian Public Administration*, vol. 22 (Summer 1979): 251–260.

Gow, Donald. *The Progress of Budgetary Reform in the Government of Canada*. Ottawa: Information Canada, 1973.

Hartle, Douglas G. *The Expenditure Budget Process in the Government of Canada*. Toronto: Canadian Tax Foundation, 1978.

Hartle, Douglas G. "Operational Performance Measurement in the Federal Government." *Optimum*, vol. 3, no. 4 (1972): 5–18.

Hartle, Douglas G. *The Revenue Budget Process of the Government of Canada: Description, Appraisal, and Proposals*. Toronto: Canadian Tax Foundation, 1982.

Hartle, Douglas G. "Techniques and Processes of Administration." *Canadian Public Administration*, vol. 19 (Spring 1976): 21–33.

Hartle, Douglas G. *A Theory of the Expenditure Budget Process*. Toronto: Ontario Economic Council, 1976.

Heclo, Hugh, and Aaron Wildavsky. *The Private Government of Public Money.* 2nd ed. London: Macmillan Press, 1981.

Hodgson, J. S. "Management by Objectives — The Experience of a Federal Government Department." *Canadian Public Administration,* vol. 16 (Fall 1973): 422–431.

Johnston, Donald J. *Guide to the Policy & Expenditure Management System.* Minister of Supply and Services Canada, 1980.

Laframboise, H. L. "Administrative Reform in the Federal Public Service: Signs of a Saturation Psychosis." *Canadian Public Administration,* vol. 14 (Fall 1971): 303–325.

LeLoup, Lance. "The Myth of Incrementalism: Analytic Choices in Budgetary Theory." In Robert T. Golembiewski and Jack Rabin, eds., *Public Budgeting and Finance: Behavioral, Theoretical, and Technical Perspectives.* New York: Marcel Dekker, 1983, pp. 61–81.

MacDonald, V. N., and P. J. Lawton. *Improving Management Performance: The Contribution of Productivity and Performance Measurement.* Toronto: Ministry of Treasury, Economics and Intergovernmental Affairs, 1977.

MacEachen, Allan J. *The Budget Process: A Paper on Budget Secrecy and Proposals for Broader Consultation.* Department of Finance, 1982.

Macnaughton, Bruce D. "Public Finance for Political Profit: The Politics of Social Security in Canada, 1941–1977." Ph.D. diss., Carleton University, 1980.

Macnaughton, Bruce D., and Conrad J. Winn. "Economic Policy and Electoral Self Interest: The Allocations of the Department of Regional Economic Expansion." *Canadian Public Policy,* vol. 7 (Spring 1981): 318–327.

Niskanen, William A., Jr. *Bureaucracy and Representative Government.* Chicago: Aldine-Atherton, 1971.

Ontario. Ministry of Treasury and Economics. *Province of Ontario: Financial Report 1985.*

Ontario. Ministry of Treasury and Economics. *Reforming the Budget Process: A Discussion Paper.* Toronto: Queen's Printer for Ontario, 1985.

Pryor, Frederic. *Public Expenditures in Communist and Capitalist Nations.* London: George Allen & Unwin, 1968.

Pyhrr, Peter A. *Zero-Base Budgeting.* Toronto: John Wiley, 1973.

Schick, Allen. "A Death in the Bureaucracy: The Demise of Federal PPB." *Public Administration Review,* vol. 33 (March–April 1973): 146–156.

Schick, Allen. "The Road to PPB: The Stages of Budget Reform." *Public Administration Review,* vol. 26 (December 1966): 243–258.

Self, Peter. *Econocrats and the Policy Process: The Politics and Philosophy of Cost-Benefit Analysis.* London: Macmillan, 1975.

Sherbaniuk, D. J. "Budget Secrecy." *Canadian Tax Journal,* vol. 24 (May–June 1976): 223–230.

Thomas, Paul G. "Public Administration and Expenditure Management." *Canadian Public Administration,* vol. 25 (Winter 1982): 674–695.

Treasury Board of Canada. *Guide on Financial Administration for Departments and Agencies of the Government of Canada.* 2nd ed. Hull: Supply and Services Canada, 1979.

Treasury Board of Canada. *Policy and Expenditure Management System Manual.*

Van Loon, Richard. "Ottawa's Expenditure Process: Four Systems In Search of Co-ordination." In G. Bruce Doern, ed., *How Ottawa Spends: The Liberals, the Opposition & Federal Priorities — 1983.* Toronto: James Lorimer & Company, 1983, pp. 93–120.

Van Loon, Richard. "The Policy and Expenditure Management System in the Federal Government: The First Three Years." *Canadian Public Administration,* vol. 26 (Summer 1983): 255–285.

Wildavsky, Aaron. "The Political Economy of Efficiency: Cost-Benefit Analysis, Systems Analysis, and Program Budgeting." *Public Administration Review,* vol. 26 (December 1966): 292–310.

Wildavsky, Aaron. *The Politics of the Budgetary Process.* Boston: Little, Brown, 1964.

Wildavsky, Aaron. "Rescuing Policy Analysis from PPB." *Public Administration Review,* vol. 29 (March–April 1969): 189–202.

Wilson, Michael H. *The Canadian Budgetary Process: Proposals for Improvement.* Department of Finance, 1985.

Young, Robert A. "Business and Budgeting: Recent Proposals for Reforming the Revenue Budgetary Process." *Canadian Public Policy,* vol. 9 (September 1983): 347–361.

CASES

In *Case Program in Canadian Public Administration* (Toronto: Institute of Public Administration of Canada):

The Elusive IPB System, by Walter Baker

Spenders, Guardians, and Policy Analysts: A Game of Budgeting Under the Policy and Expenditure Management System, by Sandford F. Borins and David A. Good

The Fiscal Framework Problem: First Steps in the Formulation of a Provincial Budget, by Paul C. Leger

Resource Allocation in a Provincial Government: The Frustration of Respecting Global Expenditure Levels, by Paul C. Leger

The Allocation of a National Housing Budget, by Barbara Carroll

24

The Management of Financial Resources

The previous chapter discussed the budgetary process, that is, the process of allocating funds to be spent on specific programs. This chapter will consider what happens to those funds after they have been appropriated. Of course, operating departments have the main role because they operate programs and therefore spend the bulk of the funds. However, there are a number of other agencies involved in the process of ensuring that funds are spent wisely and with appropriate controls. This chapter will examine in detail each of the agencies involved in the process.

THE FINANCIAL ADMINISTRATION ACT

The Financial Administration Act[1] establishes the general rules for financial management. It is the legislation which sets out the responsibilities of the Treasury Board and of the Department of Finance in the area of financial management. It establishes the general rules for the handling and safeguarding of public funds and other assets. It specifies rules for the management of the public debt and sets out procedures for maintaining the government accounting system. It also establishes the accountability regime for Crown corporations and other agencies. In sum, the Financial Administration Act provides the general framework within which the departments and agencies of the federal government must function, with respect to financial and administrative management.

PARLIAMENT

The best way to view the system is as an annual cycle, as illustrated in Figure 24.1. The process begins when Parliament appropriates funds for a new fiscal year, which begins on April 1. Most aspects of the appropriation process were covered in the previous chapter, but it is important to remember that it is a basic tenet of responsible, parliamentary government that Parliament must approve the expenditure of any funds *before* the expenditure occurs. This is the first step in the financial administration cycle.

As discussed in the previous chapter, a substantial amount of work goes into the preparation of the budget before it is tabled in the House of Commons. In this chapter, the role of Parliament in the approval of the expenditure budget will be considered.

---

[1] R.S.C. 1970, c. F-10, with numerous amendments.

Figure 24.1
ANNUAL CYCLE OF FINANCIAL ACCOUNTABILITY

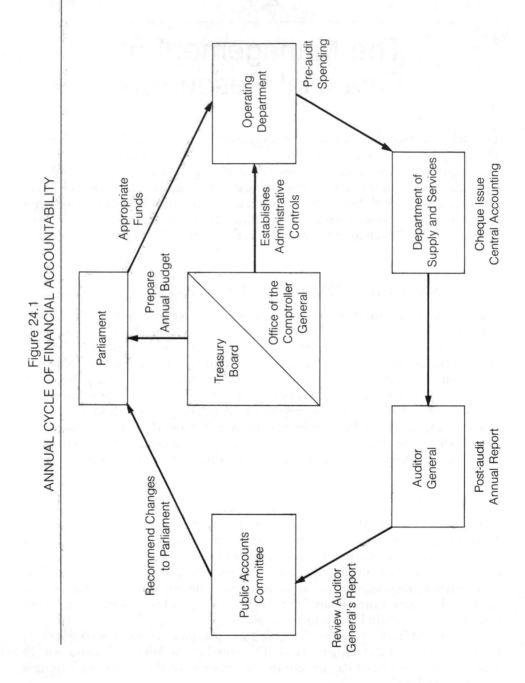

The President of the Treasury Board begins the process, usually in January or February of each year, by tabling a series of documents collectively referred to as the *Estimates*. These documents list the budget allocations requested by each department, as well as some supporting detail about the operation of the programs for which funding is requested. In recent years this supporting information has expanded, so that the estimates of each department now constitute a separate volume which provides supplementary information about programs such as the number of clients served, the number of units of service provided, and the unit cost of providing a service.[2] The *Estimates* and all other "money bills," as they are called, are always tabled and approved in the House of Commons before going to the Senate. This is a long tradition stemming from the fact that the House of Commons is the elected body of Parliament and is therefore the only body that is directly responsible to the electorate.

After the *Estimates* documents have been tabled in the full House of Commons, they are then sent to the various committees of the House for further consideration. Each committee specializes in a department, or a related group of departments, so that the *Estimates* are figuratively divided up and sent to the appropriate committees for more in-depth consideration. Since this usually takes some time, and since the *Estimates* are not tabled until a rather short time before the beginning of the fiscal year on April 1, it is unlikely that Parliament will approve the *Estimates* before the beginning of the fiscal year. Obviously, this creates a rather serious problem because departments cannot begin to spend money until Parliament has appropriated it. To circumvent this problem, Parliament provides interim supply before the beginning of the fiscal year.

Interim supply is a piece of legislation which provides for the operation of the government for the period from April 1 to June 30 by appropriating approximately one-fourth of the total budget requested. This allows departments to continue operating, even though the full budget has not yet been considered. It is customary that interim supply should include funds only for the continuation of existing programs. Funding for new programs must usually await the approval of the *Estimates*.

Shortly after the *Estimates* are tabled, the various parliamentary committees begin to hold hearings on the part of the *Estimates* that most closely concerns them. Usually, ministers and senior officials will appear before these committees to defend and explain their budget requests. The committees also like to hear from clientele groups and interested experts. The committees then recommend to Parliament what the appropriate budgetary allocation ought to be. Since these committees usually operate along highly partisan lines, it is unusual for the committee recommendation to deviate from the government's request, but that should not be taken as a sign of the committees' impotence. These budget hearings are, at minimum, an excellent place for Opposition members to learn about the activities of departments, and they can also provide an important forum for holding ministers and public servants accountable.

---

[2]The content of the *Estimates* is discussed in more detail in the appendix following Chapter 23.

After the committee reports have been received by the House of Commons, there is then a vote on the full budget as contained in the *Estimates*. This vote is very important because the expenditure budget is always a matter of "confidence," meaning that if the budget were defeated, it would be an indication that the government no longer had the "confidence" of the House and therefore, as a matter of convention, ought to resign. The rules of the House provide that if a budget has not been acted upon by the full House before June 30, then it is voted upon on that date. This means that the Opposition is free to *defeat* a budget, but it cannot hamstring the government by merely *delaying* the passage of the budget. In fact, the *Estimates* are almost always passed in exactly the form proposed by the government. When the *Estimates* document becomes law, it is known as the Appropriation Act for that year.

The government always attempts to estimate its needs as accurately as possible when it prepares its *Estimates* at the beginning of the year, but it is not surprising that sometimes these beginning-of-the-year estimates do not prove completely accurate. Since all expenditures require parliamentary approval, the government cannot unilaterally shift funds from one program to another, or spend more than was allotted by Parliament in the original Appropriation Act. In order to meet unforeseen circumstances, the government presents *supplementary estimates* to the House at various times during the fiscal year. The supplementary estimates are pieces of legislation that request either additional funds beyond those originally approved, or a shift in funds between programs. In recent years, governments typically have presented supplementary estimates from two to four times each year, usually beginning in November or December.

There is one other way of dealing with these unforeseen circumstances. *Governor General's warrants* can be issued to meet an *unforeseen need* at a time when *Parliament is not in session*. In this case the President of the Treasury Board notifies the Governor General that funds must be spent, even though there has been no parliamentary appropriation. The Governor General then issues a warrant authorizing the expenditure of these funds.

To ensure that the use of these warrants is not abused, the government is required to provide official notice whenever they are used. First, they are always announced in the *Canada Gazette*, which is the publication of the government of Canada in which all official government announcements are publicized. Then, the issuance of these warrants must be approved by Parliament when it resumes sitting before it considers any new expenditure legislation. While there is nothing that Parliament can do at this point to recapture the funds that have already been spent, it is an opportunity for the Opposition parties to question the government about the expenditure of these funds. The warrants are a limited violation of the principle that all expenditure requires prior parliamentary approval, but they are an important safety valve. For example, Governor General's warrants were used extensively during the 1979-80 period when, because of transitions in government, Parliament was not sitting for an extended period. Without some mechanism such as these warrants, absolutely no money could have been spent in that rather lengthy period.

The role of Parliament in financial administration is crucial. Legally, it is Parliament — and only Parliament — which can start the process by appropriating funds. Still, there have been criticisms of Parliament's role. Some members of Parliament have complained that they have very limited time to consider the lengthy and complex *Estimates* before they are passed. The Royal Commission on Financial Management and Accountability echoed the same concern when it suggested that individual MPs were overworked in terms of their committee activities,[3] and when it further pointed out that there was no single committee which was charged with an overview of the budget and the economy.[4] However, at this time, while it seems that most people recognize the existence of the problem, no action has been taken to resolve it.

TREASURY BOARD

Treasury Board is a Cabinet committee consisting of six Cabinet ministers including the President of the Treasury Board and the Minister of Finance. The board has been called the Cabinet committee on the expenditure budget and the Cabinet committee on management.[5] In fulfilling its first role, it assembles the budget requests of departments and recommends the budget to Parliament. This aspect of its work was covered in detail in the previous chapter. In this chapter the main focus will be on the latter role.

There are two things which distinguish the Treasury Board from other Cabinet committees. One is that there is a rather large group of civil servants working directly under the supervision of the President. In 1984, there were approximately eight hundred employees in the Treasury Board Secretariat, as the bureaucratic organization reporting to the President is properly called. The effect of this bureaucratic contingent is that the Treasury Board has a considerably higher profile as a committee touching on the day-to-day activities of public servants than other Cabinet committees.

The Treasury Board is also distinguished from other Cabinet committees in that its existence has been established by an Act of Parliament (the Financial Administration Act), unlike other Cabinet committees which are created by, and can be abolished by, a decision of the Prime Minister. The Financial Administration Act establishes the general framework for financial and administrative management in the federal government, and as a part of that framework it establishes the Treasury Board's status as a central control agency — meaning that the board has supervisory powers over certain activities of operating departments. Specifically, the board has the power to make regulations in most areas of general administrative and financial management. Some examples of the board's authority are:

---

[3]*Final Report* (Hull: Supply and Services Canada, 1979), ch. 22.

[4]Ibid., pp. 381–383.

[5]A. W. Johnson, "The Treasury Board of Canada and the Machinery of Government of the 1970s," *Canadian Journal of Political Science*, vol. 4 (September 1971), pp. 346–366.

- establishing allotments, i.e., subdivisions of parliamentary appropriations, which cannot be varied without Treasury Board approval;
- prescribing rules for the disbursement of public funds, i.e, procedures to be followed before a cheque can be issued;
- prescribing rules for the receipt and control of funds paid to the government;
- prescribing rules for the safeguarding of public property;
- ensuring coordination of administrative functions and services within departments and within government as a whole, i.e., ensuring effective interdepartmental coordination;
- prescribing the form and manner in which government accounting records will be maintained;
- establishing regulations for entering into contracts and for purchasing.

Treasury Board also has a number of responsibilities in areas other than financial management, which are discussed in other chapters.

A perusal of these activities indicates that the main role of Treasury Board is to ensure prudence and probity in government and to ensure uniformity in administration between operating departments. In a small organization, this kind of function would not be necessary, but this sort of role is frequently found in large organizations. It is necessary to have some organization to ensure that all of the diverse and centralized units of the organization are conducting their administrative activities in an appropriate and reasonably uniform manner.

In order to carry out this function, Treasury Board has prepared a number of manuals containing guidelines and regulations that are binding on all departments and agencies of the government. The regulations sometimes specify in great detail things ranging from the steps which must be followed before a government cheque can be issued, to the size of offices for officials of various ranks. In some cases, a department can obtain an exemption from following certain regulations if it is able to make a satisfactory argument to Treasury Board that special circumstances require this exemption. The staff of the Auditor General's Office is familiar with the Treasury Board regulations and uses them in the performance of audits.

The status of Treasury Board as a central control agency gives it a key role in the system of financial administration. However, it is precisely this status that frequently leads it into conflict with operating departments and raises questions about accountability. Operating departments usually feel under pressure to operate programs in such a manner that significant results are produced quickly. Officials in these departments sometimes see uniform, cross-departmental regulations as obstacles to smooth and efficient service delivery. Treasury Board is not unsympathetic to this problem, but officials in the Treasury Board Secretariat are mindful that regulations are established to serve particular purposes and should not be circumvented lightly. The operating department might see that there are ways of saving time and money by cutting certain corners, for example, by shortcutting certain purchasing procedures or by skimping on some financial control mechanisms. This raises the classic staff-line conflict, but it is exacerbated in this case because Treasury Board, unlike the classic staff agency, has *control* over some aspects of the department's work.

This raises the question of accountability. Is it really appropriate to hold the line department accountable for results if it does not have full authority to take whatever action is necessary to obtain those results? This is an old question, which really cannot be answered in the abstract. Every situation is slightly different. The important point to be made is that some controls over the activities of line departments are important, but a certain sensitivity must be employed in exercising this control so as not to hamstring unduly the activities of operating departments.

OFFICE OF THE COMPTROLLER GENERAL

The Office of the Comptroller General (OCG) is a relatively new organization. It was established by an amendment to the Financial Administration Act in 1978, which was a response to continuing pressure from the Auditor General to create a "chief financial officer" for the government of Canada. The higher profile given to financial administration by the creation of a separate office is important; but, in fact, most of the duties of the OCG were simply spun off from the Treasury Board. This is reflected in the fact that most of the OCG's initial staff complement came from the Treasury Board Secretariat.

Throughout most of the 1970s, the Auditor General was James J. Macdonell — a somewhat larger-than-life figure who will be considered in greater detail later in this chapter. When he became Auditor General in 1973 after a lengthy career in the private sector, he was surprised to find that, while Treasury Board had general responsibility for financial management, along with many other things, there was no one *individual* who could be called the "chief financial officer" of the government of Canada. This meant that there was no focal point for ensuring high quality financial management in the government of Canada. Under the terms of the Financial Administration Act, this was the responsibility of the Treasury Board. The problem was that because the board had so many other responsibilities, there was no guarantee that financial management would have the status within the board which the Auditor General felt it should have. Therefore, beginning with his 1976 report, Macdonell began urging the creation of an Office of the Comptroller General.[6] This agitation was rewarded in 1978 when the office was created.

The relationship between the new Office of the Comptroller General and the Treasury Board has always been a convoluted one, because the OCG has taken over certain responsibilities which were previously carried out by the board. The Comptroller General has the rank of deputy head — the same rank held by the Secretary of the Treasury Board — and reports to the President of the Treasury Board. Many publications bear the joint stamp of the Treasury Board and the Office of the Comptroller General. All of this makes it somewhat difficult to delineate exactly the role of the OCG, but the first Comptroller General, Harry Rogers, carved out certain areas which became his primary focus of interest.

---

[6]This story is told in Sonja Sinclair, *Cordial but not Cosy* (Toronto: McClelland and Stewart, 1979), ch. 8.

The OCG is responsible for developing government-wide policies for financial and operational management. This involves publication of the *Guide on Financial Administration for Departments and Agencies of the Government of Canada*,[7] which sets out in great detail the procedures that must be followed with regard to receipt and payment of public funds, handling inventories and other assets, internal audit procedures, and so forth. The OCG also shares with the Department of Supply and Services the responsibility for developing government accounting policy and the system of accounts used in the preparation of the *Public Accounts*.

Evaluation

The other major role which the OCG has carved out for itself is in the evaluation of government programs — a process which has been of great concern in the federal government recently. *Evaluation* involves the systematic, in-depth review of all activities of a particular program to provide information to members of Parliament which will assist them in considering the value of the program. Harry Rogers, the first Comptroller General, has defined evaluation in this manner:

> The term "program evaluation" is now widely used as an umbrella to cover a great variety of attempts to arrive at objective and coherent overviews of the effectiveness with which the tasks of government are performed. Program evaluation is no one technique, but is in effect the application of the best current empirical methods of investigation in the social sciences. The aim is to generate information about whether or not specified goals are being reached well, or at all. But if program evaluation is no one thing, I think it is safe to say that knowing how well effort translates into effect is always the objective.[8]

One of the criticisms of the federal government's former Planning-Programming-Budgeting System was that it forced all programs into one method of performance appraisal; the basic idea of "evaluation" is that any technique that is appropriate for a particular program can be employed.

The OCG does not actually evaluate the programs itself; there are important reasons why that is better left to the operating departments. However, the OCG has developed expertise in the evaluation area so that it can advise departments on undertaking evaluations and, to some extent, evaluate the evaluations. In general, it provides leadership in this area by using both moral suasion and producing publications such as *Principles for the Evaluation of Programs by Federal Departments and Agencies*.[9]

A few evaluations have been made public, but it is the government's policy that these are internal documents to be used by the department and by Trea-

---

[7](Minister of Supply and Services Canada, 1979).

[8]"Program Evaluation in the Federal Government," in G. Bruce Doern and Allan M. Maslove, eds., *The Public Evaluation of Government Spending* (Montreal: Institute for Research on Public Policy, 1979), p. 81.

[9](Minister of Supply and Services Canada, 1981).

sury Board to improve the management of programs and the delivery of services. Conceptually, they could also be used for decisions about de-emphasizing or eliminating programs, although there do not seem to be any examples of that so far.

However, a number of problems with the current system of evaluation have been identified. Some of the more straightforward, but not necessarily simple to solve, problems revolve around questions of measuring outputs of government programs, finding appropriate techniques, and overcoming the bureaucrat's normal resistance to having his or her output measured. One of the more serious problems stems from an inability to determine for whom the evaluation is being prepared — the deputy minister or the Cabinet. An evaluation geared to showing possibilities for improvements in management is radically different from one geared to determining the ultimate worth of the program. In fact, there is some question that *any* evaluation system short of the court of public opinion can do the latter.[10]

In the previous section, some of the tensions which exist between Treasury Board and line departments, and some of the problems of accountability which these cause, were discussed. Many of the same comments could be repeated with regard to the role of the OCG. As a central control agency, it has a mandate to impose certain operating rules on departments — rules which the departments sometimes find onerous. This brings it into the same kind of conflict sometimes experienced by Treasury Board, and so the same problems of line-staff relationships and muddled accountability exist here as well.

OPERATING DEPARTMENTS

The line departments are involved in actually operating most large government programs, and so it is in these departments where the bulk of government expenditure takes place. These departments are clearly in the front line in terms of making expenditure decisions, but the above discussions about the roles of the Treasury Board and the Office of the Comptroller General should make it clear that the authority of a department to act unilaterally is somewhat limited.

Departments are required to establish appropriate *pre-audit procedures* — procedures to ensure that appropriate conditions have been met *before* payment is approved. These procedures must ensure that the expenditure has been authorized by Parliament, that adequate funds still remain in the appropriation, that appropriate goods or services have been received, and that these were in line with the contract. If the payment is a grant or transfer payment, obvi-

---

[10]Rodney Dobell and David Zussman, "An Evaluation System for Government: If Politics Is Theatre Then Evaluation Is (Mostly) Art," *Canadian Public Administration*, vol. 24 (Fall 1981), pp. 420–422 and passim. For a discussion of other problems of and potential improvements in evaluation, see: J. M. Jordan and S. L. Sutherland, "Assessing the Results of Public Expenditure: Program Evaluation in the Canadian Federal Government," *Canadian Public Administration*, vol. 22 (Winter 1979), pp. 581–609; John Mayne and Robert S. Mayne, "Will Program Evaluation Be Used in Formulating Policy?" in Michael M. Atkinson and Marsha A. Chandler, eds., *The Politics of Canadian Public Policy* (Toronto: University of Toronto Press, 1983), pp. 267–283.

ously the specific procedure is different, but the general idea is the same. The department must establish procedures to ensure that the person receiving the payment is entitled to it. These procedures are called a pre-audit because they are required, by Treasury Board–Comptroller General guidelines, to occur before any public funds are paid out. These same guidelines specify similar rules for the protection of revenue received and the safeguarding of non-cash assets such as inventories.

Departments are also responsible for establishing an internal audit function. This is a group of auditors sometimes reporting directly to the deputy minister who ensure that proper financial procedures are being followed. They attempt to locate and correct developing problems *before* they are detected by the Office of the Auditor General. The Office of the Comptroller General is particularly interested in ensuring that all departments have an adequate internal audit function in place.

Departments receive a budgetary allocation and approve the payment of funds to be charged to that allocation, but they do not actually issue cheques. This is done by the Department of Supply and Services.

DEPARTMENT OF SUPPLY AND SERVICES

The Department of Supply and Services (DSS) is responsible for many common services provided to all departments and agencies such as purchasing and central accounting. It is this latter function which will be discussed in this chapter.

DSS is the central accounting agency of the government of Canada. This means that the Receiver General for Canada, which is another title that the Minister of Supply and Services always holds, is responsible for the receipt and disbursement of all public funds and for accounting for those funds in the Consolidated Revenue Fund. The *Consolidated Revenue Fund* is the one large cash account which the government maintains for all federal funds that are not earmarked for some specific purpose. The title comes from the fact that at one time there were a large number of cash funds held by a variety of different agencies and used largely for their own purposes. This created some confusion and raised the possibility of inappropriate use of, or accounting for, government funds. For this reason, it was felt desirable to consolidate all government funds in one account under the control of one minister — the Receiver General — and his or her department — the Department of Supply and Services.

DSS receives cheque requisitions from operating departments and agencies and then issues cheques as requested. Before the cheque is issued, DSS ensures that the department will not be overspending its appropriation, but it undertakes no other reviews beyond that, because it assumes that the department has conducted a proper pre-audit. DSS handles all receipts and deposits of public funds and acts as a central accounting agency; it shares with the Office of the Comptroller General responsibility for the establishment of the government accounting system. DSS is also responsible for the preparation of the government's year-end financial statements, referred to as the *Public Accounts*. These statements contain the government's balance sheet, which lists assets owned and liabilities owed, the *Statement of Revenue and Expenditure* and certain other financial statements. The *Public Accounts* also contains a great deal of detailed information about sources of revenue and objects of expenditure by program and activity. This makes it a valuable source of information for researchers.[11]

DSS is responsible for *preparing* the government's financial statements, but these statements must bear the scrutiny of an audit by an independent agency.

AUDITOR GENERAL

The Office of the Auditor General (OAG) is one of the most visible and well-known actors in the financial management system. The auditor can be seen as having two roles — one narrow and one much broader. The narrow role is the least contentious and requires the Auditor General to act in the same manner as an auditor would act in the private sector. The Auditor General's more contentious, broader role requires him or her to be something of a watchdog of government spending.

In the Auditor General's narrow role, he or she performs an attest audit. An *attest audit* is an audit performed to ensure that the financial statements accurately reflect the financial position and activities of the government. The outcome of the attest audit is the auditor's opinion, which becomes a part of the *Public Accounts*. This opinion should be read by anyone working with the *Public Accounts* to provide an insight into the level of accuracy of the statements presented.

In recent years, the Auditor General has issued an opinion indicating that the statements are not as accurate as they could be if certain better accounting principles were employed.[12] This is a rather strong statement, but it must be seen in perspective. The Auditor General is clearly not suggesting that any fraudulent or otherwise culpable activity has occurred. He has merely stated that improvements could be made in the presentation of the statements that would make them more reflective of the government's actual financial position.

In order to fulfil this attest function, the staff of the OAG must undertake a *post-audit* of a random selection of financial transactions which occurred during the year. This post-audit means that these selected transactions are traced through the accounting process to evaluate the adequacy of the pre-audit performed within departments and to determine the accuracy of the accounting records. This is how the Auditor General forms an opinion as to whether the financial statements contained in the *Public Accounts* as prepared by the Department of Supply and Services accurately reflect the financial position of the government.

In addition to the attest audit, the Auditor General also is responsible for the performance of a compliance audit. A *compliance audit* is an audit performed

---

[11]The *Public Accounts* document is described in more detail in the appendix to Chapter 23.

[12]Receiver General for Canada, *Public Accounts of Canada — 1985: Volume 1: Summary Report and Financial Statements* (Ottawa: Minister of Supply and Services Canada, 1985), pp. 2-18 and 2-19.

to ensure that all legislative enactments and government regulations have been complied with in the operation of programs. It goes beyond the attest audit in ensuring not just that expenditures have been recorded correctly, but that there was appropriate statutory authority for all expenditure, and further, that the regulations specified by the Comptroller General and the Treasury Board have been followed. This role of the Auditor General has never been very contentious because it can usually be established objectively when rules have been violated.

However, the Auditor General's broader role has always been somewhat more contentious. The Auditor General is an officer of Parliament, rather than simply an ordinary public servant. This means that he or she has the right to report directly to Parliament and has protection from arbitrary dismissal from office by the government, which will be discussed in more detail later. In this role, the Auditor General is frequently seen as Parliament's watchdog on government spending. To carry out this watchdog role, the Auditor General is required to prepare an annual report for Parliament. Different Auditors General have used this report in different ways.

Under the terms of legislation in existence prior to 1977, the Auditor General was charged with reporting on any "non-productive expenditure." Previous Auditors General who have taken this responsibility to heart have produced annual reports which contained lists of "horror stories." These were lists of specific incidents which, in the opinion of the Auditor General, indicated some sort of inappropriate expenditure by the government. This kind of report was much beloved by the media, because it provided a succession of juicy headlines. One of the most widely heralded examples was the story of the refitting of the aircraft carrier *Bonaventure*.[13] The Auditor General found numerous examples of cost overruns and excessive prices paid during the refit. Then, to add insult to injury, the ship was sold for a very low price almost immediately after the refit was complete.

These kinds of findings are important in reminding ministers and public servants that there is a check on their activities, and that they therefore must carry out their responsibilities with due care. However, not all of the Auditor General's "horror stories" were as clear-cut as the *Bonaventure*. In 1969, the government of the day became incensed over the Auditor General's criticism of its expenditure on a study of a causeway to Prince Edward Island.[14] The causeway is a continuing contentious issue between the federal government and the government of Prince Edward Island. The federal government had commissioned a feasibility study of the construction of the causeway. After considering the findings of the study, it was decided not to build the causeway at that time. At this point, the Auditor General suggested in his annual report that the cost of the study was a non-productive expenditure. The government of the day argued that this finding was unfair because it made more sense to study the feasibility of a major project first, rather than build it and then discover that it was unnecessary. This incident provides some insight into the problems which the Auditor

---

[13]Sinclair, *Cordial but not Cosy*, p. 69.
[14]*Report of the Auditor General to the House of Commons for the Fiscal Year Ended March 31, 1967* (Ottawa: Queen's Printer and Controller of Stationery, 1968), pp. 54–56.

General encounters when he or she goes beyond the narrow confines of the attest audit.

In 1977 provisions governing the Auditor General were removed from the Financial Administration Act, and the Auditor General's Office was for the first time governed by its own legislation. In this new legislation, the phrase "non-productive expenditure" was replaced by a requirement to report on any case in which "money has been expended without due regard to economy or efficiency."[15] At about this time the style of the Auditor General changed from an emphasis on individual "horror stories," to a more systematic approach to general problems in financial management. This change came about partly because of misunderstandings such as the causeway, and partly because the accounting profession was taking a more systematic approach to auditing; but mostly the change came about as a result of the coming to office of James J. Macdonell — an individual who had spent his entire career in accounting and management consulting in the private sector. Macdonell moved away from the "horror stories" approach and towards the more systematic approaches of what was first called "value-for-money" auditing and then comprehensive auditing.

Comprehensive auditing is a broader approach to auditing than the narrow attest function, because its emphasis is on the three e's — economy, efficiency, and effectiveness.[16] *Economy* is defined as obtaining the appropriate goods and services needed at the best possible price. *Efficiency* is defined as arranging resources in such a manner as to obtain the maximum output from the resources employed. *Effectiveness* is defined as maximizing the attainment of a particular objective. These three e's are obviously complementary, but it is possible to maximize some of them, but not others. For example, one could maximize economy in obtaining resources, but then employ those resources in an inefficient manner. Probably, the more usual situation is that economy and efficiency are present, but they are misdirected in some way so that effectiveness is not served, i.e., steps towards the desired objective are not maximized.

The introduction of comprehensive auditing caused a change in the style of auditing. In the former style, staff of the audit office reviewed the activities of each department and agency in as much depth as time allowed, performing mostly a post-audit, but always with an eye to uncovering horror stories.

In comprehensive auditing, there was still a concern for the ordinary attest function and post-audit. However, the random search for horror stories was replaced by a systematic and detailed review of a limited number of programs each year. An extensive, but shallow, approach was replaced by a selective, intensive approach. The style and content of the annual report also changed. The listing of horror stories was replaced by two main types of chapters. One type reported on the comprehensive audits of specific programs, and the second type dealt with government-wide reviews of a general nature, such as the use of computers or photocopy equipment. In both cases, the Auditor General's comments

---

[15]S.C. 1976–77, c. 34, s. 7(2)(d).

[16]*Report of the Auditor General of Canada to the House of Commons — Fiscal Year Ended 31 March 1983* (Ottawa: Minister of Supply and Services Canada, 1983), p. 200ff.

were not confined to dealing only with financial activities. For example, in a recent report on the operation of the Commissioner of Official Languages, the Auditor General's report referred to the lack of clearly defined roles for agencies in this area, the lack of an overall strategic plan, problems in evaluating employee performance and several other general management, non-financial areas.[17]

However, even this new approach did not deliver the Auditor General from controversy. In fact, in some ways the comprehensive audit approach increased the level of controversy. Governments ought to be concerned with all three e's, and proper accountability requires that ministers be held responsible for maximizing all three. The Auditor General can be one element in ensuring that accountability, but there is a rather difficult problem with this. It is within the appropriate sphere of the Auditor General to comment on economy and efficiency, but a consideration of effectiveness frequently requires some comment on government objectives which clearly goes beyond the mandate of the Auditor General and may venture into political territory. The Auditor General must exercise care, lest at some point he or she usurp the role of the leader of the Opposition. Comprehensive auditing attempts to avoid this dilemma by limiting its role to commenting on economy and efficiency. These are not such contentious areas. In principle, there is no attempt to comment on effectiveness as such, but Macdonell took the position that all programs should have indicators to measure their effectiveness and that his office ought to have responsibility to comment on the existence (or non-existence) and adequacy of those indicators. This attempt to define the Auditor General's role more carefully has probably limited the conflict somewhat, but Mr. Macdonell has been accused of overstepping his appropriate role.[18]

In order to carry out the audit function appropriately, the Auditor General must have what private sector auditors refer to as "independence," i.e., the auditor must not be under the direct control of the organization being audited — in this case the executive branch of government. One aspect of this independence is ensured by the fact that the Auditor General is an officer of Parliament. In practice, this means that he can deliver all reports directly to Parliament without intervention by the government; he can appeal directly to Parliament if he feels that his office is not being funded appropriately; and he can be dismissed only for cause after address of both Houses of Parliament. This last point means that an Auditor General can be dismissed only for some inappropriate behaviour, and even then, only after a majority vote of the House of Commons and Senate and the concurrence of the Governor General. This is the same procedure which is followed for the dismissal of a judge.

The method of appointment also helps ensure the independence of the Auditor General. The appointment is made by Parliament on the nomination of the

---

[17]The most complete reference on comprehensive auditing is Canadian Comprehensive Auditing Foundation, *Comprehensive Auditing in Canada: The Provincial Legislative Audit Perspective* (Ottawa: Canadian Comprehensive Auditing Foundation, 1985).

[18]Sharon Sutherland, "On the Audit Trail of the Auditor General: Parliament's Servant, 1973-80," *Canadian Public Administration*, vol. 23 (Winter 1980), pp. 616-644; and by the same author, "The Politics of Audit: The Federal Office of the Auditor General in Comparative Perspective," *Canadian Public Administration*, vol. 29 (Spring 1986), pp. 118-148.

Prime Minister. However, to help ensure the highest quality appointment, there is a tradition that, in making this nomination, the Prime Minister will rely on the advice of a committee of professional accountants. Once appointed, the Auditor General serves a fixed term of ten years or until he or she reaches sixty-five years of age, whichever comes first. The independence of the Auditor General is very important, and there is a general consensus that this independence is adequately served by the safeguards that are in place.

PUBLIC ACCOUNTS COMMITTEE

The Public Accounts Committee (PAC) is a committee of the House of Commons charged with the responsibility for reviewing the Auditor General's annual report. In most ways, it functions just as any other parliamentary committee, with the exception that, by tradition, the chairperson of the committee is a member of the Opposition. It is quite possible that the committee will be composed of a majority of members from the government party, but this does not make the chairperson powerless. The chair establishes agendas and provides leadership to the committee. The presence of an Opposition member in the chair ensures that important topics will be on the agenda and will be discussed in the presence of interested members of Parliament and the media. This high visibility does much to ensure accountability, even if the contents of the committee's reports are dominated by government input.

The committee reviews the Auditor General's annual report on a section-by-section basis. Usually, it considers the comprehensive audits of each program separately. Relevant ministers and/or senior public servants are invited to appear before the committee to comment on the findings of the Auditor General and possibly explain what steps have been taken to solve the problems. Throughout the process, the members of the PAC are advised by staff of the Office of the Auditor General. During the course of the hearings, the committee sends a series of short reports to Parliament providing its recommendations for what ought to be done as a result of each of the Auditor General's observations.

This series of reports closes the loop that was set out in Figure 24.1. Parliament will have the comments of the Public Accounts Committee before it when deciding what to do about the continued funding of a particular program in the next budget.

Speed is very important in providing the proper feedback to Parliament. It is a typical criticism of auditing, committee hearings, and similar activities that they constitute closing the barn door after the horses have escaped. This is not a valid criticism if the feedback loop is closed quickly enough. Actions can be taken to restructure or even terminate programs which are not performing as desired. In recent times this entire cycle has taken approximately eighteen months to complete. The fiscal year ends on March 31. The Auditor General is required to produce a report by the end of December — a deadline which has always been met by recent Auditors General. Then hearings by the Public Accounts Committee can begin shortly after that time. The length of those hearings obviously depends entirely upon the desires of the committee members, but in recent years the committee has usually concluded its deliberations on the Auditor General's report by the following summer. Eighteen months seems like a rather long feedback cycle, but considering the enormity of the task facing all of the actors, it is probably the best that can be expected.

It is difficult to assess the significance of the role of Parliament in this process, since it does not typically alter the *Estimates* as presented by the government. However, it is likely that the government would want to move to correct problems identified by the Auditor General and the Public Accounts Committee *before* having to take strong criticism in the House and the media. In this sense, the benefits of these organizations are sometimes more real than apparent.

BIBLIOGRAPHY

Auditor General of Canada. *Report of the Auditor General to the House of Commons for the Fiscal Year Ended March 31, 1967*. Ottawa: Queen's Printer and Controller of Stationery, 1968.

Auditor General of Canada. *Report of the Auditor General of Canada to the House of Commons — Fiscal Year Ended 31 March 1983*. Ottawa: Minister of Supply and Services Canada, 1983.

Canada. Office of the Comptroller General. *Guide on Financial Administration for Departments and Agencies of the Government of Canada*. Minister of Supply and Services Canada, 1979.

Canada. Office of the Comptroller General. *Principles for the Evaluation of Programs by Federal Departments and Agencies*. Minister of Supply and Services Canada, 1981.

Canada. Receiver General for Canada. *Public Accounts of Canada — 1985*. Ottawa: Minister of Supply and Services Canada, 1985.

Canada. Royal Commission on Financial Management and Accountability. *Final Report*. Hull: Supply and Services Canada, 1979.

Canadian Comprehensive Auditing Foundation. *Comprehensive Auditing in Canada: The Provincial Legislative Audit Perspective*. Ottawa: Canadian Comprehensive Auditing Foundation, 1985.

Dobell, Rodney, and David Zussman. "An Evaluation System for Government: If Politics Is Theatre, Then Evaluation Is (Mostly) Art." *Canadian Public Administration*, vol. 24 (Fall 1981): 404-427.

Doern, G. Bruce, and Allan Maslove, eds. *The Public Evaluation of Government Spending*. Montreal: Institute for Research on Public Policy, 1979.

Johnson, A. W. "The Treasury Board of Canada and the Machinery of Government of the 1970s." *Canadian Journal of Political Science*, vol. 4 (September 1971): 346-366.

Jordan, J. M., and S. L. Sutherland. "Assessing the Results of Public Expenditure: Program Evaluation in the Canadian Federal Government." *Canadian Public Administration*, vol. 22 (Winter 1979): 581-609.

Laframboise, H. L. "Government Spending: Grappling with the Evaluation Octopus." *Optimum*, vol. 9, no. 4 (1978): 39-52.

Mayne, John, and Robert S. Mayne. "Will Program Evaluation Be Used in Formulating Policy?" In Michael M. Atkinson and Marsha A. Chandler, eds., *The Politics of Canadian Public Policy*. Toronto: University of Toronto Press, 1983, pp. 267–283.

Rogers, H. G., M. A. Ulrich, and K. L. Traversy. "Evaluation in Practice: The State of the Art in Canadian Governments." *Canadian Public Administration*, vol. 24 (Fall 1981): 371–386.

Sinclair, Sonja. *Cordial but not Cosy*. Toronto: McClelland and Stewart, 1979.

Sutherland, Sharon. "On the Audit Trail of the Auditor General: Parliament's Servant, 1973–80." *Canadian Public Administration*, vol. 23 (Winter 1980): 616–644.

Sutherland, Sharon. "The Politics of Audit: The Federal Office of the Auditor General in Comparative Perspective." *Canadian Public Administration*, vol. 29 (Spring 1986): 118–148.

CASES

In Kenneth Kernaghan, *Canadian Cases in Public Administration* (Toronto: Methuen Publications):

Mr. Smith's Expense Accounts

V

PUBLIC ADMINISTRATION AND LOCAL GOVERNMENT

25

Structures and Politics
of Local Government
Administration

Throughout this book the focus has been mainly on the parliamentary form of government found in the federal and provincial spheres. Local governments in Canada are structured in a radically different manner from these parliamentary systems. In the first place, the constitutional and legal positions of local governments are different because they do not share in the *sovereignty* of the federal and provincial governments, but rather are creatures of the provincial governments. This means that local governments do not have any autonomous power base, but have only those powers which provincial governments decide to give to them. Second, local governments are different because their geographic boundaries are not fixed and, in some cases, have been changed rather frequently as a result of increasing urbanization. These changes have frequently been the source of great controversy. Third, the internal administrative structures of local governments differ from those of parliamentary governments rather significantly. Each of these differences will be explored in this chapter.

THE RATIONALE FOR LOCAL GOVERNMENT

It should first be considered *why* this third sphere of government is needed at all, since federal and provincial governments deliver some services in a very decentralized manner. Why do federal and provincial governments not provide all services? It is often argued that the two major values which local government alone can provide are access and service.

Access refers to "the most widespread participation possible on the part of all or virtually all individual citizens" and the maximum "capacity to influence public policy decisions and to enforce responsive and responsible administration."[1] Access is really another word for responsiveness, which was discussed earlier as one of the basic values of public administration. In this chapter, these two words will be used interchangeably.

Local government is the sphere of government closest to the people. Federal and provincial elected representatives conduct most of their affairs in federal or provincial capitals far away from the people who elected them. Local elected representatives stay in the community, where citizens have an opportunity to

---

[1] Ontario Committee on Taxation, *Report: Volume II* (Frank Fogg, Queen's Printer, 1967), p. 503.

approach them directly about local problems. This proximity to the people combined with the smaller size allows local governments to be more responsive to
citizens' desires.

> The handling of local problems through local authorities permits them to
> be disposed of with greater despatch and acceptability to the people imme-
> diately concerned, for the local authorities have a more intimate knowl-
> edge of the local conditions and can provide greater flexibility in the
> application of policies than is possible for a central authority.[2]

Service refers to "not only the economical discharge of public functions, but
the achievement of technical adequacy in due alignment with public needs and
desires."[3] Thus, local governments must not only deliver services, but to maintain credibility they must deliver them efficiently and effectively. Service then
becomes analogous to the values of efficiency and effectiveness as discussed in
Chapter 20.

The concern for service has led to two main prescriptions about the organization of local government. First, local governments must be large enough to capture economies of scale in the services they deliver. Second, cities must be large
enough in area so that they can engage in efficient and effective land use planning for the entire metropolitan area. Both of these concerns point towards the
creation of large cities.

One of the basic dilemmas of local government is that the access and service
values can be in conflict. Efficient service delivery leads to a relatively large
municipality. However, the larger the size of the jurisdiction, the more difficult
it is to provide meaningful access. The dilemma of local government is to balance these two sometimes conflicting values. One of the ways in which local
government structures ought to be evaluated is by how well they balance these
two values.

CONSTITUTIONAL AND LEGAL STATUS

The federal and provincial legislatures are supreme within their respective areas of
jurisdictions; neither order of government is superior or inferior to the other.
The British North America Act provides general mandates of power to these
governments to act in broad areas of public policy. Local governments[4] in Canada have no such general mandate. Section 92(8) of the Constitution Act, 1867,
gives provincial governments responsibility for "Municipal Institutions in the

---

[2]Kenneth Grant Crawford, *Canadian Municipal Government* (Toronto: University of Toronto
Press, 1954), p. 9.
[3]Ontario Committee on Taxation, *Report: Volume II*, p. 503.
[4]This chapter will follow a widely employed convention in that it will use "municipal government" to refer to the core governmental unit of cities, towns, etc., while "local government" will
be used more broadly to include municipal governments as well as special purpose bodies such as
boards of education, police commissions, and others.

Province." This means that local governments can do only those things allowed by provincial legislation.

> Accordingly the boundaries, functions and institutional forms of municipal government are all derived from, and sanctioned by, the over-riding authority of provincial legislatures. Local authorities can be no more and no less than what is expressly laid down in provincial statutes. . . . In addition, the provinces have unrestrained power to create, alter and abolish municipalities, and to exercise whatever degree and method of control over municipalities and their actions, as the provincial governments think fit.[5]

The fact that provincial governments exercise complete control over local governments means that the system of local government varies widely from province to province,[6] but there are some similarities at the most general level. The provincial legislature exercises its control through either one broad, supervisory piece of legislation, such as the Municipal Act, or a separate piece of legislation for each class of municipality, such as a Cities Act, a Towns Act, and a Villages Act. Larger cities sometimes have their own Act that either supplants or supplements the more general municipal legislation. In some cases this is called the municipal charter for historical reasons, but even the charters are in fact provincial legislation.

There are many other laws which have a significant impact on local government activities. Common examples are the Planning Act, the Education Act, and the Police Act. These Acts allow (or require) local governments to provide certain services and usually provide some guidance about how the service must be provided. These Acts also delegate authority to various provincial government departments and agencies to supervise certain aspects of the delivery of these services by local governments. The remainder of this section will describe the roles of these departments and agencies in supervising the system of local government.

The Department of Municipal Affairs (DMA)

Every province has a provincial department responsible for the supervision of municipalities, but the amount of detailed control and the manner in which it is exercised varies quite widely from province to province. At the extreme, the minister of municipal affairs can step in and directly take over the operation of a municipality. This is done very seldom; it usually occurs only as a result of gross misconduct on the part of municipal politicians or officials, or as a result of an inability of the government to meet its financial obligations. At a less draconian level, the minister normally has the power to issue directives to a municipality concerning some action or lack of action on its part. For example,

---

[5]T. J. Plunkett and G. M. Betts, *The Management of Canadian Urban Government* (Kingston, Ont.: The Institute of Local Government, Queen's University, 1978), p. 66.

[6]A good, quick overview of the differences is contained in the Canadian Tax Foundation's bi-annual publication — *Provincial and Municipal Finances*.

it is fairly common for the DMA to require municipalities to submit financial information in a prescribed format. In some provinces, the minister also approves municipal by-laws and budgets, including borrowing.

The DMA usually has a staff of field workers who can provide advice to municipalities in such areas as legal concerns, and financial and personnel management. Some provinces also produce extensive written material to assist municipalities. For example, the Ontario Ministry of Municipal Affairs has produced a series of monographs on the use of microcomputers in municipalities.

The DMA is also usually responsible for the provision of unconditional grants to municipalities. These have become an important source of revenue to municipalities in the last few years.

Quasi-judicial Municipal Boards

Aside from the DMAs, most provinces have a semi-autonomous agency with some responsibility for the supervision of specified municipal activities. Table 25.1 contains a list of these agencies. Unlike the DMAs, which have a general responsibility for municipal affairs, these boards deal only with certain municipal issues. However, the issues which come within the purview of these boards vary widely by province; issues which are the responsibility of the minister in one province could be the responsibility of the board in another.

Table 25.1
QUASI-JUDICIAL MUNICIPAL BOARDS

Alberta Planning Board
Local Authorities Board (Alberta)
Municipal Board (Manitoba)
Municipal Capital Borrowing Board (New Brunswick)
Provincial Planning Appeal Board (New Brunswick)
Nova Scotia Municipal Board
Ontario Municipal Board
Land Use Commission (Prince Edward Island)
Commission municipale du Québec
Commission nationale de l'Aménagement (Quebec)
Provincial Planning Appeals Board (Saskatchewan)
Local Government Board (Saskatchewan)

Source: C.E. (Ted) Clarke, ed., *1985 Corpus Almanac & Canadian Sourcebook*, vol. 2 (Don Mills, Ont.: Southam Communications, 1985), section 19; Canadian Tax Foundation, *Provincial And Municipal Finances—1983* (Toronto: Canadian Tax Foundaiton, 1983), ch. 8.

One role which seems to have devolved on boards in most provinces is a review of municipal planning decisions. The boards usually are responsible for reviewing official plans and planning by-laws prepared by municipalities. The rationale for this is that planning decisions are so sensitive and so much is at stake financially that it is sometimes felt wise to keep their review at arm's length from the influences of partisan politics. This is the same argument made in Chapter 8 for the creation of regulatory agencies.

Municipal politicians frequently object to this provincial role in local land use planning. They point out that local politicians who must be re-elected every few years are much more sensitive to local concerns than appointed civil servants who do not even live in the community. They argue that, at best, appeal to this agency slows down the development process, and at worst, it is a case of appointed civil servants with security of tenure second-guessing decisions made by local elected representatives.

Some boards are also involved in deciding about changes in municipal boundaries. Frequently, a municipality will want to increase its size by taking over some of the territory of an adjoining municipality — a process referred to as *annexation*. When a municipality requests an annexation, there is sometimes a strong objection from the municipality that would lose the territory. In this case, there is an obvious need for some outside, impartial body to review and adjudicate the dispute. Not surprisingly, municipalities are not always happy with the decisions made in annexation cases, but few would quarrel with the principle of a quasi-judicial body making the decision.

Frequently, these agencies must also approve municipal borrowing. During the Depression of the 1930s, some Canadian municipalities were unable to meet their financial obligations in the bond market. To prevent a repetition of that problem and to ensure investor confidence, these provincial agencies are responsible for examining the financial condition of a municipality and ensuring that it will be able to repay a bond issue before the municipality can commit itself to borrow funds on a long-term basis.

Some decisions of these agencies can be appealed to provincial Cabinet, but there is a reluctance on the part of Cabinet to overturn decisions very often, because this could incite a flow of new appeals. The enabling legislation of these agencies is usually structured so as to preclude review by the courts, except in unusual circumstances.

Other Provincial Departments

Most other provincial departments also have some dealings with local governments. For example, provincial highways departments are concerned about municipal roads, and provincial environment departments are concerned about municipal sewage treatment facilities. These functional departments usually use the classic "carrot and stick" approach in dealing with local governments. The "carrot" is a conditional grant which is available to any municipality that meets certain conditions in carrying out its programs. The "stick" is legislation which requires municipalities to comply with certain provincial standards. In many cases, municipal governments must obtain the approval of one or more provincial departments before they can carry out some work within the municipality. Like the DMA, these functional departments are also equipped to provide advice to municipalities with problems.

Provincial governments exercise a great deal of power over municipalities. In fact, the charge is frequently made that provincial departments and agencies exercise too much detailed control over municipalities, and that this constitutes a serious infringement on local autonomy. At the extreme, some might argue that provinces view local governments more as administrative, service-delivery arms of the provincial government than as separate autonomous bodies, established to ensure citizen access. The complex web of provincial approval requirements and conditional grants provides substantial credibility to this argument.

However, the provincial perspective is that there is a need for some level of uniformity of service provision across the province. For example, provinces allow for some level of local decision making in education, but it is a provincial concern that all young people in the province have access to some minimum level of education. A provincial government cannot simply provide grants to local governments and ignore how those grants are used; this would be very poor accountability — another of the important administrative values discussed in Chapter 20. Also, municipalities benefit from some of the standards enforced by provincial agencies. If any municipality in a province defaulted on a debt, this would have a detrimental impact on *all* municipalities in that province. Therefore, the fact that provincial governments keep a watch on levels of municipal borrowing is beneficial to all municipalities.

In sum, the charge is frequently made that provincial governments behave in an overly paternalistic manner vis-à-vis their municipalities, and there clearly are incidents which support this claim. However, the full issue is very complex, and there are some cases in which provincial involvement in municipal affairs is necessary and beneficial.

Associations of Municipalities

Constitutionally and legally, municipalities seem to be subservient to provincial governments in many ways, but in practice the situation is not as extreme as it might seem. Municipalities do have some voice and some ways of influencing provincial governments. This influence can occur through very strong and outspoken mayors, particularly in large cities, but the usual mechanism of municipal influence is the provincial municipal association. Municipalities in every province have combined to form at least one association which speaks for the municipalities of that province.[7]

These associations exercise their influence in several ways. They all have annual conferences at which they discuss matters of public policy and pass resolutions which guide the association's executive for the coming year. The executive committee of the association and some other committees meet periodically during the year with the minister responsible for municipal affairs and other relevant ministers.[8] They discuss such matters as the level of municipal grants, streamlining the provincial approvals process, and revisions in municipal legislation.

---

[7]For a discussion of the role of these associations, see: Lionel D. Feldman and Katherine A. Graham, *Bargaining for Cities: Municipalities and Intergovernmental Relations: An Assessment* (Montreal: Institute for Research on Public Policy, 1979), ch. 2; David Siegel, "Provincial-Municipal Relations in Canada: An Overview," *Canadian Public Administration*, vol. 23 (Summer 1980), pp. 312–317.

[8]Allan O'Brien describes one such meeting in Ontario in: "The Uncomfortable Partnership: A Look at the Provincial-Municipal Relationship," in Donald C. MacDonald, ed., *The Government and Politics of Ontario*, 2nd ed. (Toronto: Van Nostrand Reinhold, 1980), pp. 170–173.

Municipalities also have a national association, the Federation of Canadian Municipalities. It engages in many of the same activities as the provincial associations, but its actions are usually directed at the federal government. The federal government does not have direct control over municipalities, but many federal actions have an impact on municipalities. Among such actions are the use of federal lands within cities, such as harbours and railyards, and the criminal law with regard to prostitution.

Provincial and municipal governments have a rather awkward and sometimes tense relationship. Constitutionally and legally, the provincial government is dominant, but municipalities have a certain amount of influence over their own sphere, as mentioned above. This ambiguous relationship is framed very clearly in the making of one of the most important decisions affecting municipalities — the establishment of municipal boundaries.

THE TERRITORIAL DIMENSION OF LOCAL GOVERNMENTS

The post–Second World War period has seen an urban revolution in Canada. The rapid increase in the population of urban areas caused many severe problems as both the physical size of the urban area and the demand for urban services expanded rapidly. There were problems in both the *access* and *service* dimensions of local governments. The increases in size caused both of these values to suffer, but in particular the tension between them became more obvious. This problem was so severe that it caused major reorganizations of urban governments in virtually every province.[9]

One aspect of this reorganization was the consolidation of many small units of local government which changing technology had made obsolete. These consolidations were usually based on the idea that there are significant economies of scale to be gained by expanding the size of local governments. This tenet is dear to the hearts of some local government reformers, but the evidence on economies of scale in most local government services is mixed. Some argue that most economies are captured in even fairly small cities.

However, there are some occasions when the consolidation was clearly beneficial. For example, very small local school districts were logical when most students had to walk to school, but with the coming of all-weather roads and dependable school buses, school districts could be enlarged and better services provided. Of course, this sacrificed access for service, but the quality of the service was improved so much that this trade-off was deemed acceptable. Most of the consolidation occurred in school boards and some other special purpose bodies, although there were numerous municipal government reorganizations as well. The government reorganizations tended to take two forms — two-tier governments, or territorial expansion — although there were numerous other arrangements.

---

[9]The only recent systematic study of the many diverse forms of reorganization is in Donald Higgins, "The Processes of Reorganizing Local Government," *Canadian Journal of Political Science*, vol. 19 (June 1986), pp. 219–242. An earlier approach is T. J. Plunkett, "Structural Reform of Local Government in Canada," *Public Administration Review*, vol. 33 (January–February 1973), pp. 40–51.

Two-tier Government

When Metropolitan Toronto was created in 1954, it was considered to be the first regional or two-tier government in North America. The problem that Toronto was facing at that time was that development was expanding rapidly beyond the city's boundaries.

> With the post-war "population explosion," the rapid growth of a number of the municipalities surrounding the city of Toronto produced serious servicing difficulties. Most pressing were the problems of water supply and sewage treatment, because only six of the thirteen municipalities involved had direct physical access to Lake Ontario. Arterial road development could not keep pace with the rapidly increasing volume of traffic. Public transportation and the existing highway network were poorly integrated. There was a desperate need for new schools. Many of the outlying municipalities were particularly ill-equipped to finance these service demands since, as dormitory suburbs, they lacked industrial assessment to help relieve the tax burden of the residential taxpayer.[10]

The solution adopted by the provincial government was to establish a new local government — Metropolitan Toronto — which spanned the thirteen (later reduced to six) lower-tier municipalities.[11] Responsibilities were divided so that the upper tier had responsibility for services of a Metro-wide nature (public transit, major roads), and for services which generate significant economies of scale (sewage treatment, water purification). The lower tiers retained responsibility for functions that were related to community demands (parks and recreation), or less prone to economies of scale (garbage collection).

The two-tier approach to urban growth has proven to be very popular. It has been extended to most urbanized areas in Ontario, Quebec, and British Columbia and many places in the United States. Its strength is its attempt to balance the access and service components of local governments. Those services which could generate economies of scale were moved to the upper tier, thus providing good *service*; those which were most sensitive to citizens' desires were left at the lower tier, thus providing good *access*.

However, there have been criticisms of this form of reorganization. In some cases the service aspect has been emphasized to the detriment of access[12]; it is difficult for frugal politicians to pass up presumed economies of scale in favour of greater citizen participation, particularly when the latter frequently has made

---

[10]C. R. Tindal and S. Nobes Tindal, *Local Government in Canada*, 2nd ed. (Toronto: McGraw-Hill Ryerson, 1984), p. 66.

[11]The story of the creation of Metropolitan Toronto has been told in many places: *Report of the Royal Commission on Metropolitan Toronto: Volume I* (1977), pp. 11–17; Albert Rose, *Governing Metropolitan Toronto: A Social and Political Analysis, 1953–1971* (Berkeley, Ca.: University of California Press, 1972); Timothy J. Colton, *Big Daddy: Frederick G. Gardiner and the Building of Metropolitan Toronto* (Toronto: University of Toronto Press, 1980).

[12]C. R. Tindal, *Structural Changes in Local Government: Government for Urban Regions* (Toronto: The Institute of Public Administration of Canada, 1977), ch. 5.

their jobs more demanding. For example, the usual decision has been to centralize policing, even though citizens would like to have more community control over this function. A second criticism stems from the confusion engendered by the addition of another layer of government to the local government system, which citizens do not understand very well in the first place.

Another continuing disappointment about regional government is that it has failed to reconcile the centre city–suburban conflict. This tension can be seen in fights over the location of certain municipal facilities, or over the proper form of municipal development, e.g., downtown versus suburban shopping, urban expressways versus public transit. These are divisions which are built into the Canadian pattern of land use, and it was probably unrealistic to think that structural tinkering would solve such a basic conflict.

These and other problems, some real and some exaggerated, have caused a strong citizen reaction against two-tiered governments in most jurisdictions, particularly in Ontario. For this reason, there are no plans to create any more regional governments of this kind.

In spite of these criticisms, the two-tier system does facilitate land use planning and the provision of hard services. This is probably the reason that once it is adopted it is seldom totally scrapped, although British Columbia has recently made some revisions which significantly weaken the upper-tier governments and Winnipeg was converted from a two-tier to a one-tier city in 1971.

Territorial Expansion

Another possibility for dealing with urban expansion is to allow the central city to expand and annex adjacent territory as development occurs there. This has been the usual solution employed in cities in Saskatchewan and Alberta.[13] As development occurs outside the city's boundaries, the provincial government allows the city to expand to take in these new areas and to provide city services to them.

This policy allows cities to become very large in terms of both population and geographic area. The strength of this solution is in service delivery. It allows the city to plan for the entire area with few impediments and to establish an orderly development pattern, with lower service costs. On the negative side, the large size of these cities can cause problems with regard to access as councillors come to represent larger numbers of people and citizens feel less important in the governing process.

The Winnipeg *unicity* concept constitutes an interesting example of a city which went from a two-tier to a unitary structure, while at the same time introducing mechanisms which would help promote citizen participation.[14] This exper-

---

[13]The Calgary and Edmonton stories are told in Jack Masson, *Alberta's Local Governments and Their Politics* (Edmonton: Pica Pica Press, 1985), p. 64ff.

[14]Meyer Brownstone and T. J. Plunkett, *Metropolitan Winnipeg: Politics and Reform of Local Government* (Berkeley, Ca.: University of California Press, 1983); City of Winnipeg Act Review Committee, 1984–85, *Our City in Review: Issues Paper* (1984).

iment has been the subject of much discussion and review, not all of which has been positive.[15] However, the provincial government has not made any radical change in the unicity structure since it was established in 1971.

Incremental Change

Many areas have opted for less radical solutions to urban problems. In the older urban areas in eastern Canada there are frequently several cities in the same urban agglomeration, each with long traditions and strong loyalties making major annexations or "unicity" solutions problematic. Good examples of this are Halifax-Dartmouth in Nova Scotia and St. John's and its suburbs in New-foundland. The system adopted in Halifax[16] and other cities is to allow limited annexations while at the same time establishing intermunicipal or metro-wide special purpose bodies to provide such services as land use planning and transportation.

The strength of this solution is that it retains community identity and involves minimal disruption, while at the same time recognizing the need for some metro-wide planning and administration. Its weak point is the complexity brought about by the large number of special purpose bodies which are sometimes not properly accountable to any elected body. There are frequent disputes over who pays the bills for these agencies and who controls their activities.

The proliferation of these many special purpose bodies, each with different boundaries, complicates the overall structure of local government, makes it harder for the average citizen to understand, and so weakens accountability. The following section will discuss this problem in more detail.

INTERNAL ADMINISTRATIVE STRUCTURES

This section will first describe the overall organization of local governments (the plural is used because there are a number of different local government organizations in every urban area), and then discuss the three most common organizational structures used in the internal management of municipalities.

One sometimes hears the assertion that local government deals only with administrative matters and not with real political issues. This view is reflected in the fact that many of the structural arrangements for local government are geared to removing politics from local government administration. The phrase sometimes used by the municipal reformers who supported this view was: "There's no political way to build a road." There is a certain irony in the choice of this example in that recent acrimonious debates about expressways have highlighted the fact that road building is in fact a very political exercise.[17] The same applies to other

---

[15]Lloyd Axworthy, "The Best Laid Plans Oft Go Astray: The Case of Winnipeg," in M. O. Dickerson, S. Drabek, and J. T. Woods, eds., *Problems of Change in Urban Government* (Waterloo, Ont.: Wilfrid Laurier University Press, 1980), pp. 105–123.

[16]David M. Cameron and Peter Aucoin, "Halifax," in Warren Magnusson and Andrew Sancton, eds., *City Politics in Canada* (Toronto: University of Toronto Press, 1983), pp. 183–185.

[17]Christopher Leo, *The Politics of Urban Development: Canadian Urban Expressway Disputes* (Toronto: The Institute of Public Administration of Canada, 1977).

supposedly administrative issues such as opening new schools or closing existing ones, operating recreational programs, and finding a place to dispose of solid waste.

One of the themes mentioned throughout this book is the impossibility of separating political and administrative concerns; this is as true in local government as it is in any other sphere of government. However, this did not stop adherents to the municipal reform movement of the late nineteenth and early twentieth centuries from suggesting a number of structural reforms which attempted to do just that.[18] The influence of these reformers can be seen in the presence of special purpose bodies and in some of the internal administrative structures used in municipalities.

Special Purpose Bodies

Most people tend to think of local governments as very small, simple kinds of organizations. In fact, the local government universe, even in small urban areas, can contain many separate organizations with very complicated links with one another. To begin, most services are provided by either one or two tiers of multi-purpose municipal governments; these are the most visible entities. There is also usually at least one school board which is completely separate from the municipalities, except that their elected members are selected by the same group of voters and they draw their funding from the same property tax base. There can be other bodies elected or appointed to administer certain local services, such as hospitals or public utilities commissions. There are also organizations which are controlled jointly by municipal and provincial (or federal) governments. For example, in Ontario, police forces are controlled, not by the municipal administration, but by a three- or five-person board of police commissioners to which the municipality appoints a minority of members. Municipalities also establish on their own initiative a number of separate advisory bodies, such as committees to advise on the operation of community centres or the preservation of historic buildings. These do not create quite the same problem of divided authority because they are squarely under municipal control, but they can add to the confusion of the structure.

There is some question about how Canada came to have these bodies. They were quite common in Britain when local government was not sophisticated enough to handle certain technical services. The turn-of-the-century North American municipal reformers also supported these special purpose bodies in order to keep certain functions separate from the "evils of politics." For example, the dangers of a police force being used for political purposes are fairly clear. However, this insulation has also resulted in diminished accountability.

---

[18]This was quite an influential intellectual school of the time. Their story is told in: John C. Weaver, *Shaping the Canadian City: Essays on Urban Politics, 1890–1920* (Toronto: The Institute of Public Administration of Canada, 1977); Tindal and Tindal, *Local Government in Canada*, pp. 38-47; Plunkett and Betts, *The Management of Canadian Urban Government*, pp. 100-106.

The establishment of these boards and commissions was yet another way of reducing the authority of council . . . . Thus, almost invariably, the justification for the creation of such bodies was that they would serve as a means of shielding various municipal functions from "politics".(sic) "Politics" in this context, did not mean the process of making decisions on matters of public policy. That process obviously went on. The only effect of the creation of a special board or commission was that it helped to restrict the decision-making to a small circle of people. The "politics" from which municipal functions were being shielded was not politics per se, but democratic politics.[19]

Figure 25.1 shows the organizational structure of the city of Vancouver and its special purpose bodies. The portion at the left of the chart within the dotted lines is the part usually considered to be municipal government; everything else constitutes some kind of special purpose body. All of the different lines and letters indicate different kinds of reporting relationships.

This divided authority causes many problems and frustrations in the local government system. Citizens become confused about who controls what. If you are dissatisfied with the transit system, then do you complain to your local councillor? Not if you live in Vancouver or Victoria, where the local transit systems are operated by a provincial Crown corporation. If you need to have your street repaired, you go the municipality; but do you go to the upper tier or the lower tier? That depends on whether the road is an upper-tier or lower-tier one.

This divided jurisdiction also presents problems for the municipal manager who must attempt to coordinate many things at the service delivery level that are totally uncoordinated at the policy making level. When a new subdivision is built, the city administration must ensure that roads, parks, schools, police, public transit, and hospitals all get there at the same time, even though each of these services might be delivered by a different organization. The complexity of the situation can be appreciated by the fact that a 1968 count indicated that there were 101 separate governments in Metropolitan Toronto,[20] and a more recent count in Calgary identified seventy special purpose bodies.[21]

The municipal manager's difficulties are compounded by the fact that the elected level of municipal government does not contain anything like a Cabinet that centralizes power at the political level. Instead, the municipal manager may be required to work for a number of different individuals and committees which disagree with one another and give conflicting directions to the manager.

The difficulties caused by this fragmentation have been summarized as follows:

1. A complex and diverse local organization that makes it difficult for citizens to comprehend its structure and determine where responsibility is located.

---

[19]Plunkett and Betts, *The Management of Canadian Urban Government*, pp. 120–121. (Footnote omitted; obvious typographical error corrected.)

[20]Dominic Del Guidice and Stephen M. Zacks, "The 101 Governments of Metro Toronto," in Lionel D. Feldman, ed., *Politics and Government of Urban Canada: Selected Readings*, 4th ed. (Toronto: Methuen, 1981), pp. 267–276.

[21]Masson, *Alberta's Local Governments and Their Politics*, pp. 42–44.

Figure 25.1
CITY OF VANCOUVER, B.C., CIVIC ORGANIZATION

Source: Reprinted by permission of the City of Vancouver.

2. A weakening of the prestige and significance of the municipal council as the central governing body in the community and an inevitable decline in public interest in the problems of general government.

3. A lessening of the responsiveness of local administration to public needs and desires.

4. The creation of difficult problems in administrative integration and co-ordination.

5. The encouragement of fiscal irresponsibility on the part of public authorities, whose members do not have to account directly to the citizens they serve.[22]

However, not everyone shares this same negative view of the fragmentation of administration. The public choice approach (discussed earlier in Chapter 5) to local government is that the diversity inherent in this fragmentation is beneficial in that it allows citizens to "vote with their feet" and move to jurisdictions which provide the amenities they desire. If people want to live in an area with a very high quality recreation system, then they can do so; alternatively, if other people want to pay the lowest possible property taxes, then they can find such a jurisdiction as well. The existence of numerous special purpose bodies whose service boundaries do not coincide neatly with municipal boundaries allows people to shop for the precise geographic location which offers the exact combination of tax rates and amenities which they desire. The presence of local governments covering large areas with no special purpose bodies makes the individual the slave of the majority will.[23]

This view was developed in the United States, where the local government system is considerably more fragmented than it is in Canada; the public choice perspective has never really caught on in Canada. Most recent Canadian reforms have moved towards a consolidation of local government units and the elimination of special purpose bodies and the vesting of their powers in municipal governments. This is usually justified on the grounds of simplicity of organizational structure and better coordination of service provision.

Municipal Electoral Systems

The elected officials in municipal governments are the mayor and councillors or aldermen (the wording varies by province).[24] The mayor is elected "at large," which means that he or she runs for election in the entire city and all citizens have an opportunity to vote in the election for mayor. Councillors sometimes run "at large," usually in smaller cities, but they are frequently elected by ward. In the ward system of election, a municipality is divided into several areas, and

---

[22]Thomas J. Plunkett, *Urban Canada and Its Government: A Study of Municipal Organization* (Toronto: Macmillan of Canada, 1968), p. 67.

[23]One of the best statements of the public choice approach is found in Robert L. Bish, *The Public Economy of Metropolitan Areas* (Chicago: Markham Publishing, 1971).

[24]The material in this section does not necessarily apply to upper-tier municipalities. The names of positions and methods of election for these offices vary quite widely.

one or two (occasionally, more) councillors are elected from each ward.[25] The councils in most cities are composed of between nine and twenty councillors.[26] This is comparable to the United States situation, but fewer than many other countries.

The mayor is the head of council, but this is largely a ceremonial position, involving representing the city at important functions, greeting visitors and other important, but largely symbolic, duties. The role of the mayor should not be equated with the role of the Prime Minister or a provincial Premier.

> It is clear that the mayor, contrary to popular belief, has little legal author-
> ity. His specific duties are ill-defined and the office is largely what he makes of
> it. The mayor in Canada, unlike the pattern in the United States "strong
> mayor" systems, has neither the power to veto legislation, nor to make
> appointments on his own. He has no legislative authority to reinforce his
> role as a political spokesman for the community.[27]

In the council chamber, the mayor chairs the meeting, but he or she has no powers beyond those of any other councillor.[28] This is called the "weak mayor" system. In effect, it means that the *council as a body*, and not the mayor, controls the civic administration. This is the system usually employed in Canada.

In the United States, many cities have a "strong mayor" system, which means that the mayor functions almost like a president at the local level. Council functions like a legislative branch in that it approves the budget and other enabling legislation, but within this general framework, the mayor controls the civic administration. This system is a local government adaptation of the American principles of "separation of powers" and "checks and balances." It is an important legal point that in the strong mayor system, the civic administration works for the *mayor*; in a weak mayor system, it works for the *council*, which includes the mayor as one of its members.

The phrase "weak mayor" refers to the organizational structure and formal powers of the office, not necessarily to the real power wielded by the person holding the office. Mayors can use their force of personality and their high profile to carve out a real leadership role for themselves on council. One can think of many so-called "weak mayors" who in fact have a great deal of influence by virtue of their strong personalities and/or electoral organizations. Former mayors Jean Drapeau of Montreal and Stephen Juba of Winnipeg are two examples.

Depending on the size of council and the complexity of the administration, council is frequently divided into committees to review such functional areas as

---

[25]There can be some rather important differences in the consequences of at-large and ward voting, not all of them obvious at first glance. Tindal and Tindal, *Local Government in Canada*, pp. 102–103.

[26]Donald J. H. Higgins, *Local and Urban Politics in Canada* (Toronto: Gage, 1986), p. 325, contains information on most major Canadian cities.

[27]Stanley M. Makuch, *Canadian Municipal and Planning Law* (Toronto: Carswell, 1983), pp. 12–13. In a few provinces, the mayor does have a limited form of veto power. Tindal and Tindal, *Local Government in Canada*, p. 108.

[28]There are a few duties which place the mayor in a slightly more powerful position than other councillors. Higgins, *Local and Urban Politics in Canada*, pp. 128–130.

finance, parks, and planning. These committees hear deputations from individual citizens or groups and try to arbitrate certain issues, but they usually only *recommend* action to the full council. The full council is the sole body that can take legally binding decisions.[29]

Some cities have adopted a system employing an Executive Committee or a Board of Control, as it is called in some Ontario municipalities. This is a sort of "super committee" which has special responsibility in areas such as budget preparation, personnel, contracts, e.g., for sale or acquisition of land, and other responsibilities which vary by province and municipality. In some cases, Executive Committee recommendations can be overridden only by a two-thirds' vote of the full council; and since approximately one-third of council usually sits on this committee, that is very unlikely.

Different cities use different mechanisms to determine who will serve on these Executive Committees:
• election at large in the municipal election — Ontario Board of Control system, e.g., London;
• election by fellow councillors early in each term of office — most widely followed practice, especially in Ontario;
• selection by mayor, subject to confirmation by council — e.g., Montreal and a few other large cities in Quebec.

Cities have adopted this structure in hopes that the Executive Committee will provide a focal point for the coordination of policy making and administration. In cases where there is a strong, unified party system or where the mayor appoints committee members, the Executive Committee can function almost like a Cabinet in a parliamentary government. This means that it can be a strong focal point; in fact, in Edmonton, there was some concern that the committee was inappropriately dominating the other council committees.[30] However, the more usual situation is that there is no unifying force on a municipal council similar to that of the provincial Premier and Cabinet. This creates serious problems for municipal administrators who must be responsive and accountable to the disunited cacophony of voices emanating from the council chamber. The internal administrative structures adopted in municipalities reflect these special needs.

Management Structures
There are three basic types of organizational forms found in Canadian municipalities — council-committee, council-manager, and council-commissioner. In fact, one is more likely to find hybrids of these types in actual practice, but it is useful to know about these pure types.[31] This section will discuss these three

---

[29]Makuch, *Canadian Municipal and Planning Law*, p. 17.

[30]Masson, *Alberta's Local Governments and Their Politics*, pp. 40–42.

[31]The number of hybrids and slight deviations from the ideal types makes it difficult to settle on an exact number. The most comprehensive review of internal management structures identified a very large number of different types: Paul Hickey, *Decision-Making Processes in Ontario's Local Governments* (Toronto: Ministry of Treasury, Economics and Intergovernmental Affairs, n.d.). Donald Higgins, *Local and Urban Politics in Canada*, ch. 4, identifies five different systems, but two of these are only used in a few municipalities in Ontario.

types of administrative arrangements and provide an assessment of the advantages and disadvantages of each.[32]

The *council-committee system* is based on the British model and is the oldest form of municipal organization in Ontario. Figure 25.2 illustrates this system as employed in the borough of East York in Metropolitan Toronto. Council is divided into committees, which deal directly with heads of operating departments (usually called commissioners in municipal governments). This style provides for good accountability to committees, because committee members can develop expertise in their particular areas and can ensure accountability on the part of commissioners because of the closeness and stability of their relationship.

However, many problems have been noted with this system. Commissioners are in an awkward situation because the principle of unity of command is violated. Figure 25.2 indicates that the Works Department is responsible to the Works Committee for some things and the Traffic and Parking Committee for others, as well as the full council. These three "bosses" are not necessarily in agreement with one another.

Another disadvantage of this system is that there is no single focal point for coordinating administrative concerns. Each department develops a strong accountability relationship with "its" committee, but no one is responsible for coordinating the overall management of the municipality. In Britain, the presence of the party system at the local level tends to hold the system together. In the absence of a party system in local government in Canada, there is no similar glue for the system. This system has been very widely used and is still used in some municipalities, especially smaller ones, but its popularity is being eclipsed by a system which provides for better coordination.

The *council-manager system* was imported from the United States in the early part of this century. It was a product of the municipal reform movement which emphasized the apolitical nature of local government. The idea behind this system was to impose a business-like structure (and, it was hoped, business-like efficiency) on municipal government. The basis of the council-manager system is that the council should function like the board of directors of a corporation in that it hires a chief executive officer to administer the municipality while the board provides policy directives.

> The principles upon which the Council-Manager system is based are essentially two fold. Council possesses the authority within its jurisdiction to establish policies for the provision of public services, the regulation of persons and property, and the allocation of the financial resources of the City government. The City Manager, on the other hand, is responsible and accountable to Council for the implementation of Council's policies and

---

[32]The definitive statement of the advantages and disadvantages of the different systems is contained in Plunkett, *Urban Canada and Its Government*, chs. 3–5. The specific facts mentioned in it are out of date now, but the basic arguments are as valid as they ever were.

Figure 25.2
EXAMPLE OF COUNCIL-COMMITTEE SYSTEM,
BOROUGH OF EAST YORK

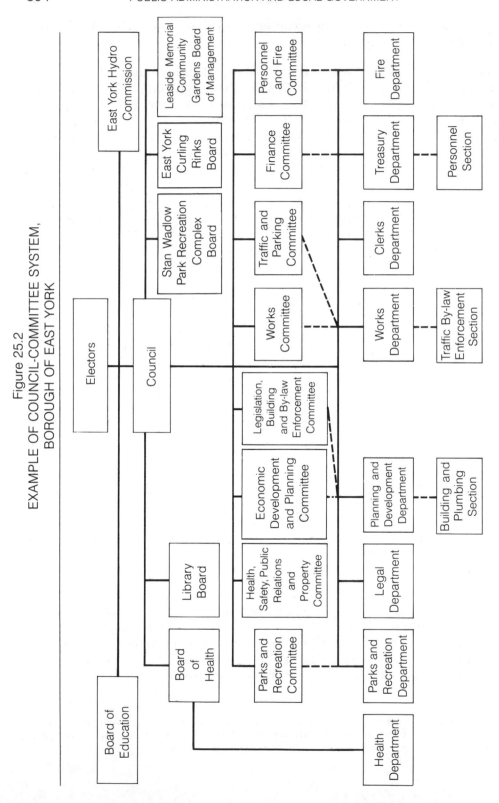

Source: Reprinted by permission of the Borough of East York.

day to day administration of its programs, as well as the management of the City's financial and personnel resources.[33]

The city manager, as the chief administrative officer of the city, is usually given authority to hire, fire, and discipline employees (subject to provisions of collective agreements with unions); negotiate collective agreements; and prepare the annual budget for consideration by council.

Other elements of the pure city manager form as employed in the United States are the at-large election of all councillors — to limit parochial political behaviour geared purely to helping one's own ward; the elimination of special purpose bodies — these would all come under the city manager; and the elimination of committees of council, because council is solely a policy-making body.

The city manager system has a number of advantages over the council-committee system:

First, it frees the council from continually having to scrutinize the administration and enables it to devote its full attention to the formulation and evaluation of short- and long-term policy. Second, it brings into the municipality a professionally trained administrator who is given the power to co-ordinate departmental activities and evaluate staff performance. More importantly, while many council members have a relatively short-term policy perspective and evaluate and formulate proposals on the basis of their effects on the upcoming electoral campaign, the manager is not as constrained by politics and tends to take a long-term view of the policy process by planning well into the next century.[34]

However, there are some disadvantages associated with the system. Most flow from the fact that the city manager system is based on the premise that politics and policy can be separated from administration. The strategic position of the city manager can isolate councillors from knowledge of administrative activities; but councillors need to be cognizant of certain administrative arrangements so that they can make political decisions intelligently and assess the performance of the city manager and the rest of the civic staff. In some cases, this has had the effect of downgrading the importance of the council and thrusting the city manager into a highly visible and political position.

Canadian cities have not generally adopted all of the trappings of the American model. Figure 25.3 shows how this system operates in Saint John, New Brunswick. This is a good example of how the city manager system has been adopted in Canada. The city manager is responsible for most areas of administration, but there are still some special purpose bodies and some administrative officials who report directly to council.

---

[33]Halifax Commission on City Government, *Report on the Structure and Processes of Halifax City Government — 1982* (Halifax: Institute of Public Affairs, Dalhousie University, 1982), p. 2.
[34]Jack Masson, *Alberta's Local Governments and Their Politics*, p. 32.

Figure 25.3
EXAMPLE OF CITY MANAGER SYSTEM,
CITY OF SAINT JOHN

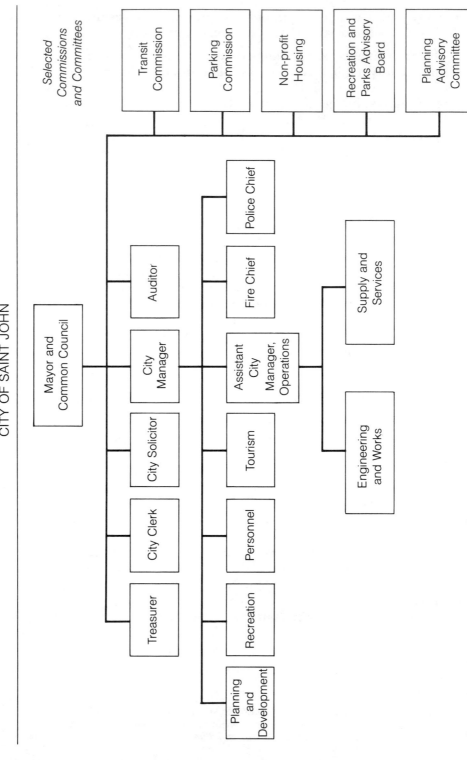

Source: Adapted from chart provided by the City of Saint John.

Another difference between the Canadian and American versions of the system is that Canadian municipalities sometimes retain a council-committee structure including an executive committee to help ensure good citizen access.

Also, Canadian municipal councils have tended to delegate less authority to city managers than their American counterparts. This might be one reason why in Canada this position is usually denoted by the weaker term *chief administrative officer* (CAO), rather than city manager. For example, Canadian councils usually retain the right to hire and fire department heads, a responsibility which is usually delegated to city managers in the United States. An experienced municipal manager has argued that the Canadian model avoids some of the defects of its United States counterpart because it limits the role of the manager.[35]

The system tends to centralize a significant amount of power in the hands of full council and the CAO. This can be beneficial to the extent that it encourages coordination of administrative activities through the CAO's office and improves accountability by pinpointing responsibility for administration. The continued presence of council committees and the limited role of the CAO in the Canadian system avoids the excessive centralization of power for which the system is sometimes criticized by U.S. commentators. However, the system still places a great deal of responsibility on the head of one individual.

The *council-commissioner system* resolves this problem by vesting the responsibility not in one individual, but in a board of commissioners. This is a western Canadian adaptation of the city manager system,[36] but it presents a number of innovations.

Figure 25.4 illustrates the system in use in Winnipeg. The chief commissioner's span of control is reduced as a result of the imposition of another organizational level between the chief commissioner and the heads of operating departments. This additional layer consists of three commissioners, each with responsibilities for a number of departments. The Board of Commissioners usually consists of the four commissioners and the mayor. (In Winnipeg, the mayor sits as a member of the board, but cannot vote.) The board is the focal point for *administration* of the city. It is usually responsible for recommending personnel appointments, preparing the budget, and managing the resources of the city in general. In cities where the mayor is a member of the board it provides an opportunity for political and administrative concerns to be represented on one committee. The committee structure of council mirrors the responsibilities of the commissioners so that each committee can develop a close and continuing relationship with "its" commissioner.

---

[35]Dennis A. Young, "Canadian Local Government Development: Some Aspects of the Commissioner and City Manager Forms of Administration," in Lionel D. Feldman and Michael D. Goldrick, eds., *Politics and Government of Urban Canada*, 3rd ed. (Toronto: Methuen, 1976), pp. 277-278.
[36]James Lightbody, "Edmonton," in Magnusson and Sancton, *City Politics in Canada*, p. 274.

Figure 25.4
EXAMPLE OF COUNCIL-COMMISSIONER SYSTEM,
CITY OF WINNIPEG

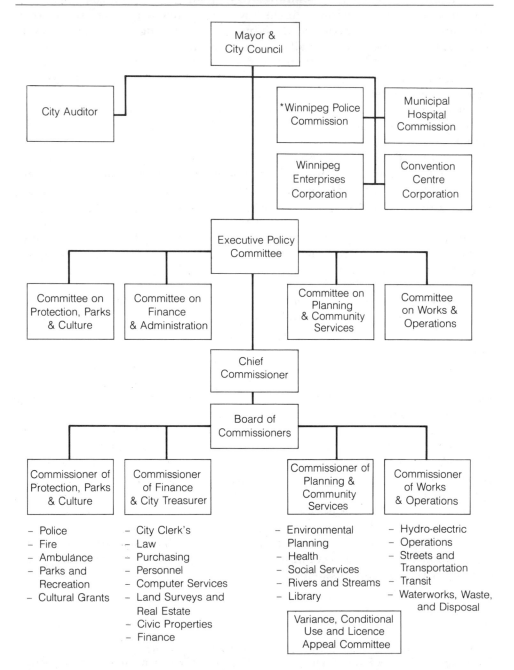

*Note: The Winnipeg Police Commission to be disbanded effective November 4th, 1986.

Source: Reprinted by permission of the City of Winnipeg.

While the council-commissioner system solves some of the problems identified with the city manager system, it also has some disadvantages. The Board of Commissioners is the focal point of a great deal of power — possibly too much power to be vested in technical experts rather than politicians.[37] It can be difficult to ensure appropriate accountability, even through the committee system. When the mayor is a member of the board it further increases the power of the board vis-à-vis other councillors and adds another problem. It can be difficult for the mayor (as politician) to scrutinize the board of which he or she is a member. It also spreads the mayor's time very thinly; the mayor must usually choose to be either a politician or an administrator — there is too little time to combine the two roles.[38]

This system has been popular in large cities in western Canada. At one time or another it has been used in Calgary, Edmonton, Regina, Saskatoon, Vancouver (with some adaptations),[39] Winnipeg, and some smaller cities. However, it has never been in favour in other parts of the country, and might even be losing favour to the city manager system in western Canada, as evidenced by the recent switch of Edmonton to a city manager system.

CONCLUSION

The kinds of problems encountered by administrators in local government are considerably different from those encountered by their federal and provincial counterparts. For one thing, the environment is considerably more turbulent; not only must local governments deal directly with many different citizens' groups, but they are also frequently on the receiving end of initiatives developed by federal and provincial governments. Many people are attracted to employment opportunities in local government precisely because of this challenge. The small size of local governments means that employees, even at junior levels, are directly involved in interesting and difficult policy decisions. Many people also find the direct contact with politicians and citizens' groups very stimulating. However, working in this kind of environment can also be very stressful; and the security of tenure is not the same as in federal or provincial governments.

Local government has traditionally been considered to be the weakest and least sophisticated sphere of government. In one sense, this is a disservice to a group of very hard-working and competent men and women in municipal service, but in another sense, it is correct. Many of the problems of local government have been alluded to in this chapter:

- weak coordination between the large number of local government units in urban areas;
- little cohesion at the political level because of structural considerations and the lack of a party system;

[37]Ibid., pp. 271-275; Higgins, *Local and Urban Politics in Canada*, p. 156; cf., Masson, *Alberta's Local Governments*, p. 38.

[38]A good discussion of the problems presented by the mayor being a member of the board is contained in Hickey, *Decision-Making Processes in Ontario's Local Governments*, pp. 218-219.

[39]Donald Gutstein, "Vancouver," in Magnusson and Sancton, eds., *City Politics in Canada*, p. 199.

- weak coordination at the administrative level because of inefficient management structures;
- overemphasis on the service aspect of local government to the detriment of its access side;
- inadequate revenue to meet financial obligations; and
- excessive provincial control over local actions and awkward approval processes.

Allan O'Brien's succinct comments about the Ontario situation could apply as well in any other province:

> Authority to plan was meaningless because authority to act was divided so many ways. Even when decisions could be made locally they were subject to ratification or reversal by the Ontario Municipal Board, a provincially appointed tribunal enjoying relative independence. Thus local government decision-making has become fractured horizontally (at the local level) and vertically (between levels of government). It has also been frustrated by lack of adequate financial resources free from provincial restrictions on their use. Together the jurisdictional and financial problems have made them unresponsive and very conservative.[40]

Local governments tend to have the lowest profile of all spheres of government; yet they affect people more directly than the others. This makes the problems identified with local governments that much more acute. In general, the system of local government works well, but some of the problems mentioned above are in need of review so that the system remains as sturdy and efficient as it has been in the past.

This chapter has emphasized the differences between local government administration and the parliamentary form of government found in the federal and provincial spheres. It is quite interesting that, while the structures of representation and governing are very different, the administrative values identified in Chapter 20 are just as important. This chapter has discussed the importance of service (efficiency and effectiveness), access (responsiveness), accountability, coordination, and power. These values hold the same significance for all spheres of government.

---

[40]"Father Knows Best: A Look at the Provincial-Municipal Relationship in Ontario," in Donald C. MacDonald, ed., *Government and Politics of Ontario* (Macmillan of Canada, 1975), p. 154.

BIBLIOGRAPHY

Bish, Robert L. *The Public Economy of Metropolitan Areas*. Chicago: Markham Publishing, 1971.

Brownstone, Meyer, and T. J. Plunkett. *Metropolitan Winnipeg: Politics and Reform of Local Government*. Berkeley, Ca.: University of California Press, 1983.

Canadian Tax Foundation. *Provincial and Municipal Finances*. Toronto: Canadian Tax Foundation, published bi-annually.

City of Winnipeg Act Review Committee, 1984-85. *Our City in Review: Issues Paper* (1984).

Colton, Timothy J. *Big Daddy: Frederick G. Gardiner and the Building of Metropolitan Toronto*. Toronto: University of Toronto Press, 1980.

Crawford, Kenneth Grant. *Canadian Municipal Government*. Toronto: University of Toronto Press, 1954.

Dickerson, M. O., S. Drabek, and J. T. Woods, eds. *Problems of Change in Urban Government*. Waterloo, Ont.: Wilfrid Laurier University Press, 1980.

Dupré, J. Stephan. *Intergovernmental Finance in Ontario: A Provincial-Local Perspective*. Frank Fogg, Queen's Printer, n.d.

Feldman, Lionel D., ed. *Politics and Government of Urban Canada: Selected Readings*. 4th ed. Toronto: Methuen, 1981.

Feldman, Lionel D., and Michael D. Goldrick, eds. *Politics and Government of Urban Canada*. 3rd ed. Toronto: Methuen, 1976.

Feldman, Lionel D., and Katherine A. Graham. *Bargaining for Cities: Municipalities and Intergovernmental Relations: An Assessment*. Montreal: Institute for Research on Public Policy, 1979.

Halifax Commission on City Government. *Report on the Structure and Processes of Halifax City Government, 1982*. Halifax: Institute of Public Affairs, Dalhousie University, 1982.

Hickey, Paul. *Decision-Making Processes in Ontario's Local Governments*. Toronto: Ministry of Treasury, Economics and Intergovernmental Affairs, n.d.

Higgins, Donald J. H. *Local and Urban Politics in Canada*. Toronto: Gage, 1986.

Higgins, Donald J. H. "The Processes of Reorganizing Local Government." *Canadian Journal of Political Science*, vol. 19 (June 1986): 219-242.

Higgins, Donald J. H. *Urban Canada: Its Government and Politics*. Toronto: Macmillan, 1977.

Kaplan, Harold. *Reform, Planning, and City Politics: Montreal, Winnipeg, Toronto*. Toronto: University of Toronto Press, 1982.

Leo, Christopher. *The Politics of Urban Development: Canadian Urban Expressway Disputes*. Toronto: The Institute of Public Administration of Canada, 1977.

Magnusson, Warren, and Andrew Sancton, eds. *City Politics in Canada*. Toronto: University of Toronto Press, 1983.

Makuch, Stanley M. *Canadian Municipal and Planning Law*. Toronto: Carswell, 1983.

Masson, Jack. *Alberta's Local Governments and Their Politics*. Edmonton: Pica Pica Press, 1985.

O'Brien, Allan. "Father Knows Best: A Look at the Provincial- Municipal Relationship in Ontario." In Donald C. MacDonald, ed., *Government and Politics of Ontario*. Toronto: Macmillan of Canada, 1975, pp. 153–170.

O'Brien, Allan. "The Uncomfortable Partnership: A Look at the Provincial-Municipal Relationship." In Donald C. MacDonald, ed., *The Government and Politics of Ontario*. 2nd ed. Toronto: Van Nostrand Reinhold, 1980, pp. 165–179.

Ontario Committee on Taxation. *Report*. Frank Fogg, Queen's Printer, 1967.

Plunkett, Thomas J. *Urban Canada and Its Government: A Study of Municipal Organization*. Toronto: Macmillan of Canada, 1968.

Plunkett, Thomas J. "Structural Reform of Local Government in Canada." *Public Administration Review*, vol. 33 (January–February 1973): 40–51.

Plunkett, T. J., and G. M. Betts. *The Management of Canadian Urban Government*. Kingston, Ont.: The Institute of Local Government, Queen's University, 1978.

Plunkett, T. J., and Katherine A. Graham. "Whither Municipal Government?" *Canadian Public Administration*, vol. 25 (Winter 1982): 603–618.

Rose, Albert. *Governing Metropolitan Toronto: A Social and Political Analysis, 1953–1971*. Berkeley, Ca.: University of California Press, 1972.

Royal Commission on Metropolitan Toronto. *Report of the Royal Commission on Metropolitan Toronto: Metropolitan Toronto: A Framework for the Future*. 1977.

Siegel, David. "Provincial-Municipal Relations in Canada: An Overview." *Canadian Public Administration*, vol. 23 (Summer 1980): 281–317.

Tindal, C. R. *Structural Changes in Local Government: Government for Urban Regions*. Toronto: The Institute of Public Administration of Canada, 1977.

Tindal, C. R., and S. Nobes Tindal. *Local Government in Canada*. 2nd ed. Toronto: McGraw-Hill Ryerson, 1984.

Weaver, John C. *Shaping the Canadian City: Essays on Urban Politics, 1890–1920*. Toronto: The Institute of Public Administration of Canada, 1977.

CASES

In *Case Program in Canadian Public Administration* (Toronto: Institute of Public Administration of Canada):

Case Studies in Government Operations and Procedures, by R. I. McLaren

La politique du transport urbain dans le région du Québec, by Louise Quesnel-Ouellet and Gilles Bouchard

The Development Dilemma: The Case of Quinpool Road, by Katherine A. Graham in conjunction with E. Grant MacDonald and T. J. Plunkett

Downtown Development or Regional Mall: Fredericton Makes a Decision, by M. C. Ircha

Winnipeg's Core Area Initiative: A Simulation, by Christopher Leo

Administration in a Fishbowl, by M. C. Ircha

Fishing in Troubled Waters or Discovering the Difference between Estimated and Actual Costs, by T. J. Plunkett and Lynn A. Freeman

APPENDIX

How to Write a Research Paper in Public Administration

One of the assignments frequently required of students in public administration courses is the writing of a major essay. This kind of assignment not only increases and reinforces a student's knowledge in the field, but it also develops research and writing skills. However, it can be a very difficult task when a student is just becoming familiar with a new field of study. This appendix provides some guidance on choosing a good topic and on doing research.

The starting point of a good essay is selecting a good topic, if a specific topic or list of topics is not provided by your instructor. The topic should interest you, and there should be an adequate amount of background material available. One obvious source of ideas is either this book, or a similar overview text such as: Richard J. Van Loon and Michael S. Whittington's *The Canadian Political System: Environment, Structure and Process*, 3rd ed. (Toronto: McGraw-Hill Ryerson, 1981); Robert F. Adie and Paul G. Thomas's *Canadian Public Administration*, 2nd ed. (Scarborough, Ont.: Prentice-Hall, 1987); G. Bruce Doern and Richard W. Phidd's *Canadian Public Policy* (Toronto: Methuen, 1983); or V. Seymour Wilson's *Canadian Public Policy and Administration* (Toronto: McGraw-Hill Ryerson, 1981). Check the table of contents and decide which chapter interests you most. Read that chapter to see the kinds of areas covered. There will always be some ideas mentioned there that could be extended or reviewed in a research paper. For example, Chapter 7 of this book discusses the accountability regime of federal Crown corporations. You could compare this regime to that of your province. Which is better? By what criteria? Chapter 10 discusses certain administrative values held by public servants. To what extent are these same values important in your province?

Another potential source of ideas for topics is articles contained in learned and professional journals. Spend some time in the library just flipping through the main journals in the field (see below) to get an idea of what topics have been covered by others. Do you see an article with which you strongly disagree? Your paper could be a detailed critique of that article. Do you see an idea applied in one context which you would like to apply in another? If you see an article which tests a hypothesis about a particular department, you could test the same hypothesis in another department.

The articles can also serve as general models for your essay. Note how the authors present their arguments and make their major points. You should also note some more technical points, such as the use of charts, tables, and footnotes.

Alternatively, your paper could take the form of a case study. This book, like most textbooks, focusses on how things *should* work. Is there some incident which occurred recently that allows you to test whether the real world operates in this manner or not? For example, Chapter 8 suggests that regulatory agencies *should* be kept at arm's length from the partisan political fray. Is there a recent example where this principle was violated? Were the consequences beneficial or detrimental? You could examine some published case studies (see below) to see what others have done.

When you have selected a topic, or had one assigned to you, your next task is to do research to determine what has already been written about it. It is dangerous to form your own conclusions before you have reviewed what experts in the field have said.

A good place to start your research is in the bibliographies at the end of the chapters of this book, or in one of the other overview books mentioned above. Note, however, that these contain only the main sources. Your research will have to be more in-depth than this. The *Canadian Public Administration Bibliography*, published by the Institute of Public Administration of Canada, is especially helpful in this regard. This bibliography was originally published in 1972; periodic supplements have been published since, the latest covering the period to 1982. It contains a complete listing of books and articles about public administration in Canada. However, the supplements are prepared approximately every three to five years, so they do not contain the latest publications.

Therefore, you should check the subject index of your library's card catalogue or computer for recent books. You should also peruse recent editions of the periodicals in the field. The main Canadian journal is *Canadian Public Administration*, published by the Institute of Public Administration of Canada. It is published four times per year and contains an annual index (as do most other journals). *Canadian Public Policy* is another valuable source of information about public policy formulation. *Optimum* is published by the Bureau of Management Consulting of the federal Department of Supply and Services. It contains very good information on the latest management innovations in the federal government. There are analogous publications in some provinces which you can locate in your university library or in provincial government libraries. *Policy Options* is a magazine published by the Institute for Research on Public Policy that contains short articles which are less weighty in an academic sense than those in the above journals, but which are more current.

In addition, there are journals which specialize in areas other than public administration, but which contain some valuable articles. The *Canadian Tax Journal* is written primarily for tax lawyers and accountants, but it is also a valuable source of information about federal and provincial budgets, and it publishes the occasional article on the revenue or expenditure budget process. The journals of the learned societies such as the *Canadian Journal of Political Science*, the *Canadian Journal of Economics*, and the *Canadian Review of Sociology and Anthropology* are all very useful in their own particular areas.

There are also many excellent journals published in other countries which can be helpful, particularly for theoretical or comparative papers. The main journal in the field in Britain is *Public Administration*; in Australia, it is the *Australian Journal of Public Administration*. *Public Administration Review* is the most widely read public administration journal in the United States, but several others, such as the *American Journal of Public Administration*, *Administration and Society*, and the *Journal of Comparative Administration*, are also useful.

You can also communicate directly with government departments to obtain information on current policy. Most governments publish a directory which provides a brief description of the responsibilities of departments and agencies. This can direct you to the agency responsible for the field in which you are interested. These directories also provide some valuable addresses and telephone numbers. The federal government publishes the *Index to Federal Programs and Services* (Ottawa: Minister of Supply and Services Canada, annual publication); the Ontario government's equivalent publication is the *KWIK Index to Services of Your Ontario Government* (Toronto: Ministry of Government Services, annual publication).

You should not overlook popular magazines and newspapers as sources of topical information. Reports in these publications do not carry the same weight in an academic paper as articles from academic journals, but they are valuable sources of information on recent events. *Le Devoir* and *The Globe and Mail* both publish lengthy analysis articles on national issues. *The Citizen* (Ottawa) provides in-depth coverage of issues concerning the federal civil service. These and other magazines and newspapers are indexed in the *Canadian Periodical Index* and the *Canadian News Index*. Some of the most useful magazines are *Saturday Night*, *Maclean's*, *L'Actualité*, and *Canadian Forum*.

If you are interested in the case approach, you should be familiar with the many cases published in the *Case Program in Canadian Public Administration*, sponsored by the Institute of Public Administration of Canada. The cases cover almost all major areas of Canadian public administration. Perusing the titles of some of these could give you some ideas for your own topic. Some of these and other cases are listed at the end of the chapters, and a free catalogue can be obtained by writing to the Institute, 897 Bay Street, Toronto, Ontario, M5S 1Z7.

Now that you have selected a topic and begun to find information, it's time to sit down and actually do the research and write the paper. Some of the books which provide general information about preparing and organizing a paper are *How to Write a Research Paper Step by Step* by Phyllis Cash (New York: Monarch Press, 1977), *A Guide to Writing Essays and Research Papers*, by Gordon Coggins (Toronto: Van Nostrand Reinhold, 1977), and *Making Sense: A Student's Guide to Writing and Style*, by Margot Northey (Toronto: Oxford University Press, 1983). Some of the best books about writing style and grammar are *The Practical Stylist*, by Sheridan Baker (New York: Harper & Row, 1981) and *The Elements of Style*, by William Strunk and Elwyn B. White (New York: Macmillan, 1979). You might also need some advice about actual preparation of the paper — typing, charts, footnotes. The best source in this area is *A Manual for Writers of Term Papers, Theses, and Dissertations*, by Kate L. Turabian (Chicago: University of Chicago Press, 1973).

Good luck!

GLOSSARY

Note: The numbers in brackets following each item refer to the page number where further elaboration on that item can be found.

Access to Information Act. A federal statute designed to provide a right of access to government information for the public. Provides for the exemption or exclusion of certain types of information from disclosure and for a review by an Information Commissioner and/or the Federal Court of decisions by ministers and public servants not to disclose certain information. Came into force July 1, 1983. (429–430)

Adjudication. In the context of employer-employee relations, the process by which an employee presents a grievance in relation to a collective agreement or arbitral award, or in relation to disciplinary action leading to discharge, suspension, or a financial penalty. (501–502)

Administrative Accountability. The obligation of public servants to be answerable for fulfilling responsibilities that flow from the authority given them. Similar in meaning to the concept of objective responsibility. (441–442)

Administrative Discretion. The element of choice or judgement left to individual public servants in their interpretation and application of laws, rules, regulations, policies, and procedures. (274–275)

Administrative Ethics. The application of moral principles to the conduct of persons in public organizations. Normally used interchangeably with the term "administrative morality." (451)

Administrative Law. The branch of public law which deals with relations between the government and individual citizens. It deals with the legal limitations on the actions of governmental officials, and on the remedies which are available to anyone affected by a transgression of these limits. (363)

Advisory Council. An organization composed of private citizens created by the government to provide an independent source of advice to a minister. It is established outside the normal departmental bureaucracy and does not ordinarily have responsibility for administering programs. (239)

Affirmative Action. An approach or program designed to identify and systematically remove employment policies, practices, and procedures which exclude or place at a disadvantage certain groups which have been historically underrepresented in the public service. (488) *See also* Representative Bureaucracy.

617

Appropriation Act. The law passed by Parliament annually which allows the government to spend public funds. (535)

Arbitral Award. *See* Arbitration.

Arbitration. In the context of collective bargaining, the procedure by which an individual or a board hears arguments from both the employer and the union sides of an interest dispute and makes a decision called an arbitral award, which is binding on both parties. In the federal government, one of the two available routes of dispute settlement; the other is the conciliation-strike route. (500)

Auditor General. The officer of Parliament who performs an annual audit of the *Public Accounts* and prepares an annual report to Parliament on the government's financial stewardship. (577)

Bargaining Agent. An employee organization (a union) that has been certified, for example, by the federal Public Service Staff Relations Board, as the organization responsible for bargaining on behalf of a particular bargaining unit. Examples include the Public Service Alliance of Canada and the Professional Institute of the Public Service of Canada. To be certified as a bargaining agent, the union must prove that it has support of the majority of employees in the bargaining unit. (498)

Bargaining Unit. A group of two or more employees which has been designated as constituting a unit of employees appropriate for collective bargaining. (498)

Blue Book. *See* Estimates.

Budgetary Transaction. A revenue or expenditure transaction which affects the government's surplus or deficit position. *See also* Non-budgetary Transaction. (547)

Bureaucratic Politics. An approach to the study of policy making which focusses on interactions among individuals, in the form of conflict, bargaining, compromise and persuasion, as determinants of the actions of a government. (114–115, 309, 392–393)

Canada Gazette. An official publication of the government of Canada in which appear official announcements such as orders in council and regulations. (143)

Captive Agency Theory. A theory which holds that regulatory agencies eventually become captive of, or controlled by, the interests they were established to regulate. (219–220)

Central Agency. An agency which has a substantial amount of continuing legitimate authority to intervene in, and direct the activity of, departments. (144–146)

Centralization. A system of organization which involves minimal dispersal of operating and decision-making units outside the centre of power. (49)

Citizen Participation. The direct involvement of individual citizens and citizens' groups in government decision making. (421)

Classical Federalism. A concept according to which the powers of government are divided "so that the general and regional governments are each, within a sphere, co-ordinate and independent." (379)

Classification Creep. The reclassification of positions so that the persons holding them receive higher pay and sometimes fancier titles for doing the same job. (473)

Classification Standard. A definition of the category within which each occupational group falls, the groups within each occupational category, and the descriptions of benchmark positions to be used as guides for assessing jobs and rating them according to their level in the group. (473)

Collective Agreement. An agreement in writing between the employer and the bargaining agent regarding terms and conditions of employment. (500)

Collective Bargaining. A method of determining wages, hours, and other conditions of employment through direct negotiations between the employer and the union. (497)

Collective Ministerial Responsibility. The responsibility of ministers as a group (that is, as members of the Cabinet) for the policies and management of the government as a whole. (307, 342) *See also* Individual Ministerial Responsibility.

Coloured Paper. *See* Green Paper or White Paper.

Comprehensive Audit. A review of a program which considers its economy, efficiency, and effectiveness. (579)

Conciliation. A process by which an impartial person tries to resolve interest disputes in collective bargaining by seeking compromise or voluntary agreement between the two parties. Unlike arbitration, the recommendations of the conciliator (or mediator) are not binding on the parties. In the federal public service, conciliation must precede legal strike action. (500–501)

Conditional Grants. Payments by the federal government to a provincial government (or by a provincial government to a municipal government) in which the receiving government undertakes programs according to conditions specified by the granting government. Often referred to as shared cost programs. (382)

Conflict of Interest. A situation in which a public employee has a private or personal interest sufficient to influence or appear to influence the objective exercise of his or her official duties. (454)

Consolidated Revenue Fund. The fund in which is recorded all receipts and expenditures of public funds which are available for general governmental purposes. (554)

Control. That form of power in which A has authority to direct or command B to do something. Sometimes referred to as "authority of position" or "position power." (252)

Cooperative Federalism. A term used to describe federal-provincial relations when the constitutional division of powers is preserved, but federal and provincial ministers and public servants engage in consultation and coordination to reach joint decisions on matters of mutual concern. (380)

Coordination. The process by which two or more parties take one another into account for the purpose of bringing their decisions and/or activities into harmonious or reciprocal relation. (263)

Council-Commission System. A method of organization of municipal government which centralizes control of administration in a Board of Commissioners consisting of a small number of civic servants and sometimes the mayor. (607-609)

Council-Committee System. A method of organization of municipal government which involves several council committees and no single focus of administrative activity. (603)

Council-Manager System. A method of organization of municipal government which centralizes control of administration in one position — the city manager. (603)

Crown Corporation. A corporation owned by the government which engages in industrial, commercial, or financial activities. (167)

Decentralization. A system of organization which involves placing actual decision-making power in the hands of units outside the centre of power, either geographically or organizationally. (49) *Contrast with* Deconcentration.

Deconcentration. The physical dispersal of operating units with only very limited delegation of decision-making authority. (49) *Contrast with* Decentralization.

Deputy Minister. The administrative head of a government department. Appointed by the Prime Minister or Premier. Also referred to as the deputy head. (152, 331)

Deregulation. The elimination of government regulatory control over an industry so that it can operate through the dictates of the private enterprise system. (222-223)

Double-image Federalism. A term used to describe federal-provincial relations characterized by a combination of interaction between the central government and the provinces and a special relationship between French- and English-speaking Canadians. (380-381)

Economy. The acquisition of goods and services at the best possible price. *See also* Effectiveness and Efficiency. (443-444, 579)

Effectiveness. A measure of the extent to which an input of resources achieves the intended objective or goal. To be distinguished from the related concept of efficiency. (443-444, 579)

Efficiency. A measure of performance that may be expressed as a ratio between input and output. The use of administrative methods and resources that will achieve the greatest results for a specific objective at the least cost. (443-444, 579)

Emergency Federalism. A term used to describe federal-provincial relations during the two world wars and the Depression; these relations were characterized by a growth in federal power vis-à-vis the provinces. (380)

''Envelope'' System. *See* Policy and Expenditure Management System.

Equalization. A program through which the federal government makes unconditional grants to provinces with a weak tax base. The program's purpose is to allow the so-called "have-not" provinces to provide adequate public services to their citizens without imposing excessively high taxes. (383)

Established Programs Financing (EPF). A transfer payment program begun in 1977 when the federal government terminated three very large conditional grants to the provinces and replaced them with a combination of cash payments and tax room. (383)

Estimates. The series of documents which contains the government's request for an annual appropriation and the necessary supporting documentation. When approved by Parliament, the *Estimates* become the Appropriation Act. (535, 546–554)

Evaluation. An in-depth analysis of a program carried out to determine its worth and to locate any needed administrative or policy changes. (574)

Executive Federalism. A term used to describe federal-provincial relations characterized by "the concentration and centralization of authority at the top of each participating government, the control and supervision of intergovernmental relations by politicians and officials with a wide range of functional interests, and the highly formalized and well-publicized proceedings of federal-provincial diplomacy." (380)

Federal-Provincial Relations Office. A central agency which is responsible for advising the Cabinet and operating departments and agencies on the conduct of federal-provincial relations. (149)

Federalism. A political system in which the powers of the state are formally divided between central and regional governments by a written constitution, but in which these governments are linked in a mutually interdependent political relationship. (378)

Finance (Department of). The central agency most concerned with macro-economic policy and preparation of the revenue budget. (151)

Financial Administration Act. The statute which governs the regime of financial accountability for federal departments and agencies and Crown corporations. (181, 469, 567)

Governor General. The representative of the Queen in Canada; functions as the head of state when the Queen is not in Canada. (137)

Governor General in Council. Refers to the Governor General acting on the formal advice of the Cabinet. When the decisions of Cabinet have been approved by the Governor General, they can be formally described as acts of the Governor General in Council. (137)

Governor General's Warrants. An authorization for the government to spend in the absence of a parliamentary appropriation; used only for unforeseen expenditures when Parliament is not in session. (570)

Green Paper. A statement prepared by government to stimulate discussion about the possibility of changing policy in a particular area. It is not a statement of government policy; rather it lists the options which the government is considering and the advantages and disadvantages of each. (244)

Hierarchy of Needs. A concept developed by Abraham Maslow which suggests that workers can be motivated by the satisfaction of a number of different needs ranging from basic shelter and food to self-actualization. As workers' lower level needs are satisfied, they are motivated by desires to satisfy higher level needs. (58)

Human Relations School of Management. An approach to management and motivation which emphasizes the dignity and needs of the workers in the workplace. Usually associated with social psychologists such as Mayo, Roethlisberger, and Dickson. (55)

Human Resources Planning. The process through which a government strives to ensure that it has the appropriate number and quality of employees to carry out its responsibilities. (475)

Individual Ministerial Responsibility. The responsibility of the minister, as the political head of the department, to answer to the legislature and through the legislature to the public both for his or her personal acts and for the acts of departmental subordinates. (342-343)

Influence. That form of power in which B conforms to A's desires, values, or goals on grounds of suggestion, persuasion, emulation, or anticipation. A more general and pervasive form of power than control. Sometimes referred to as "authority of leadership" or "personal power." (252)

Institute of Public Administration of Canada. An association of public servants from all spheres of government and of academics. Devoted to improving the study and practice of public administration in Canada. Publishes the learned journal *Canadian Public Administration*. (4)

Interest Disputes. Involve the renegotiation of an existing collective agreement. (499) *Contrast with* Rights Disputes.

Interest Groups. *See* Pressure Groups.

Intergovernmental Relations. The interactions between and among the federal, provincial, and municipal governments in the Canadian federal system. (379)

Interim Supply. A limited appropriation of funds provided by Parliament at the beginning of the fiscal year until the full *Estimates* have been approved. (569)

Interstate Federalism. "The distribution of powers and financial resources between the federal and provincial governments, as well as the relations between those two orders of government." (381)

Intrastate Federalism. "Arrangements whereby the interests of regional units — the interests either of the government or of the residents of these units — are channelled through, and protected by, the structures and operations of the central government." (381-382)

Job Classification. The process by which jobs are assigned to an occupational group within an occupational category and to a level within that group. (472)

Job Evaluation. The analysis of a job in terms of its duties, its physical and mental demands, the knowledge and skills it requires, and the conditions under which it is performed; the writing of a job description which explains the duties, working conditions, and other aspects of the job; and the assessment of these job characteristics against the classification standard established for the relevant occupational group. (473)

Lieutenant Governor in Council. The representative of the Queen in a province. (137)

Line. The part of an organization which is directly involved in producing the organization's output. (45–46) *Contrast with* Staff.

Line-item Budgeting. A style of budgeting which emphasizes the object of expenditure (salaries, stationery), rather than the purpose of the expenditure. (525)

Lobbying. A legitimate means by which groups and individuals try to influence government decisions by means of direct contact with politicians or public servants. Usually associated with the activities of pressure groups or interest groups. (400)

Main Estimates. *See* Estimates.

Management by Objectives. A system of management which emphasizes supervisors and subordinates working together to agree on sets of objectives to be attained in the coming year. Commonly associated with Peter Drucker and George Odiorne. (61)

Management Category. An occupational category in the federal public service composed of about 4,000 senior public servants with responsibility for policy development; program formulation and delivery; the design and operation of management machinery; and the management of personnel, finances, and public affairs. (474)

Memorandum to Cabinet. The key mechanism by which policy proposals are brought forward by ministers for consideration and approval by their Cabinet colleagues. The formal means by which deputy ministers provide confidential policy advice to their ministers. (321)

Merit Principle. A principle according to which (1) all citizens should have a reasonable opportunity to be considered for employment in the public service, and (2) selections must be based exclusively on qualification or fitness for the job. To be distinguished from the merit system. (277)

Merit System. The mechanism in use at any time by which the goals of the merit principle are achieved. An administrative device which can and should be adapted to changing circumstances. (277)

Minister of State for a Specified Purpose. A minister who heads a Ministry of State, e.g., for Science and Technology. (159)

Minister of State to Assist a Minister. A minister responsible for only a limited portion of a full department, e.g., for Fitness and Amateur Sport within the Department of National Health and Welfare. (160)

Minister Without Portfolio for Designated Purposes. A minister who does not have responsibility for a department, but is responsible for representing a particular interest in Cabinet, e.g., multiculturalism. (160)

Ministry of State. A small department responsible mainly for research and for coordinating the activities of other departments. (159)

Mixed Enterprise. A corporation "in which the federal government has taken a direct equity position in common with other participants for the purposes of implementing a public policy or satisfying a public need." (167)

New Public Administration. A movement of public administration scholars and practitioners in the United States in the late 1960s and early 1970s concerned with social equity, sensitivity to, and representation of, disadvantaged minority groups, increased citizen participation in government decision making, and new forms of public organization. (271–272)

Non-budgetary Transaction. An advance to or investment in some agency or corporation which is expected to be repaid; also the repayment of any of these items. These transactions do not affect the government's surplus or deficit position. (547) *See also* Budgetary Transaction.

Objective Responsibility. The responsibility of a person or an organization *to* someone else, outside of self, *for* some thing or some kind of performance. Similar in meaning to accountability or answerability. (293)

Occupational Category. Includes a broad range of occupations of the same type, distinguished by the nature of the duties performed and the education required. Examples in the federal public service are the Management and the Operational categories. (472)

Office of the Comptroller General. A central agency reporting to Treasury Board which has particular responsibility for program evaluation and financial management and internal audit in departments. (150, 573)

Ombudsman. An official authorized by statute to investigate complaints from citizens about improper, unfair or discriminatory treatment by public servants. Reports to the legislature and is independent of the political executive and the bureaucracy. (350)

Operating Department. "An administrative unit comprising one or more organizational components over which a minister has direct management and control." (137)

Order in Council. An official proclamation made by the Governor General in Council; usually a government regulation. (143)

Organizational Development. An approach to management which emphasizes the ability of members of the organization to work together in analysing organizational problems and deciding how to improve the quality of the organization. (63)

Organizational Socialization. The process through which individuals learn the expectations attached to the position they occupy in the organization and through which they selectively internalize as values certain of the expectations of those with whom they interact. (259-260)

Participative Management. A style of management which emphasizes the desirability of workers actually being involved in decision making. (61)

Partisan Mutual Adjustment. A process by which a very large measure of coordination in government takes place without any deliberate or conscious attempt to coordinate. (264-265)

Performance Budgeting. A style of budgeting which relates expenditure to specific activities to determine unit costs of providing services. (527)

Performance Evaluation. The process whereby information about the performance of employees over time is systematically collected and analysed. Also referred to as "employee appraisal." (480)

Policy and Expenditure Management System (PEMS). The current budget process of the federal government. The Cabinet Committee on Priorities and Planning divides total expenditure into "envelopes" which it allocates to other Cabinet committees for further division by program. (535-536)

Political Neutrality. A constitutional doctrine or convention according to which public servants should not engage in activities which are likely to impair — or appear to impair — their impartiality or the impartiality of the public service. (441) For example, public statements about government policies or involvement in election campaigns.

Political Parties. Organizations which seek to get their members elected to political office and to gain and maintain control of the government. Their major functions include the aggregation and articulation of interests, the recruitment and training of political leaders, and the education and socialization of the public on political matters. (413)

Political Patronage. The appointment of persons to government service or their advancement within the service on the grounds of contributions, financial or otherwise, to the governing party rather than on merit. (277)

Politics-administration Dichotomy. The idea that a sharp distinction can be made between the responsibilities of elected executives, who make policy decisions, and the responsibilities of public servants, who execute these decisions. (268-269)

Power. The capacity to secure the dominance of one's values or goals. There are two forms of power — control and influence. (252)

Pressure Groups. Organizations composed of persons who have joined together to seek their mutual interest by influencing government decisions and actions. Often referred to as interest groups. (400)

Prime Minister's Office. The central agency which provides partisan policy advice to the Prime Minister. It is most concerned with relations between the Prime Minister and the media and the party. (147)

Privacy Act. A federal statute which gives individuals access to their personal information held by the government and which protects the privacy of individuals by limiting those who may see this personal information. Also sets out principles of fair information practices. Came into force July 1, 1983. (436–437)

Privative Clauses. Statutory provisions designed to prevent judicial review of the decisions of administrative tribunals. (196)

Privatization. Turning over Crown corporations to the private sector by sale or other means. (196–197)

Privy Council Office. The central agency which provides policy advice and administrative support to Cabinet and its committees. (147)

Program Budgeting. A style of budgeting which allocates funds by program and attempts to measure the impact of expenditures on the goals and objectives of programs. (527–528)

Public Accounts. The series of documents which contains the government's year-end financial statements. (554–563)

Public Bureaucracy. The system of authority, people, offices, and methods that government uses to achieve its objectives. The means by which the practice of public administration is carried on. (5)

Public Interest Group. A form of pressure group whose members try to influence government decisions in the name of the "public interest." Distinguished from special interest groups which are primarily motivated by particular, selfish interests. (402)

Public Participation. A broad range of direct and indirect forms of participation by members of the public in government decision making. Includes such forms of participation as membership in political parties, pressure groups, and advisory bodies. A broader concept than "citizen participation." (421)

Public Policy. ". . . whatever governments choose to do or not to do." (105)

Public Service Commission. An independent agency which serves Parliament as the guardian of the merit principle in public personnel management. It is responsible for recruitment, staffing and promotion in the public service. (352)

Quasi-federalism. A term used to describe the early decades of the Canadian federation during which the federal government dominated the provincial governments, in part by making frequent use of the federal constitutional powers to disallow and reserve provincial legislation. (379)

Recruitment. The process of identifying candidates for public service positions by such methods as inviting job applications from within and from outside the public service and using a human resources inventory system. (477)

Regulatory Agency. A body which administers, fixes, establishes, controls, or regulates an economic, cultural, environmental or social activity by regularized and established means in the public interest and in accordance with general policy guidelines specified by the government. (204–205)

Representative Bureaucracy. The idea that the social composition of the bureaucracy should reflect that of the population as a whole. Also that larger numbers of persons from certain underrepresented groups (e.g., women, minority groups) should be brought into the public service. (445–446) *See* Affirmative Action.

Responsiveness. In the public service context, this term refers to the inclination and the capacity of public servants to respond to the needs and demands of political institutions and of the public. (444)

Rights Disputes. Involve disputes which arise during the term of a collective agreement with regard to matters of interpretation of either the collective agreement or some statute dealing with terms and conditions of employment. (501) *Contrast with* Interest Disputes.

Royal Commission. A temporary organization constituted to investigate either specific incidents or general policy concerns and to report to government. They usually are disbanded after they deliver their report and so are not involved in the implementation of their recommendations. (232)

Scientific Management. A management style which emphasizes tailoring the physical nature of work to the physical abilities of workers. Characterized by time-motion studies and precise work standards. Usually associated with Frederick W. Taylor. (37)

Selection. The process through which candidates for public service positions are screened by such means as application forms, written examinations, and interviews. (477)

Shared Cost Programs. *See* Conditional Grants.

Socialization. The process by which individuals learn from their environment the social patterns and values of their culture. The socializing agencies involved in this process include family, peer groups, schools, prior employment, and adult organizations. (259)

Span of Control. The number of subordinates reporting to a particular supervisor. (42)

Staff. The part of the organization which supports the line function, but is not directly involved in producing the organization's output (e.g., accounting or personnel). (46) *Contrast with* Line.

Statutory Appropriation. A continuing appropriation of funds which does not require approval in the annual *Estimates* because there is already some legislative authorization. (547)

Statutory Instruments. The rules, regulations, orders, etc. made by the executive under delegated legislative authority. (547)

Subjective Responsibility. The responsibility which a person *feels* towards others. Often described as *personal* or *psychological* responsibility. Similar in meaning to identification, loyalty, and conscience. (293)

Supplementary Estimates. A request for funds in addition to the original *Estimates*. Usually requested towards the end of the fiscal year. (570)

Systems Theory of Organization. A theory which emphasizes the position of the organization as a part of a larger system with which it must interact. Usually associated with Katz and Kahn. (69)

Task Force. *See* Royal Commission.

Tax Expenditure. A tax reduction available to a taxpayer who does (or refrains from doing) something desired by government. (535)

Theory X—Theory Y. Developed by Douglas McGregor to describe different managers' views of workers. Theory X holds that workers are basically lazy and need to be closely watched. Theory Y holds that workers are highly motivated and will voluntarily work hard. (59-60)

Transfer Payments. *See* Conditional Grants and Unconditional Grants.

Treasury Board. A Cabinet committee consisting of the President of the Treasury Board, the Minister of Finance, and four other Cabinet ministers. Responsible for preparation of the expenditure budget and for administrative management in departments. (149-151)

Treasury Board Secretariat. The central agency which assists the Treasury Board in carrying out its responsibilities. (149-151)

Unconditional Grants. Payments by the federal government to a provincial government (or by a provincial government to a municipal government) which can be used for any purpose the receiving government desires. (383)

Unity of Command. The bureaucratic principle which holds that all employees must report to one, and only one, supervisor in order to minimize confusion and misdirection. (33)

Values. Enduring beliefs that influence the choices made by individuals, groups, or organizations from among available means or ends. Values are organized into value systems in which values are ranked in terms of their relative importance. (258)

Vote (as a part of the Estimates). The basis on which Parliament appropriates funds to departments and agencies; usually, there is one vote for each program. (551)

White Paper. A statement of government policy. Usually provides a statement of policy in everyday, non-legislative language accompanied by an explanation and defence of the particular course of action chosen. (245)

Zero-base Budgeting (ZBB). A style of budgeting which emphasizes the ranking of programs in priority order and the allocation of funds on this basis. (532-533)

NAME INDEX

SUBJECT INDEX